PUBLIC ADMINISTRATION AND PUBLIC AFFAIRS

second edition

NICHOLAS HENRY

Arizona State University

PRENTICE-HALL, INC., ENGLEWOOD CLIFFS, N. J. 07632

Library of Congress Cataloging in Publication Data

Henry, Nicholas (date).
Public administration and public affairs.

Bibliography: p.
Includes index.
1. Public administration. I. Title.
JF1351.H45 1980   350   79–15414
ISBN 0–13–737296–5

Printed in the United States of America

10 9 8 7 6 5 4 3 2 1

Editorial/production supervision and interior design by Marina Harrison
Cover design by Wanda Lubelska
Manufacturing buyer: Harry P. Baisley

Acknowledgement is made to publishers and individuals for permission to reprint excerpts from the following works:

Luther Gulick, "The Twenty-Fifth Anniversary of the American Society for Public Administration," *Public Administration Review*, XV (March, 1965), pp. 1–4. Jack L. Walker, "Brother, Can You Paradigm?" *PS* V (Fall, 1972), pp. 419–422, and Evan M. Kirkpatrick, Executive Director, APSA, for the same

continued, page 502

Prentice-Hall International, Inc., *London*
Prentice-Hall of Australia Pty. Limited, *Sydney*
Prentice-Hall of Canada, Ltd., *Toronto*
Prentice-Hall of India Private Limited, *New Delhi*
Prentice-Hall of Japan, Inc., *Tokyo*
Prentice-Hall of Southeast Asia Pte. Ltd., *Singapore*
Whitehall Books Limited, *Wellington, New Zealand*

To Muriel

contents

Public Administration's Ninety Years in a Quandary   26

SECTION 2
PUBLIC ORGANIZATIONS: THEORIES, CONCEPTS, AND PEOPLE

The Threads of Organization Theory   61

Concepts of Organization Theory   89

Models of Administrative Man in Organizations   111

Toward a Bureaucratic Ethic   131

SECTION 3
NUTS AND BOLTS: THE TECHNIQUES OF PUBLIC ADMINISTRATION

The Systems Approach and Management Science   149

Program Evaluation in Public Administration   183

The Budget: Concepts and Processes   206

Public Personnel Administration   236

SECTION 4
PUBLIC AFFAIRS

Approaches to Public Affairs   297

The Urban Professions   315

13

The Urban Experience 347

14

The Federal Maze 378

15 ✓

Managing Growth 425

preface from
the first edition

In a decade in which college textbooks are, according to surveys and statistics, of declining importance in the classroom, here is a textbook. It is my contention that textbooks really are not diminishing in usefulness, but that their uses have changed. On the wane is the ponderous, two-pound tome lugged dutifully to class by student and instructor alike. On the upswing is the slimmed text, together with supplemental readings selected by the instructor. It is for this latter use that *Public Administration and Public Affairs* is designed.

The book attempts to be germane to the fast-evolving field of public administration in several ways. Each chapter contains a short selection drawn from a particularly pertinent source designed to amplify the topic under discussion. Supplemental bibliographies, in addition to a list of references, are included at the end of each chapter as a means of further aiding the student. The four appendixes are constructed to be of immediate, practical use to students and professor alike: Appendix A introduces the reader to the basic concepts of network analysis: Appendixes B and C provide an extensive listing and descriptions of information services, bibliographies, and major journals in public administration (all for the purpose of speeding research); Appendix D furnishes a list of useful organizations with addresses.

Additionally, however, there is a larger significance to this textbook. As Thomas S. Kuhn has noted in *The Structure of Scientific Revolutions*, textbooks essentially define and explicate the intellectual "paradigm"— that is, what scholars in a discipline perceive to be their proper area and focus of study—of most academic fields. True, textbooks rarely break new conceptual turf for a field; but they do define a field—they tell what, in short, the discipline itself is.

Paradigms in academic fields come and go. Changing perceptions and new discoveries bring about different viewpoints, and no field is exempt. Even in physics, as "hard" a science as one is likely to find anywhere, intellectual developments have overturned established definitions and created severe discomfiture among its practitioners. When conceptual turmoil was rife in physics some sixty years ago, and quantum mechanics was undergoing serious theoretical challenges, the brilliant physicist Wolfgang Pauli wrote, "At the moment physics is again terribly confused. In any case, it is too difficult for me, and I wish I had been a movie comedian or something of the sort and had never heard of physics."

Many public administrationists can empathize with Pauli's remark. Public administration often has been "terribly confused." A new concept for the field is needed.

This book represents an attempt to sketch such a concept. While there are few original ideas in it, the "map" of public administration it presents may strike some readers as novel.

[Section One reviews the paradigms of public administration over the last eighty years and considers why they have waxed and waned. Section One also offers a structure for the field that reflects the needs and thinking of the 1970s. In it I urge that public administration be defined as an intellectual and professional endeavor that synthesizes pertinent elements of political acuity, administrative techniques, and ethical theory.] Section Two concerns organization theory as a literature which yields insight into the political dynamics and motivations of public bureaucracies and their members. Section Three describes the applied techniques of public administration, including the more advanced methodologies stemming from systems theory and policy analysis, as well as the more traditional chapters on budgeting and public personnel administration. Finally, Section Four on "Public Affairs" considers ethical theory and the public interest by analyzing some underlying social dilemmas of the United States: the urban experience, the new federalism, and environmental administration.

The book rests on three premises: (1) "Muddling through" decision-making in government no longer is adequate in a society characterized by "future shock," and more rational policy-making is mandatory; (2) much of public administration consists of learning the languages and symbols of other people and other professions; (3) public administration is coming into its own; academically we are entering into a period of long overdue institutional expansionism and intellectual independence.

Whether or not this proposed "map" of public administration charts a topography that is useful, even if only momentarily, will be determined by time. In any event, a defining paradigm of public administration is needed for more than academic reasons. Given the rapidity of social change in American society engendered by political and technological developments, and the resulting propensity to govern the American administrative state on a crisis-to-crisis decision-making basis, the public administrator stands in acute need of an intellectual identity. In this sense, the self-view that public administration, both the theory and the profession, chooses as meaningful takes on a social significance that few other scholarly fields can claim. What government perceives as relevant to its functions and duties will be determined to a large degree by how public administration is defined. It is to this definitional chore that *Public Administration and Public Affairs* is addressed.

N. H.
Athens, Georgia

preface to
the second edition

The critical and commercial success of one's first book is always gratifying. *Public Administration and Public Affairs*, my first book, was both of these, and I am grateful to those readers of the first edition who welcomed it so warmly.

Today, five years and eight books later, I relish the revision process, as *Public Administration and Public Affairs* remains my personal favorite. The calculated risks I took in the marketplace in writing it—by strongly advocating the field's overdue breakaway from political science and administrative science—have paid off. Increasingly, academics and practitioners alike are recognizing public administration as a unique and useful field. This is as it should be.

In this second edition, the revision is substantial, but the original thrust remains.

Public administration is still changing in the last quarter of our century, and this edition reflects that change. A new introductory chapter confronts the underlying reasons for the growing popular hostility toward government and the rising autonomy of the public bureaucracy. These are serious issues, and ones that must be appreciated to properly understand public administration. A new chapter on program evaluation has been added. The rapidly developing field of evaluation may well wax into public administration's primary methodology and grant it its chief claim to legitimacy. The chapters on Public Personnel Administration, Budgeting, Federalism, and Urbanism have been so extensively reformulated that they, too, are new. The first edition's chapter on Environmental Administration has also been replaced with a new, more comprehensive one on Growth Management. The section on Organization Theory has been refined and, I hope, improved.

The strengths of the first edition have been retained, notably the discussion of the intellectual history of public administration (the reviewer for *Public Management* called it "rather heavy going in spots—but worth the time") and the analysis of bureaucratic ethics (the reviewer for *Public Administration Review* described it as "not likely to produce easy internalization . . . but is thought-provoking and different"). Despite the caveats I think the retention of both chapters is worthwhile.

The appendices of the first edition also remain, but again with alterations. Descriptions of the organizations now accompany the names and addresses of selected associations, and an appendix on appropriate forms of address to public officials has been added. Footnotes replace the references of the first edition—a concession to requests from students writing term papers, as I have never been a fan of those creatures called footnotes. The supplemental bibliographies at the end of each chapter have been retained.

In short, the second edition of *Public Administration and Public Affairs*, like the first, is designed to be useful as well as educational.

A number of people deserve my thanks for their assistance in writing this book. Professor Elizabethann O'Sullivan provided invaluable help and guidance in writing Chapter 7, Program Evaluation in Public Administration. Stan Wakefield of Prentice-Hall was always encouraging in his willingness to speed the debut of the second edition, and Marina Harrison maintained the unusually high standards of Prentice-Hall's copyediting—improving my sentence structure in the process. The secretaries in the Center for Public Affairs at Arizona State University, notably Marian Buckley, Mary Jo Curtis, Cecile Higgins, Karen Neese, Patty Phippeny, and Gwen Weaver, all labored cheerfully over humming typewriters in an effort to complete the manuscript, and Jeanne Diemunsche provided consistently prompt and pleasant research assistance; I am, of course, grateful.

As always, my wife, Muriel, and my children, Adrienne and Miles, provided the greatest support. The book is for them.

N. H.
Tempe, Arizona

THE PARADIGMS
OF PUBLIC
ADMINISTRATION

bureaucracy, democracy, and the legitimacy question

Never before in the history of the nation has the public bureaucrat been less admired and more powerful than today. Public opinion polls, politicians, and taxpayers' revolts indicate that Americans are fed up not only with their bureaucrats, but possibly with their government as well.

In light of the growing hostility towards bureaucracy, this chapter—and, indeed, this book—are attempts to explain what bureaucracy does in American life and why it does it. It reviews how bureaucracy has burgeoned and why; it considers the genuinely extraordinary power of modern public bureaucracy and the basis for that power; and finally, it examines the implications of what appears to be a significant decline in the legitimacy of government in the final fifth of America's twentieth century.

THE BURGEONING BUREAUCRACY

Despite popular antipathy toward "those bureaucrats," we now have more of them than ever before; the American governmental bureaucracy has more than 15 million people working for it, and this figure does not include soldiers in the armed services. In 1976, 2.8 million people worked

3

for the federal government, another 3.3 million worked for the state governments, and 8.8 million worked for local governments.] The recent growth of state and local governmental employment is especially staggering. Figure 1–1 indicates the increasing numbers of employees and size of monthly payrolls since 1950. As it shows the federal government has increased relatively marginally in comparison to state and local employment, which has more than tripled since 1950. In 1978 government ex-

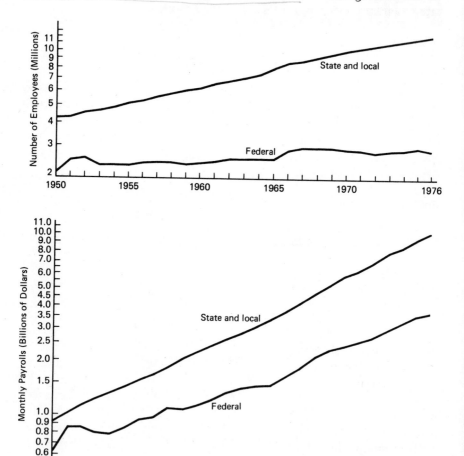

Note: Data are for month of October; 1957 data were reported for April and have been adjusted for comparability to October.

FIGURE 1–1. Government Employment and Payroll, 1950 to 1976 Logarithmic Scale. *Source:* Advisory Commission on Intergovernmental Relations.

penditures at all levels exceeded $757.2 billion, a phenomenal sum by any reckoning. Even more phenomenal is the fact that government spending had increased ten times since 1950. In that year, American governments absorbed barely one quarter of the Gross National Product (GNP), but by 1975 their expenditures accounted for an astounding 35 percent of the GNP, leaping from roughly $95 billion to $525 billion. Most of this money was consumed by the federal government, but the rate of increase was faster at the state and local levels.

WHY BUREAUCRACY?

The spectre of government expanding its influence in society by increasing its economic power is not unique to the United States; the phenomenon is universal. Why is this so? Although many explanations have been put forth (including the guile of bureaucrats themselves), we shall review only the principal ones: Political pluralism, the displacement/concentration hypothesis, and technological complexity.

Political pluralism

Our first explanation is one that is favored by political scientists.[1] Although it is not usually employed to explain the growth of government, but rather to demonstrate how the political process is supposed to work, the pluralist model nonetheless has some utility as an explanation of why government has burgeoned in society. The basic model is: Society is comprised of a number of competing groups that have a broad range of interests which may or may not be compatible with one another. Thus, blacks, for instance, may wish to wrest certain concessions from policy-makers to accomplish their own particular ends (for example, bussing children to achieve integrated school districts), but that such a gain for one group is achieved ultimately at the cost of other groups (or so it is perceived by other groups)—for instance, the inconvenience to whites that bussing may incur. Hence, in the classic pluralist model one group's gain becomes another group's loss. Pluralists believe that such a process results in a social "good" on the grounds that the majority of people benefit from this contention of interest groups—provided, of course, that the basic

---

1. The single best description of the pluralist model remains that put forth in *The Federalist*, particularly "No. 10" by James Madison, but L. Harmon Zeigler and G. Wayne Peak's *Interest Groups in American Society*, 2nd ed. (Englewood Cliffs, N.J.: Prentice-Hall, 1972), is a very good elaboration of the pluralist viewpoint in a more modern context.

human rights of a group or individual are not destroyed by the process, and government is the instiution charged with society's responsibilities to protect these rights.

But how does the pluralist interpretation of the political process relate to a theory concerning the growth of government? The intellectual jump is not a difficult one to make, but it is worth some explanation. If government has an increasingly expanding economy from which to draw resources (*i.e.*, taxes), it becomes increasingly easier for policy-makers to placate any given group, but not necessarily at the expense of other groups. With larger tax bases, more and more demands can be met by government, but without employing the traditional and necessary device of reallocating resources to do so.[2] When government's resources are scarce, and policy-makers must take away resources from one program to provide funding to another program, it follows that what one group gains in the form of a new or expanded policy, another group consequently loses. With a growing economy, however, reallocative decision-making is not required, or, at least, less required. Old programs can be maintained and new programs started by reason of an increasingly expanding resource base in the forms of growing industrialization, productivity, employment, and concomitant tax increases. Therefore, government can meet, for example, the traditional demand for adequate national defense by letting lucrative contracts to businesses in the defense industries, and simultaneously assure the adequate safety of workers in those industries by setting up such devices as an Occupational Safety and Health Administration, thus meeting the demands of other groups whose values are not necessarily profit-motivated.

A secondary consequence of such a situation is that demands for government services by various groups have resulted both in more government services that are wanted by some groups, but which are not wanted by others, and the tensions resulting from this situation may have contributed to the popular distrust and dislike of government. Nevertheless, it is this basic dynamic of competing interest groups demanding more and more resources from government—but only in the context of more resources—that serves as the basic pluralist theory explaining the growth of government.

2. As noted in the text, we are now moving slightly away from the traditional pluralist model. By introducing the notion of resources to pluralism, we implicitly are expanding the concept to include game theory. Many contributors to the theory of games, however, identify with political science. Game theory is explained more amply in Chapter 6 on "The Systems Approach," but suffice it to note here that game theorists would call the situation described in the text a "non-zero-sum game," or a "win/win scenario."

The displacement/concentration hypothesis

The traditional pluralist model of political scientists as an explanation of the growth of government is not particularly satisfying. This is not to say that the model is "wrong" but it is to say that it is awfully simple, and a more sophisticated interpretation of the growth of government is provided by economists.[3] As Alan T. Peacock and Jack Wiseman observe in this context, economists, for the most part at least, do not base their theories on "any all-embracing theory of the state," as the political scientists implicitly do. Indeed, the assumptions of the economists in explaining the growth of government are that: "Governments like to spend more money, citizens do not like to pay more taxes, governments need to pay some attention to the wishes of their citizens."[4]

Peacock and Wiseman, for example, argue cogently that the growth of government may be attributed to two distinct features in the twentieth century. One is that certain major social disturbances, such as wars, shift public revenues and expenditures to new and heretofore unimagined levels. When the disturbance has run its course, new ideas emerge of what a tolerable tax level is, and higher plateaus of government activity in the economy are achieved and maintained; invariably, these plateaus represent a higher portion of the Gross National Product than was the case prior to the social disturbance. It is this phenomenon that Peacock

3. The bulk of this discussion is drawn from Alan T. Peacock and Jack Wiseman, assisted by Jindrich Veverka, *The Growth of Public Expenditure in the United Kingdom*. A study by the National Bureau of Economic Research (Princeton: Princeton University Press, 1961), pp. xxi–xxxi.

   The displacement/concentration hypothesis as developed by Peacock and Wiseman is a refinement of the theories originated by Adolph Wagner in the late nineteenth century. Wagner set forth the "law of increasing state activity" which, to phrase it very crudely, contended that with social progress (a less than objective term in and of itself) came increased activity by government, thus intensifying the government's impact on the national economy as a whole. To quote Wagner, "Historical comparisons of different countries, at different times and places, show that in the case of culturally progressive peoples . . . we can point to a regular expansion of the activity of the state and of public agencies in general . . . The central and local governments constantly undertake new functions while they perform both old and new functions more completely and efficiently. In this way, increasingly more of the economic needs of the people . . . are satisfied more fully and in a better manner by the state and these other public agents. The clear proof of this development is seen in the increase of the financial needs of the central and local governments." (See Aldolph Wagner, *Grundlegung der Politichen Oekonomie*, 3rd ed., Leipzig: C. F. Winter'sche Verlags Handlung, 1893, p. 893, as quoted in: Frederick C. Mosher and Orville F. Poland, *The Costs of American Governments-Facts, Trends, Myths* (New York: Dodd, Mead, 1964), p. 20.

4. Peacock and Wiseman, *op. cit.*, p. xxiii.

and Wiseman call "the displacement effect." Economists do not assert that all social disturbances inevitably are accompanied by lasting increases in governmental expenditures, nor that the more permanent influences on the behavior of government, such as population shifts and growth, are irrelevant, but it is inescapable that the growth of government has been a reality in the twentieth century and can be traced, using economic statistics, to major periods of social disturbance. As Peacock and Wiseman observe, the upward displacement of government revenues and expenditures came during and after two major wars in Great Britain.

The displacement effect often is followed by an "inspection process" in society. The disturbance calls to the attention of citizens and governments new knowledge about their own society. Thus, for example, public education was seen as a desirable and social goal when the Napoleonic wars first exposed the educational deficiencies in the European lower classes. More recently, the development of British social services in World War II, which were the result of war-time bombing that had made the replacement of voluntary hospital services necessary, eventually grew into the National Health Service.[5]

Concomitant with the displacement effect and the ensuing inspection process, at least in some societies, is the "concentration process." The concentration process does not refer so much to increases in the total volume of government expenditures, but rather to the "concentration" of those expenditures at *higher* levels of government. Obviously, the concentration process can occur only in societies that have a federal form of government, such as the United States; thus, the national government acquires responsibility for public services, such as welfare, that traditionally have been the preserve of state or local governments. As we shall see in our chapter on federalism, such a concentration process has been occurring in the United States with particular rapidity during the last twenty years.

The concentration process is quite distinct from the displacement effect in the view of most economists. Economic reality, rather than social disturbance, works toward the increasing centralization of economic power by the national government relative to the state and local units. Thus, "local autonomy usually has many defenders, and its preservation is frequently a matter of political importance. At the same time, economic development produces changes in the technically efficient level of government, and also produces demands for equality of treatment (*e.g.*, in services such as education) over wider geographical areas. . . . Clearly, this

5. R. M. Titmuss, "Problems of Social Policy," *History of the Second World War*, Civil Series, London, 1950, Chapter xv, as cited in Peacock and Wiseman, *op. cit.*, p. xxviii.

evolution is distinct from the displacement effect, since the forces just described operate in normal as well as disturbed times." [6]

Even so, social disturbances which displace the level of government of expenditures upward also are going to have some bearing on the concentration process. Traditional political considerations often are swept aside during periods of major disturbance in a society, and some of these traditional political considerations may concern certain functions of government that "always" have been the exclusive preserve of sub-national jurisdictions. As Peacock and Wiseman observe, "Periods of displacement are also going to be periods of interest from the viewpoint of the concentration process." [7]

Technobureaucracy: bureaucracy as
interpreter of technology

There is a third theory (there are many more, of course, but we are considering only the major explanations in this chapter), and one that owes much of its intellectual development to the futurists as opposed to the political scientists and economists.[8] Like the pluralist and displacement/concentration models, this explanation does not contradict any of the others; instead it merely amplifies the preceding two, and it will serve as this book's primary explanation of the burgeoning bureaucracy. It holds that bureaucracy is the inescapable political expression of technology. Technology, in this sense, refers to the growing complexity of society that has been brought about not merely by scientific discoveries of profound social significance, but by the proliferating economic and social interrelationships that are associated with industrialization. Not only are purely technical complexities evident, but new and varied social relationships become apparent. "Technology," in this context, has certain conceptual relationships to what economists call "technical efficiency," and to what political scientists call "values," which are represented to policymakers by interest groups competing for resources in a pluralist political system; thus, in the political scientist's sense, both "technology" and "efficiency" are but two of many "values" to be "represented" by groups in the political process.

6. *Ibid.*, p. xxv.
7. *Ibid.*, p. xxv.
8. Actually, there is no single literature of which I am aware that explains the growth of bureaucracy in precisely the same terms that I am using in the text. Nevertheless, a number of authors identified with "futures research" seem to imply it, or state the explanation in different ways. A popular example would be Theodore Roszak's *The Making of a Counter Culture* (Garden City, N.Y.: Doubleday, 1969).

But the futurists' argument that technology lies behind the growth of government goes further, and perhaps has more power as an explanation, than either the theories of the political scientists or the economists, and among the best empirical examples of the futurists' interpretation is provided by America itself. Ours is a technological society; indeed, the United States may be the archetype of technological societies. Computers, automation, and advanced modes of transportation and communication are developed in America first. The rest of the world adopts our technologies as experiments when they are already commonplace here. But technology brings with it new and interesting political problems. ("May you live in interesting times" is considered a curse in China.) Consider a simple one—highways.

Highway technology is one that most people can understand. The Romans, indeed, understood highways as a technology supremely well 2500 years ago. Yet American society has grown so complex that highways have taken on new meanings as a technology. For example, in the late 1960s the U.S. Department of Housing and Urban Development (HUD) found that large and disproportionate numbers of urban rioters, notably in Watts and Newark, had lived in the riot areas for a year or less. Moreover, these people had recently moved to the riot-torn areas because they had been displaced from their original homes by such projects as urban renewal and highway construction. As a result, neighborhood "fabrics" were torn and former residents scattered—people became new residents in other areas; they had nothing to lose and no neighborhood to protect. Hence, building large highways through large urban areas, according to HUD officials, may have influenced the intensity of the urban riots of the late 1960s. Similarly, the interstate highway program has also spawned a major national debate over what is known as a "balanced" transportation policy. The central question in this debate is, "Do we want the automobile to remain the central mode of transportation in America at the expense of other alternative forms of transit, such as buses, trains, and subways?"

In sum, although most of us consider the highway to be relatively simple technology, it has resulted in complicated social and political problems that ultimately must be settled by the public at large. But how is the public to understand the more complex aspects of technological problems? Highways provide only one example; there are many others. Consider the problem of the computer and its role in the protection of privacy and in the gathering of social data on which to form public policy— where is the line to be drawn between the right to privacy, the need for information, and the right to know? Or consider the environment and its relationship with the energy dilemma—where does full employment end and the potential degradation of the earth begin? Still another problem is the population explosion—where does the right to life end and the rights of the individual woman begin? Of course, these are not merely technological questions; they are also deeply moral and ethical ones. Technology, in the forms of industrialization, "the pill," and electronic data processing techniques, to mention only a few, has injected new layers of complexity that are only beginning to be understood by experts in their respective fields. Yet the political questions and the public problems that these technologies and others raise require that policies concerning them be formulated in the most broadly public sense conceivable. Nevertheless, the question stands: How is the public in a democracy to understand such issues as they pertain to these extraordinarily complex and technical questions?

The answer that has emerged in fact, if not necessarily in theory, is the public bureaucracy. Bureaucrats are hired to be specialists. They are, in a sense, experts in their particular fields. Because technology requires expertise, bureaucrats have been saddled with the responsibility of interpreting complex technological and political problems so that as many Americans as possible might understand the issues involved. Whether or not the bureaucrats do a particularly good job of this chore is another question altogether. But their abilities as specialists are one reason why they are there.

We have been suggesting in the preceding paragraphs that bureaucracy grows in large part because technology requires expertise, and bureaucrats are the political actors who have been saddled with the responsibility of interpreting and translating complex technological and social problems into policy. By adopting this explanation of the *raison d'etre* of the bureaucratic phenomenon as our primary thesis, we have posited a fundamental tension between bureaucracy and democracy. On the one hand are the bureaucrats-as-experts, the specialists with knowledge about particular professions and techniques. On the other hand are "the people," those who represent what are considered human values. To carry this dichotomy even further, we have the "computers"—the "technocrats" —squaring off against "humanity." This dichotomization, which obviously is grossly overdrawn, is nonetheless representative of the root tension between "the bureaucrats" and "the people." We consider this tension in upcoming chapters on organization theory, but for now it is enough to note that there is an inherent gap in any society between expertise, including the expertise of public administration, and populist democratic values.

Regardless of why the bureaucracy exists, and irrespective of why the number of bureaucrats has grown, the fact remains that the bureaucracy has power. The founding fathers of our nation never really addressed this "fourth branch" of government, nor did most of the founding fathers of other nations. Karl Marx, for example, never comprehended the power of bureaucracy, and the Soviet Union is as fine an example as any of a nation that has created a dictatorship of the bureaucrats that will likely never "wither away" in favor of a "dictatorship of the proletariat," as Marx predicted.

Staying power

[One major form of power that the bureaucracy has is simply its staying power.]Herbert Kaufman has completed the only empirical research on the staying power of public bureaucracies and concluded, reluctantly, that it is awesome. Kaufman wanted to find out whether or not government organizations in effect "lived forever." Specifically, Kaufman determined how many U.S. government agencies had "died" (that is, were actually phased out, not just changed in name) between 1923 and 1973. He found 175 identifiably separate agencies within the government in 1923. By 1973, not only were 109 of these same agencies still going strong, but the government agency "population" had exploded to 394 separate agencies by then. Only 15 percent of the original 175 agencies had disappeared.[Kaufman concluded that "the chances that an organization in 1923 would not only be alive in 1973 but in virtually the same status were quite good."]

Kaufman also compared the "death rate" of government agencies with the rate of business failures over the fifty-year period. He found that in any given year the rate of business failure exceeded the corresponding agency death rate. In fact, when the figures were averaged, the annual rate of business failures was more than twice the annual death rate of the government agencies.

Kaufman's study is the first of its kind and has not been repeated at the state or local levels. Nevertheless, it is useful because its findings imply what many Americans already believe about government: [That government organizations are indeed "immortal" and that their growth cannot be stopped. Although Kaufman's research indicates that this con-

---

9. Herbert Kaufman, *Are Government Organizations Immortal?* (Washington: Brookings Institution, 1976), p. 34.

tention is not completely true, it is true that government organizations endure a relatively long time. Whether or not they in fact outlive their usefulness is a question that Kaufman did not address.

True, it is difficult to assess in empirical terms whether or not an agency does outlive its usefulness, but it is clear that bureaucrats have developed advanced survival skills and, as a result, may have stretched the "normal" life spans of their agencies until it is questionable whether or not some "immortal agencies" continue to serve the public interest. Consider the infamous example of the International Screwthread Commission, which one observer called the "commission that will not die." [10] Formed in 1918 by Congress with a stipulation that its life span would not exceed sixty days, it survived until 1933 when President Franklin Roosevelt ordered it abolished. The commission simply reformed itself as the Interdepartmental Screwthread Commission and eventually was re-established as the present commission. Although most observers agree that the commission's work was accomplished many years ago, it still is going strong.

Political power

Perhaps even more important than staying power is policy-making power. It is increasingly obvious in the twentieth century that bureaucracy is the major policy-making arm of government. Consider some examples: Two little black girls are sterilized by family planning officials in Alabama. The U.S. Food and Drug Administration reverses past policy and bans cyclamates because of a single but determined biologist in its employ. A vice president of the United States resigns as the unanticipated but ultimate consequence of an investigation by a lone Justice Department lawyer in Maryland. The Pentagon Papers are released by a conscience-stricken analyst in the Air Force's RAND Corporation. Watergate erupts as the result of premeditated law-breaking by members of the Cabinet, the White House staff, and a former president of the United States.

All the preceding instances are examples of public policy being made by public administrators. Some of these policies are good, others bad. Some are confined in their social impact, others are reweaving the fabric of the American polity. All of these public policies, however, were made primarily by bureaucrats, with little or no influence from legislators or judges, and all affect the lives of people.

10. Jim Clark, "The International Screwthread Commission," *The Washington Monthly*, as reprinted in Nicholas Henry, ed., *Doing Public Administration: Exercises, Essays, and Cases* (Boston: Allyn and Bacon, 1978), pp. 41–42.

Public administrators also appear to have wrested control over critical policy areas from elected officials, both legislators and chief executives. A number of empirical analyses of city council members and city managers, for example, have concluded that the city manager plays a significant policy-making role in the urban political context, despite an image of apolitical administrator. A detailed study of San Francisco Bay Area city managers found that most of the city managers responding perceived clear political roles for themselves.[11] Interestingly, the amount of education city managers have tended to determine whether they view themselves as "politicians" or as "administrators." Those managers who saw themselves in a highly political context tended to have majored in the social sciences or to have pursued masters degrees in public administration, but all of the responding managers felt that they should (and did) participate in the initiation, formulation, and presentation of policy proposals to their councils.

Bureaucrats and legislators

In a much larger national study conducted by the International City Management Association,[12] nearly 90 percent of city managers in 1,744 responding cities (a response rate of 70 percent) indicated that they always or nearly always participated in forming municipal policy, and this percentage was even higher in the larger cities. More than 60 percent of the managers felt that they played a leading role in making policy and, in an unusual aside, more than 12 percent reported that they always or nearly always gave political help to incumbent candidates up for reelection to the city council. Indeed, members of city councils often readily accept this policy-making role by a nonelected administrator. In her study of city councils, Betty A. Zisk found that most council members depended heavily upon the advice of the professional bureaucrats in making policy.[13]

Studies of other governmental bodies also tend to validate the hypothesis that public administrators are the policy makers. For example, in a classic study of policy making in school boards, which are usually

11. Ronald A. Loveridge, *The City Manager and Legislative Policy* (Indianapolis: Bobbs-Merrill, 1971).

12. Robert J. Huntley and Robert J. McDonald, "Urban Managers: Managerial Style and Social Roles," *1975 Municipal Yearbook* (Washington: International City Management Association, 1975), pp. 149–59.

13. Betty A. Zisk, *Local Interest Politics: A One-Way Street* (Indianapolis: Bobbs-Merrill, 1973), p. 58.

composed of members elected by the community, it was found that the professional school superintendent was the major formulator of board policy: "School governance has never completely fallen under the sway of the superintendent's office, but there is no question that the first half of the twentieth century saw enormous gains of power for the office." [14] In fact, the researchers concluded that in comparison to city managers in council–manager governments, superintendents exercised relatively more power over their boards than managers did over their councils. [15]

Bureaucrats and the elected executive

Just as the public bureaucrats have gained and are gaining autonomy as policy makers at the expense of legislators, public bureaucrats have also taken political independence from elected chief executives. Consider, in this light, Richard M. Nixon's effort to gain control over the federal bureaucracy between 1968 and 1974. Nixon, at least during his first term, attempted to work through the apparatus established by the Constitution for executing his duties as chief executive. He followed tradition and appointed a relatively balanced Cabinet of distinguished men and women, most of whom had their own national constituencies. Nixon had every logical reason to believe that this stratagem would be an effective means of accomplishing his program objectives. He had been elected president with the largest national vote in history and, for the most part, the people who he appointed to top Cabinet positions were persons of substantial abilities. By 1970, however, Nixon recognized that his managerial "game plan" would not work, and he began to develop what Richard P. Nathan has called Nixon's "counterbureaucracy," in an effort to "grab the reins more firmly." [16] Nixon's counterbureaucracy did not work at all well. Although Nixon enlarged his White House staff significantly (making it the biggest staff in history), his appointees "simply could not get a handle on the multitudinous field of domestic affairs. White House aides could not even keep track of each other, much less the operations of all the domestic agencies." [17] Thus the best that Nixon could hope to gain by his counterbureaucracy strategy was a holding operation until more sweeping reforms could be implemented.

Frustrated by a Democratic Congress, Nixon again tried to establish

14. Harmon Zeigler and M. Kent Jennings, with the assistance of G. Wayne Peak, *Governing American Schools: Political Interaction in Local School Districts* (North Scituate, Mass.: Duxbury, 1974), p. 27.

15. *Ibid.*, p. 251.

16. Richard P. Nathan, *The Plot That Failed: Nixon and the Administrative Presidency* (New York: John Wiley, 1975), p. 61.

17. *Ibid.*

control over "his" bureaucracy in 1971 with his announcement of "reorganization plans" that could be implemented without legislation; the objective was to dub a new "super Cabinet" as "the president's men," and the bureaucracy would report to them. This strategy, which came to its full fruition in 1972 and 1973, also entailed replacing the tradition of appointing representative, distinguished, and able people to top-level Cabinet posts with the scheme of selecting relatively little-known people who were intensely loyal to Nixon and whose dismissal or shifting to other posts would cause little publicity.

A second component of the strategy was to impound and reduce the budget; for a while, this very effectively blocked the policy intentions of Congress. Nixon was able to stop entire programs through the impoundment device and, as Nathan notes, "few more direct ways could be imagined to take on the bureaucracy." [18]

A third feature of what Nathan calls Nixon's administrative presidency was to use his reorganization plans to give the president's loyalists powerful positions in his government, and thereby to make policy choices. For example, reorganization of the executive branch was used to abolish completely the programs of the Office of Economic Opportunity that had been established under Lyndon Johnson.

Finally, the administrative presidency strategy focussed on the politics of regulation, notably rewriting standing federal regulations in various areas in such a way that certain policy programs were effectively curtailed or even abolished.

These four basic strategies to gain control over his own bureaucracy derived from a conclusion that Nixon and his chief aide for domestic policy, John Ehrlichman, had drawn as early as 1971: "Operations is policy." As Nathan observes, "Much of the day-to-day management of domestic programs—regulation writing, grant approval, and budget apportionment—actually involves policy-making. Getting control over these processes was the aim of the President's strategy for domestic government in his second term." [19] For better or worse, however, this strategy failed; Ehrlichman was dismissed by the president in 1973, and Watergate was flooding the Oval Office. As Nathan states:

> It was all for naught .... the White House hold over the domestic agencies in these final days of the Nixon Presidency was all but non-existent. ... A close aide to John Mitchell, named at the start of the second term as director of the Law Enforcement Assistance Administration in the Justice Department, was one of the few brave souls in what he thought was a private moment to speak about these new conditions.

18. *Ibid.*, p. 74.
19. *Ibid.*, p. 62.

He said he was his own boss and didn't check with anyone about his decisions. "There is no White House anymore." [20]

The point in reviewing Nixon's fervent efforts to gain control over his own bureaucracy is to illustrate the fact that public administrators can be extraordinarily independent of those who, by law, are their superiors. The bureaucracy is powerful, and bureaucrats are increasingly autonomous. It is clear that in the twentieth century the public bureaucracy has waxed into a policy-making institution of no mean proportion.

Is this development "good" or "bad" for the public? We will not attempt to answer that question here, but the point stands that bureaucratic power is real, growing, and in the views of many, worrisome.

KNOWLEDGE MANAGEMENT: THE BASE OF BUREAUCRATIC POWER

How has the bureaucracy grown so in political importance in modern America? The fundamental response must be that, in a highly complex and technologically oriented society such as ours, those who control and manipulate information gain power. The old saw that "knowledge is power" never has been more true than it is today. As Max Weber, the famous theorist on bureaucracy observed nearly a century ago:

> The pure interest of the bureaucracy in power, however, is efficacious far beyond those areas where purely functional interests make for secrecy. . . . in facing a parliament, a bureaucracy, out of a sure power instinct, fights every attempt of the parliament to gain knowledge by means of its own experts or from interest groups . . . . bureaucracy naturally welcomes a poorly informed and hence a powerless parliament—at least in so far as ignorance somehow agrees with the bureaucracy's interests. . . . [21]

More modern administrative theorists, though usually less savage in their assessments, have not seen fit to counter Weber's basic statement and, indeed, have reinforced it. As one contributor to a symposium on this very topic, published in *Public Administration Review* (the field's major journal), summarized, "Administration is knowledge. Knowledge is power. Administration is power," continuing that "this simplistic syllogism" is a major reality of our post-industrial age. [22] In a more empirical mode, in-

20. *Ibid.*, p. 76.

21. Max Weber, *From Max Weber: Essays in Sociology*, H. H. Gerth and C. Wright Mills, eds. (New York: Oxford University Press, 1946), p. 233.

22. James D. Carroll, "Service, Knowledge, and Choice: The Future as Post-Industrial Administration," *Public Administration Review* 35 (November-December 1975), p. 578. It is recommended that the reader see the Symposium on Knowledge Management, James D. Carroll and Nicholas Henry, Symposium Editors, in the same issue.

vestigators have noted the relationship between organizational complexity in political settings and the subsequent control that appointed administrators appear to gain. In the study of school boards cited earlier, it was found that the professional school superintendent had far more power relative to members of the school board in the big cities, substantially less power in the suburbs, and even less power in the small towns, indicating that, as the political system became more complex, administrators gained more power.[23]

A similar conclusion can be drawn from the study conducted by the International City Management Association of city managers and city councils. The most consistent finding in the study was that, in cities of all types, more than 60 percent of the managers voiced strong opposition to a full-time, professionally paid city council: "This item evoked the strongest expression of opinion in the entire series of questions." [24] Moreover, a majority of managers opposed the provision of a full-time separate staff for the mayor and 77 percent of the respondents reported that they always or nearly always resisted council involvement in "management issues." These strongly held opinions on the part of city managers indicate that the appointed urban chief executive is well aware that one of his major bases of political power is the control of information. A full-time professional staff for the mayor and a full-time, hard-working city council that is interested in "management issues" (recall, in this context, Nixon's and Ehrlichman's accurate observation that "operations is policy") are anathema to the typical city manager. His is an example of the politics of expertise, a peculiar kind of political control that provides the manager with an ability to have his policies adopted by elected officials primarily because he controls a major source of information, the city bureaucracy itself.

The illegitimate bureaucrat

Although some analysts (notably Peter Woll and Norton Long)[25] have argued that the growing power of the bureaucracy is in fact in the public interest, the people themselves obviously have reservations about the increase in bureaucratic power. In 1964, for example, Senator Barry Goldwater, as the Republican presidential candidate, complained about the "runaway bureaucracy;" in 1972 Senator George McGovern, as the Democratic presidential candidate, bemoaned the "faceless bureaucracy." It is

23. Zeigler and Jennings, op. cit., pp. 177–78.
24. Huntley and McDonald, op. cit., p. 150.
25. Peter Woll, The American Bureaucracy (New York: W. W. Norton, 1963) and Norton E. Long, "Bureaucracy and Constitutionalism," American Political Science Review 46 (September 1952), 651–59.

difficult to conceive of two mainstream politicians more completely in opposition than Senators Goldwater and McGovern. Nevertheless, they had one thing in common; like most people, they did not like bureaucrats. Other examples of the public's frustration over what they perceive to be an overly bureaucratized state are manifest. One poll, for instance, found that the federal government was ranked next to last among fifteen national institutions, and the only institution ranked lower was that of "the President and administration." [26]

Legislating against the knowledge monopoly

One expression of the popular distrust of bureaucracy has been the spate of legislation enacted in the 1960s and 1970s concerning "freedom of information." Although some of this legislation, such as the Administrative Procedure Act, goes back to the 1940s, it nonetheless stands that the Freedom of Information Act of 1967 and its subsequent amendments in 1974 (together with "little freedom of information acts" enacted by virtually every state), the National Environmental Policy Act, the Fair Credit Reporting Act, the Federal Advisory Committee Act, and the Privacy Act all reflect a growing popular concern over the power of the bureaucracy that has been facilitated by the bureaucrats' control over information.

Of these relatively new laws, perhaps the national and state Freedom of Information Acts are the most far-reaching, and public bureaucrats, in defending their hegemony over their files, have developed innovative strategies.[27]

These tactics to preserve bureaucratic secrecy have been effective: A requester of information can wait more than two years before all the tactics and appeals are fully played out and the case is brought to court; in 1976 more than 600 cases were pending in court under the federal act.

Related to the right to know is the practice of "executive privilege." Executive privilege refers to the president's custom of refusing to inform Congress, the courts, and the public about various matters of public importance on the grounds that it is privileged information. Executive privilege, or the "principle of confidentiality," is a "custom" because it is based on nothing more than precedent; no explicit constitutional or statutory basis for executive privilege exists.

In sum, though bureaucrats have displayed a talent for retaining their

---

26. Willard L. Rogers and Lloyd D. Johnson, *Attitudes Towards Business and Other American Institutions* (Ann Arbor, Mich.: Institute for Social Research, University of Michigan, 1974). Cited in Nathan, *op. cit.*, pp. 83–84.

27. For a cogent description of these tactics, see: Nicholas Wade, "Officials Thwart Right To Know," *Science* 175 (February 4, 1972), 498–502.

control over information (and thus their power base), they may have done so at the potential expense of their legitimacy.

The red tape hassle

The interest displayed by the people (and by the other branches of government) in breaking up the bureaucracy's control of information appears to stem not only from a widespread feeling of frustration over bureaucracy but also from an even deeper underlying belief that government no longer works for the people. And in fact, the public bureaucracy on occasion appears to hassle the people far more than seems necessary. For example, the Federal Paperwork Commission, appointed by President Gerald Ford in 1975, calculated that government-generated paperwork would cover 4.5 million cubic feet per year, at an average annual cost exceeding $100 billion; $43 billion of this sum was paid for by the federal government and more than $57 billion was borne by private industry. The commission, claiming that "a substantial portion of this cost is unnecessary," cited as examples the school that turned down a $4,500 federal grant because it would have required $6,000 in paperwork and the company that had to comply with federal demands for 8,800 reports from eighteen different agencies in a single year.[28]

The examples are as endless as the paperwork itself, but suffice it to say that, as Kaufman has observed, the impact of all this red tape on the public "is extremely broad . . . the number of different forms authorized for distribution to the public by federal agencies exceeds five thousand." [29] Hence, citizens are dismayed "because the torrent of requirements descending on them is too overwhelming for them to comply with. Conscientious, upright citizens are often distressed when they find themselves in violation of government directives, yet they simply cannot keep up with the flood." [30]

Out of control?

More serious, perhaps, than the hassling factor is a deep-rooted feeling among the people that they are losing control of their own government, although surely this sense of a loss of control is shared by public managers themselves. The president's reorganization project found in its examination of personnel management in the federal government that

28. Commission of Federal Paperwork, *Final Report* (Washington, D.C.: U.S. Government Printing Office, 1978).

29. Herbert Kaufman, *Red Tape: Its Origins, Uses, and Abuses* (Washington, D.C.: The Brookings Institution, 1977), p. 7.

30. *Ibid.*, p. 6.

firing public employees is difficult and promoting them appears to be done more by rote than by judgment. In 1977, for example, about 500,000 federal employees received within-grade increases, and only 700 were denied salary increases.[31] It perhaps is little wonder that one critic of the civil service called the federal government "the incompetent's best friend." [32]

A Parable of Mice and Men

The following incident really happened in 1977 and 1978, and it is recorded here to convey how silly the bureaucracy can be on occasion. Silliness is an innate component of legitimacy; the sillier that an institution (such as the bureaucracy) appears to the public, the less legitimacy it has. And, in the following occurrence, the federal bureaucracy was very silly indeed.

It is not only Congress but also the White House mice that have been teaching Jimmy Carter the limits of Presidential power.

When the members of the Carter entourage arrived from their country homes in Plains, Ga., they were surprised to discover that their new city mansion at 1600 Pennsylvania Avenue was plagued with mice.

Indeed, the story goes that one night when President Carter was deep in conference with Frank B. Moore, his Congressional liaison chief, in his little hideaway office, two mice scampered across the carpet. The alarm went out to the General Services Administration, which does the housekeeping for Federal buildings, and the President turned to more weighty affairs.

But the mouse problem proved intractable. Just before the Latin American heads of government arrived in Washington for the signing of the Panama Canal treaties, one small gray creature climbed up the inside of a White House hall and died. The Oval Office was bathed with the odor of dead mouse.

Desperately, the President called the G.S.A. again. But the agency insisted that it had killed all the mice inside the White House and that therefore this mouse must have come from outside the building.

According to the agency, this meant that the offensive mouse was an "outside" mouse, a wayward ward of the Interior Department, which tends the grounds around the White House.

But the Interior Department demurred. It must be an "inside" mouse, said Interior officials. Moreover, regardless of its origins, it was obviously now the G.S.A.'s worry because the carcass was imbedded inside a White House wall.

31. Alan K. Campbell, "Civil Service Reform: A New Commitment," *Public Administration Review* 38 (March-April 1978), 102.

32. Leonard Reed, "Firing a Federal Employee: The Impossible Dream," *The Washington Monthly* (July-August 1977), 36.

"I can't even get a damned mouse out of my office," the President moaned to Jody Powell, his press secretary.

In frustration, he summoned two officials from each agency and lined them up before him in the stench of the Oval Office to break the bureaucratic deadlock. As a compromise solution, one aide quipped, 'it took an interagency task force to get that mouse out of here.'

Now, vigilant against future crises, the White House has gone on the offensive. As Mr. Powell remarked, "You can't open a desk drawer around here without getting your hand caught in a rat trap."

New York Times

There also is reason to believe that people realize that the public bureaucracy is not especially representative of the people themselves. In 1977, for example, only 4.2 percent of GS-15s in the federal service (which is one of the top management levels in the federal bureaucracy) were women, and 5.8 percent were minorities.[33]

Nor are competing economic interests represented in the public bureaucracy as well as they might be. Of the 1,159 federal advisory committees—bodies that often have substantial influence on the making of public policy as it is formed deep in the bowels of the bureaucracy— nearly 3,000 of the 23,375 committee memberships available were held by employees of only twenty-eight corporations and fourteen universities. There were 173 individuals in 1977 who served on four or more of these 1,159 advisory committees (one individual was a member of eleven of the federal advisory committees), and who represented primarily corporations, organized labor, and the university community.[34]

Although the connection between such statistics and the public's distrust of the bureaucracy is sensed rather than proven, the consequences of such disillusionment with government in general and bureaucracy in particular are real, if difficult to measure. How does one assess malaise and hostility among a nation's citizens? Yet, in other respects, the consequences are all too easily measured, and perhaps the most obvious result of the public's disaffection with its governments is the rising tax revolt being felt among America's grassroots governments.

REVOLT!

In the late 1970s the often-touted but seldom substantive "taxpayers' revolt" began gaining momentum. In 1978 seventeen states enacted tax relief measures ranging from spending limitations to across-the-board

33. Campbell, *op. cit.*, p. 102.
34. William Delaney, "Business, Labor, Education Dominate Boards," *The Washington Star*, October 27, 1977, syndicated nationally.

tax slashes. All these measures were approved by popular votes of the people. The most spectacular tax reduction battle was waged in California. The Jarvis–Gann initiative, after gathering more than 1.5 million signatures, became Proposition 13 in a statewide referendum. It called for a draconian slash of all residential and commercial property taxes to 1 percent of the property's 1975–76 market value, and these taxes would be allowed to go up by no more than 2 percent a year until the property was resold. This amounted to a 57 percent decrease in property taxes; it would reduce property tax revenues from $12 billion annually to $5 billion. Howard Jarvis, chief sponsor of Proposition 13, crustily claimed that his initiative would rid California of government "of the bureaucrats, by the bureaucrats, and for the bureaucrats."

The California governor promptly labelled Proposition 13 a "meat-ax approach" to public finance and introduced Proposition 8, which would have provided "only" a 30 percent tax relief in contrast to Proposition 13's 57 percent. More importantly, Proposition 8 gave homeowners a better break than Proposition 13, which did not discriminate between homeowners and commercial interests.

Proposition 13 passed by a landslide. A record number of Californians went to the polls, and they voted nearly two-to-one (66 percent to 34 percent) in favor of it; the countermeasure, Proposition 8, was defeated handily. Most of the voters in favor of Proposition 13 were homeowners.

Proposition 13 was the fourth attempt of its kind in California during the past decade. It was also the most radical. What was its appeal?

Clearly, Californians were victims of a madly speculative real estate market (at one point, house values in some areas were increasing at the rate of 10 percent a month!) and an inflexible (and efficiently administered) property assessment system. As a result "horror stories" were rife of homeowners witnessing their property tax bills shoot to twice and even ten times the total they were paying only one to three years earlier.

It appears that many states (as Idaho and Nevada already have done) may vote in their own versions of Proposition 13 in the future, and this urge apparently is the result of a combination of skyrocketing inflation, a larger tax bite (the total tax rate rose from less than 24 percent of the Gross National Product in 1956 to more than 30 percent in 1976), and a popular resentment toward national, state, and local tax policies. As a proportion of the GNP, the national tax burden has been declining while state and local taxes have been increasing. This relationship obviously has not been lost on the average taxpayer, who no doubt is aware, at least viscerally, that the states collect more than $100 billion every year from their citizens and that many often end the fiscal year with substantial surpluses. California, for example, had more than a $5 billion surplus when Proposition 13 was enacted.

Nevertheless, it is inaccurate to conclude that the taxpayers' revolt is confined to state and local governments; it is a national phenomenon, too. Americans have favored, according to surveys, a constitutional amendment requiring a balanced federal budget for a number of years; in 1979, a Gallup poll showed that respondents favored such an amendment by nearly six-to-one.[35] By the same year, 30 of 34 states required had called for a constitutional convention to enact such an amendment.

Perhaps the mood of the rebellious taxpayers of the 1980s is best summed up by Grayce, a lady in a novel by P. G. Wodehouse. When explaining why Grayce is trying to smuggle a necklace through customs, an acquaintance states, "Grayce doesn't like the idea of paying duty. She says it's such a waste, she says the government has got more money than is good for it already and would only spend it."

EXPLORING BUREAUCRACY, UNDERSTANDING GOVERNMENT

Whether or not the government has more money than is good for it, as Grayce archly observed, is a question that, ultimately can be decided only by the taxpayers, but as this chapter emphasizes, for the better part of the twentieth century, the public bureaucracy has been not only at the center of public policy formation and the major political determinant of where this country is going, but also it expresses more articulately than any other American institution the mounting tensions between the values of technological elitism and democratic mass. The government bureaucracy also is the biggest conglomerate of organizations and employs more highly educated professional people than any other institution in the United States. It appears, therefore, that the public bureaucracy is worthy of some study, whether as an intellectual enterprise (so that we may learn more about how our country works), as an altruistic endeavor (so that we may learn how to promote the public interest more effectively), or as a self-serving investment (so that we will be more qualified for a job in government). The study and practice of public bureaucracy is called public administration, and public administration is what this book is about. We examine the peculiar nature and evolution of public administration as a field of academic enterprise in the following chapter.

SUPPLEMENTAL BIBLIOGRAPHY

APPLEBY, PAUL H., *Big Democracy*. New York: Knopf, 1945.
——— *Morality and Administration in Democratic Government*. Baton Rouge, La.: Louisiana State University Press, 1952.

35. George Gallup, "Poll Shows Tremendous Support for Balanced-Budget Amendment," *Arizona Republic* (February 25, 1979). Gallup has conducted similar polls since 1976, with comparable results.

BEER, STAFFORD, "Managing Modern Complexity," *The Management of Information and Knowledge.* Panel on Science and Technology (11th meeting). Proceedings before the Committee on Science and Astronautics, U.S. House of Representatives, 91st Congress, Second Session, January 27, 1970, No. 15. Washington, D.C.: U.S. Government Printing Office, 1970.

BURKE, JOHN G., ed. *The New Technology and Human Values* (2nd ed.), Belmont, Calif.: Wadsworth, 1972.

CHARLESWORTH, JAMES C., ed., *Theory and Practice of Public Administration: Scope, Objectives, and Methods,* Monograph 8. Philadelphia: American Academy of Political and Social Science and the American Society for Public Administration, October, 1968.

CROZIER, MICHEL, *The Bureaucratic Phenomenon.* Chicago: University of Chicago Press, 1964.

GOLEMBIEWSKI, ROBERT T., *Public Administration as a Developing Discipline, Part I: Perspectives on Past and Present; Part II: Organization Development as One of a Future Family of Miniparadigms.* New York: Marcel Dekker, 1977.

HENRY, NICHOLAS, "Bureaucracy, Technology, and Knowledge Management," *Public Administration Review,* 35 (November-December 1975), 572–78.

HILL, MICHAEL J., *The Sociology of Public Administration.* New York: Crane, Russak, 1972.

HUMMEL, RALPH R., *The Bureaucratic Experience.* New York: St. Martin's Press, 1977.

KRAMER, FRED A., ed., *Perspectives on Public Bureaucracy* (2nd ed.), Cambridge, Mass.: Winthrop, 1977.

LAMBRIGHT, HENRY W., *Governing Science and Technology.* New York: Oxford University Press, 1976.

LEWIS, EUGENE, *American Politics in a Bureaucratic Age: Citizens, Constituents, Clients, and Victims.* Cambridge, Mass.: Winthrop, 1977.

MOSHER, FREDERICK C., ed., *American Public Administration: Past, Present, Future.* Tuscaloosa, Ala.: University of Alabama Press, 1975.

ROURKE, FRANCIS E., *Bureaucracy, Politics, and Public Policy* (2nd ed.), Boston: Little, Brown, 1976.

—— ed., *Bureaucratic Power in National Politics* (3rd ed.), Boston: Little, Brown, 1978.

SCHUMAN, DAVID, *Bureaucracy, Organizations, and Administration: A Political Primer.* New York: Macmillan, 1976.

SEITZ, STEVEN THOMAS, *Bureaucracy, Policy, and the Public.* St. Louis: C. V. Mosby, 1978.

SIMON, HERBERT A., *Administrative Behavior: Study of Decision-Making Processes in Administrative Organization* (3rd ed.), New York: Free Press, 1976.

——, DONALD W. SMITHBURG, and VICTOR A. THOMPSON, *Public Administration.* New York: Knopf, 1950.

ZEIGLER, L. HARMON, and HARVEY J. TUCKER, *The Quest for Responsive Government.* North Scituate, Mass.: Duxbury, 1978.

public administration's
ninety years
in a quandary

chapter 2

∫ Public administration is a broad-ranging and amorphous combination of theory and practice. Its purpose is to promote a superior understanding of government and its relationship with the society it governs, as well as to encourage public policies more responsive to social needs and to institute managerial practices attuned to effectiveness, efficiency, and the deeper human requisites of the citizenry. Admittedly, the preceding sentence is itself rather broad-ranging and amorphous, but for our purposes it will suffice. There are, however, additional characteristics of public administration that fill out the model we shall be using in the following chapters.

As Stephen K. Bailey has noted, public administration is (or should be) concerned with the development of four kinds of theories: [1]

1. *descriptive theory*, or descriptions of hierarchical structures and relationships with their sundry task environments
2. *normative theory*, or the "value goals" of the field—that is, what

---

1. Stephen K. Bailey, "Objectives of the Theory of Public Administration," in *Theory and Practice of Public Administration: Scope, Objectives, and Methods*, James C. Charlesworth, ed. Monograph 8, (Philadelphia: American Academy of Political and Social Science, 1968), pp. 128–29.

public administrators (the practitioners) ought to do given their realm of decision alternatives, and what public administrationists (the scholars) ought to study and recommend to the practitioners in terms of policy

3. *assumptive theory,* or a rigorous understanding of the reality of administrative man, a theory that assumes neither angelic nor satanic models of the public bureaucrat

4. *instrumental theory,* or the increasingly refined managerial techniques for the efficient and effective attainment of public objectives

Taken together, Bailey's quartet of theories form three defining pillars of public administration: organizational behavior and the behavior of people in public organizations; the technology of management; and the public interest as it relates to individual ethical choice and public affairs.

In this chapter we review the successive definitional crises of public administration—that is, how the field has "seen itself" in the past. These paradigms of public administration are worth knowing, first, because one must know where the field has been to understand its present status and second, because this book represents a departure from past paradigms. We contend that public administration is unique, that it differs significantly from both political science (public administration's "mother discipline") and administrative science (public administration's traditional alter ego) in terms of developing certain facets of organization theory and techniques of management. Public administration differs from political science in its emphasis on bureaucratic structure and behavior and in its methodologies. Public administration differs from administrative science in that the evaluative techniques used by nonprofit public organizations are not the same as those used by profit-making private organizations, and in that profit-seeking organizations are considerably less constrained in considering the public interest in their decision-making structures and in the behavior of their administrators.

Public administration has developed as an academic field through a succession of five overlapping paradigms. As Robert T. Golembiewski has noted in a perceptive essay,[2] each phase may be characterized according to whether it has *locus* or *focus*. *Locus* is the institutional "where" of the field. A recurring locus of public administration is the government bureaucracy, but this has not always been the case and often this traditional locus has been blurred. *Focus* is the specialized "what" of the field. One focus of public administration has been the study of certain "principles of administration," but again, the foci of the discipline have altered with

2. Robert T. Golembiewski, *Public Administration as a Developing Discipline, Part I: Perspectives on Past and Present* (New York: Marcel Dekker, 1977).

the changing paradigms of public administration. As Golembiewski observes, the paradigms of public administration may be understood in terms of locus or focus; when one has been relatively sharply defined in academic circles, the other has been conceptually ignored and vice versa. We shall use the notion of loci and foci in reviewing the intellectual development of public administration.

THE BEGINNING

Woodrow Wilson largely set the tone for the early study of public administration in an essay entitled "The Study of Administration," published in the *Political Science Quarterly* in 1887. In it, Wilson observed that it "is getting harder to *run* a constitution than to frame one," and called for the bringing of more intellectual resources to bear in the management of the state. Wilson's seminal article has been variously interpreted by later scholars. Some have insisted that Wilson originated the "politics/administration dichotomy"—the naive distinction between "political" activity and "administrative" activity in public organizations that would plague the field for years to come. Other scholars have countered that Wilson was well aware that public administration was innately political in nature, and he made this point clear in his article. In reality Wilson himself seems ambivalent about what public administration really was. As Richard J. Stillman II concluded in a thorough and timely reconsideration of "The Study of Administration," Wilson failed

> to amplify what the study of administration actually entails, what the proper relationship should be between the administrative and political realms, and whether or not administrative study could ever become an abstract science akin to the natural sciences." [4]

Nevertheless, Wilson unquestionably posited one unambiguous thesis in his article that has had a lasting impact on the field: Public administration was worth studying. Political scientists would later create the first identifiable paradigm of public administration around Wilson's contention.

3. Woodrow Wilson, "The Study of Administration," *Political Science Quarterly* 2 (June 1887): 197–222; reprinted 50 (December 1941), 481–506.
4. Richard J. Stillman, II. "Woodrow Wilson and the Study of Administration: A New Look at an Old Essay," *American Political Science Review* 67 (June 1973), 587.

PARADIGM 1:
THE POLITICS/ADMINISTRATION DICHOTOMY, 1900–1926

Our benchmark dates for the Paradigm 1 period correspond to the publication of books written by Frank J. Goodnow and Leonard D. White; these dates like the years chosen as marking the later periods of the field, are only rough indicators. In *Politics and Administration* (1900), Goodnow contended that there were "two distinct functions of government," which he identified with the title of his book. "Politics," said Goodnow, "has to do with policies or expressions of the state will," while administration "has to do with the execution of these policies." [5] Separation of powers provided the basis of the distinction. The legislative branch, aided by the interpretive abilities of the judicial branch, expressed the will of the state and formed policy; the executive branch administered those policies impartially and apolitically.

The emphasis of Paradigm 1 was on locus—where public administration should be. Clearly, in the view of Goodnow and his fellow public administrationists, public administration should center in the government's bureaucracy. While the legislature and judiciary admittedly had their quanta of "administration," their primary responsibility and function remained the expression of the state will. The initial conceptual legitimation of this locus-centered definition of the field, and one that would wax increasingly problematic for academics and practitioners alike, became known as the politics/administration dichotomy.

The phrase that came to symbolize this distinction between politics and administration was, "there is no Republican way to build a road." The reasoning was that there could only be one "right" way to spread tarmac—the administrative engineer's way. What was ignored in this statement, however, was that there was indeed a Republican way to decide whether the road needed building, a Republican way to choose the location for the road, a Republican way to purchase the land, a Republican way to displace the people living in the road's way, and most certainly a Republican way to let contracts for the road. There was also, and is, a Democratic way, a Socialist way, a Liberal way, even an Anarchist way to make these "administrative" decisions as well. In retrospect the politics/administration dichotomy posited by Goodnow and his academic progeny was, at best, naive. But many years would pass before this would be fully realized within public administration's ranks.

---

5. Frank J. Goodnow, *Politics and Administration* (New York: Macmillan 1900), pp. 10–11.

Public administration received its first serious attention from scholars during this period largely as a result of the "public service movement" that was taking place in American universities in the early part of this century. Political science, as a report issued in 1914 by the Committee on Instruction in Government of the American Political Science Association stated, was concerned with training for citizenship, professional preparations such as law and journalism, training "experts and to prepare specialists for governmental positions," and educating for research work. Public administration, therefore, was a clear and significant subfield of political science. In 1912 a Committee on Practical Training for Public Service was established under the auspices of the American Political Science Association, and in 1914 its report recommended, with unusual foresight, that special "professional schools" were needed to train public administrators, and that new technical degrees might also be necessary for this purpose.[6] This committee formed the nucleus of the Society for the Promotion of Training for the Public Service, founded in 1914—the forerunner of the American Society for Public Administration, which was established in 1939.

Public administration began picking up academic legitimacy in the 1920s; notable in this regard was the publication of Leonard D. White's *Introduction to the Study of Public Administration* in 1926, the first textbook entirely devoted to the field. As Dwight Waldo has pointed out, White's text was quintessentially American Progressive in character and, in its quintessence, reflected the general thrust of the field: Politics should not intrude on administration; management lends itself to scientific study; public administration is capable of becoming a "value-free" science in its own right; the mission of administration is economy and efficiency, period.[7]

The net result of Paradigm 1 was to strengthen the notion of a distinct politics/administration dichotomy by relating it to a corresponding value/fact dichotomy. Thus, everything that public administrationists scrutinized in the executive branch was imbued with the colorings and legitimacy of being somehow "factual" and "scientific," while the study of public policy-making and related matters was left to the political scientists. The carving up of analytical territory between public administrationists and political scientists during this locus-oriented stage can be seen today in universities: It is the public administrationists who teach organization theory, budgeting, and personnel; political scientists teach such

6. "Report of the Committee on Instruction in Government," in *Proceedings of the American Political Science Association*, 1913–14 (Washington, D.C.: APSA, 1914), p. 264.

7. Dwight Waldo, "Public Administration," in *Political Science: Advance of the Discipline*, Marian D. Irish, ed. (Englewood Cliffs, N.J.: Prentice-Hall, 1968), pp. 153–89.

subjects as American government, judicial behavior, the presidency, state and local politics, and legislative process, as well as such "non-American" fields as comparative politics and international relations. A secondary implication of this locus-centered phase was the isolation of public administration from such other fields as business administration, which had unfortunate consequences when these fields began their own fruitful explorations into the nature of organizations. Finally, largely because of the emphasis on "administration" and "facts" in public administration and the substantial contributions by public administrationists to the emerging field of organization theory, a foundation was laid for the later "discovery" of certain scientific "principles" of administration.

PARADIGM 2:
THE PRINCIPLES OF ADMINISTRATION, 1927–1937

In 1927, W. F. Willoughby's book, *Principles of Public Administration,* was published as the second fully fledged text in the field. Although Willoughby's *Principles* was as fully American Progressive in tone as White's *Introduction,* its title alone indicated the new thrust of public administration: That certain scientific principles of administration existed; they could be discovered; and administrators would be expert in their work if they learned how to apply these principles.

It was during the phase represented by Paradigm 2 that public administration reached its reputational zenith. Public administrationists were courted by industry and government alike during the 1930s and early 1940s for their managerial knowledge. Thus the focus of the field—its essential expertise in the form of administrative principles—waxed, while no one thought too seriously about its locus. Indeed, the locus of public administration was everywhere, since principles were principles and administration was administration, at least according to the perceptions of Paradigm 2. By the very fact that the principles of administration were indeed *principles*—that is, by definition, they "worked" in any administrative setting, regardless of culture, function, environment, mission, or institutional framework and without exception—it therefore followed that they could be applied successfully anywhere. Furthermore, because public administrationists had contributed as much if not more to the formulation of "administrative principles" as had researchers in any other field of inquiry, it also followed that public administrationists should lead the academic pack in applying them to "real-world" organizations, public or otherwise.

Among the more significant works relevant to this phase were Mary Parker Follett's *Creative Experience* (1924), Henri Fayol's *Industrial and*

General Management (1930), and James D. Mooney and Alan C. Reiley's *Principles of Organization* (1939), all of which delineated varying numbers of overarching administrative principles. Organization theorists often dub this school of thought "administrative management," since it focussed on the upper hierarchical echelons of organizations. A related literature that preceded the work in administrative management somewhat in time, but which was under continuing development in business schools, focussed on the assembly line. Researchers in this stream, often called "scientific management," developed principles of efficient physical movement for optimal assembly-line efficiency. The most notable literature was Frederick W. Taylor's *Principles of Scientific Management* (1911) and various works by Frank and Lillian Gilbreth. While obviously related in concept, scientific management had less effect on public administration during its principles phase because it focussed on lower-level personnel in the organization. We consider administrative management and scientific management within the framework of organization theory in Chapter 3.

The "high-noon of orthodoxy," as it often has been called, of public administration was marked by the publication in 1937 of Luther H. Gulick and Lyndall Urwick's *Papers on the Science of Administration.* This landmark study also marked the high noon of prestige for public administration. Gulick and Urwick were confidantes of President Franklin D. Roosevelt and advised him on a variety of matters managerial; their *Papers* were a report to the President's Committee on Administrative Science.

Principles were important to Gulick and Urwick, but where those principles were applied was not; focus was favored over locus, and no bones were made about it. As they said in the *Papers,*

> *It is the general thesis of this paper that there are principles which can be arrived at inductively from the study of human organization which should govern arrangements for human association of any kind. These principles can be studied as a technical question, irrespective of the purpose of the enterprise, the personnel comprising it, or any constitutional, political or social theory underlying its creation.*[8]

Gulick and Urwick promoted seven principles of administration and, in so doing, gave students of public administration that snappy anagram, POSDCORB. POSDCORB was the final expression of administrative principles. It stood for:

8. Lyndall Urwick, "Organization as a Technical Problem," in *Papers on the Science of Administration,* Luther Gulick and L. Urwick, eds. (New York: Institute of Public Administration, 1937), p. 49.

P	lanning
O	rganizing
S	taffing
D	irecting
C ⎫	ordinating
O ⎭	
R	eporting
B	udgeting

That was public administration in 1937.

THE CHALLENGE, 1938–1947

In the following year, mainstream public administration received its first real hint of conceptual challenge. In 1938 Chester I. Barnard's *The Functions of the Executive* appeared. Its impact on public administration was not overwhelming at the time, but it later had considerable influence on Herbert A. Simon when he was writing his devastating critique of the field, *Administrative Behavior*. The impact of Barnard's book may have been delayed because, as a former president of New Jersey Bell Telephone, he was not a certified member of the public administration community.

Dissent from mainstream public administration accelerated in the 1940s in two mutually reinforcing directions. One objection was that politics and administration could never be separated in any remotely sensible fashion. The other was that the principles of administration were logically inconsistent.

Although inklings of dissent began in the 1930s, a book of readings in the field, *Elements of Public Administration*, edited in 1946 by Fritz Morstein-Marx, was one of the first major volumes to question the assumption that politics and administration could be dichotomized. All fourteen articles in the book were written by practitioners and indicated a new awareness that what often appeared to be value-free "administration" actually was value-laden "politics." Was a technical decision on a budgetary emphasis or a personnel change really impersonal and apolitical, or was it actually highly personal, highly political, and highly preferential? Was it ever possible to discern the difference? Was it even worth attempting to discern the difference between politics and administration if, in reality, there was none? Was the underpinning politics/administration dichotomy of the field, at best, naive? Perhaps the frontal answer to these questions was published in 1950: John Gaus penned in the *Public Administration Review* his oft-quoted dictum, "A theory of public administration means in our time a theory of politics also." [9] The die was cast.

9. John Merriman Gaus, "Trends in the Theory of Public Administration," *Public Administration Review* 10 (Summer 1950): 168.

In his superb analysis of "The Trauma of Politics" and public administration, Allen Schick observes that the intellectuals' abandonment of the politics/administration dichotomy in the 1940s has been overstated in more recent years, and that those advocating its abandonment never intended to argue that something called administration and something called politics were totally inseparable. The challengers of the forties only wished to emphasize that public administrators, as well as legislators, made political decisions and public policies:

> Public administration always has served power and the powerful. . . . the service of power was pro bono publico, to help power holders govern more effectively. The presumption was that everyone benefits from good government. . . the constant concern with power was masked by the celebrated dichotomy between politics and administration. But the dichotomy, rather than keeping them apart, really offered a framework for bringing politics and administration together. . . the dichotomy provided for the ascendancy of the administration over the political: efficiency over representation, rationality over self-interest. . . In the end, the dichotomy was rejected not because it separated politics and administration but because it joined them in a way that offended the pluralist norms of postwar political science.[10]

Arising simultaneously with the challenge to the traditional politics/administration dichotomy of the field was an even more basic contention: that there could be no such thing as a "principle" of administration. In 1946 Simon gave a foreshadowing of his *Administrative Behavior* in an article entitled, appropriately, "The Proverbs of Administration," published in *Public Administration Review*. The following year, in the same journal, Robert A. Dahl published a searching piece "The Science of Public Administration: Three Problems." In it he argued that the development of universal principles of administration was hindered by the obstructions of values contending for preeminence in organizations, differences in individual personalities, and social frameworks that varied from culture to culture. Waldo's major work also reflected this theme. His *The Administrative State: A Study of the Political Theory of American Public Administration* (1948) attacked the notion of immutable principles of administration, the inconsistencies of the methodology used in determining them, and the narrowness of the "values" of economy and efficiency that dominated the field's thinking.

The most formidable dissection of the principles notion appeared

10. Allen Schick, "The Trauma of Politics: Public Administration in the Sixties," *American Public Administration: Past, Present, Future*, Frederick C. Mosher, ed. (Syracuse: Maxwell School of Citizenship and Public Affairs and the National Association of Schools of Public Affairs and Administration, 1975), p. 152.

in 1947: Simon's *Administrative Behavior: A Study of Decision-Making Processes in Administration Organization* Simon showed that for every "principle" of administration there was a counterprinciple, thus rendering the whole idea of principles moot. For example, the traditional administrative literature argued that bureaucracies must have a narrow "span of control" if orders were to be communicated and carried out effectively. Span of control meant that a manager could properly "control" only a limited number of subordinates; after a certain number was exceeded (authorities differed on just what the number was), communication of commands became increasingly garbled and control became increasingly ineffective and "loose." An organization that followed the principle of narrow span of control would have a "tall" organization chart (see Figure 2–1).

Span of control made sense up to a point. Yet, as Simon observed, the literature on administration argued with equal vigor for another principle: That for organizations to maximize effective communications and to reduce distortion (thereby enhancing responsiveness and control), there should be as few hierarchical layers as possible—that is, a "flat" hierarchical structure. The logic behind this principle was that the fewer people who had to pass a message up or down the hierarchy, the more likely it would be that the message would arrive at its appointed destination relatively intact and undistorted. This, too, made sense up to a point. The "flat" hierarchy required to bring the bureaucracy in accord with this principle of administration would have an organization chart like that in Figure 2–2.

Obviously, to Simon and now to us, the two "principles" were mutually contradictory and therefore by definition could not be principles. This dilemma encompassed the whole of the traditional public adminis-

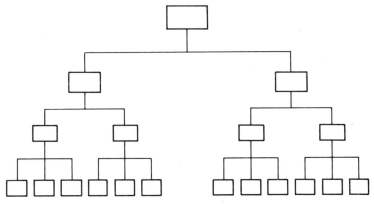

FIGURE 2–1. The Principle of Narrow Span of Control

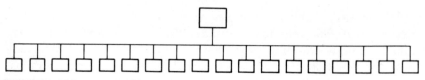

FIGURE 2–2. The "Principle" of Maximized Communications

tration literature, but it was never more than suspected of being so stark a case until Simon published his book.

By mid-century the two defining pillars of public administration—the politics/administration dichotomy and the principles of administration—had been abandoned by creative intellects in the field. This abandonment left public administration bereft of a distinct epistemological identity. Some would argue that an identity has yet to be found.

REACTION TO THE CHALLENGE, 1947–1950

In the same year that Simon decimated the traditional foundations of public administration in *Administrative Behavior*, he offered an alternative to the old paradigms. For Simon, a new paradigm for public administration meant that there ought to be two kinds of public administrationists working in harmony and reciprocal intellectual stimulation: those scholars concerned with developing "a pure science of administration" based on "a thorough grounding in social psychology," and a larger group concerned with "prescribing for public policy." This latter enterprise was far-ranging indeed. In Simon's view, prescribing for public policy "cannot stop when it has swallowed up the whole of political science; it must attempt to absorb economics and sociology as well." Nevertheless, both a "pure science of administration" and "prescribing for public policy" would be mutually reenforcing components: "There does not appear to be any reason why these two developments in the field of public administration should not go on side by side, for they in no way conflict or contradict." [11]

Despite a proposal that was both rigorous and normative in its emphasis, Simon's call for a "pure science" put off many scholars in public administration. For one thing, there already existed a growing irritation in the field with POSDCORB on the basis of its "pure science" claims; the challengers of the late 1940s had shown that the "principles of administration" were hardly the final expression of science, and consequently

11. Herbert A. Simon, "A Comment on 'The Science of Public Administration,'" *Public Administration Review* 7 (Summer 1947): 202.

public administrationists were increasingly skeptical that the administrative phenomenon could be understood in wholly scientific terms. Second, Simon's urging that social psychology provided the basis for understanding administrative behavior struck many public administrationists as foreign and discomfiting; most of them had no training in social psychology. Third, since science was perceived as being "value-free," it followed that a "science of administration" logically would ban public administrationists from what many of them perceived as their richest sources of inquiry: normative political theory, the concept of the public interest, and the entire spectrum of human values. While this interpretation may well have rested on a widespread misinterpretation of Simon's thinking (understandable, perhaps, given the wake of *Administrative Behavior*), as Golembiewski contends,[12] the reaction nonetheless was real.

The threat posed by Simon and his fellow challengers of the traditional paradigms was clear not only to most political scientists but to many public administrationists as well. For their part the public administrationists had both a carrot and a stick as inducements not only to remain within political science but to strengthen the conceptual linkages between the fields. The carrot was the maintenance of the logical conceptual connection between public administration and political science—that is, the public policy-making process. Public administration considered the "internal" stages of that process: the formulation of public policies within public bureaucracies and their delivery to the polity. Political science was perceived as considering the "external" stages of the process: the pressures in the polity generating political and social change. There was a certain logic in retaining this linkage in terms of epistemological benefits to both fields. The stick, as we have noted, was the worrisome prospect of retooling only to become a technically oriented "pure science" that might lose touch with political and social realities in an effort to cultivate an engineering mentality for public administration.

Political scientists, for their part, had begun to resist the growing independence of public administrationists and to question the field's action orientation as early as the mid-1930s. Political scientists, rather than advocating a public service and executive preparatory program as they had in 1914, began calling for, in the words of Lynton K. Caldwell, "intellectualized understanding" of the executive branch, rather than "knowledgeable action" on the part of public administrators.[13] In 1952 Roscoe Martin wrote an article appearing in the *American Political Science Review* call-

---

12. Golembiewski, *op. cit.*, pp. 20–22.

13. Lynton K. Caldwell, "Public Administration and the Universities: A Half-Century of Development," *Public Administration Review* 25 (March 1965), 57.

ing for the continued "dominion of political science over public administration." [14]

By the post-World War II era political scientists were well under
the gun, and could ill afford the breakaway of their most prestigious sub-
field. The discipline was in the throes of being shaken conceptually by
the "behavioral revolution" that had occurred in other social sciences.
The American Political Science Association was in financially tight straits.
Political scientists were aware that not only had public administrationists
threatened secession in the past, but now other subfields, such as international relations, were restive. And in terms of both science and social
science, it was increasingly evident that political science was held in low
esteem by scholars in other fields. The formation of the National Science
Foundation in 1950 brought the message to all who cared to listen that
the chief federal science agency considered political science to be the
distinctly junior member of the social sciences, and in 1953 David Easton
confronted this lack of status directly in his influential book, *The Political
System*.[15]

PARADIGM 3:
PUBLIC ADMINISTRATION AS POLITICAL SCIENCE, 1950–1970

In any event, as a result of these concerns and the icy conceptual cri-
tiques of the field, public administrationists leaped back with some alac-
rity into the mother discipline of political science. The result was a
renewed definition of locus—the governmental bureaucracy—but a corresponding loss of focus. Should the mechanics of budgets and public personnel policies be studied exclusively? Or should public administrationists
consider the grand philosophic schemata of the "administrative Platonists"
(as one political scientist called them),[16] such as Paul Appleby? Or should
they, as urged by Simon, explore quite new fields of inquiry such as sociology, business administration, and social psychology as they related to
the analysis of organizations and decision-making? In brief, this third

14. Roscoe Martin, "Political Science and Public Administration—A Note on the
State of the Union," *American Political Science Review* 46 (September 1952), 665.

15. David Easton, *The Political System* (New York: Knopf, 1953). Easton pulled no
punches in his appraisal of the status of political science. As he noted (pp. 38–40),
"with the exception of public administration, formal education in political science
has not achieved the recognition in government circles accorded, say, economics or
psychology." Or, "However much students of political life may seek to escape the
taint, if they were to eavesdrop on the whisperings of their fellow social scientists,
they would find that they are almost generally stigmatized as the least advanced."

16. Glendon A. Schubert, Jr., " 'The Public Interest' in Administrative Decision-
Making," *American Political Science Review*, 51 (June 1957), 346–68.

phase of definition was largely an exercise in reestablishing the conceptual linkages between public administration and political science. But the consequence of this exercise was to "define away" the field, at least in terms of its analytical focus, its essential "expertise." Thus, writings on public administration in the 1950s spoke of the field as an "emphasis," an "area of interest," or even as a "synonym" of political science.[17] Public administration, as an identifiable field of study, began a long, downhill spiral.

Things got relatively nasty by the end of the decade and, for that matter, well into the 1960s. In 1962 public administration was not included as a subfield of political science in the report of the Committee on Political Science as a Discipline of the American Political Science Association. In 1964 a major survey of political scientists indicated a decline in faculty interest in public administration generally.[18] In 1967 public administration disappeared as an organizing category in the program of the annual meeting of the American Political Science Association. Waldo wrote in 1968 that "many political scientists not identified with Public Administration are indifferent or even hostile; they would sooner be free of it," and added that the public administrationist has an "uncomfortable" and "second-class citizenship."[19] Between 1960 and 1970 only 4 percent of all the articles published in the five major political journals dealt with public administration.[20] In the 1960s "P.A. types" as they often were called in political science faculties, pretty much shuffled through political science departments.

At least two developments occurred during this period that reflect in

17. Martin Landau reviews this aspect of the field's development cogently in his "The Concept of Decision-Making in the 'Field' of Public Administration," *Concepts and Issues in Administrative Behavior*, Sidney Mailick and Edward H. Van Ness, eds. (Englewood Cliffs, N.J.: Prentice-Hall, 1962), pp. 1–29. Landau writes (p. 9), "public administration is neither a subfield of political science, nor does it comprehend it; it simply becomes a synonym."

18. Albert Somit and Joseph Tanenhaus, *American Political Science: A Profile of a Discipline* (New York: Atherton, 1964), especially pp. 49–62 and 86–98.

19. Dwight Waldo, "Scope of the Theory of Public Administration," in Charlesworth, *op. cit.*, p. 8.

20. Contrast this figure with the percentage of articles in other categories published during the 1960–1970 period: "political parties," 13 percent; "public opinion," 12 percent; "legislatures," 12 percent; and "elections/voting," 11 percent. Even those categories dealing peripherally with "bureaucratic politics" and public administration evidently received short shrift among the editors of the major political science journals. "Region/federal government" received 4 percent, "chief executives" won 3 percent, and "urban/metropolitan government" received 2 percent. The percentages are in Jack L. Walker, "Brother, Can You Paradigm?" *PS*, 5 (Fall 1972), 419–22. The journals surveyed were *American Political Science Review, Journal of Politics, Western Political Quarterly, Midwest Political Science Journal, Polity.*

quite different ways the gradually tightening tensions between public administrationists and political scientists: the growing use of the case study as an epistemological device, and the rise and fall of comparative and development administration as subfields of public administration.)

Case studies

The public administration case is,

a narrative of the events that constitute or lead to a decision or . . . decisions by a public administrator or . . . administrators. Some account is given of the personal, legal, institutional, political, economic, and other factors that surrounded the process of decision, but there is no attempt to assert absolute causal relationships. Psychological speculation is avoided, though repetitive patterns of behavior are cited. . . . [A]n effort is made . . . to give the reader a feeling of actual participation in the action. . . . Emphasis throughout is on decision. . . . The decision problems selected for treatment involve policy rather than technical issues. In general . . . the cases are written from the perspective of the detached observer, but with an attempt to focus on the activities of a single person or group.[21]

The development of the case method began in the 1930s, largely under the aegis of the Committee on Public Administration of the Social Science Research Council.[22] Typically, cases were reports written by practicing public administrators on managerial problems and how they solved them. This framework gave way in the mid-1940s to a new version conceived in the Graduate School of Public Administration at Harvard University, which followed the lines of Stein's definition of the public administration case. A joint, four-university program with foundation support resulted, called the Committee on Public Administration Cases. The Committee, in turn, engendered adequate interest in the case method to encourage the establishment in 1951 of the Inter-University Case Program, which continues today to publish case studies in public administration.

The significance of the case study to the development of the field of public administration is a somewhat peculiar one, quite aside from the innate value of the case method as a simulation-based teaching device and as an extraordinarily effective vehicle for illuminating questions of moral choice and decision-making behavior in the administrative milieu. Waldo believes that the emergence of the case method in the late 1940s and its growth throughout the 1950s reflect the response of public administrationists to the "behavioral revolution" in the social sciences generally. On the one hand, the traditional public administrationists, particularly those

21. Harold Stein, *Public Administration and Policy Development: A Case Book* (New York: Harcourt, Brace, 1952), p. xxvii.
22. This discussion relies largely on Waldo, "Public Administration," *op. cit.*, pp. 176–79.

who entered the field in the 1930s, welcomed the case method as a means of being empirical and "behavioral," and thus provided an additional way of reestablishing the linkages between their field and political science. The case study also offered a comfortable alternative to Simon's call for a rigorous, "pure science of administration" that could—probably would—necessitate a methodological retooling on their part. On the other hand, those public administrationists who entered the field later, and who had been academically reared in political science departments when behaviorism was very much in vogue, were not especially at home with the case study as public administration's answer to the challenge of the behaviorists, but temporarily agreed to the case method as an uneasy compromise. There was also a third grouping of public administrationists in the fifties and sixties who embraced the case study: the retired government bureaucrats, who occasionally were hired by political science departments when public administration was held in low professional esteem but in relatively high student demand. This group appreciated an academic approach to the field that identified closely with administrative experience.

The intellectual uneasiness surrounding the use of the case method reflects the condition of public administration at the time: A band of dispirited scholars, isolated from their colleagues, but trying to cope in the only way they knew how. But this generalization did not apply to one group of "P.A. types": Those who tilled the modish (and financially fertile) fields of comparative and development administration.

Comparative and development administration

Cross-cultural public administration, as the comparative approach also is called, is a fairly new development in the field. Prior to the abandonment of the principles of administration, it was assumed that cultural factors did not make any difference in administrative settings because principles, after all, were principles. As White said in 1936, a principle of administration "is as useful a guide to action in the public administration of Russia as of Great Britain, of Irak as of the United States." [23] But, as Dahl and Waldo, among others, would later point out, cultural factors could make public administration on one part of the globe quite a different animal from public administration on another part.[24] By the late 1940s, in fact,

23. Leonard D. White, "The Meaning of Principles of Public Administration," in *The Frontiers of Public Administration*, John M. Gaus, Leonard D. White, and Marshall E. Dimock, eds. (Chicago: University of Chicago Press, 1936), p. 22.

24. See, for example, Robert A. Dahl, "The Science of Public Administration: Three Problems," *Public Administration Review* 7 (Winter 1947): 1–11, and Dwight Waldo, *The Administrative State* (New York: Ronald, 1948).

courses in comparative public administration were appearing in university catalogs, and by the early 1950s the American Political Science Association, the American Society for Public Administration, and the Public Administration Clearinghouse were forming special committees or sponsoring special conferences on comparative public administration. The real impetus came in 1962 when the Comparative Administration Group (CAG, founded in 1960) of the American Society for Public Administration received financing from the Ford Foundation that eventually totaled about $500,000.

The Ford Foundation's support of comparative administration (which has since stopped) appears to have stemmed from an altruistic interest in bettering the lot of poor people in the Third World through the improvement of governmental efficiency in the developing nations, and from a political interest in arresting the "advance of communism," especially in Asia, by entrenching bureaucratic establishments composed of local elites—remember, the Ford Foundation's initial decision to support the field in a big way came at the height of the Cold War. The Foundation's emphasis on the Third World was especially enriching to a semi-autonomous sub-field of comparative public administration called development administration, which concentrates on the developing nations. Ironically, as we shall shortly see, the practical (if somewhat naive) motivations of the Ford Foundation underlying its funding of comparative and development administration were seldom shared by the recipients of the Foundation's grants.

Comparative public administration, as Ferrel Heady has explained, addresses five "motivating concerns" as an intellectual enterprise: the search for theory; the urge for practical application; the incidental contribution of the broader field of comparative politics; the interest of researchers trained in the tradition of administrative law; and the comparative analysis of on-going problems of public administration.[25] Much of the work in comparative public administration revolves around the ideas of Fred W. Riggs, who "captured" (to quote Henderson's assessment) the early American interest in public administration in the developing nations, and, finally, was simply a very prolific writer and substantial contributor to the theoretical development of the field in its early stages.[26]

25. Ferrel Heady, "Comparative Public Administration: Concerns and Priorities," In *Papers in Comparative Public Administration,* Ferrel Heady and Sybil Stokes, eds. (Ann Arbor: Institute of Public Administration, 1962), p. 3. But see Heady's excellent work, *Public Administration: A Comparative Perspective,* 2nd ed. (New York: Marcel Dekker), 1979, especially pp. 1–48.

26. Keith M. Henderson, "A New Comparative Public Administration?" in *Toward a New Public Administration: The Minnowbrook Perspective* (Scranton, Pa.: Chandler, 1971), p. 236.

From 1960 to 1970, when the sub-field dominated public administration, Riggs chaired CAG.[27]

It was and is Riggs's intention and the intention of the comparative public administrationists generally to use their field as a vehicle for stiffening and strengthening theory in public administration. To borrow Riggs's terminology, comparative public administration is to do this by being empirical, nomothetic, and ecological; that is, put crudely, factual and scientific, abstracted and generalizable, systematic and nonparochial. In this emphasis, there always was a quantum of distaste in the ranks of CAG for studies that are rooted solely in the American experience.

Aside from the fact that comparative public administration has had a problem of disciplinary identity that at least equals, if not exceeds, the general field of public administration, there have been dual tensions operating on opposite ends of comparative public administration's analytical spectrum which have compounded its problems of conceptual integration. One pressure emanates from public administration, the other from political science.

Public administration has two differences with its comparative sub-field. One is that the larger field is forthrightly and frankly culture-bound. The defense of American public administration's "parochialism" is much the same as that for "parochialism" of the behavioral sciences generally, and it is comprised of four main points:

1. that all empirical theory rests on the values of science that guide the conduct of the scientific method;
2. the choice of subjects to study usually reflects the researcher's socialization in and the needs of his or her own society;
3. since man is the object of study in the behavioral sciences, then his values, viewpoints, and culture must be included as part of the theory to be developed, notably as intervening variables in correlational analyses;
4. the uses to which public administration theory and data are put in practice inevitably must be culture-bound.

A second difference that public administration generally has with comparative public administration specifically is the question of action versus theory. From its origins, American public administration has attempted to be "practitioner-oriented" and to be involved with the "real world," while comparative public administration, from its origins, has

---

27. Heady, *Public Administration, op. cit.,* pp. 15–16. Riggs' classic work in development administration remains his *Administration in Developing Countries: The Theory of Prismatic Society* (Boston: Houghton-Miflin, 1964), but see also Riggs' *Prismatic Society Revisited* (Morristown, N.J.: General Learning Press, 1973).

attempted to be "theory-building" and to seek knowledge for the sake of knowledge. Increasingly, this purely scholarly (as opposed to professional) thrust of comparative public administration has boded ill for the sub-field. A spokesman for the chief financier of CAG, the Ford Foundation, asked what "all this theorizing and all this study will amount to" in terms of improving the practice of public administration, and no one in comparative public administration every really answered him.[28] In fact, the dominant theme among the members of CAG (although perhaps less emphatically among those involved in development administration) seemed to be a stick to their intellectual guns, and keep building theory as they perceived it. A survey of the CAG membership revealed that there was not a

> strongly stated appeal for linking the theoreticians with the practitioners ... nor for an investment of resources in stimulating empirical research nor for pursuing the work of the CAG into such practical realms as training and consulting. . . . [P]roposals to channel CAG efforts into the sphere of action received very short shrift among respondents.[29]

Not surprisingly, perhaps, the Ford Foundation terminated its support of CAG in 1971.

The tension between political science and comparative public administration results from a less identifiable source. Although there are obvious overlaps between comparative public administration and comparative politics—notably parallel rates of development in both subfields, average age of the participants, and similar outlooks and goals—the two areas of research have remained essentially apart. As Waldo has observed,

> ... despite an occasional joint conference or panel, the two movements have remained largely separate and have not much borrowed from each other. Students of Comparative Public Administration have found the most prestigious of the "models" of Comparative Politics conceptually faulty or irrelevant, and presumably the reverse is also true.[30]

To indulge in sheer speculation, it may be that because of comparative public administration's similarity with comparative politics in terms of focus, locus, methodology, and values, comparative public administrationists are concerned with a loss of conceptual identity should they work too closely with comparative political scientists; the obverse also may have

28. George Gant, as quoted in Henderson, "A New Comparative Public Administration," op. cit., p. 239.

29. CAG Newsletter (June, 1967), pp. 12–13.

30. Waldo, "Public Administration," op. cit., p. 182.

a grain of truth. Yet, what that identity is, for both subfields, often is elusive.

Comparative public administration has been productive and active as a subfield; reports of its death are premature, although comparative public administration does appear to have reached a critical point of development. Although CAG had achieved a membership of more than 500 by 1968, in 1973 it was disbanded and merged with the International Committee of the American Society for Public Administration. Relatedly, the field's major journal, *The Journal of Comparative Administration*, was terminated in 1974 after five years of publication.

Perhaps Golembiewski best sums up the dilemma (or what he calls the "fixation") of comparative and development administration in the eighties by noting, "public administration should take full notice of the fact that comparative administration's failure rests substantially on a self-imposed failure experience. It set an unattainable goal, that is, in its early and persisting choice to seek a comprehensive theory or model in terms of which to define itself." [31]

PARADIGM 4:
PUBLIC ADMINISTRATION AS ADMINISTRATIVE SCIENCE, 1956–1970

Partly because of their second-class citizenship status in a number of political science departments, some public administrationists began searching for an alternative. Although Paradigm 4 occurred roughly concurrently with Paradigm 3 in time, it never received the broadly based favor that political science garnered from public administrationists as a paradigm. Nonetheless, the administrative science option is a viable alternative for a significant number of scholars in public administration. But in both the political science and administrative science paradigms, the essential thrust was one of public administration losing its identity and its uniqueness within the confines of some "larger" concept.

The term *administrative science* is used here as a catch-all phrase for studies in organization theory and management science. Organization theory (considered in Section 2) draws primarily on the works of social psychologists, business administrationists, and sociologists, as well as public administrationists to better understand organizational behavior, while management science (considered in Chapter 7) relies chiefly on the research of statisticians, systems analysts, computer scientists, and economists, as well as public administrationists, in order to measure program effectiveness more precisely and increase managerial efficiency. As a paradigm, administrative science provides a focus but not a locus. It offers

31. Golembiewski, *op. cit.*, p. 147.

techniques, often highly sophisticated techniques, that require expertise and specialization, but in what institutional setting that expertise should be applied is undefined. As in Paradigm 2, administration is administration wherever it is found; focus is favored over locus.

A number of developments, many stemming from the country's business schools, fostered the alternative paradigm of administrative science. In 1956 the important journal *Administrative Science Quarterly* was founded by a public administrationist on the premise that public, business, and institutional administration were false distinctions, that administration was administration. Public administrationist Keith M. Henderson, among others, argued in the mid-1960s that organization theory was, or should be, the overarching focus of public administration.[32] And it cannot be denied that such works as James G. March and Herbert Simon's *Organizations* (1958), Richard Cyert and March's *A Behavioral Theory of the Firm* (1963), March's *Handbook of Organizations* (1965), and James D. Thompson's *Organizations in Action* (1967) gave solid theoretical reasons for choosing administrative science as the paradigm of public administration.

In the early 1960s "organization development" began its rapid rise as a specialty of administrative science. As a focus, organization development (considered more thoroughly in Chapter 3) represented a particularly tempting alternative to political science for many public administrationists. Organization development as a field is grounded in social psychology and values the "democratization" of bureaucracies, whether public or private, and the "self-actualization" of individual members of organizations. Because of these values, organization development was seen by many younger public administrationists as offering a very compatible area of research within the framework of administrative science: Democratic values could be considered, normative concerns could be broached, and intellectual rigor and scientific methodologies could be employed. Yale University became a major promoter of the organization development idea in public administration; its graduates often emerged with doctorates in political science but with transcripts heavy with industrial management courses.

But there was a problem in the administrative science route, and a real one. If it were selected as the sole focus of public administration, could one continue to speak of *public* administration? After all, administrative science, while not advocating universal principles, nevertheless did and does contend that all organizations and managerial methodologies have certain characteristics, patterns, and pathologies in common. If administrative science alone defined the field's paradigm, then public admin-

32. Keith M. Henderson, *Emerging Synthesis in American Public Administration* (New York: Asia Publishing House, 1966).

istration would exchange, at best, being an "emphasis" in political science departments for being, at best, a subfield in schools of administrative science. This often would mean in practice that schools of business administration would absorb the field of public administration. Whether profit-conscious "B-school types" could adequately appreciate the vital value of the public interest as an aspect of administrative science was a question of genuine importance to public administrationists, and one for which the probable answers were less than comforting.

Part of this conceptual dilemma, but only part, lay in the traditional distinction between the public and private spheres of American society. What is *public* administration, what is everything else (*i.e.*, private administration), and what is the dividing line between the two types have been gnawing dilemmas for a number of years.

"Real-world" phenomena are making the public/private distinction an increasingly difficult one to define empirically, irrespective of academic disputations. The research and development contract, the "military-industrial complex," the roles of the regulatory agencies and their relations with industry, and the growing expertise of government agencies in originating and developing advanced managerial techniques that influence the "private sector" in every aspect of American society all conspire to make *public* administration an elusive entity in terms of determining its proper paradigm. Confusion about the term *public* in the field of administration seems at least understandable. One scholar, in fact, has argued that we should begin talking about "publicadministration," since managerial organizations increasingly find themselves relating to public, governmental, and political concerns due to the growing interrelatedness of technological societies.[33]

Hence, public administrationists have recently begun to appreciate that the *public* in public administration no longer can be conceived simply in institutional terms, the terms traditionally favored by the field. *Public* instead must be cast into philosophic, normative, and ethical terms; *public* becomes that which affects the public interest. Thus, rather than concentrating on the Department of Defense as its proper *public* locus, and leaving, say, Lockheed Corporation to students of business administration, public administrationists now would examine the department's contractual and political relationships with Lockheed. Hence, the traditional definition of *public* is abandoned in favor of a more dynamic, normative definition, which would include the Department of Defense *and* its relations with Lockheed. The field is beginning to call this new dimension of the public interest *public affairs.*

The public/private, public interest/profit motive tensions repre-

33. Lynton K. Caldwell, "Methodology in the Theory of Public Administration," in Charlesworth, *op. cit.*, pp. 211–12.

sented by the administrative science paradigm do nothing to alleviate the problem of locus for public administration. Of these tensions, that of the public interest as it relates to public affairs is the most important. Without a sense of the public interest, administrative science can be used for *any* purpose, no matter how immoral. The concept of determining and implementing the public interest constitutes a defining pillar of public administration and a *locus* of the field that receives little if any attention within the context of administrative science, just as the *focus* of organization theory/management science garners scant support in political science.

If Paradigm 4 accomplished nothing else, it exposed public administrationists to some management technologies that they needed to learn and adapt to a governmental context, and, by its very disinterest in questions of values (aside from the value of economic efficiency), it started public administrationists thinking in philosophic (as opposed to institutional) terms about what the *public* in public administration really meant. Increasingly (and this applied equally to public administrationists who were functioning in the context of Paradigm 3), public administrationists were concluding that the field needed both a focus and a locus.

THE FORCES OF SEPARATISM:
"SCIENCE AND SOCIETY"
AND THE "NEW PUBLIC ADMINISTRATION," 1965–1970

Even at its nadir during the period of Paradigms 3 and 4, public administration was sowing the seeds of its own renaissance. This process—quite an unconscious one at the time—took at least two distinct but complementary forms. One was the development of interdisciplinary programs in "science, technology, and public policy" (or similar titles) in major universities, and the other was the appearance of the "new public administration."

The evolution of "science and society" curricula in universities occurred largely during the late 1960s and were the intellectual forerunners of a later and deeper scholarly interest in the relationships between knowledge and power, bureaucracy and democracy, technology and management, and related "technobureaucratic" dimensions that we touched upon in Chapter 1.[34] These programs, although broadly interdisciplinary, often were dominated by public administrationists located in political science

---

34. Representative works of the Science, Technology, and Public Policy movement that had lasting impacts include: Michael D. Reagan, *Science and the Federal Patron* (New York: Oxford University Press, 1969) and Lynton Keith Caldwell, *Environment: A Challenge to Modern Society* (Garden City, N.Y.: Natural History Press, 1970).

departments. By the late 1960s, there were about fifty such programs and they were situated for the most part in the top academic institutions of the country. It was largely this new focus of science, technology, and public policy that gave those public administrationists connected with political science departments any claim to intellectual distinction during the 1960s, and helped offset the loss of a disciplinary identity that then beset public administration. This renewed identity came in part because the focus of science, technology, and public policy did not (and does not) rely conceptually on the pluralist thesis favored by political science. Instead, the focus is elitist rather than pluralist, synthesizing rather than specializing, and hierarchical rather than communal.

The second development was that of the "new public administration." In 1968, Waldo, as Albert Schweitzer Professor in Humanities of Syracuse University, sponsored a conference of young public administrationists on the new public administration, the proceedings of which subsequently were published as a book in 1971, entitled *The New Public Administration: The Minnowbrook Perspective*. The volume remains the key work in this focus.

The focus was disinclined to examine such traditional phenomena as efficiency, effectiveness, budgeting, and administrative techniques. Conversely, the new public administration was very much aware of normative theory, philosophy, and activism. The questions it raised dealt with values, ethics, the development of the individual member in the organization, the relation of the client with the bureaucracy, and the broad problems of urbanism, technology, and violence. If there was an overriding tone to the new public administration, it was a moral tone.

In one respect, the new public administration paralleled the "new political science," a movement that was occurring simultaneously and which represented a desire by younger political scientists to call an end to the now-stultified "behavioral revolution" and broach more normative concerns. Nevertheless, with hindsight the "new P.A." can be viewed as a clarion for independence from both political science (it was not, after all, ever called the "new politics of bureaucracy") and administrative science (since administrative science always had been emphatically technical rather than normative in approach).

The science-and-society and the new-public-administration movements were short-lived. Science, technology, and public policy programs eventually devoluted into specialized courses on such topics as information systems, growth management, and environmental administration, while the new public administration never lived up to its ambitions of revolutionizing the discipline. Nevertheless, both movements had a lasting impact on public administration in that they nudged public administrationists into reconsidering their traditional intellectual ties with both political science and administrative science, and contemplating the prospects of academic autonomy. By 1970, the separatist movement was underway.

PARADIGM 5:
PUBLIC ADMINISTRATION AS PUBLIC ADMINISTRATION, 1970–?

Despite continuing intellectual turmoil, Simon's 1947 proposal for a duality of scholarship in public administration has been gaining a renewed validity. There is not yet a focus for the field in the form of a "pure science of administration," but organization theory has primarily concerned itself in the last two and a half decades with how and why organizations work, how and why people in them behave, and how and why decisions are made, rather than with how these things *should* happen. Additionally, considerable progress has been made in refining the applied techniques of management sciences, and applying them to the public sphere.

Public Administration as Neither
Administrative Science nor Political Science

The old question of whether public administration is a subfield of administrative science or political science is considered in the following two selections. The first passage discusses why public administration differs significantly from administrative science. In it, Luther Gulick, public administrationist and confidante of President Franklin D. Roosevelt, suggests that the "politico-administrative system" is unique and warrants a unique educational treatment. In the second selection, political scientist Jack L. Walker calls empirical attention to the fact that the concerns of political scientists are far removed from those of public administrationists. The quotation is from a study of the five major political journals during an eleven-year period between 1960 and 1970; a mere four percent of the articles appearing during this time dealt with "bureaucratic politics," which was the one category of fifteen that concerned public administration.

My point is best illustrated by a lesson I learned from President Franklin D. Roosevelt. In January 1937, Brownlow, Merriam and I finished our report to the President on the administrative management of the government. He sent it to the Congress in January. Some months later the hearings began and dragged on into that long, hot summer. Unfortunately, Brownlow and Merriam had to go abroad for conferences in Paris and left me with Joe Harris in Washington, to wrestle with Jimmy Byrnes and Congress over the "reorganization bill." As the only member of the committee "in residence," I had a number of sessions with President Roosevelt to test our further ideas on which we were then at work, in our search for greater efficiency and economy in national administration.

One of our technical teams had reached the tentative conclusion that the whole accounting system under social security was meaningless and highly wasteful. As you will remember, both the old age pension and the unemployment laws provided for contributions by the employer and the employee and the setting up of individual accounts under the name of each man and women covered. Millions of personal accounts were involved, with many more millions of accounts to come, and in those days, with electronic accounting still in its infancy, such accounting was very complex.

When it came to making payments to those who retired or were unemployed, however, payments were to be made on the basis of legally defined amounts, which had little or no relation to the cash balances in the individual accounts. Thus the individual cash accounts were quite superfluous for the administration of the system. Moreover the grand total of assets in the several funds were not invested as such. They were not even segregated in the Treasury.

The technical experts thus reached the conclusion that individual accounts were totally unnecessary, and were a great administrative waste. I presented the idea to Frank Bane, Arthur Altmeyer, Harry Hopkins, Henry Morgenthau, Beardsley Ruml, Alvin Hanson and others, and then to the President. He asked a number of questions, and said to come back. Something apparently troubled him about the suggestion.

Some days later he had me up to his room where he generally had breakfast in bed. He asked me to restate the proposition, and then said: "I don't see any hole in the argument, but the conclusion is dead wrong. The purpose of the accounts for Tom, Dick, and Harry is not to figure what we collect or pay. It is to make it impossible when I am gone for the . . . Republicans to abolish the system. They would never dare wipe out the personal savings accounts of millions. You can't do that in America!"

Immediately I knew he was right. His reasoning rested not solely on the dramatic political insight stated so simply, but also on the psychological impact of personal accounts on the recipients and on those who paid into the social security accounts.

The error we technical management and accounting experts almost fell into was the inadequate definition of the system which we were analyzing. We did a good job on the law, on the bookkeeping, on administrative mechanics, and the fiscal and cost analysis. But we missed two dimensions of the problem, the political and the psychological, and we overlooked the problem of strategy which was always so important in the mind of the President.

LUTHER GULICK
Public Administration Review

There may not be any ruling paradigm to shape their efforts, but political scientists still have firm ideas about what should be ignored. An inspection of political science journals during the past decade indicates that substantial agreement exists among political scientists about the subjects that demand their attention. . . . The questions being asked and political institutions being studied remain pretty much the same, year in and year out. . . . Political scientists may not agree on the validity of a fancy general theory of politics, but it seems, nevertheless, when it comes to choosing research topics, we know what we like.

Most political scientists seem to be primarily concerned with the health and well-being of democratic political institutions, the principal instruments of popular control over government. For example, if we combine the totals for articles dealing with public opinion, voting behavior and elections, political parties, pressure groups, legislative behavior, and the behavior of chief executives we have approximately 53 percent of the total, on the average, during this period, and this proportion seems to be increasing steadily. In 1970, these six-categories constituted 61 percent of the total.

By the way of contrast, if articles concerning bureaucratic politics and policy analysis, judicial behavior and constitutional law, urban and metropolitan problems, regional government and federalism are combined they constitute only 18 percent of the total, on the average, during the entire period, and this total seems to be declining. In 1970, these four categories accounted for only 13 percent of the articles published. . . .

The conclusion is inescapable that political scientists in recent years have not paid much attention to the vast new public bureaucracies emerging at all levels of the American and other Western political systems. Articles were written during the last decade analyzing the inner workings of several American congressional committees, but there was no article on the Department of Justice, the Federal Aviation Agency, the Ford Foundation, or the Institute for Defense Analysis, all prominent influences on public policy during the 1960's. Although few self-respecting political scientists would argue that sharp distinctions were possible between political, administrative, and legal processes, in practice, if not in theory, our discipline still seems to operate as if bureaucracies and courts were someone else's business. . . .

If most political scientists believe the profession's mission is to further our understanding of the means of popular control over government. . . a much broader research focus is in order—one that surges beyond the conventional system of parties and elections. In the wake of the protests and political violence of the 1960's, political scientists launched numerous investigations of unconventional efforts at social and political change, which is all to the good, but during the same period American public bureaucracies expanded rapidly, bringing into being a vast network of quasi-public corporations, foundations, consulting firms, professional societies, specialized academic degree programs, and industries dependent on government contracts. Together, all these institutions have contributed to the steady emergence of cosmopolitan, technocratic, national policy making communities whose influence on national goals and aspirations has so far virtually been neglected by students of public policy. Scattered monographs and case studies by the bushel have been completed in recent years, but there has been no comprehensive account of the development of these policy making communities, their impact on the relationship between knowledge and power in America, or their relative importance, compared to the conventional system of political parties and interest groups, in determining the broad outlines of public policy. Francis Rourke has argued that:

> . . . a variety of circumstances in modern life, including especially the growing weight of expert knowledge in policy formation, continue to push bureaucracy toward a position of preeminence in the governing process . . . this bureaucratic power rests partly on the extraordinary capacities of public agencies as sources of expertise, and partly on the fact that administrative agencies have become major centers for the mobilization of political energy and support. As a result, bureaucratic politics rather than party politics has become the dominant theater of decision in the modern state.*

If Rourke is right, the research priorities of the political science profession are seriously unbalanced. Similar assertions about growing bureaucratic power have been made with increasing frequency by journalists and political leaders in many Western countries during the past decade, and the issue is being prominently mentioned in the 1972 American presidential election campaign, yet there has been little attention paid to bureaucracy recently by political scientists. The profession runs the risk of being left out of a growing national debate over the bureaucratization of American life. Rourke's interpretation of recent political development may be an important insight into the heart of the American system, or a gross exaggeration, but relying on the empirical research of the last decade, no political scientist could be sure.

JACK L. WALKER
PS

* Francis E. Rourke, *Bureaucracy, Politics, and Public Policy* (Boston: Little, Brown, 1969), pp. 152–53.

There has been less progress in delineating a locus for the field, or in determining what the public interest, public affairs, and "prescribing

for public policy" should encompass in terms relevant to public administrationists. Nevertheless, the field does appear to be zeroing in on certain
fundamental social factors unique to fully developed countries as its
proper locus. The choice of these phenomena may be somewhat arbitrary
on the part of public administrationists, but they do share commonalities in that they have engendered cross-disciplinary interest in universities,
require synthesizing intellectual capacities, and lean toward themes that
reflect urban life, administrative relations between "public" and "private"
organizations, and the interface between technology and society. The traditional and rigid distinction of the field between the public sphere and
the private sphere appears to be waning as public administration's new
and flexibly defined locus waxes. Furthermore, public administrationists
have been increasingly concerned with the inextricably related areas of
policy science, political economy, the public policy-making process and
its analysis, and the measurement of policy outputs (considered in Chapters 8 and 11). This latter aspect can be viewed, in some ways, as a linkage between public administration's evolving focus and locus.

In this book we treat the field's focus, locus, and their linkages. Sections 2 and 3 consider the focus of public administration: organization
theory, some facts of public policy analysis, and advanced administrative techniques. Together, they represent what has been done in
answering Simon's call for a science of administration and the accom-
plishments of the "nuts-and-bolts" specialists in public administration.
Chapter 6 and Section 4 deal with the more normative locus of public
administration, bureaucratic ethics, and public affairs. Although public
affairs is still in a process of being defined, what appear to be among the
chief areas of interest for public administrationists are included. Thus, we
consider public administration within the context of its emerging paradigm: the focus of organization theory and management science, and the
locus of the public interest and public affairs.

In short, it appears that public administration as a field is at last
coming into its own. The new colleges, schools, and departments of public administration and public affairs represent clear expressions by universities of Paradigm 5. Between 1973 and 1978 the number of separate
professional schools of public administration and public affairs increased
by 21 percent and separate departments of public affairs and administration increased by 53 percent. One analysis of this trend found that across
the country "most students [in public administration] are found in programs organized in separate professional schools." [35]

Although public administration programs situated in political sci-

---

35. Michael A. Murray, "Trends in Public Administration Education," *The Bureaucrat*
(July 1975): 195.

ence departments (or the functional equivalent of Paradigm 3) continue to increase, this growth appears to be an effort by smaller colleges to build up their enrollments in an era of shrinking educational resources, rather than any planned attempt to retain a curriculum that treats public administration as a branch of political science. Generic schools of administrative sciences (or those that are roughly analagous to Paradigm 4), which usually combine business and public administration, decreased by more than half—the only category of academic units to experience a decrease over the five year period.

The scholarly calibre of those institutions at which professional schools of public management (many of them only recently established) are found is extraordinarily high. Princeton, Indiana, Wisconsin, Syracuse, University of Washington, and the University of California at Berkeley number among them. Moreover, these institutions place high priority on educating public administrators. As the president of Harvard University (which has the John Fitzgerald Kennedy School of Government) stated in a significant address:

> . . . The universities have a major opportunity and responsibility to set about the task of training a corps of able people to occupy influential positions in public life. What is needed is nothing less than the education of a new profession. . . . I can scarcely overemphasize the importance of this effort. . . . Since universities are primarily responsible for advanced training in our society, they share a unique opportunity and obligation to prepare a profession of public servants equipped to discharge these heavy responsibilities to the nation.[36]

While it is gratifying to see that the nation's preeminent institutions recognize the worth of educating public administrators and act upon that recognition, we have noted it is still uncertain what the precise shape of that education will be. Nevertheless, certain trends in public administration education are emerging.

One such trend is that of growth. The National Association of Schools of Public Affairs and Administration, the major association of such programs in the country, had more than 200 member institutions in 1980 (up from a mere sixty only a decade earlier). More than 25,000 full-time and part-time students were registered in Master of Public Administration degree programs in the late 1970s; this compares with less than 8,000 such students only five years earlier.

Another trend is the aggressive posture that public administration education has taken in recruiting minorities and women. In 1978, 11 percent of MPA degree students were blacks; almost 22 percent were women.

36. Derek Bok, "The President's Report, 1973–74," *Harvard Today*, 18 (Winter 1975): 4–5, 10.

The numbers of Latino, Native American, and foreign students also increased dramatically during the 1970s.[37]

It appears, in sum, that not only are universities recognizing public administration as a separate academic entity (and, in most cases, one that warrants not just a department but an entire college of its own), but also that the field itself is academically vibrant and on the forefront of social change. If the public is to be adequately served, to recall the words of Harvard's President Bok, then universities must take a direct hand in the process of forming the attitudes and thinking of its managing servants.

SUPPLEMENTAL BIBLIOGRAPHY

APPLEBY, PAUL H., *Morality and Administration in Democratic Government.* Baton Rouge, La.: Louisiana State University Press, 1952.

BARNARD, CHESTER I., *The Functions of the Executive.* Cambridge, Mass.: Harvard University Press, 1938.

COMMITTEE ON PRACTICAL TRAINING FOR PUBLIC SERVICE OF THE AMERICAN POLITICAL SCIENCE ASSOCIATION, Charles McCarthy, Chairman, "A Graduate School of Public Administration at Harvard University: Committee Recommendations," *American Political Science Review* 31 (April 1937), 315–20.

COMMITTEE ON PRACTICAL TRAINING FOR PUBLIC SERVICE OF THE AMERICAN POLITICAL SCIENCE ASSOCIATION, *Proposed Plan for Training Schools for Public Service.* Madison, Wis.: American Political Science Association, 1914.

CYERT, RICHARD M., and JAMES G. MARCH. *The Behavioral Theory of the Firm.* Englewood Cliffs, N.J.: Prentice-Hall, 1963.

DAVY, THOMAS J., "Public Administration as a Field of Study in the United States," *International Review of Administrative Sciences,* 64 (June 1962), 63–78.

DIMOCK, MARSHALL E., "The Study of Administration," *American Political Science Review,* 31 (February 1937), 28–40.

FAYOL, HENRI, *General and Industrial Management.* London: Pitman, 1930.

FOLLETT, M. P., *Creative Experience.* New York: P. Smith Company, 1924.

GAUS, JOHN MERRMAN, "The Ecology of Government," in *Reflections on Public Administration,* edited by John Merriman Gaus, pp. 1–19. Tuscaloosa, Ala.: University of Alabama Press, 1947.

GOLEMBIEWSKI, ROBERT T., "Public Administration as a Field: Four Developmental Phases," *Georgia Political Science Association Journal,* 2 (Spring 1974), 21–49.

KAUFMAN, HERBERT, "Emerging Conflicts in the Doctrines of Public Administration," *American Political Science Review,* 50 (December 1956), 1057–73.

37. As derived from Table 1, National Association of Schools of Public Affairs and Administration (NASPAA), *Directory: Programs in Public Affairs and Public Administration,* 1978 (Washington, D.C.: NASPAA, 1978), p. iv.

MAILICK, SIDNEY, and EDWARD H. VAN NESS, eds., *Concepts and Issues in Administrative Behavior*. Englewood Cliffs, N.J.: Prentice-Hall, 1962.

MILLETT, JOHN D., "A Critical Appraisal of the Study of Public Administration," *Administrative Science Quarterly*, 1 (September 1956), 177–88.

MOONEY, JAMES DAVID, and ALAN C. REILEY, *The Principles of Organization*. New York: Harper and Row, 1939.

MORSTEIN MARX, FRITZ, ed., *Elements of Public Administration*. Englewood Cliffs, N.J.: Prentice-Hall, 1946.

MOSHER, FREDERICK C., "Research in Public Administration," *Public Administration Review*, 16 (Summer 1956), 169–78.

NOVOGROD, R. JOSEPH, GLADYS O. DIMOCK, and MARSHALL E. DIMOCK, *Casebook in Public Administration*. New York: Holt, Rinehart and Winston, 1969.

PUBLIC ADMINISTRATION CLEARING HOUSE, *Report of a Conference on Comparative Administration*. New York: Public Administration Clearinghouse, 1952.

RIGGS, FRED W., *Administration in Developing Countries: The Theory of the Prismatic Society*. Boston: Houghton Mifflin, 1964.

—— "Relearning an Old Lesson: The Political Context of Development," *Public Administration Review*, 25 (Winter 1965), 70–79.

SIMON, HERBERT A., *Administrative Behavior: A Study of Decision-Making Processes in Administration Organization*. New York: Free Press, 1947.

WALDO, DWIGHT, "Development of Theory of Democratic Administration," *American Political Science Review*, 46 (March 1952), 81–103.

——, *Perspectives on Administration*. Tuscaloosa, Ala.: University of Alabama Press, 1956.

——, *The Study of Public Administration*. New York: Random House, 1955.

TAYLOR, FREDERICK W., *Principles of Scientific Management*. New York: Harper and Row, 1911.

THOMPSON, JAMES D. *Organizations in Action*. New York: McGraw-Hill, 1967.

WHITE, LEONARD D. *Introduction to the Study of Public Administration*. New York: Macmillan, 1926.

WILLOUGHBY, W. F., *Principles of Public Administration*. Washington, D.C.: Brookings Institution, 1927.

PUBLIC ORGANIZATIONS: THEORIES, CONCEPTS, AND PEOPLE

the threads
of
organization theory

chapter 3

In this chapter and in the remaining ones of Section 2 we shall examine various perspectives on organizations, pertinent concepts about how organizations work, and the kinds of people one finds in organizations.

MODELS, DEFINITIONS, AND ORGANIZATIONS

The notion of "models," a fairly new epistemological device in the social sciences, has considerable utility in discussing what an organization is. A model is a tentative definition that fits the data available about a particular object. Unlike a definition, a model does not represent an attempt to express the basic, irreducible nature of the object, and is a freer approach that can be adapted to situations as needed. Thus, physicists treat electrons in one theoretical situation as infinitesimal particles and in another as invisible waves. The theoretical model of electrons permits both treatments, chiefly because no one knows exactly what an electron is (that is, no one knows its definition).

So it is with organizations. Organizations are different creatures to different people, and this phenomenon is unavoidable. Thus, organizations are "defined" according to the contexts and perspectives peculiar to the person doing the defining. For example, Victor A. Thompson states that an organization is "a highly rationalized and impersonal integration of a large number of specialists cooperating to achieve some announced specific objective"; Chester I. Barnard defines an organization as "a system of consciously coordinated personal activities or forces of two or more persons"; E. Wight Bakke says an organization is "a continuing system of differentiated and coordinated human activities utilizing, transforming, and welding together a specific set of human, material, capital, ideational and natural resources into a unique, problem-solving whole whose function is to satisfy particular human needs in interaction with other systems of human activities and resources in its particular environment." [1] These models of organizations are all quite different and lead to quite different conclusions on the part of their exponents. Bakke, a social psychologist, has constructed a model of organizations that allows him to dwell on the human effects organizations engender, which he does at length and with little regard for how organizations get their tasks accomplished. Conversely, Barnard's model permitted him to write about what interested him in organizations as a retired president of New Jersey Bell Telephone Company; that is, how cooperation and coordination were achieved in organizations. Thompson's model, with its emphasis on rationality, impersonality, and specialization, ultimately leads to his taking the radical stance that organizations should have no administrators whatever, only coldly efficient "specialists." Yet, none of these models is "wrong"; they only facilitate what they are to be used to illustrate.

Even though organizations represent different things to different people, it is not enough to "define" organizations, as James G. March and Herbert A. Simon once did, with the phrase, "organizations are more earthworm than ape. " [2] As an indication of their simplicity, March and Simon are correct, to be sure, but it is possible to ascertain additional characteristics of organizations that will be useful in our model for the remainder of this book. Organizations

1. are purposeful, complex human collectivities
2. are characterized by secondary (or impersonal) relationships
3. have specialized and limited goals
4. are characterized by sustained cooperative activity

1. See the following: Victor A. Thompson, *Modern Organization* (New York: Knopf, 1961), p. 5; Chester I. Barnard, *The Functions of the Executive* (Cambridge: Harvard University Press, 1938), p. 11; and E. Wight Bakke, *Bonds of Organization* (New York: Harper & Row, 1950), pp. 8–9.

2. James G. March and Herbert A. Simon, *Organizations* (New York: John Wiley, 1958), p. 4.

5. are integrated within a larger social system
6. provide services and products to their environment
7. are dependent upon exchanges with their environment

These features make up our working model of organizations. To them we might add an eighth that is applicable only to public organizations: (Public organizations draw their resources (taxes and legitimacy) from the polity and are mediated by the institutions of the state.)

Organization theorists, using essentially this list of characteristics but stressing different features of it, have produced a vast body of literature on the nature of organizations. The literature can be trisected into these major streams: the closed model, the open model, and what the late James D. Thompson called "the newer tradition," which attempts to synthesize both models.[3] These three streams, each with its own "schools" and substreams, represent the threads of organization theory. The remainder of this chapter considers each literary stream, the thinking of its principal contributors, and the relationships and distinctions between streams.

THE CLOSED MODEL OF ORGANIZATIONS

Traditionally the closed model of organizations has perhaps had the largest influence on the thought of public administrationists. The model goes by many names. Bureaucratic, hierarchial, formal, rational, and mechanistic are some of them, and there are at least three permutations, or schools, that have thrived within its framework: bureaucratic theory, scientific management, and administrative management (sometimes called generic management).

Characteristics

Tom Burns and G. M. Stalker have provided a useful listing of the principal features of the closed model of organizations that will suffice for our purposes: [4]

1. Routine tasks occur in stable conditions.
2. Task specialization (*i.e.*, a division of labor).
3. Means (or the proper way to do a job) are emphasized.
4. Conflict within the organization is adjudicated from the top.

---

3. James D. Thompson, *Organizations in Action* (New York: McGraw-Hill, 1967).
4. Tom Burns and G. M. Stalker, *The Management of Innovation* (London: Tavistock, 1961).

5. "Responsibility" (or what one is supposed to do, one's formal job description) is emphasized.
6. One's primary sense of responsibility and loyalty are to the bureaucratic subunit to which one is assigned (e.g., the accounting department).
7. The organization is perceived as a hierarchic structure (i.e., the structure "looks" like a pyramid: △).
8. Knowledge is inclusive only at the top of the hierarchy (i.e., only the chief executive knows everything).
9. Interaction between people in the organization tends to be vertical (i.e., one takes orders from above and transmits orders below).
10. The style of interaction is directed toward obedience, command, and clear superordinate/subordinate relationships.
11. Loyalty and obedience to one's superior and the organization generally are emphasized.
12. Prestige is "internalized," that is, personal status in the organization is determined largely by one's office and rank.

So runs our closed model of organizations. One should recall that, like any model, it is what Max Weber called an "ideal type." [5] An ideal type is what an organization (or any other phenomenon) tries to be. Once we know what something wants to become (such as a little boy who wants to become a fireman), we can predict with some accuracy how it will behave (the same little boy probably will want a toy fire engine for his birthday). In this logic, closed-model organizations behave in such a way as to fulfill the twelve characteristics posited by Burns and Stalker, although this is not to say that any actual organization meets all twelve features in practice. For example, of organizations that are widely known, the Pentagon and the American military organization likely come closest to accomplishing the requisites of the closed model, but the Pentagon's exceptions to the model are obvious: Nonroutine tasks, unstable conditions, and externalized prestige are frequent facts of organizational life in the military. Nevertheless, the military behaves in such a way as to minimize these exceptions to the closed model, along which it is basically patterned.

Bureaucratic theory

The first school of the closed model that warrants consideration is that of bureaucratic theory. Its chief theorist and best known representative was Max Weber, a remarkable German sociologist who also gave us the

5. Max Weber, *From Max Weber*, H. H. Gerth and C. Wright Mills, eds. (New York: Oxford University Press, 1946).

sociology of religion, a theory of leadership and, with them, those phrases familiar to scholars and practitioners in public administration: "the Protestant work ethic" and "charisma." In what is perhaps a too succinct summary of Weber's model of bureaucracy, the features of bureaucracy amounted to

1. hierarchy
2. promotion based on professional merit and skill
3. the development of a career service in the bureaucracy
4. reliance on and use of rules and regulations
5. impersonality of relationships among career-professionals in the bureaucracy and with their clientele

Organization theorists working in the open model stream of organization theory have been most critical of Weberian bureaucratic theory, largely because it has been the most influential of all the schools in the closed model and most clearly represents the values of the closed model. Open-model theorists dislike the rigidity, the inflexibility, the emphasis on means rather than ends, and the manipulative and antihumanist overtones of Weberian bureaucratic theory. But, in Weber's defense, these criticisms often have been overdrawn and certainly have not been levelled with Weber's own social context in mind. Although the origins of bureaucracy can be traced at least as far back as Cardinal Richelieu's machinations to unify the French kingdom and Frederick the Great's project to turn poverty-ridden, land-locked Prussia into an efficient, military nation, Weber was writing at a time when "Blood-and-Iron" Bismarck was in the final stages of engineering his consolidation of the German states and when positions of public trust still were assigned on the basis of class rather than ability. To Weber, an impersonal, rule-abiding, efficient, merit-based career service provided the surest way of fulfilling the public interest in the face of a politically fragmented but culturally unified Germany and an arrogant, powerful, yet somewhat silly *Junker* class. Justice based on rational law would replace what Weber called "*Kadijustice*," or justice based on the whim of a charismatic leader; the rationalism of the bureaucracy would offset the romanticism of the polity, and this was to the good of society. In short, Weber, in a larger sense, was not antihumanist in his thinking, but the effects of the bureaucracy that he so loudly touted often were, both to the citizen clients and to the bureaucrats themselves.

Scientific management

Another major literary stream encompassed by the closed model is represented by the theories of scientific management. Scientific management refers to what is more popularly known as time-motion studies; it flourished at the beginning of the twentieth century, and remains very much in use today in industry.

Scientific management had (and has) its intellectual home in America's business schools. Its motivating concern was to improve organizational efficiency and economy for the sake of increased production. Perhaps the most firmly entrenched characteristic of scientific management was its view of humanity. Human beings were perceived as being adjuncts of the machine, and the primary objective of scientific management was to make them as efficient as the machines they operated. This view of humanity applied solely to workers on the assembly line and in the lower organizational echelons; it did not apply to upper-echelon managers—it was to them that the scientific management literature was addressed.

The key representatives of the scientific management school are Frederick Taylor (who gave scientific management its name with his 1911 volume, *Principles of Scientific Management*) and Frank and Lillian Gilbreth.[6] The man-as-machine conception, replete with all its discomfiting moral overtones, are on clear display in the writings of Taylor and the Gilbreths. A notorious example of the conception occurs in Taylor's (likely fictional) story of Schmidt, the pig-iron hauler, whom Taylor unabashedly declared to be dumb as an ox. After Taylor analyzed Schmidt's physical movements, he ordered him to change how he moved his body and, as a result of these "scientific" alterations in Schmidt's physical behaviors, Schmidt's production went up from 12½ tons of pig-iron hauled per day to 47 tons. Taylor is obviously proud of his feat in rendering Schmidt a more efficient, machine-like man, and because of such feats he was eminently successful as a time-motion expert in his day. Similarly, Frank and Lillian Gilbreth developed the concept of the "therblig," each one of which represented a category of eighteen basic human motions— all physical activity fell into a therblig class of one type or another. (The scientific management experts rarely were constrained by false modesty; try reading "therblig" backwards.)

The man-as-machine model of scientific management doubtless has a distasteful aura. Men are not machines. They do not have an array of buttons on their backs that merely need pressing for them to be machines. This distaste with the man-as-machine conception, however, has often been extended by some critics to include a distaste for the notion of efficiency, or "getting the biggest bang for the buck," to borrow former Defense Secretary Robert McNamara's phrase. Outside the realms of theory, few are against efficiency in government, least of all the governed.

6. See especially Frederick W. Taylor, *Principles of Scientific Management* (New York: Harper & Row, 1911), and Frank G. Gilbreth, *Primer of Scientific Management* (New York: Van Nostrand, 1912).

So one must be wary of dismissing the value of efficiency along with "Taylorism" (as scientific management also is called), as occasionally has been done by humanist critics of the school.

One also should be cautious of relegating Taylorism to the intellectual slag heap on the assumption that its scholar/practitioners were consciously tools of the robber barons and premeditated exploiters of the working class. To a degree they were, but Taylor and the Gilbreths would likely be shocked by the suggestion. Taylor's Schmidt, it should be recalled, was employed according to the standard industrial system of the age: the piece-work method. For every ton Schmidt hauled, he was paid accordingly. Thus, to increase his daily production meant that Schmidt, as well as his bosses, was better off. Moreover, Taylor himself had served as an apprentice workman in a steel company and knew what that side of life was like. For their part the Gilbreths applied their therbligs to surgery techniques in hospitals, and the sharply-ordered "Scalpel! Sponge!" we watch being slapped into Dr. Welby's palm by a hyperefficient nurse on television is a direct result of Gilbreth's operating-room studies. Prior to the Gilbreths' analysis surgeons rustled around for their own instruments with one hand, evidently holding open the incision with the other. Efficiency can serve humanism as well as any other value, and this aspect sometimes is overlooked by open-model critics.

As a final note, it is worth observing that Taylorism has been used—and is being used—by the federal government, occasionally in such a way as to render the man-as-machine model painfully apparent. One example is the use of "psychotechnology" by the National Aeronautics and Space Administration (NASA) in its training of astronauts. The objective of NASA's use of psychotechnology is to "integrate" the astronaut with the technological environment of his space capsule, both mentally and physically, in order to reduce his response time. Psychotechnology is essentially scientific management updated, but with the added fillip of psychoemotional as well as physical conditioning being practiced.

Administrative management

The final literature based on the closed model is administrative management, which also is called generic management. Luther Gulick and Lyndall Urwick's *Papers on the Science of Administration* is an outstanding example of administrative management in public administration, although James D. Mooney and Alan C. Reiley's *Principles of Organization* is more frequently cited as exemplary.[7]

7. See especially Luther Gulick and L. Urwick, eds., *Papers on the Science of Administration* (New York: Institute of Public Administration, 1937), and James D. Mooney and Alan C. Reiley, *The Principles of Organization* (New York: Harper & Row, 1939).

Administrative management presumed that administration is administration, wherever it was found (hence, its other title, "generic"), and therefore devoted its energies to the discovery of "principles" of management that could be applied anywhere. Once an administrative principle was found, it logically should work in any kind of administrative institution: government bureaucracies, business managements, hospitals, schools, universities, prisons, libraries, public health or international institutions—wherever. Thus, Gulick and Urwick gave us POSDCORB, and Mooney and Reiley contributed four principles of organization: the coordinative principle, the scalar principle (or hierarchical structure), the functional principle (or division of labor), and the staff/line principle. There were other exponents, of course, such as Mary Parker Follet and Henri Fayol,[8] Their impact on public administration has been detailed in Chapter 2.

Administrative management is closer in concept and perceptions to Weberian bureaucratic theory than to Taylorian scientific management. The major reason for this is that bureaucracies are less concerned with time-motion economies than are assembly lines, and both bureaucratic theorists and administrative management analysts primarily were concerned with the optimal organization of administrators rather than production workers. But, like both bureaucratic theory and scientific management, administrative management holds economic efficiency (or "rationalism") as its ultimate criterion.

The difference between traditional bureaucratic theory and administrative management largely is one of theory as opposed to implementation. Weber and his academic peers were interested in learning how bureaucracies functioned, why they functioned as they did, and what their implications for the larger society were. Mooney and Reiley, Gulick and Urwick, Follett, Fayol, and their colleagues thought they knew how bureaucracies functioned and why, and they were interested in applying the principles of administration they had derived from their knowledge to actual administrative organizations to enable administrators to operate more efficiently and effectively.

There also was a second, more subtle difference between bureaucratic theory and administrative management, one that provides a linkage between the closed and open models of organizations. Weber, like Taylor, did not think much about underlings and toilers in organizations beyond their capacities for obedience (in Weber's case) and production (in Taylor's case), and both capacities were regarded as being almost limitless, provided managers took their respective writings to heart. But with the emergence of the theorists on administrative management, a hint surfaced

8. See, for example, M. P. Follet, *Creative Experience* (New York: P. Smith Company, 1924), and Henri Fayol, *General and Industrial Management* (London: Pitman, 1930).

that underlings and toilers in organizations conceivably might have minds of their own. Indeed, it was not much of a hint, barely an inkling. But it was there, and it is noticeable in Mooney and Reiley's contention that the "indoctrination" of subordinates is vital to well-managed organizations. In fact, Mooney and Reiley attributed the durability of the Roman Catholic Church to its doctrine and its indoctrination—a function which has maintained a viable, continuing organization for nearly two thousand years and in their view is a highly praiseworthy method of organizational control and survival.

Such a grudging concession to the thinking powers of subordinates did not amount to much in terms of high esteem for the subordinates' mental prowess generally. But it represented a recognition that subordinates were people (like managers) and could think (almost like managers). It was left for certain writers using the open model to assert that underlings and toilers could indeed think, feel, and behave on their own, and often differently from the ways they were supposed to. Some of these writers would argue that subordinates could outthink, outsmart, and outfox their superordinates—and did—with ease.

THE OPEN MODEL OF ORGANIZATIONS

The open model of organizations traditionally has had a greater influence on business administration than on public administration, although this situation has been changing in recent years. Like the closed model, the open model goes by many names. Collegial, competitive, freemarket, informal, natural, and organic are some of them, and, like the closed model, three literary streams run through the model's overarching framework. These streams, or schools, are, first, the human relations school; second, the newer field of organization development and, third, the literature that views the organization as a unit functioning in its environment.

The historical origins of the open model precede the intellectual roots of the closed model, originally developed by Max Weber, by more than a century and a half. In a perceptive essay, sociologist Alvin W. Gouldner[9] attributes the open model's original conceptualization to Count Louis de Rouvroy Saint-Simon, the brilliant French social thinker, and to his protégé Auguste Comte, the "father of sociology." Saint-Simon and Comte wrote during a span of time that began in the corrupt *ancién regime* of Louis XIV, continued through the bloody French Revolution and the rule of the military despot and national hero, Napoleon Bona-

9. Alvin W. Gouldner, "Organizational Analysis," in *Sociology Today*, Robert K. Merton, Leonard Broom, and Leonard S. Cottrell, Jr., eds. (New York: Basic Books, 1959), pp. 400–428.

parte, and ended under the reign of Louis Napoleon. Partly as a reaction to the administrative stultification of the last days of the French kings and the explosiveness of the Revolution, Saint-Simon, and later Comte, speculated on what the administration of the future would be like. They thought that it would be predicated on skill rather than heredity, "cosmopolitanism" (by which Saint-Simon meant the development of new professions based on technology) would be the order of the day, and organizations themselves would be a liberating force for man. Throughout, Saint-Simon and Comte stressed the value of spontaneously created organizations that developed "naturally" as they were needed. On reflection, Saint-Simon and Comte's views on organizations and society sound like a seventeenth-century version of Alvin Toffler's concept of "Ad Hocracy" in his book, *Future Shock*.[10]

Characteristics

Once again we rely on Burns and Stalker's research for a listing of the principal features of the open model.[11]

1. Nonroutine tasks occur in unstable conditions.
2. Specialized knowledge contributes to common tasks (thus differing from the closed model's specialized *task* notion in that the specialized *knowledge* possessed by any one member of the organization may be applied profitably to a variety of tasks undertaken by various other members of the organization).
3. Ends (or getting the job done) are emphasized.
4. Conflict within the organization is adjusted by interaction with peers.
5. "Shedding of responsibility" is emphasized (*i.e.*, formal job descriptions are discarded in favor of all organization members contributing to all organizational problems).
6. One's sense of responsibility and loyalty are to the organization as a whole.
7. The organization is perceived as a fluidic network structure (*i.e.*, the organization "looks" like an amoeba: ⬭).
8. Knowledge can be located anywhere in the organization (*i.e.*, everybody knows something relevant about the organization, but no one, including the chief executive, knows everything).
9. Interaction between people in the organization tends to be horizontal as well as vertical (*i.e.*, everyone interacts with everyone else).

10. Alvin Toffler, *Future Shock* (New York: Random House, 1970).
11. Burns and Stalker, *op. cit.*

10. The · style of interaction is directed toward accomplishment, "advice" (rather than commands), and is characterized by a "myth of peerage," which envelops even the most obvious superordinate/subordinate relationships (*e.g.*, a first-name "familiarity" exists even between president and office boy, on the logic that the maintenance of an image of intimacy is somehow "friendlier").

11. Task achievement and excellence of performance in accomplishing a task are emphasized.

12. Prestige is "externalized" (*i.e.*, personal status in the organization is determined largely by one's professional ability and reputation).

So runs our open model of organizations, which, like the closed model, is an ideal type. It seldom if ever exists in actuality, although a major university might come close (which is why the open model occasionally is called the "collegial" model). A Big Ten or Ivy League university could meet many of the requisites of the open model, notably specialized knowledge located throughout the organization, largely horizontal interaction, and externalized prestige. But exceptions to the model also are apparent; tasks (*e.g.*, teaching, research, studying) are relatively routine and, at least among the faculty, one is likely to find a higher degree of loyalty to the subunit (*i.e.*, the academic department) than to the organization as a whole.

Human relations

Human relations, the first of three schools of the open model, focuses on organizational variables never considered in the closed model: cliques, informal norms, emotions, and personal motivations, among others. Paradoxically, this focus resulted from what originally was intended to be a research undertaking in scientific management, a literature at the opposite end of the continuum in terms of the values held by its theorists.

In 1927 Elton Mayo and Fritz J. Roethlisberger began a series of studies (later known as the Hawthorne studies, for the location of the plant) of working conditions and worker behavior at a Western Electric factory. Their experiment was predicated on the then-plausible Taylorian hypothesis that workers would respond like machines to changes in working conditions. To test their hypothesis they intended to alter the intensity of light available to a group of randomly selected workers. The idea—that when the light became brighter, production would increase, and when the light became dimmer, production would decrease—is all very commonsensical, of course. The workers were told they would be observed as an experimental group. The lights were turned up and production went up. The lights turned down and production went up. Mayo and Roethlisberger were disconcerted. They dimmed the lights to near darkness, and production kept climbing.

Among the explanations of this phenomenon that later came forth were:

1. human workers probably are not entirely like machines.
2. the Western Electric workers were responding to some motivating variable other than the lighting, or despite the lack of it.
3. they likely kept producing more in spite of poor working conditions because they knew they were being watched.

Mayo and his colleagues were so impressed by these initial findings that they ultimately conducted a total of six interrelated experiments over an eight-year period. In part because of the massive size of the undertaking, the Hawthorne studies number among the most influential empirical researches ever conducted by social scientists. Most notably they produced the famous term, "Hawthorne effect," or the tendency of people to change their behavior when they know that they are being observed. But even more important, the studies were interpreted both by the original investigators and succeeding generations of management scientists as validating the idea that unquantifiable relationships (or "human relations") between workers and managers, and among workers themselves, were the primary determinants of workers' efficiency; conversely, material incentives and working conditions, while relevant, were not terribly significant as motivators of productivity.

A recent re-interpretation of the Hawthorne data, using statistical techniques that were unavailable to Mayo and Roethlisberger, has turned the "human relations" interpretation upside down. In an important new analysis of the original data, Richard Herbert Franke and James D. Kaul concluded that human relations were *not* the reasons behind worker efficiency, but rather such traditional motivators as "managerial discipline," fear (in the form of the Depression), reduction of fatigue (the experimental groups were given rest periods), and money (the groups also were given group pay incentives) were the real reasons underlying increased productivity.[12]

Although the notion that workers produce more because of relations

---

12. The original Hawthorne studies are in: Fritz J. Roethlisberger and William J. Dickson, *Management and the Worker* (Cambridge: Harvard University Press, 1939). The reinterpretation of Hawthorne is in: Richard Herbert Franke and James D. Kaul, "The Hawthorne Experiments: First Statistical Interpretation," *American Sociological Review*, 43 (October 1978), 623–43.

among themselves and management has been recently and seriously questioned, the Hawthorne studies nonetheless marked the continuation of the Saint-Simonian tradition after a century-long gap, and the beginning of human relations as we know it.

Much of human relations has concerned itself with the informal work group at the assembly-line level. What makes them work or not work? How do they behave and why? Yet increasingly, human relations has had the managerial echelons as its investigative object, and this has contributed to the study of public administration.

Notable in terms of the impact of the human relationists on public administration is their research on motivation and job satisfaction. Much of this research centers around the "hierarchy of human needs" developed by A. H. Maslow. Maslow perceived human desires to be based first on (1) physiological needs, which provided the foundation for the human's next greatest need, (2) security, then (3) love or belongingness, (4) self-esteem, and finally (5) self-actualization. For the record, Maslow later added a sixth and highest need, "metamotivation," [13] but Maslow's self-actualization need has spawned the most analysis in public administration. Self-actualization refers to the individual growing, maturing, and achieving a deep inner sense of self-worth as he relates to his job and his organization. In terms of the person and the organization, Maslow wrote that these "highly evolved" self-actualized individuals assimilated "their work into the identity, into the self, *i.e.*, work actually becomes part of the self, part of the individual's definition of himself." [14]

Frederick Herzberg stimulated much of the empirical research that related to Maslow's hierarchy of needs. Herzberg developed the concepts of "motivators," which referred to direct determiners of job satisfaction (*e.g.*, "responsibility"), and "hygienic" or "intrinsic" factors, which related to psychological satisfactions derived from the task environment (*e.g.*, salary).[15] This framework (itself a derivative of Maslow's need hierarchy) and various modifications of it have produced a voluminous body of literature that attempts to test such hypotheses as "participative decision-making, interesting jobs, and related organization variables correlate positively with job satisfaction," and "job satisfaction correlates positively with job performance." But, when one reviews this literature, as Frank K. Gibson and Clyde E. Teasley have done, there is not a clear-cut body

---

13. See Abraham Maslow, "A Theory of Metamotivation: The Biological Rooting of the Value-Life," *Humanitas*, 4 (1969), 301–43.

14. Abraham Maslow, *Eupsychian Management: A Journal* (Homewood, Ill.: Dorsey, 1965), p. 1.

15. See, for example, Frederick Herzberg, "One More Time: How Do You Motivate Employees?" *Harvard Business Review*, 46 (January–February 1968), 53–62, and *Work and the Nature of Man* (Cleveland: World Publishing, 1966).

of empirical results that relates organizational effectiveness to what Gibson and Teasley call "the humanistic model of organizational motivation." [16]

Organization development

An important and new subfield of the open model is called organization development (OD). The overlappings of OD with the human relations literature are manifold, but it nonetheless can be considered a separate school because it attempts to go beyond the locus of small group theory and is almost missionary in its zeal to "democratize" bureaucracies.

Organization development is a planned, organization-wide attempt directed from the top that is designed to increase organizational effectiveness and viability through calculated interventions in the active workings of the organization using knowledge from the behavioral sciences. This intervention often is accomplished through third-party consultants. The stress in this definition of OD is on planned change, systemic analysis, top management, and the objectives of organizational effectiveness and "health." Richard Beckhard argues that these emphases distinguish OD from other kinds of efforts to change organizations, such as sensitivity training or "management development," which are not action-oriented, and operations research, which is not human value-oriented.[17]

Organization development can be viewed as having evolved along two distinct if intertwining branches, both of which owe much of their initial impetus to the social psychologist, Kurt Lewin. Wendell L. French and Cecil H. Bell, Jr., call these branches the "laboratory-training stem" and the "survey research feedback stem."[18] The laboratory approach focusses on small group methods; its origins may be traced to conferences held in 1946 and 1947, headed by Lewin, Kenneth Benne, Leland Bradford, and Ronald Lippitt. These meetings were sponsored by the Office of Naval Research, the National Education Association, and the Research Center for Group Dynamics. Elements of these organizations later formed the National Training Laboratories for Group Development, which became a significant force in the development of T-group (therapy group) and sensitivity training techniques. By the early 1960s it was becoming apparent that the laboratory approach could be used for entire organiza-

16. Frank K. Gibson and Clyde E. Teasley, "The Humanistic Model of Organizational Motivation: A Review of Research Support," *Public Administration Review*, 33 (January–February, 1973), pp. 89–96.

17. Richard Beckhard, *Organizational Development: Strategies and Models* (Reading, Mass.: Addison-Wesley, 1969), pp. 20–24.

18. Wendell L. French and Cecil H. Bell, Jr., *Organization Development: Behavioral Science Interventions for Organization Improvement* (Englewood Cliffs, N.J.: Prentice-Hall, 1973).

tions, not just small groups. Douglas McGregor, working for Union Carbide, and J. S. Mouton and Robert Blake, working for Esso Standard Oil, used the first versions of a "managerial grid" concept.[19] These efforts represented the initial attempt to involve top management in the human development of the organization, take measurements of individual behaviors, trace feedback effects, and use "third party" outside consultants to foster organizational innovation. These exercises in *intergroup* development represented a real departure from the standard T-group approach.

The survey research feedback stem can be traced to Lewin's Research Center for Group Dynamics at the Massachusetts Institute of Technology, which he founded in 1945. On Lewin's death in 1947 the center's senior staff (including Lippitt, McGregor, and Leon Festinger) moved to the Survey Research Center at the University of Michigan and formed the Institute for Social Research. The people involved in the institute began the initial studies of measuring employee and management attitudes concerning their organization. Feedback from these surveys was maximized through the use of interlocking group conferences. Thus, as these techniques developed, the individual participant in the organization was given a sense of the whole and the particular roles of himself and others as they pertained to the organization.

Since its beginnings in the late 1940s, OD has been used in a number of ways. While most of its applications have been in business organizations, its influence in public bureaucracies and the broad-ranging field of community development has been accelerating since the early 1960s. Chris Argyris applied OD techniques in 1967 to the United States Department of State in an effort to resolve intergroup conflicts between Foreign Service officers and administrative officers. OD has been used for such diverse purposes as maximizing communications between a Community Action Agency and an Indian tribe, and facilitating the organization of a new junior high school. The goals of these and many other OD projects have been and are broadly humanistic and reflect the underlying values of the field. The mission of organization development is to

1. improve the individual member's ability to get along with other members (which the field calls "interpersonal competence")
2. legitimate human emotions in the organization
3. increase mutual understanding among members
4. reduce tensions
5. enhance "team management" and intergroup cooperation

19. Douglas MacGregor, *The Professional Manager* (New York: McGraw-Hill, 1967), and Robert R. Blake and J. S. Mouton, *The Managerial Grid* (Houston: Gulf Publishing, 1964).

6. develop more effective techniques for conflict resolution through nonauthoritarian and interactive methods
7. evolve less structured and more "organic" organizations.

OD advocates strongly believe that achieving these goals of the field will render organizations more effective in the rapidly changing environment of technological societies. "The basic value underlying all organization-development theory and practice is that of *choice*. Through focused attention and through the collection and feedback of relevant data to relevant people, more choices become available and hence better decisions are made." [20] The techniques used by OD to maximize organizational choice include the use of confrontation groups, T-groups, sensitivity training, attitude questionnaires, third-party change agents in the form of outside consultants, data feedback, and the "education" of organizational members in the values of openness and participatory decision-making.

The organization as a unit in its environment

A third school of the open model is less bulky as a literature but nonetheless is separate and identifiable. Notable among its contributors are Chester I. Barnard, Philip Selznick, and Burton Clark.[21] It is characterized by use of the organization as a whole as its analytical unit (in contrast to the other schools' preference for the small group), its theme of the organizational pressures and constraints emanating from the environment, and organizational strategies designed to cope with environmentally spawned problems.

Selznick, for example, stressing the concept of environmental pressures on organizations, developed his "co-optation" concept in his book on the establishment of the Tennessee Valley Authority (TVA). Co-optation referred to the strategy employed by the TVA Board of Directors in gaining the acceptance, and ultimately the strong support, of initially hostile local interests by granting their representatives membership on the board. TVA, as a result, influenced and cajoled the local interests far more profoundly than the local interests influenced the TVA; in short, TVA co-opted the local interests, but was required to modify slightly its own purposes in so doing.

Given its relatively small numbers, the theoretical school dealing with organizations as units in their environment has had a disproportion-

20. Warren G. Bennis, *Organizational Development: Its Nature, Origins, and Prospects* (Reading, Mass.: Addison-Wesley, 1969), p. 17.
21. See, for example, Chester L. Barnard, *op. cit.*, Philip Selznick, *TVA and the Grass Roots* (Berkeley: University of California Press, 1949), and Burton R. Clark, *Adult Education in Transition* (Berkeley: University of California Press, 1956).

ate impact on public administration. This is understandable, however, for the stream is primarily concerned about the "public" (*i.e.*, the "environment"), and its political relationship with the organization. In this emphasis, the organization/environment literature is uniquely concerned with the problems of public administration.

THE CLOSED AND OPEN MODELS: THE ESSENTIAL DIFFERENCES

We have reviewed two eminently disparate models of organizations and their respective literary emphases. In essence, their fundamental differences may be reduced to four: (1) perceptions of the organizational environment, (2) perceptions of the nature of man, (3) perceptions of the use of manipulation in organizations, (4) perceptions of the role and significance of organizations in society. For purposes of review, we shall consider each of these differences.

Perceptions of the organizational environment

The closed model is predicated on a stable, routine environment, and the open model is predicated on an unstable environment, replete with surprises. Both models assume that organizations will act in order to survive and, ultimately, to thrive.

The beauty in these two differing perceptions of organizations is that both models work in the respective environments posited for them. That is, an open-model organization likely would "die" in a stable environment, and a closed-model organization probably would wither in an unstable environment. A variety of empirical studies have indicated this to be the case, notably Burns and Stalker's *The Management of Innovation*, and Michel Crozier's *The Bureaucratic Phenomenon*.[22]

Bureaucracy Versus Humanism: Two Views on the Human Being in the Closed and Open Models of Organizations

The following passages illustrate by contrast the differences between the closed and open models of organization theory. While closed-model theorist Max Weber and open-model theorist Frederick Herzberg address the plight of the bureaucrat in bureaucracies from vastly different perspectives, their basic agreement on the point that the individual remains in a genuine bind in bureaucratic settings is illuminating.

22. Burns and Stalker, *op. cit.*, and Michel Crozier, *The Bureaucratic Phenomenon* (Chicago: The University of Chicago Press, 1964).

Once it is fully established, bureaucracy is among those social structures which are the hardest to destroy. Bureaucracy is the means of carrying "community action" over into rationally ordered "societal action." Therefore, as an instrument of "societalizing" relations of power, bureaucracy has been and is a power instrument of the first order—for the one who controls the bureaucratic apparatus.

Under otherwise equal conditions, a "societal action," which is methodically ordered and led, is superior to every resistance of "mass" or even of "communal action." And where the bureaucratization of administration has been completely carried through, a form of power relation is established that is practically unshatterable.

The individual bureaucrat cannot squirm out of the apparatus in which he is harnessed. In contrast to the honorific or avocational "notable," the professional bureaucrat is chained to his activity by his entire material and ideal existence. In the great majority of cases, he is only a single cog in an ever moving mechanism which prescribes to him an essentially fixed route of march. The official is entrusted with specialized tasks and normally the mechanism cannot be put into motion or arrested by him, but only from the very top. The individual bureaucrat is thus forged to the community of all the functionaries who are integrated into the mechanism. They have a common interest in seeing that the mechanism continues its functions and that the societally exercised authority carries on.

The ruled, for their part, cannot dispense with or replace the bureaucratic apparatus of authority once it exists. For this bureaucracy rests upon expert training, a functional specialization of work, and an attitude set for habitual and virtuoso-like mastery of single yet methodically integrated functions. If the official stops working, or if his work is forcefully interrupted, chaos results, and it is difficult to improvise replacements from among the governed who are fit to master such chaos. This holds for public administration as well as for private economic management. More and more the material fate of the masses depends upon the steady and correct functioning of the increasingly bureaucratic organizations of private capitalism. The idea of eliminating these organizations becomes more and more utopian.

MAX WEBER
Economics and Society

Every audience contains the "direct action" manager who shouts, "Kick him!" And this type of manager is right. The surest and least circumlocuted way of getting someone to do something is to kick him in the pants—give him what might be called the KITA.

There are various forms of KITA, and here are some of them:

Negative physical KITA. This is a literal application of the term and was frequently used in the past. It has, however, three major drawbacks:

(1) it is inelegant; (2) it contradicts the precious image of benevolence that most organizations cherish; and (3) since it is a physical attack, it directly stimulates the autonomic nervous system, and this often results in negative feedback—the employee may just kick you in return. These factors give rise to certain taboos against negative physical KITA.

The psychologist has come to the rescue of those who are no longer permitted to use negative physical KITA. He has uncovered infinite sources of psychological vulnerabilities and the appropriate methods to play tunes on them. "He took my rug away"; "I wonder what he meant by that"; "The boss is always going around me"—these symptomatic expressions of ego sores that have been rubbed raw are the result of application of:

Negative Psychological KITA. This has several advantages over negative physical KITA. First, the cruelty is not visible; the bleeding is internal and comes much later. Second, since it affects the higher cortical centers of the brain with its inhibitory powers, it reduces the possibility of physical backlash. Third, since the number of psychological pains that a person can feel is almost infinite, the direction and site possibilities of the KITA are increased many times. Fourth, the person administering the kick can manage to be above it all and let the system accomplish the dirty work. Fifth, those who practice it receive some ego satisfaction (one-upmanship), whereas they would find drawing blood abhorrent. Finally, if the employee does complain, he can always be accused of being paranoid, since there is no tangible evidence of an actual attack.

Now, what does negative KITA accomplish? If I kick you in the rear (physically or psychologically), who is motivated? I am motivated; you move! Negative KITA does not lead to motivation, but to movement. So:

Positive KITA. Let us consider motivation. If I say to you, "Do this for me or the company, and in return I will give you a reward, an incentive, more status, a promotion, all the quid pro quos that exist in the industrial organization," am I motivating you? The overwhelming opinion I receive from management people is, "Yes, this is motivation."

I have a year-old Schnauzer. When it was a small puppy and I wanted it to move, I kicked it in the rear and it moved. Now that I have finished its obedience training, I hold up a dog biscuit when I want the Schnauzer to move. In this instance, who is motivated—I or the dog? The dog wants the biscuit, but it is I who want it to move. Again, I am the one who is motivated, and the dog is the one who moves. In this instance all I did was apply KITA frontally: I exerted a pull instead of a push. When industry wishes to use such positive KITAs, it has available an incredible number and variety of dog biscuits (jelly beans for humans) to wave in front of the employee to get him to jump.

Why is it that managerial audiences are quick to see that negative KITA is not motivation, while they are almost unanimous in their judgment that positive KITA is motivation? It is because negative KITA is rape, and positive KITA is seduction. But it is infinitely worse to be seduced than to be raped; the latter is an unfortunate occurrence, while the former signifies that you were a party to your own downfall. This is why positive KITA is so popular: it is a tradition; it is in the American way. The organization does not have to kick you; you kick yourself.

FREDERICK HERZBERG
Harvard Business Review

To elaborate, when an organization that is superbureaucratic, rigid, and routinized around long-standing patterns of well-ordered and predictable stimuli that have emanated from a habitually stable environment suddenly is confronted with a "new," unstable environment, the organization either must "loosen up" and adapt or die. For example, it is unlikely that a house of *haute couture*, which must be extremely sensitive to changes and trends in its task environment, would last long with a "tall" organizational structure staffed by Prussian officers who ran the fashion house along the lines of Kaiser Wilhelm's army.

Conversely, when an organization is superfluidic and tackles each problem emanating from its environment as something unique, new, and fresh (which indeed may be the case), with no attempt to discover commonalities among tasks and to categorize and routinize them along "rational" lines, suddenly is confronted with a highly stable and structured environment, the organization either must adapt or die from its own inefficiency and absence of structure relative to its environment. For example, it is dubious that United States Steel Corporation, which functions in a very routinized market environment, would survive long if it were staffed by flower children and organized along the lines of Students for a Democratic Society.

To summarize, in terms of matching environmental stability or lack of it, both the closed and open models make sense. From this perspective, it also makes sense that the closed model of organizations traditionally has had a greater impact on the study of public administration than the open model. When the nation was younger and simpler, the government smaller, and public bureaucracy less ambitious and complex, a closed model suited the American milieu. Lately, however, as the nation and government have grown, faced domestic upheavals, weathered technological change, and confronted future shock, the public bureaucracy has taken on new tasks, assumed new duties, and grasped new powers. The environment has changed and is changing rapidly, and the public bureaucracy must adapt to these changes or, if not die, become part of the problem. Thus, the literature of the open model seems destined to having growing influence on the thinking of public administration.

The second basic difference between the closed and open models parallels the first, in that their respective models of man match the models of organization. The late Douglas McGregor called these two models "Theory X" and "Theory Y." Theory X applies to the closed model, particularly to bureaucratic theory. Its underlying belief structure assumes that work is not liked by most people, most people prefer close and unrelenting supervision, most people cannot contribute creatively to the solution of organizational problems, motivation to work is an individual matter, and most people are motivated by the direct application of threat or punishment. It is apparent that organizations exemplifying the closed model not only would fit, but possibly might be appealing to Theory X people.

Theory Y, which goes by other titles as well, such as System 4, Self-Actualization, Intrinsic Motivation, and Eupsychian Management, has quite another underlying belief structure. Theory Y assumes that, given the right conditions, most people can enjoy work as much as play, most people can exercise self-control and prefer doing jobs in their own way, most people can solve organizational problems creatively, motivation to work is a group matter, and most people often are motivated by social and ego rewards. It is apparent that organizations predicated on the open model likely would attract Theory Y people.

There is another aspect to the nature of man posited by the open and closed models, and that is the problem of rationalism. In the closed model, *rational* means that everyone in the organization has the same goals and agrees on how to achieve those goals in an optimal fashion. Consider a hypothetical example. In International Widget, a closed model organization, we may assume that (1) everyone wants to achieve the officially stated goals of the organization, which are to make widgets and profits, and (2) everyone agrees on how widgets should be made and profits reaped with maximum efficiency and economy.

In the open model, however, *rational* has quite a different meaning—it means that everyone in the organization has his own, personal goals and has his own, personal way to achieve those goals. If we turned our example of International Widget into an open-model organization, then the production of widgets and the reaping of profits would be incidental considerations at best to most members of the organization. Their real goals (*i.e.*, their "rationality") would revolve around such values as getting ahead, acquiring status (through salary, position, and reputation), and receiving various other psychological and social satisfactions. Some of these goals are in conflict (for instance, several executives vying for the same promotion) and others are not, although they still may be quite disparate (for instance, one member of the organization may have deeply set needs for organizational prestige, while another may want nothing more than the opportunity to do his own thing, such as auditing). The point is, however, that the official goals of the organization rarely are the real goals of the organization's people.

Moreover, people with the same goals in the organization will likely differ on how those goals should be fulfilled. Two executives competing for a promotion may have quite different means for attaining the same end; one may prefer to cultivate those in influential positions and another may prefer to be judged on his merits, such as his sales record. It should be recalled, however, that in the open model even "merit" will mean different things to different people and, in certain organizational situations, "brown-nosing" may be regarded as a highly meritorious and rational activity. In sum, rationality in organization theory depends on what organization, group, or person you are talking about.

Perceptions of the concept of manipulation

Manipulation in an organizational context simply means getting people to do what you want them to do. Getting one's way, of course, may be accomplished through a wide variety of methods, ranging from brute force to no force at all, and the particular techniques of manipulation correspond with organizational perceptions on the nature of man.

The open model, most notably its organization development school, occasionally appears to argue against the practice of manipulation of men by other men. Manipulation is seen as dehumanizing, "dematurizing" (to use Argyis's term),[23] and generally nasty. Indeed, manipulation inhibits the self-actualization of organizational members and reduces their sense of self-worth. By contrast, the closed model, particularly its bureaucratic theory school, has no qualms about employing manipulative methods. It advocates "using" people for the sake of the organization's ends. Moreover, the callous use of authoritative coercion in manipulating people is seen as entirely legitimate.

The preceding paragraph may overstate the case, but it nonetheless is representative of the differing values of the two models concerning manipulation. In actuality, their difference over manipulation is one of style. In the ideal-type closed model, force is always a possibility; we can conceive of an administrator smashing the nearest chair over his subordinate's cranium in an effort to induce him to do things his way. In fact, similar incidents have happened; public administrators in the government of the Third Reich (as close to a prototype of a closed model organization

23. See, for example, Chris Argyris, *Organization and Innovation* (Homewood, Ill.: Richard D. Irwin, 1965).

as one is likely to find) were known to level Lugers at the necks of subordinates when they displayed reluctance to follow orders and be "a good German." Conversely, the use of coercion in open model organizations is considered reprehensible and is actively discouraged. Manipulation in the open model takes on a far more subtle hue; suggestions replace orders, persuasion supplants coercion, education is favored over obedience, socialization is used instead of force, and cooperation displaces authority. The fundamental idea is to so manipulate organizational members that they "want" to work for the organization.

An example of what this line of thought means in practice is Robert T. Golembiewski's discussion of the "inappropriate 'good morning'" in *Behavior and Organizations*. If administrators are to induce a feeling of supportive relationships among subordinates, goes the reasoning, then they must be aware of the more subtle requisites of the social context. It follows that one should not say "good morning" inappropriately when speaking to subordinates. An explosively cheery "good morning" is likely to put off, say, a secretary as being phony and overdrawn, while a snarled "good morning" or a grunt is likely to make him or her wary and sulky. "Good mornings" must be tailored appropriately in tone to the persons receiving them if individual self-actualization via supportive relationships is to be attained and thereby benefit organizational productivity.[24]

Not all the theorists of the open model are as straightforward in their acceptance of manipulation as Golembiewski. As Allen Schick accurately observes, Argyris, one of the intellectual leaders of organization development, "for two decades . . . has resisted his own findings that organization demands and individual needs are incongruent, and he still labors to develop models of compatibility."[25] Schick rightly perceives in this light that "The reconciliation of man and his organization has proved to be an essential but perhaps hopeless task. Either the individual is autonomous or the organization is dominant, for the very notion of individualism wars against even benevolent organization."[26]

In sum, manipulation is accepted as necessary by the open model as well as the closed model of organizations. Only the techniques of manipulation differ. The closed model theorists, in the tradition of Weber, believed in orders and obedience, rules and regulations, punctuality and punctiliousness. The human dysfunctions of these manipulative techniques are obvious; rigidity, impersonality, narrowness, and stultification number

24. Robert T. Golembiewski, *Behavior and Organizations* (Chicago: Rand-McNally, 1962).

25. Allen Schick, "The Trauma of Politics: Public Administration in the Sixties," in *American Public Administration: Past, Present, Future* (Tuscaloosa, Ala.: University of Alabama Press, 1975), p. 171.

among the human and organizational liabilities of authoritarian manipulation. But there are also human advantages to the crudities of the closed model's manipulative techniques: People in closed model organizations "know where they stand." The authoritarianism of the closed model is for persons who like things straightforward and clearcut.

Just as the disadvantages of the closed model's manipulative techniques are apparent, so the advantages of the open model's methods of manipulation are clear; humanism, openness, communication, and innovation are enhanced by the use of OD concepts. But there are also liabilities to the social-psychological brand of manipulation employed by the open model. The more refined manipulative methods stemming from small group theory, supportive relationships, myths of peerage, and appropriate "good mornings" tend to camouflage the unavoidable exercise of power in organizations. As a result people in open model organizations may never be sure "where they stand." More significantly, if they think that they do know where they stand their knowledge may be the end-product of a manipulation of their psyches so subtle as to render them analogous to the "conditioned" human shell of the protaganist in George Orwell's *1984*, who uncontrollably shrieked "Long Live Big Brother!" even as he despised him. Eric Fromm expresses this idea more succinctly with his concept of "willing submissiveness"; that is, although organizational subordinates may appear to have "team spirit" (and actually may have been so successfully manipulated as to believe they have it), the psychological techniques used to create their willing submissiveness induces in reality a subliminal and deep internal resentment toward their superiors bordering on hatred.[27]

Perceptions of the social role of organizations

The fourth principal difference between the closed and open models is particularly germane to the study of public administration, and centers on how their respective theorists have viewed the organization and its relationships with the larger society. In considering this dimension, we are examining from a different perspective the moral question of organizational manipulation.

Weber provides an especially solid example of a closed model theorist who makes his values explicit in this regard. Weber believed a highly rational bureaucracy to be essential in achieving the goals of the tumultuous, charisma-dominated society that whirled beyond its confines. Without bureaucracy, society would achieve nothing; it would not "progress," it would not replace *Kadijustice* with the rule of rational law. To exaggerate but to nontheless state the point, bureaucracy, replete with its own

27. Eric Fromm, *The Art of Loving* (New York: Harper & Row, 1956).

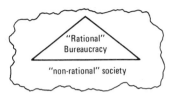

FIGURE 3–1. The Closed Model's View: Organizations *and* Society

internal injustices, dehumanizing rules, and monocratic arbitrariness, was vital in its very rigidity and rationalism to the unorganized societal lunacy that it offset. If Weber's conception of the bureaucracy's station in society could be illustrated, it would look something like Figure 3–1.

Weber was not unsympathetic to the plight of the individual bureaucrat. In fact, he deplored what the mechanization and routinization of bureaucratic settings could do to the human spirit. But, when all was said and done, Weber could accept the dehumanization of society's social servants, who were somehow apart from the other citizens, on the grounds that the bureaucracy was essential to social progress and the elimination of injustice. There was, in sum, a higher morality that provided the *raison d'être* of bureaucracy and, if a few unfortunates were hurt inside the bureaucracy, so be it.

In contrast to Weber, the open model theorists have a completely different conception of the organization's role in society. To them, virtually everyone in society is encased in some sort of organization. Thus, for the public bureaucracy to manipulate and dehumanize its own bureaucrats in order to further society's goals and establish rational social justice is self-defeating, because the bureaucrat and the citizen are one and the same. The open model's view of the role of the organization in society is a complex of interlocking and interacting organizations; society itself is a series of organizations, and there is no unorganized, nonrational society "out there," functioning beyond the organizations' boundaries. The open model's concept of society and the bureaucracy looks like Figure 3–2.

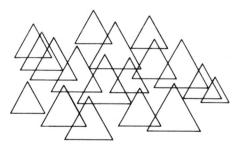

FIGURE 3–2. The Open Model's View: Organizations *as* Society

The contrast between the closed and open modelists is that the closed modelists distinguish between citizens and bureaucrats while the open modelists feel that essentially all citizens are bureaucrats—that is, all citizens belong to or are affected by organizations in some ways. The lack of distinction between citizens and bureaucrats, and between society and its organizations, has led the open model theorists to see moral choice and the concept of the public interest as essentially intraorganizational phenomena. Thus, to treat a member of an organization, particularly a subordinate, badly is immoral because there is no higher morality to excuse such treatment, as there is in Weber's construct. In the open model, what is good for the individual is also good for the society.

THE LITERATURE OF MODEL SYNTHESIS

Students of organizations may be initially confused by the fundamentally different paradigms of organization theory represented by the closed and open models. One model assumes monolithic rationality, the other model assumes nonrationality, by which is meant a pluralist system of many unique rationalities. One model assumes a stable environment, the other assumes an unstable environment. One assumes a Theory X view of man, the other assumes a Theory Y view. One assumes that society is unstructured, the other assumes that society is highly structured. These are basic differences. Can they be reconciled and, if so, how?

The answer to the first part of the question is a qualified "yes," and the attempt to do so is represented by the "newer tradition" of organization theory as exemplified by Herbert A. Simon's *Administrative Behavior,* James G. March and Simon's *Organizations,* Richard Cyert and March's *A Behavioral Theory of the Firm,* and James D. Thompson's *Organizations in Action,* although there is, of course, a much larger literature extant. Barnard's *The Functions of the Executive* also can properly be considered a key work in this stream, as well as a major contribution to the open model.

In terms of conceptually reconciling the two models, it first must be appreciated that our culture really does not facilitate our thinking of opposites as harmonious. It requires some hard concentration to think about something half closed, half open; half certain, half uncertain; half regulated, half spontaneous; and half rational, half nonrational. Yet, this is precisely what Simon, March, Cyert, Thompson, and others try to do, and they largely succeed.

The essence of the literature of model synthesis is that it starts with the open model (that is, it assumes that organizations are spontaneous collectivities of people with their own goals and drives operating in an uncertain environment), but explains organizational behavior as being motivated by a need to routinize and rationalize the organization's internal workings and its relationships with its environment whenever and wherever possible. This is essentially a Darwinian notion (adapt or die). Another way of saying the same thing is that organizations try to become rational. Consider the same concept from another perspective: Organizations try to make all variables (e.g., member behavior, technological and environmental developments) predictable. Visualized differently, we can perceive that organizations try to achieve closure. Yet another (and perhaps the best) way of expressing the same idea is to say that organizations try to reduce uncertainty.

Thus, the two models are synthesized, and the synthesis is predicated on three very reasonable assumptions:

1. Organizations and their environments can and do change.
2. Organizations and the people in them act to survive.
3. Organizations and the people in them can and do learn from mistakes.

The preceding paragraph is an important one, and we shall be referring to it implicitly in the next chapter, which is about some concepts of organization theory. Before closing this chapter, however, let us summarize the three principal models of organization theory with Table 3–1.

TABLE 3–1. The Models of Organization Theory

The Closed Model ⟶	The Literature ⟵ The Open Model of Model Synthesis: Uncertainty Reduction	
1. Bureaucratic theory (Weber).	(Barnard, Simon, March and Simon, Cyert and March, Thompson).	1. Human relations (Roethlisberger and Dickson, Maslow, Mayo, Herzberg).
2. Scientific management (Taylor, the Gilbreths).		2. Organization development (Lewin, McGregor, Bennis, Bechard, French and Bell, Lippitt, Shepard, Blake, Benne, Bradford, Argyris, Golembiewski).
3. Administrative, or generic management (Mooney and Reiley, Gulick and Urwick, Fayol, Follett).		3. The organization as a unit in its environment (Barnard, Selznick, Clark).

SUPPLEMENTAL BIBLIOGRAPHY

ARGYRIS, CHRIS, *Interpersonal Competence and Organizational Effectiveness.* Homewood, Ill.: Dorsey Press, 1962.

BOULDING, KENNETH E., *The Organizational Revolution.* New York: Harper & Row, 1953.

*CAPLOW, THEODORE, *Principles of Organization.* New York: Harcourt Brace Jovanovich, 1964.

*CLARK, BURTON R., "Interorganizational Patterns in Education," *Administrative Science Quarterly,* 10 (September, 1965), 224–37.

*GEORGE, CLAUDE S., JR., *The History of Management Thought.* Englewood Cliffs, N.J.: Prentice-Hall, 1968.

*GILBRETH, FRANK B., and LILLIAN E. GILBRETH, *Applied Motion Study: A Collection of Papers on the Efficient Method to Industrial Preparedness.* New York: Macmillan, 1909.

*GOULDNER, ALVIN W., *Patterns of Industrial Bureaucracy.* New York: Free Press, 1954.

HERZBERG, FREDERICK, BERNARD MAUSNER, and BARBARA SYNDERMAN, *The Motivation to Work.* New York: John Wiley, 1959.

KATZ, DANIEL, and ROBERT L. KAHN, *The Social Psychology of Organizations.* New York: John Wiley, 1966.

*KRUPP, SHERMAN, *Patterns in Organization Analysis: A Critical Analysis.* Philadelphia: Chilton, 1961.

LIKERT, RENSIS, *New Patterns of Management.* New York: McGraw-Hill, 1961.

*LITTERER, JOSEPH A., *The Analysis of Organizations.* New York: John Wiley, 1965.

*McGREGOR, DOUGLAS, *The Human Side of Enterprises.* New York: McGraw-Hill, 1960.

*MARCH, JAMES G., ed., *Handbook of Organizations.* Chicago: Rand McNally, 1961.

*PFIFFNER, JOHN M., and FRANK P. SHERWOOD, *Administrative Organization.* Englewood Cliffs, N.J.: Prentice-Hall, 1960.

PRESTHUS, ROBERT, *Behavioral Approaches to Public Administration.* Tuscaloosa, Ala.: University of Alabama Press, 1965.

*————,*The Organizational Society.* New York: Knopf, 1962.

*ROURKE, FRANCIS E., ed., *Bureaucratic Power in National Politics.* Boston: Little, Brown, 1966.

*————, *Bureaucracy, Politics, and Public Policy.* Boston: Little, Brown, 1969.

*SCOTT, WILLIAM G., *Organizational Theory.* Homewood, Ill.: Irwin, 1967.

*SHERMAN, HARVEY, *It All Depends: A Pragmatic Approach to Organization.* Tuscaloosa, Ala.: University of Alabama Press, 1966.

* Also pertinent to material covered in Chapter 4.

concepts
of
organization theory

chapter 4

This chapter will review briefly some of the speculations and findings generated by organization theorists about organizations. Our review is hardly definitive; it concentrates on the literature of model synthesis explained in Chapter 3, and it considers only those concepts that seem especially germane to public bureaucracies. The concepts covered are: change and innovation (particularly the roles of technology, task environment, and organizational members); information and intelligence; control and authority; decision making and administration; and organizational assessment. These are not neat categories; their many conceptual overlappings are the result of the pervasive emphasis of decision-making theory in the study of organizations.

With the preceding sketch of the chapter's structure in mind, it is important to add three caveats about organization theory generally. First, organization theory is a broad but shallow field. It melds many concepts from many fields, but occasionally the propositions generated by organization theorists do not appear penetratingly insightful. Second, organization theory does not attempt (at least, it rarely attempts) to tell you how to run your organization "better." That ability normally is the product of native intelligence, experience, and motivation. Organization theory does attempt to discover what makes organizations tick, how organizations behave, and what accounts for differences among organizations. This knowledge, it is hoped, may ultimately prove useful to students who eventually find themselves working in a public bureaucracy. Third, as we mentioned in Chapter 2, there are no "principles of organizations" that are worth anything. For every principle, there is a counterprinciple, or the principle itself may be tautological. There are, however, some enlightening perceptions in the literature about how organizations behave, and it is to a few of these that we now turn.

CHANGE AND INNOVATION

Obviously, being able to change, innovate, alter, adapt, or however one labels it is vital to any form of life, and organizations are no exception. Change in organizations is heavily influenced by at least three factors: (1) the technology of the organization (that is, what the organization does and how it does it—its official or formal goals, and its official or formal structure); (2) the task environment in which the organization must function; and (3) how the people in the organization react and interact to technology, environment, and each other.

Organizational technologies

Theorists have attempted to categorize technologies and to relate these categories to other variables in the organization. As technology changes, so will the rest of the organization.

For example, James D. Thompson [1] has classified organizational technologies into three types: long-linked technology, such as the assembly line; mediating technology, found in such institutions as the telephone company, which must deal with people and other variables both extensively and in standardized ways; and intensive technology, used by such organizations as hospitals and scientific laboratories, in which the object of the technology often is a human being and feedback from the technology itself is important to the organization. These three technologies correlate with at least three other organizational variables that are significant to change and adaptation: the cost of the operation in terms of decision, effort, and communication; the type of interdependence found among people and among parts of the organization; and the style of coordination necessary to the organization. To elaborate, a mediating technology would have low operating costs, "pooled" or "generalized" in-

1. James D. Thompson, *Organizations in Action* (New York: McGraw-Hill, 1967), pp. 14–82.

terdependence (*i.e.*, each unit of the telephone company, such as linemen, contribute to the organization, but the company could continue functioning despite the elimination of one of its units), and standardization of parts and units is the chief means of coordination. A long-linked technology would have intermediate costs, interdependence would be "sequential" (*i.e.*, no worker on the assembly line can work until the worker preceding him has completed his task), and planning is the form of coordination favored. An intensive technology would have high costs, "reciprocal" interdependence (every part and person of the organization is dependent upon every other part and person), and would be coordinated through mutual adjustment of the parts. Thompson's view of technology and change in organizations is arranged in summary form in Table 4–1.

Charles Perrow [2] is even more adamant about the significance of technology for organizational change, and he empirically illustrates how technology affects the power structure of organizations. (Thompson only implies this, but, after all, interdependence and coordination are variants of power in any social setting.) Perrow's study of hospitals is intriguing in this regard. He notes that when hospitals used relatively simple technologies, boards of trustees tended to form the central power structure, but when medical technologies became more complex, physicians dominated hospital power relationships. Moreover, as medical technologies became more sophisticated, official hospital goals changed from a "humanistic" and charitable mission to a technically proficient and professionally remunerative mission. Finally, when hospital technologies began to require the use of consultants, specialists, outside experts, and coordination,

TABLE 4–1. Technology and Organizational Variables

Type of Technology	Type of Interdependence	Type of Coordination	Operating Costs
Mediating (e.g., a telephone company).	Pooled	Standardization	Low
Long-linked (e.g., an assembly line).	Sequential	Planning	Intermediate
Intensive (e.g., a scientific laboratory).	Reciprocal	Mutual Adjustment	High

2. Charles Perrow, "The Analysis of Goals in Complex Organizations," *American Sociological Review* 26 (December 1961), 854–66; and "Hospitals: Technology, Structure and Goals," *Handbook of Organizations*, James G. March ed. (New York: Rand-McNally, 1965).

administrators became the power elite. A change of goals also accompanied this change in technology, and the official hospital mission was suddenly perceived as including the social as well as the physical aspects of medicine.

Public administration uses all three of Thompson's technological types, and its technologies are becoming increasingly sophisticated. The role of technology in the process of organizational change is a significant and largely internal factor. The chief external factor in the process of organizational change, the task environment, will now be considered.

Organizational environments

(Environmental changes can have such profound effects that organizations will radically transform themselves to survive in an altered environment.) Sheldon L. Messinger has noted how the Townsend Movement, for example, which originally was a politically activist plan to alleviate unemployment in the mid-1930s, gradually converted itself into a recreational club after the Social Security Act was enacted, which effectively knocked the ideological underpinnings from the Plan. Townsendites continued to pay lip service to their plan despite the presence of Social Security.[3]

In an effort to find out how organizational capacity for change related to the nature of the organization's task environment, Tom Burns and G. M. Stalker [4] conducted extensive empirical research at two fundamentally different organizations operating in highly dissimilar environments. Their study of a Scottish yarn factory and a Scottish electrical engineering firm indicates radically different organizational structures as a function of environmental impacts. The engineering company had virtually continuous meetings, no written job descriptions, no rule book, and an informality surpassing that of the Israeli Army, largely as the result of an unstable, rapidly changing task environment. The firm was quite successful in coping with fast-paced environmental changes because it was geared for them.

The yarn textile company was a well-established firm with a long tradition of industrial success. It had a massive rule book called the "Factory Bible" (which was followed scrupulously), highly formal and infrequent meetings, and painfully clear superordinate/subordinate relationships. But, because of recent changes in the historically hidebound task environment of the textile trade (*e.g.*, polyesters, blends, knits, and new

3. Sheldon L. Messinger, "Organizational Transformation: A Case Study of a Declining Social Movement," *American Sociological Review* 20 (February 1955), 3–10.

4. Tom Burns and G. M. Stalker, *The Management of Innovation* (London: Tavistock, 1961).

marketing techniques), the firm was in trouble. Lack of structural response to a changing environment was hurting the organization financially.

Relatedly, William R. Dill has observed how the task environment can affect the autonomy and the capacity to effect changes in top management.[5] Dill's study of two Norwegian companies, "Alpha" (a clothing manufacturer) and "Beta" (an electronics firm) concluded that the Alpha management, operating in a stable environment subject to few unexpected contingencies, had far less autonomy than the Beta management. Alpha managers had relatively less freedom to make innovative decisions either in terms of the company's owners or relative to their fellow managers.

If this book's original hypothesis—that public administration increasingly is in a time of turbulence—is valid, then it also may follow that public administrators increasingly may find themselves possessing greater latitude and exercising greater power in dealing with that turbulence, at least if Perrow's and Dill's analyses are correct. Certainly the intellectual development of the field implies that this has been and will be the case. The belated recognition by public administrationists that public administrators do make political decisions would seem to be another way of saying that public bureaucrats, confronted with an increasingly unstable task environment (*i.e.*, the society), have gained increasing autonomy with which to deal with their environment.

Organizational members

The causal relationships between technology, environment, and organizational change are obscure, but we do know that alterations in technology and environment are major factors in organizational innovation, and that these factors are "felt" by the organization through the people who make up the organization. For example, James G. March and Herbert A. Simon have noted that when an organization becomes stabilized in terms of technological and environmental change, the phenomenon of "goal displacement" often occurs.[6] That is, means become ends, or suboptimal goals become optimal goals for various parts of the organization. In the hypothetical organization of International Widget, for instance, it may happen that the advertising department perceives the optimal end of the company to be creative marketing, rather than selling widgets. But to the president of International Widget, presumably, creative marketing—or, even more to the point, effective advertising—is simply a means of selling

5. William R. Dill, "Environment as an Influence on Managerial Autonomy," *Administrative Science Quarterly* 2 (March 1958), 409–43.

6. James G. March and Herbert A. Simon, *Organizations* (New York: John Wiley, 1958), p. 38.

widgets. And to the corporation's stockholders, selling widgets is merely a means of making money. In each instance, goals have been displaced.

Change occurs in other ways, too. In an organization characterized by instability, change comes through (to borrow Richard Cyert's and March's term) organizational "drift." [7] Drift refers to the directions in which the organization flows as the result of various member coalitions being formed and reformed within its boundaries.

Of course, despite changes in technology and environment that affect human participants, organizational change can still be hindered by those members who are both powerful and conservative. Anthony Downs has noted the propensity of new organizations to be composed of "climbers," who are ambitious for the advancement that accompanies organizational innovation, and for old organizations to be dominated by "conservers," who feel more secure in stable, if possibly dying, organizations. [8] At the lower echelons, Michel Crozier has observed the inclination of French workers to resist changes that could be of obvious benefit to the organization's welfare, and ultimately their own, out of a deep psychological sense of *bon plaisir*, or the peculiarly French pride of having a recognizable, bureaucratic, and rational "place" in the organization's structure. [9]

Downs and Crozier oddly parallel each other's thoughts about how organizations change. Downs sees the process as related to an "age lump" phenomenon: Organizations grow old and stultified just as their members do, and when the conservers retire they often do so as a "lump," making way for a resurgence of change-oriented climbers. Thus, organizational change alternates between lethargic "drift" and "re-organizational catch-up."

Crozier sees essentially the same effect but with a slightly different dynamic. Because of the growing bureaucratic rigidity brought about by generally shared attitudes of *bon plaisir*, French organizations either must face collapse or revolutionary change from the top. The need to rationalize and bureaucratize is carried to the limit in French organizations, and with little regard for technological and environmental changes. Hence, change, when it comes, is revolutionary yet authoritarian, because it is long overdue and because the *bon plaisir* mentality of organizational members is one cultivated to resist cooperative innovation.

Downs's notion of an age lump in the life cycle of organizations and Crozier's concept that delayed change eventually means revolutionary change have some interesting applications in public administration. Public administration is facing an age lump of its own. The "Depression virtuo-

7. Richard M. Cyert and James G. March, *A Behavioral Theory of the Firm* (Englewood Cliffs, N.J.: Prentice-Hall, 1963).

8. Anthony Downs, *Inside Bureaucracy* (Boston: Little, Brown, 1967), pp. 92–101.

9. Michel Crozier, *The Bureaucratic Phenomenon* (Chicago: University of Chicago Press, 1964), pp. 220–224.

sos"—those talented administrators who entered government service in the 1930s because they could not find better-paying jobs in business—are in the process of retiring. Moreover, and also as a result of the Depression, there is an unusually small portion of the American population between the ages of twenty-five and forty-four, which habitually has provided the chief source of administrative personnel in government. Whether the upshot of these factors will amount to some sort of "revolutionary" change from the top in the public bureaucracy is a moot question, but it is notable that a new breed of climbers (women, ethnic groups, and highly educated youth) is knocking at the conservers' door with rising insistence.

INFORMATION AND INTELLIGENCE IN ORGANIZATIONS

How information, intelligence, and knowledge are used, distorted, and transmitted has considerable significance for what we have just considered in the preceding section: change in organizations. Cybernetist and operations researcher Stafford Beer, in fact, defines information as "what changes us." [10] Additionally, the uses of intelligence have particular significance for the understanding of public bureaucracies, for it is on knowledge and feedback that public policy decisions are made and adjusted.

Hierarchy and Information

Perhaps the most focused research in the field of organizational intelligence has been done by Harold L. Wilensky. [11] Wilensky considers both private and public organizations, but it is clear that public bureaucracies stand to gain or lose the most from how information is used or abused. Wilensky's basic contention is that organizational change and control are achieved through the control of information. He observes that organizational change is hindered by such phenomena as "the significance of slogans," "the power of preconceptions," and, perhaps paramountly, secrecy.

In Wilensky's view, organizational conflict, informational control, and personal power are inextricably intertwined. Consider Wilensky's example of Nazi Foreign Minister Ribbentrop and his use of the notorious World War II spy, "Cicero," who was the valet of the British ambassador at Ankara. Cicero sent astonishingly accurate and detailed intelligence concerning the Allied invasion plans to Ribbentrop. Although the Foreign

10. Stafford Beer, "Managing Modern Complexity," *The Management of Information and Knowledge.* Panel on Science and Technology (11th meeting). Proceedings before the Committee on Science and Astronautics, U.S. House of Representatives, 91st Congress, Second Session, January 27, 1970, No. 15 (Washington, D.C.: U.S. Government Printing Office, 1970).

11. Harold L. Wilensky, *Organizational Intelligence* (New York: Basic Books, 1967). The saga of Cicero is on pp. 68–69.

Minister had his doubts as to the authenticity of Cicero's reports, his overriding reason for sitting on most of Cicero's information appears to have been interagency rivalry. Ribbentrop was involved in a bitter power struggle with the Reich Security Office, and he loathed von Papen, the German ambassador to Turkey. Because Cicero reported directly to one L. C. Moyzisch, an attaché on von Papen's staff employed by the Reich Security Office, Ribbentrop found it most expedient to dismiss Cicero's intelligence. Wilensky concludes from this and other instances that the use of secrecy exaggerates organizational pathologies that already may be present, such as conflict, authoritarianism, lack of feedback, and excessive personal power.

Wilensky also argues that information may be distorted or prevented from reaching the people who need it and can act on it by excessive centralization or decentralization of the organization. As an example of what happens to knowledge in a decentralized (or open model) organization, Wilensky cites the surprise of American troops at Pearl Harbor during the Japanese attack. The Japanese secret code had been broken, and there is substantial evidence showing that various elements in the military and foreign services knew approximately when and where the Japanese would attack. But the information failed to reach the forces at Pearl Harbor in time.

Partly as a response to the intelligence fiasco of Pearl Harbor, the aptly dubbed Central Intelligence Agency (CIA) was established. The idea was that important messages no longer would be lost in the interorganizational shuffle, as in the Pearl Harbor incident, but would be sent directly to the people who were in a position to respond to new knowledge, including the president.

Nevertheless, information can be blocked in centralized (or closed model) organizations, too. Wilensky cites the Cuban Bay of Pigs disaster as an example. In this instance, the CIA evidently approached the freshly elected President John F. Kennedy with what it represented as a longstanding, well-formulated, and superbly-conceived (not to mention, surefire) plan for the overthrow of Premier Fidel Castro's revolutionary government in Cuba. Kennedy, who later implied he had been somewhat awed by the intelligence-gathering capabilities and expertise of the CIA and, in any event, had no comparable organization in terms of prestige to which he could turn for additional intelligence, decided to let the agency carry on, essentially in its own way. Among the other aspects of remarkably poor planning by the CIA, as it turned out, was the agency's ignorance of extensive swamps in the Bay of Pigs area, which entrapped the invasion force on the coastline and made the Cuban expatriates easy pickings for Castro's troops.

Gordon Tullock [12] has argued that organizational decentralization is more conducive than centralization to the preservation of information and the minimization of its distortion in organizations. Tullock constructs an arithmetic "model of hierarchical distortion," in which he reasons that the more an organization grows, the more effort and expense will be required for "internal" administration, to the detriment of the "external" achievement of organizational goals relative to the society. This pathology is unavoidable because the larger the bureaucracy, the more time must be devoted by its members to assuring that information reaches the right administrators relatively intact; in other words, the bigger the bureaucracy, the more people who may stop, distort, take away from, or add to the same information bit, and hence greater effort must be generated to preserve "noise"-free intraorganizational communications at the expense of accomplishing the organization's social mission. As a result of this reasoning, Tullock advocates that bureaucracies be vastly reduced in size so that the society may benefit more directly. Tullock believes that in small organizations the goal and rationality of the organization (*e.g.*, legal assistance for the poor) are more likely to complement the goals and rationalities of the individuals in the organization (*e.g.*, getting ahead) because it is far easier to see causal relationships between individual acts and mission accomplishment in small organizations than in large organizations, and the evaluation of organizational performance is thus much easier. Tullock's recommendation is a radical one relative to the rest of organization theory, which tends to regard organizational growth as a sign of health.

James G. March and Herbert A. Simon also have noticed that information tends to be distorted by multiple levels of hierarchy.[13] They note the pathology of "uncertainty absorption" in bureaucratic organizations, whereby data that initially are regarded as tentative, uncertain, and "soft" by the persons who collect them become increasingly final, certain, and "hard" as they are sent up through the decision-making hierarchy. Thus, we may assume that in the decision by Ford Motor Company to build the Edsel, the corporation's low-level market researchers concluded that there "might" be a market for a middle-range car in the United States, but by the time their findings reached Henry Ford it was being voiced in top management circles that there "was" such a market; uncertainty in the initial information had been absorbed by the various hierarchical levels that handled it on its way to upper management.

12. Gordon Tullock, *The Politics of Bureaucracy* (Washington, D.C.: Public Affairs Press, 1965).

13. March and Simon, *op. cit.*, p. 165.

It also is worth observing that organizations can collapse because of too much information. Richard L. Meier conducted an intriguing study of a university library that was in the process of administratively breaking down because of too many demands and not enough resources. He examined how institutions without the benefits of functioning in a free-market environment where information inputs could be adjusted through market mechanisms responded to communications overload.[14] He delineated fourteen strategies used by such organizations to cope with rising levels of informational stress, including queuing (e.g., keeping library patrons in waiting rooms "outside" the organization); the creation of branch facilities; creation of a mobile reserve (e.g., teams of personnel transferable to units as needed); the evolvement of specific performance standards followed immediately by a reduction of those standards; a "brain-storming" search for a "magic formula"; promotion of self-service (e.g., letting patrons into the stacks, which is a radical strategy because it represents a deliberate reduction of organizational sovereignty); the limitation of work to capacity as determined by rigid, ritualistic rules and characterized by the denial of error and the refusal of challenge; and, ultimately, the dissolution of the organization. The library, in a very real sense, had no choice but to play out this scenario. It did not have the control over demands from its environment that, say, International Widget would have had. International Widget could simply boost the price of widgets, and thereby reduce demand, or communications overload. But the library—and, presumably, any public organization—did not have this option. It had to adjust internally.

These and other studies of informational dynamics in organizations are especially relevant to public administration for a number of reasons. Public organizations tend to be bureaucratic organizations, they do not operate in free-market environments, and they "produce" policies rather than products. Information is of unusual importance to all these characteristics and functions. And recent developments in public administration indicate that information will be of even more importance to the public bureaucracy and the public. One such development is the growing professionalism and expertise of the public administrator.

Professionalism and public knowledge

The professionalization of public administration represents a second development that seems destined to affect the free flow of knowledge in the task milieu of the public bureaucrat. By *professionalization* is meant the evolvement of a core of commonly shared and recognized knowledge and

14. Richard L. Meier, "Communications Overload," *Administrative Science Quarterly* 7 (March 1963), 529–44.

expertise held by members of a group. The rise of the M.P.A. and D.P.A. degrees, the establishment of professional schools of public administration and public affairs, and the appearance of new professional journals and associations all indicate that public administration is professionalizing as never before.

Paradoxically, professionalization of the public service has both benefits and liabilities for the public. As York Willbern noted in a seminal article on the subject,[15] professionalism in public bureaucracies brings increased technical competence, increased respect for technical expertise, the enforcement of minimal ethical and technical standards, insulation from pressure to discriminate against clients, the avoidance of direct democratic control that might be of doubtful utility in some fields, greater interchangeability of personnel among governmental units, the incentive for officials to acquire more skills, the creation of in-group loyalty, and the provision of additional satisfactions to employees. Conversely, however, professionalism also brings with it

1. potential conflicts of interest between the professional group (*e.g.*, school teachers) and larger publics (*e.g.*, taxpayers)
2. the presence of undue influence wielded by special publics through professional ties (such as the medical profession's occasionally debatable impact on public health programs in some states through the American Medical Association)
3. the insulation of public servants from public control
4. the lack of internal democracy often found in professional associations
5. the limitation of public services by the professionals' insistence on the maintenance of unrealistic professional standards
6. the diminishing of transferability of personnel among agencies because of overly specialized training
7. the lack of interagency coordination because of professional specialization or jealousy
8. the discouraging of citizen participation by the presence of a professional mystique

Most if not all of the dysfunctions of professionalism listed by Willbern revolve around the control of knowledge and expertise—or what often passes for expertise. If knowledge is power, then how is professional knowledge (with its antidemocratic implications) to be used to further the goals of society? Obviously, it must be used carefully, for the

---

15. York Willbern, "Professionalization in the Public Service: Too Little or Too Much?" *Public Administration Review* 14 (Winter 1954), 13–21.

very idea of being professional carries with it a dangerous footnote for democratic values: "We know more than you, therefore do as we say."

A homely example of how professional status, mystique, and expertise exercise a control over information that prevents and undermines the manifestation of democratic values is provided by Alan Altshuler in his study of a decision to locate a freeway in the Minneapolis-St. Paul area.[16] The local highway department made a conscious, internal decision to be inflexible on the proposed freeway's route and location and based this decision on the unsophisticated but "professional" criterion of a crude cost/benefit analysis. This analysis formed the core rationale of the department's justification of its decision. More profoundly, however, the department's sole, and quite effective, justification of its decision was that it was made on the basis of professional and technical values, and who could argue with "the facts"? This argument won the day, despite very legitimate pressures brought by blacks, white residents in some of the few remaining middle-class neighborhoods in downtown St. Paul (who had the quiet support of the governor), retailers in the central business district, and the existence of an alternative route developed by the city planner that would have satisfied these many protests. Expertise and the control of information took political precedence because they were presumed to be apolitical.

James D. Carroll has extended the concept of professionalism and has called it "noetic authority," or the power that derives from knowledge. He argues that the politics and administration of the future will be based on who controls information and knowledge rather than who controls wealth and power. Carroll cites the rise of a plethora of political and administrative issues involving the press, telecommunications, urban planning, the environment, education, transportation, and consumerism, among others, as disputes in which the old "politics of greed" is being displaced by the new "politics of knowledge."[17]

CONTROL AND AUTHORITY IN ORGANIZATIONS

Organizational intelligence and noetic authority as concepts overlap considerably with organizational control and authority. He who controls information possesses genuine power in the bureaucracy.

The analyst most noted for his argument that authority is the central

16. Alan Altshuler, *The City Planning Process: A Political Analysis* (Ithaca, N.Y.: Cornell University Press, 1965).

17. James D. Carroll, "Noetic Authority," *Public Administration Review* 29 (September–October 1969), 492–500.

variable in organizational behavior is Amitai Etzioni.[18] Etzioni contends that power is all, and that virtually all characteristics of the organization are determined by the kind of authority used in the organization. For example, a prison uses "coercive" power, its method of control is physical (*e.g.*, solitary confinement); the organization acquires participants through the socialization of inmates; both officials (*e.g.*, the warden) and informal leaders (popularly respected or feared prisoners with no official position) are present; and "instrumental activities" (mechanical kinds of activities) predominate as the organization's chief technology. At the other extreme of Etzioni's power continuum, a political party uses "identitive," or "normative" power; its method of control is symbolic (*e.g.*, appeals to patriotism); the organization acquires participants both through the socialization of its members and the selection of applicants; only "formal leaders" (or leaders who have both real and official power) are present, and "expressive activities" (or interpersonal activities) predominate as the organization's chief activity. Finally, in the middle ranges of Etzioni's continuum, a business corporation uses "utilitarian" power; its method of control is material (*e.g.*, a salary); participants are acquired chiefly through a selection process; leadership comprises all types (officials, informal leaders, and formal leaders), and activities may be both instrumental and expressive. Etzioni's concept is diagrammed in Table 4–2.

Most organization theorists, however, are not so clear-cut as Etzioni in their views of control and authority. Cyert and March, Downs, and Thompson more or less share the same concept of how control and au-

TABLE 4–2. A Continuum of Organizational Power and Authority

	Type of Power	Method of Control	Acquisition of Participants	Type of Leadership	Type of Activities
	Coercive (e.g., a prison).	Physical	Socialization	Officials and informal leaders	Instrumental
Authority	Utilitarian (e.g., a business corporation).	Material	Selection	Officials, informal leaders and formal leaders	Instrumental and Expressive
	Identitive or normative (e.g., a political party).	Symbolic	Selection and socialization	Formal leaders	Expressive

18. Amitai Etzioni, *Modern Organizations* (Englewood Cliffs, N.J.: Prentice-Hall, 1964).

thority are achieved in organizations. In their view, "slack," bargaining, "side payments," and coalition formation represent the dynamics of organizational control. Slack refers to those "nonrational" interestices present in even the most rigid bureaucracies that represent opportunities for what is known in the military as "scrounging" (e.g., an unused typewriter in the accounting department mysteriously and "unofficially" finds its way to the advertising department where it receives considerable use). Side payments in organizations would not be possible without organizational slack. Side payments can be made in the form of status (e.g., a new "unofficial" carpet for an individual's office or a promotion in name only, with no increase in salary or authority) or as material rewards (e.g., a salary increment). Side payments are usually made on the basis of discreet bargaining between the representatives of coalitions (e.g., "young Turks," "old guard," whatever) in the organization, and genuine authority in the organization is determined by who represents what coalitions.

Styles of authority and control must change as the organization changes. Thus, the military sociologist Morris Janowitz [19] suggests that the old, closed model style of authority traditionally favored in the military, that of "domination," is no longer suitable for an organization characterized by such technological and environmental changes as new weapons systems, the adoption of deterrence as a strategy, the routinization of innovation, and the blurring of historic soldier/civilian distinctions. Janowitz urges that a "fraternal type authority" based on the open model's techniques of manipulation replace the domineering techniques normally used in the military.

The notion of styles of authority leads us to the problem of the legitimacy—indeed, even the morality—of authority. Chester Barnard was perhaps the first theorist to appreciate that there was more to authority than a boss giving orders to an underling; Barnard pointed out that a subordinate had to *accept* a superior's directive before that superior could ever have something called authority, or power. Even more profoundly, Barnard contended that, before an order could be accepted by a subordinate, the superior first had to penetrate the subordinate's "zone of indifference." Most of the time, Barnard said, underlings really could care less about what a boss directed. Thus, authority was conceived as a two-way process between subordinate and superior, and this "two-wayness" added to the legitimacy of authority.[20]

Herbert A. Simon, whose early work was intensely influenced by Barnard, extended Barnard's concept of authority by positing four basic

19. Morris Janowitz, "Changing Patterns of Organizational Authority: The Military Establishment," *Administrative Science Quarterly* 3 (March 1959), 473–93.

20. Chester I. Barnard, *The Functions of the Executive* (Cambridge, Mass.: Harvard University Press, 1938).

motivations of subordinates to accept the will of a superior: rewards and sanctions, legitimacy, social approval, and the subordinate's confidence in the superior's abilities.[21] Of these motivations, those of rewards and sanctions are the most interesting, if for no other reason than that Simon thought the subordinate had more rewards and sanctions at his disposal than the superior! The superior had only three: the power to hire and fire; the power to promote and demote, and certain incentive rewards. But the subordinate had at least twice that number: the power to quit, to strike, to slow down, to perform minimally, to perform "literally" (or to do only the jobs specified), and not to perform.

Although the style of authority changes as organizations change, those at the top of the organization's hierarchy still can control to a degree how the other members exercise their authority via the control of their "decision premises," to use Simon's phrase.[22] A decision premise refers to the values and perceptions held by each member of the organization, on which he bases every decision he makes regarding the organization. These individual values and perceptions are unique to the individual, but many can be altered and influenced through the use of organizational means and sanctions available to those in positions of control, the division of labor in the organization and how it affects the individual, standard operating procedures used in the organization, the socialization and training of new members of the organization, and the kinds of people who are selected to join the organization. Together, these techniques can mold each individual's decision premise in a way that reduces organizational uncertainty by making the individual's decisions predictable. When uncertainty is low (*e.g.*, "I trust Bob to do the right thing . . ."), authority and control often are relinquished or "decentralized" (". . . so I've made him responsible for the job").

Many organizations attempt to control, or at least filter, the decision premises of applicants even before they enter the organization. Some businesses prefer applicants who are business majors and fraternity members over applicants who majored in sociology and were independents. The rationale is that "B-school" joiners are more likely to cultivate a corporate team spirit than are socially aware loners. After entry, subordinates' decision premises are formed more fully by superordinates through "management training" classes and the more subtle socialization techniques extant in most large organizations.

21. Herbert A. Simon, *Administrative Behavior: A Study of Decision-Making Processes in Administrative Organization*, 3rd ed., (New York: Free Press, 1976), pp. 123–53. But see also the essay by Simon and Robert Bierstedt in *Studies in Managerial Process and Organizational Behavior*, John H. Turner, Alan C. Filley, and Robert J. House, eds. (Glenview, Ill.: Scott, Foresman, 1972), pp. 59–72.

22. Simon, *op. cit.*, pp. 48–52.

In contrast to business administration, however, public administration has been far less able to control the decision premises of decision-making participants in public bureaucracies. True, there is a selection and socialization process in public bureaucracies but, more than other bureaucracies, public bureaucracies make decisions in situations characterized by unusual degrees of participation from the task environment. The public administrator, especially in recent years that have been characterized by a social milieu advocating "power to the people" increasingly finds himself asking "client-members" of his organization to participate in the decision-making process. A client-member is a person who is both a "customer" and a member of an organization, such as a student in a university or an inmate in a prison. Examples of decision-making participation by client-members in public administration would include urban renewal, anti-poverty, and legal assistance programs, although the list might be almost endless. In any event, public administrators often find that they lack the authority and control possessed by administrators in other institutional settings, despite the power gained through the prestige that accompanies professionalization. This situation may well be to the ultimate benefit of the polity, but it often does not seem so to the frustrated public administrator confronting what occasionally appears to be organizational and environmental chaos.

DECISION-MAKING AND ADMINISTRATION IN ORGANIZATIONS

Simon's notion of decision premises provides a convenient introduction to the more general consideration of decision making and administration. Simon argues stringently for the concept that virtually all decisions in organizations are only "satisficing" decisions; that is, decisions do not maximize, they only satisfy and suffice, or (combined) "satisfice." [23] The satisficing idea ties in with the other concepts of the model synthesis literature—organizational members are limited by their own "bounded rationality," slack characterizes even the "tightest" organizations, and so forth—but it is disconcerting nonetheless to conclude that organizations simply muddle through their problems and task environments, and that their members are almost incapable of making a perfect (or maximizing) decision. Yet this may well be the most realistic view of bureaucracy, and perhaps of the human condition generally.

James D. Thompson and Arthur Tuden, [24] accepting Simon's idea of

23. *Ibid.*, pp. 38–41, 240–44.
24. James D. Thompson and Arthur Tuden, "Strategies, Structures and Processes of Organizational Decision," *Comparative Studies in Administration*, James D. Thompson, *et al.*, eds. (Pittsburgh: The University of Pittsburgh Press, 1959), pp. 195–216.

satisficing, developed a "typology of decision issues," in which they matched decision-making strategies with whether organizational members agreed or disagreed about what causes what, and whether members agreed or disagreed about what the organization should do. For example, in a bureaucracy of specialists, in theory everyone would agree about causation ("If you fill out the form, then you will get your social security check"), and they would agree about decision outcomes ("Social Security is worthwhile to society"). In such a bureaucracy, decisions would be made "computationally"; that is, with little or no internal debate about values and with decisions made on the basis of shared technical perceptions. Other kinds of organizations necessitate other kinds of decision-making strategies; the matrix in Table 4–3 summarizes them.

In all these situations, however, the art of administration rests on the concept of ("coalition management." Every organization is a complex of coalitions and, while technologies, environments, and perceptions will always be unique, politically motivated coalitions will always be common. Thus, one way of expressing what an administrative decision-maker does is to say that he manages coalitions that are contending, cooperating, and coalescing inside his organization.

Public administration has both contributed to and borrowed from the literature of decision-making theory, and these concepts shall be referred to as we discuss other facts of public administration in later chapters. For instance, in Chapter 6, where we consider administrative decision-making from the perspective of individual ethics, or in Section 3, where we discuss some quantitative administrative techniques and analysis, the overriding if implicit questions are: Can satisficing decisions be made

TABLE 4–3.   A Typology of Decision-Making Strategies

| | Preferences about Outcomes | |
	Agreement	Disagreement
Agreement	Computational decision-making (e.g., an organization of specialists).	Compromising decision-making (e.g., Congress agrees that it facilitates social change, but disagrees about how society should be changed).
Beliefs about Causation		
Disagreement	Judgmental decision-making (e.g., a college agrees that students should learn, but disagrees on how to cause learning).	Inspirational decision-making (e.g., An "anomic" organizational, such as France in 1958— De Gaulle's Fifth Republic represented inspirational and authoritarian decision-making).

more maximal? Can we afford satisficing decisions much longer? Part and parcel of this pastiche of questions is that of making decisions about how effectively the organization as a whole is performing. We consider this aspect next.

Herbert A. Simon and the Theory of "Bounded Rationality"

In 1978, Herbert A. Simon became the first scholar closely associated with public administration to win the Nobel Prize in Economics (and, in the process, inspiring the academic joke, "What's a successful public administrationist?" "An economist."). In the following selection, a long-time collaborator of Simon's explains in unusually lucid language Simon's major contribution to decision-making theory.

In company with most economists, Simon began with the assumption that human choice behavior was intendedly rational. That is, he assumed that decision-makers had a set of criteria known to them in advance of their actions, and that they made choices by measuring estimates of the consequence of alternative actions against the criteria. What Simon added was an awareness of the informational and computational limits on rationality within human institutions. Where most theories of rational choice assumed that all relevant alternatives were known, Simon suggested that alternatives had to be discovered through search and that typically only a relatively few alternatives were considered. Where most theories assumed that information on the consequences of alternatives was known, at least up to a probability distribution, Simon suggested that information had to be sought through some kind of search. Where most theories assumed that decision-makers optimized—that is, looked until they found the best alternative from the point of view of their preferences—Simon suggested that decision-makers "satisficed"—that is, chose the first alternative that was "good enough."

The perspective was behavioral. Simon argued that the rationality demanded of human beings by classical theories of rational choice was not observed in actual human behavior and was inconsistent with what was known about human capabilities for processing information. The argument was narrow. Most rational theories of choice already assumed that choice was constrained by factors of availability, cost, technology, time, and the like. Simon added the idea that the list of constraints of choice should include not only external factors in the environment but also some properties of human beings as processors of information and as problem-solvers. He called attention to human limits on memory and computing power, viewing them as obvious restrictions on full rationality. Thus, he initiated a string of related developments by others that have come collectively to be called a theory of limited, or bounded, rationality. In a proper sense, these developments comprise not a theory but a collection of behavioral complications for conventional theory. The number of such complications has grown considerably . . . but Simon's formulation remains the core.

Simon focused on three aspects of bounded rationality. The first was the extent to which information was sought through search in response to a problem rather than simply given. He assumed a search process stimulated by a failure or a need, and characterized by working backward from a desired outcome to a set of antecedent actions sufficient (but not necessary) to produce it. The second was the conception of preferences. He proposed substituting two-valued utility functions for the more complete preference orders familiar to decision theory. Alternatives were assumed to be judged sequentially and to be defined as either satisfactory or unsatisfactory, with much less attention to finer discriminations within those categories. The third was the importance of ordinary rules of behavior. Decisions were seen as the result of combining premises and rules that were modified through a long-term process only marginally affected by a current choice.

The standard metaphor for the theory reflects both the simplicity of the ideas and the memories of a Wisconsin boyhood. Consider a farmer confronting a haystack and deciding what to do with it. To make a decision in purely classical form, he would want to know (among other things) all of the contents of the haystack, all possible uses of each of the contents and combinations of them, and the probability distribution over all possible consequences of each. Simon observed that few farmers behave in such a way. A more typical farmer reduces the size of the problem. He notices that his shirt needs a button, and considers looking for the sharpest needle in the haystack. That seems a difficult thing to do, so he decides to look for any needle good enough to sew a button. But then he remembers an old family rule that shirts needing buttons should be hung in the laundry. So he does that. Simon's great contribution was to point out that decision-making in economic organizations is more like hanging a shirt in the laundry than looking for the sharpest needle in the haystack.

JAMES G. MARCH
Science

ASSESSING THE PERFORMANCE OF PUBLIC ORGANIZATIONS

Meier's article on the tribulations of a university library undergoing pressures from its environment was cited earlier as an example of the difficulty that a public organization has in dealing with a task environment that lacks the benefit of a market mechanism. On another plane, Meier's dilemma is one of how to assess the performance and efficiency of all public organizations. Unlike business corporations, government agencies normally cannot measure their performance by the fatness of their profits.

James D. Thompson has framed the organizational assessment problem in a more rigorous manner. He observes that organizations may be evaluated according to one of three "tests"; the appropriateness of any one of these tests depends on the nature of the organization. Thompson posits efficiency, instrumental, and social tests as ways of assessing organizational performance,[25] and, in several ways, these tests represent a conceptual extension of Thompson and Tuden's earlier work on decision issues (see Table 4–3).

The *efficiency test* relates to Thompson and Tuden's notion of "computational decision-making," and is applicable to organizations that have "crystallized standards of desirability," and whose members believe they fully comprehend the relationships between causes and effects. For example, executives in our hypothetical corporation of International Widget have a solid notion of what they want to do and how to do it: maximize profits (*i.e.*, their standards of desirability are quite firm and clear, or "crystallized") and manufacture widgets as cheaply as possible (*i.e.*, there is a clear causal connection between high profits and cheap production). Thus, assessing the performance of International Widget as an organization is both objective and easy; efficiency, or economic, tests are applicable.

The *instrumental test* is less objective, less easy to apply, and less optimal in evaluating organizational performance than the efficiency test. But it is the only kind of test that is appropriate for certain kinds of organizations, notably organizations that use "judgemental decision-making." Instrumental tests are applicable to organizations that, like International Widget, have crystallized standards of desirability (*e.g.*, high profits) but, unlike International Widget, the organizational members are uncertain about what causes what. As a result of this situation, the efficiency test no longer is a suitable evaluative tool, because when no one is sure about causality there is no way of assessing the effects of what the organization is doing.

An example of such an organization might be a public bureaucracy. The Department of Defense, for instance, has a crystallized standard of desirability (adequate deterrent), but its officers are unsure about whether their programs actually are establishing that deterrent. None of them knows if their defense policies are sufficient to deter a nuclear attack (until and unless, of course, one comes). Thus, unlike the officials of International Widget, the Pentagon brass always will be uneasy about whether its programs are maximizing its mission achievement. Hence, we see Defense asking for more money as a means of maximizing its standard of

25. Thompson, *op. cit.*, pp. 83–98.

desirability (*i.e.*, its unproven deterrent capacity), but International Widget attempting to reduce its operational costs as a means of maximizing its standard of desirability (*i.e.*, profits).

The *social test* also is applicable to public bureaucracies, particularly those agencies that have ambiguous, rather than crystallized, standards of desirability. Whether or not members believe they understand cause-and-effect relationships does not matter, so the decision-making strategies of such an organization could range from one of compromise to inspiration. Such an agency might be a social service or a university; often, no one in these organizations can quantify, even remotely, the impact of their activities. What, for instance, is meant by "breaking the cycle of poverty"? What is "learning"?

Instrumental, but more especially social, tests of organizational performance are the kinds of evaluational tools that public bureaucracies find themselves using. Neither test is especially effective, but at least the reasons for their ineffectuality are fairly clear; public organizations, like the polity they administer, lack specificity in expressing their goals and in comprehending the most efficient way to achieve those goals.

Because of this dilemma, organizations that are unclear about causality or standards of desirability have developed a number of variants of instrumental and social tests in an attempt to assess themselves and to prove their worth to their audience outside. Public organizations have been especially adept at this because their very survival depends on the monies and legitimacy that they draw from the polity. Put crassly, this means acquiring prestige. For an organization faced with the necessity of using instrumental or social tests as a method of assessment, prestige and status often become the operational yardsticks of performance.

One way of measuring prestige is by calculating the historical improvement of the agency. This may be done in a number of ways: an increase in organizational visibility, budget increments, ratings by outside observers, proliferation of programs, size of the clientele served, and so forth. Universities, for example, rely to a large degree on accrediting associations, faculty publications, and research grants (all of which are ratings by outside observers) as social tests of performance, while public agencies often rely on the relative size of their annually appropriated budget as an indication of prestige. It is not surprising that organizational growth is associated with high organizational prestige, which in turn relates to an inferred favorable assessment of organizational performance. This is an especially telling point for public bureaucracies. It indicates that we can expect public officials to try to acquire fatter budgets for their agencies in an effort to "prove" their agencies' high level of performance, and then rationalize that their fat budgets represent a measurement of high performance that already was there. Either way, it is the prestige factor that determines how public bureaucracies normally are assessed.

Unfortunately, the prestige factor can be carried to ludicrous lengths as a yardstick of organizational efficiency. Joseph W. Eaton found that the in-house research units in two "treatment-oriented" organizations were used primarily as a method of acquiring prestige rather than as a method of discovering more objective measurements of true organizational performance.[26] Any "substantive" research projects regarding organizational performance that could be potentially embarrassing were discouraged, while "symbolic" research—noncontroversial research that did not question the organizations' traditional goals nor threaten established power patterns and was essentially useless—was encouraged in the organizations. In this light, it is worth recalling that government generally has less prestige than business organizations among the American populace. This situation can affect relative organizational performance in the two spheres. A study by Ray H. Elling and Sandor Halebsky of a public government hospital and a private volunteer hospital concluded that the private institution was better able to fulfill its official mission than the government hospital because of greater prestige in the community. The private hospital received more financial contributions, patients, and popular support.[27]

This section on organization theory would be incomplete without an inspection of those who populate the organization. The following chapter asks: What kinds of people are found in pubic bureaucracies? Are they geniuses or jerks, saints or satans? Regrettably, Chapter 5 does not answer these questions. It indicates, nonetheless, the ways in which the mentality and behavior of people may be changed by the organizations that they are in, and what you might expect from your fellow bureaucrats as a result.

SUPPLEMENTAL BIBLIOGRAPHY *

APPLEBY, PAUL, *Policy and Administration*. Tuscaloosa, Ala.: University of Alabama Press, 1949.

DIMOCK, MARSHALL E., *A Philosophy of Administration*. New York: Harper & Row, 1958.

MARTINDALE, DON, *Institutions, Organizations, and Mass Society*. Boston: Houghton Mifflin, 1966.

MILLETT, JOHN D., *Organization for the Public Service*. Princeton, N.J.: Van Nostrand, 1966.

MOUZELIS, NICOS P., *Organization and Bureaucracy*. Chicago: Aldine, 1968.

26. Joseph W. Eaton, "Symbolic and Substantive Evaluation Research," *Administrative Science Quarterly* 6 (March 1962), 421–42.
27. Ray H. Elling and Sandor Halebsky, "Organizational Differentiation and Support: A Conceptual Framework," *Administrative Science Quarterly* 6 (September 1961), pp. 185–209.
  * See also *Supplemental Bibliography* in Chapter 3.

models of administrative man in organizations

chapter 5

In this chapter, we shall examine some "bureaucratic types"—that is, various models of people used by organization theorists. There are considerably more models of people than those represented by Theory X and Theory Y, although all would more or less fall into one or the other of these two broad categories.

The more useful and more recent theorists attempt to analyze and classify all participants in the organization, but earlier writers often addressed themselves only to particular levels of the hierarchy, such as "leaders" or workers. We shall review some of the earlier models to achieve perspective, and then concentrate on what seem to be the more germane analyses of why some people behave as they do in public organizations. First, however, we will consider the question: Do organizations change people?

WHAT CAN ORGANIZATIONS DO TO YOU?

We saw in the last chapter that organizations are changed according to the ways in which technologies, task environments, and other people interact with one another in the organization. We know that people change organizations and this, in its way, is a comforting thought. Less comforting, however, is the thought that organizations change people—that organizations somehow, over time, alter personalities. Was *The Organization Man* described by William Whyte [1] the same rigid automaton before he joined "the team," or was he originally a normal human being who was drastically altered by the organization once he was under its influence?

It appears that some organizations—what Erving Goffman calls "total institutions," such as prisons, orphanages, barracks, ships, asylums, sanitariums, monastaries, and certain types of schools—can change the people in them.[2] This is logical; the technology (*i.e.*, what the organization does) of total institutions is people, and the mission of total institutions is to change the "client-members" inside them. The technology of prisons, for instance, is rehabilitation; the technology of schools is education.

Goffman has delineated the characteristics of total institutions as follows:

1. All aspects of life are separated from the larger society and are conducted in the same place and under the same authority.
2. The activities of client-members generally occur in "large batches" (*i.e.*, they do most things together, and client-members are treated equally).
3. Each day's activities are tightly scheduled and regulated.
4. Each activity is perceived as being part of an overall plan designed to achieve official goals.
5. There is a staff/inmate (*e.g.*, guard/prisoner) split.

In his study of prisons, Goffman observed that life in the "inmate world" was characterized by (1) a "mortification process" that often was perpetrated unconsciously by the staff as the result of managing many people in a small space with limited resources, (2) a "privilege system" that amounted to nothing more than a lack of sanctions, and (3) various forms of adaptation by inmates to the mortification process. These adaptations could include situational withdrawal; rebellion; "colonization," in which inmates grew to prefer prison to the society outside; and "conversion" by those inmates who came to be known as "square johns" because of their total acceptance of the official prison system. In the "staff world," Goffman noted that prison officials, who were pulled between the desires to main-

1. William H. Whyte, *The Organization Man* (New York: Simon and Schuster, 1956).
2. Erving Goffman, "The Characteristics of Total Institutions," in *Symposium on Preventive and Social Psychiatry,* sponsored by the Walter Reed Institute of Research (Washington, D.C.: U.S. Government Printing Office, 1957), pp. 43–84.

tain both humane standards and organizational efficiency, often developed a "theory" of human behavior that rationalized the inmates' hostility toward them.

Another kind of total institution may be closer to home to most readers: colleges and universities. Not all colleges, of course, have totalistic features, but many do. S. M. Dornbusch has written of the ethos prevalent in the United States Coast Guard Academy, which was designed to develop a "bureaucratic spirit" and a sense of solidarity in its students.[3] In this light, voluntary student resignations were speeded and hushed by academy officials, and questionable practices, such as hazing, were justified with such slogans as "separating the men from the boys."

Charles E. Bidwell and Rebecca S. Vreeland [4] have developed a "typology of socializing organizations" for colleges that classifies a college's probability for successfully indoctrinating students for life according to the kinds of goals professed by college officials and the scope of student involvement in the institution. For instance, a "doctrinal-administered communal" college (*i.e.*, a residential college with the goal of inculcating certain ethical and philosophic beliefs in its students) would have a very strong and homogeneous moral impact on its client-members. An example might be Bennington College, which was set up in 1932 with the idea of liberalizing the daughters of wealthy and often conservative families. Studies by Theodore M. Newcomb [5] at Bennington indicated that, indeed, the college's students adopted more politically liberal attitudes during their college careers and retained these attitudes well into later life. Conversely, a "procedural-administered associational" college (*e.g.*, a commuter college with "technical" goals, such as teaching its students a particular trade) would have no significant moral impact on its client-members. An example might be any public junior college.

Bidwell and Vreeland's conception of how organizations change their client-members is shown in Table 5–1.

If it is true that total institutions alter their client-members (and this contention is by no means conclusively validated by evidence), it does not necessarily follow that bureaucracies somehow change their members. Many (but not all) total institutions acquire their client-members by force, or at least by the application of social pressure (*e.g.*, "Don't you

3. Sanford M. Dornbusch, "The Military Academy as an Assimilating Institution," *Social Forces* 33 (May 1955): 316–321.

4. Charles E. Bidwell and Rebecca S. Vreeland, "College, Education and Moral Orientations: An Organization Approach," *Administrative Science Quarterly* 8 (September 1963): 166–191.

5. Theodore M. Newcomb, "Attitude Development as a Function of Reference Groups: The Bennington Study," *Readings in Social Psychology* 3rd ed., Eleanor E. Maccoby, Theodore M. Newcomb, Eugene L. Hartley, eds. (New York: Holt, Rinehart & Winston, 1958), pp. 265–275.

TABLE 5–1. A Typology of Socializing Organizations

| | | Scope of Involvement | |
		Communal	Associational
Goals	Moral	Doctrinal-administered community: strong, homogeneous moral impact on client-members.	Doctrinal-administered association: moderate, homogeneous moral impact on client-members.
	Technical	Procedural-administered community: strong, heterogeneous moral impact on client-members.	Procedural-administered association; no significant moral impact on client-members.

want to go to Dad's *alma mater?"*) Bureaucracies rarely add to their memberships in these ways; people join bureaucracies relatively voluntarily. And when they do join, they are not client-members, such as a prisoner or a student. They are full-fledged members of the organization, such as a guard or a faculty member.)

(Some theorists, however, do argue that bureaucracies, particularly public bureaucracies, change the bureaucrats inside them.) Perhaps the classic statement of this argument is Robert K. Merton's essay on the "bureaucratic personality." By the very drive of the bureaucracy to rationalize (and thus rigidify) its administrative techniques, the bureaucrats in it must be trained and socialized so that they begin to think along the lines and patterns mandated by those techniques. Thus, in Merton's words, the bureaucrat grows to personify "Veblen's concept of 'trained incapacity,' Dewey's notion of 'occupational psychosis' or Warnotte's view of 'professional deformation.' " [6] Yet, after such training, a way of seeing also becomes a way of not seeing. It is an inescapable outcome that bureaucrats become methodical and prudent persons because they must if they are to survive in a bureaucracy that places "tremendous symbolic significance" on rules and their adherence. In fact, the pressures to rationalize the bureaucracy work to produce "overconformity," because that assures a margin of safety in terms of reducing uncertainty in the organization. Additionally, the stress in bureaucracies to depersonalize relationships, combined with the "professional deformation" brought about by socialization, results in the unsympathetic, disinterested, and often uncomprehending bureaucrat perceived by the client who is concerned with his special problem and its several unique features. Because of such dynamics

6. Robert K. Merton, "Bureaucratic Structure and Personality," *Social Forces* 18 (1940):563.

between social and organizational forces, the notorious, petty, dense, and arrogant bureaucratic personality has emerged.

Other analysts are less positive that organizations change their members. Ivar Berg, in a methodologically careful empirical study, attempted to ascertain if organizations changed people by examining the attitudes and behavior of "old" and "new" organizational members; in Berg's words, "I tried to measure employees' propensities to accept and act upon their impulses." [7] After much analysis, Berg was forced to concede that he could not draw any final conclusions, although there was a "close fit" between senior members and their organizations. Problems involving personality change, self-selection, and organizational selection were too difficult to separate as intervening variables, and the thesis that the organization caused changes in its people was methodologically impossible to "prove." Although research is continuing, whether or not bureaucracies change people must still remain a moot point.

We do know, however, that there are many different kinds of people in organizations, regardless of the forces that may have shaped their personalities. It is to some of these models that we now turn, in an effort to learn what our implicit assumptions about the nature of administrative man really are.

MODELS OF ADMINISTRATIVE MAN: THE CLASSICAL VIEW

Under the "classical view," we consider those early theorists who tended to ignore social and psychological variables in the constitutions of members of organizations, and instead stressed their "rational" and physical dimensions. The classical model of man was not drawn entirely from Theory X, but it was largely predicated on that concept. Max Weber, for example, perceived the key to getting things done in a bureaucracy to be primarily a matter of "rationalizing" the behavior of bureaucrats—getting each member to do his job in such a way that he optimally expedited the official goals of the bureaucracy. Frederick Taylor had essentially the same idea, but his theory rationalized the physical behaviors of workers.

Although the classical theorists had more highly refined models of man than the preceding paragraph may indicate, they nevertheless were drawn from the basic conception that it expresses. Classical models of administrative man, in keeping with the closed model of organizations' focus, dwelt on the notion of leadership. What made a leader? What were the qualities of leadership?

7. Ivar Berg, "Do Organizations Change People?" *Individualism and Big Business*, Leonard Sayles, ed. (New York: McGraw-Hill, 1963), p. 62.

Weber, for example, delineated three kinds of leadership: *charismatic, traditional,* and *legal/rational.* A charismatic leader was a primitive, *Volksgeist* (folk spirit) sort, who embodied the spirit of the people. He led a *Gemeinschaft* type of society, or a society characterized by irrational romanticism. A traditional leader represented what Weber was resisting in the Germany of his day, that is, a person who was a leader by dint of heredity and class. A legal/rational leader was a monocrat, or any other bureaucratic leader who fulfilled Weber's criterion of impersonal and rigid rationalism. A legal/rational leader led a *Gesellschaft* type society, or a society characterized by rationalism, regulations, impersonality, and bureaucracy. The monocrat (or the omniscient bureaucrat who headed the bureaucracy) was a legal/rational leader who should, in Weber's view, displace the incompetent, traditional leaders of German society and would counter, with his *Gesellschaft* organization, the revolutionary tendencies represented by charismatic leaders that were rife in the larger, *Gemeinschaft* culture.[8]

Similarly, James D. Mooney and Alan C. Reiley delineated three leadership types, although, unlike Weber's typology, their distinctions were more directly applicable to organizations than to society generally. Mooney and Reiley described leaders as being *titular leaders, controllers,* and *true organizers,* and these types were related to their staff/line principle of organization. A titular leader followed his staff's advice undeviatingly and hence was not much more than a figurehead; a controller was at the other extreme, he refused to delegate authority to line officers, and usually ignored staff advice; a true organizer was a leader who simply did everything right—including, of course, the correct application of Mooney and Reiley's principles of organization.[9]

It also is in the classical tradition that Amitai Etzioni and Philip Selznick develop their views on leadership. To Etzioni, leaders may be typed according to personal and positional power: *Officials* have authority only by virtue of their hierarchical position, *informal leaders* command because of their personal and charismatic qualities, and *formal leaders* combine the power features of both.[10] Selznick relates leadership to levels of political and social interaction. *Leaders* coalesce and mold elements of the society at an "institutional level" and are rather grandiose figures generally, while *administrators* fritter away the hours doing the mundane

8. Max Weber, *From Max Weber,* H. H. Gerth and C. Wright Mills, eds. (New York: Oxford University Press, 1946).

9. James D. Mooney and Alan C. Reiley, *The Principles of Organization* (New York: Harper & Row, 1939).

10. Amitai Etzioni, *Modern Organizations* (Englewood Cliffs, N.J.: Prentice-Hall, 1964).

but necessary chores of a bureaucratic and technical nature that keep the organization running on a day-to-day basis.[11]

MODELS OF ADMINISTRATIVE MAN:
THE SOCIAL-PSYCHOLOGICAL VIEW

In contrast to the classical theorists, theorists relying principally on the open model of organizations and the Theory Y conception of personality focussed on all members of organizations and rarely distinguished "leaders" as a special group. Representatives of a "pure" social psychological view of the organization man would include Chester I. Barnard, Herbert A. Simon, James G. March, Richard M. Cyert, and James D. Thompson.[12] In this literary stream, man is seen as a biological, physical, emotional, behavioral, and social creature who possesses limited cognitive abilities, but nonetheless has an occasional capacity to perceive and act on his self-interest, solve problems, and bargain.

Simon provided a useful description of the social-psychological view in his *Models of Man*.[13] On the one hand, Simon posited *psychological man*, or *Freudian man*, who represented the model used by psychologists to predict the behavior of individual persons. Psychological man was beset by insecurities, quirks, motivations, and emotional needs; "rational" behavior was a totally individual phenomenon; every person had to do his own thing. On the other hand, Simon posited *rational man*, or *economic man*, who represented the model used by economists to predict the behavior of the economy as a whole. Economic man was totally rational in the sense that he not only understood thoroughly his own self-interest (*i.e.*, the acquisition of money), but was fully cognizant of all the options available to him and would act on the choice that brought him the most money. Thus, in contrast to psychological man who had his own unique and highly personal goals that were rational only to him, economic man

---

11. Philip Selznick, *TVA and the Grass Roots* (Berkeley: University of California Press, 1949).

12. See, for example, the following works: Chester I. Barnard, *The Functions of the Executive* (Cambridge: Harvard University Press, 1938); Herbert A. Simon, *Administrative Behavior*, 3rd ed. (New York: Free Press, 1976); James G. March and Herbert A. Simon, *Organizations* (New York: John Wiley, 1958); Richard M. Cyert and James G. March, *Behavioral Theory of the Firm* (Englewood Cliffs, N.J.: Prentice-Hall, 1963); and James D. Thompson, *Organizations in Action* (New York: McGraw-Hill, 1967).

13. Herbert A. Simon, *Models of Man, Social and Rational* (New York: John Wiley and Sons, 1957).

had precisely the same goal as every other man in the economy, and would behave just like every other man to achieve it.

Administrative man, in Simon's view, provided a conceptual bridge between psychological man and economic man. While administrative man had his own private goals and rationality, he also understood the official goals and formal rationality of his organization. Moreover, he knew that his welfare and that of the organization were somehow related, although this was not to say that he believed what was good for the organization was necessarily good for him. Finally, administrative man could seldom if ever see all his possible options in making a decision, nor could he predict their consequences.

All these models of man work—that is, they yield accurate predictions—in their respective disciplines. The social-psychological model of man posited by the Barnard-Simon-March-Cyert-Thompson stream of literature works for organization theory. But the social-psychological model has at least two submodels of man that stress variables of special significance to public administrators: cultural models and political models.

Cultural models of man

Although there is a vast literature on comparative and development public administration, which we mentioned in Chapter 2, relatively few theorists have considered the specific impact of national cultures on organizational behavior, but two who have deserve mention. Harold L. Wilensky, for one, has considered how cultural variables relate to attitudes about organizational uses of information and patterns of bureaucratic secrecy.[14] In his view, modern totalitarian governments based on technology (*e.g.*, Stalin's Russia, Hitler's Germany) were and are the most fully organized to protect secrecy. Information pathologies attained their ultimate expression in both states: Huge sums were passed to "experts" of various kinds, antiintellectualism was rife, an immense intelligence-gathering apparatus was created, interagency sabotage was commonplace, and the general dysfunctions of bureaucracy were exaggerated. When these pathologies were combined with a dogma, such as proletarianism or racism, "grotesque intrigues," official paranoia, and spectacular intelligence failures (such as Hitler's strategy for the conduct of World War II) were the result.

Wilensky compares the administrative methods of developing radar employed by the British and Germans during World War II as an illustration of how differing sociopolitical cultures can affect organizations. Although the Germans may have had an earlier start than the British, they soon felt it necessary to bureaucratize their system of radar research

14. Harold L. Wilensky, *Organizational Intelligence* (New York: Basic Books, 1967), pp. 110–29.

by creating a Plenipotentiary for High Frequency Techniques. The Plenipotentiary established himself as a coordinator between a chain of new research laboratories that he had built and the Air Ministry. Abstract specifications of what the *Luftwaffe* wanted then were sent to the Plenipotentiary by the Ministry, who checked his list of available laboratories and mailed the data to the one needing work. Because of an absence of interaction between fliers and scientists, German radar development eventually ground to a halt. In contrast, the British effort was characterized by continuous discussions between members of the Royal Air Force and the Telecommunications Research Establishment. A feature of this relatively open model approach was the frequent use of "Sunday Soviets," in which officials and experts of all ranks and designations discussed various aspects of radar development. Needless to add, it was the British use of radar that was instrumental in winning the Battle of Britain.

Wilensky believes that the parliamentary democracies with traditions of aristocracy, such as Britain and France, fall midway between the pathologically secretive totalitarian nations and the publicity-hungry United States, which he feels has organizations that are the least constrained by secrecy. In the United States, news "leaks" are a common strategy of interagency rivalry, exposés of public figures are encouraged by the press, congressional investigations are favored, and the libel laws are loosely construed. In England, however, an administrator's first loyalty is to the Cabinet, and the Official Secrets Act is an effective cork on the leakage of secret information.

Unfortunately, in Wilensky's view, Americans display a love/hate syndrome for secrecy. Pressures for publicity provoke counterpressures for the reestablishment of "national security," and it is Wilensky's worry that the publicity consciousness of America's culture may strengthen the power of secrecy via a kind of rebound effect; *i.e.,* "Let's not go too far with this publicity stuff, because we may sell ourselves down the river to our enemies abroad." The various investigations of the Watergate affair provide an example of Americans' love/hate syndrome for secrecy, particularly when the intense publicity that surrounded them is contrasted to the political defense of the accused: that a cover-up of the Watergate break-in was necessary for the sake of national security.

Unlike Wilensky, Michel Crozier has focused his research less on the effects of national culture on the organization's relationship with its political environment, and more on the influences that culture has on the internal workings of the organization.[15] Crozier's thesis is that each national culture has a unique effect on organizations operating in that culture, and this effect ultimately will constitute the primary pathology of

15. Michel Crozier, *The Bureaucratic Phenomenon* (Chicago: University of Chicago Press, 1964).

the organizations. In France, as noted in Chapter 4, the culturally derived pathology is *bon plaisir*—that is, to quote Crozier, "it is considered better to restrict oneself and to remain free within the narrower limits one has fixed or even those one has had to accept." [16] *Bon plaisir*, a symptom long ingrained in the French culture, is a stubborn insistence on personal autonomy that inhibits cooperation in French organizations.

The Soviet Union, however, has quite an opposite cultural phenomenon that impinges on the workings of bureaucracy. This is the *blat*, which refers to an informal network of complicity entered into by middle managers as a means of assuring that the national production quotas set by the state are met. The *blat* is characterized by a high degree of mutual, almost familial, trust among middle managers. Middle managers are quite willing to enter into "illegal" deals with one another in order to fulfill the demands of "the plan," which rarely if ever provides the methods of its own success. As a result, hierarchy, suspicion, and control are emphasized by the top echelons of the Soviet bureaucracy, but often the otherwise destructive consequences of these pathologies do little to undermine the functioning of the *blat*.

In extreme contrast to Soviet organizations American organizations are characterized by divisions of labor and due process of law. These twin cultural factors bring about organizational pathologies unique to American bureaucracies. Functional specialization (which is almost another way of saying professionalization) results in an abnormally high number of jurisdictional disputes within and among American organizations, while Americans' passion for due process of law produces a plethora of impersonal bureaucratic rules designed to protect the individual from injustices. Both cultural traits tend to magnify the role of lawyers, or any official who is in a position to interpret organizational rules, jurisdictions, and prerogatives, and this aspect often impedes change in American organizations. British organizations, on the other hand, are permeated by a deference system emanating from their culture that makes the use of impersonal rules to assure compliance by subordinates unnecessary, since the authority of superordinates possesses greater legitimacy than in American organizations. In France peer-group resistance to authority acts as a substitute for impersonal rules and due process of law.

In Crozier's view, American organizations, on the whole, tend to protect the rights of individuals more effectively, are better attuned to reality, are characterized by more cooperation, and are generally more open than French, Russian, or British organizations. But the existence of many centers of authority in American organizations, and the difficulties that must be surmounted in coordinating them, pose problems of change for American organizations. Although American organizations are likely

16. *Ibid.*, p. 223.

more open to innovation than the French, British, and Russian, Crozier notes that "Willful individuals can block the intentions of whole communities for a long time; numerous routines develop around local positions of influence; the feeble are not protected so well against the strong; and generally, a large number of vicious circles will protect and reinforce local conservatism." [17] These pathologies, like the bureaucratic dysfunctions of a differing nature in other countries, are the result of cultural factors unique to America that no organization can escape.

Political models of man

A second theme on the nature of administrative man that falls within the social-psychological framework deals with how administrators behave politically in organizations. The findings and speculations extant in this field of research have particular relevance to public administration, for politics influences the public administrative sector as no other. Three studies that are of particular note in this area are by Gordon Tullock,[18] Alvin Gouldner,[19] and Victor A. Thompson.[20]

Culture and the Organization Man

The following selection discusses how national culture affects public bureaucrats. Its author is an Englishman and professor of English literature who is also Assistant Director-General of the United Nations Educational, Scientific, and Cultural Organization.

People, we assume, are much the same everywhere; personality will out, and the ups-and-downs of life are much the same everywhere too. Sure, but the ways these qualities and experiences express themselves differ in different societies. Each society has several ranges of typical face, and the distinctions between them become finer and finer as you look at them. There is a lean, quizzical, face one finds among clever men on the Eastern seaboard of the United States, the face of an intelligent man in a wide-open, mass-persuasive society who is not to be taken in, who has kept his cool and his irony. Such a face is not so likely to be found among its counterparts in Eastern Europe; the winds

17. *Ibid.*, p. 236.

18. Gordon Tullock, *The Politics of Bureaucracy* (Washington, D.C.: Public Affairs Press, 1965).

19. Alvin W. Gouldner, "Cosmopolitans and Locals: Toward an Analysis of Latent Social Roles," *Administrative Science Quarterly* 2 (December 1957 and March 1958): 281–306 and 444–480.

20. Victor A. Thompson, *Modern Organization* (New York: Knopf, 1961).

which beat on these men are different. Their faces are graver, more direct, and yet more reserved.

Because I have met them at some cross-roads in my own life, I am particularly interested in a range of faces which cluster round the idea of a public man in Britain. At his most characteristic, this man is in his middle-fifties. His appearance is what the whisky advertisements, giving it more of a gloss than it really has, call distinguished. His face is well-shaven but not scraped; it has a healthy bloom, but not an outdoor roughness; it is smooth, but not waxy. What is by now quite a full face is as solid as leather club-armchairs, and as decently groomed; it smells as good as the public rooms of those clubs. The hair is often marked by the appearance of Cabinet Minister's wings, that is, it is brushed straight back above the ears to plump out at the sides; it has a silvery sheen. The teeth are strong, one sees when the lips, as they readily do, curl back into a full, firm smile. They suggest someone who is used to talking in public and to deciding, to biting firmly into problems. They are wonderfully communicative teeth, and remarkable evidence that from all the possible ways of using teeth, the ways we smile or grimace, we select only some: we select from the codebook of tooth-signals in our society.

The coherence of the style is rarely breached. I remember one occasion which, because of its oddness, underlined how consistent that style usually is. One such public man—one who was apparently such a man—said to me, as we stood around in the intervals of a meeting: "You see, Hoggart, I believe in the English people." As he said it, it sounded naive, a little self-important, touching, generous; but not sayable by a native English intellectual, least of all in that particular ambience. But he was a first generation European immigrant intellectual. His son is hardly likely to strike a false note like that.

Among the most striking in the line of public figures is the old-young man; and they are most often found in the higher reaches of education. These men are slim, with little trace of a paunch even at fifty-five; their faces still show the outlines formed when they were Head boys at their public schools or good day-schools. There is a French public type of about the same age who is in some ways similar; but the differences are interesting and, to me, unexpected. The French type is even leaner; he is also more elegant, better groomed, and more professional-looking than the Englishman. He is likely to have close-cropped hair and glasses with thin gold rims. It all fits with being called a "haut fonctionnaire." The English type is more casual, looser in the limb. . . .

Not long ago I was lost before a new kind of face. Or rather, I mistrusted my own reading of it; it was too easy and dismissive. This was a politician from the United States, a man who had been successful in oil or insurance well before he was forty and who now, in his middle forties, had an assured, thrusting, mercantile, tanned, smoothly smiling but tough look. To me the face, the whole manner, was two-dimensional, unmarked. It was like the face of a well-groomed dog. It said only: "Public acquaintance . . . manipulation . . . action"; not: "Friendliness . . . thought . . . feeling." Had such a man, you wondered, ever felt shabby or insecure? Oddly, it was easier to imagine him crying. There was probably within the rhetorics available to him a form of crying that would do. But I was probably wrong, unable to read the signals in a way which got me near his character, which made him three-dimensional, capable of real grief and joy, unpublic. I couldn't easily imagine him in his underwear, and when I did he looked like an advertisement in *Esquire*.

RICHARD HOGGART
On Culture and Communication

Bureaucrats as Medieval Politicians. Tullock posits an overarching conceptualization of how power is distributed in bureaucracies relative to a hypothetical reference politician. Tullock writes directly to the reader; he attempts to inform him how he (the reference politician) can survive and thrive in the bureaucratic power setting.

Tullock visualizes bureaucracies in terms of modified feudal societies. The reference politician is surrounded by "spectators" (who watch him but do not affect him), "allies," a "sovereign" (who is comparable to Weber's monocrat, but who lacks his omniscience), "peers" (his hierarchical equals), "courtiers" (who make it a point to curry favor with organizational power figures), "followers" (who add to the reference politician's power, but in a way different from that of his allies), and "barons" (powerful individuals in the bureaucracy who have cut out their own organizational domains and who operate within their domains quite independently from the rest of the organization—for example, J. Edgar Hoover, as Director of the Federal Bureau of Investigation during the mid-1960s, relative to the Justice Department and much of the rest of the federal bureaucracy). A reference politician may play any one or several of the roles that Tullock lists; few of them are mutually exclusive. But any reference politician will confront and deal with spectators, allies, sovereigns, peers, courtiers, followers, and barons in any public bureaucracy.

Locals vs. Cosmopolitans. Gouldner also has itemized organizational roles, but along a different political dimension. In an empirical analysis of a small college's faculty and administration, Gouldner distinguished between "locals" and "cosmopolitans." Locals derived their power and sense of personal identity (their self-actualization, if you will), from internal organizational factors. There were several kinds of locals: the "dedicated," who had a deep loyalty to the college, were committed to the idea of interdisciplinary studies, and were deployable from department to department; the "true bureaucrats," who were satisfied with everything about the organization, including their own salaries, were suspicious of "outsiders" such as the American Association of University Professors (AAUP), and were prone to favor the strict use of rules and regulations; the "homeguard," who were the least specialized and trained of the faculty, and were likely to be women administrators in the lower ranks; finally, the "elders," who were oriented toward a particular faculty clique and a time period in the past.

Conversely, cosmopolitans related to factors external to the organization, such as their professional association. In contrast to the locals, cosmopolitans were measurably more likely to believe that lighter teaching loads would result in greater research productivity, valued their research time more, in terms of their professional interests were more alienated from their colleagues, were more likely to have a doctoral degree, published more, were less sociable, were less loyal to the organization, were acquainted with fewer of their fellow faculty members, were friendlier toward the AAUP, were likelier to be intellectually stimulated by sources outside the college, and were more dissatisfied with their salaries. There were two kinds of cosmopolitans: the "outsiders," who were committed to specialization and were not particularly close to either students, colleagues, or the administration; and the "empire builders," who perceived themselves as being economically independent, had a high commitment to their departments, preferred departmental autonomy, and disliked such checks as student ratings of faculty teaching and the central administration generally.

In terms of how localism and cosmopolitanism affected the organization directly, Gouldner found that central administrators tended to be high on the homeguard, dedicated, and true bureaucrat dimensions, and low on the outsider and empire builder dimensions. On the other hand, empire builders had considerable power in the organization (in the sense that they were comparable to Tullock's "barons"), and were less likely than locals to emphasize rules and regulations.

The notion of cosmopolitanism and localism is increasingly significant to public administration because of the field's growing reliance on and use of expertise. As public bureaucracies fill with more highly trained and specialized experts, new patterns of personal loyalties, perceptions, and commitments may evolve that will present new kinds of organizational contingencies to the public administrator. It is probable that the functions of the public administrator will change as the personnel in his organization professionalize. We consider the implications of this development more thoroughly in Chapter 10.

Bureaucrats as Sycophants. Thompson argues that precisely because of the growing social necessity for highly educated specialists in organizations, private as well as public, the political power of the administrator ought to be reduced radically. In fact, Thompson thinks that bureaucrats and administrators should be exorcised altogether from organizations because they are dysfunctional. In Thompson's opinion only specialists, such as scientists, lawyers, engineers, and accountants, get things done in organizations; bureaucrats only get in the way. Bureaucrats, or administrators, are nothing more than sycophants and parasites in any organization, and Thompson urges that we recognize this fact for what it is and toss out the rascals before it is too late. (A third type also is posited by Thompson: "bureautics," or those persons who cannot accept organizations of any kind and drop out. Thompson does not think highly of bureautics and concentrates on bureaucrats and specialists.)

Thompson then asks rhetorically how bureaucrats have managed to featherbed so effectively in organizations for as long as they have and offers three explanations. One reason that bureaucrats have maintained their organizational power position is their shrewd use of "dramaturgy," or, to put it in the vernacular, their capacity for manufacturing "snow jobs." Bureaucratic dramaturgy is designed, like the other two strategies used by bureaucrats to justify their positions, to camouflage their lack of any knowledge that is truly useful to the organization. Dramaturgy consists of personal aloofness, firm handshakes, an unwavering eye, confidence, and winning smiles—in short, the Dale Carnegie School's method of executive development personified. Dramaturgy has gone far in keeping bureaucrats inside organizations, but in reality the image that it creates is insubstantial froth and fluff.

Equally insubstantial but nonetheless effective in the preservation of bureaucratic power is the bureaucrats' reliance on "ideology" and "bureaupathology" to justify their organizational existence. Ideology is simply tradition. Bureaucrats always have been around, and it has become an ideological rationale that they should stay around. Bureaupathology refers to the excessively rigid, even by bureaucratic standards, roles assumed by bureaucrats to maintain their power positions. Rules, obedience, loyalty (to themselves), and subservience are stressed as a means of heading off embarrassing, uncomfortable, and probing questions from the dispossessed specialists about why the organization is run in the way it is.

Thompson takes a radical stance on administrators: He considers them useless at best and dangerous at worst. He thinks administrators should be eliminated from organizations in order that the skill-possessing specialists can get together without interference and get the organization's job done more efficiently and effectively.

Obviously, in a book about public administration we cannot bring ourselves to accept Thompson's thesis. If we did, I would not have bothered writing this tract, and you (hopefully) would not have bothered taking this course. But the notion that Thompson articulates so straightforwardly—that administrators play psychological roles and political games in bureaucracies for their own ends—is well worth amplification, if for no other reason than that you might stand a better chance of recognizing some roles and games for what they are and react to them accordingly. Two analysts who have pursued this line of thought are Anthony Downs [21] and Dwaine Marvick.[22]

Zealots, Advocates, and Statesmen. It was mentioned in the preceding chapter that Downs posited "conservers" and "climbers" in organizations and related these personality types to an "age lump" phenomenon that he associated with organizational change. Conservers and climbers are "pure" types in Downs's construct, but he also forwards three "mixed motive" types that blend elements of the two in differing ways: "zealots," "advocates," and "statesmen." These personalities are distributed along a continuum that relates to the breadth or narrowness of their perceptual scope.

Zealots tend to have the most shallow perceptual base, they are effective founders of organizations but not very effective managers once the organization is established. They espouse the most narrow policy set, such as a particular pet project, and promote it with a zeal that warrants, in Downs's mind, the title with which he has dubbed them.

Advocates articulate broader policy sets than do zealots. They tend to see the organization whole and to understand its components; occasionally this results in advocates having a magnified view of themselves and their organizational roles. They believe in the organization and generally occupy its higher, nonroutinized offices. While advocates are highly partisan in defending the organization relative to its environment, they often are impartial arbiters of internal disputes and are sensitive to the long-range implications of organizational policies.

Statesmen have the broadest perceptual abilities of the three types; they see their society as a whole and their organization's role in it. Because of their greater loyalty to the entire society, however, statesmen often are misfits in their organizations. In theory, anyway, statesmen would be willing to sell their organization down the proverbial river if they believed that their society would benefit as a result. Needless to say, there are few

21. Anthony Downs, *Inside Bureaucracy* (Boston: Little, Brown, 1967).
22. Dwaine Marvick, *Career Perspectives in a Bureaucratic Setting*, University of Michigan Governmental Studies, No. 27 (Ann Arbor: University of Michigan Press, 1954).

statesmen around, although they may be particularly needed in public organizations.

Career Types and their Political Motivations. A similar but more empirical study of the roles bureaucrats play in public organizations was undertaken by Marvick. Marvick asked, "what must management do in order to cope with persons having different career perspectives?" Marvick tried to place in broad categories the individual goals and rationalities of public bureaucrats that are assumed to exist in the open model.

This was an eminently worthwhile project, and his study has manifold uses for public administrators. It is one thing merely to say, as the open model theorists often do, that everyone is unique in organizations and then stop. True enough, one must retort, but so what? How far can such a statement carry us in terms of understanding our organization and our colleagues? Not very far. Yet it is quite another matter when we can type, no matter how roughly, the individual rationalities according to certain broad commonalities. This gives us an insight and a theory to work with. The writers who we have reviewed in this chapter have tried to do just that and are therefore useful. But Marvick's study is especially useful, empirical, and not very well known.

Marvick trisected public bureaucrats by career style: "institutionalists," "specialists," and "hybrids." Institutionalists were believers in the organization, but their career commitments were "a matter of 'sublimated' interest—ends in themselves." That is, institutionalists received their psychoemotional gratifications from the organization on the bases of very superficial criteria, such as unwarranted optimism and shallow status rewards granted by the organization. As a group, institutionalists were relatively high in their demands for organizational advancement and unqualifiedly high in their quest for organizational prestige. They tended not to stress the task-oriented features of their jobs, but preferred to emphasize its benefits and had spent most of their career-lives in government, often in the military. Institutionalists generally were found to be mid-level bureaucrats, encumbered by few family ties, had relatively low formal educational attainments, and had short job histories—that is, they had changed positions (though had not necessarily advanced) within the government frequently.

Institutionalists were very sociable people within the organization, and were extremely loyal to it and to their co-workers. In that light they preferred being in on group decisions, wanted their decisions buttressed by their peers, and tended to compare their job performance with others on an *ad hominem* basis. In sum, institutionalists were "place-bound" (like Gouldner's locals), committed to an executive career in the government, had a superficial concern with achieving their agency's goals, were optimistic concerning their agency's performance (and their own), were gregarious and preferred working with others, felt relatively uninfluential in terms of their agency (and probably were), but nevertheless were complacent about their organizational role.

Specialists were at the opposite end of the spectrum from institutionalists. Unlike institutionalists, who occupied generalized managerial slots, specialists tended to be highly educated professionals, such as lawyers, scientists, engineers, and accountants. Specialists were not particularly concerned about personal advancement in the organization and had virtually no interest in organizational status rewards. What they did want very badly, however, was the freedom to do their own thing, to be in jobs that allowed them to use their professional skills on a daily basis. In terms of career histories, specialists tended to have experience both in public and private bureaucracies, had less military experience than institutionalists and, while they were fairly well advanced in terms of their careers, specialists were seldom interested in executive positions, in stark contrast to institutionalists. Whereas institutionalists revealed a sublimated need for organizational status, specialists displayed an unconscious demand to use their specialties. Task-orientation rather than place-orientation was a key difference between specialists and institutionalists; specialists, like Gouldner's cosmopolitans, had no particular loyalty to the organization, nor did they indicate a desire for prestige as defined by position in the organization.

Interestingly, specialists resembled institutionalists in that they preferred to have their opinions supported by their peers, although they favored working alone and were less likely to be involved in group decisions than institutionalists. Yet, as individuals, specialists had more influence within the organization than did institutionalists. Finally, specialists were by far the most critical of the agency's performance and of bureaucratic methods generally; in this sense, Marvick felt that specialists were "manifestly maladjusted" in their working relationships.

Hybrids, or "politicized experts," drew their characteristics from both institutionalists and specialists. Like specialists, hybrids were highly educated professionals, were advanced in organizational rank, had experience in both the public and private sectors, and were disinterested in organizational prestige. Like institutionalists, hybrids were very concerned with acquiring executive positions and charting a career in government. If there was a single group that could be called the realistic loners, it was the hybrids. They were very keen on executive advancement and generally divorced themselves from any strong identification with particular groups in the organization. Marvick calls them "free agents," that is, they thought of both place and skill in quite detached terms. Hybrids were unconcerned with peer groups, organizational prestige, and the exercise of their skills;

they were committed neither to their agency nor to their profession. Nevertheless, hybrids were very committed to money and advancement. Interestingly, in this light, hybrids tended to have far heavier family responsibilities than either institutionalists or specialists. Also of interest is the fact that hybrids had relatively low levels of influence in the bureaucracy, which may reflect their propensity for working alone; although their influence equalled that of institutionalists, it was lower than that of specialists. Hybrids, like institutionalists, were not especially critical of meetings and similar bureaucratic paraphernalia and were well adjusted to their jobs; on the other hand, they were likely to be disgruntled when they felt that they were being distracted from their work. Finally, hybrids had no sublimated goals, unlike either of the other two types. Hybrids' goals were explicit and personal, and they were quite amenable to using either place or skill criteria to advance their goals. Because of this, hybrids often were the organization's realists in Marvick's view.

All three groups possess perils and potentialities for public organizations. Institutionalists can become rule-oriented and inflexible; their sociability can degenerate into cliquishness, their loyalty into recalcitrance to change, and they resist performance evaluation along quantitative, measurable scales. Yet, institutionalists provide the bureaucracy with genuine organizational stability and furnish the needed lubrication among interpersonal relationships in the agency.

Specialists tend to displace the agency's goals because their individual, professional projects are more important to them than the organization's welfare. This propensity can affect organizational performance generally. Moreover, their highly critical cast and lack of place commitment can cause sinking morale, disharmony, and high rates of turnover. In view of Marvick's findings, we might recall Thompson's advocacy of organizations staffed entirely by specialists and speculate on what such organizations might really be like. Yet, when properly placed, specialists can get things done in a most effective way, and they are not inclined to compete politically with other members of the bureaucracy.

Hybrids bring the most dangers and benefits to the organization. Their chief danger lies in their instability. Hybrids are fair-weather friends, "superficial and showy performers." Their lack of both place and skill commitments render them unpredictable. Yet, hybrids are the most likely people to assess accurately and holistically the dynamics and problems of the organization. Unlike the other two groups, they possess no sublimated personal needs that might interfere with their realistic evaluation of the organization and where it is going. Nevertheless, hybrids must be watched, for they are prone to change the organization purely for their own self-betterment.

Marvick's typology has clear parallels with the constructs of Downs,

Gouldner, Tullock, and others, but it is notable in that Marvick has associated his classifications with variables that can be found in any personnel file—educational attainments, job histories, family responsibilities, and so on. This is useful administrative knowledge, particularly when amplified by the analyses that have been reviewed in this chapter. Together, these studies aid us in understanding the people we deal with in organizations.

But what about ourselves? Is it not also useful to understand the bases on which we make organizational decisions? In the final chapter of this section, we consider some rationales of individual decision-making in public organizations. As we shall see, these rationales are ethical, not social-psychological.

SUPPLEMENTAL BIBLIOGRAPHY

ARGYRIS, CHRIS, *Personality and Organization*. New York: Harper & Row, 1957.

BENNIS, WARREN S., "A New Role for the Behavioral Sciences: Effecting Organizational Change," *Administrative Science Quarterly*, 8 (September 1963), 125–63.

BOULDING, KENNETH E., *The Organizational Revolution*. New York: Harper & Row, 1953.

BUCKLEY, WALTER, *Sociology and Modern System Theory*. Englewood Cliffs, N.J.: Prentice-Hall, 1967.

GOLEMBIEWSKI, ROBERT T., *Men, Management, and Morality: Toward a New Organizational Ethic*. New York: McGraw-Hill, 1965.

———, *Renewing Organizations*. Itasca, Ill.: F. E. Peacock, 1972.

———, *The Small Group*. Chicago: University of Chicago Press, 1962.

HERZBERG, FREDERICK, BERNARD MAUSNER, and BARBARA SYNDERMAN, *The Motivation to Work*. New York: John Wiley, 1959.

KATZ, DANIEL, and ROBERT L. KAHN, *The Social Psychology of Organizations*. New York: John Wiley, 1966.

LIKERT, RENSIS, *New Patterns of Management*. New York: McGraw-Hill, 1961.

———, *The Human Organization*. New York: McGraw-Hill, 1967.

PERROW, CHARLES, *Organizational Analysis: A Sociological View*. Belmont, Calif.: Wadsworth, 1970.

PRESTHUS, ROBERT, *Behavioral Approaches to Public Administration*. Tuscaloosa, Ala.: University of Alabama Press, 1965.

toward a
bureaucratic ethic

chapter 6

We noted in the preceding chapter that public administrators often make decisions on the bases of subliminal needs. In this chapter, we resurrect conscious, decision-making rationality, but with a difference. It is not our intention to recapitulate the economic rationalists of the closed model of organizations (*e.g.*, Weber, Taylor, Gulick and Urwick, and others), but rather to introduce the philosophic, moral, and ethical rationales on which public administrators make decisions. We do this on the logic that an awareness of ethical choice is essential to the lone bureaucrat who possesses considerable discretionary power, and who is charged with making decisions that somehow must be in "the public interest." Such a chapter does not draw on the usual literature of organization theory, but it does seem to be appropriate to our larger discussion in this section devoted to "Public Organizations."

The notion that the public bureaucracy stands in need of ethical sensitivity in order to serve the public interest is a fairly new one. Prior to the abandonment of the politics/administration dichotomy and the principles of administration, the public administrator needed morality no more than a hotel clerk carrying out his daily duties. After all, of what use was morality to a person who did no more than execute the will of the state according to certain scientific principles? Provided the public administrator accomplished his given tasks efficiently and economically, he was, by definition, moral in the sense that he was responsible. Morality, after all, necessitates ethical choice, and, as the literature was wont to stress, ethical choice simply was not a function of the functionaries.

PUBLIC ADMINISTRATION'S ETHICAL EVOLVEMENT

The demise of the politics/administration dichotomy

Three developments have been instrumental in the emergence of the concept that ethics are, in fact, pertinent to public administration. One, of course, was the abandonment of the politics/administration dichotomy. When this naive bifurcation was eliminated, when politics and administration were recognized as being part of the same parcel, it was also admitted implicitly that morality had to be relevant to the bureaucracy. Now the public administrator was forced to make decisions not on the comfortable bases of efficiency, economy, and administrative principles, but on the more agonizing criteria of morality as well. He had to ask himself: What is *the* public interest?

The emergence of decision-making theory

The second development was the new role of decision-making theory in public administration. Herbert A. Simon had called for the rigorous analysis of decision-making behavior as central to the future study of administration; he simultaneously decimated as simplistic the "proverbs of administration" in his *Administrative Behavior*.[1] Simon argued that administrators made decisions on bases other than those of economy and efficiency. He contended that social and psychological factors had a significant effect on the decisions that decision makers made. And, before the appearance of *Administrative Behavior*, Harold Lasswell in *Psychopathology and Politics*[2] and Chester I. Barnard in *The Functions of the Executive*[3] had made essentially the same argument. The contention that decision makers made decisions on the bases of feeling, emotion, and mental sets, as well as on "rationality," implied that public adminis-

1. Herbert A. Simon, *Administrative Behavior: A Study of Decision-Making Processes in Administration Organization* (New York: Free Press, 1947).
2. Harold Lasswell, *Psychopathology and Politics* (New York: Viking, 1930).
3. Chester I. Barnard, *The Functions of the Executive* (Cambridge: Harvard University Press, 1938).

trators could make highly questionable, even immoral, public policies that possibly would affect whole populations. This was a serious matter. Public administrationists became increasingly cognizant of the disquieting notion that a sense of ethics—a sense of the public interest—was a genuine need in the practice of public administration.

This concern was exacerbated by the appearance of a new body of literature that addressed the topic of morality in public administration in a different manner. Paul H. Appleby, in *Morality and Administration in Democratic Government*, took on the ethical problems posed by the tensions between pluralistic politics and bureaucratic hierarchy. In Appleby's view, the pressures of politics and hierarchy forced moral dilemmas "up" to the highest appropriate policy-making levels in legislatures and bureaucracies and simultaneously simplified the number of choices available to public bureaucrats, usually leaving them with only two options. This was a realistic appraisal of the moral situation of the public bureaucrat; it emphasized the lack of ethical subtlety that the bureaucrat was permitted in making decisions. Although a situation might have "gray" areas in reality, decisions usually had to be either "black" or "white." [4] Similarly, Norton Long explained the connections between moral choice and administrative decision making in the public bureaucracy by his survival thesis. In Long's opinion, all decisions made by public administrators could be explained by their desire that their agencies survive. Long perceived this situation as beneficial to the public interest more often than not, but his reasoning did not rest easily with many of his colleagues as one that cultivated moral rectitude in government. [5] Likewise, Joseph Harris, in *Congressional Control of Administration*, implied that federal public administrators made their decisions primarily on the basis of satisfying a few men who headed powerful committees in Congress; his logic did not strike many as a sound rationale for promoting the public interest. [6]

Perhaps the most shattering analyses of the public administrator's relationship to the public interest were Gordon Tullock's *The Politics of Bureaucracy* [7] and Dwaine Marvick's *Career Perspectives in a Bureaucratic Setting* (1954). [8] Although we reviewed their contributions in the last chapter, a brief consideration of their works' implications for bureaucratic

4. Paul H. Appleby, *Morality and Administration in Democratic Government* (Baton Rouge: Louisiana State University Press, 1952).

5. Norton Long, *The Polity* (Chicago: Rand McNally, 1962).

6. Joseph P. Harris, *Congressional Control of Administration* (Washington, D.C.: Brookings Institution, 1964).

7. Gordon Tullock, *The Politics of Bureaucracy* (Washington: Public Affairs Press, 1965).

8. Dwaine Marvick, *Career Perspectives in a Bureaucratic Setting* (Ann Arbor: University of Michigan Press, 1954).

ethics is warranted. By arguing that all decision making in bureaucracies is predicated on the individual "reference politician" getting ahead in the hierarchy, Tullock implied that, among public administrators, what is good for the public, or even for the organization, is at best an incidental consideration. Marvick's empirical study of public administrators hypothesized that all individual behavior in public organizations was a matter of conscious or sublimated self-interest. Some participants had deep security needs that obstructed organizational innovation. Others needed simply the opportunity to "do their own thing" and had no commitment beyond protecting that opportunity. Still others were consciously willing and able to disrupt, disorient, and undermine the organization if they felt such behavior would advance their own career goals. In brief, research such as Tullock's and Marvick's was disconcerting not only to public administrationists, but to democratic theorists as well. As Ferrel Heady observed, with the experiences of France and Germany chiefly in mind, public bureaucrats "have obediently and even subserviently responded to whatever political leaders have gained power." [9]

The counter-culture critique

A third development that has led scholars and practitioners in public administration to dwell more acutely on the meaning of the public interest is the emergence in America of the "counterculture." The term *counterculture* is here used to refer to that body of literature that criticizes the American administrative state as being inhumane, technocratic, impersonal, and "faceless." The counterculture's critique of the public bureaucracy is an especially fundamental one: It states that the typical public administrator is not *immoral* but *amoral*—that is, he has been so seduced in this thinking by the values, pressures, and propaganda of the technocratic state that he no longer is capable of comprehending what morality is or is not. Thus, even if he wanted to do the "right" thing—indeed, even if he thought that he was doing the right thing—he neither would be able to make the proper moral decision nor recognize it should he happen to stumble on it.

The counterculture's argument is essentially a linguistic one. It holds that the symbols and values of technological society prevent individual men and women from choosing the life styles that they in fact would probably choose if they were not propagandized by the technocracy to be aggressive, amoral, competitive, even war-like "consumer hedonists." Herbert Marcuse, for example, stresses the symbolic aspects of this view. He contends that the media and institutions of society represent a pro-

9. Ferrel Heady, *Public Administration: A Comparative Perspective* (Englewood Cliffs, N.J.: Prentice-Hall, 1966), p. 45. But see Heady's new edition released in 1979 through Marcel Dekker.

found kind of authoritarianism, one that co-opts protest via the continual repetition of certain phrases over the mass media that restrict, by their drilling meaninglessness, alternative thinking; for example, the Soviet Union's unending repetition of the phrase, "warmongering capitalist imperialism" over its media squelches the objective analysis of Western economic and foreign policies on the part of its citizens while encouraging popular paranoia.[10]

Likewise, Jacques Ellul states that citizens in technological societies dwell on "technique" to the exclusion of "reality"; thus, moral choices are "defined out" of administrative problems, and technical means become far more important than ethical ends.[11] Similarly, Theodore J. Roszak argues that "scientism" is inadequate as a way to analyze social problems because it "hexes" our thinking on moral issues. As Roszak states:

> . . . we have produced the scientized jargon which currently dominates official parlance and the social sciences. When knowledgeable men talk, they no longer talk of substances and accidents, of being and spirit, of virtue and vice, of sin and salvation, of deities and demons. Instead, we have a vocabulary filled with nebulous quantities of things that have every appearance of precise calibration, and decorated with vaguely mechanistic-mathematical terms like "parameters," "structures," "variables," "inputs and outputs," "correlations," "inventories," "maximizations," and "optimizations." . . . The more such language and numerology one packs into a document, the more "objective" the document becomes—which normally means the less morally abrasive. . . .
>
> Thus to bomb more hell out of a tiny Asian country in one year than was bombed out of Europe in the whole Second World War becomes "escalation." . . . A comparison of the slaughter on both sides in a war is called a "kill ratio." Totaling up the corpses is called a "body count." Running the blacks out of town is called "urban renewal." Discovering ingenious new ways to bilk the public is called "market research." Outflanking the discontent of employees is called "personnel management." . . . On the other hand, one can be certain that where more colorful, emotive terms are used—"the war on poverty," "the war for the hearts and minds of men," "the race for space," "the New Frontier," "the Great Society,"—the matters referred to exist only as propagandistic fiction or pure distraction.[12]

Charles Reich dubs this situation "Consciousness II" and lists its characteristics as a critique of the administrative state: the reduction of personal freedom via the amalgamation and integration of the public and private interests of society; the value-neutral, even value-less, bureaucracy

10. Herbert Marcuse, *One Dimensional Man: Studies in the Ideology of Advanced Industrial Society* (Boston: Beacon Press, 1964).
11. Jacques Ellul, *The Technological Society* (New York: Knopf, 1964).
12. Theodore J. Roszak, *The Making of a Counter Culture* (New York: Doubleday, 1969), pp. 142–44.

that is consistently biased in favor of existing policy; the autonomy of the administrative bureaucracy, which makes particular decisions untraceable to particular sources; the displacing of traditional private property, such as land owned by people, by "the new property" of people belonging to organizations—thus, status and identification conferred by the organizations replace private property in man's traditional structure of values; and, finally, law as an "inhuman medium" that relates to classes and categories in society, but not to individual people. These features combine to produce the major symptoms of the administrative state, the essence of which "is that it is relentlessly single-minded; it has just one value . . . technology as represented by organization, efficiency, growth, progress." The effect on the individual public administrator of this relentless single-mindedness is the development of "a profound schizophrenia." Not only is his working self separated from his private self by the creation of unwanted needs and status drives via advertising, but there also is a split between his public self and his private self, which is accomplished through the nourishment of his "liberal" feelings of elitist paternalism for the dispossessed as well as cultivating his own needs for status and identity in a consumer-oriented society.[13]

PUBLIC ADMINISTRATION AND THE RECOGNITION OF THE PUBLIC INTEREST: TWO INTELLECTUAL ATTEMPTS

The counterculture critique of the moral dilemma of the public administrator (*i.e.*, that he is amoral because of the obfuscation of his language and symbols and the fractionalization of his sense of identity) is a profound one. Public administrationists, while increasingly concerned with administrative ethics and decision-making, have not yet addressed themselves to the necessary chore of defining a workable framework of moral choice for the public administrator.

Bureaucratic "responsibility"

In fact, public administrationists have avoided this task by implying that a moral framework is really not needed when they examine instead the various ways in which "responsibility" and "accountability" are assured in public bureaucracies.[14] For example, some scholars, such as Carl

13. Charles A. Reich, *The Greening of America: How the Youth Revolution is Trying to Make America Livable* (New York: Random House, 1970).

14. The following works are germaine to this paragraph: Carl J. Friedrich and Taylor Cole, *Responsible Bureaucracy* (Cambridge: Harvard University Press, 1932); Norton Long, *The Polity* (Chicago: Rand McNally, 1962); Charles S. Hyneman,

Friedrich and Norton Long, contend that the normal scruples and professional commitments that public administrators glean from being socialized into the public service, along with the "representative elite" nature of their bureaucracies, act as internal constraints against the perpetration of antidemocratic policies. Most public administrationists, however, argue that a plethora of external checks exist as well, assuring compliance with the public interest. Charles Hyneman and Herbert Finer, for instance, believe that legislative surveillance is an adequate check. J. D. Lewis and L. Von Mises contend that citizen participation in bureaucratic decision making accomplishes the task of matching bureaucratic behavior with the public interest. Henry J. Abraham makes a case for the use of the Ombudsman (a figure in Scandanavian governments and elsewhere who has no official power but great personal prestige, which he uses to rectify unjust bureaucratic decisions on an individual basis) as an effective means for assuring administrative responsibility. Dwight Waldo, John M. Pfiffner, and Robert Presthus have stated that decentralization of the bureaucracy provides an effective means of implementing the public interest. Gordon Tullock and Harold Wilensky urge the use of publicizing bureaucratic information to insure accordance with the public interest. And K. C. Davis believes that judicial review of administrative decisions checks policies not in the public interest. In a very real sense, however, these efforts miss the crucial point: that public administrators do make political decisions, but that no effective moral and philosophic guidelines (as opposed to *mechanisms* for correcting "bad" decisions) exist for their making these decisions in the public interest.

"Radical humanism"

Eugene P. Dvorin and Robert H. Simmons have confronted the dilemma head-on. They observe that "little of the literature of public administration reflects on the nature of the public interest, and virtually none

Bureaucracy (New York: Harper and Row, 1950); Herbert Finer, "Administrative Responsibility in a Democratic Government," *Public Administration Review* 1 (Summer 1941): 335–350; J. D. Lewis, "Democratic Planning in Agriculture," *American Political Science Review* 35 (April and June 1941): 232–249, 454–469; L. Von Mises, *Bureaucracy* (New Haven, Conn.: Yale University Press, 1944); Henry J. Abraham, "A People's Watchdog Against Abuse of Power," *Public Administration Review* 20 (Summer 1960): 152–157; Dwight Waldo, "Development of a Theory of Democratic Administration, *American Political Science Review* 46 (March 1952): 81–103; John M. Pfiffner and Robert Presthus, *Public Administration*, 5th ed. (New York: Ronald Press, 1967); Gordon Tullock, *The Politics of Bureaucracy* (Washington, D.C.: Public Affairs Press, 1965); Harold L. Wilensky, *Organizational Intelligence: Knowledge and Policy in Government and Industry* (New York: Basic Books, 1967); K. C. Davis, *Administrative Law* (St. Paul: West Publishing, 1951).

reflects belief in the dignity of man as the ultimate value." Conversely, they add, the other branches of the government do have operational conceptualizations of the public interest. Both the legislative and adjudicative branches "have their myths and techniques by which they serve these myths." In the legislature, the operational concept is majority rule as the fundamental precondition of democracy. In the judiciary, the concept is *stare decisis,* judicial precedent, by which the evolutionary development of legal principles is perceived as the basic method for obtaining a system of justice that reflects the public interest. In both of these examples there are, of course, flaws. As Dvorin and Simmons say, the "myths" of majority rule and *stare decisis* in reality "serve several functions—to meet the psychoemotional needs of the society and to protect and defend both legislators and judges." Nevertheless, the point stands that these concepts do not pretend to be value-neutral, and they do go far toward defining the abstract notion of the public interest in workable terms that meet the needs of the legislative and adjudicative institutions of society. Not so, however, with the executive branch, which has no such operational definition.

Dvorin and Simmons urge that "radical humanism" constitutes the public bureaucracy's functional concept of the public interest. In their words:

> "Radical humanism" forwards the proposition that the ends of man are the ends of man. . . . Radical humanism is radical because it is not willing to compromise its human values on any grounds. . . . Radical humanism calls for the ultimate capitulation of operational mechanics and political strategies to a concept of the public interest based on man as the most important concern of bureaucratic power.[15]

This statement is fine as far as it goes. Regrettably Dvorin and Simmons go no further, and a serious problem arises in terms of what "radical humanism" means when it is applied to particular administrative problems.

AN EXAMPLE OF APPLIED ETHICAL CHOICE
IN PUBLIC ADMINISTRATION

Consider, for an example, a growing dilemma in that traditionally mundane field of public personnel administration: hiring members of socially disadvantaged groups. There are two positions. One is that government

---

15. Eugene P. Dvorin and Robert H. Simmons, *From Amoral to Humane Bureaucracy* (San Francisco: Canfield Press, 1972), pp. 60–61.

should make special efforts, including the reduction of entrance standards, to hire members of those segments of American society that have endured various forms of racial, religious, ethnic, or sexual discrimination. The reasoning is that, because of cultural bias in testing, lack of educational opportunity, and general social prejudice, government owes those people who have suffered these injustices a special chance to get ahead. If this should entail some bending of the civil service regulations (as is done for veterans), so be it. Such rule-bending will, after all, only balance the social equities for those applicants who have had to suffer bigotry in the past, and this is only as it should be since government is the single institution most responsible for assuring equality of opportunity in society.

The other position is that no "lowering of standards" should be considered, regardless of the applicant's past tribulations. The logic for this viewpoint is that government owes the best governance possible to all the governed. To hire applicants who do not score as well on tests as other applicants, or who do not have comparable educational attainments, or who are just less qualified, irrespective of the tough breaks in their backgrounds, is to do a disservice to the populace generally, deprived groups included. Governmental economy, efficiency, effectiveness, and responsiveness will deteriorate to the detriment of us all, unless only the top applicants are hired. (It must be noted here that both arguments, pro and con, have been simplified considerably in order to emphasize the ethical aspects of each. Other pertinent facets, such as the efficacy of tests in measuring administrative ability and the role of strict civil service standards in protecting applicants from disadvantaged groups against discrimination, among others, are considered in Chapter 10.)

It is reasonably apparent from this example that radical humanism does not offer much of a guide to the public administrator in formulating a decision in terms of promoting the public interest. Radical humanism states that man should be the ultimate end in bureaucratic decision-making, but which option should the public administrator choose in the case cited? Is man best served by hiring or promoting a deprived group member who may not execute his duties especially well, or is man best served by not hiring (or by holding back) the same disadvantaged group member, thus never permitting him to try realizing his full human potential nor aiding the cause of his people? This dilemma can be rendered even more exquisite by making the hypothetical deprived group member in question an applicant to an agency designed to end discrimination against deprived groups, such as the Equal Employment Opportunity Commission; thus, to hire him or not to hire him implies a lack of sincerity in advancing the cause of disadvantaged groups, depending on one's point of view. In any event, radical humanism would seem to lack a viable framework of clearcut referent points for a public administrator in making an ethical choice that is in "the public interest."

JUSTICE-AS-FAIRNESS: A VIEW OF THE PUBLIC INTEREST

What is needed for the public administrator is a simple and operational articulation of the public interest that permits him to make a moral choice on the basis of rational thinking. It is forwarded in this book that such a useful concept may exist in the form of a theory of justice offered by philosopher John Rawls.

Rawls extends the notion of a social contract formulated by John Locke, Jean-Jacques Rousseau, and Thomas Hobbes, and contends implicitly that the public interest can be discerned in most situations by applying two "principles of justice": (1) that "each person is to have an equal right to the most extensive basic liberty compatible with a similar liberty for others" and (2) that "social and economic inequalities are to be arranged so that they are both (a) reasonably expected to be to everyone's advantage, and (b) attached to positions and offices open to all." Should these principles come into conflict, the second is expected to yield to the first; thus, just as in radical humanism, the dignity of man is considered to be of paramount importance.[16]

Rawls's theory of justice goes further, however. His principles necessarily lead to the conclusion that inequalities of wealth, authority, and social opportunity

> are just only if they result in compensating benefits for everyone, and in particular for the least advantaged members of society. These principles rule out justifying institutions on the grounds that the hardships of some are offset by a greater good in the aggregate. It may be expedient but it is not just that some should have less in order that others may prosper.

In short, as Rawls observes, his principles in essence are a rigorous statement of the traditional Anglo-Saxon concept of fairness.[17]

INTUITIONISM, PERFECTIONISM, AND UTILITARIANISM

The usefulness of Rawls's justice-as-fairness philosophy can be elucidated by contrasting it with other philosophies of the public interest. One is the *intuitionist* philosophy, expressed by Brian Barry, Nicholas Rescher, and

16. John Rawls, A *Theory of Justice* (Cambridge: Belknap Press of Harvard University Press, 1971), p. 60.
17. *Ibid.*, pp. 14–15.

W. D. Ross, among others.[18] Intuitionist theories expound a plurality of first principles, which may conflict when applied to particular situations but which offer no precise method for choosing the principle that should take precedence in cases of conflict. Such dilemmas are resolved by intuition, by what seems most nearly right. Intuitionist philosophies do not help the conscientious public administrator to make a rational decision in light of an explicit theory of the public interest, other than rendering him some solace in justifying his present practices. In other words, public administrators already make decisions on the basis of intuitionist theories —that is, they do what seems to be to them most nearly right on an individual basis and given particularistic circumstances. The view here, however, is that this practice—an ethical "muddling through"—is increasingly inadequate for a society in which rapid change is the only constant.

A second major philosophical school that addresses the public interest is *perfectionism*. The first and sole principle of perfectionism is to promote via society's institutions, the attainment of excellence in art, science, and culture. There are, however, two forms of perfectionism. In its relative form, as advocated by Aristotle, the perfectionist principle is one among many first principles, and thus overlaps with intuitionism. In its absolutist form, however, there are no problems of ambiguity: The public administrator should always strive to support the upper intellectual crust of his society; any misfortune for society's least fortunate segments that accrues from the necessary allocation of resources and that results from implementing the perfectionist principle is morally justified by the benefits incurred by the best members that the society has. As Nietzsche put it so pithily, the deepest meaning that can be given to the human experience is "your living for the rarest and most valuable specimens." [19]

Perfectionism is a counterpoise to the egalitarian notions rife in a democratic society, and for that reason we shall not dwell on it as an appropriate ethical decision making framework for American public administrators. Nevertheless, this is not to imply that perfectionism has not been used as an operating premise by American bureaucrats in making decisions. The National Science Foundation's traditional criterion for financing "pure" scientific research (which has been the only kind of research that the foundation financed)—that science should be funded for the sake of science—would appear to be an implementation of the

18. See, for example: Brian Barry, *Political Argument* (London: Routledge and Kegan Paul, 1965); Nicholas Rescher, *Distributive Justice* (New York: Bobbs-Merrill, 1966); and W. D. Ross, *The Right and the Good* (Oxford: Clarendon Press, 1930).

19. Friedrich Nietzsche, as quoted in J. R. Hollingsdale, *Nietzsche: The Man and His Philosophy* (Baton Rouge: Louisiana State University Press, 1965), p. 127.

perfectionist principle, although this emphasis has been changing in recent years.

A third ethical framework for the determination of the public interest is *utilitarianism,* as represented by Jeremy Bentham, Adam Smith, David Hume, and John Stuart Mill.[20] Of the philosophies that have had the most influence on public administrators in terms of intellectual rigor and social appropriateness, utilitarianism holds first place in theory, if not in actual practice.

The reasoning of utilitarianism is both democratic in values and systematic in thought. It holds that a public policy will be in the public interest provided the policy increases the net balance of social satisfaction summed over all the individuals belonging to the society. In other words, if a public policy makes everybody slightly better off, even if some individuals are left slightly worse off in other ways as a result of that policy, then the policy is just and the public interest is served. An example of a utilitarian public policy would be one that increased the income of medical doctors by raising everyone's taxes, thereby increasing everyone's net balance of health by inducing a greater net balance of individuals to enter the medical profession. Even though society's least well off individuals would lose money under this arrangement, the policy nevertheless would be just and in the public interest under a utilitarian theory because everyone's net balance of health would be increased, including that of the least well off. The logic behind this justification of such a public policy is that since individuals try to advance as far as possible their own welfare in terms of net increases, it therefore follows that the group should do the same, and the society likewise. The ethical theory of justice-as-fairness, however, would hold that such a public policy was not just and not in the public interest because it reduced the welfare of the least well off people in society, even if it is for the net benefit for the whole society. With some alterations, our hypothetical policy could be made just under Rawls's principles, however; for instance, by not taxing the poor but still letting them take part in the overall health benefits that derive from the policy. It is on the same logic that the United States has a mildly "progressive" income tax structure which is supposed to tax the rich proportionately more than the poor, rather than a "regressive" income tax structure that taxes the poor proportionately more than the rich.

---

20. See, for example: Jeremy Bentham, *An Introduction to the Principles of Morals and Legislation,* J. H. Burns and H. L. A. Hart, eds. (London: Athlone, 1970); Adam Smith, *The Wealth of Nations,* Edwin Cannan, ed. (New York: Modern Library, 1937); David Hume, *Theory of Politics,* Frederick Watkins, ed., (Edinburgh: Nelson, 1951); and John Stuart Mill, *Essays on Politics and Culture,* Gertrude Himmelfarb, ed. (New York: Doubleday, 1962).

APPLYING THE JUSTICE-AS-FAIRNESS THEORY

Intuitionism, perfectionism, and utilitarianism illuminate by contrast the usefulness of justice-as-fairness as an ethical framework for public administrators in making decisions that are in the public interest. But how would justice-as-fairness help the public administrator in deciding our original dilemma, that of hiring "less qualified" applicants from disadvantaged groups in society? It would, by the inevitability of its logic, argue for the hiring of these applicants on these grounds:

1. *Not* hiring them would be further depriving society's most deprived groups for the sake of the whole society.
2. Hiring them would facilitate the full realization of their "basic liberty" (or personal dignity) without encroaching on the basic liberty of others.
3. Hiring them helps assure that all positions and offices are open to all.
4. Hiring them helps assure that privileges innate to such offices continue to work toward the advantage of all in a reasonably equal way, because the privileges and positions are being extended to the least well off in society.

Moreover, of the ethical frameworks considered, only justice-as-fairness would by its logic permit the public administrator the decisional choice of making a special effort to hire members from disadvantaged groups. Utilitarianism would demand that the good of the whole be the first priority, regardless of consequences for society's least well off. Perfectionism, in effect, would say to hell with society's least well off since they are not considered at all in its value structure. Intuitionism, which most public administrators practice, permits the choice of hiring members of minority groups, but only as a coincidental happenstance and not by the force of its theory.

Justice-as-fairness offers the public administrator a workable way for determining the public interest. So, for that matter, does utilitarianism and perfectionism, but we are rejecting those frameworks in this book, the former because it logically permits the least advantaged persons in American society to be disadvantaged further and thus is "unfair" and not in the public interest in all instances, and the latter because its antidemocratic values are incompatible with the dominant values of American society. The choice in this book of justice-as-fairness as an operating logic for the public administrator is, of course, a value choice by the author and should be recognized as such by the reader. But it is believed to be a reasonable one under the circumstances.

On The Moral Dilemma of the Public Administrator

The following passage illustrates a typical (aside from the attendant publicity) ethical situation confronted by the public administrator. Former Beatle John Lennon and his wife Yoko Ono wished to remain in the United States for several reasons, notably their cultural attachment to New York City and Yoko's child by a previous marriage, whom they would lose if they were deported. A number of luminaries testified on behalf of their staying in the country—the president of the United Auto Workers, the mayor of New York, and the curator of the Metropolitan Museum of Art, among others—and there were reasons to believe that the charge being used to deport the Lennons—that John Lennon had been indicted in England for possessing marijuana—was an incidental consideration in the minds of top Immigration Service officials.

The hearing ended, the Lennons disappeared briefly to be finger-printed for their visa applications, and the flock of reporters waited for them in Mr. [Vincent] Schiano's office. Mr. Schiano [Chief Trial Attorney for the New York District of the United States Immigration Service] was not trying particularly hard to conceal his lack of enthusiasm for deporting the Lennons—he is, he said, another Beatle fan among millions—but, as the reporters idly asked him questions to pass the time, he grew a trifle uncomfortable. Someone asked him if he thought it was really such a good idea to kick John Lennon out of the country, and he said, "What I think isn't the point. I feel that the law bars him from becoming a permanent resident. The law allows no discretion at this point, and that's it. Even if we loved the Lennons, we couldn't do anything about that."

"Maybe the law should be changed, then," a reporter suggested.

"Well, a bill was introduced in Congress to give us the right to choose between the good guys and the bad guys on something like this. I mean, if we know a guy is a big drug dealer but the only conviction on his re-cord is for possession of marijuana, we ought to be able to deport him. But if it's just a kid who got himself busted for a joint, that's something different."

The reporters asked more questions, and finally Mr. Schiano mum-bled, as if to himself, "You know the old saying—sometimes the best guarantee of civil liberties is the inefficiency of government." Then he said, "I think I'd better stop talking. I'm still healing from some old wounds. I've had to sue for every promotion I've gotten."

The Lennons entered, and Mr. Schiano looked relieved. "Tell you what," he said to John. "I'll go to Tittenhurst"—Tittenhurst is the Lennons' country house in England—"and you take my job."

"Maybe you got a deal there," said John. . . .

HENDRIK HERTZBURG
The New Yorker

CONCLUSION

We may have assumed too much in this chapter; it is not likely, after all, that the public administrator is typically confronted with decision choices that involve the conscious application of the thinking of Aristotle, Nietzsche, or whomever. One reason why this is so is that (as Herbert Simon pointed out) choices seldom are very clear in organizational decision-making. The clarification of options thus has some importance, and public administrationists have devoted substantial effort to the development of quantitative techniques that can assist decision-making by clarifying alternatives. We consider some of these techniques in the following section.

SUPPLEMENTAL BIBLIOGRAPHY

Downs, Anthony, *Inside Bureaucracy*. Boston: Little, Brown, 1967.

Edgeworth, F. Y., *Mathematical Psychics*. New York: A. M. Kelley, 1961.

————, *A Levy on Capital for the Discharge of Debt*. Oxford: Clarendon Press, 1919.

Moore, G. E., *Principia Ethica*. Cambridge: Cambridge University Press, 1903.

Nietzsche, Friedrich, *On the Genealogy of Morals*, trans. Walter Kaufman and R. J. Hollingdale. New York: Random House, 1967.

Peabody, Robert L., and Francis E. Rourke, "Public Bureaucracies," In *Handbook of Organizations*, ed. James G. March, pp. 802–37. Chicago: Rand McNally, 1965.

Pigou, A. C., *The Economics of Welfare*. London: Macmillan, 1920.

NUTS AND BOLTS:
THE TECHNIQUES
OF
PUBLIC ADMINISTRATION

the systems approach
and
management science

chapter 7

Public administration always has been concerned with the techniques of management—what Stephen Bailey has called "instrumental theory" [1] and what political scientists occasionally have referred to as the field's predilection for "nuts and bolts." Like any social science public administration has its own corpus of methodologies, and lately the field's methods have developed in an increasingly separatist and unique way.

There are reasons for this trend. One is that government has been in the forefront of management science in recent years. Planning-Programming-Budgeting received much of its impetus during the early 1960s in the Defense Department under Robert McNamara. Computer-based information storage and retrieval systems have been at least partially developed with the concentrated sponsorship of the National Science Foundation. Systems analysis and management science have been applied in new ways by the National Aeronautics and Space Administration. Operations Research and the Critical Path Method were originated largely as the result

---

1. Stephen K. Bailey, "Objectives of the Theory of Public Administration," *Theory and Practice of Public Administration: Scope, Objectives, and Methods*, James C. Charlesworth, ed. (Philadelphia: The American Academy of Political and Social Science, Monograph 8 (October 1968), pp. 128–39.

149

of interest displayed by the U.S. Navy. While the talents of business administrators, psychologists, and scientists have contributed significantly to the development of new and more refined administrative techniques, public administrators have been a key element in their evolution.

A second reason for this trend is that public administrationists have become increasingly (if belatedly) aware that the central methodologies of the "mother discipline," political science, usually are irrelevant to practicing government bureaucrats. True, some of the methodologies of political science have minor utility; an acquaintance with the rudiments of public opinion polling, for example, could conceivably be of some use. But it is difficult to see what possible use a public administrator would have for such techniques as legislative roll call analysis, content analysis, or international aggregate data analysis.

An underlying thesis of this book is that an effective public administrator needs to learn the languages and symbols of other people. By this reasoning, a white administrative analyst in the Equal Employment Opportunity Commission would be well advised to try to understand the languages, symbols, and cultures of blacks and Chicanos if he wishes to be effective. Similarly, an administrator in the Office of Education would benefit both his agency and himself by learning the argot of education.

Equality of opportunity and education are fairly particularistic examples, however. When we approach the interrelated topics of systems theory, management science, budgeting, public personnel administration, performance assessment, and public policy analysis, we are dealing with new languages and symbols that *all* public administrators would be well advised to learn. Not to learn them, or attempting to ignore them, renders the public administrator very vulnerable indeed. He can be placed in the unenviable position of trying to hide his ignorance (and probably making a fool of himself in the process). He becomes a victim of "snow jobs" and jargon by those who are more facile in the idiom of the hour. To resurrect an old but nonetheless valid cliché, knowledge is power. It follows that, while an ability to synthesize and generalize always will be vital to the public administrator, he can ill afford to permit administrative power to devolve to technical specialists by dint of his own ignorance of their technologies, languages, and symbols.

This is not to say that every public administrator should be as fully steeped in Operations Research, systems theory, statistical analysis, computer science, or whatever, as are the full-time professionals in those fields. But the public administrator should know at least some of the basics of these subjects so that he will be able to cut through the verbiage of technical analysis and recognize the underlying value choices that the jargon often obscures. Politics pervades all endeavors, and to recognize the politics of expertise requires an understanding of the languages and the symbols of the experts. All too frequently public administrators have hidden behind the phrase, "We can leave that to the engineers." They can no longer afford to be so flippant, or if they are, then public administrators must accept the consequences of their having taken such a position: the social deficiencies that result when "engineering mentalities" are placed in positions of political power, the dangers of technocracy, the political disregard for human problems by a new managerial elite trained in science but not in social science, and—last but not least—the undermining of their own usefulness in the governmental hierarchy.

The nuts-and-bolts techniques of public administration that we shall consider in the four chapters of Section Three are not only sophisticated but increasingly vital to the efficient and effective management of the public sector. As society becomes more complex, so must the methods used to regulate it. Indeed, biological, neurological, and cybernetic theories support this contention. Information theorist W. Ross Ashby's "law of requisite variety" states that regulatory mechanisms must equal in complexity the systems they are designed to control.[2] Thus, the growing sophistication of public administration's traditional nuts-and-bolts orientation is hardly surprising in view of the country's growing social and technological variety.

A consideration of the methodologies of public administration follows. The emphasis accorded systems theory, its permutations, and the emerging area of program evaluation in public administration is unusual but needed; it indicates the recent surge of intellectual effort by public administrationists to develop the tools they need to cope with the American social ecology. Budgeting and public personnel administration also are included in this section. Budgeting is perhaps the most traditional administrative technique of the field, but treating public personnel administration as a methodology may strike some readers as novel. Yet, it really is a methodology, a technique, an area of professionalized expertise, and one unique to public administration. Finally, these methods have their own politics and values, and these facets shall be considered throughout the section.

THE SYSTEMS IDEA

A system is an entity in which everything relates to everything else. To put it another way, systems are comprised components that work together for the objectives of the whole, and the systems approach is merely a way of thinking about these components and their relationships.

---

2. W. Ross Ashby, *Introduction to Cybernetics* (London: Chapman and Hall, 1961).

In an extraordinarily lucid essay on the topic, C. West Churchman has noted that the management scientist keeps in mind five basic considerations when he thinks about systems:[3]

1. the total *objectives* of the system and, relatedly, the measures of performance of the system (in a private corporation, the performance measure might be net profit)
2. the system's *environment*—its fixed constraints (in the same example, the environment would consist of the constraint on capital, the price per product, the demand for the product, and the number of items of each product that can be produced per unit of resources)
3. the system's *resources* (the dollars and personnel in the private corporation)
4. the system's *components*, and their activities, goals, and performance measures (the product lines—*i.e.*, those subsystems that manufacture and sell each product)
5. the *management* of the system (the decision-making concerning the amount of resources to make available to each product-line)

Each of these concepts requires some hard, analytical thinking. Although, in one sense, the systems approach is simply common sense made rigorous, successfully analyzing a system is not always easy.

Consider, for example, the first concept, that of objectives. As we noted in the preceding section on organization theory, determining the goals (or the rationality) of a system can become complicated. A person who proclaims his dedication to public service, for instance, yet seems to be found more often in private enterprise earning money, represents a "system" with two different kinds of objectives. His *stated*, or *official*, objective is public service; his *real*, or *operational*, objective is earning money. Measuring the performance of his operational goal would consist of counting how much money he has earned. Such, at least, is the way a management scientist would view the situation.

In terms of public administration, one defines the system according to the problem that one wishes to resolve. Often this entails considerable coordination among and revision of disparate systems that have been developed for other kinds of problems. Daniel P. Moynihan, former director of the President's Urban Affairs Council, confronted this dilemma in trying to formulate welfare policies for the poor.[4] After considerable analysis, Moynihan and his advisers concluded that the "system" of wel-

---

3. C. West Churchman, *The Systems Approach* (New York: Dell, 1968).
4. Daniel P. Moynihan, *Maximum Feasible Misunderstanding: Community Action and the War on Poverty* (New York: Free Press, 1969).

fare worked against its own objective—that of making the country's deprived population less deprived. In fact, Moynihan believed that the War on Poverty, the Aid to Families with Dependent Children program, the Office of Economic Opportunity, and the entire "service-dispensing class" of welfare's big bureaucracy worked far more beneficially for the middle class than for the lower class. The middle class received the jobs spawned by the numerous welfare programs, while the lower class paid, at least in part, the salaries of the welfare bureaucrats with their income taxes. Moreover, the welfare programs stigmatized the recipients, in Moynihan's opinion, by reducing their self-esteem, increasing their psychological and economic dependency on government, and encouraging (albeit unwittingly) an attitude of outright loathing toward welfare "bums" among lower-middle-class whites. Moynihan concluded that a more disastrous piece of social engineering could not have been designed had one tried.

To alleviate this situation, Moynihan, in effect, redefined the "system" of social deprivation in America. He did so by including the income tax as a newly recognized variable in the system and by redefining poverty more as a matter of money and less as a matter of life style, which had been the usual emphasis of the welfare bureaucrats and social workers. By redefining America's system of social deprivation to include these variables, Moynihan was able to see the problem in a new light. He proposed that the tax structure be so rigged as to provide every citizen with a minimum annual income. Partly as a result of his analysis, those citizens with annual incomes under the so-called poverty line were exempted from paying any income tax whatsoever. Moynihan also proposed a complicated negative income tax (the Family Assistance Plan), which would have had the Internal Revenue Service supplementing the income of those citizens under the poverty line so that they would have a guaranteed annual income.

The negative income tax was a radical idea; the systems approach tends to come up with politically radical notions on occasion. A Yugoslav Marxist stated that, were the guaranteed annual income to be enacted, it might become the most important piece of social legislation in history. (Partly because of its radicalism, Moynihan's Family Assistance Plan was defeated twice in the Senate, with the help of both parties.)

Nevertheless, the point stands that very new and fresh solutions to very old and distressing problems can emerge as a result of analysis via the systems approach. Moreover, the example also indicates that any system inevitably is embedded in some larger system. Thus, while a system may work superbly as a discrete entity, in terms of a larger system it may not work at all. This is a common problem, for instance, in computer-based information storage and retrieval systems. Occasionally, an information system, by the nature of its programming, will "define out" variables that can be of considerable importance to the organization as a larger system. This situation can produce severe organizational dysfunctions.

This leads us to the *Weltanschauung* problem. *Weltanschauung* is a German word meaning "world view," or the underlying belief structure held by a person about how the world works and what makes it go. For example, Theory X and Theory Y represent two different, partial *Weltanschauungen*. Similarly, the personnel in the Community Services Administration may have a different *Weltanschauung* than a majority of the members of Congress. The advantage of the systems approach is that it forces us to formally delineate the differences and similarities between world views. To do this aids in rationalizing the means and ends in an organization. Goals are clarified, and efficiency and effectiveness are improved.

THE SYSTEMS DEBATE

The idea of defining the parameters of a system and the notion of a *Weltanschauung* lie at the center of the larger debate about systems theory generally. While we have been discussing the systems approach from the viewpoint of the management scientist (who obviously favors it), there are other points of view and other kinds of analysts who question its utility—who, indeed, are concerned about its dangers. Churchman has categorized these analysts as efficiency experts (primarily the scientific management crowd we reviewed in Chapter 3), humanists, and anti-planners.[5] We shall consider their arguments in turn.

The efficiency approach

The crux of the notion behind efficiency is that there must be one best way to do a job. The words *a job* imply that the overriding concern of the efficiency expert is to complete a subsystemic task with maximum efficiency, and such, in fact, is the case.

The management scientist has no argument with the time-motion expert as far as he goes. Conflict arises when what is good for the subsystem becomes bad for the total system. In other words, the management scientist has the broader perspective, and the limited rationale of the efficiency approach is frequently in direct contradiction with the more comprehensive rationality of the systems approach. When the efficiency approach is favored over the systems approach under these circumstances, organizational dysfunctions can result.

5. Churchman, *op. cit.*

Consider Churchman's example of the airport as a case in which the efficiency expert's cost-reduction policy leads to an increase in the total cost of the system. The objective of the efficiency expert is to reduce "wastage" by keeping every piece of equipment in continual operation; to let an airplane sit idle is "waste" in the efficiency expert's terms. Thus, the time-motion expert will try to schedule an airplane take-off and landing every minute (assuming such scheduling would be safe) on each airstrip; such a schedule would maximize the efficient use of airstrips, airplanes, and airport personnel. The subsystem that occupies the efficiency expert's attention in this case is the schedule for airplane use of each airstrip.

A problem exists beyond the vision of the time-motion expert, however, that will cause systemic inefficiency. The efficiency expert is assuming that planes are taking off and landing *every minute*, but in reality they are taking off and landing every minute *on the average*. It is this situation that concerns the management scientist. He realizes that wind conditions, differences in the engines of planes, and so forth cause certain delays and speedups, and that, therefore, airstrip idleness must be balanced against airplane idleness. In the management scientist's view, the efficiency expert fails to note that one inefficiency in the system must be offset by another. Thus, the management scientist brings in probability theory and, by applying it to the airstrip/airplane mix, concludes that if the efficiency expert's one-plane-per-minute recommendation were to be followed, the waiting line of airplanes on each airstrip eventually would increase without limit. Although the airstrip is being used "efficiently," the waiting-time per plane grows increasingly inefficient. As a result, the management scientist might suggest the construction of a new airstrip, even though the existing one is not in use during certain times of the day. Probability theory indicates that the efficiency of the total system would be improved by such an addition.

The humanist approach

It is the larger systemic outlook that distinguishes the systems analyst, or management scientist, from the time-motion expert. With the humanist approach, we get the reverse effect. The humanist argues that it is the management scientist who is too narrow in his definition of "the system" —or any system. At root in this dispute is a question of values. This aspect distinguishes it from the fundamental difference between the management scientist and the efficiency expert; in that case, the difference was one of systemic size, but both sides agreed that economic efficiency and effectiveness were the prime values.

The humanist suggests that there is more to "life" (which is essentially the humanist's "system") than economics. He argues for human genius, triumph, despair, and all those uniquely human conditions that the system of life encompasses. These variables can never be included in the management scientist's system, and it is therefore incomplete.

Robert Boguslaw has extended this argument to warn us of the dangers that accompany the application of the systems approach to social problems. He states that the management scientists and the systems analysts are "the new utopians"—that is, they intend to create a theoretically "perfect" world, but one that may define out human problems in the process. The new utopians are concerned with "people-substitutes" that have neither "souls nor stomachs." Machines will limit human behavior; at best, the individual will become a conditioned, humanoid shell, molded by the use of economic and behavioral data, and designed to fit in ever more tightly with the ever rationalizing system being perfected by the systems analysts who manage it.[6]

To this the management scientist can but reply: I have to analyze on the basis of data that I can use. True, systems analysis works best when the data are quantifiable, measurable, or weightable, and this condition by itself renders economic (and, to a lesser degree, behavioral) questions important. Economic and behavioral data are more feasible to examine, analyze, and reshuffle than are the less measurable, more elusive humanistic values represented by Boguslaw. In this sense, the planner and management scientist ultimately are concerned with—and limited by—what is feasible. It is not that the new utopians are necessarily antihumanist; rather, they cannot yet quantify those values that the humanist would like them to include as part of the system. When this is tried, the results can be somewhat pathetic. For example, a computer-based college search service once included "campus beauty" as a variable in finding "the right college for the right applicant." Beauty, however, was determined by the number of trees per acre. That may be one person's definition of beauty, but it is not necessarily everyone's.

The antiplanning approach

There are several variants of the antiplanning approach; they all represent a repugnance toward the notions of both systems and analysis. In this aspect, the antiplanners differ from the efficiency experts and the humanists. The efficiency expert values both ideas of systems and analysis, but simply goes about it in a more limited way than the management scientist. The humanist also values the concepts of systems and analysis, but wants more variables, usually nonquantifiable variables, included in the

---

6. Robert Boguslaw, *The New Utopians: A Study of System Design and Social Change* (Englewood Cliffs, N.J.: Prentice-Hall, 1965), pp. 1–28.

process. Not so the antiplanners, but at least they are easily identified. The most common variety is "Mr. Experience." He believes that experience in the organization, combined with natural ability, native intelligence, and personal leadership, beats management science every time. This may be true occasionally, but it would be a difficult contention to "prove" either way. There are examples in industry of "experienced" men who climbed to the top of their corporations (which often were characterized by rigid seniority rules), only to reject newfangled management science techniques and lead their companies into bankruptcy.

A somewhat more serious version of antiplanning is held by the skeptic. The skeptic is a relativist who asks if anything is really "true." For instance, do Americans have a "better" quality of life now than fifty years ago, or vice versa? Is planning "better" than antiplanning? Both are worthy questions, but they also are sophomoric ones. While skepticism suggests good questions, it does not provide good answers. Perhaps in time answers will be found to these questions, but until that day skepticism does not go very far as an argument for (or against) antiplanning.

Still another proponent of antiplanning is the determinist. The determinist argues that any system is the result of various, often unidentifiable, social forces, and it therefore follows that decision makers in a system do not really make decisions at all, but merely ratify the inevitability of determinism as it affects their organization. Determinism relates to a number of concepts concerning decision-making in public administration —e.g., satisficing, muddling through, disjointed incrementalism, intuitionism, nondecision making, and the "technostructure." These notions basically argue that systemic decision making is not a reality in public bureaucracies and attempt to describe the policy-making process as it really is; incremental, fragmented, unanalytic, limited, and disjointed.

From this viewpoint, however, determinism is a statement of fact, not an argument against the systems approach. The determinist argument thus is not an argument *against* planning (as are the experiential and skeptical arguments); rather it merely asserts that the systems approach is not here yet. This, of course, may change and, while it is a dubious proposition at best that human decision makers ever will become computers capable of measuring all systemic variables, it nonetheless is fair to state that many decision makers would like to become more analytical in their work.

With these concepts about the systems approach in mind, we now can turn to some of the more specific techniques of management science. We shall consider Operations Research, Performance Evaluation and Review Technique/Critical Path Method, simulations and games, and electronic data processing, with emphasis on how they pertain to the systems approach.

Operations research

E. S. Quade has observed that Operations Research (OR) differs from systems analysis in that it focuses on "efficiency problems in which one can maximize some 'payoff' function that clearly expresses what one is trying to accomplish," rather than trying to clarify alternative policy choices within the system as a whole.[7] OR, in other words, comes into play only *after* value choices have been made. It is used to maximize systemic efficiency and effectiveness within the subsystems represented by those choices. Our prior example of the optimal airstrip/airplane mix problem is also an example of how the management scientist would apply Operations Research, for OR relies on the use of probability theory, queuing techniques, and mathematical model building to allocate and utilize resources maximally within a designated subsystem.

OR got its start and its name in England, primarily during the development of British radar in the late 1930s. Later OR was brought into the analysis of other kinds of war-related problems. In 1940 an early and elementary Operations Research analysis of British fighter plane losses over France persuaded the English to make the significant decision not to send any more fighters to France. Soon OR was being applied by the Allies in the analysis of bombing runs and their effectiveness and in how to boost the "kill ratios" of Nazi submarines.

In the submarine analysis, it was simply a matter of applying rudimentary probability theory. The British were having considerable difficulty with German U-boats in the English Channel. Operations researchers observed that the depth charges of British submarine hunters never exploded until they had sunk at least thirty-five feet below the surface. As Churchman has noted, "what is especially interesting about this story is that the scientists kept asking stupid questions" and in the process recommended that the charges be set to go off closer to the surface. This was done, and the number of destroyed Nazi submarines in the English Channel rose significantly.

Because of these kinds of successes on a variety of battlefronts, by 1945 there was no major Allied command without an OR group of one kind or another. Since World War II, OR has been applied to problems of bus scheduling, the U.S. Post Office, the Department of Defense, waste management, land use, urban planning, highway safety, education,

7. E. W. Quade, "System Analysis Techniques for Planning-Programming-Budgeting," *Planning-Programming-Budgeting: A Systems Approach to Management,* Fremont J. Lyden and Ernest G. Miller, eds. (Chicago: Markham, 1972), p. 246.

agriculture, and even birth control. With the advent of computers possessing enormous analytical capacities, the uses and refinements of Operations Research have burgeoned, and its potential application to a variety of problems in public administration is almost limitless.

OR is used most fruitfully in the solution of public administration problems that repeat themselves. Russell L. Ackoff and Patrick Rivett, while noting that there is no "one way" to classify these kinds of managerial problems, nonetheless provide a useful guide. They state that OR may be applied to at least eight kinds of problems.[8]

1. *Inventory,* which involves problems of idle resources—most training problems, for example, can be viewed as inventory problems.
2. *Allocation,* or finding the optimal mix of resources available, jobs to be done, and ways to do those jobs—most budget problems are problems of allocation.
3. *Queuing,* which considers how to get people or material through a service facility in the fastest, most efficient, and most effective way possible—problems relating to bus-stop scheduling are an example.
4. *Sequencing,* which attempts to solve problems relating to performance in a queue—for example, minimizing the total time needed to service a priority group of waiting clients in a queue.
5. *Routing,* or the effort to minimize the distance, time, or cost involved between points. "The traveling salesman problem" is the classic expression of a routing dilemma, and the objective is to find the shortest, most efficient route for a salesman to take between cities. It is a simply stated problem, but a difficult one to solve: while there are only six possible routes between four cities, for eleven cities there are 3,700,000 possible paths.
6. *Replacement,* which is the attempt to minimize the costs of replacing items that degenerate or fail with the passage of time—such items may include everything from light bulbs to lathes to labor wastage.
7. *Competition,* or the problems of maximizing returns for one decision maker in the face of rivalry from other decision makers—in terms of public administration, competitive problems arise in the area of foreign policy.
8. *Search,* which involves the optimal method for finding the opportunities and resources needed by a decision maker. OR has been

8. Russell L. Ackoff and Patrick Rivett, *A Manager's Guide to Operations Research* (New York: John Wiley, 1963), pp. 21–34.

used to routinize search procedures and reduce costs in auditing, geological explorations, and inspections, among other areas.

Most OR problems involve mixes of these classifications, and operations researchers have developed or adapted a number of statistical and computer techniques to solve them. Inventory problems, for instance, often employ the use of matrix algebra (in linear programming), the calculus of variations (in dynamic programming), and computer-based simulations for their resolution. Mathematical programming also is used in the solution of allocation problems, notably linear, nonlinear, stochastic, parametric, and dynamic programming. Queuing problems also require some sophisticated mathematics, particularly probability theory and the use of differential and integral equations. Sequencing problems involve simulation, Performance Evaluation and Review Technique (PERT), and the Critical Path Method (CPM). Dynamic programming and relatively simple calculus often are used for replacement problems, and gaming is a favored type of simulation used in the analysis of competitive problems. We shall consider PERT, CPM, simulation, and game theory in greater detail in this chapter because they have been used to a significant extent in the solution of public administration problems.

Before continuing this brief review of Operations Research, it is worth reemphasizing that OR is "value-free." That is, it can be and virtually has been used for any purpose. While mail deliveries have been speeded by OR, Sir C. P. Snow has observed that Sir Winston Churchill used Operations Research to optimize the effects of British bombing strikes on the civilian population of Germany.[9] (Churchill wanted revenge. Fortunately for the German people, his operations researchers overestimated the effects of British bombing levels.) Similarly, operations researchers were asked to calculate the effects that the first "firestorm" bombs would have on Tokyo. (Unfortunately for the Japanese, and because the OR workers neglected to consider adequately the frailties of Japan's wood-and-paper architecture among other variables, operations researchers underestimated the awesome destruction wrought.) Finally, "kill ratios," "body counts," "overkill," and the other unsavory phrases of the more recent Vietnam conflict were derived from the concepts of Operations Research. Amorality is an inescapable facet of efficiency, and it is Operations Research that is used to maximize efficiency scientifically. Thus, it is useful to comprehend some of the overlapping techniques of OR and management science in order to enhance our capability of per-

9. C. P. Snow, *Science and Government* (Cambridge: Harvard University Press, 1961), pp. 47–53.

ceiving the values that underlie the argot of administrative techniques. PERT and CPM provide a useful example in this regard.

On Efficiency in Public Administration

Rudolph Hoess was a Nazi SS captain who, in his own words, "personally arranged the gassing of two million persons" during a two-and-a-half year period in the Auschwitz concentration camp. The following passage concerns Hoess's feelings about being "a good German," following orders, and being efficient in the execution of his duties. It illustrates that "value-free" management science can be used for any purpose.

So, as Hoess himself has written, "by the will of the Reichsfuhrer SS, Auschwitz became the greatest human extermination center of all time." He considered that Himmler's order was "extraordinary and monstrous." Nevertheless, the reasons behind the extermination program seemed to him to be right. He had been given an order, and had to carry it out. "Whether this mass extermination of Jews was necessary or not," he writes, "was something on which I could not allow myself to form an opinion, for I lacked the necessary breadth of view." Hoess felt that if the Fuhrer himself had given the order for the cold calculated murder of millions of innocent men, women, and children then it was not for him to question its rightness.

What Hitler or Himmler ordered was always right. After all, he wrote, "Democratic England also has a basic national concept: 'My country, right or wrong!'" and what is more, Hoess really considered that was a convincing explanation. Moreover he thought it strange that "outsiders simply cannot understand that there was not a single SS officer who could disobey an order from the Reichsfuhrer SS." . . . His basic orders, issued in the name of the Fuhrer, were sacred. They brooked no consideration, no argument, no interpretation. . . . it was not for nothing that during training the self-sacrifice of the Japanese for their country and their Emperor, who was also their god, was held up as a shining example to the SS. . . .

Hoess's own account of his misdeeds is not only remarkable for what he has described but also for the way in which he has written it. The Nazis, Hoess among them, were experts in the use of euphemisms and when it came to killing they never called a spade a spade. Special treatment, extermination, liquidation, elimination, resettlement, and final solution were all synonyms for murder, and Hoess has added another gem to the collection, "the removal of racial-biological foreign bodies." . . .

Hoess was a very ordinary little man. He would never have been heard of by the general public had not fate decreed that he was to be, perhaps, the greatest executioner of all time. Yet to read about it in his autobiography makes it all seem quite ordinary. He had a job to do and he carried it out efficiently.

Although eventually he appears to have realized the enormity of what he did, he nevertheless took pride in doing it well. . . .

LORD RUSSELL OF LIVERPOOL
Commandant of Auschwitz

*Performance evaluation and review technique
and the critical path method*

PERT, CPM, "network analysis," or whatever it might be called, goes by many names, but essentially the same techniques are used regardless of title. PERT was developed in the late 1950s by the Booz, Allen, and Hamilton consulting firm for the U.S. Navy as a method of assuring that the incredibly complex task of constructing the first Polaris missiles and their nuclear submarines would be completed on schedule. PERT more than fulfilled expectations; the Polaris system was completed almost two years ahead of the scheduled target date. Since then, PERT has been and is used by a variety of government agencies (particularly the research-and-development oriented agencies) for a variety of systems analysis and scheduling purposes. In fact, it has been reported that the Soviet government uses a variant of PERT for developing its five-year economic plans. All of our military services, the National Aeronautics and Space Administration, the Federal Aviation Agency, the Nuclear Regulatory Commission, and the Office of Management and Budget among others, had adopted PERT by the early 1960s.

PERT is an effort to specify for the administrator how various parts of a particular project interrelate, especially what parts of the project must be completed before the remaining parts of the project can be started. For instance, before we can open our front doors for a cocktail party, we first must have glasses and liquor. A PERT chart not only specifies and clarifies this sequence, but gives us the times in which each portion of the overall sequence must be finished in order to keep the whole project on schedule. In its most sophisticated (and computerized) form, a PERT chart can give the administrator the time *and* cost for each part of the project; it is simply a matter of developing a formula of the cost per each time unit (*e.g.*, days, hours, whatever).

Rather than review here the arithmetical concepts of PERT, which would take an undue amount of time, we shall go on to simulations and games. Nevertheless, because an understanding of PERT and CPM is useful for the public administrator, a simple but fairly detailed example of how it works has been included as Appendix A to this book.

Simulations and games

Another aspect of systems theory and management science involves simulations and games. Both are models of variables and their behavior in the system, and like PERT they attempt to clarify for the decision maker how the system works by abstracting and simplifying it.

Modern simulations and games got their start in the early war games —chess may have been such a war game.[10] The first true war game was originated in 1798 in the German state of Schleswig, and during the course of the following century two forms of the *Neue Kriegspiel* (as the game was called) evolved: the rigid and free. Both versions became popular in the Prussian military academies and had spread to the rest of Europe and to West Point by the end of the nineteenth century.

By World War II, all the major international powers were playing war games, and Japan and Germany were becoming especially adept. At the Total War Research Institute and Naval War College of Imperial Japan, Japan's future actions for 1941–1943 were gamed during a period of days. Roles were played by members of the military and government elite, and represented the Italo-German Axis, the Soviet Union, the United States, England, and various eastern powers including Japan, which, interestingly, was played as a fragile coalition of military, government, and industrial interests. Japan's military groups proved more aggressive than the others in this game, winning most of the internal disputes, and plans for controlling Japan's consumer goods in wartime were developed during the course of the games that were identical to those actually put into effect in Japan on December 8, 1941. Similarly, prior to Hitler's ascension in 1933, the German Reichswehr gamed Germany's future relations with Poland, which was of grave concern to the Germans since their military strength was limited to 100,000 troops by the Versailles Treaty. Previously, in 1929, Erich von Manstein (later General von Manstein) proposed that the standard war game be expanded to include a political game. The inventiveness of the player representing Poland in alleging German provocations dumbfounded the player representing the German Foreign Ministry, while the procrastination of the League of Nations in coming to Germany's diplomatic defense also was gloomily enlightening.

By the 1950s similar games and simulations were being played in the Soviet Foreign Office and the U.S. Air Force's RAND Corporation. The

10. The following discussion on war games is drawn largely from John R. Raser, *Simulation and Society: An Exploration of Scientific Gaming* (Boston: Allyn & Bacon, 1969), pp. 46–49.

U.S. Joint Chiefs of Staff now have a Joint War Games Agency which has developed TEMPER, for "Technological, Economic, Military, and Political Evaluation Routine," indicating the broadened scope of the historic *Neue Kriegspiel.*

More recently, the use of games and simulations has been extended to a diversity of new fields. Herbert A. Simon and Richard C. Snyder have used it to refine decision-making theory.[11] The American Management Association developed the first popular management game in 1956 after some of its members discovered the use of gaming at the Naval War College, and a number of private corporations since have developed their own variants. Sociology, education, psychology, law, and anthropology also have developed simulations. Simulations in economics have been particularly successful in generating accurate predictions. Economists have been working on computer simulations of the national economy since 1957. They now can generate reasonably precise predictions about the economy for up to six months or even a year—which outdistances any other social science easily.

Political science also has been active in simulations work. Perhaps the most notable example is the Simulmatics Project, created by Ithiel de Sola Pool for the Democratic Party during the 1960 presidential election. Pool delineated 480 "voter types," computer-simulated how they would respond to the salient issues of the campaign, and predicted the outcome of the vote. Pool's Simulmatics Project predicted the actual vote in 1960 far more accurately than any other method used (polls, surveys, and so forth) to which it was compared.[12] Similarly, simulations work done by Michael J. Shapiro and Cleo H. Cherryholmes accounted for approximately 90 percent of the variance in the voting pattern of members of the U.S. House of Representatives.[13]

These kinds of simulations in political science have some discomforting overtones. In the Simulmatics Project, it is probable that other issues could have been substituted for those that actually arose in the campaign, with exactly the same results. In other words, there is a potential peril here that political issues could be selected and marketed so adroitly through simulation techniques that genuine dangers of mass persuasion in

11. See, for example, Herbert A. Simon, Donald W. Smithburg and Victor A. Thompson, *Public Administration* (New York: Knopf, 1950); and Richard C. Snyder, H. W. Bruck, and Burton Sapin, eds., *Foreign Policy Decision-Making: An Approach to the Study of International Politics* (Glencoe, Ill.: Free Press, 1962).

12. Ithiel de Sola Pool, Robert P. Abelson, and Samuel Popkin, *Candidates, Issues, and Strategies: Computer Simulation of the 1960 and 1964 Presidential Elections* (Cambridge: MIT Press, 1965).

13. Cleo H. Cherryholmes and Michael J. Shapiro, *Representatives and Roll Calls: A Computer Simulation of Voting in the 88th Congress* (Indianapolis: Bobbs-Merrill, 1969).

a democracy may emerge. This danger is compounded when the voting behavior of the voters' representatives also is reduced to a series of computer games.

Public administration has been using simulations peripherally for a number of years. The field of Organization Development (described in Chapter 3), in fact, relies on the use of person-to-person simulations and games in a major way as a means of "democratizing" and "opening up" organizations. But public administration's direct use of simulations and games has been fairly recent, although they now are a standard feature at the national conferences of the American Society for Public Administration. Such games have included the "Health Game," involving role-playing the field of providing health services, and "I'm OK—You're OK," which approaches bureaucratic problem-solving through transactional analysis.

In sum, the development and expansion of games, simulations, and their uses have burgeoned, and public administration has been affected. Although the methodology is less than thirty years old, a report by Abt Associates in 1965 stated that between $3 and $6 million was spent on economic, political, and social simulations in 1965 alone.[14]

As we have observed, simulations and games are the playing out of scenarios and involve abstraction, simplification, and substitution; their advantages are economy, the clarification of the phenomena being simulated, reproducibility and safety. Beyond these features, simulations and games can be categorized according to three distinct types: simple two-person games, computer games, and man-machine games. Each of these games has its own kind of usefulness, although, as we shall see, man-machine games would appear to combine and add to the best of both worlds.

Two-person games grew out of social science research in small group theory. As an area of study, small group theory has had a notable impact on public administration, and many of its propositions have been used by organization theorists in human relations and organization development. Small group theory also has provided a good deal of information concerning the dimensions of "leadership."

An early researcher in this area was Kurt Lewin, who, by observing small groups of people, developed his notion of "affective" and "instrumental" leaders; that is, a friendly, outgoing person tends to emerge first as a leader in a group by establishing intragroup communications and a trusting atmosphere and, having paved the way emotionally, then is eventually supplanted by a more aggressive, let's-get-things-done type, who mobilizes the group for the sake of accomplishing some task.[15] Simi-

14. Abt Associates, *Survey of the State of the Art: Social, Political and Economic Models and Simulations* (Cambridge: Abt Associates, 1965).

15. Kurt Lewin, *A Dynamic Theory of Personality* (New York: McGraw-Hill, 1935).

larly, the experiments of Muzafer Sherif, among others, indicated the impressive effect peer-group pressure could have on individuals in the formation of their own perceptions and viewpoints.[16] It is also in this vein that R. F. Bales developed his frequently used scale for measuring the kinds of behaviors with which group members interact with one another.[17]

Perhaps the most formal, mathematical statement of "the games people play" in small groups is the two-person game as developed by Anatol Rapoport.[18] Two-person games may be either "zero-sum" (one person may win only at the expense of the other), or "non-zero-sum" (both players win or both players lose). This is not quite so simple as it may sound, however, because there are a variety of mixes in terms of relative costs and benefits that are possible, and calculating the maximum win and minimum loss per player often requires the use of some fairly sophisticated mathematics. Thus, we hear such terms used in game theory as "maximin" or "minimax" (which mean the same thing) to denote these kinds of strategic thinking. As Sam Spade put it in *The Maltese Falcon*, "That's the trick, from my side . . . to make my play strong enough so that it ties you up, but yet not make you mad enough to bump me off against your better judgment."

The classic example often used to illustrate how this works is provided by "the prisoner's dilemma," which can be seen as either a zero-sum or non-zero-sum two-person game. A prosecutor is convinced that two prisoners are partners in a crime, but cannot prove the guilt of either one on the basis of the existing evidence and needs a confession of their mutual complicity. To get it, the prosecutor separates the prisoners and points out to each of them individually that they may confess or deny the crime. If neither prisoner confesses, both will be booked on some minor charge. If both prisoners confess, the prosecutor will recommend a lighter sentence. If one prisoner confesses and the other does not, the confessor will be freed for turning state's evidence, while the other will be prosecuted to the full extent that the law allows.

Thus, each prisoner can get a maximum payoff by double-crossing the partner—i.e., by confessing—but only if the other prisoner does not also confess; this would be a zero-sum game, or one player winning at the expense of the other. But if both prisoners should elect to double-cross, both lose—hence, a non-zero-sum game. If both stand fast (i.e., if they have adequate faith in one another to cooperate with each other), then

16. Muzafer Sherif and Carolyn Sherif, *Groups in Harmony and Tension* (New York: Harper & Row, 1953).

17. Robert F. Bales, *Interaction Process Analysis: A Method for the Study of Small Groups* (Reading, Mass.: Addison-Wesley, 1950).

18. Anatol Rapoport, *Fights, Games, and Debates* (Ann Arbor: University of Michigan Press, 1960).

TABLE 7–1. The Payoff Matrix of Prisoner's Dilemma

| | | Prisoner B | | | |
		Deny Everything		Confess Everything	
		I		II	
Prisoner A	Deny Everything	2a	2b	10a	0b
		III		IV	
	Confess Everything	0a	10b	5a	5b

both win something, but each wins less than if he or she had been the only double-crosser. This, too, is a non-zero-sum game. The prisoner's dilemma can be illustrated more formally by the payoff matrix posited in Table 7–1.

The sub-*a*'s and sub-*b*'s next to each number in the matrix represent the payoff (or lack of it) to Prisoner A and Prisoner B, respectively. Each number stands for years in prison that the prisoner must face for each alternative. For example, if Prisoner A confessed everything and Prisoner B denied everything. Prisoner A would get off scot-free and Prisoner B would get the book thrown at him, as quadrant III indicates. Conversely, if both prisoners confessed everything, each would get five years (quadrant IV), and if both denied everything, each would get only two years (quadrant I).

We get more sophisticated in this kind of game when we talk about "non-zero-sum, n-person games"—that is, life. With more than two people, the possibility of coalitions, deals, and bargains emerges, and our matrix waxes infinitely more complex. W. H. Riker [19] has done some of the theoretical work in this area, although Anthony Downs has considered the possibilities of non-zero-sum, n-person games in terms of organizations and in largely nonquantitative language. Downs brings in the "size principle" and contrasts it with the "information effect." The size principle refers to the desirability of the leader of a coalition acquiring only the bare majority needed to win. Such a coalition is optimal, because any members beyond those needed for a winning majority simply make the coalition less easily controlled; thus, the notion arises of "minimum winning coalition." The information effect relates to the need for "padding": since information is distorted in organizations, the coalition leader can never be sure that his coalition will be big enough to win, so he accepts

19. W. H. Riker, *The Theory of Political Coalitions* (New Haven: Yale University Press, 1962).

the control costs of adding members to his coalition for the sake of assuring victory.[20]

These ways of thinking play a large role in the newly resurgent field of political economy, or public choice. Political economists ask, how do we measure what the polity "wants"? How do we determine what choice is in the public interest? How do we measure that choice and its alternatives? In this perspective, public policy making can be viewed as a theory of games, just as the choices that the individual makes in terms of his organization may be seen as an array of zero-sum and non-zero-sum options. Public choice is considered in more detail in Chapter 10.

In the last two paragraphs, we have been digressing from our original two-person game and instead have been considering more complicated situations. This is easy to do, because the two-person game does not take us very far when it comes to developing theoretical models that pertain to real life. In other words, the chief disadvantage of the simple two-person game is just that—it is too simple; it cannot handle more than one or two propositions at once.

To simulate more complex models of society and organizations requires the enormous analytical capacities of the computer. Computer simulations often are used in connection with the problems and techniques associated with Operations Research. Instead of working with problems of human behavior and personality, computer games deal with the operation of large and complicated systems. The simulations of the national economy are of this type, as are the Simulmatics Project and a variety of OR-related simulations involving managerial problems. Occasionally, the formal theorems of game theory are programmed on a computer, such as in foreign policy questions: If the United States does this, will the Common Market do that? Obviously, the notions of zero-sum and non-zero-sum games play a significant role in such computer simulations.

Two-person games and computer games both have their uses. A two-person game has the great advantage of dealing directly with real life situations. Although there are elements of artificiality in the laboratory approach to people, the techniques of sensitivity training, T-groups, and role-playing nonetheless are more likely to evoke "real" emotions and responses from players simply because they deal with real people. In this sense, the simulation—the model—gains in accuracy and predictive power.

Unfortunately, human-to-human games cannot cope with very complicated models. They cannot consider the nonhuman variables extant in any administrative system, such as office rules or an unanticipated urban riot. A computer simulation, however, can. The "traveling salesman" simulation, for example, can tell us that there are 3,700,000 different ways

20. Anthony Downs, *Inside Bureaucracy* (Boston: Little, Brown, 1967), pp. 112–131.

to travel among eleven cities and the characteristics of each of them. These variables are too rich to be included within the limited theoretical confines of a simple person-to-person game. On the other hand, a computer simulation cannot tell us with very much accuracy just how human beings would react to such data—or, more importantly, how human and nonhuman variables would interact in the total system. Since all administrative systems include both kinds of components, the ability to model their interactions becomes a critical task for simulations, and it is for this task that man-machine games have been designed. Man-machine games represent an attempt to combine the best features of human-based and machine-based games.

An example of a man-machine game is provided by the American air defense system. In refining this system, a man-machine game was used that simulated both the hardware complex (*i.e.*, radar, interceptor planes, communications, and so forth), and a team of men whose mission it was to decide whether or not to launch the interceptors on the basis of receiving and judging incoming signals under a variety of conditions. As a result of this simulation, the optimal conditions for the correct player response were discerned, and some of the hardware was modified.

Man-machine games also have been used for sensitizing public policy makers to their administrative environments. The Massachusetts Institute of Technology has, since 1959, conducted such games for high-ranking officials in the Departments of Defense and State, and a man-machine game has been developed at the University of North Carolina for training Peace Corps volunteers.

In sum, simulations and games are a technique of management science (as well as of social science) that can be used to clarify the interrelationships of variables in an administrative system and to expand the awareness of administrators in that system. In this orientation, simulations and games relate to and overlap with the other variants of the systems approach and management science.

The computer and electronic data processing

The final major aspect of management science that we shall consider concerns information theory and electronic data processing (EDP), also known as automatic data processing (ADP)—in short, the computer. Perhaps more than any other of the new management sciences, the computer is shrouded by the greatest mystique. Some of its aspects are worth considering here.

The computer has been bought by administrative organizations everywhere. There are more than one hundred thousand computers operating in the United States, and the machines probably are responsible for the employment of at least one million people. State governments own about 10 percent of the nation's computers, and the federal government has more than four thousand of the machines.

Assets. The computer is extremely well suited for certain kinds of functions. It can repeat itself precisely, thus taking over many routine duties in an organization; it does its complex duties, such as calculating and tabulating social security checks, with awesome rapidity; it can manipulate models, thus enhancing the value of other management sciences, such as OR, PERT, and simulations; and it can control other machines. An example of EDP's usefulness in performing the chores of public administration is provided by the Internal Revenue Service (IRS). In 1966 the twenty-seven computers (worth roughly $12 million) of the Service did the work of twelve thousand employees, produced additional revenues of $27 million, held back $61 million in refunds to cover debts owed from back taxes, noted seven hundred thousand missing income tax returns (which potentially could amount to an additional $156 million in federal revenues), yielded $19 million by discovering errors in arithmetic, and caught 416,000 duplicate refund claims.[21]

It should be noted that the success experienced by IRS officials with the computer relates to the kind of organization that IRS is. Some organizations, particularly those in which the volume of clerical operations is heavy, can use EDP more beneficially than can others. The military forces, the Social Security Administration, the Veterans Administration, as well as IRS, number among those that use the computer with dramatic benefits.

Limitations. Even with these many managerial benefits that the computer brings to organizations, EDP cannot perform many of the functions that many people seem to think it can. For instance, while the computer can "remember" every data bit programmed into its memory banks, it cannot perceive relationships among data bits. Put crudely, and imprecisely, a computer cannot think. Another deficiency of computers is they have not yet learned a human language. One must talk to them in FORTRAN, COBOL, or whatever. While a computer easily can be programmed with a ten thousand-word human vocabulary, the humans in turn must be careful to use those words exactly as they originally were programmed, or the computer will not understand them. COBOL (Common Business Oriented Language), in fact, does just this; while it resembles English and represents quite a step forward in this regard, it

21. Frederick G. Withington, *The Real Computer: Its Influence, Uses, and Effects* (Reading, Mass.: Addison-Wesley, 1969), p. 5.

nevertheless remains a very precise computer language that a human being must learn as well as the computer.

Another weakness of the computer is that it does not have much in the way of a personality. To put it another way the computer cannot respond to variables that do not fit its program, such as the special problems of an individual client. In this sense the computer is the ultimate expression of Robert K. Merton's "bureaucratic personality." The lack of a human touch by computers can have unfortunate consequences for public organizations. Consider another example drawn from the IRS experience with EDP.

A seventy-eight-year-old woman in Maine, seriously ill and subsisting on her pension, filed her income tax form on schedule with IRS. She received no reply and assumed all was well. Then several months later she received a bill on an IBM form demanding an absurd amount of additional tax payment, plus interest, and payment within twenty days. The woman, shocked, responded that no exemption had been credited. She received no reply from IRS, other than a second bill for the same amount, but with more interest added. Again the woman wrote IRS to explain her situation, but received in response only a third bill. She felt that she had to hire a lawyer to file an amended report, which she did. Then she received a very snippish letter from IRS, threatening to place a lien on her property—which, in her case, consisted solely of her house.[22]

This episode made the *Congressional Record* as an example of a "monster computer" ripping off a little old lady. Although there is more to the case than the impersonality of a computer (obviously, the IRS had some programming problems at the very least), what comes across to the public is the indignity of corresponding with a machine whose only human attribute is arrogance.

Finally, EDP costs a lot. Although the cost-per-computation has been declining radically over the last few years, the "software" side of EDP— the programmers and analysts—is characterized by zooming costs. While these costs, too, can be shaved by various methods, they seem likely to keep climbing fairly steadily.

In sum the managerial advantages of the computer consist in its rapidity, precision, repetitiveness, manipulative ability, and its capacity for performing complex calculations and controlling other machines. The managerial disadvantages of the computer consist in its inability to perceive relationships and to handle human languages, its lack of personality, and high (and rising) overall costs.

---

22. *Congressional Record,* September 12, 1967, as cited in Withington, *op. cit.,* pp. 35–36.

These benefits and liabilities of the computer concern only how EDP functions as a technique, as a management science. The organizational and human implications of EDP, the systems approach, and management science run much deeper, and "The Computer" symbolizes the threat of these techniques for many people. The concluding portion of this chapter will consider some of the ramifications of technology for organizations and decision-making.

TECHNOLOGY, THE PUBLIC BUREAUCRACY, AND THE PUBLIC

Herbert A. Simon has observed that popular views on the implications of computers and automation for human beings can be classified according to "economic" and "technological" dimensions, and by "conservative" and "radical" interpretations.[23] These are shown in Table 7–2.

Simon considers himself to be a technological radical and an economic conservative in his perceptions of computers and automation; that is, he foresees employment patterns similar to today's, and computers taking over the more mundane activities of mankind—in short, the best of both worlds. In this view, Simon argues that the computer will free man from the dispiriting and deadly routine chores that have burdened bureaucracies for too long and release the energies of human beings in more fulfilling enterprises. Notably, men no longer will have to be clerks and assembly-line workers; instead they can work in jobs involving face-to-face, human-to-human interaction. In Simon's view this will be a far more gratifying experience than is possible in the unautomated present. Already, in fact, computers have taken over the solving of "well-structured problems" (such as sending and collecting telephone bills), rapidly are usurp-

TABLE 7–2.   Views on the Human Implications of Computers and Automation

	Economic Dimension	Technological Dimension
Radical Perception	A "glut" of goods, widespread unemployment, the rise of a technocracy.	Computers can do anything that human beings can do, including thinking.
Conservative Perception	Rising production, full employment, with employment patterns similar to today's.	Computers can do only what human beings program them to do.

23. Herbert A. Simon, *The Shape of Automation for Men and Management* (New York: Harper and Row, 1965).

ing "ill-structured problems," and slowly are developing heuristic problem-solving techniques for application to supervisory duties.

Moreover, Simon contends, the fears of a "technocracy" (or a ruling class possessing the skills demanded by a technologically advanced society) developing along with the expansion of computers are unfounded. As a technological radical Simon argues that computers can be programmed to program themselves, thus preventing programmers and mathematicians from evolving into a powerful elite. He contends that as automation progresses, maintenance problems decrease.

Similarly, full employment should accompany automation, and as an argument Simon offers an analogy: The horse disappeared because of automation (in the form of the automobile), but man did not; the horse corresponds to the machine, but man does not. Thus, technology will increase real wages and capital per worker. In brief, Simon urges that we recognize the enormous significance of the computer in forming man's image of himself. Galileo and Copernicus showed us that man is not at the center of the universe; Darwin enlightened us with the knowledge that man is not created by God, not especially endowed with soul and reason; Freud demonstrated that man is not completely rational; and the computer will yield us the insight that man is not uniquely capable of thinking, learning, and manipulating his environment.

There is, of course, a less optimistic view concerning computers and automation. Boguslaw, Jean Meynaud,[24] and Jacques Ellul,[25] among others, argue that technology will dehumanize mankind and possibly create economic chaos if carried to its automated extreme. Boguslaw phrases this view particularly succinctly. He suggests that "the automation revolution has *not* led to a world of happier and more vital people" because a basic tenet of the technological value structure is that work is stupid. This tenet goes against the grain of traditional Western (especially American) thought. "For example, fundamental to Max Weber's Protestant Ethic is the notion that hard labor—sweat-of-the-brow-type labor—is essentially a good and desirable thing." But the values of automation and technology contradict this historic value, and

> have turned Max Weber's ethic on its head to read, "Hard work is simply a temporarily unautomated task. It is a necessary evil until we get a piece of gear, or a computer large enough, or a program checked out well enough to do the job economically. Until then, you working stiffs can hang around—but, for the long run, we really don't either want or need you." [26]

24. Jean Meynaud, *Technocracy* (London: Faber and Faber, 1968).

25. Jacques Ellul, *The Technological Society* (New York: Knopf, 1967).

26. Boguslaw, *op. cit.*, p. 25.

This value dissonance, combined with the on-going popular glamorization of science, quantitative techniques, and professionalism, work to provoke deep-set anxiety and alienation among workers and managers alike. Boguslaw wonders what the successor to the Protestant work ethic might be:

> Will the unspoken creed, which once could be verbalized as "I may not be a brain but I can always make a living with these hands; I am fundamentally the producer," be replaced by another, which when verbalized might say, "All these hands (or all this mind) can do is what some machine hasn't yet gotten around to doing. ... I am the one, in effect, who is doing the exploiting—why not do it deliberately and systematically?" [27]

Simon and Boguslaw are sufficiently representative of the two poles of the computer/planning/automation/technology/humanism/organization/management debate. What is worth examining further at this juncture are the potential effects of the new technologies on the managerial echelons of organizations, particularly public organizations, and there are a few studies that have attempted to do this. In them, the investigative missions of the authors revolve around such questions as: Will middle management be displaced by machines? Will top management control all variables in the organization via computer technologies and management science, or will it, too, be displaced by automation? Will administrators generally be alienated by the new machinery, or will they become "true believers"? Will the authority relationships and controlling abilities of administrators be altered by the use of computers? It is these kinds of concerns that characterize the studies that we shall review briefly in terms of the computer's impact on authority and control, organizational structure, "dehumanization" and alienation, and the role of computers in government.

Authority and control

A frequent premise of investigators is that computers facilitate the concentration and centralization of authority in organizations. Although empirical findings are mixed in this area, the bulk of the research tends to support the proposition but with some interesting variations. A study by Thomas L. Whisler of twenty-three large insurance companies indicated that where computers were introduced in the organization, decision-making loci tended to move upward in the hierarchy; indeed, the most commonly reported phenomenon in the study was the centralizing of control after the introduction of computers. Computers tended to displace

27. *Ibid.*, p. 26.

clerks in the companies; it was estimated that without EDP, the companies would have required a 60 percent increase in their clerical staff, only a 9 percent hike in supervisory personnel, and a mere 2 percent increase in managerial jobs.[28] Simon's observation on the propensity of EDP to solve well-structured, ill-structured, and supervisory problems in an ascending order of rapidity and accuracy would seem to be substantiated by Whisler's research.

From another viewpoint, however, managers report a "decentralization" of authority attributable to computers, but only in the sense that managers are released from routine chores and are able to spend more time on authoritative decision making. In a study of fifty state employment agencies (plus Puerto Rico, the Virgin Islands, and Washington, D.C.), S. R. Klatzky observed a "cascade effect" in terms of authority as a result of computers. Computers created a "vacuum" of activity at the lowest managerial levels by freeing these managers from many routine jobs; if top-level managers then *decided* to let their authority devolve after the introduction of EDP, the resulting "new" authority granted to each level of the hierarchy could be handled more effectively since computers had taken over routine tasks.[29] Thus, computers, together with a decision by top management to decentralize their authority, created a "cascade" of authority to lower levels that increased the mission effectiveness of the organization generally.

The cascade effect can also be seen in a study conducted by Donald R. Shaul of fifty-three middle managers and fourteen top managers in eight companies. Shaul found that after EDP had been adopted, 60 percent of the managers reported an increase in planning activities, a "high percentage" increased their directing activities, and a greater propensity by managers to relinquish certain kinds of authority was observed. Interestingly, two-thirds of the managers reported less need to bother with "controlling" subordinates because the computer kept an adequate check on misuse of budgetary funds and work time, while opportunities for engaging in coordination activities increased.[30]

Withington observes in this regard the phenomenon of "flickering authority" in organizations enabled by the advent of EDP. Because the computer frees all managers from a plethora of mundane duties and furnishes them with information that they can use more potently than ever before, they have more time to develop their ideas and more information

28. Thomas L. Whisler, *The Impact of Computers on Organizations* (New York: Praeger, 1970).

29. S. R. Klatzky, "Automation, Size, and Locus of Decision-Making: The Cascade Effect," *Journal of Business* 43 (April 1970): 141–151.

30. Donald R. Shaul, "What's Really Ahead for Middle Management?" *Personnel* 41 (November–December 1964): 9–16.

to substantiate them, and authority thus becomes more accessible to all managers. In Withington's words, "The effect is that the authority for originating and testing ideas for change 'flickers' within the management structure of the organization. He who has the idea is the one who temporarily has the authority to proceed with its analysis. . . ." [31]

Organizational structure

If computers have an effect on the exercise of authority in organizations, they have an equal impact on hierarchical structure. Most analysts agree that EDP will pressure the hierarchical pyramid to "flatten," and this pressure would appear to be the result of increased organizational control made possible by computer technology. John Pfiffner and Robert Presthus, for instance, speak of the bureaucratic pyramid evolving into a "bell" formation because of EDP and the related techniques of systems analysis.[32]

EDP-resultant changes in organizational structure present difficulties for public administrators. A study by Marshall W. Meyer, using data gathered from 254 state, county, and city finance departments and comptrollers' offices, found that tensions arose between superordinates inexpert in EDP and subordinates proficient in computer science, because electronic data processing requirements forced superordinates and subordinates to cooperate in ways not provided for by the traditional bureaucratic structure. If the organization was able to adapt to the use of EDP, Meyer found, horizontal interaction increased and the normal vertical interaction of the closed model decreased; if the organization was too stultified to change, administrative pathologies quickly surfaced.[33] In this light, Whisler noted a blurring of traditional line/staff distinctions in organizations as a result of EDP; staff members with computer skills gained new organizational prestige.[34]

"Dehumanization" and alienation

If clerks are the bureaucrats most often displaced by automation, those clerks who remain frequently find that their jobs become rigidly routinized, and occasionally they are transformed into key punch operators. Such, at least, was the conclusion of Albert A. Blum in a study of EDP

---

31. Withington, *op. cit.*, p. 203.
32. John M. Pfiffner and Robert Presthus, *Public Administration*, 5th ed. (New York: Ronald Press, 1967), p. 247.
33. Marshall W. Meyer, "Automation and Bureaucratic Structure," *American Journal of Sociology* 74 (November 1968): 256–264.
34. Whisler, *op. cit.*

and white-collar workers.[35] On the other hand, the promotion possibilities for those clerks remaining are about the same as they were prior to the introduction of EDP, and Whisler found that, while clerical responsibilities were not enlarged, salaries went up with the increased need for clerical precision.[36]

Older bureaucrats occasionally experience a sense of alienation when EDP is introduced. Meyer's findings imply this, but a study by H. S. Rhee specifically noted the presence of conflict between older, bureaucratically oriented locals and younger, professionally oriented cosmopolitans over the automation issue.[37]

Generally, most investigators seem to agree that EDP does not affect top-level decision makers very much one way or another. Rodney H. Brady, after interviewing more than one hundred top managers and examining in detail the decision-making process in more than a dozen large companies, concluded that the computer has not had much impact on decision making at the top.[38] On the other hand, EDP has speeded the overall decision-making process in organizations by making more information more readily available to top managers. Rhee found that the concern over a computer-oriented technocratic elite eventually displacing top administrators to be a view not shared by top administrators themselves; in fact, highest-level decision makers did not consider a technical background to be a prerequisite for their positions.[39] Whisler reported that the organizational centralization accompanying the introduction of computers tended to increase the responsiveness and power of the topmost echelon,[40] while Shaul concluded that middle managers, too, believed that their responsibilities and capabilities had increased after the advent of EDP.[41] In fact, when one considers the findings of Brady, Whisler, and Shaul together, one infers that all officials of all administrative levels in the organizational hierarchy feel that their personal status rises after the switch to EDP. While not all studies support this conclusion, it is a significant counterargument to the dehumanization hypothesis.

Still, one wonders. There have been reports in business magazines of "deskless offices" in the presidential stratum of "progressive" multina-

35. Albert A. Blum, "White Collar Workers," *The Computer Impact*, Irene Taviss, ed. (Englewood Cliffs, N.J.: Prentice-Hall, 1970).

36. Whisler, *op. cit.*

37. H. A. Rhee, *Office Automation in Social Perspective* (Oxford: Basil Blackwell, 1968).

38. Rodney H. Brady, "Computers in Top Level Decision-Making," *Harvard Business Review* 45 (July–August 1967): 67–76.

39. Rhee, *op. cit.*

40. Whisler, *op. cit.*

41. Shaul, *op. cit.*

tional corporations. In these poshest of quarters, there are no desks, only chairs, lounges, and coffee tables. The underlying assumption is that the topmost corporate decision maker should be only that; he should do no more than listen, confer, and decide; he should be relieved of anything resembling paperwork; the brain is all. Similarly, the growing "fetish of the clean desk" refers to the propensity of top-level administrators to have no more than one sheet of paper on their desks at any one time, and betokens an emphasis on "thought" and decision making rather than on "paper shuffling"; the presidents of private foundations seem to favor this clean desk affectation. Continuing this line of thinking, a major company recently introduced a "waterbed room" for use by its top-level executives (presumably on a one-at-a-time basis); the idea is that an executive floats, meditates, and ultimately decides about the grand issues facing the company.

Do these developments reflect anything other than a desire to make the decision-making process more effective and, probably, more pretentious? It seems possible, at least, that top executives may be trying to manipulate their images (their "dramaturgy," to recall Victor Thompson's term) in such a way as to distinguish their functions from the functions of the computer. The more they are unlike the computer, the less paper they handle, the more they "think," the more essential they become as human beings. This, of course, is only speculation, but the increasing obsequiousness displayed for the decision-making function in organizations may reflect a subliminal fear over the awesome, if as yet unrealized, cognitive powers of The Computer.

Computers and government

As with other administrators, computers and the many overlapping techniques of management science have had an impact on public administrators. Paul Armer observes that governmental use of EDP could facilitate interagency sharing of information, reduce expensive duplication of information systems, improve planning, upgrade auditing (thus increasing revenues), and bring about more responsive services to the public generally. In Armer's view, EDP will increase the pressures for the consolidation of national, state, and local government, starting only with the consolidation of files through information-sharing systems but ultimately consolidating and centralizing governmental authority as well: Cities will defer power to counties, counties to states, states to regions, and regions to the nation.[42]

Nevertheless, Armer desponds that governments are beset by factors

42. Paul Armer, "Computer Applications in Government," in Taviss, *op. cit.*

that inhibit the optimal use of computer-based information storage and retrieval systems. Notable in this regard are the unfamiliarity of top-level government executives with EDP and management science, a lack of qualified personnel to perform the necessary kinds of systems analysis, the need to rewrite laws in order to permit the integration of files and information-sharing arrangements, a general lack of coordination among government agencies, the parochialism of many agencies, and finally, popular and official fears of invasions of privacy and of a 1984 variety of technocratic state.

Armer's final caveat regarding EDP is worth additional examination; the computer-and-privacy/computer-and-policy issue is one unique to *public* administration, and the now-deceased proposal for a National Data Center brought many of these problems to the public's attention. The Center would have been a mechanism for integrating government files, with the goal of gathering statistics for purposes of more sensitive public planning. The proposal was defeated in Congress as a result of fears over possible government invasions of privacy.

As Arthur R. Miller notes, the Center's demise may have been a Pyrrhic victory for the advocates of citizen privacy because federal agencies have been establishing since the mid-1960s (and are continuing the practice) their own centers for exchanging information that they feel they need, sans the public scrutiny that a National Data Center likely would have received.[43]

An even more susceptible area involving the potential invasion of privacy via government data banks occurs at the local level. Albert Mindlin has observed that EDP and federal program requirements for local coordination in federally financed projects have spurred the sharing of confidential data among local agencies. But, unlike federal data-sharing activities, which affect people of all social classes, local information-sharing programs tend to single out the dispossessed, such as the poor and various kinds of social deviants. Under these circumstances, the opportunities for misusing private information are magnified.[44]

In a useful summary of the computer-and-privacy/computer-and-policy issue, Alan F. Westin has observed that there are at least five kinds of data bank systems emerging in American society: statistical systems for policy studies, executive systems for general administration, systems designed to centralize data gathered by other agencies, individual agency

43. Arthur R. Miller, "Personal Privacy in the Computer Age: The Challenge of a New Technology in an Information Oriented Society," *Michigan Law Review* 67 (April 1969): 1091–1246.

44. Albert Mindlin, "Confidentially and Local Information Systems," *Public Administration Review* 28 (November–December 1968): 509–518.

data-bank systems, and mixed public/private systems.[45] All these data-bank systems bring with them new problems of public policy. If we are to learn more about our citizenry in order to develop more responsive and effective public policies, where do we draw the line? At what point does the collection, storage, retrieval, and sharing of social information become an invasion of the citizen's privacy? Emerging from this fundamental dilemma of the government's use of computers are delicate political issues: Who will control this new technological capacity? Will new knowledge of old problems inspire brand-new problems in society (as may be the case with improved crime statistics, which have served to frighten many a formerly complacent citizen)? Where does the expertise and planning enabled by the computer end, and where does democratic participation by the public in public policy making begin?

In any event, it seems unavoidable that new knowledge of problems will undermine the justifications of past government inaction in attempting to resolve those problems. Knowledge is pressure, with or without pressure groups, and the computer makes all of us, whether private citizen or public bureaucrat, more knowledgeable about government, society, and our problems. In short, computers, systems analysis, and management science may serve not merely to centralize the administration of government, but to widen the scope of government activities beyond anything yet envisioned.

CONCLUSION

In this chapter, we have reviewed briefly the scientific techniques and political potentialities of the systems approach, management science, and the implications of technology and technique for public administrators, public organizations, and government. In so doing, some arbitrary conceptual distinctions and emphases necessarily have been made. In reality, systems analysis, Performance Evaluation and Review Technique, Operations Research, Critical Path Method, queuing theory, cybernetics, game theory, prisoner's dilemma, simulations, computer science, budgeting theory, linear and dynamic programming, information theory, and all the rest of it represent variations on the same theme: the efforts to clarify decision options and to measure program effectiveness. In reality, the overlappings between the techniques and technologies of public administration are manifold, just as are the overlappings between what is policy

45. Alan F. Westin, "Civil Liberty and Computerized Data Systems," *Computers, Communications and the Public Interest*, Martin Greenberger, ed. (Baltimore: Johns Hopkins, 1971), pp. 151–168; and "Information Systems and Political Decision-Making," in Taviss, *op. cit.*, pp. 130–144.

and what is program, what is politics and what is administration, and what is value and what is fact.

Many of these techniques have been bundled into a package called "program evaluation," which we consider in the next chapter.

SUPPLEMENTAL BIBLIOGRAPHY

American Society for Public Administration, *Automation in Government.* Washington, D.C.: American Society for Public Administration, 1963.

ASHBY, W. Ross, *Design for a Brain.* London: Chapman and Hall, 1960.

BATTERSBY, A., *Mathematics in Management.* Middlesex, England: Penguin, 1968.

BURCK, GILBERT and the Editors of *Fortune, The Computer Age and Its Potential for Management.* New York: Harper & Row, 1965.

Federal Electric Corporation, *A Programmed Introduction to PERT.* New York: John Wiley, 1963.

FITE, HARRY H., "Administrative Evaluation of ADP in State Government," *Public Administration Review,* 21 (Winter 1961), 1–7.

————, *The Computer Challenge to Urban Planners and State Administrators.* New York: Spartan Books, 1965.

GOLEMBIEWSKI, ROBERT T., FRANK GIBSON, and GEOFFREY Y. CORNOG, eds., *Public Administration: Readings in Institutions, Processes, Behavior,* 2nd ed. Chicago: Rand McNally, 1972.

HEIN, L. W., *Quantitative Approach to Managerial Decisions.* Englewood Cliffs, N.J.: Prentice-Hall, 1967.

JOHNSON, DAVID L., and ARTHUR L. KOBLER. "The Man-Computer Relationship," *Science,* 138 (November 23, 1962), 873–79.

KANTER, J., *The Computer and the Executive.* Englewood Cliffs, N.J.: Prentice-Hall, 1967.

KELLEHER, GRACE J., ed., *The Challenge to Systems Analysis: Public Policy and Social Change.* New York: John Wiley, 1970.

MACKENZIE, W. J. M., *Politics and Social Science.* Baltimore: Penguin Books, 1967.

PARSONS, TALCOTT, R. F. BALES, and E. A. SHILS, *Working Papers in the Theory of Action.* New York: Free Press, 1953.

Public Automated Systems Service, *Automated Data Processing in Municipal Government.* Chicago: Public Administration Service, 1966.

————, *Automated Data Processing in State Government.* Chicago: Public Administration Service, 1965.

————, *Automation in State Government, 1966–1967: A Second Report on Status and Trends.* Chicago: Public Administration Service, 1967.

SCHUMACHER, B. G., *Computer Dynamics in Public Administration.* New York: Spartan Books, 1967.

SCOTT, ANDREW M., WILLIAM A. LUCAS, and TRUDI LUCAS, *Simulation and National Development.* New York: John Wiley, 1966.

TAVISS, IRENE, and JUDITH BURBANK, eds., *Implications of Computer Technology: Research Review 7*. Cambridge, Mass.: Harvard University Program on Technology and Society, 1971.

U.S. Bureau of the Budget, *Report to the President on the Management of Automatic Data Processing in the Federal Government*, 89th Congress, 1st Session, Senate Document No. 15. Washington, D.C.: U.S. Government Printing Office, 1965.

VON BERTALANFFY, L., *Problems of Life*. London: Watts & Co., 1952.

WIENER, NORBERT, *The Human Use of Human Beings: Cybernetics and Society*. New York: Doubleday, 1954.

program evaluation
in
public administration

chapter 8

THE ROOTS OF EVALUATION RESEARCH

One of the more exciting developments in public administration during
the last few years has been the intellectual and professional evolution
of what has come to be called program evaluation, evaluation research,
or productivity improvement. Although the field is relatively new, its
roots can be traced back at least as far as the early part of this century
when Frederick Taylor began his time-motion studies, and later when
Elton Mayo conducted his experiments among workers at the Western
Electric plant, described in Chapter 3.[1] In the 1940s groundbreaking
evaluative research was conducted on such topics as the effects of work
relief programs and public housing,[2] and some observers have contended
that Theodore Newcomb's research at Bennington College (reviewed in

1. See, for example, Frederick W. Taylor, *Principles of Scientific Management* (New
   York: Harper & Row, 1911) and Fritz J. Roethlisberger and William J. Dickson,
   Management and the Worker (Cambridge: Harvard University Press, 1939).
2. F. Stuart Chapin, *Experimental Designs in Sociological Research* (New York:
   Harper & Row, 1947).

Chapter 5) is an early example of evaluative research.[3] It was also during the 1940s that the work of the pioneering experimenters in organization development (noted in Chapter 3) embodied some of the basic theoretical precepts of program evaluation, particularly in the initial work by Kurt Lewin, Ronald Lippitt, Leon Festinger, and Harold Kelley.[4]

With the inauguration of Lyndon Johnson's Great Society legislation in the 1960s, social scientists rediscovered poverty, education, and similar domestic issues, and evaluation researchers focused on public programs in these areas.[5] The Office of Economic Opportunity (now the Community Services Administration) was especially aggressive in encouraging an evaluation research component in its sundry projects, and the Elementary and Secondary Education Act of 1965 did much to promote evaluation research in education.

PROGRAM EVALUATION'S IMPACT ON PUBLIC ADMINISTRATION

Nevertheless, it was only in the 1970s that public administrators became aware of (and started using) evaluation research in any comprehensive sense. Indeed, as late as 1971 a leading public administrationist could ask, as the title of an editorial in the field's leading journal, "Why Does Public Administration Ignore Evaluation?" The question was entirely justified; as the editorialist understated, "our literature, teaching, and research have not been overtly concerned with it," [6] and even four years later this author could accurately observe that "the practice of evaluation in public administration remains in its formative stages." [7]

A 1970 study of federal evaluation practices conducted by the Urban Institute concluded that "the whole federal machinery for making policy

3. Theodore Newcomb, *Personality and Social Change* (New York: Holt, Rinehart & Winston, 1943).

4. See for example, Kurt Lewin, *Resolving Social Conflicts* (New York: Harper & Row, 1948); Ronald Lippitt, *Studies in Experimentally Created Autocratic and Democratic Groups*, University of Iowa Studies: Studies in Children's Welfare, vol. 16 (No. 3), pp. 45–198, 1940; and Leon Festinger and Harold Kelley, *Changing Attitudes through Social Contact* (Ann Arbor: University of Michigan Press, 1951).

5. The best single synopsis of the state of the art in evaluation research through the mid-1960s is contained in: Edward Suchman, *Evaluative Research* (New York: Russell Sage Foundation, 1967).

6. Orville F. Poland, "Why Does Public Administration Ignore Evaluation?" *Public Administration Review* 31 (March–April 1971): 201.

7. Nicholas Henry, *Public Administration and Public Affairs* (Englewood Cliffs, N.J.: Prentice-Hall, 1975), p. 222.

and budget decisions suffers from a crucial weakness: it lacks a comprehensive system for measuring program effectiveness." [8] Similarly, program evaluation efforts at the state and local levels still were in their embryonic stages in the early seventies. A national survey of all cities and counties with more than 50,000 people conducted in 1971 found that only 38 per cent of the 354 responding governments had some form of program evaluation unit in even one agency or more,[9] while a poll of state governments conducted the following year ascertained that only half of the forty-two responding states had a full-time program analyst in at least one agency.[10] Respondents in both surveys displayed a strong desire to learn more about program evaluation and to implement it more widely.

By the mid-1970s there were clear signs that public administrators in all levels of government were determined to use evaluation research in a significant way. In 1974 the Office of Management and Budget created its Evaluation and Program Implementation Division, which was specifically designed to evaluate federal domestic programs,[11] and the Congressional Budget Act of the same year directed the Comptroller General, as head of the General Accounting Office, to "develop and recommend to Congress methods for reviewing and evaluation of government program carried on under the existing law." [12]

At the state and local levels evaluation research as a function frequently was expressed in the effort to improve "productivity," or the attempt to direct "attention to methods of accomplishing desired program results with a savings in manpower and total cost." [13] Florida, Illinois, New York, Vermont, Washington, Wisconsin, and Washington, D.C. all initiated state- or district-wide productivity improvement programs in the mid-1970s, but local efforts were considerable, too. In 1977

8. Joseph S. Wholey, *et al.*, *Federal Evaluation Policy: Analysing the Effects of Public Programs* (Washington, D.C.: Urban Institute, 1970), p. 23.

9. Richard E. Winnie, "Local Government Budgeting, Program Planning, and Evaluation," *Urban Data Services Report* 4, No. 5 (International City Management Association, May 1972).

10. Unpublished report conducted by the Council of State Governments and the Urban Institute, 1972; cited in Harry P. Hatry, *et al.*, *Practical Program Evaluation for State and Local Government Officials* (Washington, D.C.: Urban Institute, 1973), p. 17.

11. For a description see: Susan Salasin and Laurence Kivens, "Fostering Federal Program Evaluation: Current OMB Initiatives," *Evaluation* 2 (July–August 1975): 37–41.

12. For a description see: U.S. General Accounting Office, *Evaluation and Analysis to Support Decision-Making*, PAD–75-9, September 1, 1976, pp. 1–2.

13. George A. Bell, "State Administrative Organization Activities, 1974–75," *Book of the States, 1976–77* (Lexington, Ky.: Council of State Government, 1976), p. 111.

a major study conducted by the International City Management Association, which analyzed responses from all cities of more than twenty-five thousand people and which had a response rate of 43 percent, found that local governments are working at improving productivity. Although the notion of productivity is easily understood, defining it in operational terms is not always easy. The survey takers in this particular poll defined a city as actively engaged in improving its productivity if it was employing such managerial techniques as zero-base budgeting, cost accounting, management by objectives, management information systems, and performance auditing. The survey found that almost half of the cities, 46 percent, had organized special staffs to evaluate productivity in their cities and to identify better methods to improve the delivery of services. Most of these staffs were located in the cities' budget offices, and 338 cities reported that they were using outside resources, as well as their own employees, to improve productivity: 46 percent were using local university personnel, 68 percent were using student interns, 42 percent were getting help from citizen volunteers, 82 percent hired consultants, 18 percent borrowed executives from business or industry, and 14 percent were employing public interest groups to help improve productivity. The survey concluded that "cities are actively pursuing ways to reduce costs, to improve organizational performance, and to increase the impact of services." [14] Indeed, 379 of the 404 cities responding reported that they used at least one of the improved productivity improvement methods just cited.

The motivations behind this kind of activity in the fields of evaluation research and productivity improvement by all levels of government appear to stem from an underlying disaffection among citizens with the disappointing results of public programs. As Francis G. Caro notes,

> there is every reason for dissatisfaction with the current state of intervention on problems of health, economic security, education, housing—indeed on the entire range of social disorders that confront our urban communities. Neither the rhetoric of politicians nor the pleas of do-gooders of various persuasions are sufficient to guide program development. Similarly, neither the theories of academicians nor the exaggerated statements of efficacy by practitioners are adequate bases for the support and expansion of various human service activities. Evaluation research, not a new but nevertheless an increasingly robust enterprise, can have a major impact on social problems.[15]

14. Rackham S. Fukahera, "Productivity Improvement in Cities," 1977 Municipal Yearbook (Washington, D.C.: International City Management Association, 1977), pp. 196–197.

15. Francis G. Caro, "Evaluation Research: An Overview," Readings in Evaluation Research, Francis G. Caro, ed. (New York: Russell Sage Foundation, 1971), p. 1.

WHAT IS PROGRAM EVALUATION?

True, evaluation research seems to be making a political comeback in governmental circles, but what is it? Evaluation research has a number of possible definitions,[16] but perhaps the most useful one is provided by the U.S. General Accounting Office:

> *Evaluation and analysis covers a wide range of activities designed to support the on-going decision-making process. These activities include reviews known as program charting, budget examination, management analysis, planning, institutional research, program budgeting, systems analysis, engineering, economic analysis, program evaluation, policy analysis, cost benefit analysis, etc.*[17]

One review of the literature on the evaluation process noted that the more recent attempts to define evaluation reflect "concern with both information on the outcomes of program and judgments regarding the desirability or value of programs." [18]

A final note: It is important to observe in defining evaluation research that *evaluation research* differs from *basic research*. Evaluation research is a form of applied or "action research" because it may contribute to social action, but without assessing the effects of specific interventions in a program by researchers. It is concerned with basic theory and research design, but its chief function is to evaluate comprehensively a particular activity and, importantly, to meet an agency deadline.

The purposes of program evaluation

The emphasis that current definitions of evaluation research place on the effectiveness of programmatic outcomes and on the desirability of even having those programs as social policy in the first place leads us to ponder the real purposes of program evaluation. At one level program evaluation allows policy makers to confront the problem of resource allocation. Policy makers obviously must choose among competing social objectives and among competing ways of achieving those objectives; moreover, these choices must give full consideration to the somewhat abstruse principles of justice, equity, and political reality. Thus, certain social questions can

16. See for example, Suchman, *op. cit.*, pp. 31–32; Michael Scriven, "The Methodology of Evaluation," *Perspectives on Curriculum Evaluation* (Chicago: Rand McNally, 1967), pp. 40–41; Michael Brooks, "The Community Action Program as a Setting for Applied Research," *Journal of Social Issues* 21 (1965): 34.

17. U.S. General Accounting Office, *op. cit.*, p. 6.

18. Caro, *op. cit.*, p. 2.

be raised that evaluation research often can clarify.[19] These policy queries include: What is the appropriate level of achieving a particular objective? Are there choices for reaching that level? What resources will be required to attain the program objective? Are there obstacles to the implementation of a particular alternative and what would be the costs of attempting to overcome the obstacles? And finally, are there equity considerations connected with the leading alternative?

If resource allocation questions were the only purpose underlying program evaluation research, they would provide more than adequate justification for conducting it, but there is a deeper motivation initiating program evaluations, a motivation that is more political than economic. As one analysis notes,

> evaluation research can be invoked for a variety of purposes, not only as a means of improving programs. Sometimes evaluation is undertaken to justify or endorse an on-going program and sometimes to investigate or audit the program in order to lay blame for failure, abolish it, change its leadership, or curtail its activities.[20]

Kinds of program evaluation

Analysts have attempted to delineate various kinds of evaluation research and to match these techniques with the most suitable types of social programs. Among the most basic distinctions in the literature of evaluation research is that made between summative and formative research.[21] Summative evaluation is designed to assess a program's result after the program has been well established. Formative evaluation is meant to improve a program while it is still on-going and fluid. These very basic distinctions have since been refined, and a variety of taxonomies have been developed by specialists in evaluation research. For example, the Community Services Administration distinguishes between *program impact evaluation*, which assesses the impact and effectiveness of a program; *program strategy evaluation*, which evaluates the program strategies that are the most effective in delivering services; and, finally, *program monitoring*, which assesses the individual project to determine operational efficiency.[22] The Urban Institute modified these distinctions formulated by the Community Services Administration to include *project ranking*, which is an effort to rank the *relative* achievements of local projects.[23]

19. See U.S. General Accounting Office, *op. cit.*, pp. 4–5.
20. Henry W. Riecken, "Principal Components of the Evaluation Process," *Professional Psychology* 8 (November 1977): 395.
21. Scriven, *op. cit.*, p. 43.
22. See Wholey *et al.*, *op. cit.*, p. 62.
23. *Ibid.*, pp. 24–26.

Conversely, the RAND Corporation developed a somewhat different series of distinctions for the Department of Health, Education, and Welfare; it separated evaluation from compliance control and capability building. *Compliance control* is defined as "monitoring for compliance with legislative intent and administrative regulations," while *capability building* is attained through efforts to make a program more subject to evaluation techniques, including "increasing state and local decision-makers' ability to carry out their own evaluations." [24]

Perhaps the most useful categorization of the evaluation literature is that devised by Orville F. Poland, in which the schemata of effectiveness evaluation, efficiency evaluation, and eclectic evaluation is offered.[25] *Effectiveness evaluation* uses controlled experiments to determine how well programmatic goals have been achieved. *Efficiency evaluation* uses cost-effectiveness approaches to determine what the cost of the goals being achieved are. *Eclectic evaluation* analyzes a program's secondary criteria, such as its inputs, outputs, and processes, in an effort to identify programs needing greater attention; it can lead to a better understanding of how the program really works.

Effectiveness evaluation, although not an easy task, is nonetheless appealing because it attempts to identify a program's real achievements. Thus, the achievements are especially visible to and appreciated by top agency executives and legislators, who have the authority to act on the continuation or funding of a particular program. Effectiveness evaluations have the greatest immediate impact when they are applied to social experimental programs or pilot projects.

Efficiency evaluations are valued by policy makers because they measure whether or not a program's resources are being consumed effectively. Normally, cost-benefit analysis and cost-effectiveness measures are used to determine a program's real cost. The difference between cost-benefit analysis and cost-effectiveness measures is that the former attaches a monetary value to program outcomes, while the latter attempts to employ broader, more qualitative yardsticks of efficiency. As Elizabethann O'Sullivan points out, "cost-benefit analysis can require a researcher to try to measure the unmeasurable; commonly a quantifiable aspect of the program's effects will be used as a substitute measure," going on to mention that the earliest calculations of the benefit of saving a human life were based on a person's earning potential.[26] In contrast to cost-

24. R. A. Levine and A. T. Williams, Jr., *Making Evaluation Effective: A Guide*, R–788–HEW ICMUO (Santa Monica, Calif.: RAND Corp., 1971).

25. Orville F. Poland, "Program Evaluation and Administrative Theory," *Public Administration Review* 34 (July–August 1974): 333–334.

26. Elizabethann O'Sullivan, "The Current Status of Program Evaluation: A Review," unpublished paper, 1978. For two thorough discussions of cost-benefit analysis.

benefit analysis, cost effectiveness skirts the moral dilemmas of attaching a monetary value on program outcomes. This admirable effort, however, can make validity problems a real issue in cost-effectiveness evaluations and, as O'Sullivan observes, cost-effectiveness analysis is "particularly limited in its ability to handle multiple outcomes, especially the combined occurrence of desirable and undesirable consequences." [27]

The real advantages of efficiency evaluations are teased out when they are used in conjunction with effectiveness evaluations, if for no other reason than efficiency evaluations can identify a program that is effective although its cost may be far more than is desirable. An agency's top administrators are most likely to find efficiency evaluation useful; such cost-related information can improve program management and enhance the presentation of agency programs to legislators and the public. Because of this dimension, efficiency evaluations appear to be waxing into a genuine budgetary strategy.

Two variants of efficiency evaluation that have gained popularity in recent years are program monitoring and discrepancy evaluation. *Program monitoring* is a type of formative evaluation; it assesses whether the target population is being affected, whether staff performance matches program objectives, and whether policies are in accordance with preestablished standards and regulations.[28] *Discrepancy evaluation* often is used profitably in conjunction with management-by-objectives (MBO). Program achievements are compared to a set of standards, such as an outline of how a program should be managed to accomplish its objectives. The technique is not unlike MBO's attempt to define standards centrally while decentralizing how those goals are met.[29]

Finally, Poland's notion of eclectic evaluation relies on concepts from a variety of disciplines; it is predicated on the premise that, with relatively low investment of time and money, policy makers can identify program weaknesses and assess to some degree the impact of program delivery systems. Eclectic evaluations investigate input, process, or output criteria that are assumed to be associated with the program's effects.

see E. S. Quade, *Analysis for Public Decisions* (New York: American Elsevier, 1975); and Alice M. Rivlin, *Systematic Thinking for Social Action* (Washington, D.C.: Brookings Institution, 1971), p. 56.

27. O'Sullivan, *op. cit.*, p. 11. For a more thorough discussion of cost effectiveness, see Henry M. Levin, "Cost Effectiveness Analysis in Evaluation Research," *Handbook of Evaluation Research*, Vol. 2, Marcia Guttentag and Elmer N. Streuning, eds. (Beverly Hills, Calif.: Sage, 1975), pp. 89–122.

28. Erwin Epstein and Tony Tripodi, *Research Techniques for Program Planning, Monitoring, and Evaluation* (New York: Columbia University Press, 1977), p. 55.

29. Malcolm Provus, *Discrepancy Evaluation for Educational Program Improvement and Assessment* (Berkeley, Calif.: McCuttchan, 1971).

O'Sullivan describes what is meant by these terms: "For example, to study a job training program, the number of trainees (input), the content of the training program (process), or the number of participants placed in jobs (output) could be measured." [30] Techniques favored in eclectic evaluation are needs assessment, identifying social indicators to develop rankings, and productivity studies. Eclectic evaluations are a type of formative evaluation, and among their attractions is the fact that a variety of program participants can become eclectic evaluators; agency personnel, outside consultants, and academic researchers—all could be suitable for conducting an eclectic study.

THE EVALUATION PROCESS

As noted, the process of evaluation is far from simple, and Figure 8–1 illustrates this process. The chart shows four basic fundamentals of the evaluation process: ascertaining decision makers' needs; defining the nature

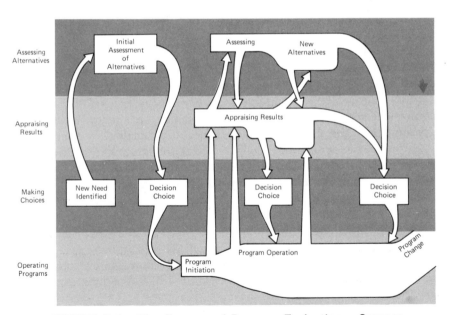

FIGURE 8–1. The Process of Program Evaluation. *Source:* U.S. General Accounting Office, *Evaluation and Analysis to Support Decisionmaking.* Washington, D.C.: U. S. Government Printing Office, 1976, p. 8.

30. O'Sullivan, *op. cit.*, p. 15.

and scope of the problem; determining valid objectives; and specifying comprehensive measures.[31] Let us consider these in turn.

Four fundamentals of program evaluation

To determine a decision maker's needs, we must ask what the decision maker's perceptions of the problem are. Is he or she dissatisfied with the effectiveness or the results of the program—or with the lack of a program—to meet a particular social mission? How will the information be used and when is the final report needed?

Defining the nature and scope of the problem also is important, and it is vital that the people who are to use the results of the study (in other words, the decision makers themselves) understand the nature and scope of the issues at stake at least as thoroughly as the people responsible for conducting the study. This means that all persons involved in the evaluation should be aware of the study's origin, review legislative hearings and reports associated with the topic, be informed about the history of the program designed to deal with the problem, and examine together the past analyses and evaluations of the issue. The General Accounting Office (GAO) has noted that "there is often a trade-off between the breadth of a study and the precision of the results." [32]

Determining valid objectives is a third area of importance. To the extent possible, a statement of objectives should include a complete understanding of the intended benefits. It should include how many of those benefits are expected to be attained, identify possible recipients of adverse consequences or unintended benefits that cannot be avoided, include important qualitative features (although measuring qualitative attainments is hardly an easy task), and finally, account for multiple objectives that may conflict with or support one another. As the GAO again notes in this regard, "the importance of taking such a comprehensive view of objectives cannot be overstated. Oversimplified statements (1) will not capture all essential aspects of the effects intended and (2) may contain implied conflicting consequences for groups other than the intended beneficiaries (e.g., to eliminate hunger or to achieve energy sufficiency)." [33]

The final area of importance is specifying comprehensive measures. It should include quantifying the extent to which the program's goals are met—in other words, effectiveness measures. These comprehensive measures should involve capturing qualitative aspects of the consequences,

31. U.S. General Accounting Office, *op. cit.*, p. 11.
32. *Ibid.*, p. 13.
33. *Ibid.*, p. 14.

or those *intangible measures;* quantifying to the degree possible unintended consequences, or *side effect measures;* and quantifying as much as possible the differences of impact on the beneficiaries and the bearers of the cost, or what are known as *distribution measures.*

Conducting a program evaluation

Once these fundamentals of the evaluation process are established, certain basic steps must be taken to successfully execute a program evaluation.[34] Among the first is *preparing a detailed study plan.* The plan should include a clear statement of the problem and a careful listing of built-in constraints and assumptions to be used in evaluating the problem. It should state the methods to be used and elaborate the resources to be committed in the study. It should include a report schedule, specified procedures for amending the study plan, and finally, a time frame for completing the major components of the study, including a final deadline.

Next, *a study team should be selected, lines of communication established, and appropriate methods to conduct the study determined.* We shall return to the problem of methods later, but suffice to note here that in selecting appropriate methods the following criteria should be used: *level of validity* (how much confidence can a program manager have in the results of the study?); *relevance* (will the results be useful to decision makers?); *significance* (will the study results show the program manager substantially more than can be deduced from direct observation?); *efficiency* (does the value of the study exceed the cost?); and finally, *timeliness* (will the analytical information be available in time to meet program objectives and legislative schedules?).

All evaluation plans should *specify procedures for using the results.* In other words, the evaluation's results must be communicated if they are to have any effect, and this means specifying the nature of the reports and to whom they are to be made; communicating those reports with clarity and with conciseness; and following up. The follow-up should include interpreting the report to decision makers, responding to questions that have not been answered by the report, and generally helping decision makers develop a logical reaction to the report.

This review of the nuts and bolts of evaluation research in public administration does not delve into the human problems encountered in conducting a program evaluation. These problems are scientific and technical, administrative and political, and moral and ethical. We consider these next.

---

34. The section on conducting a program evaluation is drawn from *ibid.*, pp. 17–41.

As Henry Riecken accurately observes,

> The central scientific problems in evaluation are (a) the segregation of treatment effects per se from random variation on the one hand and from systematic biasing through uncontrolled factors that are extraneous to treatment on the other hand, and (b) the reliable measurement of these effects.[35]

✓ *Problems of validity and measurement*

The first part of the problem, as Riecken phrases it, deals essentially with the question of validity. Evaluation researchers can use a number of methods to assure validity—selecting the appropriate experimental methods, using a nonrandom comparison group method, comparing similar programs using time series analysis, and similar approaches.[36]

The other portion of Riecken's dilemma is that of measurement. Before a program evaluator can measure anything, however, he or she must identify the objectives of the program in a way that permits valid measuring. Such an identification of program goals includes the content of the objective (in other words, what is to be changed by the program), the target of the program, the time frame within which the change is expected to occur, the number of objectives if there are more than one, and finally, the extent of the expected effect.[37]

Once objectives are so defined, then distinctions can be made between immediate, intermediate, and ultimate objectives, and measurements can be developed accordingly. One type of measurement, for example, is input measurement: What are the resources allocated by an agency for a particular program relative to the services actually received by the clients of that program? In this case, the resources would be the inputs. Original and secondary data also need to be measured. As Caro observes, "identification of variables is, of course, only a first step in the measurement process. Evaluators are often confronted with serious obstacles in seeking the valid, reliable, and sensitive measures they need," going on to note that agency records often are seriously deficient and the evaluator must collect his own original and secondary data; such data collection "may add enormously to the cost of evaluation." [38]

35. Riecken, *op. cit.*, p. 398.

36. U.S. General Accounting Office, *op. cit.*, pp. 17–20.

37. Edward Suchman, "A Model for Research and Evaluation on Rehabilitation," *Sociology and Rehabilitation*, Marvin Sussman, ed. (Washington: Vocational Rehabilitation Administration, 1965), pp. 64–65.

38. Caro, *op. cit.*, p. 22.

Caro also observes that the subjects of the evaluation (*e.g.*, public administrators) may try to redirect their behavior in an effort to affect the evaluation's outcome, and that detecting this attempt becomes particularly difficult when evaluative criteria and data are incomplete. An example of the evaluative problems posed by incomplete data is provided by higher education. Who has not heard of the "publish or perish" dictum in universities and not wondered if the number of a professor's publications actually has anything to do with his or her teaching abilities? Relatedly, do grades indicate the real level of learning by a student?

Problems of research design

A final major problem of a scientific and technical nature in evaluation research is that of dealing with program research design. Caro notes that the design problem can be broken down into the components of controlled interaction between program practitioners, interactions between recipients of the program, and the fact that many programs are both diffuse and unstable.[39]

Achieving control over the variables in a program for purposes of evaluating that program is unusually difficult in an action setting. When a control group (that is, a group of clients who are excluded from receiving the benefits of a particular experimental program designed to improve services) is set aside for purposes of comparing it with an experimental group (a group of clients who do receive the benefits of a particular program innovation), there is often a great deal of social and political pressure to provide the benefits of that experiment to both groups. Thus, both the program's administrators and the program's clients are reluctant to withhold services from a particular group that might benefit from those services, even though the evaluation might be ruined by doing so. Relatedly, self-selection is a problem in program evaluation in an action setting; "it is difficult to refuse service to those who seek it and provide service to those who resist it."[40]

In short, action settings simply inhibit evaluators from using a well-controlled experimental design. However, one of the real problems in developing a research design for program evaluation is more political than social; hidden motives on the part of the evaluators can interfere with accurate measurement. For example, private consultants, who must make a living by securing contracts from public agencies, may promise too much in writing their research design. Perhaps the most vivid example of this in recent years was provided by a program evaluation attempted

39. *Ibid.*, pp. 23–27.
40. *Ibid.*, p. 24.

by the Office of Economic Opportunity in 1972, in which 120 drug treatment centers in six cities were evaluated in a study involving interviews with nine thousand present and former drug abusers. The purpose of the study was to assess client characteristics and behavior, the delivery system, the relationship of the project to the communities themselves, and the program's cost-effectiveness. All of this was to be accomplished in thirteen months. After seven months of rather grotesque trial and error, the project was abandoned. During that time, the program evaluators (a private consulting firm) had collected data on nine treatment centers and 1,270 clients at a cost of more than $2 million.[41]

Avoiding such fiascoes as OEO's abortive attempt to evaluate drug abuse treatment programs can be enhanced by asking certain basic questions about the research design itself.[42] Is the research design explicit about important constraints in the study? Does it use standard evaluation procedures as much as possible? Have the evaluators adjusted expectations to known data reliability and availability? Does the evaluation rely on opinions as measures only if the program is intended to change opinions? Does it mandate a clear separation between the results of the data collection and analysis and the evaluators' judgments and beliefs? Does it specify at least one acceptable measure of accomplishment? Does it keep the questions relatively few in number? Does it establish priorities? And does the design require as few formal reports from the evaluators as possible, depending instead on frequent and informal contacts? While such questions may seem elementary, the sad fact is that they are rarely asked in many research designs.

ADMINISTRATIVE AND POLITICAL PROBLEMS IN EVALUATION RESEARCH

A second major problem in conducting evaluation research, apart from the scientific and technical ones, is the administrative and political difficulties to be surmounted in conducting an evaluation. Riecken observes that "in comparison with the vast amount of scholarly examination of the design and measurement features of evaluation, the matter of day-to-day execution of these tasks has received scant attention," noting further

41. Don Messer, "Drug Abuse Treatment: An Evaluation That Was Not," *Case Studies on Evaluation HEW Programs for the Student and Practitioner of Evaluative Research,* James G. Abert, ed. (New York: Marcel Dekker, prepublication manuscript).

42. The following paragraph is drawn from Donald R. Wideman, "Writing a Better RFP: Ten Hints for Obtaining More Successful Evaluation Studies," *Public Administration Review* 37 (November–December 1977): 714–717.

that political realities complicate evaluation management because evaluation "is always undertaken in a context of decisions about the use of resources and, accordingly, has implications for the acquisition, distribution and loss of social or political power." [43]

Who are the evaluators?

To understand the administrative and political implications of evaluation research, we must first know who the evaluators are. Program evaluators play many social roles, and the roles they assume affect the ways they discharge their responsibilities. In his excellent study of policy analysts in the federal government Arnold Meltsner identified four separate roles played by program evaluators: the *entrepreneur*, who has excellent analytical and political skills; the *politician*, who has reasonable political skills but who is less impressive in intellectual analysis; the *technician*, who has good analytical skills but is apolitical; and finally what Meltsner calls the *pretender*, who is weak both analytically and politically.[44] Similarly, K. A. Archebald has observed three roles: *academics*, or evaluation researchers who typically are funded by grant monies and conduct a study with minimal contact with the program's clients; *clinicians*, who respond only to their own interpersonal dynamic and who treat (quite paternally) the client as a patient who needs help to cure a sickness; and *strategizers*, who use the management consultant approach and who work with clients as if they were colleagues. Archebald contends that in an evaluation that blends all three evaluator roles, it is the program's clients who often have the ultimate responsibility for decisions regarding research and their consequences.[45]

Managers against evaluators?

Because of the social and political roles that program evaluators frequently play, tensions can develop between the evaluators and the line managers of an agency. As a result, it is unfortunately not unusual for conflict to erupt between the program managers and the program's evaluators, whom the managers may see as self-anointed prophets passing judgment on the managers' efforts to solve real and long-standing social problems. Mutual perceptions aside, evaluators often do have different perspectives, purposes, and values from the on-line practitioners. Conflict can occur if

43. Riecken, *op. cit.*, pp. 401–402, 405.
44. Arnold J. Meltsner, *Policy Analysis in the Bureaucracy* (Berkeley: University of California Press, 1976), Chapter 2.
45. K. A. Archebald, "Alternative Orientations to Social Science Utilization," *Social Science Informant* 9 (April 1970): 7–35.

the practitioners feel themselves threatened—and objective analysis in and of itself, irrespective who is conducting it, often can be perceived as such a threat. Often, however, tensions between evaluators and managers result simply from the evaluators' failure to make a clear distinction between the administrative and personal qualities of the managers and the actual effectiveness of the treatment they happen to be using.

As a result of these problems, most experts in the field of evaluation agree that the evaluation of a program ought to be commissioned and sponsored by the highest level in an organization that has program responsibility and, on balance, evaluation that is conducted by an external agency or by a third-party consultant probably is preferable.[46] By commissioning an evaluation by the upper-most level of an organization and by using outside evaluators, some of the natural strains between practitioners and researchers are avoided. Notably such an approach can avoid those tensions that emanate from such diverse values as: specificity versus generality (researchers are more likely to be interested in long term problem-solving, while practitioners are more likely to be concerned with solving immediate problems); status quo versus change (practicing administrators, on the one hand, may attempt to conceal badly managed programs and to resist any change that they perceive as being potentially disruptive, while academic evaluators, on the other hand, often claim a superior knowledge of human affairs that predisposes them to dramatize the inadequacy of the administrators); and finally, academic knowledge versus practical experience (because the evaluator is, in fact, usually an academic, the practitioner views him as having no "real world" experience in or awareness of such practical problems as limited budgets and personnel resources).[47]

Assessing People: What Really Counts?

When administrators evaluate the performance of other administrators in public organizations, one cannot help but wonder what cues and standards they actually use. In this selection on "Injelititis," the formulator of "Parkinson's Law" suggests that gross incompetence can be more highly valued than any other "qualification" when it comes to assessing individual performance and handing out promotions and demotions.

We find everywhere a type of organization (administrative, commercial, or academic) in which the higher officials are plodding and dull,

46. Riecken, *op. cit.*, p. 405.
47. Caro, *op. cit.*, pp. 13–15.

those less senior are active only in intrigue against each other, and the junior men are frustrated or frivolous. Little is being attempted. Nothing is being achieved. And in contemplating this sorry picture, we conclude that those in control have done their best, struggled against adversity, and have finally admitted defeat. It now appears from the results of recent investigation that no such failure need be assumed. In a high percentage of the moribund institutions so far examined the final state of coma is something gained of set purpose and after prolonged effort. It is the result, admittedly, of a disease, but of a disease that is largely self-induced. It is the disease of induced inferiority, called Injelititis. It is a commoner ailment than is often supposed, and the diagnosis is far easier than the cure. . . .

The first sign of danger is represented by the appearance in the organization's hierarchy of an individual who combines in himself a high concentration of incompetence and jealousy. Neither quality is significant in itself and most people have a certain proportion of each. But when these two qualities reach a certain concentration—represented at present by the formula I^3J^5—there is a chemical reaction. The two elements fuse, producing a new substance that we have termed "injelitance." The presence of this substance can be safely inferred from the actions of any individual who, having failed to make anything of his own department, tries constantly to interfere with other departments and gain control of the central administration.

The next or secondary stage in the process of the disease is reached when the infected individual gains complete or partial control of the central organization. In many instances this stage is reached without any period of primary infection, the individual having actually entered the organization at that level. The injelitant individual is easily recognizable at this stage from the persistence with which he struggles to eject all those abler than himself, as also from his resistance to the appointment or promotion of anyone who might prove abler in course of time. He dare not say, "Mr. Asterisk is too able," so he says, "Asterisk? Clever perhaps—but is he sound? I incline to prefer Mr. Cypher." He dare not say, "Mr. Asterisk makes me feel small," so he says, "Mr. Cypher appears to me to have the better judgment." Judgment is an interesting word that signifies in this context the opposite of intelligence; it means, in fact, doing what was done last time. So Mr. Cypher is promoted and Mr. Asterisk goes elsewhere. The central administration gradually fills up with people stupider than the chairman, director, or manager. If the head of the organization is second-rate, he will see to it that his immediate staff are all third-rate; and they will, in turn, see to it that their subordinates are fourth-rate. There will soon be an actual competition in stupidity, people pretending to be even more brainless than they are.

The next or tertiary stage in the onset of this disease is reached when there is no spark of intelligence left in the whole organization from top to bottom. This is the state of coma we described in our first paragraph. When that stage has been reached the institution is, for all practical purposes, dead. It may remain in a coma for twenty years. It may quietly disintegrate. It may even, finally, recover. Cases of recovery are rare. It may be thought odd that recovery without treatment should be possible. The process is quite natural, nevertheless, and closely resembles the process by which various living organisms develop a resistance to poisons that are at first encounter fatal. It is as if the whole insitution had been sprayed with a DDT solution guaranteed to eliminate all ability found in its way. For a period of years this practice achieves the desired result. Eventually, however, individuals develop an immunity. They conceal their ability under a mask of imbecile good humor. The result is that the operatives assigned to the task of ability-elimination fail (through stupidity) to recognize ability when they see it. An individual of merit penetrates the outer defenses and begins to make his way toward the top. He wanders on, babbling about golf and giggling feebly, losing documents and forgetting names, and looking just like everyone else. Only when he has reached high rank does he suddenly throw off the mask and appear like the demon king among a crowd of pantomime fairies. With shrill screams of dismay the high executives find ability right there in the midst of them. It is too late by then to do anything about it. The damage has been done, the disease is in retreat, and full recovery is possible over the next ten years. But these instances of natural cure are extremely rare. In the more usual course of events, the disease passes through the recognized stages and becomes, as it would seem, incurable. . . .

C. NORTHCOTE PARKINSON
Parkinson's Law

While the general thrust of the evaluation literature tends to favor the use of outside consultants, arguments can be made for either inside or outside evaluators. Contentions favoring the use of outside consultants include: they are more objective; they are more likely to question the basic premises of the organization; they would be more effective mediators because of their objectivity; and they are more likely to devote their time more fully to the research problem at hand. Still, insiders have certain advantages, too, including a more detailed knowledge of the organization, and the probability that they are in a better position to be able to do continuing, long-term program evaluation.[48]

ETHICAL AND MORAL PROBLEMS IN EVALUATION RESEARCH

Finally, evaluators should be cognizant of some basic ethical and moral problems associated with the conduct of evaluation research. Principal

48. *Ibid.*, p. 17.

among these are problems involving privacy, confidentiality, and informed consent.

The issues of privacy and confidentiality are not unique to evaluation research, but they do assume a somewhat different tenor in this context. In program evaluation projects, *privacy* refers to the state of the individual; *confidentiality* refers to a state of information. Thus, privacy becomes a matter between the evaluator and the respondent. It hinges on the degree to which the evaluator's questions, in and of themselves, are perceived by the respondent to be prying or embarrassing. Hence, privacy is not a matter of *who* knows the answer, but of whether certain kinds of knowledge are known to *anyone* other than the respondent himself. The test of an invasion of privacy is to ask if the respondent will voluntarily furnish answers under conditions that appear to appropriately restrict the use of those answers.

Confidentiality refers to the question of whether an investigator's promise of confidentiality to a respondent is either sufficient or even necessary. The evaluator's promise, no matter how solemnly given, may not be sufficient because, under certain legal situations, the investigator must yield the information he or she has collected or go to jail. The legal fact of the matter is that social science research records are not protected under statutory law as a privileged communication, as are the records of lawyers and physicians.

Central to the ethical issues of privacy and confidentiality is the problem of *informed consent*, which refers to whether or not a respondent understands what he or she is consenting to. Such an understanding, of course, is particularly important in cases of human experimentation, but it also has a bearing on program evaluation studies. As Riecken observes,

> lawyers have questioned the legality as well as the ethicality of experimental designs and random assignment of participants to treatment for purposes of program evaluation. The grounds for such questioning include the issues of informed consent, equal protection, and the statutory (or other) authority of the agency to conduct experimental evaluations.[49]

DOES EVALUATION MATTER?

We have reviewed a number of difficulties regarding program evaluation, but we have not asked what Republicans in the White House used to call the "big enchilada"—that is, is evaluation research used by anyone? Carol H. Weiss observes in this connection that

49. Riecken, *op. cit.*, p. 408.

there is a pervasive sense that government officials do not pay much attention to the research their money is buying. The consensus seems to be that most research studies bounce off the policy process without making much of a dent in the course of events. Support for this notion surfaces in many quarters—among social scientists, executive branch officials, and members of Congress.[50]

Examples to support Weiss's assessment are plentiful, and perhaps the most notorious instance of program managers resisting program evaluation has occurred over the years in elementary and secondary education. Because the education establishment in the United States is a highly decentralized one, local educators have successfully resisted attempts to evaluate such basic programs as whether or not pupils are learning to read. Under Title I of the Elementary and Secondary Education Act of 1965, for example, the U.S. Office of Education requested achievement test data from local school officials; the data were wanted both by Congress (which sought such data as a means of reforming education) and federal executives (who wanted the data as a management tool). Local school officials, however, thought these federal attempts at rather rudimentary program evaluation to be threatening and, although student scores on national tests have been declining since the early 1960s, local educators still have successfully resisted efforts by the federal government to find out more about student achievement in the nation.[51]

The example of public education indicates in broad strokes the basic problems to be overcome in getting governments to use program evaluations. At one level the reasons why program evaluations are used less frequently by policy makers than they might be are fairly straightforward. Often the research cannot produce results early enough to be employed in short-term policy decisions. The evaluator is, after all, often only an advisor, and policy makers are under no particular obligation to accept the evaluator's recommendations. Disagreements between evaluators and practitioners contribute to the fact that the evaluation is not used; occasionally, for instance, administrators will claim that the "real goals" of the project were not accurately measured.[52]

At a deeper level, however, a lack of use of evaluation by policy makers stems from the different perceptions between practitioners and evaluators reviewed earlier. Evaluators generally tend to place the most importance on a study, and sometimes the demand for an evaluation is a signal that a program is in trouble. Adding to this problem is the fact

50. Carol H. Weiss, "Research for Policy's Sake: The Enlightenment Function of Social Research," *Policy Analysis* 3 (Fall 1977): 532.

51. M. McLaughlin, *Evaluation and Reform: The Elementary and Secondary Education Act of 1965*, Title I, Report R-1292-RC (Santa Monica, Calif.: RAND Corporation, 1974).

52. Caro, *op. cit.*, pp. 12–13.

that scarce staff may have to be reallocated to compile data (which may not be wanted by top administrators in the first place), leading to complaints by staff that they have less time, as a consequence, to carry out their assigned responsibilities. Thomas V. Bonoma suggests that the prior relationships between the evaluators and administrators whose program is being evaluated largely determines the nature of the evaluation that is subsequently conducted, the level of resistance to initiating changes recommended by the evaluation, and the strategies to be used by evaluators in overcoming bureaucratic resistance to their findings. Bonoma ranks these strategies for overcoming administrative resistance to organizational changes that are recommended by evaluation research along a continuum ranging from coercion and inducement, to rational persuasion, and finally to "consensual cooperation." [53]

Although the often-observed resistance of government executives to initiating recommended changes may be frustrating to the evaluators, it nonetheless should be recognized that the very act of program evaluation often serves a purpose that is both important and underrecognized by social scientists. Weiss calls this hidden purpose "the enlightenment function," citing as evidence for its existence three major studies on the uses of evaluation research that indicate, in Weiss's words, that "some other process is at work." [54] This process, according to Weiss, is not the conventional wisdom of the social researcher, which holds that

> to the extent that he departs from the goals and assumptions adhered to by policy-makers, his research will be irrelevant to the "real world" and will go unheeded. [Therefore, for maximum research utility,] the researcher should accept the fundamental goals, priorities, and political constraints of the key decision-making group. He should be sensitive to feasibilities and stay-within the narrow range of low cost, low change policy alternatives.[55]

Weiss argues that this perception by the evaluation researcher is both cynical and naive. The real utility of evaluation research, according to Weiss, is that it is a form of social criticism and should be viewed by social scientists as such. "The enlightenment function" of evaluation research is based on assumptions that are quite at odds with the conventional wisdom of the social scientists. The enlightenment model

> does not consider value consensus a prerequisite for useful research. . . . it implies that research need not necessarily be geared to the operating feasibilities of today, but that research provides the intellectual background of concepts, orientations, and empirical generalizations that

53. Thomas V. Bonoma, "Overcoming Resistance to Change Recommended for Operating Programs," *Professional Psychology* 8 (November 1977): pp. 451–463.

54. Weiss, *op. cit.*, p. 535.

55. *Ibid.*, p. 544.

inform policy. As new concepts and data emerge, their gradual cumulative effect can be to change the conventions policy-makers abide by and to reorder the goals and priorities of the practical policy world.[56]

The enlightenment model posited by Weiss is perhaps the most succinct and useful view of the role that program evaluation plays in modern public administration. Although not rigorously scientific, it does appeal to the basic precepts of how knowledge is used (i.e. information theory). In this view evaluation research sensitizes policy makers. It opens new options that, over time, they are more likely to adopt because of the background data provided by an evaluation research project. Evaluation research may not be used as immediately and radically as the evaluation researcher might wish, but in the long run program evaluations are employed by policy makers, and perhaps on a broader plane than evaluation researchers realize.

Evaluation research is likely to reach the position that public administration has reached in the final fifth of the twentieth century. In many ways, the current intellectual revival of evaluation research among public administrationists represents a return to the golden era of the 1930s when the "principles of public administration" paradigm was dominant. Fortunately, evaluation research has sidestepped the intellectual pitfalls of the "principles" period and has simultaneously provided the field of public administration with much of its long-needed scholarly focus. Like the "principles" of yore, evaluation research is a major means of demonstrating the legitimacy of government. Government has no profit margin by which it can demonstrate to the taxpayers a reason for existing. Instead, government must demonstrate more difficult concepts to justify itself, such as efficiency, effectiveness, and social worth in carrying out its programs. Evaluation research, in its sophisticated but deeply rooted appeal to Western beliefs in scientific method, may provide one such means of demonstration and, as such, it is going to become an increasingly important aspect of public management in an age when government consumes more economic resources than ever before in history.

In its effort to demonstrate the efficient and effective use of public funds, evaluation research provides a graceful introduction to our next chapter on the public budget and how to use it.

SUPPLEMENTAL BIBLIOGRAPHY

CAMPBELL, DONALD T., "Validity of Experiments in Social Settings," *Psychological Bulletin*, 54 (1957), 297–312.

56. *Ibid.*, p. 544.

COLEMAN, JAMES S., "Evaluating Educational Programs," *The Urban Review*, 3, No. 4 (1969), 6–8.

FREEMAN, HOWARD E., and CLARENCE C. SHERWOOD, *Social Research and Social Policy*. Englewood Cliffs, N.J.: Prentice-Hall, 1970.

FROMAN, LEWIS A., "Some Perspectives on Evaluating Social Welfare Program," *The Annals of the American Academy of Political and Social Science*, 385 (September 1969), 143–156.

GLUECK, ELEANOR, *Evaluative Research in Social Work*. New York: Columbia University Press, 1936.

HERZOG, ELIZABETH, *Some Guidelines for Evaluation Research*. Washington, D.C.: U.S. Government Printing Office, 1959.

HOROWITZ, IRVING, "The Academy and the Polity: Interaction Between Social Scientists and Federal Administrators," *Journal of Applied Behavioral Science*, 5 (1969), 309–335.

MAYO, ELTON, *The Human Problems of an Industrial Civilization*. New York: Macmillan, 1933.

MERTON, ROBERT, "Role of the Intellectual in Public Bureaucracy," in *Social Theory and Social Structure*, pp. 207–224. New York: Free Press, 1957.

MILLER, S. M., "Evaluating Action Programs," *Trans-action*, 2 (March–April 1965), 38–39.

RIVLIN, A. M., and P. M. TIMPANE, eds. *Ethical and Legal Issues of Social Experimentation*. Washington, D.C.: Brookings Institution, 1975.

ROSSI, P. H., and W. Williams, *Evaluating Social Programs*. New York: Seminar Press, 1972.

WEISS, C. H., ed., *Evaluating Action Programs*. Boston: Allyn & Bacon, 1972.

WEISS, C. H., *Evaluation Research: Methods of Assessing Programs*. Englewood Cliffs, N.J.: Prentice-Hall, 1972.

the budget: concepts and processes

Of the many variants of systems theory that have been applied to problems of public administration, budgetary concepts have had the longest
and most pronounced impact on the field. Like the other nuts-and-bolts
techniques reviewed in the preceding chapters, the budget represents a
technique of administrative control that has been extended conceptually
from a negative to a positive function.

In this chapter, we shall trace the evolvement of budgetary concepts
in government. We shall also consider the impact, or lack of it, of budgeting concepts on various levels of American government, and the political
significance of the budgetary process.

THE HISTORY OF BUDGETARY CONCEPTS

Bertram Gross and Allen Schick have broken down, in slightly differing
ways, the evolvement of budgetary thinking by public officials.[1] Briefly, the

1. See: Bertram M. Gross, "The Ney Systems Budgeting," *Public Administration Review* 29 (March–April 1969): 113–137, and Allen Schick, "The Road to PPB,
The Stages of Budget Reform," *Public Administration Review* 26 (December
1966): 243–258.

past development of the budget can be categorized into five periods: (1) traditional, or line-item budgeting, with its control orientation; (2) performance, or program budgeting, with its management orientation; (3) Planning-Programming-Budgeting (PPB), with its economic planning orientation; (4) Management-by-Objectives (MBO), with its emphasis on budgetary decentralization; and (5) zero-base budgeting (ZBB), with its stress on ranking program priorities.

In each of these thrusts, the idea of what a budget is, could be, or should be, has assumed a different cast. Nevertheless, the essential meaning of the word *budget* has remained unaltered. To borrow Aaron Wildavsky's definition, a *budget* is "a series of goals with price tags attached." [2] There are, of course, other and lengthier definitions of *budget*, but Wildavsky's pithy one-liner has the blessed advantage of being unmysterious, accurate, and short, so we shall rely on it.

Line-item budgeting (1921–1939)

Most people know what a budget looks like. Each line on a piece of paper has an item (for example, pencils, 112) on the left side followed by a cost ($5.00) on the right side, Hence, the traditional budget acquired its descriptive title of "line-item," or "objects-of-expenditure."

Of course, all governments have always had some form of line-item budget. From the days of the ancient courts of Egypt, Babylon, and China, something was needed to keep track of expenses. But in American public administration, the refinement of the line-item budget was a product of national political and reformist pressures. One such pressure was the drive to establish a consolidated "executive budget." The value behind this drive was one of ousting financial corruption in government, and the way to accomplish this goal was to consolidate public financial management bureaus under the chief executive.

This thrust related to a second pressure, which was the administrative integration movement. The proponents of administrative integration advocated the functional consolidation of agencies, the abandonment of various independent boards, the enhancement of the president's appointive and removal powers, and the short ballot, among similar reforms designed to assure efficiency and coordination in government.

The third pressure was the desire of political reformers to build in administrative honesty by restricting the discretionary powers held by public administrators. Thus, innovations such as competitive bidding for contracts, centralized purchasing, standardized accounting procedures, and expenditure audits emerged. All related directly to the notion that

2. Aaron Wildavsky, *The Politics of the Budgetary Process*, 2nd ed. (Boston: Little, Brown, 1974), p. 4.

the budget was a useful device for controlling public administrators (if in a purely negative way) and ensuring morality in government. Among other results of these forces, the Budget and Accounting Act of 1921 was enacted. This act centralized federal budget formation in the Bureau of the Budget (BOB), and established the General Accounting Office (GAO) as the congressional check on federal expenditures.

The line-item budget rapidly became associated with governmental honesty, efficiency, and less propitiously, inflexibility. In 1923 Charles G. Dawes, as first director of the Bureau of the Budget (now the Office of Management and Budget), wrote: "The Bureau of the Budget is concerned only with the humbler and routine business of government. . . . it is concerned with no question of policy, save that of economy and efficiency." [3] As a result of these very limited objectives, the line-item budget emphasized such factors as skilled accountancy, the objects needed to run an office or program and their costs, incremental policy making throughout government, dispersed responsibility for management and planning, and a fiduciary role for the budget agency. Technical definitions of items were stressed (for example, pencils, 112, with ½-inch erasers, wood, No. 2 grade lead, 6″ × ¼″), and the use of such phrases as "watchdog of the treasury" and "balanced budget" were common, indicating the mentality of the control-oriented stage of budgetary thought.

Gross observes that the line-item budget covered *inputs* only, meaning that it dealt only with what it took to make a project continue— typewriter ribbons, erasers, paper, and secretaries.[4] Consider two examples, paperclips and parks. Under a line-item budget, the only policy-related questions that a public administrator would be channeled into asking are: (1) How many paperclips do we need and what will they cost? or (2) How many parks do we have and what will it cost to maintain them? We shall refer again to paperclips and parks as examples of how each successive concept of the budget changed the policy-related questions that pertained to them. The point is that the budget represents a way of thinking about, measuring, and evaluating public policy.

Performance budgeting (1939–1960)

As early as 1913, budget officers displayed a recognition that the budget could be used for more than merely controlling the public's fiscal accounts. In that year, the Bureau of Municipal Research of New York City urged, in its officials' words, "a classification of costs in as many different ways as there are stories to be told." Practically speaking, the bureau developed

3. Charles G. Dawes, *The First Year of the Budget of the United States* (Washington: U.S. Govt. Printing Office, 1923), p. ii, as cited in Schick, *op. cit.*

4. Gross, *op. cit.*

a threefold scheme of classifying expenditures: by administrative units, by functions, and by items. Such an analysis was an extraordinarily far-sighted concept of the uses of the budget, but it was ultimately rejected by the city on the ground that inadequate accounting information was available.

Although lone voices were heard throughout the 1920s and 1930s advocating a budget attuned to government performance as well as objects of expenditure, the meaningful shift to this kind of thinking came with President Franklin D. Roosevelt's New Deal. A number of historical factors influenced this movement. One was the firm establishment of the control techniques advocated by the line-item budgeters. With the setting up of accurate accounting, purchasing, and personnel practices, budgeting as a concept was released from many of its traditional watchdog duties. Second, the government was expanding enormously, and there emerged a corresponding need to centralize and coordinate managerial activities more effectively. The budget provided the obvious salient tool for systematically coordinating government management. Third, government was increasingly perceived as an institution that delivered benefits, and the budget in turn was seen as a means by which the appropriate managerial delivery systems could be measured.

With the New Deal, these factors congealed. Between 1932 and 1940 federal spending more than doubled. The President's Committee on Administrative Management recommended (in the form of Luther Gulick's and Lyndall Urwick's oft-mentioned report of 1937) that the Bureau of the Budget shed its control orientation in favor of a managerial emphasis, and that BOB be used to coordinate federal administration under presidential leadership. In 1939, BOB was transferred from the Treasury Department to the newly founded Executive Office of the President. The bureau's staff was increased by a factor of ten, it developed new methods of statistical coordination and budgetary apportionment, and it increasingly drew its personnel from the ranks of public administration rather than from accounting. Executive Order 8248 officially expressed the new managerial role of BOB.

> ... to keep the President informed of the progress of activities by agencies of the Government with respect to work proposed, work actually initiated, and work completed, together with the relative timing of work between the several agencies of the Government; all to the end that the work programs of the several agencies of the executive branch of Government may be coordinated and that the monies appropriated by the Congress may be expended in the most economical manner possible to prevent overlapping and duplication of effort.[5]

The managerial orientation of the budget was reified by the preeminence of administrative management in public administration and, to

5. Executive Order 8248, as quoted in Schick, *op. cit.*, p. 250.

a degree, by scientific management in business administration. This general emphasis was known as "Operations and Management" (O & M), and government bureaucracies, particularly BOB, became preoccupied with originating measures of work performance and performance standards. In 1949 the Hoover Commission's report gave this thrust the name by which we know it: performance budgeting. Prior to 1949 performance budgeting (which in some circles came to be known as program budgeting) was called functional or activity budgeting. Although the federal government had in fact been practicing performance budgeting, largely under the aegis of Harold D. Smith, director of BOB (1939–1946), the Hoover Commission more or less clinched its worth by dramatizing the problems that the government faced under line-item budgeting. The commission observed that the federal budget for fiscal year (FY) 1949–1950 was 1625 pages long with approximately 1.5 million words and questioned its utility as a document that facilitated more coordinated and effective public management.[6] In 1950 President Harry S Truman sent Congress the first full-fledged federal performance budget.

In sum, performance budgeting covered more administrative activities than had the traditional line-item budget. Now *outputs* as well as *inputs* were considered. Budget officers saw their mission not only as one of precise and controlled accounting, but the development of activity classifications, the description of an agency's program and its performance, and the exploration of various kinds of work/cost measurements. Administrative, as opposed to accounting, skills were stressed, activities of the agency were given precedence over the purchase of items required to run the office, management responsibility became newly centralized, although planning responsibility remained dispersed, policy making remained incremental, and the role of the budget agency evolved from a fiduciary to an efficiency function.

What did this new role of the budget signify for our original examples of paperclips and parks? Under a line-item budget, an administrator asked only input-related questions: How much will it cost next year to assure an adequate supply of paperclips for the office? How much will it cost next year to assume adequate maintenance of the parks for the public? Under a performance budget, an administrator was pushed into asking not only input-related questions, but output-related questions as well: How many papers will be clipped? How many people will be served by the parks? In other words, the *performance* of the objects of expenditure became important and, as a result of output-related queries, we might anticipate administrative studies to be generated that would survey the average

---

6. Commission on Organization of the Executive Branch of Government, *Budgeting and Accounting* (Washington, D.C.: U.S. Government Printing Office, 1949), p. 8.

number of papers clipped per paperclip, or the average number of persons visiting each park. In short, how did paperclips and parks *perform?*

Planning-programming-budgeting (1960–1970)

While performance budgeting represented a step forward in budgetary theory, it did not delve into the deeper levels of government. Unquestionably, performance budgeting made a significant contribution in attempting to devise measurements of an agency's effectiveness, and this was to the public's good. But, as one New York state legislator exclaimed after looking over his state's performance budget, "Who the hell cares how much a pound of laundry costs?" [7] Such data represent needed knowledge, to be sure, but ultimately the more important issue is: How should funds be allocated among various programs? Which programs are the most important? After this issue is resolved, then we can begin evaluations of a program's performance.

There were other problems with performance budgeting. It was becoming increasingly subjective. The description of various programs that accompanied an agency's budget to the legislature were beginning to serve a justificatory function for the bureaucracy. Also, the management emphasis of performance budgeting was viewed increasingly as an impediment to effective public planning. Performance budgeting (like line-item budgeting) tended to increase the purview and costs of an agency's programs incrementally. This "keep-on-truckin'" attitude impaired the articulation of the single essential question of planning: Why? Why do we need this or that program? Instead, performance budgeting merely stated: We've got the program, so let's do it efficiently.

These concerns eventually led to the displacement of performance budgeting concepts in government by Planning-Programming-Budgeting. PPB-related notions had their origins in industry. As early as 1924 General Motors Corporation was using variants of PPB, and during World War II the Controlled Materials Plan of the War Production Board relied on PPB concepts. By the 1950s the U.S. Air Force's RAND Corporation began applying systems analysis to the evaluation of weapons systems and recommended the institution of "program packages" as budgeting units in Air Force planning. The Air Force rejected the idea, but later found it expeditious to retrench when Robert McNamara became Secretary of Defense in 1960.

McNamara had been trained as an executive in the confines of Ford Motor Company. The Defense establishment that he entered was beset by almost cut-throat competition between the services, each of which

7. Allen Schick, *Budget Innovation in the States* (Washington, D.C.: Brookings Institution, 1971), p. 127.

was vying for control of as many new weapons systems as it could acquire. Each service viewed its particular programs not only as vital to the defense of the nation, but also as essentially the nation's only defense. Hence, each service defined the country's defense problems in ways that suited their peculiar capabilities. Combined with the competitive milieu of the Pentagon, this viewpoint produced a situation in which the Air Force was preparing for a brief, nuclear war (which would be air-centered), and the Army was girding for a long, conventional war (which would be ground-centered). Thus, it was contended in 1961 before the Senate Subcommittee on National Security and International Operations that because "the land and tactical air force were being planned for different kinds of wars, they were not ready to fight either."

McNamara and his "whiz kids" (a not entirely affectionate appellation given the McNamara team by the military) shook up the services. They felt the services were autonomous to a possibly dangerous point of inefficiency and uncoordination. McNamara's method for reestablishing central control of the military services was systems analysis, and the primary expression of this analysis was PPB. By FY 1964, PPB was standard operating procedure in the Defense Department. President Lyndon B. Johnson was sufficiently impressed that in 1965 he ordered PPB to be applied throughout the federal government. By 1967 the Bureau of the Budget had instructed the use of PPB in twenty-one agencies, with a final goal of thirty-six agencies.

What precisely is PPB? Taking its component concepts one by one, *planning* is the defining and choice of operational goals of the organization and the choice of methods and means to be used to achieve those goals over a specified time period. *Programming* is the scheduling and implementation of the particular projects designed to fulfill an organization's goals in the most favorable, efficient, and effective way possible. *Budgeting* is the price estimate attached to each goal, plan, program, and project. By way of example, one *official goal* of the United States government is the attainment of the people's welfare. When this goal is made operational, a variety of subgoals result. One such *operational goal* is the achievement of a certain minimum income level for every American family. One *plan* for achieving this operational goal is unemployment assistance. A *program* is distributing welfare checks. A *project* is the setting up and managing of the various welfare bureaucracies in the United States.

Beyond simple definitions, however, PPB represents a systemization of political choice in the format of budget formulation. PPB is an effort to render decision making by public administrators as rational as possible. PPB represents a *rapprochement* between budgeting and planning. Its major characteristics are listed below:

1. PPB is an effort to integrate budgetary formulation with Keynesian economic concepts; that is, it attempts to consider the effects of government spending on the national economy.
2. PPB is an effort to develop and use new informational sources and technologies to bring more objective and quantitative analysis to public policy making.
3. PPB is an effort to integrate systems-wide planning with budgeting.

With the preceding characteristics defining its basic conceptual form, PPB also is associated with budget officers who have skills in economic analysis, as well as in accountancy and administration. The purposes of various programs become the chief concern, as opposed to their objects of expenditure or activities. Decision making becomes less incremental and more systemic throughout the bureaucracy. Management responsibility grows more supervisory in nature, while planning responsibility becomes increasingly centralized. Finally, the budgetary agency is seen more than ever before as a policy making body—a far cry from Dawes's statement in 1923 about the Budget Bureau being concerned with the "humbler and routine business of government."

Another way of phrasing the preceding paragraph is to say that PPB is concerned not only with inputs and outputs, but also with *effects* and *alternatives*. How does this broadened conceptual scope of the budget affect the questions that we have been asking about our original examples of paperclips and parks? With inputs, you recall, we ask only: How much will a year's supply of paperclips or a year's program of park maintenance cost? With outputs, we must ask: How many papers will our paperclips clip, or how many people will visit the parks?

With effects and alternatives, however, our budget-related questions become considerably more sophisticated and penetrating. For example, in order to determine the effects of our paperclips, we must ask: What effect do the clipped papers have on the agency and its mission? Does paperclipping them facilitate the achievement of agency goals? Does the process expedite anything, or should paperclips be abandoned as an item on the budget? How do we measure the effects of the paperclips program on agency goals? After determining paperclips' effect on the accomplishment of the agency's mission, we then must ask about alternatives. Should we use staples instead? Is there an optimal paperclip/staple mix? Do other alternatives exist?

Parks present a similar dilemma. When we ask about the effects of parks, we also must ask: What are parks really meant to do? The answer, of course, is that the purpose of parks is to provide recreation to the public—to allow citizens to "re-create." Yet, we soon discover that recreation is not much of an answer, particularly when we try to measure the effects of the park program. It is no longer enough to count visitors per day to each park—that is, to measure the park's performance, or output. Now we must ascertain whether or not each visitor is "re-creating" in the park—whether he is having fun. That chore is not only difficult, but it may be impossible. For instance, we may discover that after midnight the park is visited entirely by muggers, rapists, and victims—not an entirely unwarranted assumption, given urban crime patterns. Under these conditions, we may assume that only half of the park's visitors from midnight to four in the morning—the muggers and rapists—are having fun and it is not even good, clean fun. The other half of the park's twelve-to-four A.M. population—the victims—presumably are not.

This kind of thinking, which is enabled by PPB, also forces us to consider more systemic questions about parks. We may find out that the recreation function of a city affects other urban functions, such as crime control. If it is discovered that parks correlate positively with crime, we may wish to reconsider the utility of parks in light of the total urban system. At the very least, the role that parks play in the larger urban system will be clarified by asking questions about the effects of parks, and planning for public policy presumably will be made more precise, responsive, and rigorous.

Finally, we can consider alternatives to parks. Would public libraries provide more opportunities for re-creating among the citizenry, and should monies allocated for parks be used instead for libraries? Might not many neighborhood miniparks provide more effective recreation than a few superparks? These and other alternatives would come up for evaluation under a PPB budget.

PPB met with mixed welcomes in various American governments. Despite President Johnson's executive order in 1965 that PPB be adopted by virtually all federal agencies, the *Rouse Report* of 1968 indicated that there was substantial resistance to its implementation in many agencies, including the Bureau of the Budget.[8] Much of this recalcitrance stemmed from the need for new information that the use of PPB required. A number of agencies simply had neither the information nor the ability to acquire it, and they fell back on generating largely useless reports as a means of bureaucratic compensation. This early emphasis by topside on procedures fostered some resentment concerning PPB in the minds of many federal administrators, and the implementation of PPB concepts was not aided by the Johnson Administration's premature insistence for unavailable data. Nevertheless, the *Rouse Report* did indicate some progress. Five of the sixteen agencies surveyed (Health, Education, and

8. Edwin L. Harper, Fred A. Kramer and Andrew M. Rouse, *Implementation and Use of PPB in Sixteen Federal Agencies* (Washington, D.C.: U.S. Bureau of the Budget, April 1969).

Welfare; Agriculture; Office of Economic Opportunity; Atomic Energy Commission; and the Corps of Engineers–Civil Works) were receiving substantial support from above in developing genuine PPB systems, and one (Commerce) was in the process of beginning development. But, as is indicated later, federal progress in PPB was undermined after 1968 with the advent of the Nixon Administration.

State and local governments had mixed reactions regarding PPB. By 1968, 28 states and 60 local governments reported that they were in the process of implementing PPB and 155 additional localities were considering its adoption.[9] Once state and local officials decided that they liked PPB, however, other obstacles prevented its adoption. The principal hurdles were lack of local resources or lack of authority. Also in 1968, 73 local governments reported that they had decided against using PPB largely for those reasons.[10] New York and California, both early proponents of the notion, ultimately abandoned it.

Implementing PPB in American governments was unusually controversial. Nevertheless, its impact on public management has been more profound and ongoing than any other budgetary concept, so a review of its uses and misuses is appropriate. Two Senate subcommittees that conducted hearings on PPB in government evidenced slightly differing opinions concerning its utility. The Jackson Subcommittee hearings of 1967 tended to warn of the potentially hazardous preconceptions that accompanied PPB, while the Proxmire Subcommittee hearings of the same year indicated greater hope for more responsive government via PPB. In sum, the following points about PPB were made by both subcommittees.[11]

Favorable aspects of PPB. PPB's main advantage is to sharpen and clarify the policy options available to administrative decision makers. In this vein, PPB caused many agencies to reconsider their missions and how they have been defined, with a broader range of policies being opened. It also is felt that coordination is enhanced by the use of PPB

9. Harry P. Hatry, *Status of PPBS in Local and State Governments in the United States* (Washington, D.C.: Urban Institute, 1974).

10. *Ibid.*

11. See: U.S. Congress, Joint Economic Committee, Subcommittee on Economy in Government, *The Planning-Programming-Budgeting System: Process and Potentials*, 90th Congress, First Session (Washington, D.C.: U.S. Government Printing Office, 1967); and U.S. Congress Senate, Committee on Government Operations, Subcommittee on National Security and International Operations, *Planning-Programming-Budgeting Inquiry of the Subcommittee on National Security and International Operations*, Parts I through IV (Hearings of August 23, September 20, October 18, 1967, and March 26, and July 11, 1968) (Washington, D.C.: U.S. Government Printing Office, 1970).

because the hard analysis that it forces brings out the interrelationships among the various programs of the agency.

Unfavorable aspects of PPB. Most of PPB's liabilities revolve around its misuse or misinterpretation. One hazard is the question of values. PPB cannot make value choices; PPB can do no more than illuminate those choices, although some persons occasionally appear to argue that PPB somehow is actually making political decisions. This notion relates to the stress that PPB places on the use of quantification. Sometimes the quantification used by PPB is mindless; numbers are tacked onto issues purely for the sake of tacking on numbers, not because they in any way clarify the issues. This is particularly true for agencies with social welfare missions. Consider again our examples of parks. Assuming that we could quantify "fun" in some fashion, is it really necessary? Beyond that question, however, is it not actually dangerous? For example, are we willing to administratively define the park pastimes of muggers and rapists as "fun" in measuring the effects of our park program? Indeed, muggers and rapists likely do consider their park activities fun, but is it in the public interest to include this kind of evidence as a justification for the park program?

This question, in turn, relates to what Anatol Rapoport has called "the seduction of technique." [12] Numbers, measurements, quantification, and sophisticated methodologies somehow make any program more politically saleable. By this rationale, PPB's use of quantification actually might becloud value issues. For example, in an effort to justify the city's park program to higher-level decision makers, an unscrupulous bureaucrat might argue that "50 percent of our midnight-to-four A.M. parkland users indicated a 100 percent fulfillment on the Likert-type Recreation/Fun Gratification Scale." While the statement sounds positive and "tough-minded," our bureaucrat would not mention that this 50 percent was comprised wholly of muggers and rapists, nor indicate how muggers and rapists got their "recreation/fun gratifications," nor state that the other half of the park's users (the victims) were rated negatively by the same measure.

For these reasons PPB often seems to be used most effectively in organizations centered around "hard" technology, such as the Department of Defense. Measuring a new aircraft's costs and benefits is considerably easier and more accurate than measuring the costs and benefits of recreation, and those agencies that have missions centering on client-member technologies, such as the Department of Health, Education, and Welfare, are less likely to be able to use PPB with comparable efficacy. This

12. Anatol Rapoport, *Fights, Games, and Debates* (Ann Arbor: University of Michigan Press, 1960).

is not to imply that PPB is not useful in the more humanistic agencies—any technique that facilitates the clarification of choice and responsive policy making has utility anywhere, and PPB is such a technique. But its limitations—and potential perils—also must be recognized by public administrators.

Another hazard of PPB brought out in the Senate hearings was its potentially "centralizing bias" and the corresponding diminution of legislative control over policy making. PPB's stress on planning, goal-clarification, and systematic and scientific decision making tends to force decisions "up" the hierarchy. Once decision choices are clear, the highest appropriate level of the bureaucracy is in a rational position to make a rational decision. The upper echelons are less likely to be "removed" from the problem with PPB than they are without it, and hence are more likely to make an optimal decision without relying as much on subordinates for input into the decision-making process: That input is provided by PPB. Moreover, because PPB emphasizes that a knowledge of the entire system is desirable before a decision should be made, it is increasingly evident that decision making becomes centralized for the sake of systems analysis and comprehensive planning. As with the other techniques of management science, PPB assumes that it can help make the ideal, Weberian omniscient monocrat a reality.

It also is felt that a corresponding deemphasis of the legislature's role in policy making could result from the use of PPB. It was noted in the Senate hearings that agencies had not given Congress a full set of the internal PPB documents that agency bureaucrats had used in making their own policy choices, and this practice was seen as an undermining of congressional control over policy making. Bureaucrats prefer to avoid embarrassing probes whenever possible. Although complete intra-agency program-evaluation studies are available to a congressman on his specific request (except for national security documents), such requests are rare. But this possibly genuine diminution of legislative control over policy making is not necessarily attributable to PPB. It is attributable to bureaucratic secrecy, which could be significantly cracked open by aggressive action on the part of Congress, if Congress so desired. Moreover, PPB presumably aided in clarifying the issues as they were presented in those intra-agency working papers that Congress seldom saw, and thus potentially could aid in increasing legislative policy-making control, had Congress felt the need to do so.

The demise of PPB. In light of the kinds of policy questions engendered by PPB as articulated by the concept of a counterbudget, it is of note that the Nixon Administration decided to move steadily away from the policy-planning orientation of PPB. In the late 1960s, for example, then Secretary of Defense Melvin Laird spoke of instituting "participatory budgeting" in the Department of Defense. By this he meant that the admirals and generals would be able to participate more fully in budget formation, although participatory budgeting was seen by many outside critics as a method of dismantling the well-controlled and highly centralized PPB system established in the Pentagon by Robert McNamara.

Also during this period, President Nixon revamped (for virtually the first time since its founding in 1939) the Executive Office in accordance with the recommendations of the President's Advisory Council on Executive Reorganization (the Ash Council). A Domestic Council was established as a new unit that in effect undercut the programmatic and planning responsibilities of the Bureau of the Budget. In 1970, the bureau was retitled the Office of Management and Budget (OMB), indicating its new, managerial orientation. According to former President Nixon, "The Domestic Council will be primarily concerned with *what* we do"— that is, with policy and planning; "the Office of Management and Budget will be primarily concerned with *how* we do it and how *well* we do it"— that is, with management and effectiveness.[13] The effect of this shift has been to create additional layers of authority between budgeters and policy makers, and to demote the function of the budget examiner.

In 1971 a memorandum to all federal agencies from OMB concerning their budget preparations stated, "Agencies are no longer required to submit with their budget submissions the multi-year program and financing plans, program memoranda and special analytical studies . . . or the schedules . . . that require information classified according to their program and appropriation structures." Schick has written that "by these words, PPB became an unthing."[14]

Whether or not PPB is an unthing in the federal bureaucracy, the budgetary concepts it represents and its conceptual predecessors are still viable within OMB: control, management, and planning. Under the Nixon Administration, OMB displayed a growing predilection for the notion of management as a preeminent budgetary concept. Prior to 1970 OMB (then BOB) was a bifurcated organization; there was a budget branch and a management branch that worked rather separately on policy problems. After BOB's metamorphosis into OMB, this dual chain of command was replaced by four powerful associate directors and a number of upper-echelon "management associates."

13. Reorganization Message of President Richard M. Nixon to Congress, March 12, 1970. Quoted in Allen Schick, "A Death in the Bureaucracy: The Demise of Federal PPB," *Public Administration Review* 33 (March–April 1973): 151.
14. Schick, "A Death in the Bureaucracy," *op. cit.*, p. 146.

With the abandonment of Program-Planning-Budgeting by the federal government and by many state and local governments in the late 1960s, budgeters turned to a new concept of budgeting (or, more precisely, to a variant of budgeting): Management-by-Objectives. Management-by-Objectives got its start in the private sector, and in 1954, Peter Drucker wrote a book entitled *The Practice of Management*, which generally is thought to be the first major expression of the MBO concept.[15] Management-by-Objectives may be defined as "a process whereby organizational goals and objectives are set through the participation of organizational members in terms of results expected."[16] With this kind of definition, McGregor's Theory Y becomes an important component of the budgetary process. Management-by-Objectives encourages "self-management" and decentralization, advocates an integrated approach to total management, stresses the concepts of communication and feedback, encourages organization development and change, and emphasizes policy research and the support of top management. MBO, in short, is an attempt to set objectives, track the progress of the appropriate program, and evaluate its results. Through this process, an organization decentralizes by operationalizing its objectives and letting the individual managers most concerned with the appropriate aspects of the program achieve those objectives in the most effective fashion possible.

We have seen how PPB was concerned with inputs, outputs, effects, and alternatives as a budgetary posture. By contrast, MBO is in many ways a return to the world of performance budgeting. MBO is concerned with inputs, outputs, and effects, but not necessarily with alternatives. It deals primarily with agency performance and the effectiveness of governmental programs, but when it comes to forcing policy makers to ask what else—or what "other"—might government do to accomplish a particular social mission, MBO appears to be at somewhat of a loss. MBO has a managerial orientation that stresses, in terms of personnel skills, something called "common sense." It is concerned paramountly with program effectiveness, and its policy-making style is decentralized and participatory. In terms of planning—and very much *unlike* PPB—MBO is comprehensive in one sense (*i.e.*, it sets operational goals centrally), but it allocates the implementation of that comprehensive planning responsibility to on-line managers. Thus, the budgetary agency becomes

15. Peter Drucker, *The Practice of Management* (New York: Harper & Row, 1954).
16. Jong S. Jun, "Management by Objectives and the Public Sector, Introduction," *Public Administration Review* 36 (January–February 1976): 3.

concerned chiefly with program effectiveness and efficiency, much in the style of program budgeting of the 1950s.

In relating MBO to our previous example of paperclips and parks, we do not ask what the alternatives to paperclips and parks might be in accomplishing the mission of the agency. Instead, we merely ask: How effective are paperclips in achieving the agency's mission? How effective are parks in achieving society's objectives? We do not ask, however, what alternatives there are to paperclips or to parks.

The advantages of an MBO system are obvious. It gives those people closest to the problem some latitude in dealing with that problem and simultaneously measures their performance according to criteria developed by policy makers at the highest level. An MBO system that works should permit individual initiative and innovation, but Management-by-Objectives is no administrative panacea and, like any quantitatively based system, MBO can be used to obscure efficient and effective management as well as to enhance it.

Even so, MBO has been used in a number of governmental contexts, and it is perhaps somewhat surprising, given MBO's emphasis on decentralization and on subordinates' implementing policy, that the federal government embraced Management-by-Objectives in a big way under the Nixon Administration—an administration, as we noted in Chapter 1, not known for its trust of bureaucrats beyond the immediate confines of the White House. Frank P. Sherwood and William J. Page, Jr., have noted in an article on MBO that "the attitude of the Nixon top management was one of low trust and contempt towards civil service." [17] It was, however, partly because of this distrust of civil servants that Nixon introduced MBO to government through the Office of Management and Budget, which he had staffed with officials who were closely associated with the business community.

Many federal administrators, as we noted, were becoming disillusioned with Program-Planning-Budgeting in the early 1970s, particularly because of what one observer called PPB's "unfortunate association with a passion for uniformity and detail," [18] and MBO looked like a flexible alternative. In 1975 OMB issued Circular A–11, which required the submission of agency objectives with the fiscal year budget estimates. This, in effect, was a new budgetary format, and OMB was implementing an MBO concept. Soon afterwards, President Gerald Ford endorsed MBO, and the notion rapidly was adopted by a number of federal agencies.

17. Frank P. Sherwood and William J. Page, Jr., "MBO and Public Management," *Public Administration Review* 36 (January–February 1976): 5.

18. Chester A. Newland, "Policy/Program Objectives and Federal Management: The Search for Government Effectiveness," *Public Administration Review* 36 (January–February 1976): 20.

As implemented in its short duration in the federal government, MBO emphasized productivity measurement, program evaluation, and the effort to establish social indicators of program effectiveness. As Jerry McCaffery points out,

> *MBO presents an interesting contrast to PPB. The latter is primarily a policy choice mechanism, operating periodically, with results in dis-aggregated down-the-line managerial decisions, while MBO could be classified as an administrative decision-making mechanism, operating continuously, which intermittently aggregates data for top level policy choices. In theory, the decision flow is opposite—PPB down and MBO up. The outstanding difference seems to lie in PPB's ability to compare programs across departmental lines. But PPB's weakness was its lack of flexibility, whereas MBO has great flexibility in system design and application.[19]*

It was this flexibility, in contrast to PPB's alleged inflexibility, that made MBO attractive to many federal administrators under Nixon.

State and local governments have been adopting MBO in relatively creative ways.[20] In 1974 New York City introduced MBO into almost one hundred of its schools. Goals were set in the school district's central office and were operationalized as the percentage of pupils who fell below the national level of minimum scholastic achievement; annual measures were established showing how much progress each school was making with its students, and it was up to the individual school to decide how they would achieve these measurable goals. In Michigan, a multimillion dollar compensatory education program based on an MBO precept was launched in the early 1970s. A "performance pact" between the state and local school districts was developed in which the state set a basic objective for each child in the program, defined as a month's gain in achievement for each month's instruction in the areas of reading and arithmetic. Again, each school district could decide the most expeditious way of meeting this objective and, if it failed to achieve at least 75 percent of the objective, it would lose its funding for the following year. Similarly, the University of Pennsylvania adopted MBO to administer the university's twenty-two schools and institutes, which it dubbed "responsibility centers." A success in all programs, at least initially, was gratifying and much of the success was due to the propensity of MBO to decentralize administrative responsibility.

19. Jerry L. McCaffery, "MBO and the Budgetary Process," *Public Administration Review* 36 (January–February 1976): 35.
20. The following examples are drawn from George E. Berkley, *The Craft of Public Administration*, 2nd ed. (Boston: Allyn & Bacon, 1978), pp. 337–342.

Zero-base budgeting (1976–present)

Although President Ford had warmly embraced Management-by-Objectives, a new face in the White House brought in a new budgeting concept. The new face, obviously, was President Carter, a nonestablishmentarian fresh from Georgia who had had a good experience with a concept called zero-base budgeting (ZBB) when he was governor. Indeed, Carter was the first elected executive to introduce ZBB to the public sector. Carter, as governor of Georgia, contended that ZBB was instrumental in making his government more cost-effective, noting

> The services provided by Georgia's state government are now greatly improved and every tax dollar is being stretched farther than ever before. There has not been a general statewide tax increase during my term. In fact there has been a substantial reduction in the ad valorem tax.[21]

Peter Pyhrr, perhaps the proponent most often associated with zero-base budgeting, has stated that ZBB forced some major reallocations of resources in Georgia under the aegis of Jimmy Carter. Notably, as governor Carter allegedly was able to reduce agency budget requests anywhere from 1 percent to 15 percent by using ZBB, while the corresponding program reduction within each agency ranged from no change whatever to the total elimination of the agency itself.[22] Because of this thrust ZBB is closely associated with sunset legislation. A *sunset law* provides that, unless the legislature specifically acts otherwise, public programs or agencies are disbanded after a set period of time, for example, five to ten years. Programs and agencies are reviewed periodically by the legislature under this threat of termination, with the idea that overlapping jurisdictions and inefficient programs can be eliminated or possibly reworked.

Sunset laws are increasingly popular among American governments. The federal government has been considering such legislation since the mid-1970s and about thirty states have enacted such laws. Common Cause is a strong supporter of such legislation and has identified a number of criteria to be met in developing a workable sunset law. The criteria included the termination of programs and agencies at a set date unless re-created specifically by the legislature, the institutionalization of a pro-

21. Jimmy Carter, "Planning a Budget from Zero." *Innovations in State Government* (Washington, D.C.: National Governors Conference, 1974), p. 42.

22. Peter A. Pyhrr, "The Zero Base Approach to Government Budgeting," *Public Administration Review* 37 (January–February 1977): 7. It is probable, however, that Pyhrr is overstating the case, especially since Georgia was also undergoing a governmental reorganization. See also: Thomas P. Lauth, "Zero-Base Budgeting in Georgia State Government: Myth and Reality," *Public Administration Review* 38 (September–October, 1978), pp. 420–430.

gram review process, the gradual phasing in of sunset legislation throughout state and local governments, the strengthening of a program evaluation
capacity in government (in other words, is the program really doing the
job well, and is it doing a job that still is necessary to do?), and genuine
public participation in the sunset process, among other items.[23]

Both sunset laws and zero-base budgeting, in essence, mandate that
the entire budget of an agency be reevaluated and that all programs be
justified periodically. In practice, ZBB employs two steps. The first step
is the development of "decision packages" for each agency with each
package containing a summary analysis of each program within the agency.
These packages are ranked by the agency head in accordance with his
or her perception of overall agency priorities. The second step requires
that each decision package be evaluated by top management to determine whether it is justified for further funding. Programs that are
considered ineffective or to have outgrown their usefulness are discarded,
modified, or combined in other agencies. In short, zero-base budgeting
gets its name from the fact that each year's budget is computed from a
hypothetical "zero base." It asks, what would we do with this agency's
funds if they were not already committed? To determine such options,
practitioners of ZBB identify each decision unit, analyze each decision
unit within a decision package, evaluate and rank all decision packages
to develop the appropriations request, and finally prepare a detailed
operating budget that reflects those decision packages approved in the
budget appropriations. In short, and like Management-by-Objectives,
zero-base budgeting is in many respects a throwback to performance budgeting of the 1950s in that, to quote Pyhrr, "Zero base means the evaluation of all programs." [24] Thus, to return to our original examples of paperclips and parks, we would find zero-base budgeting approaching these problems in very much the same way that Programming-Planning-Budgeting
would have approached them as a budgetary concept. In other words, ZBB
considers inputs, outputs, effects, *and* alternatives; it focuses on the decision-making process; it demands managerial and planning skills of its
personnel; it regards as critical information about the purposes of the
program or agency; and its policy-making style can be characterized as
cautiously systemic, utilizing a decentralized planning concept, and rein-
stating the budget agency in its role of a policy-making body.

When President Carter came to Washington, zero-base budgeting
came with him; as one high ranking officer in the Office of Management
and Budget noted, "Never has any management fad so completely taken

23. Thomas J. Culhane, John R. Dunne, and Meyer S. Frucher, *Sunset Laws: A Tool
For Reappraisal of Government Programs and Regulations* (Albany: State of New
York, January 1977), pp. 1–2.

24. Pyhrr, *op. cit.*, p. 7.

over this town." [25] By mid-1977, OMB had issued its Bulletin No. 77–9, stating that agencies had to rank their decision packages and submit the required documents in support of those packages. This bulletin was, in effect, the beginning of zero-base budgeting in the federal government. Schick, perhaps the most astute observer of the federal budgetary scene, noted that, with the introduction of ZBB to Washington, agency heads were notably speedy to adopt the concept. To quote Schick,

> ZBB was introduced quickly and painlessly because it did not alter the rules of evidence for budgeting or the structure for budget choices. There is not a single bit of budgetary data unique to ZBB. . . . Agency after agency accommodated ZBB to its existing budgetary framework. If an agency had a program budget, it selected programs as decision units; if its budget still was oriented to organizational lines, these became its ZBB categories.[26]

Schick points out that the key to the acceptance of ZBB by the bureaucrats in Washington rested with the notion of decision units and how to rank those decision units in terms of establishing priorities for budgetary choices. Because of this, an agency head was given an unusual opportunity to define what a decision unit is, and in effect, to fool around with how that decision unit is ranked with other units.

Although zero-base budgeting remains a useful budgetary concept, how useful it will be to the vast sprawl of the federal government will be determined only by time. As Schick points out, "with ZBB, upwards of 75 percent of the budget will continue to be uncontrollable under existing law; upwards of 95 percent will continue to be de facto uncontrollable." [27] As one veteran of the Office of Management and Budget perceptively noted,

> Introducing ZBB in a state with 5 million people, 79,000 state employees, and a $5 billion budget with 14 budget analysts is one thing. However, designing and implementing a ZBB system for a nation of 203 million people, 5 million civilian and military personnel, a $460 billion budget and doing this with 180 budget examiners—all in six months—is quite another.[28]

Thus, it may be that ZBB is more easily implemented in state and local governments than it is in the federal government.

25. Quoted in: Donald F. Haider, "Zero Base: Federal Style," *Public Administration Review* 37 (July–August 1977): 401.
26. Allen Schick, "The Road from ZBB," *Public Administration Review* 38 (March–April 1978): 178.
27. *Ibid.*, p. 10.
28. Quoted in Haider, *op. cit.*, p. 401.

Does zero-base budgeting actually work? Does the method result in a comparative evaluation of every major program in the agency by explicitly rejecting reliance on the program's historical base, as zero-base budgeting is designed to do? In a study of the U.S. Department of Agriculture's (USDA) effort to inaugurate zero-base budgeting, it was concluded that the department's attempt was not only very costly, but ineffectual. Zero-base budgeting tends to grossly overestimate an administrator's capacity to calculate program effectiveness, and vastly underestimates "the importance of political and technological constraints." [29] Because USDA officials were unable to make the calculations needed for substantial programmatic changes in the department's policies, few specific changes in the Department of Agriculture could be attributed to the use of zero-base budgeting.

Nevertheless, the use of the method did result in some unexpected dividends for USDA. In particular, it produced a "Hawthorne effect" among some of the participants in the experiment, in that they felt more important to the organization for having taken part. Top administrators were pleased at having been able to display their expertise to coworkers, and lower-ranking officials also were pleased by the opportunity to educate their superiors. Generally speaking, most USDA bureaucrats were gratified by the chance to use an apparently more rational method of budgeting and program evaluation that substantially vindicated (in their own eyes) what they already had been doing. Thus, many administrators concluded that, while zero-base budgeting helped a lot of other USDA officials to correct and refine their policies, it did not have much effect on their own policies.

Despite its potential drawbacks, zero-base budgeting should not be dismissed as another fad of the budgeteers. Reevaluating public programs on a regular schedule, as ZBB attempts to do, is a solid concept, and the basis of ZBB's solidity appears to be its simplicity. When all is said and done, ZBB does try to force agency heads to justify their programs and rank them on the basis of quantifiable criteria. As Schick observes "for budget watchers who have seen a parade of innovations and fashions over the past thirty years, the road from ZBB might lead back to PPB." [30]

In summary, each budgetary form not only forces the bureaucrat to ask increasingly basic questions about the agency's programs, but each form connotes different patterns and functions for the whole of government as well. The principal features of and differences between the line-

---

29. Aaron Wildavsky and Arthur Hammond, "Comprehensive versus Incremental Budgeting in the Department of Agriculture," *Administrative Science Quarterly* 10 (December 1965): p. 334. As the perceptive reader will note from the date of the publication, the term "zero base budgeting" is not all that new.

30. Schick, "The Road from ZBB," *op. cit.*, p. 180.

TABLE 9-1. Some Differences between Budgetary Concepts

Feature	Line-Item (1921–1939)	Performance (1939–1960)	PPB (1960–1970)	MBO (1970–1976)	ZBB (1976–)
Basic orientation	Control	Management	Planning	Management	Decision making
Scope	Inputs	Inputs and outputs	Inputs, outputs, effects, and alternatives	Inputs, outputs, and effects	Inputs, outputs, effects, and alternatives
Personnel skills	Accounting	Management	Economics and planning	Managerial "common sense"	Management and planning
Critical information	Objects of expenditure	Activities of agency	Purposes of agency	Program effectiveness	Purpose of program or agency
Policy-making style	Incremental	Incremental	Systemic	Decentralized and participatory	Cautiously systemic
Planning responsibility	Largely absent	Dispersed	Central	Comprehensive, but allocated	Decentralized
Role of the budget agency	Fiscal propriety	Efficiency	Policy	Program effectiveness and efficiency	Policy prioritization

item, performance, Planning-Programming-Budgeting, Management-by-Objectives, and zero-base budgeting concepts are summarized in Table 9–1.

THE BUDGETARY PROCESS

Regardless of what form of budgeting is used by a government, the methods through which an agency gets money remain essentially the same. Those methods, according to a critique by the National Urban Coalition, are characterized by secrecy, lack of a comprehensive review procedure, and inadequate decision criteria.[31]

Whether or not the National Urban Coalition is correct in its assessment, in 1974 Congress took the unprecedented step of revising substantially the budgetary process of the United States.[32] This revision was the Congressional Budget and Impoundment Control Act of 1974, which represented a unique effort by Congress to consider total federal expenditures and revenues together and determine their effects on the economy. This meant that Congress was trying to focus directly on national budget priorities in the light of national goals and the performance of individual policy programs.

The act brought about budgetary reforms that were needed for a number of reasons. For example (and somewhat incredibly), neither the House of Representatives nor the Senate had committees that were charged with reviewing the president's annual budget proposals as a whole. Consequently, Congress voted only on individual portions of the budget, and there was no process for reviewing what the total effects of such actions could do to the economy. Often individual appropriations bills were passed by Congress only after a considerable portion of the fiscal year to which the bills applied already had ended. Compounding this problem were the facts that a one-year time frame for the execution of the budget process was unrealistic in terms of having any impact on the national economy; that a number of spending patterns had developed over the years that were not subject to the normal appropriations process; that the president could—and often did—impound funds that were appropriated on the basis of his own priorities; and that Congress really did not

---

31. National Urban Coalition, *Counterbudget: A Blueprint for Changing National Priorities, 1971–1976*, Robert S. Benson and Harold Wolman, eds. (New York: Praeger, 1971), p. xii.

32. Most of the following discussion on the Congressional Budget and Impoundment Control Act of 1974 is drawn from Committee for Economic Development, *The New Congressional Budget Process and the Economy* (New York: Program Committee, CED, December 1975).

have the analytical and staff capacities needed to properly analyze the president's budgetary request and to develop worthwhile policy alternatives within the context of the federal budget.

The Budget and Impoundment Control Act rectified these problems in several ways. First, it inaugurated a new institutional structure in Congress by establishing for each house a budget committee responsible for developing overall fiscal priorities among major programs.

Second, the act coordinated decision making by requiring that, on two prescribed dates every year, Congress must vote explicitly on the budget as an entire package and on budget priorities; all subsequent decisions concerning the budget, in effect, must relate to these two votes. To facilitate this process, the entire fiscal calendar was changed from beginning on July 1st to starting on October 1st, beginning with fiscal year 1977.

Third, the act established a time table for scheduling different phases of action by Congress on the budget. In effect, the act set up a PERT chart for the budgetary process; thus, appropriations bills, for example, cannot be considered by either house until authorizations have been passed and the first concurrent budget resolution has been adopted. Similarly, Congress is not allowed to adjourn under the act until it has ironed out all differences on budgetary matters.

Fourth, the Congressional Budget and Impoundment Control Act improved budgetary control across the board. For example, those patterns of spending that had developed which were not subject to the regular appropriations process (known as "backdoor spending") were largely wiped away and the president's capacity for impounding funds appropriated by Congress was stringently limited under the act.

Finally, the act established a Congressional Budget Office to improve Congress's analytical base and required it to make five-year projections of the budget, thus assuring a greater degree of economic planning for the nation.

The act has been considered a success by most observers, although in the view of some it has not accomplished all of the far-reaching reforms originally envisioned. Nevertheless, the House and Senate budget committees have been established and are working smoothly, the Congressional Budget Office has proven to be successful, and overall fiscal targets have been developed. Figure 9-1 illustrates the structure of the new federal budgetary process as prescribed by the Congressional Budget and Impoundment Control Act of 1974.

Although understanding the process in its formal aspects is necessary, it is important to realize that the essence of the budgetary process is political. Aaron Wildavsky, Richard F. Fenno, Jr., and Jesse Burkhead, among others, have addressed what it means for a budgeteer to be a

THE FEDERAL BUDGET PROCESS *

INFORMATION GATHERING, ANALYSIS, AND PREPARATION OF 1ST BUDGET RESOLUTION	ADOPTION OF 1ST BUDGET RESOLUTION	CONGRESSIONAL ACTION ON SPENDING BILLS	ADOPTION OF 2ND BUDGET RES. AND RECONCILIATION

Months: OCTOBER | NOVEMBER | DECEMBER | JANUARY | FEBRUARY | MARCH | APRIL | MAY | JUNE | JULY | AUGUST | SEPTEMBER | OCTOBER

Key dates: Nov 10 · Dec 31 · Jan (Approx. last week) · Mar 15 · Apr 1 / 15 · May 15 · 7th day after Labor Day / Sep 15 · Sep 25 · Oct 1

- Previous Fiscal Year Begins (Oct 1)
- President Submits Current Services Budget (Nov 10)
- CBO 5 Year Projection Report (As soon as possible after Oct. 1)
- Jt. Economic Committee Reports Analysis of Current Services Budget to Budget Committees
- President Submits Budget (15 days after Congress convenes) — Approx. last week in Jan
- All Committees and Jt. Committees Submit Estimates and Views to Budget Committees (Mar 15)
- BUDGET COMMITTEES HOLD HEARINGS BEGIN WORK ON 1ST BUDGET RESOLUTION
- BUDGET COMMITTEES REPORT 1ST BUDGET RESOLUTION (ON OR BEFORE APR. 15)
- CONGRESS ENACTS APPROPRIATIONS AND SPENDING BILLS
- CBO Issues Periodic Scorekeeping Reports Comparing Congressional Action with 1st Budget Resolution
- CBO Report to Budget Committees
- HOUSE AND SENATE CONSIDER 1ST BUDGET RESOLUTION
- CONGRESS COMPLETES ACTION ON 1ST BUDGET RESOLUTION (May 15)
- Deadline for Committees to Report Authorization Bills (some exceptions, and waiver procedure)
- CONFERENCE ACTION AND ADOPTION OF CONFERENCE REPORT (Sec. 305)
- Conference Report Joint Explanatory Statement Allocates Total Levels of Budget Authority and Outlays Among Committees
- After Adoption of 1st Budget Resolution, Each Committee Subdivides Its Allocation Among Its Subcommittees, and Promptly Reports such Subdivisions to Its House
- Legislation Providing Contract or Borrowing Authority Must Be Made Subject to Amounts Provided in Appropriation Acts
- Reports on New Budget Authority and Tax Expenditure Bills Must Contain Comparisons With 1st Budget Resolution, and 5 Year Projections
- As Possible, CBO Cost Analyses and 5 Year Projections Will Accompany All Reported Public Bills, Except Appropriation Bills.
- Before Adoption of 1st Budget Resolution, Neither House May Consider New Budget Authority or Spending Authority Bills, Revenue Changes, or Debt Limit Changes (some exceptions, and waiver procedure)
- Before Reporting 1st Regular Appropriation Bill, House Appropriations Committee to Extend Practicable Marks up all Regular Appropriations Bills and Submits Summary Report to House, Comparing Proposed Outlays and Budget Authority Levels With 1st Budget Resolution
- If a Committee Reports New Entitlement Legislation that Exceeds Appropriate Allocation in Latest Budget Resolution, It Shall Be Referred to the Appropriations Committee with Instructions to Report Its Recommendations Within 15 Days.
- BUDGET COMMITTEES PREPARE 2ND BUDGET RESOLUTION AND REPORT
- Congress Completes Action on All Budget and Spending Authority Bills (7th day after Labor Day)
- CONGRESS COMPLETES ACTION ON 2ND BUDGET RESOLUTION (Sep 15)
- CONGRESS COMPLETES ACTION ON RECONCILIATION BILL OR RESOLUTION (Sep 25)
- Thereafter, Neither House May Consider Any Bill or Amendment, or Conference Report, That Results in An Increase Over Budget Outlay or Authority Figures, or a Reduction in Revenue Level, Adopted in 2nd Resolution
- Congress May Not Adjourn Until it Completes Action on 2nd Budget Resolution and Reconciliation Measure, If Any
- FISCAL YEAR BEGINS (Oct 1)

Note: CBO means Congressional Budget Office.

politician in securing an agency's funding, and a review of some of their thinking on the topic is worthwhile.[33] Although they broach the federal budgetary process almost exclusively, the same basic rules apply to state and local governments as well (governments of big cities play some variations of this process, however, and these leitmotifs are considered in Chapter 11). Politics requires the use of strategies and the politics of the budgetary process is no exception. As Wildavsky observes in his classic essay on the topic:

> What really counts in helping an agency get the appropriations it desires? Long service in Washington has convinced high agency officials that some things count a great deal and others only a little. Although they are well aware of the desirability of having technical data to support their requests, budget officials commonly derogate the importance of the formal aspects of their work as a means of securing appropriations. . . . But, as several informants put it in almost identical words, "It's not what's in your estimates but how good a politician you are that matters." [34]

STRATEGIES FOR BUDGETARY SUCCESS

To be a good budgetary politician requires the use of "ubiquitous" and "contingent" strategies.[35] Ubiquitous strategies are pervasive in nature and are required on a continuing basis by any agency. They are designed to build outside confidence in the agency and to add to its clientele. Contingent strategies are more particular, and depend on circumstances. They are designed to take advantage of unusual opportunities presented to the agency for the sake of defending or expanding its base. Budgetary strategies can be categorized as follows.

Ubiquitous strategies

(1) *Find, serve, and use a clientele for the services you perform.* The thought here is that an agency, when threatened, mobilizes its clientele. A case in point is the Office of Economic Opportunity (OEO). When the Office was budgetarily emasculated under the Nixon Administration, various organizations representing the poor rose to its defense, fighting a remarkable rearguard action in the courts in an effort to preserve OEO.

33. Wildavsky, *op. cit.*; Richard F. Fenno, Jr., *The Power of the Purse: Appropriations Politics in Congress* (Boston: Little, Brown, 1966); and Jesse Burkhead, *Government Budgeting* (New York: John Wiley, 1956).

34. Wildavsky, *op. cit.*, p. 64.

35. The following discussion of budgetary strategy is drawn from *ibid.*, pp. 63–127.

Although OEO can be faulted on other strategy counts, the Office unquestionably had found and used a clientele. A number of observers felt that OEO had politicized and organized "the forgotten fifth" in this country to a point at which the poor could adequately fend for themselves when it came to passing and implementing federal legislation, with or without OEO.

(2) Establish confidence in the mind of the reviewer that you can carry out the complicated program (which he seldom understands) efficiently and effectively. Here, the key notion is that if legislators believe in your abilities, you can get just about anything you want. Exemplary in this regard is the National Science Foundation (NSF), founded in 1950. An early fear held by a number of citizens was that NSF would become an all-powerful "science czar" of the United States. Through the strategic use of a low administrative profile, academic trappings, and capitalizing on a popular romanticism concerning science, the foundation not only eliminated this worry but eventually was operating in a budgetary environment that permitted an awesome degree of latitude: science could (and should) be funded solely for the sake of science, and fellow-scientists were deciding who among them should be awarded NSF grants.

The foundation's premise—that science should be funded according to what happened to interest scientists rather than for the achievement of larger social goals—ultimately (in the late 1960s) came under some hard questioning in Congress. But for many years NSF enjoyed an impressive degree of budgetary success despite a virtual absence of accountability in terms of what it did with the money.

(3) Attempt to capitalize on the fragmentary budgetary review process. A notable example of this strategy is provided by the Air Force. Throughout most of the 1950s, the Air Force practiced "phased buying." This meant that the Air Force bought parts for a larger number of weapons than its appropriations request indicated it intended to purchase. As a result, Congress and the president were left with little choice but to authorize the purchase of the remaining parts if any of the weapons were to be useful. For many years, this questionable use of the fragmentary review process worked handsomely, but in 1957, after a public furor arose, Secretary of Defense Charles Wilson ended the practice.

Contingent strategies

(1) Guard against cuts in the old programs. There are a number of ways for an agency to do this; a favorite strategy is to cut the most popular program that the agency has, on the logic that citizen complaints will get

back to congressmen more speedily. Thus, the National Institutes of Health has been known to start a dental research program by cutting heart, cancer, and mental health research in its proposed budget. Because of constituent pressure, Congress restored these funds and approved the whole package.

(2) *Attempt to inch ahead with old programs.* It is always easier to get new appropriations if they are made to look like old programs. A favored device for accomplishing this is the numbers game. The National Institutes of Health, for example, long has engaged in this strategy by reducing the number of its research grants ("Look! We're economizing!"), but increasing their size (thus inching ahead).

On the Financing of Government

In the following passage, a public administrator discusses how bureaucrats decide how to spend money. While satirical, his point is not entirely fictional.

In spite of evidence to the contrary, the System *isn't* free. There are dollars that are attached and because of this, many tyrocrats impede Program progress by their reluctance to spend the huge sums necessary to finalize a Program. So inhibiting, sometimes, is this feeling that by the time the money is requested, the Project for which it is intended is no longer required.

However, spending will come naturally and easily once it is understood that there are really *two entirely different kinds of legal tender in use by the System!* One counts; one doesn't.

The first type of money is the day-to-day or "real" kind that everybody uses to pay the bills. This type is rare, and always in short supply when needed most.

The other type is the tender used for bureaucratting; i.e., Money of Unspecified Denomination, or MUD.

MUD is produced by a special process. Real money is sent to governments in the form of taxes and is immediately machine processed to remove all the amount marks from both sides. Then when Bureaucracy wants to buy something, the proper number of blanks are selected and appropriate amount marks reinserted until there is enough to cover costs and still keep the pile to a manageable size. Since there are enormous amounts involved, the basic counting unit is the million, which Bureaucracy calls a *megabuck*. Below one megabuck, in the petty cash range, the unit is the thou or the K. . . .

Once the money is put through the marks remover, any connection it had with its original owner is severed. With the last trace of value removed, and all pecuniary restraints with it, the Bureaucrat is free to function with maximum efficiency. That is, he can charge ahead to the extent that he is not delayed by a mispricked conscience or the tight-fistedness associated with "real" money.

For example, the head of a large government agency sent an aide to see to the printing of a sizable Report. In the interest of haste, it was taken to a private firm with the request that it be finished "by Friday morning. We need it for distribution." The printer pointed out some diffi-culties and a number of needed corrections, and told the aide that it couldn't be finished until the following Monday without spending a fortune for overtime. The aide, being totally uninhibited, replied, "To hell with the expense. The boss wants this on Friday, and money is no object!" Thanks to the aide's decision, the report—exploring the meth-ods whereby the Agency could save money—was available for study on Friday as planned.

The advantages of effortless spending are clear and the MUD theory can be substantiated to promote it. A piece of hard evidence became available in the early 1960s when the United States wanted to borrow 500 megabucks from the International Monetary Fund to strengthen the dollar which was under heavy attack by foreign interests. The loan was approved, of course, since we are the heaviest contributor to the IMF. And were it not for the two different types of money, we would have been in the impossible position of borrowing our own money.

JOHN KIDNER
The Kidner Report

(3) *Adding new programs.* The final contingent strategy used by budgetary officers is the incremental addition of new programs. Because the new and novel often are distrusted by those empowered to distribute money, every effort is made in the agency to make its new program look as old as possible. Variants of this strategy include the contention that the new program is only temporary, that it is exceedingly small and thus hardly worth examination, that it is merely a logical continuation of an old program, that it is an attempt to reduce some sort of backlog in the agency, and that it will save money.

On the other hand, an agency occasionally will try to make the pro-gram look as new and "with-it" as possible. This variant also has its uses. A favored strategy is christening the new program with an inspiring title—for example, the "War on Poverty," "Polaris," "Titan," and "Mission 66" (which was a park improvement program). Salesmanship is not neglected; congressmen, on occasion, have been irritated by the use of "Peter Rabbit" presentations—simple graphs, fancy brochures, and lots and lots of pic-tures. Salesmanship often is used in conjunction with the recognition of some new crisis. Witness the effects of such drama-ridden salesmanship on a member of one appropriations committee:

> A week ago, Mr. Chairman, after this hearing about cancer, I went home and checked all the little skin flecks and felt for bumps and bruises. I lay awake that night and could have convinced myself I had cancer. And then more recently I lay awake listening to my heart after hearing the heart-trouble talk. . . . And here I am listening to all this mental health talk. . . . and I wonder what I am going to dream about tonight.[36]

If the foregoing strategy review sounds cynical, it is. To be cynical, however, is not necessarily to be scrofulous. Bureaucrats-as-politicians are capable of using cynical means for the sake of noble ends, and this phenomenon is well exemplified by the budgetary process.

An alternative always is possible, however. Cynical means can be used to attain cynical ends. As an administrative technique, the budget has its own combination of means and ends, methods and values. The ways in which these variables are interrelated by administrators are in essence political and affect programs and people.

So it is, too, with another management technique, public personnel administration. Like budgeting, public personnel administration is draped with the trappings of professionalism, technology, and expertise, but it is primarily a system of values and politics. We consider this subject in the next chapter.

SUPPLEMENTAL BIBLIOGRAPHY

Buchanan, J. M., *Public Finance in Democratic Process*. Chapel Hill: University of North Carolina Press, 1967.

Cohn, G., and P. Wagner, *Federal Budget Projections*. Washington, D.C.: Brookings Institution, 1966.

Commission on Budget Concepts, *Report to the President's Commission on Budget Concepts*. Washington, D.C.: U.S. Government Printing Office, 1967.

Committee for Economic Development, *Budgeting for National Objectives*. New York: Committee for Economic Development, 1966.

Comptroller General of the United States, *Report to the Congress, Survey of Progress in Implementing the Planning-Programming-Budgeting System in Executive Agencies*. Washington, D.C.: U.S. Government Printing Office, July 29, 1969.

Council of State Governments, *Budgeting by the States*. Lexington, Ky.: Council of State Governments, 1967.

Eckstein, Otto, *Public Finance*. Englewood Cliffs, N.J.: Prentice-Hall, 1967.

36. *Ibid.*, p. 120.

FISHER, GENE H., "The Role of Cost-Utility Analysis in Program Budgeting," in *Program Budgeting: Program Analysis and the Federal Government*, ed. David Novick, pp. 61–78. Cambridge, Mass.: Harvard University Press, Copyright by The RAND Corporation, 1965.

HAVEMAN, ROBERT H. and JULIUS MARGOLIS, eds., *Public Expenditures and Policy Analysis*. Chicago: Markham, 1970.

JERNBERG, JAMES E., "Information Change and Congressional Behavior: A Caveat for PBB Reformers," *Journal of Politics*, 33 (August 1969), 722–40.

LUTHER, ROBERT A., "PPBS in Fairfax County: A Practical Experience," *Municipal Finance*, (August 1968), 34–42.

MOSHER, FREDERICK C., *Program Budgeting: Theory and Practice*. Chicago: Public Administration Service, 1954.

MOSHER, FREDERICK C., and JOHN E. HARR, *Programming Systems and Foreign Affairs Leadership, An Attempted Innovation*. New York: Oxford University Press, 1970.

OTT, J., and A. F. OTT, *Federal Budget Policy*. Washington, D.C.: Brookings Institution, 1969.

Senate Subcommittee on National Security and International Operations, *Planning-Programming-Budgeting Inquiry of the Subcommittee on National Security and International Operations*, United States Senate. Washington, D.C.: U.S. Government Printing Office, 1970.

SHARKANSKY, IRA, *The Politics of Taxing and Spending*. Indianapolis: Bobbs-Merrill, 1970.

TURNBULL, AUGUST B., III, *Government Budgeting and PPBS: A Programmed Introduction*. Reading, Mass.: Addison-Wesley, 1970.

WALDO, DWIGHT, ed., "Planning-Programming-Budgeting System: A Symposium," *Public Administration Review*, 26 (December 1966), 243–310.

———, "Planning-Programming-Budgeting System Re-examined: Development, Analysis, and Criticism: A Symposium," *Public Administration Review*, 29 (March–April 1969), 111–202.

public personnel administration

chapter 10

It is our purpose in this chapter to review four public personnel systems, to trace the development of the public personnel profession, to sketch the nuts and bolts of public personnel administration (PPA), and to consider some value dilemmas in the field. Public personnel administration concerns the management of and policy-making for people and positions in the government bureaucracy. It long has been a mainstay in the field of public administration; its scholars traditionally have seen themselves as grappling with "people problems" and wrestling with the stuff of politics and the public interest. In recent years, however, PPA has undergone some serious questioning of its basic intellectual premises and has been buffeted by new developments in the public merit systems. Many public administrationists now favor dealing with "people problems" within the conceptual framework of organization theory, and the whole notion of "merit" has received new and bizarre meanings, at least in the opinion of numerous public personnel practitioners and academicians. While this chapter does not represent an attempt to "straighten things out" in PPA, we shall consider some of the difficulties and challenges confronting public personnel administration.

PUBLIC PERSONNEL SYSTEMS

Frederick C. Mosher has observed that there are at least four broad types of personnel systems functioning concurrently in American government: the political appointee system, the general civil service, professional career systems, and the collective system.[1] Often, every one of these personnel systems can be found within the same agency.

The political appointee system

"Political executives" are those public officials appointed to an office without tenure, who have policy-making powers, and who are outside the civil service system. There are only approximately sixty-five hundred of these positions available at the federal level, and they have been called "the true nexus between politics and administration." About the only job-related commonalities that these political executives share is their lack of job security and their high level of rank.

As a group of men and women in the public employ, however, they exhibit certain systemic tendencies. Most notably, perhaps, is the growing emphasis on intellect—partisan political experience may be of declining importance in the selection process. This is not to imply that partisan sympathies and willingness to be a "team player" are not vital considerations in the appointment process, but it appears to be increasingly recognized that, in the words of the late President John F. Kennedy, "you can't beat brains." To pick an admittedly dramatic example, the Cabinet in 1966 had six college professors and only two secretaries with significant political experience; contrast this fact with the Cabinet's average composition during the mid-1800s, when approximately 90 percent were lawyers, a profession almost synonymous with partisan politics at that time. At the assistant secretary and deputy agency administrator level, Dean E. Mann and Jameson W. Doig found that 90 percent of this group in the Kennedy administration were college graduates, a figure that has risen with every administration since that of Franklin D. Roosevelt.[2] At the federal administrative level just below that of assistant secretary, a study by W. Lloyd Warner and others revealed that the political appointees in this group had more formal education than their counterparts in the military, civil

---

1. The following discussion is drawn largely from Frederick C. Mosher, *Democracy and the Public Service* (New York: Oxford University Press, 1968), pp. 99–201.
2. Dean E. Mann with Jameson W. Doig, *The Assistant Secretaries: Problems and Processes of Appointment* (Washington, D.C.: Brookings Institution, 1965).

service, and Foreign Service.[3] Thus, education and brains count in the political, "nonmerit" personnel system.

A second tendency of the political appointment process is a growing emphasis on generalism as opposed to specialism. Education in the social sciences is increasingly represented among political executives, while the ratio of lawyers in this group (at least in the lower echelons) is only about 25 percent and declining. Of 108 assistant secretaries intensively studied by Mann and Doig, only 30 percent were appointed on the basis of a particular specialization, and the remainder because of "general experience." [4]

Finally, although there may be a declining emphasis on partisanship in the political executive personnel system (Mann and Doig concluded that a mere 10 percent of their sample of 108 assistant secretaries were appointed primarily by dint of "service to party"), there is a growing reliance on prior experience in government. Between 1933 and 1961, 80 percent of the Cabinet and sub-Cabinet political appointees had had some professional experience at the national level, and a third had devoted a major portion of their careers to the federal service.[5]

The political appointee system of public personnel administration at the state and local levels is more pervasive and less "executive" in tone than in the federal bureaucracy. Here the political appointments resound more of an effort to pay off political debts than to assure political responsiveness. The state systems vary greatly in pervasiveness; the governor of Oregon controls less than a dozen patronage jobs, while the governors of Illinois and New York have the power to make thousands of such appointments. Moreover, the majority of these positions are below executive level, with clerical and lower positions going to party loyalists.

The civil service system

The general civil service system comprises those white-collar, generally nonprofessional, personnel who have tenure and who are administered according to traditional civil service practices. Its overriding characteristic is the emphasis that is placed on the *position:* its description of duties, responsibilities, requirements, qualifications, and so on. As a public personnel system, the civil service has been the historic locus of public administration and, of course, PPA. We shall concentrate more amply on the civil service in the following section of this chapter; it is sufficient to observe for the moment that the civil service values the notions of "neutrality," "merit," and being removed from "politics."

3. Lloyd W. Warner *et al., The American Federal Executive* (New Haven: Yale University Press, 1963).
4. Mann and Doig, *op. cit.*
5. *Ibid.*

Professional career systems

The various career systems of the public service are made up of white-collar personnel, generally professionals and paraprofessionals, who are tenured in a de facto (*i.e.*, in actuality) if not always in a de jure (*i.e.*, in a legal) sense. The system's principal feature is the emphasis that is placed on the *person*, rather than on the position, as in the civil service system. In a career system an individual's career is administered in a planned manner; he is expected to advance upward through several hierarchical positions in which he can use his professional expertise in increasingly responsible and effective ways. As with the civil service system, we shall examine career systems more fully in the following sections of this chapter. It is sufficient for now to note that career systems place high value on the concepts of "professionalism," "specialization," and "expertise," and that their rise in the public service has had a profound and disquieting impact on the more traditional civil service system.

The collective system

The collective public personnel system refers to the problems of collective bargaining by and unionization of government employees. It comprises primarily blue-collar workers (with growing influxes of white-collar workers from the civil service and career personnel systems) whose jobs are administered via agreements between management and workers. The collective "system" is more an issue in public personnel administration than a system, so we shall treat it in more detail later in the chapter.

The four public personnel systems that have been described represent fundamental value differences in the practice of public personnel administration. What we shall do now, therefore, is trace briefly the evolution of public personnel administration in the United States, stressing the kinds of values represented by proponents of these systems. In this regard we shall concentrate especially on the thinking underlying the civil service and career systems, since the concepts that they represent have historically had the greatest impact on PPA.

THE DEVELOPMENT OF AMERICAN PUBLIC PERSONNEL ADMINISTRATION

The evolution of American public personnel administration can be divided into six phases: the guardian period of a relatively high sense of administrative ethics; the period of unmitigated "spoils"; the reform period; the scientific management period with its concern for efficiency; the administrative management period with its centralizing bias; and the professional period. We shall consider these phases in turn, although none of them is actually as discrete and clear-cut as the following review may imply.

Phase 1: The guardian period, 1789–1829

Mosher calls the guardian period "government by gentlemen," [6] and it corresponds principally to George Washington's influential administration as president. Washington set the moral tone of the early federal bureaucracy by appointing men to office who were reputed to be persons of character as well as competence. Character was synonymous with merit, and merit during the administrations of Washington, John Adams, and Thomas Jefferson meant a respected family background, a high degree of formal education, and substantial loyalty to the president—in short, being a member of the establishment. Sidney H. Aronson's statistical analysis of the early public service in the United States shows that it was of a highly elitist nature, with roughly 65 percent of the highest level appointees being drawn from the landed gentry, merchant, and professional classes.[7]

Moreover, the early public service was highly political. While ability and integrity were valued, it did not hurt to be a "team player." Aronson's analysis indicates that of the 87 major political appointments made by Adams, 60 were new appointments. In other words, more than two-thirds of Washington's original appointments to top-level positions were tossed out by the new administration. Similarly, of the 92 top appointments made by Jefferson, 73 were original appointments; stated another way, four-fifths of Jefferson's top administrators were team players.[8] Today, these kinds of turnovers among the federal elite simply do not happen. Nevertheless, the notions of character, ethical conduct, and public trust commanded considerable respect in making appointments to the public service during the first half-century of the American experiment.

Phase 2: The spoils period, 1829–1883

With the inauguration of Andrew Jackson as president in 1829, the United States government was put on a paying basis. That is, the government (and the taxpayers) paid the party that won. The period acquired its name from a remark made in 1832, attributed to Senator William L. Marcy of New York: American politicians "see nothing wrong in the rule that to

6. See Mosher, *op. cit.*, p. 55.
7. Sidney H. Aronson, *Status and Kinship in the Higher Civil Service* (Cambridge: Harvard University Press, 1964), p. 61.
8. *Ibid.*

the victor belong the spoils of the enemy." [9] The rationale underlying the spoils system was that if presidents were to emerge, like Jackson, from the class that earned its own living, then politics had to be made to pay. And history indicates that it did.

While Jackson symbolizes the ascension of the spoils system in the public bureaucracy, a more accurate assessment is that Jackson simply fostered the democratization of the public service. The percentage of top administrators appointed by his predecessor, John Quincy Adams, that Jackson removed so that he could appoint his own people to top posts was very similar to that of Jefferson; for Jefferson, approximately 80 percent were original appointments, and for Jackson the figure was closer to 90 percent.[10] Nevertheless, Jackson likely started the process of making the public service a system redolent of bribes and graft. Power was transferred from one group (the gentry) to another (political parties), but never to the people as a whole.

Phase 3: The reform period, 1883–1906

The corrupt excesses of the spoils systems during this period eventually resulted in a reform movement determined to rid government of those bureaucrats who owed their office to no more than party hackwork. From 1865 to 1883, a small group of intellectual idealists agitated for thoroughgoing reform of the entire public personnel system. Notable in this respect were George William Curtis, Carl Schurz, Richard Henry Dana, and Thomas Jenckes. Largely as a result of their efforts, the New York Civil Service Reform Association, the nation's first, was founded in 1877. In 1881 thirteen state associations modeled after the New York group merged to form the National Civil Service Reform League, now known as the National Civil Service League. British concepts of merit in the public service were of considerable interest to the civil service reform movement, and Dorman B. Eaton's report to President Rutherford B. Hayes (1877–1881) on the English civil service (published as a book in 1879) enhanced their influence.[11] The assassination of President James A. Garfield by a mentally ill, dissatisfied office-seeker in 1881 effectively assured national legislation of civil service reform. In 1883 Congress passed the Civil Service Act (the Pendleton Act), which created a bipartisan Civil Service Commission (which was replaced in 1978 by the Office of Personnel Management and the Merit Systems Protection Board) responsible to the president and charged with the duty of filling government positions by a process of open, competitive examinations.

9. Quoted in Leonard D. White, *The Jacksonians* (New York: Macmillan, 1954), p. 320.

10. Mosher, *op. cit.*, pp. 52–63.

11. See *ibid.*, p. 65.

Although the Civil Service Act had been influenced by the British system of public service (notably the principles of competitive examinations and a "neutral" civil service free from partisan pressures), the Senate inserted some major provisos into the act that were uniquely American in character. One such clause was that the Senators required civil service examinations to be "practical in character." While talented essayists of an academic sort might be nice to have floating around in the federal bureaucracy, it was far more important that the bureaucrat be able to do his job. This requisite provided the basis for a detailed system of position classification several years later; to be able to administer "practical" entrance tests, one first had to know what the job was all about.

Second, the Senate omitted the requirement that an applicant could enter the federal service only at the lowest grade. This permitted an "open" civil service with "lateral entry" as a possibility for all administrators (for example, a GS-13 level official in the Commerce Department could execute a "lateral arabesque" into a GS-13 position in the Transportation Department if he so desired).

Third, no special tracks were laid between the public service and the universities, unlike Great Britain. Indeed, initially it was preferred that the service be as highly "democratic" in character as possible. Only in 1905 did the Civil Service Commission first observe that "the greatest defect in the Federal Service is the lack of opportunity for ambitious, well-educated young men," and only in the 1930s was a major effort begun to upgrade the educational level of the national bureaucracy.[12]

Finally, the Pendleton Act set up no special "administrative class," no "permanent undersecretaries," contrary to the practice in England and Western Europe generally. Thus, the idea of political neutrality was not upheld at the potential expense of social responsiveness; instead the top bureaucratic echelon was occupied by *political* executives.

The crusade for reform of the public service had three dominant characteristics. First, the reform movement had been negative. That is, the reformists wanted to do away with the spoils system and its attendant evils. Second, the movement had been highly moral in tone. In Mosher's words,

> it associated what we now refer to as personnel administration with morality, with a connotation of "goodness" vs. "badness," quite apart from the purposes for which people were employed or the nature of the responsibilities they would carry.[13]

Third, and not too emphatically, the reform movement had been concerned with efficiency in government, and the reformers believed that the

---

12. U.S. Civil Service Commission, 22nd Report (Washington, D.C.: U.S. Government Printing Office, 1905), quoted in Mosher, *op. cit.*, p. 66.
13. Mosher, *ibid.*, p. 65.

merit system would help assure more efficient (*i.e.*, less corrupt) practices. These characteristics, combined with the antielitist sympathies of the Civil Service Act itself, acted to create what Mosher has called a period of "government by the good"; ethics and egalitarianism were prized.[14] Managerial effectiveness, however, was an incidental consideration at best.

There were two lasting effects that this phase of moral rectitude had. The first was its influence on the study of public administration. Only four years after the passage of the Pendleton Act, Woodrow Wilson wrote his seminal essay on "The Study of Administration" (recall Chapter 2). The moral tone of Wilson's article reflected the mental set of the reform period, and it has been a continuing undercurrent in the study of public administration. Wilson, an ardent reformer and later a president of the Civil Service Reform League, facilitated the expansion of an ethical sense of public duty beyond the conceptual confines of the civil service and into the entire intellectual terrain of public administration. Relatedly, the old politics/administration dichotomy, long favored as an academic focus in the field of public administration, received much of its initial legitimacy and acceptance as a result of the thinking that dominated the reform period of PPA. "Politics" was "bad" in the civil service, and "administration" was "good." Frank Goodnow's *Politics and Administration*, published in 1900, both reflected and strengthened the prevalent intellectual view that administration not only was different from politics, but also was somehow better.

The second effect of the reform period related more to the practice of public administration: The continuing independence of the Civil Service Commission was fostered, and its use as a model in the reform of state and local governments was encouraged. The commission evolved into a buffer against political pressures brought on by both the Congress and the president. In this development during the reform period, not only was morality increasingly identified with public personnel administration, but PPA as a field gradually was disassociated from the substantive and managerial functions of government. To put it far too crassly but clearly: The bureaucrats responsible for getting a job done and the bureaucrats responsible for keeping government moral became increasingly distinct entities.

Phase 4: The scientific management period, 1906–1937

Increasingly, the academic field of public administration was being influenced by developments in business administration, which then was dominated by the time-motion, scientific management school represented by Frederick Taylor and Frank and Lillian Gilbreth (recall Chapter 3). The ultimate value of this period was efficiency—in other words, doing

14. *Ibid.*, p. 64.

the job with the least resources. The values, concepts, and structure of the civil service were most compatible with the notion of efficiency. During the reform period, efficiency had been associated with morality and lack of corruption. Efficiency also was "neutral," another traditional value of the civil service and public personnel administration. Thus, a somewhat inconsistent but soothing amalgam of beliefs emerged that packed goodness, merit, morality, neutrality, efficiency, and science into one conceptual lump. Of these values, efficiency came to represent the best of the rest, a value "more equal" than the others—what "good" public personnel administration was all about.

The drive for scientific management in government began at the local level, largely because American government was concentrated at this level at the beginning of the twentieth century. In 1902 aside from the national defense budget, nearly 75 percent of public expenditures were at the local level. Moreover, because the functions of local governments at that time were mostly to provide routine, physical services (e.g., garbage collection, fire protection, water supplies, and so forth), local government tasks often were receptive to improved efficiency via the techniques of scientific management. Scientific management generated a concern in governments for such topics as planning, specialization, quantitative measurements, standardization, and the discovery of the "one best way" to perform a duty. Instrumental in inaugurating the scientific management period of public personnel administration was the founding in 1906 of the New York Bureau of Municipal Research. Mentioned in the preceding chapter for its advanced thinking on budgetary concepts, the bureau was the prototype of numerous bureaus that later sprang up in cities throughout the country, most of them endowed with philanthropic funds and offering gratis their not-always-appreciated services to local officials.

The municipal bureaus provided the linkage between the techniques and values of scientific management and the public sector. Their staffs were enthusiastic developers of quantitatively oriented and detailed job descriptions, productivity measurements, training programs, examinations keyed to job-related abilities, and efficiency ratings. Science and technique were stressed, particularly in the field of testing applicants for employment qualifications.

There were some notable effects of the scientific management period in public personnel administration, both intellectual and practical. The intellectual effect was to strengthen the politics/administration dichotomy, already popular as a partial result of the reform period, in the study of public administration. PPA was where the quantitative action was in public administration, and "hard-nosed" public administration largely meant the application of scientific management for the sake of governmental efficiency.

The practical effects of the scientific management period were to widen the scope of the merit system in the federal government and to aid in the development of the city manager profession in the United States. Because of the considerable effort expended on the development of job descriptions, tests, and measurements, the informational basis for position classification was broadened significantly. Once a thoroughgoing system of position classification was capable of being implemented, it was only a matter of time for the civil service system to extend its control of the public personnel system. This it did. Although civil service regulations applied to less than 46 percent of the federal government's non-military employees in 1900, by 1930 almost 80 percent of these employees were under its auspices. Much of this expansion can be attributed to the focus of the civil service system on the *position* as opposed to the *person*, and the success of scientific management in rendering many public positions quantifiable, measurable, and susceptible to classification.

During the scientific management period, the city manager profession received its initial impetus. The justification of the city manager idea reflected the politics/administration dichotomy in public administration as it was enhanced by scientific management: that the city manager would administer the policy formed by the city council in an expert, scientific, and efficient fashion. The first genuine city manager plan was adopted in this country in 1914, and the early literature on the topic almost exclusively related to the notion of the "professional manager," removed from, unresponsive to, and, indeed, contemptuous of local politics. Proposals were even made during this period to have for each state a state manager, who would be an administrative counterweight to the political/policy-making governor. Indeed, although its stance has been modified substantially in recent years, the International City Management Association remains a relative bastion of belief that public administration is separable from politics.

Phase 5: The administrative management period, 1937–1955

The advent of the New Deal in 1932 brought with it a new view of the role of government: that the public sphere should be active, aggressive, and positive in the rectification of public problems. This attitude was reflected in public personnel administration. "Management" became the new goal of PPA, and although it never displaced efficiency as a major value of the public service, the concept of management waxed and worked in tandem with efficiency.

The objective of management implied that there was something more to public personnel administration than mere efficiency. In reality—and more broadly—the traditional politics/administration dichotomy that had provided the essence of the field's focus was being questioned. Increasingly, people in the public service were perceived as having a political as well as an administrative function, and "management" served as a convenient codeword with which to express this new dimension.

The benchmarks for the administrative management period are the report of President Roosevelt's Committee on Administrative Management (known as the Brownlow Committee) in 1937, and the report of President Dwight D. Eisenhower's Commission on Organization of the Executive Branch of the Government (known as the second Hoover Commission)in 1955.[15] The clear thrust of the Brownlow Committee's report was one of centralizing the powers and responsibilities of the president: agency functions should be consolidated, lines of authority and communication should be clarified, and the president's administrative authority should be enhanced. Although the committee favored extension of the civil service system "upward, outward, and downward," it nonetheless was critical of the Civil Service Commission's past attitudes as encouraging a narrow, specialized, and technically-oriented breed of public bureaucrat. Generalism, too, was a clear value of the Brownlow Committee. Not only did the committee's predilection for generalist public administrators challenge the civil service system's long-standing emphasis on the position as the basis for personnel administration, but it blurred the distinction between politics and administration that dominated the whole of public administration as well. Although the committee rationalized the politics/administration dichotomy as valid, it hardly dwelled on it, and considered far more thoroughly those "positions which are actually policy-determining. . . ." A series of executive orders beginning in 1938 on public personnel administration (notably Roosevelt's order of that year requiring the establishment of professionally staffed personnel offices in each major agency), the first Hoover Commission (1949), and the development of "little Hoover commissions" in the states extended and amplified the values of the administrative management period as represented by the Brownlow Committee throughout the federal structure: Public personnel administration was a part of the general managerial function (just like budgeting, planning, organizing, reporting, coordinating, and so forth), and the goal of PPA was to enhance the effectiveness of management.

With Eisenhower's election as president in 1952, the comfortable

15. See Committee on Administrative Management (Louis Brownlow, Chairman), *Personnel Administration in the Federal Service* (Washington, D.C.: U.S. Government Printing Office, 1937) and Commission on Organization of the Executive Branch of the Government, *Personnel and Civil Service* (Washington, D.C.: U.S. Government Printing Office, 1955).

separation between politics and administration that had served Democratic appointees to the federal service for so long as a rationalization of their personal policy preferences suddenly received a stark challenge. During the preceding twenty years of Democratic rule, the federal government had burgeoned to many times its size under Herbert Hoover. Few seasoned Republicans were available for duty in the new regime as a result of their long isolation from the federal bureaucracy, and many positions (and the Democrats in them) that entailed major policy-making powers were protected by civil service regulations (thus aggravating Republicans). At the same time many New Deal public administrators felt themselves threatened by a rising tide of McCarthyism that they associated with the Republican party. The problems of transition were severely exacerbated and highlighted the quintessential dilemma: how to render a theoretically neutral public service responsive to the political and policy preferences of a fundamentally new administration. As a result of this problem, a second Hoover Commission was created in 1953. Its report two years later included the first thorough analysis of the relations between political appointees and career administrators.[16]

The second Hoover Commission revitalized the faltering politics/administration dichotomy, which was by then under intellectual attack. It assumed that the distinction was valid, but that it should be made more operational, in terms of government personnel, than it was. Thus, the commission recommended that no more than eight hundred presidentially appointed political executives should fill top public positions and went on to propose a new upper-echelon administrative class of approximately three thousand persons to be called the "senior civil service." These officials would be politically neutral career types and, significantly, transferrable from one post to another. For both groups, the abilities of the person would outweigh the requisites of the position. The proposal for a professional senior civil service à la the model of Western Europe died a quiet death in the late 1950s, but the idea that public administrators could and should be transferrable from agency to agency lived on and prospered by practice.

In terms of its overall impact, the administrative management period of public personnel administration integrated PPA with other administrative functions under the value/rubric of "management." Administrative management was perceived as an area of research and learning that was a needed profession for good government regardless of the specialty of any particular agency. Thus, the period witnessed the development of personnel directors in each agency who were responsible to (and a part of) the centralized managements of the agencies themselves. This intraagency personnel function was an effective agency counterforce to the quasi-

16. Commission on Organization of the Executive Branch of the Government, *op. cit.*

autonomous Civil Service Commission; it proved especially useful as a means of selecting persons for agency positions on the basis of those individual talents that agency managements valued more than did the civil service system.

Phase 6: The professional period,
1955–the present

The report of the second Hoover Commission in 1955 on public personnel administration indicated a new awareness of professional education as a contributing factor to government effectiveness. Although the report represented the zenith of the administrative management period in PPA, management itself was viewed as a profession in the report, and thus it marks the beginning of our present, professional period of public personnel administration.

THE MEANING OF PROFESSIONALISM AND ITS RISE IN PUBLIC BUREAUCRACIES

A profession may be defined as an easily identifiable and specialized occupation, normally requiring at least four years of college education, which offers a lifetime career to the persons in it. Professions are beset by status problems. They attempt to maintain their public visibility, yet they prefer accomplishing this task with dignity. (Surgeons, for example, seldom offer cut-rate prices to potential clients.) Professions try to achieve status by refining their work content; the body of knowledge and expertise that must be learned (along with the manifold modes of acceptable behavior) in order to be "professional" grows with each passing year and becomes increasingly academic in character. Hence, professions and being professional are identified closely with the university and the professional association—institutions well removed from the usual circles of government. In this light, professionals also prefer autonomy, the right to do their own thing in their own way. Finally, and stemming fairly logically from the values of status, education, expertise, specialization, and autonomy already mentioned, professionals do not like politics. Nor, for that matter, do they like bureaucracy. This aversion is reasonable enough, given the historical struggles of many professions (*e.g.*, the city manager, the social worker, the librarian) to develop a corpus of knowledge and skill purged of detrimental influences from nonscientific, emotional, and ignorant outside sources. Put bluntly, professionals who choose the public service often must overcome their antipathy for its two major features: politics and administration.

The entrance of professionals into the public service is accelerating and its impact is deepening.[17] Between 1960 and 1976 the number of "professional, technical, and kindred" ("ptk") personnel who worked for government doubled from 2.6 million to 5.4 million. In the mid-1970s, 40 percent of *all* "ptk" civilian workers in the United States were employed by a government. This figure excludes military personnel and people employed by the government on grants, such as research scientists; if they were included, "ptk" personnel would account for nearly half of all public sector employment; without them such personnel still amount to 36 percent of all public employees. In 1976, "ptk's" accounted for 21 percent of all federal civilian employees, 39 percent of all state employees, and 42 percent of all local employees. More state and local personnel than federal workers are designated "ptk" employees by the Census Bureau primarily because more than half of the state and local personnel are educators. Nevertheless, even when educators are deleted from the "ptk" statistics, 26 percent of all government civilian employees still are "ptk"— a figure that is more than double the proportion of "ptk's" in the private sphere, which is 12 percent. A surprisingly large number of these publicly employed professionals (40 percent) are women, although this is largely attributable to the fact that women are overrepresented in teaching (71 percent of all teachers are women).[18]

Who are these professionals? The federal government tends to favor the use of professionally trained military officers, Foreign Service officers, foresters, and scientists from virtually all the disciplines, while state and local governments employ social workers, psychiatrists, and professors; all American governments hire civil engineers, public health physicians, lawyers, and educators. Additionally, new, exclusively governmental professions are making an impact via vastly improved or totally new programs in higher education: examples are police, assessors, penologists, employment security officers, public health paraprofessionals, recreation specialists, computer technicians, purchasing experts, librarians, environmental scientists, and, of course, graduates of public administration programs.

Although the Brownlow Committee report and the reports of the two Hoover Commissions barely considered professions other than that of administrative management, within ten years after publication of the second Hoover Commission's Report it was apparent that government managers were becoming concerned over the need for them; the 1962 analysis by the Municipal Manpower Commission concentrated entirely

---

17. The bulk of the following discussion is drawn from Frederick C. Mosher and Richard J. Stillman, II, "Introduction to Symposium on the Professions in Government," *Public Administration Review* 37 (November–December 1977): 631–632.

18. Frederick C. Mosher, "Professions in Public Service," *Public Administration Review* 38 (March–April 1978): 147.

on "APT" personnel, an acronym for administrative, professional, and technical.[19] Similarly, studies of diplomatic personnel, public health personnel, and urban governance personnel all reflect an overriding awareness of the new role of the professional specialist in government. Yet, public personnel administration as a field has been curiously slow in recognizing the implications of professionalism. As Mosher has stated, few specialists "have recognized them—few even of the authors of books about public personnel administration." [20]

The professional paths to power

While the growing importance of professionals in public administration seems clear, the precise channels of professionals' influence on government remains somewhat clouded. Mosher has identified some of these paths to power, and certainly the most obvious is that of being elected or appointed to high office. This route is, of course, dominated by the legal profession, which has "monopolized the judiciary, accounted for a majority of legislators above the local level, provided nearly two-thirds of American presidents and probably an equal proportion of state governors, and accounted for a plurality of top officials in the executive branches." [21] Professors, too, favor this road, with Cabinets becoming increasingly dominated by academics since 1960.

Another route is the capture by individual professions of significant managerial positions in administrative agencies, such as military units by career officers, the State Department by the Foreign Service, the Office of Education by educators, and public works agencies by engineers. Mosher believes that "this pathway of professions to policy is probably the most important of all," since so many public policies of consequence are made in the bowels of these agencies.[22]

A third channel is the presence in all agencies of certain professions, which, while they do not control the agency, can influence its policies. For example, most bureaus have staff lawyers, personnel specialists, budgeteers, planners, accountants, and so on; all of these and other agency professionals bring their own perspectives to bear on policy formation within the agency.

Professionals also can bring political pressure to bear from the outside, often working through their professional associations. Frequently, a "Mr. Inside"/"Mr. Outside" double play can be used to pressure public

19. Municipal Manpower Commission, *Governmental Manpower for Tomorrow's Cities* (New York: McGraw-Hill, 1962).
20. Mosher, *Democracy and the Public Service, op. cit.*, p. 124.
21. Mosher, "Professions in Public Service," *op. cit.*, p. 145.
22. *Ibid.*

policy formulation—Pentagon brass working with veterans' organizations, for example, or lawyers teaming up with bankers.

Finally, professionals are able to use the very structure of federalism to further their power, largely by tinkering with the grants-in-aid system. Thus, state health professionals, for instance, may argue in tandem with federal health professionals for certain adjustments in intergovernmental funding formulas that subtly could accrue to the advantage of the health profession.

The impact of professionalism

While the effects of professionals on public personnel administration may be profound, precisely what those effects are and the patterns they may take are open to speculation. We have already considered the impact of professionals on organizations in Chapters 4 and 5, but the more general significance of professionalism on the public bureaucracy is worth some discussion in its own right.

Rivalry with the civil service system. Perhaps the most striking feature of professionals in the public service is the direct challenge that they pose to the traditional values of the civil service system. Professionals make up the emergent and increasingly competitive career system (mentioned earlier in this chapter), which is characterized by its focus on the person rather than the position. These foci are fundamentally at odds. The civil service system is egalitarian by tradition, whereas the career system is elitist; what one does in a job is of paramount importance in the civil service system, whereas how one does it is of major significance in the career system; neutral and autonomous control of the entire public personnel system is valued by the civil service system, whereas planned and autonomous control of the individual professional is the concern of the career system. Although the merit system technically controls almost 90 percent of the federal employees in the public service, pressures from the various career systems throughout the government in fact have weakened the hold of the traditional, position-centered system on the careers of many professionals. Indeed, the Office of Personnel Management officially has excepted approximately ninety different professions from its purview. What appears to be happening is the evolvement of new operational definitions of what "merit" means, and these definitions reflect the value differences between professionalism and traditional public personnel administration.

In addition to the rivalry that the career systems pose to the civil service system, there are at least three other effects which professionals have on the public service: the growing influence of professional elites inside government agencies, the growing influence of private professional associations on government, and the indirect but growing influence of universities on the personnel policies of public agencies.

Elitism.   Professional elitism appears to be an expanding source of conflict in some agencies. Research conducted among government agencies in California by Frederick Mosher and Keith Axtell indicates that the more established and recognized a profession is in society, and the scarcer the professionals available to a particular agency for hire, the more probable that the professional elite in question will exercise real and effective control over agency policies, standards, actions, and its entire personnel system, irrespective of the de jure control over personnel practices supposedly exercised by the civil service system. Mosher and Axtell found this to be the case regardless of governmental level—whether national, state, or local.[23]

Professional societies.   Professional societies are increasingly exercising considerable power in public affairs; the intimate connection between them and public personnel career systems enhances this power. Studies indicating this growing and discomfiting influence by the profession in government, mostly by political scientists, are too numerous to list, and the variations and subtleties that their influence can assume are limitless. It will suffice to note that the control professions possess over a particular sliver of knowledge enables these private professional associations to have considerable input vis-a-vis those public decisions made in their sphere of expertise. Studies of the decision process in regulatory agencies, the politics of professional licensing procedures in the states, the raw power and generously funded political activity of some "apolitical" professional societies, such as the American Medical Association, indicate the gravity of this problem not only for public personnel administration but for the public generally. For instance, Corinne Lathrop Gilb, in *Hidden Hierarchies: The Professions and Government*, has questioned the special interest nature of the professions' impact on public decisions; Jethro K. Lieberman, in *The Tyranny of the Experts*, has scored licensing practices as monopolistic; and Guy Benveniste in *The Politics of Expertise* has warned public administrators of relying too heavily on the supposedly apolitical advice of professionals in making policies.[24]

23. Frederick C. Mosher and Keith Axtell, Unpublished studies cited in Mosher, *Democracy and the Public Service, op. cit.,* p. 127.
24. See: Corinne Lathrop Gilb, *Hidden Hierarchies: The Professions and Government* (New York: Harper & Row, 1956); Jethro K. Lieberman, *The Tyranny of the Experts; How Professional Are Closing the Open Society* (New York: Walker, 1970); and Guy Benveniste, *The Politics of Expertise,* 2nd ed. (San Francisco: Boyd & Fraser, 1977).

Universities and colleges. Finally, the universities, those accreditors and sanctifiers of established and emerging professions, exercise an oblique influence on the dynamics of public personnel administration. Increasingly, academic standards (*e.g.*, university attended, grades, and faculty references) count more heavily in getting into the public service than does the traditional, position-centered entrance examination; more often than not, governments defer to universities the responsibilities for filtering applicants to administrative positions. The sheepskin is becoming the symbol of merit, and the more sheepskins the more meritorious the applicant.

Professionalism and "the great training robbery"

There is increasing reason to question the long-standing conventional wisdom of Americans that high educational levels correlate positively with high income levels and job success, in public or private employment. In an analysis of an extensive survey taken by the U.S. Civil Service Commission of 7,867 randomly selected male federal employees, grades 5 through 15, Ivar Berg found that essentially education mattered only when an applicant was being hired for a relatively high-level administrative position (grades 11 through 14). After having been in the federal employ for a period of time, the effects of high educational attainment on advancement were negligible. Similarly, in a study conducted by the Federal Aviation Administration of 507 male air traffic controllers, grades 14 and 15, Berg found that "neither amount of education nor managerial training was related to higher grade." Berg terms this situation "the great training robbery." [25]

Moreover, there is a growing and symbiotic relationship between the universities and the professional associations in the form of accreditation procedures. Professional societies self-appoint themselves with ever-increasing frequency as judges of a particular academic department's qualifications to certify graduates as members of the pertinent profession. The probable consequence of this trend is to require more specialization in the field, at the expense of general education.

In this connection, the universities tend to be rivals of the government as attractive employers of those candidates with substantial educational credentials. The landmark 1964 study, *The Image of the Federal Service*, by Franklin P. Kilpatrick, Milton C. Cummings, Jr., and M. Kent Jennings, indicates that the more one progresses over educational hurdles, the less attractive government employment becomes; universities appear to

---

25. Ivar Berg with the assistance of Sherry Gorelick, *Education and Jobs: The Great Training Robbery* (Boston: Beacon Press, 1971).

have surpassed business corporations as the chief employment competitor for advanced-degree graduates.[26]

While professionalism is a new and major factor in public personnel administration, it nonetheless stands that the traditional civil service system dominates the field. With this in mind, the following section of the chapter briefly reviews the nuts and bolts of PPA, for the field's techniques and procedures have evolved, in the main, within the context of position-oriented concepts.

THE NUTS AND BOLTS OF PPA

The federal "merit system," which normally is taken to mean the general civil service system including general merit and special merit personnel systems (e.g., the Public Health Service, Foreign Service, Federal Bureau of Investigation), encompasses nearly 90 percent of all federal employees. Among the fifty states thirty-five now have comprehensive merit systems, a trend that appears to be accelerating (in 1958 only twenty-three states could make this claim), and the remaining states have some form of a more limited merit system. The Social Security Act amendments of 1939, which mandated the use of merit systems in state agencies that managed federally assisted programs in health, welfare, employment security, and civil defense, and the Intergovernmental Personnel Act of 1970, which initiated a program of grants administered by the U.S. Office of Personnel Management to inaugurate and improve merit systems in states and localities, have been instrumental in the development of state and local merit personnel systems. Merit systems are prevalent in American cities as well. Excluding education, civil service protection covers about 75 percent of all municipal employees. Only in county governments has the merit personnel system been effectively curtailed; there it covers less than 10 percent of the nation's county employees and the spoils period continues supreme.

These figures are open to interpretation, and the various merit systems themselves are vulnerable to circumvention. Nevertheless, the scope and expansion of the general civil service system in American governments is impressive. We shall concentrate on its structure and functions in this portion of the chapter.

Structure of the civil service

The basis of the civil service, irrespective of governmental level, is the position classification system. Public personnel classification techniques

26. Franklin P. Kilpatrick, Milton C. Cummings, Jr., and M. Kent Jennings, *The Image of the Federal Service* (Washington, D.C.: Brookings Institution, 1964).

received their impetus during the scientific management period of PPA. In 1923, as a result of increasingly vocal dissatisfaction over the lack of rigor in federal personnel classification policies and an ongoing belief in the "equal work for equal pay" ideology, Congress passed the Classification Act, which established the Personnel Classification Board to group public positions into rational classes on the basis of comparable duties, responsibilities, and skills of each function. A new and more comprehensive Classification Act was enacted in 1949.

The Classification Acts provide the foundation for the salary structure of the federal government. At present there are four major pay systems in the federal government for civilian employees: the General Schedule (which applies to almost half of federal civilian personnel), the wage board system, the postal field service system (these two are the lowest paying systems), and various remaining pay systems of limited scope, such as that of the Foreign Service. The General Schedule (GS) has eighteen levels, each level having a number of steps within it. The salaries of most top federal executives(*e.g.*, Cabinet members, agency heads, undersecretaries, assistant secretaries, bureau chiefs, and members of independent commissions) are regulated under the procedures of the Federal Executive Salary Act of 1964. The Pay Comparability Act of 1970 delegated authority to the president to set salaries for General Schedule and Foreign Service employees; the president is assisted in this function by the director of the Office of Personnel Management, the director of the Office of Management and Budget, the Federal Employees Pay Council, and his Advisory Committee on Federal Pay. Their advice to the president is based on annual reports from the Bureau of Labor Statistics, which is charged with maintaining federal rates of pay that are comparable to those of private industry, a policy that was established by the Federal Salary Reform Act of 1962.

The General Schedule is the mainstay of the federal personnel structure; it has influenced the design of pay scales in state and local governments. GS-5 through GS-15 are considered to be the major professional and administrative grades; college graduates tend to enter the federal service at GS-9 or better, and, after a brief probation period, generally advance to GS-12 or therabouts without inordinate difficulty and at a relatively rapid rate. GS-16 through GS-18 are the "supergrades" of the career service. Generally the supergrades are officially recognized as policy-making positions, and only about 25 percent of them are filled by political appointees.

Recruiting able administrators into the public service has long been a problem. A traditional hindrance is the low prestige that government bureaucrats have among the American populace. The first survey on the social status of public administrators, published by Leonard D. White in

1932, concluded that they had little prestige.[27] Later surveys have failed to indicate a reversal in attitude relative to other professions, although there seems to have been an overall rise in the prestige of public administration as an occupation. Taken together, the major 1964 study of Kilpatrick, Cummings, and Jennings and related surveys of high school and university students indicate that working for the government is most appealing to those persons with relatively little education and low income levels and least appealing to those respondents with relatively high educational attainments and income levels. Blacks appear to favor working for the government more than whites, and the majority of all respondents rank employment by federal, state, and local governments in a descending order of desirability.[28]

Salaries can pose another recruitment problem. In most states and localities, salaries for public officials are relatively low, although the federal wage rates compare favorably with those of the private sphere as a result of the 1962 legislation. In an effort to attract executives for those top federal positions not covered by the Federal Salary Reform Act, in 1967 Congress established the Commission on Executive, Legislative, and Judicial Salaries, which recommends salary levels to the president for executive-level personnel in all three branches. The president has more discretionary authority in determining salary rates for these officials than he does for those administrators covered under the General Schedule and Foreign Service systems; thus far presidents have tended to resist recommendations by the commission for substantial wage hikes in this group.

Most recent college graduates enter the federal government service by taking the Professional and Administrative Careers Examination (PACE), which tests verbal and quantitative abilities. Veterans, as a result of the Veterans' Preference Act of 1944 and continuing political activity by the American Legion, receive an automatic five points on the examination (ten points for disabled veterans). Only a few states and localities have a test comparable to PACE, although many use more specialized written examinations and grant extra points to veterans.

Once inside the bureaucracy, a variety of in-service executive training programs are offered to public administrators, particularly at the federal level. In-service training is a relatively new development in public bureauc-

27. Leonard D. White, *Further Contributions to the Prestige Value of Public Employment* (Chicago: University of Chicago Press, 1932).

28. See, for example, H. George Frederickson, "Understanding Attitudes Toward Public Employment," *Public Administration Review* 27 (December 1967): 411–420 and Frank K. Gibson and George A. James, "Student Attitudes Toward Government Employees and Employment," *Public Administration Review* 27 (December 1967): 429–435.

racies; most of it, in fact, emerged when the Government Employees Training Act was enacted in 1958. The act required federal agencies to provide training for their personnel, using both public and private facilities. As a further stimulus President Lyndon B. Johnson issued Executive Order 11348 in 1967, which encouraged the U.S. Civil Service Commission to work more actively with agency heads to develop in-service personnel training programs. Johnson's Executive Order resulted in the creation of the commission's Bureau of Training and Regional Training Centers nationwide and, a year later, Johnson followed this up with the inauguration of the Federal Executive Institute in Charlottesville, Virginia. The institute is designed for the enrichment of supergrade federal administrators, and similar centers have been established in New York, California, and Tennessee for mid-range administrators, grades 13 through 15. As the result of a presidential memorandum in 1969, a provision in the Equal Employment Opportunity Act of 1972, and the Labor Department's Public Service Careers Program, all federal agencies have begun to develop in-service training programs designed to encourage the upward mobility of lower-echelon personnel, with special emphasis to assuring the advancement opportunities of minority groups.

In-service training programs in the states and cities are less developed than in the federal bureaucracy. Traditionally, most such programs were conducted by state or local universities, particularly those with institutes of government, institutes of public administration, or well-established continuing education programs. This remains largely the case today, although the Intergovernmental Personnel Act of 1970 represents a breakthrough of sorts in that it opens up federal in-service training programs to state and local employees and authorizes grants to enable states, localities, and certain nonprofit organizations (including universities) to develop their own training programs.

The civil service dynamic: hiring, promoting, demoting, and firing

How does one get a job in government? According to merit principles, all one should have to do is possess the proper educational and professional credentials and score well on a test. But more is involved, particularly when a personal interview is required. Employers in government (and presumably in private enterprise as well) would rather hire someone who is professionally less able and personally more amiable. Consider the following passage from Frank J. Thompson's study of personnel politics in Oakland.

> The attitudes of the statistical service officer show how important amiability can be. He would rather hire a mediocre programmer who is

easy-going and pleasant, than a very able one who is abrasive—who "makes waves and stirs up trouble." On one occasion, he served on an oral board, which was interviewing a young lady. In terms of the applicant's computer knowledge, she was clearly superior to all the other applicants. But he and the other board members felt that she was too "aggressive and dynamic." There was too much "hostility" in her replies and, consequently, they flunked her.[29]

So much for merit principles in hiring.

Some evidence suggests that the test-based merit system does not work even when judged by its own standards. In a 1970 study of the New York City civil service, which had roughly 250,000 out of a total of 400,000 employees who were considered "competitive class" employees (that is, they were hired and advanced on the basis of competitive tests), it was found that the "merit" system discriminated *"against those applicants who are most qualified according to its own standards.* Candidates with low passing grades are actually *more* likely to be hired than those with high passing grades! Furthermore, this perverse result seems to hold true for all skill levels."[30] How so? The investigators found that the city had a lengthy waiting period between the date that an applicant took the examination and the date of hire—a median of seven months—and that, during this period, the best qualified were skimmed off by other employers. Conclusion: "*New York City's civil service system functions as an inverse merit system* (something the public at large has cynically assumed for years)."[31]

Once inside the civil service, many public administrators find that seniority counts when it comes to being promoted. In his analysis of the U.S. Civil Service Commission (now the Office of Personnel Management) Berg found that when "age and length of service are considered together, as a surrogate measure of experience [and as a genuine measure of seniority], the combination becomes the strongest factor in accounting for the promotion rates of the highest level, the GS 11–14 category. . . ."[32]

The considerable advantages of seniority are a fact of life in virtually any organization, but the efforts made in the field of public personnel administration to reward ability rather than more time-in-grade are worth a brief observance. The Office of Personnel Management first required formal promotion plans from federal agencies in 1959, and since 1969 the

29. Frank J. Thompson, *Personnel Policy in the City: The Politics of Jobs in Oakland* (Berkeley: University of California Press, 1975), p. 106.

30. E. S. Savas and Sigmund G. Ginsburg, "The Civil Service: A Meritless System?" *The Public Interest* 32 (Summer 1973): 76. Emphasis is in original.

31. *Ibid.*, p. 77. Emphasis is in original.

32. Berg and Gorelick, *op. cit.*, p. 107.

office has been notably more aggressive in trying to minimize the detrimental effects of the seniority factor by emphasizing intraagency ranking procedures based on job-related standards and by broadening the scope of promotional searches within the agency. State and local governments are more prone to rely on written tests as a basis for promotion than are federal agencies.

Service ratings are a device favored for determining not only promotions but also pay increases, decreases, demotions, and dismissals. The first Hoover Commission initially proposed the use of service ratings in government;[33] often they amount to little more than adjectival descriptions (*e.g.*, excellent, average, poor) by a supervisor of his employee. There are two principal kinds of service ratings, "trait rating" and "performance rating." Trait rating attempts to evaluate such personality features as industry, intelligence, tact, and courtesy, while performance rating tries to judge how effectively the employee is fulfilling the duties of his position. In point of fact, however, the difficulties of distinguishing personality traits from job performance in the evaluation of individual administrators may be insuperable, especially given the nature of administration itself.

It is important to note that service ratings symbolize a fundamental aspect of administration that, though obvious, is often overlooked. Administration affects people's lives. An administrative act can alter a person's self-concept, for good or ill, as well as influence the course of his occupational future. Administration is power, and public administration can be very powerful indeed.

The ways in which administration affects the lives of those in it are usually most dramatically visible when demotions and dismissals are being processed. Dismissal, of course, means being fired for cause. It does not refer to those employees who are (to use the current parlance) "riffed"—a derivative of the phrase "reductions in force"; these government workers often are the victims of economizing measures and have relatively low service ratings.

But this is not always the case, and occasionally talented administrators are fired for reasons other than low service ratings. An incident that dramatized this phenomenon occurred in late 1973 when A. Ernest Fitzgerald, a GS–17 Deputy for Management Systems in the Office of the Assistant Secretary of the U.S. Air Force, was reinstated to his original civilian position by a ruling of the U.S. Civil Service Commission. Fitzgerald had effectively been fired by the Air Force for his candid testimony before Congress on a $2 billion cost overrun incurred by the C-5A cargo

33. Commission on Organization of the Executive Branch of the Government, *Personnel Management: A Report to the Congress* (Washington, D.C.: U.S. Government Printing Office, 1949).

transport plane development project—testimony that did not rest easily with the Pentagon brass.[34]

On the other hand, the procedures that must be followed to dismiss genuine incompetents can be time-consuming and costly. The appeals procedure can be wearing for everyone involved (the Fitzgerald case took about five years from start to finish), and due process of law must be observed so stringently that a class of lawyers that specializes in defending public employees fired from government has emerged.

Public Personnel Administration: How to Be Fired "For Cause"

Despite efforts to assure that due process of law and the rights of the individual are protected in government, public employment does not always work the way it is supposed to. In the following incident, which occurred in 1973, a top-level career public administrator was fired in a less than exemplary fashion, at least if we are to believe the literature of the Office of Personnel Management.

A former patent commissioner testified yesterday that a Commerce Department assistant secretary coerced him into quitting recently, telling him on the day he was to depart for an international convention that he was forbidden to leave the country unless he submitted his resignation first.

Appearing as a surprise witness on Capitol Hill, former Commissioner Robert Gottschalk said he had no idea why he had to resign. But he charged that Commerce Department leadership has for years exerted improper influence on the Patent Office, which processes about 100,000 applications annually.

He rejected assurances to the contrary given earlier this week by Commerce Department, Patent Bar and other witnesses at a hearing held by Sen. Philip A. Hart (D-Mich.) for a Senate Judiciary subcommittee considering legislation for basic reform of the Patent Office.

Gottschalk alluded to a "specific situation" of undue influence, testifying that he was "directed to follow a course of action contrary to what I and the general counsel thought sound."

He gave no details, on grounds that the situation is pending. Another source, however, said this issue arose out of a directive handed down last January by Richard O. Simpson, then acting assistant secretary of commerce for science and technology and now chairman of the Consumer Product Safety Commission.

---

34. For a description of the Fitzgerald episode, see Barbara Newman, "The Cost of Courage," and A. Ernest Fitzgerald, "Fitzgerald on Fitzhugh," in *Blowing the Whistle: Dissent in the Public Interest*, Charles Peters and Taylor Branch, eds. (New York: Praeger, 1972), pp. 195–206 and 207–221.

Simpson ordered that a decision by the U.S. Court of Customs and Patent Appeals be appealed to the Supreme Court, the source said. Gottschalk and his general counsel believe the decision should not be appealed.

Gottschalk further disclosed to the subcommittee that the Commerce Department has regularly siphoned off substantial sums that Congress had appropriated specifically for the Patent Office. . . .

Gottschalk testified that he was forced out by another presidential appointee, Dr. Betsy Ancker-Johnson, who became assistant secretary for science and technology after Frederick B. Dent became Secretary of Commerce early this year. She was in her office yesterday but was unavailable to a reporter.

Gottschalk, 62, who has been involved in the patent system in one capacity or another for 40 years, resigned effective June 29 after three years in the Patent Office—as deputy and acting commissioner, and finally as the commissioner, paid $36,000 a year.

"In truth, I do not know why I was fired," he testified.

But on May 7, he said, Dr. Ancker-Johnson told him he had "a fatal fault or flaw," as a result of which she wanted his resignation.

He tried to pin down the "fatal fault," but, he said, could elicit nothing from her but the "vaguest reference" to a purported inability to get along with key subordinates.

Gottschalk testified that Dr. Ancker-Johnson asked him to draft a resignation letter expressing to President Nixon a desire to return to private life, and to return with the draft on May 14!

As it turned out, she was out of the city that day. The following day, Gottschalk was planning to leave for Vienna, where he would head the American delegation to an international trademark and treaty convention.

He testified, however, that before he could leave, the assistant secretary relayed this message to his office: "Mr. Gottschalk is not to leave the country without seeing Dr. Ancker-Johnson. Please be sure that he understands this."

In a subsequent brief phone conversation, he told the subcommittee, she insisted that, treaty or no treaty, "she had to have my resignation that day." She got it, and Gottschalk went to Vienna.

MORTON MINTZ
The Washington Post

Because firing a clearly incompetent public employee can take a notoriously long time, it is perhaps not too surprising that one of the major arguments that has emerged against civil service systems is that they provide a sinecure for life to public bureaucrats. Because their jobs cannot be threatened, they are responsible and responsive to no one. Nevertheless, it is unclear how firmly ensconced in their positions public bureaucrats really are. O. Glenn Stahl contends that, although it is difficult to compare the proportionate number of dismissals between the public and private sectors because of different data bases, it nonetheless appears that

> There is every reason to believe that the annual rate of removal, ranging from a little less than one to about one and a half percent of public jurisdictions in the United States as a whole, is exceeded, if at all, in certain categories of private employment, such as a few areas of manufacturing.[35]

In other words, according to Stahl, the proportionate numbers of people fired in both private enterprise and in government are about the same.

If these figures are accurate, then it is surprising that the rate of dismissal in the public sector is as high as it is, considering how inordinately difficult it is to fire a public employee. In California, for example, a teacher may demand a hearing upon receiving notice of dismissal and the school board, unless it rescinds its action, must file a complaint in Superior Court requesting the court to make an inquiry and to determine if the basis of dismissal is supportable. Then court-appointed referees hold hearings and report back to the court. A trial is held by the court itself, and a decision is made on whether the board may, in fact, dismiss the teacher. In effect, any contested dismissal of a California teacher brings the judiciary into the act. Stahl contends that this is "perhaps the most extreme instance of abridgement of executive power in American school administration." [36]

But even reaching the point of firing a public employee is difficult and it is much more difficult to adjudge an employee's performance in some types of jobs than it is in others. Thompson has observed that the standards used in local government to evaluate performance can themselves be unclear, and the visibility of a subordinate to his or her supervisor can vary from agency to agency. For example, it is relatively clear whether or not a secretary is producing typing quickly and accurately, and a secretary is relatively visible to his or her supervisor. But in police departments, patrolmen are not very visible to their supervisors, nor is their standard of performance a particularly clear one.[37] Table 10–1 indicates the differences among public agencies in terms of a manager's ability to judge his or her subordinates' performance.

To compensate for these problems of assessing personnel in agencies where employees are relatively on their own, supervisors develop complicated performance forms and rating systems. As Thompson observes, these

35. O. Glenn Stahl, *Public Personnel Administration*, 7th ed. (New York: Harper & Row, 1976), p. 309.
36. *Ibid.*, p. 390.
37. Thompson, *op. cit.*, pp. 142–143.

TABLE 10–1. Evaluating On-the-Job Performance of Public Employees: Problems of Visibility and Standards

		Visibility of Employee Performance to Supervisor	
		Low	High
		---	---
	Clear	e.g., Building Inspectors	e.g., Secretaries Sanitation Workers
Standards of Performance			
	Unclear	e.g., Police Patrolmen Recreation Directors	e.g., City Planners

Source: Derived from: Frank J. Thompson, *Personnel Policy in the City* (Berkeley: University of California Press, 1975), p. 142.

forms seldom follow function, and to presume that the form is actually evaluating the performance of an employee is to likely be wrong. Nevertheless, bureaucrats are not spending their time ritualistically filling out useless pieces of paper. As Herbert Kaufman has stated in his classic study of *The Forest Ranger*, the forms actually are used to prevent problems from arising and to justify to outsiders a disciplinary action or decision to remove an employee. A record is kept by the forms, although the forms are seldom read by the supervisor when they are received.[38]

The employee, once dismissed or demoted, has extensive rights of appeal, and the example in California cited by Stahl is an excellent illustration of how far this appeal can go—and how precipitously. Employees who are fired often attempt to bring in outsiders and to apply public pressure to be reinstated. The ploy of expanding the scope of conflict between the employee and the employer, either in the courts or with the public, is a classic one in public employment circles. Thompson observed that in Oakland, while dismissals of the Oakland work force averaged less than 1 percent a year, almost two-thirds of those fired were on probation and therefore had no right of appeal to the city's civil service commission; however, at least one-third of those persons who were dismissed as regular, nonprobationary employees appealed their dismissal to the commission.[39] In short, a supervisor can expect problems if he or she fires someone in the public bureaucracy.

On the other hand, far more public administrators leave the bureaucracy on their own than are fired. Although relatively few of those who have made it to the top (such as city managers) voluntarily leave the public service, judging from the Oakland data considerably more of those

38. Herbert Kaufman, *The Forest Ranger* (Baltimore: Johns Hopkins, 1960), p. 158.
39. Thompson, *op. cit.*, p. 156.

at the lower levels leave. Young professionals in Oakland often found better options elsewhere; assistant planners had a turnover rate of 55 percent in a single year; junior accountant auditors, 19 percent; and recreation directors, 22 percent.[40]

Although state and local civil service systems may be both perverse and perverted by bureaucrats and elected officials alike, their presence does affect the politics of patronage. For example, in Oakland, a city that is virtually the archetype of reformed governments and council–manager rule, the city manager and various appointed bureaucrats conduct the politics of personnel. But in boss-rule cities the mayor takes over. For instance, the late Mayor Richard Daley of Chicago was known to review the applications for even the lowest-level positions throughout the city.[41] Although Daley's chief concern was loyalty to himself and the Democratic party, even he could not totally ignore minimal professional competence as a requisite for an appointment. Similarly, we may expect state legislators and city council members to be much more interested in public appointments in states and cities where civil service traditions are not strong than in states and cities where a civil service system has been entrenched for some years.

Regardless of the internal dynamics of government personnel systems, it is clear that some very basic concepts of the "merit" system are being challenged by various social developments. These include the issues of political neutrality in the civil service, affirmative action, unionism and collective bargaining, and reforming the civil service for the sake of enhanced managerial control. We consider these issues in turn.

POLITICIZING PUBLIC PERSONNEL:
THE CHALLENGE OF POLITICAL NEUTRALITY

The notion of separating partisan politics from the administration of the public's business has long been a value of public personnel administration. As early as 1801 Thomas Jefferson urged his small band of public administrators to be nonpartisan in their administrative decisions, but it was not until the passage of the Pendleton Act eighty-two years later that the concept of political neutrality was codified into law. President Theodore Roosevelt strengthened the role of political neutrality in 1907 with his Civil Service Rule I, which barred the collection of involuntary political contributions from government workers and prohibited their taking part in political campaigns. The U.S. Civil Service Commission took Roosevelt's rule very much to heart, refining its application in the course of

40. *Ibid.*, p. 161.
41. Mike Royko, *Boss* (New York: Signet, 1971), pp. 21–23.

considering more than three thousand separate cases on the political activities of federal employees during the next thirty-three years. Because Rule I covered only 69 percent of federal personnel, the Political Activities Act (the Hatch Act) was enacted in 1939, extending the effects of Rule I to all federal employees. Since then, the Hatch Act has been broadened to cover state and local employees working in federally funded projects and personnel in private organizations working in community action programs funded under the Economic Opportunity Act. "Little Hatch Acts" have since been enacted in a number of states.

The framers of the original Political Activities Act wanted to protect more federal workers from partisan abuses, but the debates of the time indicate that they also wished to liberalize the increasingly restrictive policies of the U.S. Civil Service Commission and to assure freedom of speech on the part of government personnel. The crux of the argument against the Hatch Act is that it turned public officials into second-class citizens by denying them the rights of political expression common to all Americans. For example, in its zeal to purge politics from the public service the Civil Service Commission ruled over the years that federal employees may be punished for disparaging the president during private conversations, failing to discourage the political actions of a spouse, and criticizing the government's handling of veterans during a closed session of the American Legion.[42]

The constitutionality of the Hatch Act was first tested in the U.S. Supreme Court in 1947 (*United Public Workers of America (CIO)* v. *Mitchell*). The Court upheld its constitutionality by dint of a four-to-three decision, and it was not until 1971 that the federal judiciary permitted the issue to be reopened. In that year, federal circuit courts in Georgia and Rhode Island ruled that the *Mitchell* case was no longer valid, and in 1972 a federal appellate court declared the Hatch Act unconstitutional. This decision was overturned in 1973 by a six-to-three vote of the U.S. Supreme Court (*U.S. Civil Service Commission* v. *Letter Carriers*), and this ruling appears destined to stand for some time. In its opinion, the Court stated that the

> restrictions so far imposed on federal employees are not aimed at particular groups or points of view, but apply equally to all partisan activities. . . . They discriminate against no racial, ethnic or religious minorities nor do they seek to control political opinions or beliefs.

In 1974 the first and only national liberalization of restrictions on political activity that affected public employees was passed by Congress, and it

---

42. Philip L. Martin, "The Hatch Act in Court: Some Recent Developments." *Public Administration Review* 33 (September–October 1973): 443–447.

applied not only to federal employees, but to those state and local public workers who were engaged in federally financed programs. This was a clause in the Federal Election Campaign Act Amendments of 1974, which continued many basic political prohibitions, but did extend permissible political activities by authorizing the free expression of opinions on political issues and candidates, permitting the solicitation and collecting of party contributions without coercion or pressure, permitting active participation in parties (short of holding an office in the party) and, finally, allowing the active campaigning by government workers on behalf of partisan candidates. In 1976 Congress really moved and repealed the Hatch Act, sent it to then-President Ford, who promptly vetoed the repeal measure.

The Hatch Act affects a lot of people; more than 5 million federal and federally related civilian employees have been discouraged from political participation beyond voting in elections by the act. These employees make up roughly 2.5 percent of the nation's population, about 7 percent of the voting population, and about 16 percent of the civilian work force.[43] In some jurisdictions, the Hatch Act bars large proportions of voters from political activity. Alaska's 17,000 federal workers, for example, make up 21 percent of the state's voting population.[44]

Proponents of prohibitions on political activity by government workers argue that, without such legislation, it would be possible to subvert the federal bureaucracy for political purposes because employees could be pressured, threatened, or fired for refusal to cooperate in partisan politics. Patronage unchecked could destroy the merit system as we understand it. The arguments that eventually may sweep such laws under the rug revolve around the fact that the government employee has no independent political rights other than voting, and that he or she has been left unprotected and at the mercy of the legislature and various civil service commissions. Their vagueness and ambiguity permit wide latitudes of discretion on the part of personnel specialists in determining whether or not a public employee has violated prohibitions against political activities.

Would abandonment of the Hatch Act and "little Hatch Acts" have an impact on the levels of political participation by government employees? It is an impossible question to answer but, judging by a study of 976 federal employees, the political activities of government workers would probably not increase as governments reduced their restrictions on political activity. The survey indicated that only 8 percent of the respondents said they would be "a lot more active" if they were permitted

43. Philip L. Martin, "The Hatch Act: The Current Move for Reform," *Public Personnel Management* 3 (May–June 1974): 180–184.

44. Martin, "The Hatch Act in Court: Some Recent Developments," *op. cit.*

a greater degree of political freedom, only 14 percent stated they would become "somewhat more active," and 18 percent said they would become "a little bit more active." Sixty percent of those polled stated that, even if permitted to do more in politics, their own level of political activity would "stay about the same," and 71 percent maintained that they have never wanted to take part in certain kinds of political activities, rather than that they refrained from doing so because they were civil servants.[45]

Nevertheless, while public employees as individuals may not wax suddenly political as soon as the ban on partisan activities is lifted, public employees as union members may feel differently. Some 5.4 million government employees are organized in some fashion, and if they were freed of restrictions on their political activities, their leaders in their unions and professional associations could channel this vast political resource toward raising salaries and benefits at the taxpayers' expense. What ambitious legislator would spurn the campaign money and manpower that a well-heeled union could offer? And what union of public employees would not expect the legislator it backed to come through with hefty wage increases at appropriations time? Such are the dilemmas surrounding the proposed rescinding of limitations on the political freedom of public employees.

RACE, SEX, AND JOBS:
THE CHALLENGE OF AFFIRMATIVE ACTION

One of the myths of American democracy is that jobs, especially public jobs, are open to all. They are not. Prejudice is still with us and working against both women and members of minority groups. Women, for example, often are disqualified from public jobs (such as fire fighting and police work) on the basis of physical "qualifications" that may not be necessary to do the work. Similarly, increasingly more rigorous requirements concerning formal education works against those minorities who already are disadvantaged in society since, as a group, they are less likely to have attained as much formal education as whites; yet few people seriously argue that a high school diploma ever made its recipient intelligent or a quick learner. This argument is persuasive and as a result the public bureaucracy has witnessed the rise of "affirmative action." *Affirmative action* is a policy that argues for the hiring of members of disad-

---

45. Jeffrey C. Rinehart and Lee E. Brenick, "Political Attitudes and Behavior Patterns of Federal Civil Servants," *Public Administration Review* 35 (November–December 1975): 603–611.

vantaged groups on the grounds that government positions should be open to as many people as possible.

The federal impact

Affirmative action is a highly sensitive issue in public administration today. We shall not review the ethical arguments for and against affirmative action since we did that in Chapter 6. Suffice to note that the federal government favors hiring members of deprived groups and consequently has implemented affirmative action policies that have had and are having a profound effect on the national employment picture. The major legislation in this area is the Civil Rights Act of 1964, which paved the way for the more specific efforts that followed. These included tougher executive orders by the president; prohibitions of discrimination in federal agencies and by private contractors on the federal payroll; more positive antidiscrimination policies by local, state, and federal civil service commissions; and some significant court decisions.

An especially important new law, the Equal Employment Opportunity Act of 1972, has for the first time brought state and local governments under the provisions of the Civil Rights Act. The act also provides the first statutory grounds for the federal government's equal employment opportunity programs. The act prohibits discrimination based on race, religion, sex, and national origin and directly affects some 3 million federal and 10 million state and local government employees. The U.S. Equal Employment Opportunity Commission (EEOC), which the act established, may investigate charges of employment discrimination in state and local governments and, if no conciliation is achieved, the U.S. Department of Justice may bring suit against the alleged offender. On top of that, the person in question may also initiate his or her own private litigation. This kind of federal legislation, plus significant court cases, has made state and local governments extremely aware of the demands of minority groups and women.

A landmark court case that has had a major impact on state and local public personnel practices was the 1971 U.S. Supreme Court case, *Griggs* v. *Duke Power Company*. On the face of it, the *Griggs* decision had nothing whatever to do with governments. The Court ruled that the Civil Rights Act banned discriminatory employment practices against blacks in a private company. Nevertheless, this decision has had considerable relevance for public personnel administration, because it effectively bars those employment practices (notably intelligence tests and minimum education requirements) that operate to exclude members of disadvantaged groups when those practices cannot be shown to relate to job performance. The ruling did not demand the institution of flat quota systems in the employment of minority group members, nor did it preclude the use of tests in performance measurements. It did require that any such device actually indicate levels of employee performance and individual potential objectively.

Quotas or "quality"?

These realities in national policy bring us quickly to the question of quotas. Quotas in public personnel administration refer to the argument that the traditional entry and promotion qualifications of the civil service, such as high test scores, should be reduced or waived for the disadvantaged until the number of women and minority group members working in government at all ranks at least equals their proportion of the population at large. In brief, each group, such as blacks, would have a quota, or a percentage, of the public jobs allotted to it which equals its percentage in the state's or city's population. If a city, for instance, had 10 percent blacks in its population, it would then follow that blacks should be allocated 10 percent of the jobs available in city hall.

Pressure generated for the establishment of quota systems in state and local governments has met with some success. In 1972, for example, a federal district court ordered that one black be hired for every newly hired white until the all-white Alabama State Police Force was 25 percent black, a figure corresponding to the percentage of blacks in Alabama according to the 1970 census. Again in 1972, while the federal court denied the legitimacy of an outright quota system, it nonetheless ordered the Minneapolis Fire Department to hire at least one minority applicant for every two whites in its next sixty openings.[46] In 1973 the federal court ordered the San Francisco Civil Service Department to establish two separate lists of candidates for entry-level positions and promotions, one for minorities and one for nonminorities, and to hire three minority candidates for every two nonminority candidates until the number of minority police patrolmen was brought up to at least 30 percent of the total. The court also ordered the department to promote one minority and one nonminority candidate until the total number of minority sergeants in the department reached at least 30 percent of the total number of sergeants. Similarly, openings in the Chicago police force were ordered to be filled in groups of two hundred, with one hundred positions to be filled by blacks and Spanish-surnamed males, thirty-three to be filled by women, and sixty-seven to be filled by other men.[47] Victor A. Thompson

---

46. Charles S. Rhyne, "The Letter of the Law," *Public Management* 57 (November 1975): 9–11.

47. *Ibid.*

contends that the Chicago Police Department had more than six hundred vacancies in 1974 "as a result" of such court orders.[48]

The "reverse discrimination" dilemma

Such court orders and public policies have resulted in the accusation of "reverse discrimination," a charge usually levelled by organizations composed largely of white males. White policemen in Dayton, Ohio, for example, sued that city in 1973 charging racial discrimination in promotions.

The earliest well-known reverse discrimination case was that of *DeFunis* v. *Odegaard*, which involved a white male who applied to the University of Washington Law School in 1971. His application was rejected by the law school and he filed a suit contending that the school's admissions procedure had admitted minority applicants with test scores and grades lower than his. A trial court ordered him admitted in 1971, the decision was appealed by the University of Washington Law School, was overturned, and DeFunis then appealed his case to the U.S. Supreme Court, which adjudged his case moot in 1974.

The most famous reverse discrimination case, however, is *Regents of the University of California* v. *Bakke*, in which Allan Bakke, a white male, was denied admission to the University of California's Medical School at Davis because that institution had set aside a portion (16 percent) of each entering class for blacks and other "approved minorities." In 1977 the California Supreme Court upheld a lower court's ruling, and with it Bakke's position, by refusing to endorse racial quotas, arguing that doing so "would call for the sacrifice of principle for the sake of dubious expediency," going on to note that people should "be judged on the basis of individual merit alone." Both the lower court and the California Supreme Court, in deciding against the university, had ruled that the university had violated the Civil Rights Act of 1964 and, significantly, the Fourteenth Amendment of the Constitution, which forbids states to "deny to any person . . . the equal protection of the laws." The University of California appealed to the U.S. Supreme Court, which agreed to hear the case.

In 1978 the Supreme Court, in a five-to-four decision, ruled against the university, thus upholding the California Supreme Court. But the Court's ruling was not clear-cut. Justice Lewis Powell, Jr., writing the Court's main opinion, stated that the medical school had gone too far in considering race as a criterion for admission, but Powell also said (if

48. Victor A. Thompson, *Without Sympathy or Enthusiasm: The Problem of Administrative Compassion* (University, Ala.: The University of Alabama Press, 1975), p. 79.

rather vaguely) that affirmative action programs could properly be a factor in admitting students. Powell stated that, "Preferring members of any one group for no reason other than race or ethnic origin is discrimination for its own sake," holding that such discrimination, as expressed by rigid racial quotas, was in violation of the Fourteenth Amendment and thus was unconstitutional.

Importantly, each of the remaining four justices in the majority wrote their own separate opinions, and none of them took Powell's position that quotas were unconstitutional. Instead, they held that Bakke should have been admitted to the University of California medical school on the basis of the Civil Rights Act of 1964. Justice John Paul Stevens stated, in words reflecting this tack, that the act prohibited "in unmistakable terms . . . the exclusion of individuals from federally funded programs because of their race."

The distinction between ruling racial quotas unconstitutional (as Powell did) or illegal (as the other four justices did) is significant. If the majority had held that the University of California had violated the Constitution, then affirmative action programs across the country would likely have faced dismantling. Fortunately for these programs, however, all the nine justices agreed that affirmative action programs per se were neither unconstitutional nor illegal, and that being from a minority group could "be deemed a 'plus' in a particular applicant's file," to quote Justice Powell, although it would "not insulate the individual from comparison with all other candidates. . . . "

Justice Thurgood Marshall, the Court's only black, wrote the dissenting opinion, stating that "If we are ever to become a fully integrated society, one in which the color of a person's skin will not determine the opportunities available to him or her, we must be willing to open those doors" that have been shut to blacks in the past.

The *Bakke* decision, although limited to education admissions policies, had obvious ramifications for affirmative action programs in all sectors and for that reason was greeted with demonstrations across the country calling for its overturn. Clearly, the judiciary's wrestling with the dilemma of reverse discrimination is far from over.

Regardless of how reverse discrimination suits will be decided in the courtroom, it is clear that the problem is both real and divisive not only for public administrators but for the citizenry. A review of public opinion polls on the topic concluded that "Americans are sensitive to the distinction between *compensatory action* and *preferential treatment*" in the hiring and promotion of minorities and women.[49] In other words, vast majorities of whites in various surveys conducted from 1972 on respond

---

49. Seymour Martin Lipset and William Schneider, "An Emerging National Consensus," *The New Republic* (October 15, 1977): 8. Emphasis is in original.

that they approve of such actions as government job training programs for minorities, but draw the line in suspending normal merit standards as a means of hiring and promoting minorities. Indeed, blacks and women also respond in this way; in a 1977 Gallup poll, for example, blacks endorsed promoting minorities on the basis of "ability" over "preferential treatment" by 64 to 27 percent, and 71 percent of the women respondents favored the same distinction.[50]

Nevertheless, whose ox is getting gored remains a valid political principle, and the discrimination issue is no exception. College faculty members, for example, heavily favor using affirmative action criteria in deciding the admission of undergraduates to college (62 percent in 1975), but are not nearly so positively disposed toward the notion when it comes to deciding their own careers; less than 35 percent of the nation's professors favor giving preferential treatment to women and minority applicants for faculty positions.[51]

In responding to the dilemma of reverse discrimination, some state and local governments seem to have gone overboard—perhaps in part because of the wiliness of their employees. For example, in 1977 fifty-three San Francisco police officers claiming that they were American Indians were hauled before the Equal Opportunity Commission, and all were officially reclassified as white.[52]

In Los Angeles, a city long under federal pressure to desegregate its schools, both white and minority teachers began claiming they were of a different race in order to avoid being sent to another school district as part of the school board's effort to attain faculties in each school that were at least 30 percent minorities. To counter this ploy Los Angeles established "ethnic review committees" that investigated "ethnic discrepancies" among teachers.

In New York both teachers and pupils are "visually confirmed" by the board of education for racial identification purposes—and the subsequent assignment to a school.

If all this sounds a bit like springtime in Hitler's Germany, it is. Racial certification, regardless of motivation, is unpalatable to most Americans. Nevertheless, racial review boards may be a standard component in the state and local governments of the future as public employees of all races try to "pass" for the sake of enhancing their work location and promotion prospects.

| Perhaps the best single augury for accommodating both the demands

50. *Ibid.*, p. 9.
51. *Ibid.*
52. The following examples of "reverse passing" are in: "Disadvantaged Groups, Individual Rights," *The New Republic* (October 15, 1977): 7 and Eliot Marshall, "Race Certification," in *ibid.*, p. 19.

of disadvantaged groups and the demands of those who are qualified according to traditional civil service criteria but who are not members of disadvantaged groups is the fact that public employment is increasing at an almost incredibly rapid rate. As a consequence there is a fair amount of slack in the system. This growth is put in perspective when we realize that between 1961 and 1975, government employment in this country grew more than twice as fast as employment in the private sector. While public employment grew by 70 percent, the private non-agricultural work force increased by only 27 percent and the nation's population grew by only 16 percent. In 1961 there was 1 government employee for every 21 inhabitants in the country. By 1975, the number was 1 government employee for every 14 inhabitants. Similarly, there was 1 government employee in 1961 for every 5.9 in private, non-farm labor force. By 1975, this ratio was 1-to-4.4. If this growth in government employment increases in the next fifteen years at the same rate as the past fifteen years, by 1990 there will be 1 government employee for every 3.3 workers in private non-farm employment. With some 15 million people already employed by the government work force, there may be room to accommodate both sets of seemingly irreconcilable demands pertaining to "discrimination" and "reverse discrimination," but admittedly this may be only a hope.

Tests: Problems of validity and bias

The questions of discrimination, quotas, reverse discrimination, and the whole issue of affirmative action relate fundamentally to the concept of "the test" for job entry and promotion in the public service, and the implications of the Supreme Court's decision in 1971 concerning *Griggs* v. *Duke Power Company* lead us directly to the issue of test validity. *Test validity* means: Do the several kinds of tests administered by the public bureaucracy for determining entry and promotion really indicate how well-qualified an employee is for a job? Test validity is determined by comparing "successful" employees with their scores on tests that are thought to be job-related. High job performance should correlate with high test scores. Yet, validating public personnel examinations is done inordinately rarely. A survey taken by the National Civil Service League of every major state and local public personnel system (outside of education) indicated that only 54 percent of them validate any tests in any way regardless of type—written, oral, or whatever.[53] Thus, it appears that a public employee or applicant is being judged on the basis of his or her performance on an examination that may or may not—and probably does not—reflect his or her ability to do a job.

53. Jean J. Couturier, "Court Attacks on Testing: Death Knell or Salvation for Civil Service System," *Good Government* 88 (Winter 1971): 12.

The growing controversy over test validity relates to another problem of public personnel examinations, that of cultural bias in testing. _Cultural bias_ refers to the tendency of those highly educated people who write examinations to unwittingly slant the phrasing and nuances of their test questions in a way that reflects their own culture. Thus, people taking an examination who are not members of the dominant culture (_i.e._, who are not white) are unfairly handicapped in their chances to score as well as those examinees who have been reared in the prevailing culture. After investigating the phenomenon of cultural bias in testing, the California State Personnel Board concluded that "written tests were more of a barrier to employment of minorities than any other phase of the selection process." Accordingly, the board instituted greater use of nonverbal aptitude tests, tried to root out culturally biased language in written examinations, and placed more members of minority groups on oral examination boards.[54]

Reflecting this concern over cultural bias in testing are a spate of recent court cases. In 1975 a federal court held (in _Davis_ v. _Washington_) that the fact that black applicants failed a written test given to all applicants to a local police force at a rate of more than four times that of whites was adequate evidence to prove that the examination had a "racially disproportionate" impact, and that blacks were therefore being discriminated against in police force hiring.

The problems of validity and cultural bias in personnel testing have cast doubt as to the use of tests to measure job-related ability as a means of controlling entry and promotion in public personnel administration. Yet, tests represent a cardinal tenet of the field, perhaps the principal operational determinant of what "merit" means. One thing is clear, however: Any tests used in the public service increasingly will be scrutinized to determine whether or not the tests actually relate to the job in question and whether or not the test, by design or accident, discriminates against members from disadvantaged groups.

The politics of affirmative action:
The Oakland experience

How governments respond to the question of affirmative action has been detailed in Thompson's case study of Oakland.[55] In 1969 spokesmen for minority job hunters challenged Oakland's personnel director over his policies concerning affirmative action. The challenge came as the result of a report in 1969 issued by the U.S. Commission on Civil Rights, which

54. Vernon R. Taylor, "Cultural Bias in Testing: An Action Program," _Public Personnel Review_ 29 (July 1968): 170.

55. Thompson, _op. cit._, pp. 112–130.

observed that Oakland was the only major jurisdiction among seven metropolitan areas studied in which the three main minority groups were substantially underrepresented in the city's job rosters; with a minority population of almost 50 percent in Oakland, only 15.3 percent of city hall employees were black, 1.5 percent had Spanish surnames, and 1.6 percent were Asian-Americans.

Oakland's minority leaders focussed on two strategies; they attempted to "bang Oakland officials over the head" with its own dismal record of minority employment, and they also tried to involve themselves in the recruitment structures of the city. A major target of the minorities was the police force: Minority leaders felt that its written tests were culturally biased, and a suit was duly filed. Minorities also pressured for a Citizens' Advisory Committee for the force, which was resisted by the police chief and the personnel director, who saw it as a front for a community control board.

Oakland city officials were quick to construct their own version of a domino theory on affirmative action; that is, if one department "fell" to minority pressure, then all the departments would become more susceptible to affirmative action demands. Although Oakland officials had the legal and actual power to flatly deny the demands of minorities, they elected not to be so direct and thus avoid an image of unresponsiveness. Delay was a major tactic in this strategy. Because recruitment authority in Oakland's city hall was widely dispersed, officials had great deal of opportunity to pass the buck. One frustrated minority spokesman compared the bureaucracy of Oakland to a "monolithic multi-headed hydra—when we approach one head, it always tells us that the other head is responsible." Or, as another minority member stated, "In Oakland the buck never stops." [56]

City officials marshalled a variety of tactics designed to justify their own positions and throw the blame on the minorities. For example, the personnel director warned that, "The city was responsible to the taxpayer and can't afford to hire people not capable of doing their jobs."

Not all of Oakland's officials were so recalcitrant on the issue. Some procedures were changed to encourage minority applicants, and the use of oral examinations was expanded to facilitate the entrance of minorities into city government. As Thompson observes, "Orals make favoritism feasible both in structuring the mechanism and scoring applicant responses. Furthermore, racial preference in the oral is not as visible within the bureaucracy as other adjustments aimed at helping minorities (for example, lowering credential requirements). Consequently, manipulation of the oral is less likely to precipitate organized opposition." [57] Thompson

56. *Ibid.*, p. 120.
57. *Ibid.*, p. 136.

concludes that, in the face of demands from minorities to expand minority representation in the city, a personnel director generally will put more pressure on those city departments that have hired few minorities, have made little effort to recruit them, have jobs that require simple skills (at least in the opinion of the personnel director), and that have a substantial number of open slots.

The effects of the efforts

The city of Oakland is a microcosm of the problem of representation of deprived groups in state and local government across the country. In 1969, the last year for which data are available, both minorities and women were underrepresented and underpaid in city government.[58] Of the more than 3 million employees, excluding teachers, who were working in local governments in 1969, fewer than five hundred thousand were blacks. Of these, fewer than 5 percent of the black males were among the higher-paid managerial and administrative categorized. By contrast, more than 12 percent of the white males and more than 6 percent of the white women were in these classes. Slightly more than 113,000 city employees during that year were of Spanish origin, yet fewer than 5 percent of the Spanish males were categorized as managers and administrators and fewer than 3 percent of the Spanish women were so classified.

When we look at the status of women in state and local government, quite aside from race, we find that their salaries are substantially lower than those of males in the same kinds of jobs; moreover, black women and women of Spanish origin earn substantially less than white women. Table 10–2 summarizes these findings at the local level, and unpublished data for the states are very similar.

In a 1973 survey of more than two thousand chief administrative officers in cities across the country, it was found that even less progress had been made in the upper echelons of local government. Of the city managers

---

58. Actually, more recent data are available, but they are considerably less comprehensive than those cited in the text. Data on the employment of women and minorities in state and local governments have been collected since 1970 by the federal government, but only as such employment pertains to federally-assisted programs in public welfare, health, and employment security. In 1976, these programs accounted for 418,800 full-time employees, or less than a tenth of non-education employees in state and local governments. Employment patterns in these programs indicate that "the proportion of women and minorities . . . substantially exceeded their proportion in state and local employment generally and in the total labor force." See Intergovernmental Personnel Programs, Office of Personnel Management, *EEO Statistical Report on Employment in State and Local Government: Comparison of 1970, 1974, 1976* (Washington, D.C.: U.S. Government Printing Office, 1979), p. 3.

TABLE 10-2. Local Government Employees by Occupation, Ethnicity, and Sex: 1969

		White					
		Male			Female		
Occupation	Total employees [1]	No. of male employees	% of total male employees	Median salary ($)	No. of female employees	% of total female employees	Median salary ($)
Total, all occupations [2]	2,299,039	1,585,388	100.0	8,386	713,651	100.0	5,962
Professional and technical	354,432	185,152	11.7	10,053	169,280	23.7	7,287
Managers and administrators	241,593	195,652	12.3	10,769	45,941	6.4	6,571
Sales workers	8,352	5,330	0.3	8,181	3,022	0.4	4,362
Clerical and kindred workers	436,116	86,830	5.5	7,521	349,286	48.9	5,183
Craftsmen and kindred workers	250,865	245,710	15.5	7,765	5,155	0.7	6,041
Operatives, except transport	49,810	39,341	2.5	7,315	10,469	1.5	4,188
Transport equipment operatives	100,873	95,355	6.0	6,661	5,518	0.8	4,316
Laborers, except farm	118,347	115,901	7.3	6,306	2,446	0.3	4,645
Farm workers	3,423	3,219	0.2	6,127	204	—	5,707
Service workers [3]	735,228	612,898	38.7	8,194	122,330	17.1	3,873

TABLE 10–2 (cont.)

Black

Occupation	Total employees[1]	Male			Female		
		No. of male employees	% of total male employees	Median salary ($)	No. of female employees	% of total female employees	Median salary ($)
Total, all occupations[2]	339,342	205,076	100.0	6,614	134,266	100.0	5,381
Professional and technical	42,846	16,097	7.8	8,703	26,749	19.9	7,121
Managers and administrators	14,143	9,600	4.7	9,597	4,543	3.4	8,269
Sales workers	1,419	785	0.3	6,888	634	0.5	4,393
Clerical and kindred workers	53,430	11,480	5.6	6,878	41,950	31.2	5,296
Craftsmen and kindred workers	22,270	21,309	10.4	6,745	964	0.7	4,900
Operatives, except transport	14,092	10,220	5.0	6,428	3,872	2.9	4,065
Transport equipment operatives	28,119	27,129	13.2	7,046	990	0.7	3,969
Laborers, except farm	39,646	38,610	18.8	5,005	1,036	0.8	4,032
Farm workers	465	418	0.2	4,676	47	—	—
Service workers[3]	53,481	69,428	33.8	6,168	53,481	39.8	3,895

Spanish origin

Occupation	Total employees[1]	Male			Female		
		No. of male employees	% of total male employees	Median salary ($)	No. of female employees	% of total female employees	Median salary ($)
Total, all occupations[2]	90,128	67,090	100.0	6,686	23,038	100.0	4,969
Professional and technical	10,114	6,094	9.1	8,726	4,020	17.4	7,022
Managers and administrators	3,904	3,243	4.8	9,226	661	2.8	5,637
Sales workers	458	330	0.5	—	128	0.6	—
Clerical and kindred workers	14,152	3,662	5.5	6,233	10,490	45.5	4,267
Craftsmen and kindred workers	10,426	10,180	15.2	7,351	246	1.1	—
Operatives, except transport	4,155	3,054	4.6	6,084	1,101	4.8	3,744
Transport equipment operatives	6,375	6,235	9.3	6,268	140	0.6	—
Laborers, except farm	10,777	10,585	15.8	5,443	192	0.8	—
Farm workers	201	201	0.3	—	—	—	—
Service workers[3]	29,566	23,506	35.0	6,394	6,060	26.3	3,767

Source: U.S., Bureau of the Census, *1970 Census of Population: Government Workers*, PC(2)-7D (Washington, D.C.: Bureau of the Census, 1973) pp. 171–73.

Dashes (—) indicate not applicable or that the figure is too small to be shown.

[1] All data apply for employees who worked 30 hours or more in sample week and 50–52 weeks during 1969.

[2] Excludes teachers but includes school administrators.

[3] Excludes household workers.

responding 98 percent were white and 99 percent were male. Fifty-four percent of the city managers responding said that their jurisdictions had no plans concerning affirmative action for women. Of the 46 percent of those cities that had taken such action, the action was initiated by the city manager himself in 84 percent of the cases; in only 52 percent of the cases did the manager have the support of his own city council.

The percentage of cities initiating affirmative action plans for minorities was a little higher; 55 percent of the cities surveyed had initiated an affirmative action plan for minorities, a substantially higher proportion than had initiated plans for women. In 84 percent of those cases the initiative had been taken by the city manager, and in 56 percent of those cases the manager had the support of his city council. Huntley and MacDonald conclude that, "While managers and chief administrators exhibit no strong personal commitment to such [equal opportunity] goals, they are far away the principal initiators of affirmative action in their governments."[59] Indeed, of all the cities surveyed, Huntley and Mac-Donald found that council-manager cities tended to be the most positive in establishing employment goals and objectives for minorities and women and in temporarily relaxing civil service requirements to increase minority employment. Nevertheless, the clear majority of city managers resisted even a temporary relaxation of civil service requirements to increase the employment of women and minorities.

At the federal level, the effects of the efforts are about the same as the grassroots. On first glance, the statistics seem encouraging.[60] Members of the principal minority groups in the United States, who altogether numbered 16.9 percent of the population, held 19.5 percent of all federal jobs in 1971. This is a slight rise from 1967 figures (18.9 percent), although the percentage hovered at 19.5 from 1968 through 1971 (the latest year for which data are available). Blacks, with 11 percent of the American

59. Robert J. Huntley and Robert J. MacDonald, "Urban Managers: Organizational Preferences, Managerial Styles, and Social Policy Role," *The Municipal Yearbook, 1975* (Washington, D.C.: International City Management Association, 1975), p. 157.

60. The following data are drawn on federal Affirmative Action results from the following sources: U.S. Civil Service Commission, *Minority Group Employment in the Federal Government* (Washington, D.C.: U.S. Government Printing Office, November 30, 1971); U.S. Civil Service Commission, *Pay Structure of the Federal Civil Service* (Washington, D.C.: U.S. Government Printing Office, June 30, 1971); U.S. Civil Service Commission, *Study of Employment of Women in the Federal Government, 1966* (Washington, D.C.: U.S. Government Printing Office, 1968); U.S. Department of Labor, *Final Report of the Public Sector Task Force* (Washington, D.C.: U.S. Government Printing Office, November 15, 1972); and U.S. Department of Labor, *Final Report on the Status of Minorities and Women in the Department of Labor* (Washington, D.C.: U.S. Government Printing Office, October 1971).

population according to the 1970 census, held 15 percent of all federal jobs in 1971. Latinos, with 5 percent of the population, held 2.9 percent of the federal jobs. Native Americans, with 0.4 percent of the population, held 0.7 of the positions. Asian-Americans, with 0.5 percent of the population, held 0.8 percent. Women, who made up 51 percent of the American population and 36.4 percent of the nation's labor force in 1970, occupied 27 percent of all federal jobs in 1971, a percentage that has remained constant since 1968. Judging by these figures, only Hispanics and women have suffered from discrimination in the federal service.

Unfortunately, these statistics do not tell the entire story, and on second glance the picture is less than comforting. It is painfully obvious that minority groups and women occupy virtually no positions of power in the federal service. In the General Schedule in 1971 minorities held 28 percent of the lowest GS-1 through GS-4 positions, which are essentially clerical and menial jobs, but only 4.9 percent of the GS-12 through GS-18 positions. In the lowest-average-pay wage board system, minorities held 59.6 percent of the three lowest brackets, but only 6.6 percent of the three top brackets. Similarly, in the postal field service system, minorities constituted 24.7 percent of the lowest five grades, but only 7.7 percent of the highest eight grades. And in the fourth category encompassing all remaining pay systems operative in the federal government, minorities held 29.5 percent of all positions paying less than $6500 a year, but only 3.8 percent of the jobs with a salary of more than $18,000.

Of the 23 major federal departments and agencies, which accounted for 95 percent of all federal civilian employees in 1971, 10 of the 23 fell below the 16.9 percent level of the country's total minority population. Nine departments and agencies employed proportionately fewer blacks than are living in the nation, 22 had fewer than 5 percent of their positions occupied by Spanish-surnamed, 20 employed fewer native Americans than would be indicated by the total native American population, and 3 fell below the mark in terms of Asian-Americans.

Less data are available for women than for minorities. The information that does exist shows a bleak picture. In 1970 women held 46.1 percent of the GS-1 through GS-6 positions of the General Schedule and equivalent grades or, phrased another way, 76.7 percent of all women working for the federal government worked in the six lowest grade groups. In the GS supergrades and their equivalents in other pay systems, less than one-half of 1 percent of the positions were held by women. At the middle management levels 21.7 percent of grade groups 7 through 12 were filled by women, and only 1.1 percent of grade groups 13 and above (including the supergrades) were women. Ten of the 23 departments and agencies accounting for 95 percent of federal employees in 1971 had less than 36.4 percent women employed—or a level which corresponds to women's share of the national labor force.

A remaining question concerning the status of women and minority groups in public administration is: How much of their poor pay and lack of representation at the higher levels is due to discrimination? After all, as some have argued, other factors beyond the personnel system's control are surely to blame and, besides, governments are likely to be fairer to women and minority groups than private industry. In a sophisticated regression analysis of its own personnel practices by the U.S. Department of Labor (which is relatively outstanding in terms of according opportunities to persons from deprived groups), researchers concluded that "Minority and female employees in the department do earn less than all employees, and a major portion of this salary gap exists just because of their race or sex." Moreover, in a comparative analysis of public and private personnel practices, Harry Kranz, an official in the Department of Labor, found that

> federal minority employment ratios trail private employment minority ratios in 20 states; private employment of minorities exceeds their population ratios in 20 states; and in only 24 states do federal employment ratios exceed minority employment percentages in both the population and private enterprise. Thus, in roughly half the states, minorities do poorly in the federal government, compared to their population ratios or private employment.[61]

In sum, if the field of public personnel administration in the United States accepts the notion that it should lead the way in the hiring and promoting of persons from disadvantaged groups, then it has a long way to go. Blacks, Latinos, native Americans, Asian-Americans, and women are excluded from the positions that matter in public administration.

BLUE-COLLAR BUREAUCRATS:
THE CHALLENGE OF PUBLIC UNIONISM

The unionization of public employees is a relatively new, rapidly developing, and occasionally discomfiting phenomenon in public administration. Of the less than 3 million civilian employees in the federal work force, more than 1.2 million (or 53 percent of the nonpostal workforce) are represented by 78 unions or very similar organizations.[62] The major unions

61. Harry Kranz, "How Representative is the Public Service?" *Public Personnel Management* 2 (July–August 1973): 249.

62. The following data on the size of the public sector union movement are drawn from Eugene C. Hagburg and Marvin J. Levine, *Labor Relations: An Integrated Perspective* (St. Paul: West Publishing, 1978), pp. 176–177 and 133–138, and James W. Singer, "The Limited Power of Federal Worker Unions," *National Journal*, 10 (September 30, 1978), pp. 1547–1551.

of federal workers are the American Federation of Government Employees (AFGE), with 266,000 members in 1978 and which is an affiliate of the American Federation of Labor-Congress of Industrial Organizations (AFL–CIO); the National Federation of Federal Employees (NFFE), which is independent of the AFL–CIO and boasts a membership of more than 34,500; and the National Treasury Employees Union (NTEU), with 63,000 members, and the National Association of Government Employees (NAGE), both of which are independent. Significantly, these and other unions in the federal sector represent and negotiate for far greater numbers of employees than their membership rosters indicate; only about 30 to 35 percent of the 1.2 million workers represented actually are union members. The AFGE, for example, represents nearly 680,000 federal workers; NFFE bargains for more than 133,000; NTEU speaks for nearly 93,000; and NAGE represents more than 81,000. Moreover, there are unions representing public employees (both state and local as well as federal ones), but whose members are drawn mostly from the private sector; for example, about one-third of the AFL–CIO's Service Employees' International Union's membership is public workers. It also should be noted that the nation's 600,000 postal employees are organized under the unique guidelines of the Postal Reorganization Act of 1970 and are not directly affected by other federal policies.

The major associations and unions of state and local government employees are the American Federation of State, County, and Municipal Employees (AFSCME) with more than 750,000 members in 1975; the American Federation of Teachers (AFT) with 475,000 members; the recently militant National Education Association (NEA) with 1.8 million teachers in its ranks; and the International Association of Fire Fighters (IAFF) with 175,000 members. Both the AFSCME (now the sixth largest union in the country) and the AFT tripled their membership rosters between 1964 and 1976. Although membership in federal unions declined in the 1970s, Big Labor sees its real growth opportunities for the future in public employment. In fact, organized labor's share of employees in the private sector has declined sharply in recent years while its share of public employees, overall, has jumped dramatically, especially at the state and local levels, where more than half of all government employees are organized.

Although proportionately more federal workers (roughly 50 percent) belong to unions than state and local workers, proportionately more government workers (approximately 75 percent) work for state and local governments. Although union membership (excluding teachers) does not exceed more than a third of the state and local employees in any one state, state and local governments nevertheless are the fields worth tilling insofar as organized labor is concerned. If we include the one million state and local government workers who belonged to professional associations (again excluding teachers) that bargain on behalf of employees (but that technically are not considered unions), the number of "unionized" public workers amounts to 20 percent of all the people who work for state and local governments. When teachers are included in the calculations we find that 56 percent of the nation's full-time local employees and nearly 21 percent of the nation's state employees were organized in 1974. The most heavily organized government workers nationally at the state and local levels are fire fighters, with nearly 77 percent of their members organized; second are teachers with almost 70 percent; and third are police with almost 56 percent.

Efforts to organize public employees are not new, and early attempts at organizing go back to the 1830s. In fact, the National Education Association was founded in 1857, roughly thirty years before the birth of the American Federation of Labor. And in the 1800s public employees had good reason to organize. Police and fire fighters, for example, who are among the most heavily unionized public employees today, traditionally have tolerated among the worst working conditions. In 1907 the New York Health Department condemned thirty of the city's eighty-five police stations as uninhabitable, and the police worked from seventy-three to ninety-eight hours a week. Fire fighters, who commonly were paid low salaries, worked twenty-one hours *a day* and had only one day off in eight.[63] Despite such conditions, there was considerable resistance to the unionization of public employees, mostly for ideological reasons, but also for economic ones. As merit systems developed in state and local governments, job security became more assured and working conditions did improve. There were (and are) also a spate of state and local laws forbidding or discouraging any kind of union activity by government workers (the constitutionality of which are at least questionable). White-collar workers, as a class, had never really identified with unionization and, finally, there was a considerable weight of public opinion against the notion of government workers being allowed to disrupt vital public services by resorting to the strike.

Securing the right to collective bargaining

Although federal employees had secured the right to organize in 1912 with the passage of the Lloyd–La Follette Act, the rights to negotiate collectively and to strike were resisted until the 1960s, and the initial indications that attitudes were shifting on these issues came not from Wash-

---

63. Hugh O'Neill, "The Growth of Municipal Employee Unions", in *Unionization of Municipal Employees*, Robert H. Connery and William V. Farr, eds. (New York: Academy of Political Science, 1970), p. 4.

ington but from the state and local governments. In 1959 Wisconsin passed the first law requiring its local governments to bargain collectively and by 1971 twenty-one states had similar statutes. In 1974 thirty-five states had laws on collective bargaining for their employees, and only seven states prohibited strikes by their workers. A special study of local governments conducted during the same year by the U.S. Census Bureau, however, found that only 15 percent of the country's eighty thousand local governments had any kind of labor relations policy that addressed organized public employees.[64]

State and local governments are only beginning to approach sophistication in their collective bargaining with organized employees. Generally, state and local policies on government negotiations with organized employees are of two types. The *collective bargaining* approach permits decisions on salaries, hours, and working conditions to be made jointly between employee and employer representatives. The *meet-and-confer* tack says only that both sides must meet and confer over these issues, but that management has the final decision. Judging by their written policies, the great majority of states and localities prefer the collective bargaining approach.

State and local governments are becoming increasingly innovative in bargaining with their employees. Englewood, Colorado, for example, has passed a city ordinance that stipulates that an impartial fact-finders' recommendation will be put on the ballot with the best offer of the union and management alongside it; then Englewood lets the voters decide the issues. Sam Zagoria refers to the increasing use of "goldfish-bowl bargaining," noting that the public is being brought increasingly into the negotiation process, a process that has traditionally, particularly in the private sector, gone on behind closed doors. In this way the public's right to know is protected, and the bargaining is opened up at a time when the public's knowledge can affect the outcome of the negotiation process. Goldfish-bowl bargaining is now a fact of public life in the state of Florida; Kansas City, Missouri; San Rafael, Walnut Creek and Sacramento County, all in California; Fairfax County, Virginia; and Sioux City, Iowa.[65]

Federal activity in the field of collective bargaining is marked by President Kennedy's Executive Order 10988 of 1962. The order stated that certain conditions of employment could be bargained for collectively between agency managements and employees; wages, hours, and fringe benefits, however, were excluded because these topics were subject to

64. U.S. Department of Commerce, Bureau of Census, *Labor Management Relations in State and Local Governments, 1974,* Special Studies No. 75 (Washington, D.C.: U.S. Government Printing Office, February 1976), p. 9.

65. Sam Zagoria, "Attitudes Harden in Governmental Labor Relations," *ASPA News and Views* 26 (December 1976): 1, 21, and 22.

regulations of the various agencies and the Civil Service Commission. Employee representatives found these limitations restrictive, and, in 1969, President Richard Nixon issued Executive Order 11491 in response to growing discontent. This order attempted to rectify a plethora of negotiating problems that had emerged since 1962: multiple labor representatives competing to bargain with management, the absence of third-party machinery, and the abuse of power by some agency heads in determining bargaining units, exclusive agents, and unfair employment practices. These latter decision-making areas were transferred from the agency heads to the Assistant Secretary of Labor for Labor-Management Relations, and appeals from his decisions could be made to the Federal Labor Relations Council, a board comprised of the chairman of the Civil Service Commission, the Secretary of Labor, and a representative of the Office of the President. A Federal Service Impasse Panel also was created by the order, empowered to resolve bargaining impasses.

Within a few months of the issuance of Executive Order 11491 the first major strike by federal employees occurred. In March 1970 about two hundred thousand postal workers staged an unprecedented walkout. For the first time federal representatives bargained on salaries (subsequently ratified by Congress), and later Congress legislated the right of postal employees to bargain collectively for wages. This incident, in the eyes of many observers, rendered Executive Order 11491 obsolete, and as a result Executive Order 11616 appeared in 1971, amending minor portions of the previous order. Collective negotiations on salaries and fringe benefits remained off limits, however, and labor representatives did not consider Executive Order 11616 to be a substantial improvement. In 1978, President Carter's Reorganization Plan No. 2 created the Federal Labor Relations Authority as an independent agency. The new authority (whose functions were enacted into law later in 1978 with the passage of the Civil Service Reform Act) took over the responsibilities of the Federal Labor Relations Council, and its creation represented an attempt to clarify the role of organized labor in government. As formalized by the Civil Service Reform Act, federal employees had the right to join unions, but strikes and slowdowns were prohibited. Federal agencies which issue government-wide directives that affect all federal employees now must consult with labor representatives before major directives are issued.

Collective bargaining: The record in dollars

The basic dilemma of collective bargaining in the public sector is the fact that, unlike the private sector, neither side is bargaining with its own money. Public labor is demanding tax monies that may or may not be in the public till, and public management is negotiating with tax money that likewise may not be in the public till. The person who pays is the taxpayer. With this reality in mind it is not too surprising that public laborers have made considerable financial gains in their negotiations with public management. Currently personnel costs account from 50 percent to 80 percent of a typical city budget, and much of this proportion stems from the gains that workers have made in collective bargaining. From 1962 to 1967 the number of city employees grew by only 19 percent while municipal payrolls burgeoned by 46 percent; major gainers during this period were the heavily unionized employees. Between 1960 and 1968 the average salary of schoolteachers increased by almost 66 percent. The pay of police and fire fighters in cities with more than one hundred thousand people went up by 38 percent in the five years between 1964 and 1968.[66] Sterling D. Spero and John M. Capozzola, noting these kinds of salary boosts, conclude that "collective bargaining undoubtedly was a significant cause in the rise in per pupil costs in New York City from slightly over $500 in 1960 to more than $1,500 in 1970".[67]

A major negotiating area between public employers and employees is that of pensions. In the case of police department, for example, the national tendency has been to permit retirement at half-pay after twenty years service. Such arrangements, of course, aggravate urban financial problems. New York City probably is the most outstanding example of what a pension plan can do to urban finances. In the city transit workers, police, fire fighters and other workers are allowed early retirement with generous benefits. Spero and Capozzola quote "the pension specialist" of the American Federation of State, County, and Municipal Employees to the effect that its "members are just beginning to realize that pensions can be negotiated." When queried where the money for higher pensions is coming from, the pension specialist for AFSCME replied, "That's government's problem. Just because there is a pinch for money, it's no excuse to make the employees do without." [68]

Collective bargaining has given public employees a relatively good deal in comparison with workers in the private sector, and evidence of this is provided by a 1971 study conducted by the U.S. Bureau of Labor Statistics in twenty-two large and middle-sized representative cities. In a report that covered the eleven largest cities (Atlanta, Boston, Buffalo, Chicago, Houston, Kansas City, Los Angeles, New Orleans, Newark, New York, and Philadelphia), it was found that in nine of them government workers in clerical jobs were paid more than their counterparts in both private industry and in federal government. Most of these cities also

66. Sterling Spero and John M. Capozzola, *The Urban Community and Its Unionized Bureaucracy* (New York: Dunellen, 1973), p. 218.

67. *Ibid.*, p. 223.

68. *Ibid.*, p. 219.

showed higher pay scales for computer-related jobs and janitorial jobs. Employees in skilled and semi-skilled blue-collar jobs earned more than their counterparts in industry, mainly because their jobs were steadier than those in the private sphere.[69] The Bureau of Labor Statistics did not address the issue of whether or not collective bargaining was a reason behind these kinds of increases relative to the private sector, but a study by the Institute of Labor Relations of twelve Michigan school districts concluded that collective bargaining appeared to have given teachers 10 percent to 20 percent more in wage increases than unilateral school board action would have furnished.[70]

The public strike: The public record

Because of the potential fiscal impact that collective bargaining can have on state and local governments, states and cities are often reluctant to "come across" to union demands. The result of such reluctance can be, and occasionally is, a strike. It used to be that sanitation workers were the most frequent public employees to walk picket lines, but more recently it has been teachers who are more inclined to strike. In 1973 there were 117 teacher strikes involving 51,400 workers; in the following year the number soared to 133 strikes of teachers involving 60,100 people. In 1974 there were 384 strikes by public employees. Of these, 348 occurred at the local level, thirty-four at the state level, and two at the national level; 106,700 workers were involved and 1,404,200 days lay idle during the year. Compare these figures with 1956, when there were only twenty-seven such strikes involving only 3,460 people and 11,100 days idle.[71] Table 10–3 indicates the types of work stoppages in government by the issues involved. It is clear from the table that wages are the paramount issue in strikes of public employees, followed closely by supplementary benefits such as pensions.

Strikes are realities and are with us, regardless of whether or not there are laws permitting or prohibiting them in the public sector; nonetheless, the emotional issue of the public employees' right to strike runs

69. Stephen H. Perloff, "Comparing Municipal Salaries with Industry and Federal Pay," *Monthly Labor Review* 94 (October 1971): 46–50 and Spero and Capozolla, *op. cit.*, pp. 219–220.

70. Charles N. Rehmus and Evan Wilner, *The Economic Results of Teacher Bargaining: Michigan's First Two Years* (Ann Arbor, Mich.: Institute of Labor and Industrial Relations, 1958).

71. U.S. Department of Labor, Bureau of Labor Statistics, *Analysis of Work Stoppages, 1973* (Washington, D.C.: U.S. Government Printing Office, 1975), p. 31: *Analysis of Work Stoppages, 1974* (Washington, D.C.: U.S. Government Printing Office, 1976), pp. 5–6; *Handbook of Labor Statistics* (Washington, D.C.: U.S. Government Printing Office, 1975), p. 407.

TABLE 10–3. Types of Work Stoppages in Government by Issue

Item	1973			1974		
	Number of stop-pages	Workers involved	Days idle	Number of stop-pages	Workers involved	Days idle
Total	387	196.4	2303.9	384	160.7	1404.2
Issue:						
Wages	235	159.0	2005.1	255	131.3	1207.9
Supplementary benefits	4	.6	2.7	5	1.2	2.6
Wage adjustments	5	.4	2.4	10	1.6	5.3
Hours of work	3	.4	1.7	3	.7	3.9
Other contractual matters	5	1.8	23.7	7	1.0	2.4
Union organization & security	42	10.7	123.7	41	5.8	56.1
Job security	26	13.1	91.9	25	10.2	92.2
Plant administration	52	8.2	37.8	33	8.1	22.7
Other working conditions	7	1.0	6.9	3	.4	10.2
Interunion or intraunion matters	4	.9	7.5	—	—	—
Not reported	4	.4	.6	2	.3	.8

Source: U.S. Department of Labor, Bureau of Labor Statistics, *Work Stoppages in Government, 1974* (Washington, D.C.: Government Printing Office, 1976) p. 6.

deep. One viewpoint holds that a strike by public employees amounts to an act of insurrection because such strikes are directed against the people themselves; the opposing view contends that the right of government workers to strike is a basic freedom protected under the Constitution. To deny public employees a right granted to workers in private corporations is to treat public personnel as second-class citizens. The courts thus far have held that there is no constitutional right of public workers to strike, but neither has the judiciary prohibited the enactment of laws permitting government employees to strike.

Unions versus "merit": The basic differences

The future of collective bargaining, unionization, and the right to strike bode ill for the traditional merit standards of the civil service personnel system. At root, there are two differences between the "collective system" and the "civil service system." One difference concerns the notion of *sovereignty*. The civil service system holds that a public position is a privilege, not a right, and that each public servant is obliged to uphold the public trust accorded to him or her by a paternalistic government. Conversely, the collective system holds that employees are on an equal footing with employers, and that they have a right to use their collective powers as a means of improving their conditions of employment. The civil service system sees this contention as a threat to the sovereignty of the state. At the same time the collective system views the traditions of the civil service as redolent of worker exploitation.

The second difference concerns the concept of individualism. The American civil service system long has valued the ideal that the individual worker be judged for a position on the basis of his or her unique merits for performing the duties of a particular job; the collective system argues that the identity of the individual should be absorbed in a collective effort to better the conditions of all workers. Hence, the relations of the individual with his or her government employer are replaced by a new set of relations that exists between the government employer and a collective "class" of employees. Among the conflicts that result from these fundamental differences between the two systems over sovereignty and individualism are these: disputes over employee participation and rights (equal treatment versus union shop); recruitment (competitive tests versus union membership); promotion (performance versus seniority); position classification and pay (objective analysis versus negotiation); working conditions (determination by legislatures and managements versus settlement by negotiations); and grievances (determination by civil service commissioners versus union representation to third party arbitrators).

REFORMING CIVIL SERVICE REFORM:
THE CHALLENGE OF MANAGERIAL CONTROL

The latest challenge to public personnel administration is President Carter's far-reaching and radical reform of the federal personnel system, as expressed in the Civil Service Reform Act of 1978. Without doubt, part of the impetus for reform derived from the abuses of the civil service system suffered under President Richard M. Nixon in the early 1970s. Among the more notorious examples of these abuses was the so-called Malek Manual, named after Fred Malek, a major official in the Office of Management and Budget who encouraged the appointing of high-level federal executives on the basis of partisan politics.[72] With the prestige of the federal civil service at a particularly low ebb when President Carter assumed office, Carter placed reform of the federal personnel system high on his list of national priorities, remarking in his 1978 State of the Union address that he considered the reform of the civil service "to be absolutely

---

72. The "Malek Manual" is published in *The Bureaucrat* 4 (January 1976): 429–508. One reviewer has said it "stands as the best guide to how the federal civil service works as well as a monument to a concerted attempt to achieve political control over large sections of the federal bureaucracy." See: H. Brinton Milward, "Politics, Personnel and Public Policy," *Public Administration Review* 38 (July–August, 1978): 395.

vital," and that it was his intention to form "a government that is efficient, open, and truly worthy of our people's understanding and respect." [73] To implement these goals, the president inaugurated two rather bold initiatives. One was a Reorganization Plan that assigned the functions performed by the U.S. Civil Service Commission to two separate agencies, the Merit Systems Protection Board and the Office of Personnel Management. The effect of this reassignment was the abolition of the Civil Service Commission. The second initiative was the Civil Service Reform Bill. Proposed early on in President Carter's administration, the bill was designed, in the president's words, to "restore the merit principle to a system which has grown into a bureaucratic maze. It will provide greater management flexibility and better rewards for better performance without compromising job security." [74]

These two initiatives embodied a number of basic reforms of the national civil service system. One was the total overhaul of the appeals system through which federal employees could appeal dismissals or demotions. Under the former law an employee had three rather ambiguous bodies to which he or she could appeal an adverse decision by his or her supervisors: the Federal Employee Appeals Authority; the Appeals Review Board; and the Civil Service Commissioners. Under President Carter's reforms these bodies were abolished and replaced, first, by converting the Civil Service Commission to the Merit Systems Protection Board, which now has both appellate and investigatory responsibilities, and, second, by establishing an Office of Personnel Management for personnel policy making. The Merit Systems Protection Board was established as an independent agency that also had an appeals function. In addition to the Board, an Office of Special Council appointed by the president was created and given responsibilities for investigations and prosecutions within the civil service.

An Office of Personnel Management was also created to act as the president's major agent for managing the federal work force; it is the policy-making office for the federal civil service. Of particular note is the fact that the Office of Personnel Management may delegate authority to separate on-line agencies (*e.g.,* the Department of Energy), a function that had been the exclusive prerogative of the Civil Service Commission. In other words, the central managements of individual agencies have more control over certain basic personnel functions such as recruitment and demotion than they had in the past. This is a very basic reform, and one which could have far-reaching implications for federal personnel practices.

73. Jimmy Carter, State of the Union Message, January 19, 1978.
74. *Ibid.*

Perhaps the most intriguing aspect of the Civil Service Reform Act is the fact that a Senior Executive Service was established. This represents an adoption of the professional values of the present personnel period in that "grade and rank for both career and non-career executives would be assigned to persons rather than to positions." [75] Not only is this development representative of the present professional period of public personnel administration, but it also signifies a return to the values of the administrative management period by adopting the notions expressed by the second Hoover Commission; as we noted, the second Hoover Commission represented an attempt to revitalize the faltering politics/administration dichotomy by suggesting the appointment of a Senior Civil Service in the European tradition.

Among the more controversial proposals made by President Carter was the eventual abolition of veterans' preference. Veterans' preference, the policy that gives veterans a five- to ten-point edge on federal employment tests, has led to a disproportionate representation of veterans in the federal work force. To quote the director of the Office of Personnel Management,

> though veterans are 25 percent of the national labor force, they fill 50 percent of all federal jobs. Even more significant, 65 percent of the top jobs in the federal government are filled by veterans. In 1976, of competitors for the Professional and Administrative Careers Examination, 19 percent of those scoring in an eligible range were veterans but 29 percent of those hired were veterans.[76]

President Carter, himself a veteran, came out against the traditional veterans' preference, but it nonetheless was retained by Congress.

An effort was also made to add incentives for productivity in the federal work force, and clearly incentives are needed. To quote again the director of the Office of Personnel Management, "The current system provides few incentives for managers to manage or for employees to perform. . . . For example in FY 1977, while one-half million federal employees received within-grade increases 700 were denied them." The director went on to note that "the compensation system for senior federal managers is less motivational than that for lower ranking employees. . . . a GS-15, step 10, currently receives the same salary as a GS-18 executive, despite considerably less responsibility." [77]

In brief, problems such as the traditional veterans' preference and the lack of incentives for superior service in the federal service led Presi-

75. Alan K. Campbell, "Civil Service Reform: A New Commitment," *Public Administration Review* 38 (March–April 1978): 101.

76. *Ibid.*, p. 102.

77. *Ibid.*, p. 101.

dent Carter and Congress to enact sweeping reforms of the federal civil service system. Clearly they were needed, both for the public good and the legitimacy of government itself.

CONCLUSION: TURMOIL IN THE PUBLIC SERVICE

The problems reviewed here are complex and massive. Public personnel administration, like any other form of public administration, has large dollops of politics as part and parcel of it. The historic efforts of "good government" reformers to rid public personnel systems of "politics" have traditionally been based on the introduction of "merit principles" in the management of the public bureaucracy. Merit principles, as they normally have been understood, are now under considerable attack. The efforts to include more minorities and women in government, the attempts to expand freedom of political expression for government employees, the drive to bring more professionals into government (who often do not identify with the public service in the same sense that traditional personnel specialists have related to it), the reality of strikes, unionism, and collective bargaining, and the drive to overhaul the civil service all lead one to wonder what "merit" in public personnel administration really means.

SUPPLEMENTAL BIBLIOGRAPHY

American Assembly, Sixth, *The Federal Government Service* (2nd ed.), ed. Wallace S. Sayre. Englewood Cliffs, N.J.: Prentice-Hall, 1965.

APPLEBY, PAUL H., *Big Democracy*. New York: Knopf, 1945.

BYERS, KENNETH T., ed., *Employee Training and Development in the Public Service*. Chicago: Public Personnel Association, 1970.

CASE, HARRY L., *Personnel Policy in a Public Agency: The TVA Experience*. New York: Harper & Row, 1955.

DIMOCK, MARSHALL E., *Administrative Vitality*. New York: Harper & Row, 1959.

DIMOCK, MARSHALL E., and GLADYS O. DIMOCK, *Public Administration* (4th ed.), New York: Holt, Rinehart & Winston, 1969.

DONOVAN, J. J., ed., *Recruitment and Selection in the Public Service*. Chicago: Public Personnel Association, 1968.

GRAVES, W. BROOKE, *Federalism and Public Employment*. Washington, D.C.: Federal Professional Association, 1965.

HARVEY, DONALD R., *The Civil Service Commission*. New York: Praeger, 1970.

International City Management Association, *Municipal Personnel Administration* (6th ed.), Washington, D.C., 1960.

JONES, CHARLES O., "Reevaluating the Hatch Act: A Report on the Commission on Political Activity of Government Personnel," *Public Administration Review*, 29 (May–June, 1969), 249–54.

MAINZER, LEWIS C., *Political Bureaucracy*. Glencoe, Ill.: Scott, Foresman, 1973.

PEGNETTER, RICHARD, *Public Employment Bibliography*. Ithaca, N.Y.: New York State School of Industrial and Labor Relations, Cornell University, 1971.

STAHL, O. GLENN, *The Personnel Job of Government Managers*. Chicago: Public Personnel Association, 1971.

United Nations, Public Administration Branch, *Handbook of Training in the Public Service*. New York, 1966.

U.S. Commission on Civil Rights, *For All the People—By All the People: A Report on Equal Opportunity in State and Local Government Employment*. Washington, D.C., 1969.

VAN RIPER, PAUL P., *History of the United States Civil Service*. New York: Harper & Row, 1958.

PUBLIC AFFAIRS

approaches to public affairs

chapter 11

In this concluding section of the book, we shall consider public affairs, a new dimension of public administration that continues to develop rapidly. Public affairs deals with the substantive issues of public problems. We shall discuss three such problems: urban governance, intergovernmental relations, and growth management. There are many others of equal worth—indeed, Dwight Waldo has noted more than a dozen "areas of activity" in the "external environment of public administration." [1] The selection of the three areas of public affairs that are included in this section (urbanism, federalism, and energy and the environment) are conceptually broad-ranging and indicate the emerging locus of public administration that was discussed in Chapter 2.

Chapter 11 introduces our discussion of public affairs with a review of the literature of public policy. *Public policy* is an amorphous and developing field that, like organization theory, spans political science, economics, sociology, psychology, business administration, social psychology, and anthropology, as well as public administration. The field of public policy analysis can be bisected into two broad thrusts. The first is the

1. Dwight Waldo, "Developments in Public Administration," *Annals of the Academy of Political and Social Science* 404 (November 1972): 217–254.

attempt to analyze the *process* of public policy making; it endeavors to be descriptive rather than prescriptive in tone. In terms of models of public policy, the elite/mass, group, systems, and institutionalist models would fall crudely under the rubric of processually-oriented, descriptive literature on public policy making.

The second basic thrust is of somewhat more use to public administrators. It attempts to analyze the *outputs* and *effects* of public policy and is more prescriptive than descriptive. A related tangent is the effort to prescribe ways to improve the content of public policy by improving the way public policy is made. Using this schemata the incremental and rational (or political economy) models of public policy making would represent this thrust.

In reviewing briefly both the processual and the output-oriented thrusts of public policy analysis, our purpose is simply that: to review. One ought to be aware of public policy analysis as a literature. With the possible exception of the political economy and public choice emphasis, it is a broad field whose principal utility is one of clarification about how the public policy-making process works.

MODELS OF PUBLIC POLICY MAKING AS A PROCESS

The elite/mass model

Of the four emphases we shall consider under this heading (elitism, groups, systems, and institutions), the emphasis represented by the elite/ mass model may be the most germane to public administrators. Increasingly, public administrators appear to be perceived less as "servants of the people" and more as "the establishment." In cursory form the elite/mass model contends that a policy-making/policy-executing elite is able to act in an environment characterized by apathy and information distortion and thereby govern a largely passive mass. Policy flows downward from the elite to the mass. Society is divided according to those who have power and those who do not. Elites share common values that differentiate them from the mass, and prevailing public policies reflect elite values, which may be summed up as: preserve the status quo. Finally, elites have higher incomes, more education, and more status than the mass. Perhaps the classic expression of elite theory can be found in C. Wright Mills's *The Power Elite.*[2]

A diagrammatic version of elite theory that relates it to public administration is found in Figure 11–1.

2. C. Wright Mills, *The Power Elite* (New York: Oxford University Press, 1956).

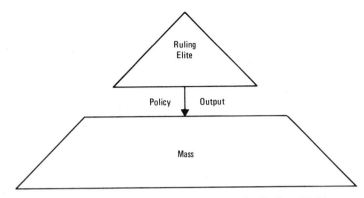

FIGURE 11–1. The Elite/Mass Model of Public Policy Making

The group model

A second model of public policy is the group model. In these days of illegal campaign contributions, powerful vested interests, and the "military-industrial complex," the notion of pressure groups and lobbies also has relevance. Another way of describing the group model is the "hydraulic thesis," in which the polity is conceived of as being a system of forces and pressures acting and reacting to one another in the formulation of public policy. An exemplary work that represents the group model is Arthur F. Bentley's *The Process of Government.*[3]

Normally, the group model is associated with the legislature rather than the bureaucracy, but it also has long been recognized by scholars that the "neutral" executive branch of government is buffeted by pressure groups, too. The numerous studies by political scientists on federal regulatory agencies, for example, all point to the same conclusions: that the agency ultimately is "captured" by the group that it is meant to regulate, and its administrators grow increasingly unable to distinguish between policies that are beneficial to the interests of the public and policies that are beneficial to the interests of the groups being regulated. What is good for the group is good for the nation, in the eyes of the regulators. (An excellent overview of this phenomenon is provided by Louis M. Kohlmeier's *The Regulators,*[4] and a superb theoretical explanation of why it works the way it does can be found in Murray Edelman's *The Symbolic Uses of Politics.*[5]) Figure 11–2 illustrates the group model.

3. Arthur F. Bentley, *The Process of Government* (Bloomington, Indiana: Principia Press, 1949). First published in 1908.
4. Louis M. Kohlmeier, *The Regulators: Watchdog Agencies and the Public Interest* (New York: Harper & Row), 1969.
5. Murray Edelman, *The Symbolic Uses of Politics* (Urbana, Ill.: University of Illinois Press), 1964.

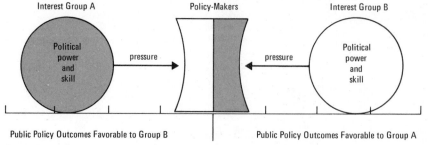

Political power and skill   pressure   pressure   Political power and skill

Public Policy Outcomes Favorable to Group B | Public Policy Outcomes Favorable to Group A

FIGURE 11–2. The Group Model of Public Policy Making: I

Bureaucracies, particularly in regulatory agencies, seldom encounter the countervailing pressures illustrated in Figure 11–2. In other words, Interest Group A might be the drug manufacturers, the Policy Makers might be the Food and Drug Administration, and Interest Group B might be the unorganized public. This situation might be diagrammed more accurately as in Figure 11–3.

The systems model

A third emphasis in the processual public-policy literature is the systems model. The systems model relies on concepts of information theory (*e.g.*, feedback, input, output) and conceives of the process as being essentially cyclical. The systems model is concerned with such questions as: What are the significant variables and patterns in the public policy-making system? What constitutes the "black box" of the actual policy-making process? What are the inputs, "withinputs," outputs, and feedback of the process? A representative author of this literary stream would be David

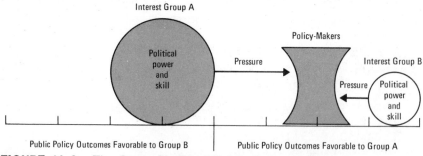

Interest Group A

Political power and skill   Pressure   Policy-Makers   Interest Group B   Pressure / Political power and skill

Public Policy Outcomes Favorable to Group B | Public Policy Outcomes Favorable to Group A

FIGURE 11–3. The Group Model of Public Policy Making: II

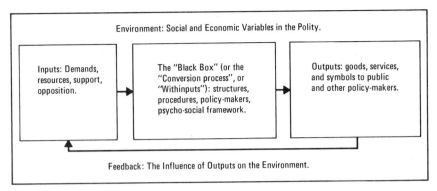

FIGURE 11-4. The Systems Model of Public Policy Making

Easton, particularly in his *The Political System*.[6] The emphasis is diagrammed in Figure 11-4.

The institutionalist/neo-institutionalist model

Finally, we include in the public-policy-making-as-a-process literature the traditional institutionalist model. The institutionalist model focuses on the organization chart of government; it describes the arrangements and official duties of bureaus and departments, but customarily it has ignored the linkages between them. Historically, constitutional provisions, administrative and common law, and similar legalities were the objects of greatest interest; the connections between a department and the public policy emanating from it were of scant concern. Carl J. Friedrich's *Constitutional Government and Democracy* is a representative work.[7] Illustratively, an institutionalist model would look like the diagram in Figure 11-5.

With the onrush of the "behavioral revolution" in political science, institutional studies of the policy process were swept aside in favor of studies that relied more heavily on the group, systems, and elite/mass models, in about that order of emphasis. Yet the institutionalist model had a use, and it may experience a resurgence of favor in the future. The "new federalism," revenue sharing, and executive reorganization plans, among the other actual and potential rearrangements of the government bureaucracy, necessitate a renewed understanding of how the structure of government works before the public policy-making process can be analyzed fully.

6. David Easton, *The Political System* (New York: Alfred A. Knopf, 1953).

7. Carl J. Friedrich, *Constitutional Government and Democracy* (Boston: Little, Brown, 1941).

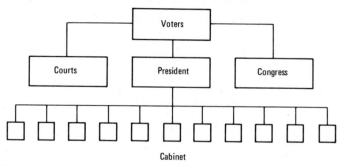

Cabinet

FIGURE 11–5. The Institutionalist Model of Public Policy Making

However, a recent stream of public policy literature has surfaced that might best be described as neoinstitutionalism, and it is on a considerably more sophisticated analytical plane. Theodore J. Lowi, Randall B. Ripley, Robert Salisbury and John Heinz, and Dean Schooler, Jr., number among the major contributors, and they attempt to categorize public policies according to policy-making subsystems.[8] For example, Lowi classifies policies by four "arenas of power": redistributive, distributive, constituent, and regulative. In a redistributive arena of power, for instance, power is *redistributed* throughout the polity on a fundamental scale. Redistributive policies tend to be highly ideological and emotionally charged for particular groups, involving a fight between "haves" and "have-nots" but having low partisan visibility. Usually they are centered in the bureaucracy. Lowi, in fact, considers redistributive policies to be concerned with "not use of property but property itself, not equal treatment but equal possession, not behavior but being," and believes, because of the secrecy enshrouding the redistributive policy process, that the policy process which takes place primarily in the government bureaucracy has received the least study by social scientists.[9] Thus, neoinstitutionalism is concerned

8. See, for example, Theodore J. Lowi, "Decision-Making versus Policy-Making: Towards an Antidote for Technocracy," *Public Administration Review* 30 (May–June 1970): 134–139; Randall B. Ripley, "Introduction: The Politics of Public Policy," *Public Policies and their Politics: An Introduction to the Techniques of Government Control*, Randall B. Ripley, ed. (New York: Norton, 1966), pp. i–xv; Robert Salisbury and John Heinz, "A Theory of Policy Analysis and Some Preliminary Applications," *Policy Analysis in Political Science*, Ira Sharkansky, ed. (Chicago: Markham, 1970), pp. 39–60; Dean Schooler, Jr., *Science, Scientists, and Public Policy* (New York: Free Press, 1971).

9. Theodore J. Lowi, "American Business, Public Policy, Case Studies, and Political Science," *World Politics* 16 (July 1964): 691. But see also: Theodore J. Lowi, "Population Policies and the American Political System," *Political Science and Population Studies*, Richard L. Clinton, William S. Flash, and R. Kenneth Godwin, eds. (Lexington, Mass.: D. C. Heath, 1972), pp. 25–53.

chiefly with political institutions, but with an eye toward generating theoretical predictions about how policy types relate to the branches of government and the polity generally.

MODELS OF PUBLIC POLICY MAKING AS AN OUTPUT

Our second major thrust of public policy analysis tends to stress the policy itself. In this stream analysts appear to be more normative and prescriptive, and less "value-free" and descriptive. They are more concerned with how to improve the content of public policies themselves and how to improve the ways in which public policies are made, with the objective of forming better policies. There are essentially only two models, incrementalism and rationalism. The former attempts to describe how the public policy-making process "really works" and what is good or bad about it; the latter explains how the process of incrementalism could or should work and offers suggestions toward this end. Thus, the incrementalist and rationalist models really are two poles of the same continuum; that is, they are both concerned with the "black box" of policy making.

The output-oriented literature of public policy analysis has been of more significance to public administration than has the processually oriented literature, which largely has been favored by political scientists. For this reason, we shall spend a bit more time on the incrementalist and rationalist models, especially the latter. Under the rationalist model we also shall consider briefly the developing fields of public choice, political economy, and technology assessment.

The incrementalist model

In many ways, the incrementalist model of public policy already has been considered in Section Two on organization theory. "Satisficing," organizational "drift," "bounded rationality," and "limited cognition," among other terms of the literature of model synthesis in organization theory, reflect the basic idea of the incrementalist paradigm.

The various writings of Charles E. Lindblom are associated most closely with incrementalism and, in fact, it was he who is as responsible as anyone for the notion's name, *disjointed incrementalism*, as a description of the policy-making process.[10] *Disjointed*, in this context, means that analysis and evaluation of conditions and alternative responses to perceived conditions occur throughout society, while *incrementalism* means that only a limited selection of policy alternatives are provided to policy makers, and

10. Charles E. Lindblom, *The Policy Making Process* (Englewood Cliffs, N.J.: Prentice-Hall, 1968).

that each one of these alternatives represents only an infinitesimal change in the status quo. Before Lindblom made the incrementalist idea more academically legitimate (and pompous) by dubbing it "disjointed incrementalism," he called the concept "muddling through." [11] Muddling through, as a term, not only is a more colorful description of the policy-making process, but is also clearer and self-explanatory.

Basically, the incrementalist model posits a conservative tendency in administrative decision making; new public policies are seen as being variations on the past. The public policy maker is perceived as a person who does not have the brains, time, and money to fashion truly different policies; he accepts the policies of the past as satisficing and legitimate. There are also certain "sunk costs" in existing policies that probably would be impossible to retrieve if a radically new course were taken, and this discourages innovative action from the standpoint of political economy. And because social goals are devilishly difficult to operationalize, an incremental approach is certainly an easier row to hoe than a rational, systemic approach would be. Finally, incrementalist policies are nearly always more politically expedient than are rationalist policies that necessitate fundamental redistributions of social values. As Ralph Huitt concluded in his study of political feasibility, "what is most feasible is incremental." [12] In short, there are reasons (*rational* reasons, given the nature of the political system) for the prevalence of the incrementalist model. An illustration of the incrementalist model is shown in Figure 11–6.

The rationalist model

Rationalism attempts to be the opposite of incrementalism. As an intellectual endeavor, rationalism tries to learn *all* the value preferences extant in

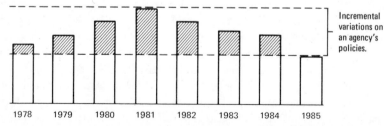

FIGURE 11–6. The Incrementalist Model of Public Policy Making

11. Charles E. Lindblom, "The Science of Muddling Through," *Public Administration Review* 19 (Spring 1959): 79–88.
12. Ralph K. Huitt, "Political Feasibility," in *Political Science and Public Policy*, Austin Ranney, ed. (Chicago: Markham, 1968), p. 274.

a society, assign each value a relative weight, discover all the policy alternatives available, know all the consequences of each alternative, calculate

Public Administration and the Policy Process

The following passage attempts to "place" the role of the public bureaucracy in the policy-making process. As it indicates, to so "place" the bureaucracy may necessitate a basic reconsideration of traditional democratic theory.

It is remarkable how unappreciated the significance of the bureaucracy is among America's political thinkers. It is evident from reading *The Federalist* that the country's most original contributors to the world's political literature did not anticipate the rise of the public bureaucracy, much less its institutional dominance in the public policy-making process, nor the fact that by the middle of the 20th century there would be more Americans earning their livelihoods by working for it than there were Americans living when the Constitution was written. Less understandably, our current generation of political thinkers . . . also have failed to appreciate the importance of the public bureaucracy, despite its awesome magnitude, its growing administrative reliance on the techniques of social science, and its financial support of their own academic research. . . .

Is there a reason behind the disregard for and disinterest in the public bureaucracy that is exhibited by the bulk of modern political thinkers? One can conjure several possibilities, including that of rampant stupidity, but . . . I shall offer only one hypothesis. It is: The bureaucracy, as a public policy-making institution in a technological society, is antithetical to the pluralist paradigm of the democratic process originally conceived by James Madison and perpetrated by most of his intellectual progeny. . . . More pointedly, the Madisonian notion that the interests of the public will be best served in a democracy by the policy of compromise emerging from the contentions of interest groups (which "represent" those "publics" affected by the policy resolution) is of dubious validity in a techno-bureaucratic state. In brief, two overwhelming factors of modern culture—technology and bureaucracy— undermine what one political scientist has described as the "hydraulic theory" of the democratic process. The hydraulic thesis constitutes the basis of the pluralist paradigm shared by mainstream political scientists, and it is apparent, given the short shrift accorded the public bureaucracy, public administration, and technology assessment by political scientists as objects of study, that few scholars interested in politics are capable of denying interest-group pluralism as an apologia for how the public interest is achieved in a democracy.

Perhaps the hydraulic thesis still "works" (*i.e.,* interest group compromises are indeed in the public interest) in legislative and adjudicative policy settings, and perhaps its "provability" in these settings accounts for why political scientists much prefer studying voting behavior, legislative committees, lobbyists, and the judicial process in contrast to "bureaucratic politics." But in order to "work," the hydraulic thesis by necessity rests on at least three implicit assumptions concerning the political process: that (1) all publics affected by a particular policy question are aware that its resolution will affect them, (2) all affected publics have a reasonable understanding of the policy question, and (3) if the affected publics are unaware of the policy question, it is only a matter of time before they find out about it and join in the policy-making fray in order to protect their interest.

These assumptions, combined with some strictly enforced rules of the game, such as freedom of the press, provided a rational foundation on which the hydraulic thesis could be constructed as an explanation of the policy-making process in a democracy—at least in the 18th century. Yet, in the 20th century, the interlaced forces of bureaucracy and technology deny these assumptions. For its part, bureaucracy denies assumptions #1 and #3. The well-documented penchant of bureaucrats for secrecy, and the mounting evidence that neither bureaucrats nor the citizenry always act on their "most rational" self-interest undercut the premises that people *know,* that people are *informed,* of what matters, and that they will act on what matters.

Technology denies assumption #2. Technology, or what is perceived by the people as being science "applied" for the rectification of their problems, is not simple. Technology is complicated, and it becomes more complicated when, as public bureaucrats are wont to do, technology is cast into the context of systems analysis in an effort to inhibit the proliferation of its socially dysfunctional side effects. Technology and its social assessment, by their very complexity, deny understanding to the people of what their problems are. Such concepts as "technocracy," "professionalism," "politics of expertise," "technipol," "systems politics," "noetic authority," and "participatory technology" represent intellectual efforts to address the enormous political problems of bureaucracy and technology not considered in the Madisonian pluralist paradigm—nor, for that matter, in the Constitution that Madison largely wrote. Yet, if democratic political processes are to be retained under the Constitution, bureaucracy and technology must be integrated into its framework, for the twin factors may be, in their essence, antithetical to democratic values.

Nicholas Henry
Public Administration Review

how the selection of any one policy will affect the remaining alternatives in terms of opportunity costs, and ultimately select that policy alternative that is the most efficient in terms of the costs and benefits of social values. Whether or not these goals can be realized, the point is that the rational model works toward their achievement, and toward the reduction of incrementalism.

Much of the rationalist model deals with the construction of public policies that assure better public policies. Yehezkel Dror (as good a representative as any of the rationalist model) calls this concern "metapolicy," that is, policy for policy-making procedures.[13] In this emphasis the rationalist model dwells on the optimal organization of the government structure that will assure undistorted information flow, the accuracy of feedback data, and the proper weighting of social variables.

Diagrammed, the rationalist model renders public policy formation into a linear flow chart, reminiscent of Operations Research, Performance Evaluation and Review Technique, Critical Path Method, and the related computer programming techniques of the systems approach and information theory. While Figure 11-7 may remind one of the systems model (Figure 11-4), the rationalist model actually deals only with the "black box" of the systems model. (So, for that matter, does Figure 11-6, the incrementalist model.) That is, the rationalist model articulates how public policy should be formed within government, or how the elements of the conversion process that change environmental inputs into environmental outputs should be arranged optimally. This is what makes the rationalist model so useful to public administration because, in one sense at least, making policy better is what the field is concerned with.

Public choice and political economy. A significant variation of the rationalist model is the literature dealing with public choice and political economy. The public choice field has been of growing importance to public administration since at least 1963, when a small collection of scholars met to discuss, in their words, "developments in the 'no-name' fields of public administration." [14] Since then, *public choice* and *political economy* are the terms most frequently used in describing this literature.

Public choice has a variety of intellectual directions. Besides the overarching emphasis on the rationalist model as a policy-making tool, public choice is concerned with the nature of public goods and services (Otto Eckstein, Robert L. Bish, and L. L. Wade and R. L. Curry, Jr.,[15]

13. Yehezkel Dror, *Public Policy Making Reexamined* (San Francisco: Chandler, 1968), p. 8.
14. Vincent Ostrom and Eleanor Ostrom, "Public Choice: A Different Approach to the Study of Public Administration," *Public Administration Review* 31 (March–April 1971): 203.
15. See Otto Eckstein, *Public Finance*, 2nd ed. (Englewood Cliffs, N.J.: Prentice-Hall, 1967); Robert L. Bish, *The Public Economy of Metropolitan Areas* (Chicago:

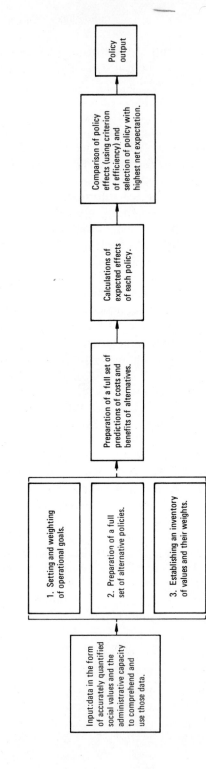

FIGURE 11-7. The Rationalist Model of Public Policy Making

would be representative of this literary emphasis), the relationships between formal decision making structures and human propensities for individual action (*e.g.*, Gordon Tullock, Anthony Downs [16]) and for collective action (*e.g.*, Mancur Olson [17]), the requisites of constitutional government and corresponding patterns of collective action (*e.g.*, James M. Buchanan and Gordon Tullock [18]), and the interstices between producers, performance, consumer interests, and the provision of public goods and services (*e.g.*, Garrett Hardin, Joseph J. Seneca [19]).

Using the concepts of political economy, we can assess public policy in new ways. Consider, for example, the problems of air pollution, the energy crisis, and the role of the automobile, which accounts for roughly 60 percent of the air pollutants in this country and almost 40 percent of its fuel consumption. Rather than passing a flatly stated law that says little more than "Thou shalt not pollute nor use too much gas," a political economist would likely turn instead to the tax structure. He or she would reason that if a particular citizen chose to buy a Cadillac rather than a Volkswagen, the general citizenry should not have to bear the common costs of the choice (*i.e.*, the extra pollutants emitted and fuel consumed by the Cadillac), but neither should citizens be denied the Cadillacs if they really want them. Thus, a special tax should be established that taxes cars according to the pollutants they emit and the energy resources they consume; the more pollutants and gas, the higher the tax. In this method, the individual citizen still can buy a Cadillac, but the costs of the purchase to the general citizenry will be offset by the special tax that the owner is forced to pay by using that tax for pollution abatement and energy research programs. Such is the nature of assessment in the public choice literature.

On a more sophisticated plane, public choice is concerned with *Pareto optimality*, a concept originally developed by the economist Vilfredo Pareto. Or, more exactly (and because optimality is supremely

---

Markham, 1971); and L. L. Wade and R. L. Curry, Jr., *A Logic of Public Policy: Aspects of Political Economy* (Belmont, Calif.: Wadsworth, 1970).

16. Gordon Tullock, *The Politics of Bureaucracy* (Washington, D.C.: Public Affairs Press, 1965) and Anthony Downs, *An Economic Theory of Democracy* (New York: Harper & Row, 1957).

17. Mancur Olson, *The Logic of Collective Action* (Cambridge: Harvard University Press, 1965).

18. James M. Buchanan and Gordon Tullock, *The Calculus of Consent: Logical Foundations of Constitutional Democracy* (Ann Arbor: University of Michigan Press, 1962).

19. Garrett Hardin, "The Tragedy of the Commons," *Science* 162 (December 13, 1968): 1243–48, and Joseph J. Seneca, "The Welfare Effects of Zero Pricing of Public Goods," *Public Choice* 7 (Spring 1970): 101–10.

difficult to achieve in any context), public choice concerns "Pareto improvements," and the notions of tradeoffs and externalities. To borrow E. J. Mishan's definition, a Pareto improvement is "a change in economic organization that makes everyone better off—or, more precisely, that makes one or more members of society better off without making anyone worse off." [20]

Pareto optimality may be illustrated with reference to public choice in graphic form. Figure 11–8 posits a hypothetical social value (X) relative to the accomplishment of all other social values. The *indifference curve* refers to the combination of values about which society is indifferent (at least up to a point); the *value achievement curve* indicates the optimal combination of values that it is possible for government to encourage given limited resources. The point of optimal achievement of Value X and optimal achievement of all other social values constitutes the point of Pareto optimality. The closer that society gets to the point of Pareto optimality is considered a Pareto improvement.

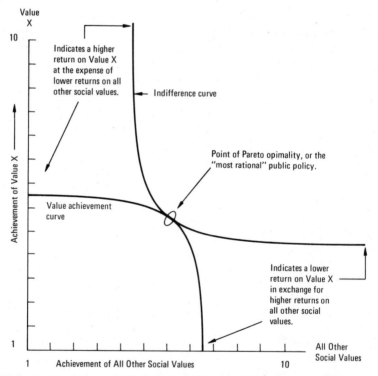

FIGURE 11–8. Pareto Optimality and Public Choice

20. E. J. Mishan, *Economics for Social Decisions: Elements of Cost-Benefit Analysis* (New York: Praeger, 1972), p. 14.

Figure 11–8 also illustrates what the public choice writers mean by *tradeoffs*. A tradeoff refers to what value is being traded (and the social costs and benefits incurred in such a trade) for what other value. In other words, every time Value X is achieved more fully, all other values are correspondingly reduced in achievement; the benefits gained by increasing resource input into Value X must decrease resource input into all other values.

A related term common to the public choice literature is *externality*, or *spillover effect*. When a public policy in one sphere of social action affects other spheres of social action, the manner in which the other sphere is affected is called an *externality*; that is, the effects of a public policy in one sphere "spill over" into other spheres. Externalities may be positive or negative, intended or unintended. For example, a positive, intended spillover effect of reducing corporate taxes might be to raise employment levels. A negative, unintended externality of the same public policy might be to reduce the financial resources available to the government for welfare programs.

Technology assessment. The notion of externalities leads us into our final topic of this chapter, technology assessment. Technology assessment is an effort to evaluate new technologies in light of their spillover effects throughout society. Thus, public policies for new technologies become the objects of analysis. A variant of technology assessment is technological forecasting, which is the attempt to predict what effects very new technologies might have on society. For instance, medicine may be viewed as a technology that, in its success in extending life, has been more responsible than any other factor for the population explosion.

Consider another example, one perhaps more modest but also more germane to most readers: the Xerox machine. Photocopiers have lived up to all the original hopes that were held for them. As an information technology, photocopiers have facilitated research, record keeping, and decision making. They have probably reduced the inclination of patrons to vandalize volumes in libraries. They have eased the process of education throughout society and have made life far more convenient for innumerable people who handle paper as part of their jobs. They may even have contributed to more responsive policy making in public organizations because they speed the information flow in the bureaucracy. They have made some people a lot of money. But the photocopier also has brought with it certain unintended negative externalities. Roughly 30 billion photocopies are made every year in the United States, and empirical research indicates that approximately 60 percent of these copies may be of materials protected by copyright.

Some questions inevitably come to the fore: If photocopies were unavailable, would sales of copyrighted books and periodicals rise? Is popular use of photocopying technologies cutting into the royalty payments of authors and publishers? And if so, are royalties being reduced to a point sufficient to undermine the financial incentive of authors to write and of publishers to risk capital to publish? Ultimately, have these machines contributed to a less creative society? Or will they? Is the incentive to develop new ideas in science, social science, and literature decreased by the emerging photocopier/copyright relationship, or is there more incentive because of the added convenience provided by photocopiers in transmitting new ideas? Although there are many opinions, many of them heated, among authors, publishers, librarians, and educators, the impact of the technology of photocopying on society has yet to be adequately assessed.[21]

Presumably, a more rigorous system of technology assessment and technological forecasting by the government could aid in achieving a more rationally planned society. As a significant step in this direction, Congress passed a bill in 1973 establishing an Office of Technology Assessment with a mission of advising Congress on matters of technology assessment. The office is seen by some observers as representing a congressional effort to offset the almost total monopoly of scientific and technical information held by the executive branch.

Regardless of how the Office of Technology Assessment performs, the function of technology assessment remains a new and important aspect of public policy analysis generally and of the rationalist model particularly. Many agencies of government can use it in evaluating their programs. Gabor Strasser has stated that technology assessment actually has a rather broad meaning:

> A systematic planning and forecasting process that delineates options and costs, encompassing economics as well as environmental and social considerations that are both external and internal to the program and/or product in question, with special focus on technology-related "bad" as well as "good" effects.[22]

With this definition in mind, look at Figure 11–9, which illustrates the elements of technology assessment.

The notion of public policy provides a natural stepping-stone to our next chapter. While the field of public policy analysis that we have just

21. For additional information on this complex topic, see Nicholas Henry, *Copyright/ Information Technology/Public Policy, Volumes I* and *II* (New York: Marcel Dekker, 1975 and 1976), and Nicholas Henry, ed., *Copyright, Congress, and Technology: The Public Record, Volumes I, II, III,* and *IV* (Phoenix: Oryx, 1978 and 1979, and 1980).

22. Gabor Strasser, "Technology Assessment: A Fad or a New Way of Life?" *Science Policy Review* 5 (1, 1972): 7.

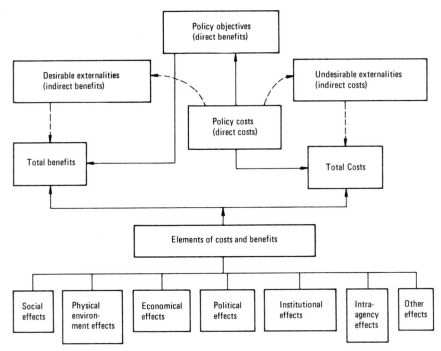

FIGURE 11–9. Technology Assessment in Public Administration

reviewed deals with how to analyze and upgrade the process of public policy making, the topic of public affairs considers the actual content of public policies. Thus, in public affairs the emphasis is on substance and output, rather than on procedure and process.

SUPPLEMENTAL BIBLIOGRAPHY

BATEMAN, WORTH, "Assessing Program Effectiveness: A Rating System for Identifying Relative Project Success," *Welfare in Review,* 6 (January–February 1968), 1–10.

CHASE, SAMUEL B., JR., ed., *Problems in Public Expenditure Analysis.* Washington, D.C.: Brookings Institution, 1968.

DENISTON, O. L., I. M. ROSENSTOCK, and V. A. GETTING, "Evaluation of Program Effectiveness," *Public Health Reports,* 83 (April 1968), 323–35.

DORFMAN, R., ed., *Measuring the Benefit of Government Investments.* Washington, D.C.: Brookings Institution, 1965.

HATRY, HARRY P., RICHARD E. WINNIE, and DONALD M. FISK, *Practical Program Evaluation for State and Local Government Officials.* Washington, D.C.: Urban Institute, 1972.

HAVEMAN, R. H., and J. V. KRUTILLA, *Unemployment, Idle Capacity, and the Evaluation of Public Expenditure.* Washington, D.C.: Resources for the Future, 1968.

LEVINE, ABRAHAM S., "Cost-Benefit Analysis and Social Welfare Program Evaluation," *Social Service Review,* 42 (June 1968), 173–83.

LEVINSON, PERRY, "Evaluation of Social Welfare Programs, Two Research Models," *Welfare in Review,* 4 (December 1966), 5–12.

the urban
professions

chapter 12

This chapter and the one following introduce the section on public affairs with a review of the dilemmas of urban man. They are many. In this chapter we consider some selected realities of urban areas: the implications of recent demographic and economic shifts in the nation's Standard Metropolitan Statistical Areas (SMSAs); major forms of urban governance; the rising impact of the urban planning process; and finally, the urban fiscal scene, focussing on that paragon of budgetary virtue, New York City.

THE SUBURBANIZATION OF CITIES

Since mid-twentieth century, Americans have been suburbanizing more than urbanizing.[1] At least 76 million Americans live in places like Levittown and Park Forest and, depending on how one defines *suburb*, as many

1. For a lucid discussion of recent urban demographic trends, see President's Urban and Regional Policy Group, *A New Partnership to Conserve America's Communities: A National Urban Policy* (Washington, D.C.: U.S. Department of Housing and Urban Development, 1978).

as 90 million people may be living in the nation's twenty thousand suburbs. Projections indicate that there certainly will be more than 100 million people living in America's Levittowns by 1985, and it is estimated that roughly 40 percent of our population now lives in the suburbs. This is a plurality, as only about 30 percent of Americans live in cities and another 30 percent in rural areas. Suburbia is where the action is—not only in population growth, but in economic growth as well.

Between 1960 and 1970 the number of people living in urban fringe areas grew 36 percent while the core cities expanded by only 8.4 percent. Table 12–1 indicates the growth in both metropolitan and suburban areas in the United States.

Suburbia: richer and whiter

Statistics substantiate, at least in part, the suburban image that those who live in the suburbs are indeed "whiter," richer, and more educated than

TABLE 12–1.   U.S. Population, by Metropolitan Residence: 1970–1974 (Numbers in Thousands)

Type of Residence	1970	1974	Numerical Change 1970– 1974	Percent Change 1970– 1974
U.S. total	199,819	207,949	8,130	4.1%
Metropolitan areas, total	137,058	142,043	4,985	3.6
Central cities	62,876	61,650	−1,226	− 1.9
Suburban rings	74,182	80,394	6,212	8.4
Metropolitan areas of 1 million or more	79,489	81,059	1,570	2.0
Central cities	34,322	33,012	1,310	− 3.8
Suburban rings	45,166	48,047	2,881	6.4
Metropolitan areas of less than 1 million	57,570	60,985	3,415	5.9
Central cities	28,554	28,638	84	0.3
Suburban rings	29,016	32,347	3,331	11.5

| | Percent Distribution | | | |
	1950	1960	1970	1975
U.S. total	100.0%	100.0%	100.0%	100.0%
Metropolitan	62.5	66.4	68.6	68.0
Central city	35.5	33.3	31.5	29.2
Suburban	27.0	33.1	37.1	38.8
Non-Metropolitan	37.5	33.6	31.4	32.0

Source: George Sternlieb and James W. Hughes, "New Regional and Metropolitan Realities of America," *Journal of the American Institute of Planners,* Vol. 43 (July 1977), p. 235.

TABLE 12–2. Social and Economic Status Index for Urbanized Areas Based on Measures of Occupation, Education, and Income

Place of Residence and Race	Percentage of Population with Status Scores of:			
	80–99	50–79	20–49	0–19
Total				
Central cities	13.7	42.4	35.2	8.6
Urban fringe	22.8	50.1	23.4	3.7
White				
Central cities	16.0	46.8	31.1	6.1
Urban fringe	23.7	51.3	22.0	3.0
Nonwhite				
Central cities	3.0	21.9	54.5	20.6
Urban fringe	3.6	25.2	52.7	18.4

Source: U.S. Bureau of the Census, *Current Population Reports, Technical Studies*, Series P–23, No. 12 (Washington, D.C.: U.S. Government Printing Office, July 31, 1974). The urban fringe is that portion of the urbanized area (which is the SMSA excluding its sparsely settled parts) outside the central city.

those who live in large central cities. Table 12–2 shows that nearly 23 percent of those who reside on the outer fringes of cities are within the highest status category; fewer than 4 percent are in the lowest status category. When we view these status categories in terms of the inner cities, only 14 percent are in the highest level and 9 percent are in the lowest (*Status categories* are determined by the Census Bureau according to socioeconomic measures based on occupational type, level of education, and amount of income.)

Still, such figures should be viewed within the proper context. Dramatic disparaties between the income levels of central city residents and suburban residents are more apt to be found in the larger SMSAs than in the smaller ones. "The stereotype portraying the flight of white, middle-class families from low income, ethnic dominated cities to the miniature republics of suburbia is generally appropriate only for the larger SMSAs." [2] Nevertheless, as of 1970 about 30 percent of the nation's poor, or 8.2 million, lived in the core cities; only 21 percent, or less than 5.2 million, lived in the suburbs.[3]

Just as money is fleeing to the suburbs, the races are also dividing along suburban and urban lines. In every region of the country, blacks now constitute a higher proportion of metropolitan populations than they did ten years ago, and the changes are most dramatic in the larger cities, those with more than half a million people. During the 1960s the growth in the black population in SMSAs rose 3.7 million, and 60 percent of

2. John C. Bollens and Henry J. Schmandt, *The Metropolis: Its People, Politics, and Economic Life*, 3rd ed. (New York: Harper & Row, 1975), p. 69.

3. Samuel Kaplan, *The Dream Deferred* (New York: Seabury Press, 1976), p. 212.

TABLE 12–3. Percentage of Blacks in Central Cities of Twelve Largest SMSAs, 1950–1970

City	1950	1960	1970
New York	10	14	21
Los Angeles	9	14	18
Chicago	14	23	33
Philadelphia	18	26	34
Detroit	16	29	44
San Francisco	6	10	13
Washington, D.C.	35	54	71
Boston	5	9	13
Pittsburgh	12	17	20
St. Louis	18	29	41
Baltimore	24	35	38
Cleveland	16	29	46

Source: U.S. Bureau of the Census, *Census of Population; 1960 and 1970, General Population Characteristics* (Washington, D.C.; U.S. Government Printing Office, 1971).

this increase was concentrated in the twelve largest metropolitan areas. Table 12–3 lists these proportions. The central cities gained 6.5 million blacks between 1950 and 1970. The number of white residents in the central cities of eleven of the twelve most populous metropolises (the exception is Los Angeles) declined by more than 2.5 million between 1960 and 1970. In New York City alone, more than 600,000 whites fled to the suburbs or to other states while 579,000 blacks came in. In Chicago another half million whites left while the number of blacks in the city rose by 300,000. With less than 11 percent of the national population, blacks make up 28 percent of the total population of the central cities in metropolitan areas of more than two million people, an increase of 8 percent since 1960. Table 12–4 amplifies these relationships.

The number of blacks who reside in the suburbs is also increasing.

TABLE 12–4. Population Distribution and Change Inside and Outside SMSAs, by Race, 1950–1970 (in Millions)

	Black			White		
	1950	1960	1970	1950	1960	1970
United States	15.0	18.9	22.6	135.1	158.8	177.6
Metropolitan areas	8.8	12.8	16.8	85.1	106.3	121.3
Central cities	6.6	9.9	13.1	46.8	50.1	49.5
Outside central cities	2.2	2.8	3.7	38.3	56.3	71.8
Nonmetropolitan	6.2	6.1	5.8	50.0	52.5	56.3

Source: U.S. Bureau of the Census, "General Demographic Trends for Metropolitan Areas," *Census of Population and Housing: 1970* (Washington, D.C.: U.S. Government Printing Office, 1971).

Although the proportion of black population in the suburbs is considerably lower than in the central cities, the number of black suburbanites nonetheless increased by 900,000 during the 1960s, and 60 percent of this increase was within the twelve largest SMSAs. Even so, and as Karl and Alma Taeuber have shown in their study of *Negroes in Cities*, these suburbanization trends hardly indicate that blacks are at long last weaving themselves into the fabric of American society. The Taeubers' statistical analysis indicated that "Negroes are more segregated residentially than are Orientals, Mexican-Americans, Puerto Ricans, or any nationality group. In fact, Negroes are by far the most residentially segregated urban minority in recent American history." [4]

Latinos also display similar trends, though not as dramatically as those of blacks. Latinos are the second largest minority in the United States, numbering 11 million or almost 5 percent of the population. Latinos are made up primarily of Mexican-Americans, who are concentrated largely on the West Coast in such barrios as East Los Angeles; Puerto Ricans, who are found mostly in New York City; and Cubans, mostly in Miami. Nationwide, people of Spanish origin are found mostly in California, Texas, New York, Arizona, Florida, Illinois, and New Mexico; most are concentrated in the metropolitan areas.

It seems that people of all races (but particularly whites) want to get out of the city and get into the suburbs. The reasons why are not entirely clear. Some sociologists argue that it is simple racism, a polite form of white supremacy, that motivates the drive toward the suburbs, although most suburban respondents tell poll takers that they live in the suburbs "for the children." A patch of grass to play on and a good school to attend are major factors for parents seeking the suburbs.

Money and metro

Considering people's motivations for moving to the suburbs it is ironic that the suburbs are urbanizing as never before. Businesses have been shifting their central offices to the suburbs at a rate equal to that of families since the mid-1940s. Indeed, it is possible that businesses are relocating to the suburbs even faster than families, as suburbs begin to encourage businesses to move to their jurisdictions to strengthen the tax base. The 278 SMSAs contain more than 70 percent of the nation's labor force, 70 percent of the country's taxable assessed valuation, and they have higher per capita incomes than other sections of the nation; but nonetheless, since World War II the central cities within those

4. Karl E. Taeuber and Alma F. Taeuber, *Negroes in Cities* (Chicago: Aldine, 1965), p. 68.

SMSAs have been losing manufacturing jobs to their surrounding suburbs.[5] As Table 12–5 indicates, these trends are continuing: It has been estimated that 80 percent of new jobs created in the major SMSAs during the last decade have been in suburbia.[6]

TABLE 12–5. Change in Central City Jobs and Population for 10 Large SMSAs Between 1960–1970

SMSA	Change in Jobs (%)	Change in Population (%)
New York	− 1.9	1.4
Chicago	−12.1	− 5.1
Philadelphia	− 4.1	− 2.6
Detroit	−18.8	− 9.4
Boston	−14.2	− 8.0
St. Louis	−14.2	−17.0
Baltimore	− 4.6	− 3.5
Cleveland	−12.9	−14.2
Newark	−12.5	− 5.6
Milwaukee	−10.2	− 3.2

The Big Move

The decision by a corporation to move from an inner city to a neighboring suburb is a big one, affecting metropolitan jobs, taxes, and people. How are such decisions made? In the following passage, a noted urbanist sketches a cynical, but perhaps accurate, picture of how corporate executives decide to abandon cities.

The decentralization of manufacturing and retailing to suburbia has hurt the cities economically. But given the production and market factors that must be considered in the locating of manufacturing and retailing concerns, the moves have made sense to both management and consumer. Less rational and more disturbing has been the relatively recent phenomenon of corporations relocating in suburbia. If the cities have any functions left other than to house the poor and minority groups locked out of suburbia, it is their traditional role as the centers of business management, finance and professional and governmental services. The loss of corporations, the taxes they pay and the thousands of white-collar workers they bring into the center cities daily, cuts deeply into the foundation of metropolitan America.

The advertisements luring corporations to suburbia in *The Wall Street Journal* and the financial sections of *The New York Times* and

5. Bollens and Schmandt, *op. cit.*, 86.
6. Kaplan, *op. cit.*, 189.

other large metropolitan dailies present the proposition bluntly. "Join the Great Corporate Getaway to Connecticut," stated an ad in the *Times,* though it also could have been to Westchester, Santa Clara, or Orange counties, Elk Grove, Long Island, or any other suburban area in need of tax ratables and jobs, or where a speculator might have put together an office campus and was now seeking buyers or renters.

The ads look good to the weary executive reading them for a second time as his train limps along the New Haven tracks in the Bronx, or waits in the Jersey Meadows for a Penn Central drawbridge to unstick, or is sidetracked in the Sunnyside Yards again by a faulty Long Island Railroad switch. And at last as the executive stumbles off his train at Pennsylvania and Grand Central Stations hours late to fight his way into a crowded subway, or to try to catch an elusive cab, or even walk, the ads look even better and the city worse. Though less dramatic, the situation is similar for other executives in other cities, except instead of being stuck in a train, they might be stuck in their car on some freeway, or in city traffic, or backed up on street waiting to get into a parking lot. Chaotic commuting, air pollution, noise pollution, crime, power shortages, bombs, strikes, payroll taxes—the list of city ills has become a litany to be recited over drinks at executive luncheons, the business clubs and in the commuter bar cars. Caustic comments become conversations, become company inquiries, become consultant studies, and soon another corporation is considering leaving a city for suburbia. . . .

The cities are now worried, very worried, prompting many to establish agencies to counter the lure of suburbia by using high pressure sales techniques, public opinion and such "sweeteners" as additional police protection and more convenient parking. New York City . . . Economic Development Administrator, D. Kenneth Patton, . . . [has] warned that if . . . firms continue to locate at random in the suburbs and ignore regional transportation, housing, labor, and tax problems, "we will Los Angelize our land, Balkanize our region's finances and South Africanize our economy."

Strong words and a stern warning, which has been echoed by city politicians, professors, and planners at perpetual seminars and unending conferences sponsored by good-government groups. But when the words and warnings are filtered through corporate decision-making processes and paraphrased in memoranda and in deep tones in the anonymous board rooms high above city streets, they are dismissed as grandstanding. Private enterprise—what is best for the corporation —comes before public interest. "A few of our execs sit on this city board and that, and we support things like the Urban Coalition," confided a top corporation executive, "but if you look behind our corporate posture, we really don't give a damn about the city. In fact, some of our guys, especially the Midwest and South transfers, really hate it. They were big wheels in their towns, and here they are nothing." An executive with a company that moved from Midtown Manhattan to an office campus in White Plains, Westchester, put it more positively: "We were darn near lost in New York. Here we are an important part of the community." The discussion then in most corporations considering leaving the city is not whether their move is good for the city and the region—those are questions for their public relations men to deal with—but rather where to relocate and what they can expect to find in suburbia.

Corporations leaving the city generally relocate near the homes of their top executives, or in a community where the executives want, and can afford, to live. Of course, expensive studies are conducted by relocation consultants, but most persons in the business know the studies are shaped by subtle, and sometimes not too subtle, suggestions of the executives directing the studies. "What we are told, usually after the third drink at the contract lunch, is that so-and-so-lives in, say Greenwich or Scarsdale, and wants to be within 10 easy minutes of his home and golf club," confided one relocation specialist who did not want to be identified for obvious reasons. "What we are asked is to survey the surrounding area and, with nice maps and charts, justify the selection, and to hell with any regional plans and projections."

Other consultants confirmed the approach. One even told of having his contract broken by a corporation president who lived in New Jersey when he strongly recommended an office location in Fairfield. He added that the corporation eventually moved to New Jersey—upon the strong recommendation of another consultant. . . .

"I say that the principal reason we have 500 new companies in Elk Grove Village is that it is close to where the boss lives," said Marshall Bennett, a partner in Bennett & Kahnweiler, industrial real estate brokers. His firm developed Centex Industrial Park in Elk Grove Village, the largest of its kind in the nation. . . .

The consequences of the corporate exodus to suburbia are obvious in the cities, which are losing taxes and jobs. The once thriving downtown stores that catered to the lunchtime and five o'clock shoppers also are hurting, as are the thousands of allied concerns that serviced the corporations.

Samuel Kaplan
The Dream Deferred

Industries and retail businesses have been moving to the suburbs since the 1950s, but between 1965 and 1976 the trend accelerated. For example, during this period New York City's share of the nation's one hundred largest corporations dropped from nineteen to ten and its portion of the one thousand largest corporations declined from 198 to 120—figures that represented a loss of more than 420,000 jobs for New York. An estimated seventy-five major firms left Boston during a two-year period in the mid-1970s; forty-three left St. Louis. Cleveland and Detroit each said adieu to about two dozen major firms during a similar period.

"The worse things get, the worse things get"

These shifts of metropolitan populations and jobs are being felt by the nation's cities. In a sophisticated analysis of "urban hardship" in fifty-five major cities, the Brookings Institution ranked the disparities that existed between inner cities and their suburbs on the logic that "such disparities often lead to the population movement and economic decline typical of distressed central cities." [7] As the authors observe:

> The picture is familiar. As more residents and businesses move to the suburbs, the city's tax base is driven down. Property or other tax rates must be raised to compensate, in turn causing more people and industries to leave. A natural law seems to govern these high-disparity cases: "The worse things get, the worse things get." It is a continuous process, feeding on itself.[8]

The Brookings study concluded that forty-three of the cities were worse off economically and socially than their surrounding suburbs, two were about equal, and ten inner cities were actually better off than their suburban rings. Table 12–6 lists the fourteen "worst off" cities and the ten "best off" as defined by Brookings' "hardship index" (*i.e.*, the third column from the left). A score of 100 on this index means that a city is roughly equal socially and economically with its suburbs; a score of more than 100 means that the city is worse off, and a score of less than 100 means that the city is better off than its suburbs. The table's last column on the right gives the percentage of urban housing built before 1939, because this is a major criterion by which the federal government allocates community development block grants to cities; the more pre-1939 housing, the bigger the grant.

Brookings' fourteen worst-off cities are in bad shape by any measure. They lost, on the average, 4.2 percent of their people between 1960 and 1970. By contrast, Brookings' Top Ten gained in population by an average of 18.5 percent during the decade. The Foundering Fourteen have almost 10 percent less per capital income than the Top Ten, lower median house values, and lower tax bases.

The Brookings researchers have uncovered some fascinating patterns of urban hardship, concluding that "The most important differences

---

7. Richard P. Nathan and Paul R. Dommel, "Understanding the Urban Predicament." *Brookings Bulletin* 14 (Spring–Summer 1977): 9.
8. *Ibid.*

TABLE 12–6. Central Cities Ranking Above 200 and Below 100 on an Index of City-Suburban Disparity ("Hardship Index") in 1970, with Selected Data on Their Standard Metropolitan Statistical Areas, 1960–70

Primary central city of SMSA	Region [1]	Index of city-suburban disparity	SMSA population, 1970		Percent change, 1960–70		Pre-1939 housing in 1970
			Total (thousands)	Percent in central city	Population	Land area	(percent)
Central cities worse off than their suburbs							
Newark	NE	422	1,857	20.6	− 5.7	—	68.4
Cleveland	NE	331	2,064	36.4	−14.3	—	73.3
Hartford	NE	317	664	23.8	− 2.6	—	67.0
Baltimore	NE	256	2,071	43.7	− 3.5	—	60.0
Chicago	NC	245	6,975	48.2	− 5.1	—	66.5
St. Louis	NC	231	2,363	26.3	−17.0	—	73.9
Atlanta	S	226	1,390	35.8	2.0	3.2	30.3
Rochester	NE	215	883	33.6	− 7.0	—	79.5
Gary	NC	213	633	27.7	− 1.6	—	43.7
Dayton	NC	211	850	28.6	− 7.4	12.3	52.1
New York	NE	211	11,572	68.2	1.5	—	62.1
Detroit	NC	210	4,200	36.0	− 9.4	—	61.8
Richmond	S	209	518	48.2	−13.4	60.0	44.8
Philadelphia	NE	205	4,818	40.4	− 2.6	—	69.5
Central cities better off than their suburbs							
Omaha	NC	98	540	64.3	15.0	60.2	46.1
Dallas	S	97	1,556	54.3	24.2	4.7	18.1
Houston	S	93	1,985	62.1	31.4	35.2	17.3
Phoenix	W	85	968	60.1	32.4	32.3	11.2
Norfolk	S	82	681	45.2	1.0	0.5	30.5
Salt Lake City	W	80	558	31.5	− 7.2	6.5	52.1
San Diego	W	77	1,358	51.3	21.6	62.8	21.7
Seattle	W	67	1,422	37.3	− 4.7	2.2	47.6
Ft. Lauderdale	S	64	620	22.5	66.9	39.0	7.6
Greensboro, N.C.	S	43	604	23.9	20.5	9.7	20.7

Index calculated from data in U.S. Bureau of the Census, *County and City Data Book, 1972* (Government Printing Office, 1972), tables 2, 3, 6; population from Bureau of the Census, *1972 Census of Governments,* vol. 1, *Governmental Organization* (GPO, 1972), table 19; pre-1939 housing data from *1970 Census of Housing,* Series HC(1)B, *Detailed Housing Characteristics,* table 35.
[1] *Northeast* (NE): New England states, New York, New Jersey, Pennsylvania. *North Central* (NC): Michigan, Ohio, Indiana, Illinois, Wisconsin, Minnesota, Iowa, Missouri, North and South Dakota, Nebraska, Kansas. *South* (S): Kentucky, Tennessee, Georgia, Florida, Alabama, Mississippi, Arkansas, Louisiana, Oklahoma, Texas. *West* (W): Montana, Wyoming, Colorado, New Mexico, Idaho, Utah, Arizona, Washington, Oregon, Nevada, California.
Source: Richard P. Nathan and Paul R. Dommel, "Understanding the Urban Predicament," *The Brookings Bulletin,* 14 (Spring–Summer, 1977), p. 20.

among big cities are regional."[9] The cities decomposing most rapidly are found largely in those midwestern and northeastern states in the northeastern quarter of the country; the more viable metropolises are in the Sunbelt and West.

Another important factor is that of municipal boundaries. Those cities whose boundaries have not been changed for some time—sixty to one hundred years in some cases—are the most likely to be troubled and suffering from a diminishing resource base. It does not follow, however, that a city with political boundaries that have not been altered for years is also geographically small. In fact, Brookings concluded that "while the public often associates urban problems with city size, it is not necessarily size but other factors that produce the problems."[10]

The upshot of the black/white, poor/rich imbalance between cities and suburbs is that those local governments with the greatest demand for public services are least able to afford them because of inordinately weak tax bases. Funds for education, fire protection, police protection, zoning, public health, and other basic functions of government are lacking for significant portions of the population.

Coping with these realities of urban demography and economy is not a simple task. To do so, localities have devised a variety of ingenious forms of governance; we consider the four major forms next.

GOVERNING CITIES

Municipalities use two major kinds of government: the "weak executive" model and the "strong executive" model. Included in these two categories are various forms of municipal government, notably the mayor–council form which may rely on either a "weak mayor" or a "strong mayor" system, the commission form, and the council–manager plan.

The "weak executive" form of urban governance

There are two principal models of the "weak executive" form of municipal administration: "Weak mayor" government and the commission plan. Both are characterized by their integration of the executive and legislative functions.

The weak mayor form of government is usually associated with a *mayor-and-council* arrangement in city hall. The mayor has inconsequential powers, most of the managerial perquisites being parcelled out to a

9. *Ibid.*
10. *Ibid.*

substantial number of elected officials or already vested in the members of the city council who generally are elected by ward. The long ballot of municipal elections, characteristic of weak mayor governments, assures that administrative powers are splintered among a number of council members and other electer officers and that the mayor is not much more than a chairman of the city council.

The problems of a weak mayor form of government are those classic to any overly decentralized administrative system. Comprehensive planning, especially comprehensive financial planning, becomes a virtual impossibility. Such liabilities are compounded by the areal decentralization prevailing in most Standard Metropolitan Statistical Areas—that is, a plethora of districts and jurisdictions, each with its own powers and administrative responsibilities.

It should be noted that it often is difficult to adjudge whether or not a city government uses a weak-mayor or strong-mayor form (although Los Angeles and Minneapolis clearly are examples of the former). Perhaps the classic example is the late Richard Daley's Chicago. Mayor Daley inherited a weak mayor form of municipal government and, in fact, that remains the structure, at least on paper, of Chicago's government. For example, Chicago has a city council of fifty members to whom Daley "reported," numerous independent boards (including those that dealt with such important areas as education and housing), and other features that are found in a weak mayor form of government. Nevertheless, there is no question in anyone's mind that Mayor Daley was a strong mayor and implemented, if never on paper, a strong mayor form of government.

The *commission plan* initially was a reaction against the weak mayor form of government, yet ironically it shares many of its underlying disadvantages. It was created by a local disaster. In 1900 Galveston, Texas, was flooded by a raging Gulf of Mexico. Within twenty-four hours, a sixth of the population was dead or injured, fresh water supplies were gone, food dwindling, sanitation nonexistent, and looting rampant. The mayor called together Galveston's leading citizens—the city's "real" leaders—and from their ranks formed a Central Relief Committee, which became Galveston's operational government. The unique feature of this plan was that each member of the committee was "commissioned" to accomplish a particular task and to make policy on how that task was to be accomplished. Thus, the committee possessed both an executive and a legislative function and, in terms of restoring order out of chaos, the committee worked.

Galvestonians were convinced that they had discovered a revolutionary form of municipal government. They petitioned the Texas legislature to legitimate it, which was done, and the commission form of government was inaugurated.

City commissioners generally are elected at large rather than by wards in an attempt to reduce parochialism, and the short ballot predominates. Each member of the council formally is both a legislator and administrator. Policy is set collectively and executed individually, and the mayor is little more than an important commissioner. Indeed, in some cities commissioners rotate the office of mayor among them. The initiative, referendum, and recall generally are features of the commission plan, and the value of nonpartisan elections is salient. Unfortunately, each commissioner, because he is both legislator and administrator, often is predisposed to protect his individual "barony," and to do so he must "go along to get along" with his fellow commissioners. To do otherwise means that he will be singled out and necessarily have his power base undercut as a minority player in a game that can be won only by a majority.

Ten years after the Galveston flood the commission plan was in use in 108 cities, but by 1970 only 37 cities of more than 50,000 people plus a number of smaller towns, mostly in the south, were using it. Currently, only about 5 percent of the nation's cities use this form; the lack of administrative integration and the belief of many citizens that the commission plan amounted to government amateurs has led to its decline.

The "strong executive" form of urban governance

While the mayor-and-council form of urban governance can employ a weak mayor variant, more frequently the form favors the use of the *strong mayor and council form.* Nine of the ten largest cities in the United States use a strong mayor government and, in fact, all American cities with more than one million people in them have a mayor-council form. Only five of the nation's twenty-six largest cities, or those with more than 500,000 people, use a council-manager system. They are Dallas, San Antonio, Kansas City, San Diego, and Phoenix.

The use of a strong mayor form of government in the big cities is predictable for a number of reasons. The media tend to focus on the mayor as the representative spokesman of power in city hall; the size and complexity of big cities mandate the presence of a political executive who is more than a figurehead; and, because of the city's legal subserviency to the state, a strong mayor option offers a major means by which able persons who can deal effectively with the governor and state legislature may be attracted to municipal service.

Political patterns in strong mayor cities are similar to the basic patterns of the national and state governments. A skilled mayor can become a chief legislator as well as chief executive under a strong mayor form just as can an adept president or governor. The city council is usually small, elected by wards, and is relatively "pure" in its legislative function. The partisan short ballot is common, and often only the mayor, councilmen, and auditor are subject to election. The mayor has the sole power to form budgets, administer municipal departments, and make most of the policy decisions. The council, of course, must approve budgets, appointments, and policies, and it has the power to launch potentially embarrassing investigations of the mayor's administration.

Besides being associated with big cities, strong mayor-council forms of government also relate positively to such factors as relatively older citizenries, more blue-collar workers, less education, and slower economic growth rates. The obverse of these characteristics in a city tends to be associated with council-manager and commission forms of government. Mayor-council governments are also clearly associated with the eastern and midwestern cities.[11]

The last remaining major form of urban government is the *council–manager form*, which, like the commission form of government, has an unusual history. In 1908 the city councilmen of Staunton, Virginia, frustrated with the welter of "administrivia" of city government that tends to crop up under any weak executive model, decided to hire a professional manager: The council was to decide policy, and the city manager was to execute it. Although the commission plan was then the national rage, Staunton's idea gradually began taking root. In 1913 the influential National Municipal League approved the plan in its model city charter. But the decision in 1914 of Dayton, Ohio (which recently, like Galveston, had been badly damaged by flood) to alter its governmental form and switch to a council–manager system provided the real impetus for the novel plan. With its new city manager Dayton centralized, economized, and enlarged a number of municipal functions rebuilding and improving a largely destroyed town in record time.

The essence of the council–manager form is that while legislative (city council) and executive (city manager) powers are clearly separate, administrative powers are highly unified under the aegis of a professionally trained city manager. The council controls only the manager whom it hires and may fire; the manager controls the administrative apparat of the city. Elections in council–manager municipalities usually are nonpartisan (unlike strong mayor governments), characterized by the short ballot, with the electorate having the initiative, referendum, and recall.

Since its inauguration in 1914 the council–manager plan has been growing in municipal popularity. By 1970 more than 50 percent of American cities of more than ten thousand population had city managers, 47 percent of towns with less than five thousand people had a council–manager plan, and it was encroaching on big cities, which traditionally

11. Leo Schnore and Robert Alford, "Forms of Government and Socioeconomic Characteristics of Suburbs," *Administrative Science Quarterly*, vol. 8 (June 1963): 1–17.

have favored a strong mayor form of government. Less than one hundred American cities have adopted and then permanently abandoned the plan by popular vote, and its use is making significant inroads in Canada and Europe.

Just as the mayor–council form of government is associated with big cities in the East and Midwest, with heterogeneous working-class populations, and with stable growth rates, the council–manager form of government is associated with relatively medium-sized cities, usually with populations of 25,000 to 250,000 people, in the Sunbelt. The use of the council–manager form also is correlated with the middle-class, white-collar workers, relatively low proportions of foreign-born residents, and comparatively high levels of educational attainments. In other words, council–manager government normally walks hand-in-hand with middle-class values, whereas mayor–council forms appear to be associated more with working-class values. Hence, council–manager forms of government are found mostly in the suburbs.

It is interesting to note that in some ways the council–manager and the mayor–council variants of urban government appear to be blending in the form of a new office, the popularity of which is on the rise in cities. The office is that of chief administrative officer, also known as city administrator, city administrative officer, or managing director. This position is usually held by a professional administrator (such as a city manager) who is accountable only to the mayor, and not responsible to the city council. Figure 12–1 summarizes our discussion about forms of urban government.

Aside from the city manager and the chief administrative officer, perhaps the "urban professional" who is having the greatest impact on the local polity during this century's last quarter is the urban planner. Increasingly, as we shall see, the planning process is becoming important to city hall.

THE PLANNING PROCESS

The structure of local planning

Planning is an intergovernmental process, but it has local roots. Approximately 75 percent of all American communities with more than five thousand people have some sort of published plan.[12] Almost eleven thousand municipalities have planning boards (a figure representing more than half of the local governments that might be expected to have such boards), and virtually all the large cities, those with fifty thousand or more

12. Allen D. Manvel, *Local Land and Building Regulations* (Washington, D.C.: U.S. Government Printing Office, 1968), p. 31.

"Weak Executive" Forms.

1. Weak Mayor-Council Form

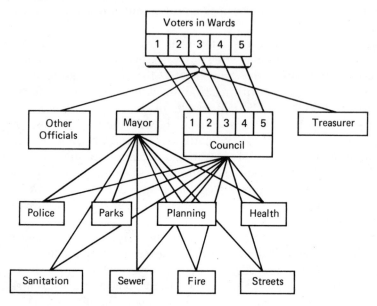

2. Commission Form

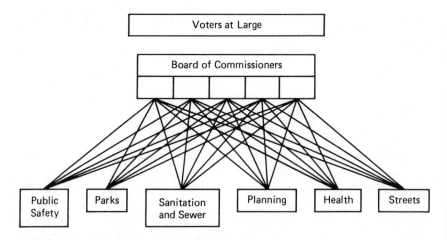

FIGURE 12–1. Forms of Urban Government

"Strong Executive" Forms.

1. Strong Mayor-Council Form

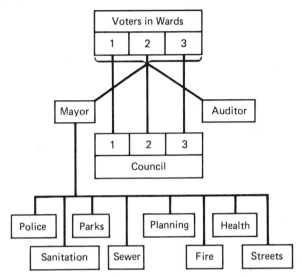

2. Council-Manager Form

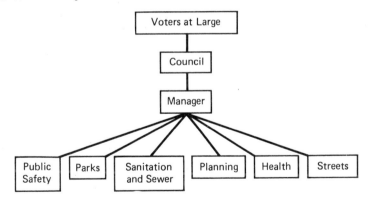

FIGURE 12–1. (cont.)

people, have planning boards. Ninety percent of cities and towns in the five thousand to fifty thousand population range have planning boards, and all state governments have planning agencies and programs.[13]

Although planning boards are being integrated into the standing city bureaucracy at an increasingly rapid rate, they nonetheless operate somewhat autonomously as governmental units. Members of planning boards usually are appointed or elected for specific terms on a staggered basis, a device that contributes to the independence of the local planning commission (since their terms of office do not necessarily coincide with that of the mayor or council members), and boards have an average size of eight to nine members. A highly educated planning staff generally serves the board, and political reality is such that board members usually follow the advice of the professional staff.

Community planning commissions are generally responsible for revising and updating the comprehensive plan, making rezoning decisions, drawing a zoning map, administering community subdivision regulations, and suggesting changes of the laws in these areas. Planning commissions have particular power in formulating the comprehensive plan and developing land use controls, the most notable authority here being zoning. Local planning commissions rarely have programs of their own, but they are involved in the programs of a number of other agencies, notably such federally sponsored programs as urban renewal, model cities, community development, and mass transit, but they also are involved in local building and housing code programs.

The real clout that local planning commissions have in these programs varies. Allensworth points out, for example, that the staff director of Philadelphia's Planning Commission was a "crucial participant in the urban renewal process for years,"[14] while Scott Greer found that the local planning commissions functioned as a "rubber stamp of approval" in urban renewal programs in many communities.[15]

The use of the urban plan

While the official plan of a community does not have any legal weight as such, professional planners nonetheless have a variety of tools at their disposal with which to implement their plans. Among these tools are zoning ordinances (perhaps the most significant single tool), regulations concerning subdivisions, the power to draw official maps of the area, building and construction codes, decision-making authority on the location

13. Don Allensworth, *Public Administration: The Execution of Public Policy* (Philadelphia: J. B. Lippincott, 1973), p. 33.

14. Allensworth, *op. cit.*, p. 38.

15. Scott Greer, *Urban Renewal in American Cities* (Indianapolis: Bobbs-Merrill, 1965), p. 76.

of public facilities and buildings, and devising a capital improvement program. Communities increasingly are developing *comprehensive plans,* which are land use plans for an urban area that include relevant aspects of the system. More commonly used is the *functional plan,* a term which refers to the specialized planning done by such agencies as urban renewal authorities, health departments, highway departments, recreation agencies, and so forth. In this chapter we are more concerned with the comprehensive aspect of planning, since comprehensive plans are being used increasingly by local policy makers.

A survey taken in 1972 of all cities with more than 150,000 people found that comprehensive planning documents were used by city governments "frequently" to set priorities in the budget process—54 percent of the responding cities reported such a use. On the other hand, about a third of the cities reported they used their planning document only "to qualify for federal grants," particularly when it came to the use of an economic development plan and, to a lesser degree, land use plans.[16]

National pressure is a major aspect of developing rational planning among America's plethora of governments, and it can be traced back at least to 1928 with the enactment of the U.S. Department of Commerce's model planning act known as the Standard City Planning Enabling Act. Designed to serve as a guide to state legislatures in permitting their localities to engage in planning, it was this act that encouraged the establishment of independent planning commissions at the local level.[17]

Since that time a number of federal laws have encouraged (or even forced) states and localities to engage in more comprehensive and rational public planning, and certainly among the more significant of these acts is the Urban Planning Assistance Act of 1954. Under its Section 701, federal grants were allocated to regional, state, and local planning agencies to promote coordinated planning. Now known as the "701" program, these funds are administered by the Department of Housing and Urban Development (HUD), and HUD has granted almost $200 million to subnational planning agencies under its auspices. Later the Demonstration Cities and Metropolitan Development Act of 1966 (*i.e.,* model cities), the Intergovernmental Cooperation Act of 1968, and the National Environmental Policy Act of 1969 were enacted, and all encouraged the development of Councils of Governments and regional planning agencies. In 1974 the Housing and Community Development Act was passed, Title IV of which authorizes grants to local and regional governments for planning purposes, and eligibility for "701" comprehensive planning assistance was expanded to include activities leading to the development and carry-

16. Thomas Thorwood, "The Planning and Management Process in City Government," *Municipal Yearbook, 1973* (Washington, D.C.: International City Management Association, 1973), pp. 28–38.
17. Allensworth, *op. cit.,* p. 33.

ing out of comprehensive plans, improving management skills to implement such plans, and developing policy planning and evaluation capacities. It is hoped that these changes will permit local governments to use "701" grants to improve planning management.[18]

The planning elite

The planning profession is growing increasingly political and, in the process of recognizing the needs of other kinds of people, planners as professionals are beginning to learn that to get along they must go along. Still, the field's acceptance of politics as legitimate is by no means total, as no professional planner wishes to "prostitute" his or her values for the sake of politics. A survey taken for the International City Management Association (ICMA) confirmed that planners are very professionally oriented indeed. All cities of one hundred thousand people or more have professional planners, and more than one-third of the planning directors in big cities come directly from an educational background in planning, followed by educations in engineering, landscape architecture, and public administration, respectively. Seventy percent of all planning directors have planning as their chief work background; most of the remainder have backgrounds in enforcing zoning and code ordinances, engineering, and public administration. Planning directors are extremely well-educated, considerably more so than the typical city council member, with 39 percent holding master's degrees and another 48 percent having bachelor's degrees.[19]

The politicization of planners

Given these kinds of educational and professional backgrounds, it is not surprising that some planners elect not to participate in the political process to get their plans implemented. A number of studies have shown that planners adopt three distinctly different kinds of professional roles. Francine Rabinowitz, for example, has categorized these roles on a professional/political continuum ranging from the *technician*, who develops plans purely on the basis of professional values and who does not get involved in whether or not the plan is accepted by the local government, to the *broker*, who plays the role of a confidential advisor to local officials and is concerned over whether or not a plan is "marketable," to the

18. Mavis Mann Reeves and Paris N. Glendening, "Congressional Action Affecting Local Government," *The Municipal Yearbook, 1976* (Washington, D.C.: International City Management Association, 1976), p. 55.

19. B. Douglas Harman, "City Planning Agencies: Organization, Staffing, and Functions," *The Municipal Yearbook, 1972* (Washington, D.C.: International City Management Association, 1972), p. 63.

mobilizer, who goes out and seeks support in the community for the comprehensive plan and solicits the backing of various local interest groups.[20] Corresponding roles are posited by David C. Ranney, who used the same concepts but dubbed them *political agnostic, confidential advisor,* and *political activist.*[21]

In the 1960s the planning profession itself began to recognize that politics did play a role in urban planning. An example of this recognition was the rise of "advocacy planning," by which was meant that planners legitimately could be overtly political in getting their plans accepted by the community. Advocacy planning clearly was a departure from the normal, staid, and middle-class perspective of professional planning in that most "advocate planners," as they call themselves, were and are consciously in favor of achieving the goals of the poor, the black, and the dispossessed.[22]

Although the concept of advocacy planning has declined in recent years, it is nonetheless clear that the planning profession is becoming increasingly political in its viewpoints and is accepting politics as a legitimate component of the planning process. Increasingly, urban planning programs are found in schools of public administration rather than in schools of architecture, and planning agencies themselves are becoming integrated into the political workings of city hall and state capitol. Moreover, such a trend long has been advocated by scholars of urban affairs. Herbert J. Gans, for example, has urged that planners see themselves as—and become—policy makers, arguing that to remain "technicians" or "political agnostics" will keep planners in ineffectual positions at a time when they are sorely needed if metropolitan growth is to be intelligently managed.[23] As Allensworth has observed, "The planning bureaucracy is enmeshed in politics, and planning policy can normally be traced to a political base. The planning administrator cannot escape this reality." [24]

FINANCING URBAN GOVERNMENTS

Urban governments perform most of the essential tasks of the American polity. It is in cities and towns that health, education, safety, sanitation, recreation, transportation, and crime control are the duties of government.

20. Francine Rabinowitz, *City Politics and Planning* (New York: Atherton, 1959).

21. David C. Ranney, *Planning and Politics in the Metropolis* (Columbus, Ohio: Charles E. Merrill, 1969), pp. 147–150.

22. See, for example, Paul Davidoff, "Advocacy and Pluralism in Planning," *Journal of the American Institute of Planners* 31 (December 1965): 331–338.

23. Herbert J. Gans, "The Need for Planners Trained in Policy Formulation," *Urban Planning in Transition,* Ernest Erder, ed. (New York: Grossman, 1970), pp. 239–245.

24. Allensworth, *op. cit.,* p. 52.

In 1975 municipal governments spent more than $54 billion and collected in revenues more than $53 billion.[25] The chief objects of expenditure were education, the criminal justice system, and highways, though large amounts of public cash went to fire protection, public welfare, sewage, health, hospitals, parks and recreation, housing, and urban renewal.

Most of the revenues of local governments come from the property tax, which amounts to more than 80 percent of all urban income. Increasingly, state and federal aid is making a major contribution to city revenues and in the mid-1970s such aid accounted for more than 40 percent of local revenues. The sales tax also is a major source of revenue for local governments, especially in the big cities. While the average revenues collected by the sales tax amount to about 6 percent of all local tax revenues, in the larger cities it can amount to as much as 60 percent. Certain kinds of use taxes are also becoming a major source of local revenue, notably use taxes for such specific services as hospitals, parks, sewerage, and even education. In the mid-1970s, use charges accounted for more than 17 percent of locally generated revenues, and urban governments are growing increasingly reliant on them.[26]

It is clear from recent events that America's urban governments are increasingly in a monetary bind. We recounted in Chapter 1 the taxpayers' revolt that erupted in California in 1978 as an example of the dimensions of this bind, but it is also worth noting the trials and tribulations of New York City in its faltering effort to match expenditures with revenues.

THE MANHATTAN MONEY SQUEEZE: HARD TIMES IN FUN CITY

In early 1975, New York City discovered that it no longer could borrow money in the municipal bond market. Investors no longer believed in the city's ability to pay back the bonds, and thereby began a long saga.[27]

In March of 1975 the first of a series of stopgap measures was enacted when the state advanced the city some $800 million. In June the Municipal Assistance Corporation, known as "Big Mac," was established to serve as a borrowing agency for the city. Despite the fact that Big Mac was backed by the state of New York and was offering an unprecedented tax-

25. *Municipal Yearbook, 1978* (Washington, D.C.: International City Management Association, 1978), p. 6.

26. James A. Maxwell and J. Richard Aaronson, *Financing State and Local Governments* (Washington, D.C.: Brookings Institution, 1977), pp. 92–165.

27. The following discussion is drawn largely from: Congressional Budget Office, *New York City's Fiscal Problem: Its Origins, Potential Repercussions, and Some Alternative Policy Responses.* Background Paper No. 1, October 10, 1975 (Washington, D.C.: U.S. Government Printing Office, 1975).

exempt interest rate of up to 9.5 percent, it still could not sell the bonds, and eventually tax-free interest rates were forced up to 11 percent. By September 1975 New York was unable to find a syndicate that would underwrite its borrowing, a situation that led to the next stopgap measure, the enactment by the New York legislature of the Financial Emergency Act, which provided the city with $2.3 billion—enough to meet its pressing cash requirements. The act also set up the Emergency Financial Control Board, which was dominated by state officials; in effect, the city was being managed by the state on an increasingly wide scale.

Still, this was not enough. Standard and Poors, which rates the risk associated with various municipal bond issues, warned the state that it would be jeopardizing its own finances if it poured much more money into the city, and Moody's Investor Service, which also rates bonds, reduced the state's bond rating from A to B, thereby further discouraging investment in the city. In November 1975 then-President Gerald R. Ford agreed to back the city with federal money, although for two months he had been stridently maintaining that New York was not the nation's responsibility. (The New York *Daily News* had headlined the president's position with its now notorious headline: "Ford to City: Drop Dead.") Ford offered New York short-term loans of up to $2.3 billion, terminating in 1978, and to be channelled through the Emergency Financial Control Board of the state of New York. The offer was readily accepted.

New York City, of course, had to do its share, and the budgetary slashing became savage at points. Within the first year of the fiscal emergency, $500 million in taxes were imposed on what already were the most heavily taxed citizens in the country. The city income tax for New Yorkers was increased an average of 25 percent, and taxes on corporations, property, and cigarettes were raised. The city's work force was reduced by 55,000 people to 239,000, the lowest level in more than a decade. Wages of most remaining workers were frozen, and wages previously promised were deferred for a year. The illustrious 129-year-old policy of free tuition at the City University of New York was ended abruptly. The transit fare was hiked; seventy-seven day care centers were closed, excluding about five thousand children who had relied on them; the number of city hospitals was reduced from nineteen to seventeen, with plans to close two more; and thirty-two public schools were closed.

Budgets, demographics, and politics

How did "Fun City" get in such sad shape? Certain short-term factors clearly were a problem, notably the immediate crisis in investor confidence, the recession of 1974, which reduced city revenues sharply, and the severe inflation of the same period. However, the long-term factors were

of greater consequence; the poor are, and have been for some time, moving into New York City, particularly from the rural South and Puerto
Rico. There is an out-migration of the middle class to the suburbs, and
the city's population is growing both older and poorer. Between 1950
and 1970 the portion of the city's population over sixty-five years of age
grew from 8 percent to more than 12 percent, and the proportion of the
city's families with incomes below the nation's average income level rose
from 36 to 49 percent. While New York's population has remained relatively
constant, New York rapidly lost jobs between 1970 and 1975. Meanwhile,
taxes went up. A glance at Table 12–7 indicates the steep rise in New
York City taxes and their relationship to the personal income of New
Yorkers between 1969 and 1975.

Beyond these relatively uncontrollable events, however, New York
suffered from mismanagement, and among the most notable aspects of this
mismanagement was the city's relationship with public unions. U.S.
Treasury officials estimate that it costs New York City an average of
$30,000 every year to pay and provide fringe benefits for each municipal
employee; this compares with an average of $13,000 to $14,000 for each
federal civil service employee. New York City's payroll in 1976 exceeded
$7 billion, and $2 billion of this went to civil service pensions alone, which
ranged from $12,000 to $30,000. New York paid in 1976 more than $35,000
for the average fire fighter, and almost $19,000 for the average senior
clerk.

Moreover, the fringe benefits were phenomenal. Victor Riesel wrote
in his syndicated column that a good portion of the city's employees had
contracts which, in effect, permitted them to work only half a year for a
full year's pay.[28] In 1976 police officers in New York had twenty-seven

TABLE 12–7. The New York City Tax Burden, 1969–75

Fiscal Year	Personal Income ($ billions)	Taxes [1] ($ billions)	Taxes as Percent of Personal Income
1969–70	39	2.958	7.5
1970–71	41	3.178	7.7
1971–72	43	3.736	8.7
1972–73	45	4.017	8.9
1973–74	48	4.506	9.4
1974–75	50	5.111	10.2

Source: New York City Finance Administration
[1] Excludes fees and charges, stock transfer taxes and nonresident income taxes.

28. The following discussion of New York City's retirement pensions is drawn from
Victor Riesel, "Years Pay, Six Months Work, The Fun City Way," syndicated
column, October 15, 1975.

days' vacation, eighteen days off in return for a fifteen-minute early arrival for briefings, three days off for giving blood, three days off for "good arrests," an average of ten days of sick leave, eleven annual holidays, and two regular days off on the seven-day swing shift. Employees in the Sanitation Department had the same type of arrangement, and both calculated out to about six months off every year. Teachers, with summer holidays, the Easter and Christmas weeks off, school closure days, sick leaves, sabbaticals, "short-days," early breaks, and election days off, amounted to five to six months off annually. One hundred percent of each employee's health insurance costs was paid for by the city, including, in some cases, free dental care and eyeglasses for retired workers.

A married employee in New York who retired at sixty-five with twenty-five years service received an after-tax income equal to 125 percent of his or her take-home pay during the last year on the job. By comparison the retirement rate in Atlanta was 43 percent of the last year's salary; in Chicago, 47 percent; in Dallas, 53 percent; and in Los Angeles, 54 percent.

By 1975 New York City workers were earning consistently higher salaries than their counterparts in virtually every major city in the country. A major reason why New York's benefits are so high is that the city employees and their families cast about a half million votes in city elections, and Fun City's politicians have been duly responsive. In the 1960s city employees' salary and fringe benefits increased by 15.7 percent and 19.4 percent respectively in each of the city's two election years. Table 12–8 indicates the salaries of New York's employees and also itemizes the percentage of the city's population receiving welfare payments, per capita expenditures of city government, local government employment per ten thousand population, and debt outstanding per capita, and compares these data with other major central cities in the nation. With a debt of more than $14 billion, New York's outstanding debt per capita in 1972–1973 was almost $1,700; the next largest was Boston with a debt of almost $1,400 per person.

New York and the wonders of "creative accounting"

Other than bad bargaining with unions, New York also relied extensively on another system of mismanagement, known in some circles as "creative accounting." Steven R. Weisman has described how New York became a "fiscal junkie," relating how New York relied on the "expense fix," the "revenue fix," the "capital fix," and the "outright deficit fix." [29] Basically,

29. Steven R. Weisman, "How New York Became a Fiscal Junkie," *New York Times,* August 17, 1975.

TABLE 12–8. Major U.S. Cities by Welfare Recipients, Per Capita Expenditures, Public Employment, Employee Salaries, and Per Capita Debt, 1975

City	(2) Fraction of Population Receiving Welfare Payments [1]	(3) Per Capita Expenditures 1972–1973	(4) Local Government Employment Per 10,000 Population 1974	(5) Public Employee Average Salaries 1974				(6) Debt Outstanding per capita 1972–73 [1]	
				(a) Teacher	(b) Police	(c) Fire	(d) Sanitation	(a) Total	(b) Short-term
New York City [2]	12.4	$1,224	517.1	$17,018	$14,666	$16,964	$15,924	$1,676	$352
Boston	16.9	858	378.0	13,938	14,352	13,844	10,666	1,385	334
Chicago	11.1	267	140.0	17,409	14,146	15,525	11,956	733	169
Newark	14.4	692	391.1	13,720	13,282	13,282	8,473	616	112
Los Angeles	8.0	242	162.2	13,058	15,833	21,180	13,168	650	14
Philadelphia [2]	16.2	415	163.8	12,800	14,354	13,869	13,337	1,015	101
San Francisco [2]	9.1	751	312.5	14,855	15,529	17,765	13,023	1,225	151
New Orleans [2]	11.4	241	177.3	8,715	10,746	10,645	4,170	770	39
St. Louis [2]	15.8	310	241.9	14,894	11,748	13,185	9,593	731	49
Denver [2]	7.2	473	237.0	13,505	12,907	14,198	10,258	786	52
Baltimore [2]	16.3	806	434.1	10,488	10,098	10,980	8,126	609	45
Detroit	11.1	357	194.8	18,836	15,636	16,107	13,814	658	63

[1] Central County

[2] Boundaries of the city are coterminous with those of the central county

Source: Derived from Congressional Budget Office, *New York City's Fiscal Problem*, Background Paper No. 1, October 10, 1975, Washington; U.S. Government Printing Office, 1975, pp. 16, 17, and errata sheet

these "fixes" amounted to treating current costs as next year's costs, treating anticipated revenues as current revenues, diverting capital expenditures to day-to-day operating costs, and simply borrowing against anticipated revenues for daily operating expenses. Of these the revenue fix, which had been initiated very quietly by Mayor Robert Wagner in 1965 as a means of financing a $100 million deficit that the city then had, was ultimately perhaps the most damaging.

In 1977 the U.S. Securities and Exchange Commission (SEC) charged that the city's financial practices had gone beyond the bounds of creative accounting and that Mayor Abraham Beame and six major banks had arranged the sale of $4 billion in municipal bonds to an unsuspecting public in 1975, knowing full well that the city was about to go down the fiscal tubes. While some of these banks were pushing the sale of New York bonds, they simultaneously were dumping their own holdings on the marketplace before the financial roof caved in. Duped investors lost 45 percent of their bonds' face value when New York's monetary plight was exposed later that year.

Beame called the SEC's one thousand pages of charges "a shameless, vicious political document," since it was released shortly before New York's Democratic mayoral primary. The banks also denied any impropriety. Nevertheless, the SEC maintained that New York "employed budgetary, accounting and financial practices which it knew distorted its true financial condition"—such as listing city-owned property on tax rolls, even though no city taxes its own property.

Beame, who had been New York's chief financial officer for eight years before he was elected mayor in 1973, was defeated by relatively conservative Edward Koch in 1977. During Beame's tenure, the city had managed to repay all its emergency loans from the federal Treasury on time or before they were due, although the city's debt actually was slightly higher when Koch became mayor than it was at the height of the fiscal crisis in 1975—chiefly because of the city's annual debt service charge of an almost unbelievable $2 billion. Still, New York's financial *chutzpa* persists; in 1978 Mayor Koch asked Washington for more emergency funding (the city still was frozen out of the municipal bond market) just as he announced that he was raising the salaries of 2,100 city executives by $3,000 to $7,000 a year! [30] Congress came through with a guarantee to back New York bond issues with another $1.65 billion in 1978 to stave off municipal bankruptcy.

What if? the impact of bankruptcy

New York City is one of the second largest governments in the country. Therefore, when a government of its magnitude runs into financial snags,

30. Andy Logan, "Around City Hall," *The New Yorker*, January 23, 1978, pp. 98–103.

the effects may not be limited to the municipal boundaries. If the city had been, or ultimately were, forced to default on its obligations, a number of investors could be hurt. The Congressional Budget Office observed,

> While it is possible that the collapse of New York would precipitate a storm of bankruptcies in the private sector, and a wave of municipal defaults, it is also possible that the default by the city would generate but a ripple on the nation's financial waters.[31]

The large New York banks held roughly $2 billion of the $14.6 billion in outstanding debt in 1975, or only 5 percent of their total assets. Approximately 60 percent of the nation's nine thousand banks that do not belong to the Federal Reserve System have more than half of their capital in New York city securities, and a similar number of city securities are held by the five thousand banks that are members of the Federal Reserve System. Nevertheless, the Federal Reserve has agreed to back these non-member banks in the event of a New York default, thereby lessening the economic impact.

Ultimately, however, the impact of New York City going bankrupt would depend on the psychology of the bond market, which no one really can predict, although there are indications that investors are getting nervous over New York. In 1975 bonds were rejected in three states—Ohio, New Jersey, and New York—by large margins at the polls, and these defeats were linked by experts to the New York City financial crisis. Larger, older cities, particularly those in the North Central area and in the East, have already been forced to pay unusually high rates of interest, and the Congressional Budget Office has linked this situation to their "superficial fiscal resemblance to New York." [32] The interest rates paid by Philadelphia, Detroit, and New York State, for example, all were forced up substantially in 1975, largely because of the fiscal albatross of New York City.

Just as the investment community is concerned about New York City, so is the public at large. A sampling of public opinion polls taken in 1975 indicated that between 18 and 35 percent of Americans really did not want to do anything for New York City, while somewhere between 24 and 42 percent definitely favored an effective cash aid to help New York.[33] By 1977, however, a national survey indicated that 44 percent of the nation opposed aid to major cities in fiscal trouble, while 43 percent

---

31. Congressional Budget Office, *op. cit.*, p. 19.
32. *Ibid.*, pp. 20–21.
33. Kevin Phillips, "New York Bail Out, Polls Only Confuse Issue," syndicated column, November 27, 1975.

favored it; in the Northeast, not surprisingly, 58 percent favored such aid.[34]

Is New York unique? not likely

American cities have gone bankrupt in the past; Mobile, Alabama, was the first, gaining that dubious distinction in 1838. The Advisory Commission on Intergovernmental Relations reports that most municipal defaults on obligations occurred right after the Civil War, then again during the Depression of the 1930s. Four hundred thirty-one American cities defaulted on obligations after World War II, but at least 306 of these were technical and temporary defaults. Defaults totaled less than one-half of 1 percent of all municipal debts outstanding in 1970.

Other cities are facing New York's experience, if in less traumatic terms and considerably less precipitously. In 1978 the Advisory Commission on Intergovernmental Relations released startling data indicating that ten of America's most depressed big cities (not including New York) had become dramatically more dependent upon Washington to make ends meet than only two years earlier. The cities, on the average, received thirty-one cents from the federal government for every dollar they raised from their own sources in 1976, but only two years later were receiving more than 54 cents for each local tax dollar. The cities were Atlanta, Baltimore, Boston, Buffalo, Chicago, Cleveland, Detroit, Newark, Philadelphia, and St. Louis.[35]

There are exceptions to such dismal statistics, however. Seattle provides a fine example of a city that has maintained fiscal control despite some tough economic sledding. Seattle underwent terrific economic disruptions as a result of massive cutbacks in aircraft production by Boeing Corporation in the early 1970s. Seattle countered this turmoil by raising taxes and reducing its workforce. Moreover, the city's unions, in the view of many, have become a conservative force for fiscal responsibility and this attitude has been of considerable help in keeping Seattle financially viable, which it largely is today.

Nevertheless, a majority of major American cities are potentially headed for financial trouble, and it is little wonder that the National League of Cities, the nation's largest group of city officials, has requested President Carter to create a Council of Urban Advisors and to channel $10 billion in immediate federal aid to meet the economic requirements of the cities.

34. Advisory Commission on Intergovernmental Relations, *Changing Attitudes on Government and Taxes* (Washington, D.C.: U.S. Government Printing Office, 1977).

35. Advisory Commission on Intergovernmental Relations, cited in Associated Press, April 2, 1978, syndicated nationally.

When cities have revenues to expend (an increasingly rare phenomenon, it appears), the urban budgeteers take over. In cities with strong executive governments, the mayor has an unusual degree of control over budgetary priorities relative to the governor and the president; the council, while technically in charge of final authorizations, generally defers to the mayor or city manager. John P. Crecine, in his computer simulation of urban budgetary processes in Detroit, Pittsburgh, and Cleveland, observes that the municipal chief executive forms his budget primarily around the values of, first and foremost, balancing it (hardly a problem at the national level), maintaining existing levels of services, increasing the salaries of city employees, and avoiding tax hikes, particularly property tax increases on the assumption that high taxes will induce big taxpayers, such as employers, to move to the suburbs and thereby reduce the city's tax base.[36]

If budget cuts are called for, reductions in spending usually (at least in strong executive governments) are negotiated between the mayor or manager and agency heads; the council waits on the sidelines for the final document, which it rarely questions. Crecine notes that in terms of either budgetary cuts or increases, there generally is a clear list of priorities: administrative wages are attended to first, followed by nonadministrative salaries, operating expenses, equipment expenditures, and maintenance, in that order.

"Rational" budgeting, as exemplified by Programming-Planning-Budgeting techniques in contrast to "incremental" budgeting based on past expenditures, appears to be a less likely eventuality in urban governments than in state governments and the national government. There are unique reasons for the paramountcy of incremental budgeting in city hall. One is the sheer complexity of the urban budget and the lack of administrative, professional, and technical personnel trained to function exclusively as budgeters. Crecine has observed that Pittsburgh, with an extraordinarily complicated budget in excess of $75 million annually, had a budget staff of four people. Another reason is an absence of information and inadequate cost/effectiveness measurements, which obstruct rational policy choices. While hardly unique to urban governments, these deficiencies are unusually salient in the operations of the municipal public sector.

Metropolitan governments also have an unusually low degree of control over their expenditures; most urban budgets are previously committed to ongoing programs, such as police and fire protection which, because

36. John P. Crecine, *Governmental Problem-Solving: A Computer Simulation of Municipal Budgeting* (Skokie, Ill.: Rand McNally, 1969).

of their vital importance to the very idea of government, cannot be de-emphasized in favor of more modish social programs. Finally, urban governments must function, or attempt to function, in the face of con-straints on their revenues that do not apply to officials of the federal and state governments. One of these constraints is the necessity of balancing the local budget; unlike the national government, and more so than in state governments, urban expenditures must match revenues. The other major constraint on local revenues is "Judge Dillon's rule," which is the phrase commonly used to express the complete subservience of the city to the state. Because most cities may neither initiate new methods of taxing, nor adapt administrative innovations, nor tap new sources of revenue without the explicit consent of the state legislature, cities are further constrained in the implementation of rational budgetary strategies.

Clearly, managing money is a major problem for urban governments, and we examine fiscal matters from another perspective in Chapter 13, "The Federal Maze." But we have not yet completed our review of the urban experience, and we do so in the next chapter.

SUPPLEMENTAL BIBLIOGRAPHY

ADRIAN, CHARLES and CHARLES PRESS, *Governing Urban America* (5th ed.), New York: McGraw-Hill, 1977.

BANFIELD, EDWARD C. and JAMES Q. WILSON, *City Politics*. New York: Vintage Books-Random House, 1963.

CLAWSON, MARION and PETER HALL, *Planning and Urban Growth: An Anglo-American Comparison*. Baltimore: Johns Hopkins University Press, 1973.

DANIELSON, MICHAEL, ed., *Metropolitan Politics: A Reader*. Boston: Little, Brown, 1966.

FESLER, JAMES W., ed., *The 50 States and Their Local Governments*. New York: Knopf, 1967.

GANS, HERBERT, *The Levitowners: Ways of Life and Politics in a New Sub-urban Community*. New York: Pantheon, 1967.

International City Managers Association, *Techniques of Municipal Adminis-tration* (2nd ed), Chicago: I.C.M.A., 1969.

JACOB, HERBERT, *Justice in America*. Boston: Little, Brown, 1965.

JACOB, PHILIP E. and JAMES V. TOSCANO, eds., *The Integration of Political Communities*. Philadelphia: J. B. Lippincott, 1964.

LOCKARD, DUANE, *The Politics of State and Local Government* (2nd ed.), New York: Macmillan, 1969.

LOUIS, THEODORE, *At the Pleasure of the Mayor*. New York: Free Press, 1964.

SAYRE, WALLACE and HERBERT KAUFMAN, *Governing New York City*. New York: W. W. Norton, 1960.

SENGSTOCK, FRANK S., *et al.*, *Consolidation: Building a Bridge Between City and Suburb*. Worcester, Mass.: Heffernan Press, 1964.

TALBOT, ALAN R., *The Mayor's Game*. New York: Harper & Row, 1967.

U.S. Advisory Commission on Intergovernmental Relations, *Alternative Approaches to Governmental Reorganization in Metropolitan Areas*, Report A–11. Washington, D.C.: U.S. Government Printing Office, 1962.

———, *Factors Affecting Voter Reactions to Governmental Reorganization in Metropolitan Areas*, Report M–15. Washington, D.C.: U.S. Government Printing Office, 1962.

VOSE, CLEMENT E., "Interest Groups, Judicial Review, and Local Government," *Western Political Quarterly*, 19 (March 1966), 85–100.

WILSON, JAMES Q., ed., *City Politics and Public Policy*. New York: John Wiley, 1968.

ZIMMERMAN, JOSEPH F., ed., *Government of the Metropolis*. New York: Holt, Rinehart and Winston, 1968.

the urban
experience

chapter 13

In the last chapter, we approached the problems of the municipal management from a professional perspective—that is, we considered demographics, economics, governance, planning, and finance. In this chapter, we view the urban experience from a policy perspective, focussing on some of the major issues confronting the urban administrator in the 1980s: crime, housing, and transportation.

CRIME IN THE STREETS

Urban crime is pervasive, frightening, and widespread. Consequently, controlling crime has become a principal concern of public administrators, and in this portion we review the roots of urban rioting (and its results a decade later), the fear and reality of street crime, the effectiveness of the police, and the problems of the courts.

The race riots of the 1960s

The 1960s were a decade of urban riots, and these riots were race riots. One reason why the riots were *race* riots is that the poor and uneducated also are more likely to be black and brown. In the 1970s the median income of a black family was almost half that of a white family and, while 80 percent of white women and 81 percent of white males between twenty-five and twenty-nine years of age in 1971 had completed four years of high school or more, only 63 percent of black women and only 59 percent of black males in the same age bracket could make the same statement.[1]

Most of the race riots of the 1960s occurred in the big cities of the North. In the five years between 1963 and 1968 there were 283 racial disturbances of varying degrees of intensity in cities of more than 25,000 people, compared to only 76 major racial disorders during the fifty years between 1913 and 1963. The Watts riot of 1965 in Los Angeles scorched an area of more than forty-five square miles, killing thirty-four people, of whom thirty-one were black, and damaging or destroying more than six hundred buildings. Newark, New Jersey, erupted in 1967, requiring more than four thousand police and troops to restore order and killing twenty-three people, of whom twenty-one were black. Detroit, the worst, blew up in the same year with five days of concentrated rioting, killing forty-three people, of whom thirty-nine were black, levelling more than thirteen hundred buildings, looting more than twenty-seven hundred businesses, and deploying fifteen thousand peace officers and soldiers to quell the riot. In 1967 alone, the most explosive year of the riots of the sixties, 139 riots or serious racial incidents in 114 cities and towns erupted in virtually every section of the country, killing 95 people, maiming more than 1,700, and resulting in more than 12,000 arrests. The National Guard and Army paratroopers were brought in to restore order in fifteen cities in 1967, and property damage in eight communities alone that year totalled more than $250 million.[2]

Virtually all the disturbances in the 1960s occurred in black neighborhoods. They were usually directed against symbols of white authority. Normally, no single incident precipitated the riots but, rather, they were preceded by a series of tension-heightening occurrences culminated by a final incident (usually police-related) that led to violence. Riots occurred, however, only in those cities with large black populations, and particularly in cities with high levels of population density that had experienced recent upsurges in the size of their black population. The "typical" rioter was a young black male, a life-long resident of the city in which he rioted, underemployed or working in a menial job, hostile to whites and

1. Bureau of the Census, *Social and Economic Status of Negroes in the United States,* Current Population Report Series No. 29 (Washington, D.C.: U.S. Government Printing Office, 1976), p. 23.
2. David L. Langford, "Black Plight Changed Little Since Turbulent '67 Summer," United Press International, July 10, 1977, syndicated nationally.

middle-class blacks alike, racially proud, politically informed, alienated, and better educated than blacks in his neighborhood who did not riot. In a survey taken after the major Detroit riots of 1967, 11 percent of the residents admitted to participating in the riots; 20 to 25 percent identified themselves as counterrioters who urged other blacks to "cool it." Counterrioters typically had more formal education and higher incomes than either the rioters or the people who did not participate in the riots.[3]

Why did they riot? A survey taken by the National Advisory Commission on Civil Disorders[4] of twenty riot-torn cities of the 1960s indicates that although at least a dozen reasons could be listed, they varied markedly in degrees of intensity. Included in the first order of intensity—in other words, the major "causes" of the riots—were, first and foremost, police practices, followed by unemployment or underemployment, and inadequate housing. In the second order of intensity were inadequate educational opportunities, poor recreational facilities, and ineffectual police review structures and complaint mechanisms for residents. The third level of intensity included "disrespectful" white attitudes, a discriminatory administration of justice, inadequate federal programs and municipal services, discriminatory consumer and credit practices, and inadequate welfare programs. The available evidence indicates that black perceptions of reality were largely accurate.

Did the riots work?

Did the riots of the sixties accomplish anything for blacks? During the 1960s, for example, Benjamin L. Hooks, now National Director of the National Association for the Advancement of Colored People, told a white audience that, "Pragmatically, riots work"[5] and, to be sure, during the decade between 1967 (the peak year of black rioting) and 1977, blacks made substantial political gains. In 1967 only 400 blacks in the whole country held an elected political office (although this was four times the number of only three years earlier); by 1977, 4,311 held office. In 1967 there were no black mayors; by 1977 there were 130. The number of blacks in Congress increased from three in 1967 to sixteen in 1977, and political scientists largely feel that blacks were responsible more than any single group for electing Carter president in 1976.[6]

Blacks also made significant overall strides economically and educa-

3. Seymour Spilerman, "The Causes of Racial Disturbances," *American Sociological Review* 35 (August 1970): 617–649.

4. National Advisory Commission on Civil Disorders, *Report* (Washington, D.C.: U.S. Government Printing Office, 1968).

5. Quoted in Langford, *op. cit.*

6. *Ibid.*

tionally during the decade following the riots. The average income of black families, less than $5,000 in 1967, had risen to more than $9,000 in 1975; the proportions of blacks eighteen to twenty-one years old who were in colleges more than doubled from a modest 10 percent in 1966 to 23 percent in 1976.[7]

But what have these gains meant to blacks on the streets, the poor blacks? Blacks still do not earn nearly as much money as whites, are not educated as well as whites, and make up disproportionate numbers of the welfare rolls. Employment levels fell off precipitously for nonwhites between 1967 and 1977 with nonwhite unemployment rising from more than 7 percent in 1967 to nearly 14 percent ten years later. These layoffs have hit the poor black and brown people far more forcefully than middle- and upper-class minorities.

In the riot areas themselves the ruins of destruction persisted ten years later. Although the riots brought federal, state, and local aid to the Twelfth Street neighborhood in Detroit, the Fourteenth and Seventh Street corridors in Washington, D.C., and the Watts area in Los Angeles, these and other riot centers of the sixties clearly are worse off than they were in 1967. Of the 200,000 people who left Detroit between 1967 and 1977, 12,000 were from the Twelfth Street area alone and vacant lots that once supported small businesses abound. Along Washington's Fourteenth Street only ten stores that were in operation before 1967 are still doing business, and the percentage of poor people in the neighborhood has increased since the rioting. Blacks have fled Watts since the devastation, leaving behind the poorest families, and unemployment is estimated at more than 25 percent—considerably higher than it was in the mid-1960s.[8]

Moreover, blacks may be in even worse shape emotionally than they were in the 1960s. The national president of Operation PUSH, the Reverend Jessie Jackson, has stated, "As opposed to the politics of confrontation, right now we are in the politics of escapism. Blacks today are doing something that's more destructive than external riots, they are beginning to self-inflict riots upon their bodies with extreme alcoholism, heroin, cocaine, marijuana, and premature pregnancy." [9] The United Nations Fund for Drug Abuse estimates that there are more than 620,000 drug addicts in the United States, most of whom live in big city ghettoes and who commit more than half of the nation's street crimes—not surprising, since a heroin habit now costs more than $50 a day. One thousand addicts are

---

7. "Those Riot Torn Cities: A Look at Progress Ten Years Later," U.S. News and World Report, August 29, 1977, p. 51.

8. Ibid., pp. 50–51.

9. Quoted in Langford, op. cit.

born every year in New York City alone, and about two thousand people across the country die each year from heroin overdoses.[10]

The phrase no longer is, as it was in 1967, "Burn Baby Burn!" It is now, "Not enough jobs and too many junkies." The Department of Health, Education and Welfare estimates that there are at least forty thousand heroin addicts in Detroit alone, which has a population that is 60 percent black. On the other hand, Detroit's forty-five hundred-man Police Department, which was only 5 percent black in 1967, was 25 percent black ten years later and the mayor, Coleman A. Young, also a black, expressed himself as committed to doubling that figure.[11]

Although blacks have made some major political gains and some less dramatic social and economic advances, the problem of the black poor is little changed and may have become worse since the 1960s. Indeed, some have argued that upper class blacks may have been co-opted—that is, because members of their race have made significant inroads politically, it is easier for blacks to keep the lid on the dispossessed and downtrodden, who also happen to be black. In sum, Hooks may be wrong; rioting did not work, at least not for the very poorest members of society. To quote one Willie Alexander of Rochester, New York ". . . I threw a few stones, but I don't think it did no good, though. I didn't have a job then and I'm still not workin'. . . ." Or, as another participant noted, "In some ways it might have been better then. At least then we had decent places to shop. What's there now? A big hole in the ground." [12]

This frustration exploded in 1977 when New York City experienced a major power failure. During the blackout hundreds of stores were sacked by residents of their own neighborhoods, an action in stark contrast to the city's power failure of 1965; roughly thirty-five hundred people were arrested in 1977 as a result of looting during the power failure, whereas only around one hundred were arrested in 1965 on similar charges. A conclusion one might draw from this contrast is that, as frustration in the ghetto mounts, the poor have turned on themselves.

The fear of crime

The urban race riots of the 1960s and the massive looting in 1977 in New York are instances of spectacular crimes. Far more pervasive and insidious is the "normal" street crime, such as robbery, burglary, murder, and rape. It is these kinds of crimes that have had a far greater impact on the

10. United Press International, November 2, 1977, syndicated nationally.

11. Langford, *op. cit.*

12. Quoted in *ibid.*

American psyche than the occasional, if more violent and spectacular, riot. Polls conducted by the Urban Observatory, Gallup, and Harris all indicated that people increasingly are afraid of being violated or killed in their own neighborhoods.[13]

Moreover, the fear of crime in America is intensifying. In 1949 Gallup found that only 4 percent of big city residents saw crime as their community's worst problem; by 1965 crime had emerged as a vital issue; and by 1975 Gallup found that nearly half of Americans—a record 45 percent—were afraid to walk in their own neighborhoods at night and in the nation's largest cities, those of half a million people or more, the figure was 56 percent. Among women in large urban areas, 77 percent were afraid to go out at night and 19 percent were afraid of household intruders. By contrast in 1968 only 31 percent of the respondents were fearful of walking in their own neighborhoods at night.

The overall fear of crime as measured by such polls has remained essentially constant since 1972, but there has been some radical attitude changes among segments of the population, notably among black and brown citizens, who have grown increasingly fearful over walking in their own neighborhoods at night. Forty-nine percent of the respondents in 1975 believed that the crime situation had worsened in their own communities during the last year, and only 12 percent said they had less fear than a year ago.

The reality of crime

Fears of the citizenry over crime against their persons and their property, especially among the poor and minorities, are well founded. The United States has more crime, according to its own statistics, than any other Western industrialized nation. More people are murdered (more than ten thousand a year) in America than in any other country in the world. According to the Federal Bureau of Investigation's Uniform Crime Reports, crimes have been increasing almost exponentially between 1960, when Uniform Crime Reports first were maintained, and 1975. During that fifteen year period (in which the U.S. population went up by only 16 percent), the number of murders and manslaughters doubled, forceable rapes tripled, robberies more than tripled, and assaults, burglaries, larcenies, and car thefts all more than doubled by substantial margins. The total crimes against persons (by which is meant murder, manslaughters,

---

13. The following data concerning polls on the fear of crime are drawn from: Gene A. Fowler, *Citizen Attitudes Toward Local Government, Services and Taxes* (Lexington, Mass.: Ballinger, 1974), pp. 147–150; George Gallup, Associated Press, July 28, 1975, syndicated nationally; and "Crime Scene Top Problem for Cities," *The Washington Post*, July 27, 1975, for the Harris Survey.

rapes, and assaults) soared from 160 such crimes per 100,000 population in 1960 to 459 in 1975. The total crimes against property (by which is meant burglary, larceny, robbery, and auto theft) shot up from 1,716 per 100,000 people in 1960 to 4,363 in 1975.[14]

These are only the official statistics; the "unofficial" statistics reveal a far bleaker picture of crime in America. In recent years a number of surveys of criminal victims have been conducted in several cities and states, and they indicate that the FBI Uniform Crime Reports tell only half, or even only a third, of the crime actually committed in the seven standard categories just listed. According to one of the more recent such polls conducted by the Gallup organization, one household in every four in the United States was hit by some crime at least once during the twelve months between 1974 and 1975. In the big cities, those with more than five hundred thousand people, the ratio is even more staggering, with one household in three being struck by some criminal act.[15]

Lately, it has been unclear whether or not the crime rate in America is increasing or levelling off. The FBI, in its Uniform Crime Reports for 1975 and 1976, indicated that there was a decline in violent crimes, although thefts were increasing in certain large cities. On the other hand the Law Enforcement Assistance Administration (LEAA) issued its own report during the same year which countered the FBI's findings. As the result of a "victim's survey" that questioned the occupants of roughly sixty thousand households and twenty-four hundred businesses, the LEAA concluded "no significant changes in victimization rates from 1974 to 1975 were recorded for any of the major crimes measured," which excluded murders (it is, after all, difficult to survey murder victims), although the FBI had reported the same year that there was a 9 percent increase in overall crime.[16]

It has been contended that one reason the FBI's Uniform Crime Reports show such dramatic increases in crime every year is that the report is a conscious effort to fan public fears so that police department budgets might be increased. Nevertheless, it probably is true that crime has been increasing in this country for the past fifteen years, and that most of the crimes are never reported.

Particular groups show an alarming propensity both for committing crimes and being the victims of crimes. The President's Commission on Crime found that young people are most prone to commit crimes, particularly the fifteen- to seventeen-year-old age group which constitutes less

14. Federal Bureau of Investigation, *Uniform Crime Reports 1960–1975* (Washington, D.C.: U.S. Government Printing Office, 1976).

15. Associated Press, July 3, 1975, syndicated nationally.

16. Law Enforcement Assistance Administration as quoted by Associated Press, May 25, 1975, syndicated nationally.

than 6 percent of the population but which has the highest arrest rate, accounting for almost 13 percent of all arrests. Projections by the commission forecast that approximately 40 percent of all male children in our nation eventually would be arrested for a nontraffic offense sometime during their lives.[17] The President's Commission on Law Enforcement and Administration of Justice sketched the "typical" perpetrator of urban robberies, rapes, and murders in America as under twenty-five years of age, poorly educated, extremely deprived economically, likely unemployed, unmarried, reared in a broken home, and probably having a prior criminal record.[18] Between 1960 and 1975 arrests of youths for violent crimes increased 246 percent, a rate twice that of the adult rate. Overall, young people between ten and seventeen years old, which accounted for only 16 percent of the population, made up nearly 50 percent of *all* arrest for thefts and criminal violence between 1960 and 1975.[19] Given the facts that roughly half of American blacks are under twenty-five, about 14 percent of blacks of all ages are unemployed or underemployed, and nearly 40 percent of black teenagers are in similar straights, it follows that a disproportionate share of street crimes are committed by blacks against blacks. Moreover, victims resemble criminals in terms of the sociological characteristics just listed.

What is being done?

Maintaining law and order is, by definition, essential to the very concept of government. What has government done about both the rise in the fear of crime and the rise of real crime? The evidence indicates, given the increases in crime, not much. Part of the reason is because the police still rely on very traditional methods of crime control.

The local constabulary: who are the cops?

The towns and cities of America, with their more sophisticated police departments, have been relatively responsive to the dynamic of social change and its relationship to the rise in crime. There are 17,464 local police agencies in America, and most of these are very small—in fact, more than half of these departments have less than five full-time employees. It has been estimated that about one-half of the country's more

17. President's Commission on Crime, *Report of the President's Commission on Crime* (Washington, D.C.: U.S. Government Printing Office, 1967).
18. President's Commission on Law Enforcement and the Administration of Justice, *The Challenge of Crime in a Free Society* (New York: Avon, 1969).
19. Associated Press, May 23, 1976, syndicated nationally.

than 38,000 local jurisdictions have law enforcement agencies, and that almost 70 percent of these departments have fewer than ten sworn officers.[20] The National Advisory Council on Criminal Justice Standards and Goals recommended in 1975 that police departments with fewer than ten employees be consolidated as a major means of upgrading the war against criminals.[21]

What kinds of people inhabit these almost 17,500 police departments across the country? The typical police officer comes from a working-class background; very few hail from the middle class. According to a survey conducted in 1976 by the International City Management Association (ICMA) of all cities with more than ten thousand people, 90 percent of the nation's police departments require a high school diploma or the equivalent, 4 percent of the departments require some college education, and another 4 percent require a degree from a community college; only a tenth of 1 percent require a bachelor's degree, and 2 percent of the localities do not have formal educational requirements. Nevertheless, the National Advisory Commission on Criminal Justice Standards and Goals recommended that all police departments require four years of college by 1982, and roughly 23 percent of American cities do provide incentive programs for their officers to further their educations.[22]

Of course, cities and towns get what they pay for, and in the early 1970s the U.S. Bureau of Labor Statistics concluded that the cities did not pay much for their policemen. The average patrolman's pay in major cities was 33 percent less than what was needed to support a family of four in urban areas, and it appears that the situation may have grown even worse over time. Fifty years ago policemen earned higher salaries than nearly all other trades and there were more qualified applicants than positions. Some experts estimate that from a third to a half of all metropolitan policemen moonlight. The ICMA survey of 1976 indicated that 97 percent of American cities permitted their police to take on outside employment. Eighty-one percent of the cities imposed some sort of restriction regarding the type of job that a policeman could take, but more than 60 percent had no restrictions on the number of hours of outside employment permitted per week.[23] It would appear that cities recognize the fact

20. S. Emphany McCann, "Law Enforcement Agencies in Urban Counties," *County Yearbook, 1975* (Washington, D.C.: National Association of Counties and the International City Management Association, 1975), pp. 110–113.

21. As quoted in *ibid.*, p. 112.

22. As cited in James R. Mandish and Laurie S. Frankel, "Personnel Practices in the Municipal Police Service: 1976," *Municipal Yearbook, 1977* (Washington, D.C.: International City Management Association, 1977), pp. 160–161.

23. Madish and Frankel, *op. cit.*, pp. 160–161.

that they themselves underpay their police officers, and that the police officers often have to support a family.

Similarly, training programs for the police are minimal at best, quite aside from formal educational attainment. In terms of the average minimum training hours required by state governments, physicians must put in eleven thousand hours, embalmers five thousand hours, barbers four thousand hours, beauticians twelve hundred hours, and policemen an almost paltry two hundred hours. Yet, these are the people on whom society straps a pistol and expects, at least officially, to react to dangerous and disorienting human situations as if they were combinations of Sherlock Holmes, Sigmund Freud, Perry Mason, and Sergeant Preston of the Mounties.

Perhaps it is not too surprising, then, that surveys indicate that police across the country increasingly are adopting a siege mentality relative to their own communities. A 1964 study of the Oakland, California, police force indicated that 70 percent of 282 randomly selected officers felt their work commanded only a very limited amount of respect from other people. Surveys of Chicago police sergeants in 1960 and 1965 showed that a majority of the respondents believed that the public did not respect the police and resisted cooperating with them. In a 1969 poll of the attitudes of experienced policemen in 286 state and local departments across the country, 83 percent of the policemen felt that most people looked upon a policeman as an "impersonal machine" rather than as a fellow human being. Only half of the officers felt that public support of the police was improving, and almost 75 percent felt they were not receiving enough support from city hall.[24] In fact, studies of police opinion have revealed that some policemen hide their occupations from their neighbors because they think that many people do not like to be friendly with policemen.

If the police do indeed have siege mentality relative to people in their own communities, then this condition may be at least partially the result of their own attitudes. Survey after survey has shown that blacks are far more distrustful of the police than whites. A Harris poll conducted in 1969 found that almost one-fifth of the whites and four-fifths of the blacks felt that there were discriminatory patterns in the relations of police with minority groups. A 1971 Harris survey found that nearly two-thirds of the white respondents were "deeply skeptical" about the dangers of alleged police brutality, but that more than 50 percent of the blacks felt that accusations of police brutality were more likely than not to be true. The same poll found that whites, in contrast to blacks,

24. Nelson A. Watson and James W. Sterling, *Police and Their Opinions* (Washington, D.C.: International Association of Chiefs of Police, 1969), p. 55.

tended to accept the idea of a conspiracy afoot to kill policemen.[25] The Urban Observatories' survey of ten cities found in 1970 that "the most obvious issue with respect to citizen attitudes toward the police was the feelings of blacks in cities," and concluded that "a major factor in this perception was the feeling among blacks that police did not respond adequately to calls for help." [26] This finding supports the finding in the same survey that blacks were far more fearful of crime than whites.

Traditionally, and regrettably, black perceptions of the police have been largely accurate, although this factor may be changing with the relatively rapid influx of blacks into the nation's police forces. Past studies, for example, have indicated that disproportionate numbers of policemen supported Senator Barry Goldwater in the 1964 presidential election, were members of the rightist John Birch society during the 1960s, or belonged to the then-powerful Klu Klux Klan through the 1940s. Interviews with policemen in the cities that experienced the major riots of 1967 indicated that policemen perceived accurately the hostility that was directed toward them by blacks.[27] Policemen felt that very few blacks saw them as friends, while the great majority of whites were likely to view them that way. The survey found that the hostility toward blacks among white policemen was fairly pronounced, with 49 percent of the police not approving of "socializing" between blacks and whites in residential neighborhoods.[28]

Are the police effective?

In the light of soaring crime rates, a burgeoning popular paranoia over crime, and hostility between the police and the community (at least insofar as the poor minority races are concerned), how well have the police fared in their fight against crime?

Two studies of consequence have concluded that greater levels of police activity do not result in less crime. E. Terrence Jones studied crime rates and related them to police manpower levels and expenditures in 155 cities from 1958 through 1970 and was unable to find any evidence to support the thesis that more and better equipped police results in less

25. The surveys are cited in: Advisory Commission on Intergovernmental Relations, *State and Local Relations and the Criminal Justice System* (Washington, D.C.: U.S. Government Printing Office, 1971). Reprinted in: W. P. Collins, ed., *Perspectives on State and Local Governments* (Englewood Cliffs, N.J.: Prentice-Hall, 1974), pp. 120–121.

26. Fowler, *op. cit.*, p. 170.

27. National Advisory Commission on Civil Disorders, *Supplemental Studies* (Washington, D.C.: U.S. Government Printing Office, 1968), p. 44.

28. *Ibid.*

crime.[29] Similarly, a behavioral study that is in many ways more intriguing, was the famous Kansas City Patrol experiment, which was conducted with a particularly rigorous methodology between 1972 and 1973. In this study the Kansas City Police Department, with assistance from the Police Foundation, divided certain of its beats into three categories. In one area no patrols were sent out at all, and police responded only on specific call for help. In the second area patrols were strengthened substantially, often to the point of being doubled or tripled, and in the third area, the control group, the patrols were maintained at previous levels. The results indicated that there were no statistically significant differences in crime rates among the three types of beats. There also were no differences in citizen attitudes, the number of reports of crimes, citizen behavior, or even in the rate of traffic accidents.[30]

In short, it may be that no matter what the police do, and no matter what society does to support its police, crime may continue unabated.

The overloaded dockets

Certainly one of the overriding problems in facilitating urban justice is that of overloaded courts. The nation's courts have more criminals than they can adequately process. The New York City blackout of 1977, which resulted in the arrest of almost 4,000 people on looting charges, also caused a massive overload in the city's court systems; many of the accused were freed simply because the city's courts and jails did not have adequate facilities, and the police, judges, district attorney, and public defenders would not cooperate with one another to expedite the process.

Although the New York example is an extreme one, it is not unique. In some sections of the country the overload problem is almost as severe on an everyday basis as it was in New York after the 1977 blackout, although the situation has improved in the 1970s. In the Cook County Circuit Court (i.e., Chicago), for example, the average waiting time from the first step in a personal injury trial that involved the court to the trial's termination was almost sixty months (nearly five years) in 1970, and in the New York Supreme Court of Bronx County, the average waiting time was almost fifty-nine months.[31]

29. E. Terrence Jones, "Evaluating Everyday Policies: Police Activity and Crime Incidents," *Urban Affairs Quarterly* 8 (March 1973): 267–279.

30. George Kelling et al. *The Kansas City Preventive Patrol Experiment: Summary Report* (Washington, D.C.: The Police Foundation, 1974), pp. v–vi.

31. Congressional Quarterly, *Crime and the Law* (Washington, D.C.: Congressional Quarterly, 1971), p. 36; and Mark W. Cannon, "Administrative Change and the Supreme Court," *Judicature: The Journal of the American Judicature Society* 57 (March 1974): 1–6.

Because many of the people held in jails awaiting trial are poor, they cannot make bail and must stay there. Not too long ago a survey of prisoners found that court delays resulted in prisoners being held without trial for an average of ninety-one days; some had been waiting six months or a year in jail, and one prisoner in the survey, who had been charged with murder, had been waiting for his trial for three years.[32]

When these kinds of delays occur, and they do all too frequently, the constitutional rights of the accused to a speedy trial are violated. And the accused seldom are granted a quick trial.

America is founded on the unique idea that the individual is supreme, and that his or her rights must be protected. Nevertheless, protection cannot be extended merely to the accused in a crime; it also must be extended to the victims of the crime and to those citizens who are potentially susceptible to future crimes. Thus, even in America, something called "society" must also be protected.

The prevalence of plea bargaining

How well is society being protected by the courts? The record is not an outstanding one, and one reason why is that the overloaded dockets of the judiciary, particularly at the state and local levels, have resulted in the widespread practice of plea bargaining. *Plea bargaining* is the negotiating that takes place between the accused's lawyer and the public prosecutor. The defense lawyer argues for a reduced charge while the prosecutor pushes for a conviction. Massive case overloads and resultant delays in local courts make it expeditious for all sides that the defendant plead guilty (usually to a lesser crime) since, in this manner, precious court time is not consumed, the defendant receives a minimal sentence, and the district attorney gets his sought-after conviction.

While expeditious, the almost total reliance on plea bargaining in state and local courts is hardly justice. Considerable pressure is placed on the accused to plead guilty, and many observers feel that judges tend to hand out harsher sentences to guilty defendants who have demanded their constitutional right to a trial. The all-too-frequent, exceptionally long waiting period before a defendant's trial provides additional pressure on the accused to plead guilty so that he or she at least may be released from jail. A survey by the Law Enforcement Assistance Administration showed that, of the 160,863 people in local jails on March 15, 1970, 52 percent had not been convicted, and there are instances of defendants waiting for months in municipal jails before they ever see a lawyer.[33]

32. Henry Robert Glick and Kenneth N. Vines, *State Court Systems* (Englewood Cliffs, N.J.: Prentice-Hall, 1973), p. 26.
33. Congressional Quarterly, *op. cit.*, p. 11.

It is not surprising, therefore, that most defendants plead guilty. Some educated estimates calculate that at least 90 percent of all convicted defendants in state and local courts were never proven guilty because they never went to trial.

The consequence of plea bargaining practices is to undermine popular respect for the criminal justice system in two ways. If the accused really is guilty, then the victim of the crime watches the criminal "get off" with an extraordinarily light sentence; thus the victim does not receive justice. Recall, in this regard, the controversy surrounding the dramatically minimized sentence granted to former Vice President Spiro T. Agnew relative to the bribery and corruption charges against him. Or the total pardon of all crimes, past and future, given out by President Gerald Ford to former President Richard Nixon after he resigned the Presidency. Many Americans—the effective "victims" of both politicians—wanted far more severe punishments meted to both the vice president and the president, and they felt that the Justice Department and President Ford, through some remarkable plea bargaining, had "let off" a couple of crooks. Conversely, if the accused is not guilty, but succumbs to the pressures brought to bear upon him to plead guilty—often including pressure from his own defense lawyer if appointed by the court—then the innocent citizen is saddled with a criminal record for the remainder of his or her life; thus, the accused does not receive justice.

Locking up the few

Another area of protecting society involves the percentage of people actually incarcerated who are found guilty. The proportion of imprisonments to crimes committed in society is dismally small. Of the known offenses (that is, reported crimes) in 1970, in only 20 percent of them was an actual arrest made, in only 17 percent of them was a person charged with a crime after the arrest was made, only 5 percent of those charged pleaded guilty as charged and, of the offenses known, in only 2 percent of the cases was a convicted felon sent to jail. If we use as a base the findings of various victim surveys, in which "real" crimes are estimated to be two-and-a-half times the number of reported crimes, the percentages would be less than half of these figures. Hence, we can conclude that the number of people jailed as a percentage of real crime probably is less than 1 percent.[34]

There is also reason to believe that many American judges are something less than Learned Hands. In an investigation of Boston's crim-

34. U.S. Bureau of the Census, Department of Commerce, *Statistical Abstract of the United States, 1970* (Washington, D.C.: U.S. Government Printing Office, 1970), p. 146.

inal courts by Richard Harris (he selected Boston because he thought it would probably have the most "civilized" municipal court system), Harris found some patterns of heavier sentences being dealt to blacks than to whites who had been convicted for comparable crimes. Harris concluded that in many of Boston's courts, the law was what the judge (often a political appointee) said it was.[35] In an effort to alleviate the problem of unfit judges, California in the late 1960s instituted a system by which judges could be removed through a panel of their peers, a method which since has been adopted by several other states.

Finally, the efficient administration of the courts is becoming a growing concern among public administrators. It is believed in many quarters that some traditional practices in courtrooms (such as the rather lackadaisical schedules of certain judges) are unnecessary impediments to speedy trials and that administrative analysis could result in faster trials. In response to this Congress established the Federal Judicial Center in 1967 as an agency designated to improve management in federal courts. All states have established an office of court administration, and in 1970 Congress authorized the appointment of "circuit executives" to administer the eleven federal courts in conjunction with each chief judge.

HOUSING AND CITIES

A second issue confronting urban administrators is not located, like crime, in the streets, but is found in the home: housing policy. (It should be recalled, however, that a major factor behind the urban race riots of the 1960s was inadequate housing.) Housing urban dwellers is at least as complex a problem as combatting crime, and in this discussion we review the federal-urban linkage in housing policy, local initiatives in public housing, the dismal suburban "war of resistance" to public housing, and the encouraging phenomenon of "urban homesteading."

The federal role:
making homes for middle America

Housing people is essentially a state and local matter, but the federal government has long been involved in planning housing policy. The creation in 1934 of the Federal Housing Administration (FHA), which provides federal insurance and low down payments on long-term home mortgage loans, and the passage of the first national Housing Act in the same year, which authorized the formation of private secondary mortgage

35. Richard Harris, "Annals of Law in Criminal Court Part I," *The New Yorker* 49 (April 14, 1973): 45–88; Part II, 49 (April 21, 1973): 44–87.

markets, marked the entrance of the federal government into state and local housing policy in a big way. In 1938 the Federal and National Mortgage Association ("Fannie Mae") was set up as a conduit between idle savings and people who needed to borrow funds for new construction. The Housing Act of 1937, however, created the first permanent and direct subsidy program for low-income families. Under the act the federal government pays the annual principal and interest on long-term, tax-exempt bonds that are used to finance the construction of new housing by local housing authorities, which are set up by state law. In 1949 Congress passed another Housing Act that represented the first comprehensive housing and community development law. It provided substantial increases in funding for low rent public housing and was the basis of the urban renewal program. In 1954 yet another Housing Act was enacted; it expanded earlier programs and was aimed at fostering total community development. The act mandated for the first time the preservation of existing structures, relocating families that were displaced by urban renewal projects, and some community-wide citizen participation in the planning of urban renewal.

The 1960s witnessed a spate of federally initiated activities in the area of planning for new housing. The Housing Act of 1961 was aimed toward finding new and rehabilitated housing for low-income families and the elderly, and in 1965 Congress wrote a variation into the public housing program that allowed local housing authorities to lease dwellings in privately owned buildings and to make them available to families that were eligible for regular public housing; it was also in that year that Congress created the Department of Housing and Urban Development. In 1967 two major presidential commissions on housing were established: the National Commission on Urban Problems and the President's Commission on Urban Housing. In response to the recommendations of both commissions, Congress passed the Housing and Urban Development Act of 1968. It called for the production or rehabilitation of 26 million housing units within ten years, including 6 million units for low- and moderate-income families. The act marked the first time that Congress had specified a housing goal in terms of real housing units within an established time frame.

In 1974 Congress passed the first Housing and Community Development Act. Under the act the Secretary of HUD is authorized to make assistance payments on behalf of lower-income families who are living in new or substantially rehabilitated rental units, but it does not provide assistance for new construction or rehabilitation; the cost of these projects must be borne by the developer or owner. The 1974 act (and its 1977 extension) also reflects a desire on the part of federal officials to begin a foundation for a national housing allowance plan; thus, the rental subsidy is tied to the *family* rather than to the *housing unit*. This innovation represents a real departure from past federal housing policies, although, in a more traditional mode, the act called for the construction or rehabilitation of 400,000 units annually for the next two years.

In 1977 Congress passed a second Housing and Community Development Act, and substantially increased the funding of the 1974 act by signing into law a $14.7 billion program. The rent subsidies alone, together with additional financial aid to cities, helped 345,000 more families to find housing at rents they could afford. Also in the Carter administration legislation was a $400 million Urban Development Action Grant Program designed to encourage economic development in the nation's most troubled cities, particularly in the Northeast and Midwest, and a slight increase in the amount of money going to the Sunbelt cities.

Though it may appear that the federal role in housing is aimed at helping the poor, in reality national policy has helped the middle class far more than any other economic group. The creation of the FHA and "Fannie Mae" in the 1930s were major boons to middle-class home purchasers, and the urban renewal programs consistently were oriented toward middle-class business interests located in the downtowns of metropolises. For example, the Housing Act of 1949, which initiated urban renewal, specified that any new developments replacing slums in cities must be "predominantly residential." Yet the Housing Act of 1954 added a 10 percent exception to this requirement; in 1959 the exception was increased to 20 percent; in 1961 the exception went to 30 percent; and in 1965 it was hiked to 35 percent. In short, businesspersons were and are the object of concern in urban renewal.

Federal income tax policy also favors middle-class housing through the device of tax deductions on mortgage interest. Thus, in 1962 the federal government spent an estimated $820 million to subsidize housing for the poor, including savings resulting from income tax deductions as well as public housing and other forms of public assistance. But during the same year it spent an estimated $2.9 *billion* to subsidize housing for those with middle-class incomes, including savings from income tax deductions.[36] Relatedly, an analysis of the 1976 federal budget indicated that the highest 1 percent of the top income earners in the nation received 10 percent of all housing subsidies (including tax breaks), while the lower half of income earners received only 25 percent of all housing subsidies; more than two-thirds of housing subsidy recipients have incomes above $10,000. In 1973 only 8 percent of new housing was available to the 29 percent of all American families with incomes below $8,000.[37]

36. U.S. Commission on Civil Rights, *Twenty Years After Brown: Equal Opportunity in Housing* (Washington, D.C.: U.S. Commission on Civil Rights, 1975), p. 24.
37. Cushing Dolbeare, "Let's Correct the Inequities," *ABA World* 30 (April-May, 1975): 9, 35.

Although housing policy in America is essentially designed for the middle class, it nonetheless is true that an effort has been made to encourage the development of housing for the poor, and this attempt has occurred primarily at the grassroots. Even so, the effort has not been easy, and the political brawls over public housing have taken their toll of state and local officials.

Public housing: planners against people?

Public housing in this country generally is associated with an unmitigated disaster. When they hear the phrase *public housing*, many people think of "monolithic high-rise buildings filled with fatherless black welfare families, some of the most savage and dangerous spots on this continent— places like Providence's Chad Brown, Chicago's Robert Taylor Homes, New York's Fort Greene and St. Louis's infamous Pruitt-Igoe." [38]

The examples are indeed depressing. Consider, for instance, the high-rise of Cedar-Riverside in downtown Minneapolis. Built in 1971, it was part of the U.S. Department of Housing and Urban Development's "new-town in-town" program and was hailed by architects and urban planners as a major contribution to the community cityscape; in fact, Cedar-Riverside won a major architectural design award. In three years, Cedar-Riverside was broke and HUD had been brought into a landmark suit to desist from funding the project's second stage. [39]

An even more serious failure of public housing was the Pruitt-Igoe complex in St. Louis, which was once also considered a national example of the best in public housing. Today it is sixty acres of rubble and weeds surrounded by a chain-link fence, evocative of Berlin after World War II. The thirty-three buildings of Pruitt-Igoe cost more than $35 million to build in 1954, and housed almost twelve thousand poor people. In 1973 federal and local officials agreed that the project was a flop and ordered it razed simply to save the city's Housing Authority $12 million in annual operating costs; many of the residents displaced by the destruction of Pruitt-Igoe were forced to move into nearby tenements. [40]

There are exceptions to such dismal stories as Pruitt-Igoe and Cedar-Riverside, and these exceptions seem to revolve around the notion of "small is beautiful." Public housing projects such as Valley View Homes, occupying eleven acres in Providence, LaClede houses in St. Louis, West Bluff in Kansas City, New York's Wise Houses and Twin Towers West,

38. Neal R. Pierce, "Public Housing Projects Need Not be Jungles," syndicated column, November 2, 1977.
39. Paul Goldberger, *New York Times* News Service, November 17, 1976, syndicated nationally.
40. United Press International, October 10, 1976, syndicated nationally.

and San Francisco's North Beach are among those successful housing projects that seem to share certain common themes, such as being relatively small, staying clear of areas that patently cannot be rehabilitated, putting a strong manager in charge with considerable authority, promoting an effective tenant council, and providing adequate maintenance funds on a regular basis.[41]

Placing public housing:
the suburban war of resistance

If urban analysts are correct in their perception that a number of inner-city ghettos cannot be rehabilitated by even the most advanced public housing, then policy makers must start looking elsewhere for public housing sites. This search has resulted in some of the most bitter community controversies in recent years. Middle-class suburbanites have shown themselves willing to fight to the last tax dollar in their effort to preserve the status quo of their neighborhoods by keeping out public housing. Poor blacks and browns—and poor whites as well—are less than welcome in many white middle-class and working-class suburbs.

The federal government has played an on-again, off-again role in the locating of public housing. Up until 1968 federal regulations required that all federally subsidized housing receive approval by the appropriate local government before being built, and the effect of this requirement was to assure that public housing was kept out of the suburbs. With the passage of the Housing and Urban Development Act of 1968, however, the requirement of gaining local approval for public housing projects was effectively abandoned.

With direct control of where public housing could be built wrested from their hands by federal legislation, localities responded with more subtle forms of resistance. In Cleveland, for example, the city fathers in effect cancelled plans to build a major public housing project when they found out that, for the first time, the housing would be situated in a predominantly white area; in the past, Cleveland had permitted the construction of such projects in the minority areas of the city. In *Cuyahoga Metropolitan Housing Authority* v. *City of Cleveland* the district court ruled in 1972 against the city, stating that the policy smacked of racism.[42]

In a significant case that took ten years of litigation, the U.S. Supreme Court ruled in 1976 that the Chicago Housing Authority was guilty of racial discrimination by selecting sites for public housing largely

41. Pierce, *op. cit.*
42. U.S. Commission on Civil Rights, *Twenty Years After Brown: A Report of the United States Commission on Civil Rights* (Washington, D.C.: U.S. Government Printing Office, 1975), p. 135.

in minority areas and by assigning minority tenants to apartments located in minority areas. The Court noted in its decision on *Hills* v. *Gautreaux* that Chicago's public housing policies appeared to be based on race rather than income and were therefore in violation of the Constitution.[43]

This was an important distinction, because only five years earlier the U.S. Supreme Court had ruled in *James* v. *Valtierra* that a California law requiring approval by the local voters before low-rent public housing could be built was not in violation of the Fourteenth Amendment. The logic used by the Court was that economic, not racial, discrimination was allowed by the Constitution, even though minorities often constitute the larger number of applicants for public housing.[44]

These and other court cases reflect the grimness of the war over public housing that is occurring in American cities and, as noted, the federal government has likely confused the issue even further with its go/no-go posture on where to locate public housing. For example, the Nixon administration, whose political base was largely suburban, backed away from any kind of enforcement of fair housing requirements and in 1973 the Nixon administration officially terminated all federal public housing programs. Moreover, it was clear from the behavior of HUD officials under Nixon that affirmative action requirements for localities that were attached to such federal programs as urban renewal and model cities were going to be enforced less than rigorously.

Since Nixon's departure from Washington, federal public housing policy has changed. As noted, the first Housing and Community Development Act, which was enacted in 1974 and expanded in 1977, placed public housing, model cities, and urban renewal programs, among others, under its aegis and decentralized much of Washington's longstanding control of these programs to state and local governments. In 1976 the Carter administration announced plans to finance some thirty thousand additional housing units for the country's poorest families at a cost of almost $4 billion;[45] the plan represented a resurrection of the federal government's public housing programs, which Nixon had effectively cancelled in 1973. Nevertheless, it remains to be seen if a commitment by Washington to public housing also means a commitment to breaking up racial segregation in neighborhoods, and the odds are that those in Wash-

43. Richard P. Fishman, ed., *Housing for All Under Law: New Directions in Housing, Land Use, and Planning Law*, A Report of the American Bar Association Advisory Commission on Housing and Urban Growth (Cambridge, Mass.: Ballinger, 1978), Appendix to Chapter 3.

44. U.S. Commission on Civil Rights, *Twenty Years After Brown*, *op. cit.*, p. 138.

45. "U.S. Planning Thirty Thousand Housing Units for Four Billion Dollars," *The Washington Post*, November 20, 1976.

ington, as always, will tread very carefully—and in different directions— when decisions are needed on where housing for poor people will be built.

Unlike Washington, some state and local governments have taken the initiative in placing public housing. The Housing Development Commission in Missouri and the New York Urban Development Corporation, for example, both are deeply involved in "new-town in-town" redevelopment programs. The new-town in-town movement represents an effort to rehabilitate housing in the core cities by encouraging families of all levels of income, but especially the poor and families of moderate incomes, to move back to the downtown areas.[46]

Urban homesteading

An aspect of the new-town in-town movement is the "urban homesteading" drive, which is among the more exciting of urban housing programs. The states, particularly California, Connecticut, Minnesota, and Rhode Island, have taken a major role in urban homesteading, although cities initially took the lead, notably Wilmington, Baltimore, and Philadelphia.[47]

In 1975 the federal government got into urban homesteading by providing low-interest loans to homesteaders to renovate their purchases. A homesteader may buy a run-down townhouse from the city for a dollar, but because it costs several thousand dollars more to renovate it, the loan program is important. By the late 1970s about forty communities had federally sponsored urban homesteading programs involving nearly two thousand homes, and a number of additional cities were running homesteading efforts without federal help.[48] Urban homesteading often is used as a means of preserving cultural areas, as well as for revitalizing downtown commerce, by bringing young professionals back to the core cities. An analysis by Anne Clark and Zelma Rivin of urban homesteading programs in a dozen cities found that success of an urban homesteading program depended upon the local availability to homesteaders of both financial counseling and technical counseling on how to improve the physical structure of a house.[49]

46. Anne D. Stubbs, "Community Development and Housing," *Book of the States, 1976–77* (Lexington, Ky.: Council of State Governments, 1976), p. 449.
47. Stubbs, *op. cit.*, pp. 449–451.
48. Ward Morehouse, "Urban Homesteading," *Christian Science Monitor* News Service, May 28, 1978, syndicated nationally.
49. Anne Clark and Zelma Rivin, "The Administrative Models of Urban Homesteading," *Public Administration Review* 37 (May-June 1977): 286–290.

URBAN TRANSIT POLICY

One reason behind the move back to the inner cities, as typified by the
urban homesteading phenomenon, is the convenience of living closer to

---

On the Human Costs of Urban Administration

*Interstate Highway 95 in Boston symbolizes what it can mean to
people when a city is "improved." Urban renewal, highway construction, and the several other public programs that are predicated on the
notion that cities must be destroyed before they can be saved often
disorient the lives of city dwellers. The following passage concerns
I-95, and what it meant to a few families in its way. Their experience
has been replicated in the execution of numerous such projects designed to "serve the public interest."*

Lamartine Street in the working-class district of the Jamaica Plain
neighborhood in the city of Boston, Ground Zero of the Federal Interstate Highway System.

A scattering of blacks and Puerto Ricans are here, but mostly there
are white Catholics, who make up the bulk of Boston's population.
Ask them where they live, and they'll as likely tell you the parish before
the name of the street. And if you're not familiar with the parish, they'll
think it strange. You'll call their neighborhood parochial, and some will
call it colorful. Whatever you call it, those who plan, design, and construct America's highways call it a rite-of-way.

To find out what Lamartine Street was like, you have to look on the
odd-numbered side of the street, because that's not part of the rite-of-
way. It ranges from well kept two- and three-story houses to somewhat
shabby three-deckers to a mix of commercial and residential red brick
in the style of Late Industrial Revolution.

Some houses on the even-numbered side also remain. Number 260,
for example, is a yellow house with brown trim and a neat garden. Its
occupants are an elderly couple. Their home is not needed for the
highway. But they have seen and heard the bulldozers and the earth
movers rip up their neighbors' homes and leave a flat dirt wasteland
all the way to No. 226, a vacant space two blocks long and a block
from the street to the railroad tracks.

The old man and his wife want to be left alone. They watched the
machines at work and then saw vandals rip the plumbing and pipes and
all the other vital organs out of the abandoned houses, and finally, they
smelled the stench of arson and heard the almost nightly wail and
clanging of fire engines.

From No. 226, a dilapidated house with its door ajar, to No. 216 is
more vacant land. Both No. 216 and the house behind it are gutted.

Here, in the yard adjoining No. 216, is one of the last links in the chain reaction set off by the approach of an interstate highway. A man's personal life, from the kind of beans his family ate and milk they drank, to the frame of their television set, is strewn all over the lawn. His wife owned a Maytag washer; they had a red scatter rug; he wore size 10 French Shriner black shoes, and he read *Field and Stream* and *American Rifleman*.

In back, in the large field that was once a neighborhood, you find other artifacts. A grisly torso of a plastic monkey in a soldier's suit; a mangled tricycle with one wheel missing; the heart of a record, with jagged edges ("Unbreakable," the label insists), that once featured "Blue Barron and His Orchestra in 'Cruising Down the River' with Vocal Ensemble"; and two-thirds of another record, this one a collection of Christmas carols by Bing Crosby. Bing Crosby and Blue Barron and the *American Rifleman*. It may not be your life style, but it was somebody's. It was from the civilization known as White Urban Ethnic American, a local colony of which was being plowed under for Interstate 95.

Do you know that if I-95 is ever completed, it will take you from Houlton, Maine, to South Miami, Florida, a distance of 1,866 miles, without one traffic light? Not one traffic light.

ALAN LUPO
Rites of Way

work—a convenience that is related directly to the inconvenience of urban transportation. Urban transit policy, like criminal justice and public housing, is complex. In this section we review highway finance, the "imbalance" of current transportation policy in favor of the car, mass transit policies, paratransit, the social justice of transportation policies, and the dynamics of the transit planning process.

In the mid-1970s the federal, state, and local governments spent more than $15.4 billion for their 3.8 million miles of roads and highways. Highway expenditures for state and local governments alone, as opposed to other kinds of transportation expenditures (such as aviation, waterways, and mass transit), is the third largest consumer of local funds, after education and public welfare.[50]

Financing highways

Highways in America are financed from five major sources of revenues: toll roads, property taxes, special assessments, user taxes, and federal aid. The most important of these sources are user taxes and federal aid, and

---

50. James F. Runke and Charles G. Whitmire, "Transportation," *The Book of the States, 1976–77* (Lexington, Ky.: Council of State Governments, 1976), p. 348.

significant among the user taxes are the state taxes on gasoline and motor vehicle licenses; approximately half of all state and local highway revenues is derived from user taxes levied on vehicle owners. The federal government also collects gasoline taxes to the tune of four cents per gallon, generating almost $6 billion a year, and these revenues are deposited in the Federal Highway Trust Fund. The Federal Highway Trust Fund, known to some as the "ever-normal trough," is a device set up under the Federal Highway Act of 1956, and it absorbs the lion's share of all federal gasoline taxes. The fund is *earmarked* (that is, set aside) specifically for paying for the interstate highway system. Currently, the federal government pays 90 percent for the interstate highway construction costs across the country; the states chip in a nominal 10 percent.

The feds and highways

The federal government long has had an impact on the state and local system of roads, but its impact is greatest in the area of interstate highways. Initially the federal role in transportation policy was primarily rural, as expressed by the Federal Aid Road Act of 1916, which provided the first regular funding for public highway construction. A departure from this rural orientation was signalled in 1944 when the Federal Highway Act was passed. This act assisted in the development of roads designed to help farmers get to markets, but it also provided for the extension of primary roads in urban areas; this latter innovation, known as "ABC funds," still is continued today, and federal funds are given to the states on a matching basis.

The Federal Highway Act of 1944 also promoted the development of the national system of interstate highways, under the logic that such highways were necessary for national defense, but it was only in 1956 that a new Federal Highway Act authorized enormous amounts of money to develop the interstate highway system. It was the 1956 act that stipulated that highways could be developed with 90 percent federal funding and 10 percent state funding, an opportunity that the states could not resist. The act called for the completion of the interstate highway system by 1972, but the system was only 87 percent complete by that year. Thus, Congress in 1973 enacted the Federal Aid Highway Act. As amended in 1974 the act will continue and complete the 42,500 miles of the interstate highway system with authorizations of $3 billion and more for each year through 1979. The rationale behind the legislation is that official projections indicate that motor vehicle travel may increase by nearly 50 percent above 1975 levels by the year 1990. Such use of the highways, no doubt, will depend upon the availability of fuel, which may or may not be forthcoming.

An incredible 135 million motor vehicles travel on America's nearly 4 million miles of tarmac. Highway travel dominates the nation's transportation by a ratio of more than ten to one. In fact, approximately 94 percent of all "person-miles" of travel in the United States is accomplished exclusively by highway vehicles (both automobiles and buses) and, within cities, the proportion is even greater—98 percent; only 4 percent of this figure represents travel by bus as opposed to car. In the large urban areas where rail travel, such as subways and trains, is available, the combined travel on these two transportation modes amounts to only 11 percent of all daily trips; the remaining 89 percent is done by car.[51]

Eighty percent of all households in America have at least one car and 30 percent have two or more. Americans spend about twice as much each year just to register their cars in their states as they do to ride buses or subways. Consumers paid more than $103 billion to buy and maintain cars in 1973, in comparison with $1.6 billion for public transit.[52]

One reason for this clear preference is the convenience of automobiles. Car drivers who travel ten miles to work average twenty-four minutes in commuting time, while public transportation riders average fifty minutes for the same distance; similarly, the average time for trips to work is twenty-one minutes for the car driver in comparison with thirty-seven minutes for the transit rider. Moreover, the cost difference between rapid transit systems and the car is not great. In 1973 the full economic cost of urban driving was calculated at something more than 26 cents per mile, while rapid transit cost the consumer 25 cents per mile; the bus, however, cost the consumer between eight and nine cents per mile.

In the big cities the reliance on urban transit is considerably greater. In New York 61 percent of the city's residents use public transit to and from work; in Boston, the figure is 38 percent; in Philadelphia, 37 percent; and in Chicago, 36 percent. Fourteen major metropolitan areas account for 70 percent of *all* the nation's public transit passengers, and New York City alone accounts for 38 percent.

National policies for mass transit

The fact that America's urban transit policy is tilted to favor the car is so obvious that even Congress has begun to notice. Before 1964 the federal government spent no money whatever on public transit, and in

---

51. *1974 National Transportation Report*, quoted in *ibid.*, p. 350.
52. The data in this and the following two paragraphs are drawn from Wilfred Owen, *Transportation for Cities* (Washington, D.C.: Brookings Institution, 1976), pp. 5–6, 10.

that year total federal support was a nominal $30 million; by contrast, total federal support for urban mass transit is now approaching $5 billion a year.[53]

Although the Federal Aid Highway Act of 1973 extended the controversial Highway Trust Fund, for the first time the act also permitted funds that had traditionally been earmarked exclusively for highways to be used for urban mass transportation. This victory for the friends of mass transit was not a particularly auspicious one, but it was a qualitative change. Under the act $780 million from the Federal Highway Trust Fund for fiscal 1974 and some $200 million for each of the years thereafter are allocated to cities and towns to use for developing public transit systems, including buses, railroads, and highways; these projects are to be selected by appropriate local officials in concert with state governments. The act also established an 80 percent federal and 20 percent local matching ratio for urban mass transportation administration grants.

In 1974 the National Mass Transportation Assistance Act was passed, expanding state and local opportunities for developing public transit systems. Under this act $11.8 billion was provided over a six-year period from 1975 through 1980.[54]

The legislation, though not entirely adequate, is needed to develop mass transportation facilities. For the past thirty years the number of people carried by public transportation has declined from 23 billion passengers a year in 1945 to less than 7 billion in 1974. The public clearly prefers the automobile, but one reason for that preference may be the lack of alternative means of transportation. In the 1940s and the 1950s big cities (Los Angeles is a representative example) tore up trolley car tracks and discarded bus lines in the face of pressure from organized interest groups such as automobile manufacturers and oil companies, and it seems clear that state and local transportation officials still prefer the automobile. During the first year that the Federal Aid Highway Act was in effect, only two cities, New York and East St. Louis, Illinois, actually applied for and received funds; in both cases the funds were used to purchase additional buses.[55] Moreover, a survey conducted by the *New York Times* concluded that transportation officials in a number of states were heavily biased in favor of more road construction and did not favor the idea of developing public transportation facilities.[56] It is perhaps because of these attitudes held by state and local officials, plus a disadvantageous funding ratio relative to highway construction, that only fifteen cities in

53. *Ibid.*, p. 1.
54. Runke and Whitmire, *op. cit.*, p. 353.
55. Ralph Blumenthal, "Mass Transit Use of Fund Lags," *New York Times*, April 21, 1975.
56. "Transit Funds Weaken Review," *New York Times*, April 27, 1975.

the mid-1970s had rapid transit systems that either were operable or under construction.

"Paratransit" and the small-is beautiful movement

Another possible reason why state and local administrators are reluctant to embrace rapid transit may be because they recognize that such systems are not the proper solution to the problems of urban mobility. In this light, an interesting new wrinkle on transportation policy is the adoption of the "small-is-beautiful" philosophy, which is beginning to make an impact on the thinking of transportation planners. The idea is called *paratransit*, and it refers to independent car pools, van pools, jitnies, and taxis, in contrast to such large mass transit concepts such as subways, trains, and buses.[57] The Twin Cities (Minneapolis and St. Paul) are among the leading cities in the development of paratransit. Local officials determined that only 17 percent of the jobs in the Twin Cities area were located in downtown Minneapolis and St. Paul, so transportation planners concluded that to push increased busing and rail service to the downtown made little sense. In 1977 the Minnesota legislature appropriated $5.5 million to experiment with paratransit in both urban and rural areas. The objective is to lift legalisms that often discourage or prohibit paratransit operations, notably restrictions that are the result of pressure from big labor, which perceives such efforts as a threat to union employment. Indeed, it has been estimated that regulatory obstacles prohibit 99.7 percent of drivers and 99.8 percent of vehicles on the road from providing transportation services for a fee to others. Yet, given the fact that rapid transit systems cost the consumer almost as much as a private automobile (buses, as noted, are the exception), paratransit could be a solid alternative—provided that public policy permits it to flourish.

Public transit as social justice

Public transportation, whether small or large in scale, is needed for reasons other than simple convenience and economy (projections indicate that raising the average number of occupants in cars going to and from jobs from its present 1.2 persons per car to 2 persons can save more than one million barrels of oil a day).[58] Public transit also is a matter of social justice. The old, the young, the poor, and the deprived stand out as groups that have been denied the necessary right of physical mobility because of lack

57. The discussion on paratransit is drawn from Neal R. Pierce, "Transportation Planners Thinking Smaller," syndicated column, June 17, 1977.

58. Runke and Whitmire, *op. cit.*, p. 351.

of access to a car. In 1968, 32 percent of all households in the central cities did not have a car, while only 13 percent of the households in the suburbs did not. Forty-four percent of Americans over sixty-five years of age had no car. In riot-torn Watts in Los Angeles, only 38 percent of 538 males interviewed in 1967 had access to usable automobiles; the remainder had to rely on mass transit services, such as they were, or car pools. Currently, nearly 55 percent of all households with incomes of $3,000 to $5,000 a year have no cars.[59] The point of reeling off these statistics is that, without cars, the people who need jobs most cannot get to places of employment because of the absence of mass transit systems in urban areas. Thus, a balanced transportation policy becomes a matter of social justice.[60]

The great game of transportation politics

A major reason why we have an imbalanced transportation policy is the nature of the political transportation game. At the national level some of the most powerful interest groups in the United States have done battle over the continuation of the Highway Trust Fund. Arguing that it be continued and used solely for highway construction are the oil industry, the automobile interests, the rubber industry, the road construction interests, the trucking industry, and the American Association of State Highway Officials. Aligned against the fund are interest groups who are less powerful (with the exception of the railroad industry), notably the environmental interests, busing interests, and generalized urban lobbies, such as the United States Conference of Mayors and the National League of Cities. Thus, perhaps it is not too surprising that the real impetus for rectifying the policy of imbalance in transportation politics has come from the big cities rather than from Congress.

The cities as transit innovators

Although studies indicate that federal policies are a major influence on local transportation policy making, it also is increasingly clear that the central cities are taking the lead in developing mass transit systems rather than highways. Robert S. Friedman, for example, has found that there is

---

59. Melvin M. Webber and Shlomo Angel, "The Social Context for Transport Policy," *Science and Technology in the Cities.* A Compilation of Papers prepared for the Tenth Meeting of the Panel on Science and Technology, Committee on Science and Astronautics, U.S. House of Representatives (Washington, D.C.: U.S. Government Printing Office, 1969), pp. 57–72.

60. *Ibid.*

little evidence of a relation between the wealth or industrialization level of the states and their emphasis on highway expenditure. There is, however, a significant relation between highway expenditure and metropolitanism in which the states with the highest proportion of their population living in standard metropolitan statistical areas, devote the smallest proportion of state and local expenditure to highways.[61]

Similarly, in a significant analysis of the politics of transportation in eight big cities, Alan Lupo, Frank Colcord, and Edward P. Fowler concluded that there was reason to believe that local policy making for urban transit was becoming increasingly democratic, systematic, and rational, although the structure and process for local transportation needs remain fragmented and characterized by disparities.[62] Colcord, in that and other studies, has noted a lack of any local leaders, public or private, who are concerned with the whole urban area and who are inclined to confront transit issues only when they reach crisis proportions, the presence of competition among various municipal units, and an inordinate suspicion of the city held by the suburbs.[63]

The "logics" of transit planning

More critical, perhaps, as impediments to cohesive public planning of urban transportation policy are the relationships among the various "logics" of transportation politics in metropolitan areas. Despite the fact that urban transportation planning undoubtedly is the cities' single most powerful tool for attaining land use goals, Colcord has identified at least three conflicting logics of transportation policy making that represent competing professional and political values: the logic of the technician, the logic of the planner, and the logic of the politician.[64]

The technician's logic continues to dominate the decision-making process in transportation of all levels of government in Colcord's view, and it guides the thinking behind the present highway program. The technician assumes that his field, the highways, offers a "final solution" to a narrowly defined technical problem, that of transporting people and

61. Robert S. Friedman, "State Politics and Highways," *Politics in the American States*, 2nd ed., Herbert Jacob and Kenneth N. Vines, eds. (Boston: Little, Brown, 1971), p. 518.

62. Alan Lupo, Frank Colcord, and Edward P. Fowler, *Rites of Way: The Politics of Transportation in Boston and the U.S. City* (Boston: Little, Brown, 1971).

63. Frank C. Colcord, Jr., "Decision Making in Transportation Policy: A Comparative Analysis," *Southwestern Social Science Quarterly* 28 (December 1967). Reprinted in *Politics in the Metropolis*, Thomas R. Dye and Brett W. Hawkins, eds. (Englewood Cliffs, N.J.: Prentice-Hall, 1971), pp. 205–222.

64. Frank C. Colcord, "The Nation," in Lupo, Colcord, and Fowler, *op. cit.*, pp. 204–237.

products from point A to point B with optimal efficiency. Unfortunately, the technician's logic fails to take into account such values as ripped-up neighborhoods, razed homes, marred urban landscapes, displaced people, environmental degradation, and a politically alienated urban citizenry. These variables do not enter the calculations of an engineering mentality and are irrelevant to the logic of the technician.

The planner's logic is broader in scope but, though the planner has the potential for considering the larger mission for the metropolitan community, this mission is nearly always unexpressed. This is not to imply that community goals larger than that of getting efficiently from one point to another are not present. In fact, it is the current preeminence of the technician's logic in transportation planning circles that has served to express more forcefully than ever before the planner's logic in terms of the broader community mission. Occasionally this is done within the framework of advocacy planning, as exemplified by the successful citizen's campaign in Boston to stop Interstate Highway 95 dead in its tracks.

Finally, the politician's logic can be compatible with the planner's logic when it comes to fostering the broader values of the community, but the politician is also susceptible to the short-range objectives of the technician. For example, temporarily relieving downtown traffic congestion by slapping down a new freeway may be a most appealing alternative in the absence of expressed objections from various citizen groups or alternative policy choices offered by other planning groups. The logic of the politician, in brief, is supremely one of staying in power and this is achieved by responding to the pressures of the moment as they relate to the politician's perception of a "good record" over time.

These distinctive logics of transportation planning coexist in metropolises and each has its uses. What is needed is to establish legitimate patterns of relationships among them. The planner must express the community's goals, present and future, and offer creative solutions; the politician must cooperate with and beneficially influence the planning process, provide leadership, and yield legitimacy; the technician must find efficient, novel, and effective means for implementing community goals as identified by the planner and the politician. According to Colcord, there may be a renewed trend in establishing a harmonious relationship among these traditionally discordant transportation logics in urban areas.

CONCLUSION

As our discussions of crime, housing, and transportation have implied, urban policy often is not really "urban" at all. More frequently, "urban" policy is intergovernmental policy. In the next chapter we review the dynamics and complexities of the intergovernmental maze, a labyrinth that is of unique significance to public administrators.

SUPPLEMENTAL BIBLIOGRAPHY

CAMPBELL, ALAN K. and SEYMOUR SACKS, "The Fiscal Zoning Game," *Municipal Finance*, 65 (1964), 140–49.

CHRISTIAN, CHARLES M. and SARI BENNETT, "Industrial Relocations from the Black Community of Chicago," in Michael R. Greenberg, ed., *Readings in Urban Economics and Spatial Patterns*, chap. 9. New Brunswick, N.J.: Rutgers University Center for Urban Policy Research, 1974.

DOIG, JAMESON W., *Metropolitan Transportation Politics in the New York Region*, chap. 2. New York: Columbia University Press, 1966; and Frank C. Colcord, Jr., "Decision-making and Transportation Policies: A Comparative Analysis," *Social Science Quarterly*, 48 (December 1967), 383–398.

DOWNS, ANTHONY, *Opening Up the Suburbs*. New Haven, Conn.: Yale University Press, 1973.

HOWARD, EBENEZER, *Garden Cities of Tomorrow*. Cambridge, Mass.: MIT Press, 1965; first published as *Tomorrow* in 1898.

JACOB, HERBERT, *Urban Justice*. Englewood Cliffs, N.J.: Prentice-Hall, 1973.

LINDSEY, ROBERT, "Mass Transit, Little Mass," *New York Times Magazine*, 19 (October 1974), 17ff.

LOGAN, CHARLES, "Evaluation Research in Crime and Delinquency," *Journal of Criminal Law, Criminology, and Police Science*, 63 (1972), 378–387.

NIEDERHOFFE, ARTHUR, *Behind the Shield*. Garden City, N.Y.: Doubleday, 1967.

SKOGAN, WESLEY G., "Crime and Crime Rates," chapter 6 in Skogan, ed., *Sample Surveys of the Victims of Crime*, Cambridge, Mass.: Ballinger, 1976.

STERNLIEB, GEORGE et al., *Housing Development and Municipal Costs*. New Brunswick, N.J.: Rutgers University Center for Urban Policy Research, n.d.

TITTLE, CHARLES R., and CHARLES H. LOGAN, "Sanctions and Deviance: Evidence and Remaining Questions," *Law and Society Review*, 7 (Spring 1973), 371–392.

WEBBER, MELVIN M., "San Francisco Area Rapid Transit—A 'Disappointing' Model," *New York Times*, 13 (November 1976), 23.

WILLIAMS, OLIVER P. et al., *Suburban Differences and Metropolitan Policies*, Philadelphia: University of Pennsylvania Press, 1965.

WILSON, JAMES Q., "Police Morale, Reform, and Citizen Respect: The Chicago Case," in David Bordua, ed., *The Police*, pp. 137–162, New York: Wiley, 1967.

WILSON, JAMES Q., *Varieties of Police Behavior*, chap. 4. Cambridge, Mass.: Harvard University Press, 1968; and in Albert J. Reiss, Jr. *Police and the Public*. New Haven, Conn.: Yale University Press.

the federal maze

chapter 14

Federalism, or *intergovernmental relations,* concerns the relations among governments, but *intergovernmental relations* can be defined more formally as the series of legal, political, and administrative relationships established among units of government and which possess varying degrees of authority and jurisdictional autonomy.

FEDERALISM IN TURMOIL

Reasonable as the foregoing definition is, the concept, structure, and practice of federal relations in the United States have been in turmoil for the last decade, to a degree seldom appreciated by the social scientists. Michael D. Reagan, after a perusal of a number of textbooks, found only one which acknowledged that the meaning of federalism had changed.[1]

1. Michael D. Reagan, *The New Federalism* (New York: Oxford University Press, 1972).

And change it has. The late President Lyndon B. Johnson characterized many of his social programs as exercises in "creative federalism." President Richard M. Nixon preferred the term "new federalism" for much the same purpose. Don K. Price has studied "federalism by contract," or the immensely complex system of research and development that is co-managed by the public and private sectors.[2] The late Morton Grodzins popularized the phrase "marble cake federalism" (in contrast to the conventional wisdom of "layer cake federalism"), emphasizing the fluidity of the governmental process.[3] Reagan has urged the advent of "permissive federalism." "Cooperative federalism" became a modish phrase after the New Deal, supplanting the earlier concept of "dual federalism," which stressed the separateness of state and national governments. Joseph F. Zimmerman has observed the phenomenon of "the federated city" in sizeable urban areas, in which "neighborhood governments" function in relative autonomy from city hall.[4]

Authorities differ on the effects of new forms of federalism on the public and its interests. Theodore J. Lowi has attacked new variations of federalism, particularly those of the Johnson administration, as overly decentralized, inducing a "crisis of public authority" antithetical to the national interest, and indicative of "the end of liberalism."[5] Lowi's attack is devastating, particularly his real-life account of urban renewal in "Iron City," in which federal administrators knowingly permitted and financed what amounted to a "Negro removal" program by local officials. Conversely, Vincent Ostrom has applauded the decentralizing overtones of new ventures in federal relations as beneficial to the assurance of a "compound republic"—that is, one in which there are multiple and jurisdictionally overlapping administrative units extant that promote a polity maximally responsive to the needs of the individual citizen.[6] In view of the honest and differing opinions of the nature of intergovernmental relations held by both politicians and political scientists, it is not

2. Don K. Price, *Government and Science* (New York: Oxford University Press, 1962).
3. Morton Grodzins, "The Federal System," from *Goals for Americans* (New York: Columbia University Press, 1960), p. 265.
4. Joseph F. Zimmerman, *The Federated City: Community Control in Large Cities* (New York: St. Martin's, 1972).
5. Theodore J. Lowi, *The End of Liberalism* (New York: W. W. Norton, 1969), pp. 250–266.
6. Vincent Ostrom, *The Intellectual Crisis in American Public Administration* (University, Ala.: University of Alabama Press, 1973).

surprising to learn that we are dealing with an extraordinarily complex system.

The crises of federalism

Given the complexity of the federal system, it is not surprising that the crises of federalism are many. These crises are administrative, jurisdictional, and financial, and in this chapter we will concentrate on these problems of intergovernmental relations. Table 14–1 delineates the 80,179 governments in the United States by type—that is, nation, states, counties, townships, municipalities, school districts, and special districts—and indicates their fluctuations between 1967 and 1977.

The table indicates that American governments are many. The U.S. Task Force on Land Use and Urban Growth, in its report on the *Use of Land,* noted that much of this fragmentation goes back to "a long American tradition of localism in land use control, dating at least to the issuance of the Standard State Zoning Enabling Act of 1924, an act which most states copied and which viewed land use controls as a matter of local rather than state control." [7] Much of the proliferation of units of local government occurred in the years following World War II, particularly around the fringes of big cities; it was largely due to the trend of white flight from the inner cities and unplanned metropolitan growth. The lack of prior planning for urban regions is particularly noticeable when we consider that forty-four new suburban governments were created between 1945 and 1950 around St. Louis by builders desirous of escaping strict municipal building codes, or when we consider that new towns were formed around Minneapolis solely as a means of taxing a newly arrived industry, including one village that was incorporated for the

TABLE 14–1. American Governments by Type, 1967, 1972, and 1977

Type of government	1977	1972	1967
Total	80,171	78,269	81,299
U.S. Government	1	1	1
State governments	50	50	50
Local governments	80,120	78,218	81,248
Counties	3,042	3,044	3,049
Municipalities	18,856	18,517	18,048
Townships	16,822	16,991	17,105
School districts	15,260	15,781	21,782
Special districts	26,140	23,885	21,264

Source: U.S. Bureau of the Census, Census of Governments, 1977.

7. Task Force on Land Use Urban Growth, *The Use of Land* (New York: Crowell, 1973).

single purpose of issuing a liquor license. There are still more examples: Bryan City, California, was created so that a circus owner could zone for animal populations. The town of New Square, New York, was established so that a Kosher slaughterhouse could be operated. Gardenia, California, was incorporated so that its residents might play poker legally.[8] But though Americans appear to be eager to set up small towns, they are wary of creating large ones. Community efforts to merge urban and suburban governments (considered later in this chapter) have generally failed, despite frequently intensive efforts by urban political elites. With the exception of school districts, which have been diminishing in number since the 1930s, and special districts, which have been slowly multiplying, the numbers of governmental units in all categories have remained essentially the same since 1900.

Although the jurisdictional crises of federalism are real and severe, governments at most levels in the United States have been making genuine strides during the last twenty years in trying to reduce the adverse effects of governmental fragmentation. We shall consider some of these efforts in turn, first by approaching the federal government's role in intergovernmental relations, then moving to the states' role, and finally considering some aspects of interlocal cooperation.

THE REVIVAL OF REGIONALISM

Federal regional councils

One result of state and city lobbying activity in Washington, at least indirectly, has been the development of Federal Regional Councils. President Johnson, increasingly concerned that the delivery of his "Great Society" program was becoming mired in the interstices of federalism and a red-tape jungle of bureaucracy, appointed a secret task force to recommend a reorganization of the executive branch. Ben W. Heineman, a railway executive, headed the high-level group, and in 1967 it turned over its "administratively confidential" report to the president. The Heineman report urged "far more decentralization of operational program decisions" on a nationwide basis by appointing powerful "field representatives" of the President's Office of Program Coordination. These officials would head ten administrative regions in the United States.

Johnson let the report die, but it was resurrected by President Nixon, who had it reconsidered by his own task force. The Heineman report clearly influenced the creation of ten federal administrative re-

8. Henry S. Reuss, *Revenue Sharing: Crutch or Catalyst for State and Local Governments?* (New York: Praeger, 1970).

gions in 1969, each headed by a Federal Regional Council. Little political controversy was stirred, no new federal buildings were built, and a minimum of government personnel was transferred—about 2300 federal employees had to move to the new headquarters.

The ten Federal Regional Councils are designed to bring greater order, efficiency, and effectiveness to the administration of federal programs at the state and local level. They are made up of regional officials representing the Departments of Health, Education, and Welfare, Housing and Urban Development, Transportation, Labor (in the form of its Manpower Administration unit), the Environmental Protection Agency, and others.

One major goal of the Federal Regional Council idea seems likely to be put into effect: reducing the time taken to process grant requests for federal funds from state and local officials. John Fischer reported that, while HUD used to take an average of ninety-six days to decide on a mayor's application for a rehabilitation loan, it soon was taking only five days. Overall, time for processing applications of all kinds had been cut by almost half, and the application forms had been reduced by hundreds of thousands of pages.[9]

More significantly, however, the Federal Regional Councils were created to identify conflicting agency policies in regions, to design coordinated agency programs that would give maximum agency effectiveness, and to direct their component agencies in ways that would strengthen program monitoring, evaluation, and coordination. Clearly, the core value of these goals (which were expressed in a 1970 memorandum from the Office of Management and Budget) is to reduce interagency conflict and enhance program coordination. In Melvin B. Mogulof's view, formulated after a systematic investigation, Federal Regional Councils have not fulfilled expectations in terms of coordinating their member agencies' activities. Council members tend to defer to each other in cases of conflict, leaving significant issues of interdepartmental coordination unresolved. Mogulof urges that Federal Regional Councils be increasingly brought under the purview of the Office of Management and Budget so that genuine programmatic coordination might be achieved.[10]

Federally encouraged districts

Closely related to Federal Regional Councils, though not directly created by the federal government, are what some call "federally encour-

9. John Fischer, "Can The Nixon Administration Be Doing Anything Right?" *Harper's Magazine* 103 (November 1970): 22–24, 32, 34, 35, 37.

10. Melvin B. Mogulof, *Federal Regional Councils* (Washington, D.C.: The Urban Institute, March, 1970).

aged districts." These districts have grown over the years and are unique in that they administer federal area-wide programs, which vary substantially in both purpose and form. In 1964 there were five federally encouraged districts; by 1972 this number had grown to twenty-four. Some of these programs have several purposes; others deal only with a single function, such as urban and rural development, economic development, providing public facilities and services, transportation, health, water, solid waste disposal, and so on. The number of geographic areas incorporated by these twenty-four federal areawide programs is 4,045, and about 1,800 new districting organizations were created as a result of these programs. David B. Walker and Albert J. Richter conclude that "These federal programs in most instances have established inconsistent and confusing requirements which necessitate major grantsmanship efforts by area-wide organizations," and it is these area-wide programs that the federally encouraged districts broach.[11] Table 14–2 itemizes the federal area-wide programs.

Agency coordination

More than a dozen federal agencies have responsibility for urban programs and, in fact, the year after the Department of Housing and Urban Development (HUD) was created (1965) the Secretary of HUD was authorized to convene meetings of appropriate officials to promote cooperation among federal departments for those programs that affected urban areas. This effort was not as successful as it might have been, and subsequently the practice developed of negotiating jurisdictional arrangements among agencies at the top levels. By way of example, the Office of Economic Opportunity (now the Community Services Administration) and HUD worked out a number of working relationships relative to the Community Action and Model Cities programs.[12]

Creating new agencies

Since the late 1950s the federal government has made a concerted effort to strengthen coordination between the national government and state and local agencies. In 1959 the Advisory Commission on Intergovernmental Relations was established. The commission comprises representatives of national, state, and local governments and the public. This in-

11. David B. Walker and Albert J. Richter, "The Counties and Regionalism," *The County Yearbook, 1975* (Washington, D.C.: National Association of Counties, 1975), p. 16.
12. John C. Bollens and Henry J. Schmandt, *The Metropolis*, 3rd ed. (New York: Harper & Row, 1975), p. 60.

TABLE 14–2. Federal Areawide Programs

Program	Federal agency	Year of enactment/ major amendment
Areawide comprehensive planning grants ("701")	HUD	1954/1965
Open space grants	HUD	1961
Urban transportation planning grants	DOT/FHWA	1962/1970
Resource conservation and development loans	USDA/SCS	1962/1966/1970/1972
Urban mass transportation planning grants	DOT/UMTA	1964/1970
Community action grants (CAP)	OEO	1964
Water and sewer facilities grants	HUD	1965
Water and sewer planning grants for rural communities	USDA/FHA	1965/1972
Water and waste disposal systems grants for rural communities	USDA/FHA	1965/1972
Regional medical program grants	HEW	1965
Economic development planning grants	Commerce/EDA	1965
Appalachian local development district grants	ARC	1965
Solid waste planning grants	EPA	1965
New communities	HUD	1965/1970
Land development mortgages		
Loan guarantees		
Supplemental grants		
Comprehensive areawide health planning grants	HEW	1966/1967/1970
Process notification and review process (A-95)	OMB	1966/1968
Air pollution control grants	EPA	1967
Manpower planning grants (CAMPs)	Labor	1968
Law enforcement planning grants	Justice/LEAA	1968/1970
Airport system planning grants	DOT/FAA	1970
Water quality management planning grants	EPA	1970/1972
Rural development planning grants	USDA/FHA	1972
Rural industrialization loans and grants	USDA/FHA	1972
Areawide waste treatment management	EPA	1972

Source: Advisory Commission on Intergovernmental Relations, *Regional Decision Making* (1973), p. 169.

Note: Key to abbreviations: ARC = Appalachian Regional Commission; Commerce = U.S. Department of Commerce; DOT = U.S. Department of Transportation; EDA = Economic Development Administration; EPA = Environmental Protection Agency; FAA = Federal Aviation Administration; FHA = Farmers Home Administration; FHWA = Federal Highway Administration; HEW = Department of Health, Education, and Welfare; HUD = Department of Housing and Urban Development; Justice = U.S. Department of Justice; Labor = U.S. Department of Labor; LEAA = Law Enforcement Assistance Administration; OEO = Office of Economic Opportunity; OMB = Office of Management and Budget; SCS = Soil Conservation Service; UMTA = Urban Mass Transportation Administration; USDA = U.S. Department of Agriculture.

creasingly influential commission studies and makes recommendations on common intergovernmental problems. In 1967 the president issued Circular No. A–85 through the Bureau of the Budget, which established consultation procedures between federal, state, and local officials. In 1969 former President Nixon set up under the vice president, the Office of

Intergovernmental Relations, which combined into a single staff the various people who had been working in the area of federal relations.

Councils of governments (COGs)

Perhaps the best known result of the federal government's effort to co-ordinate regional policy-making and implementation are Councils of Governments. COGs were originated in 1954 in Detroit, but by 1965 only nine were in operation. Since 1965, however, and largely as the result of several pieces of federal legislation, the number of COGs has expanded dramatically. There are more than 300 COGs, and every one of the nation's SMSAs has its own Council of Government.

At least three pieces of federal legislation have aided the development of Councils of Governments: The Demonstration Cities and Metropolitan Development Act of 1966, the Intergovernmental Cooperation Act of 1968, and the National Environmental Policy Act of 1969. These acts, combined with the ongoing administration of federal planning grants to state and local governments by the Department of Housing and Urban Development under its "701" program and, more significantly, Circular A–95 of the Office of Management and Budget (OMB), are the cornerstones of Councils of Governments.

Section 204 of the Demonstration Cities and Metropolitan Development Act facilitated the growth of COGs by requiring that applications for federal grants and loans for purposes specified in the act be submitted "for review to any area-wide agency which is designated to perform metropolitan or regional planning for the area within which the assistance is to be used. . . ." The applicant must show that the comments of the review agency have been considered before the grant or loan can be granted.

Title IV of the Intergovernmental Cooperation Act also encouraged the development of COGs by specifying that the president may establish rules for the evaluation and review of federal programs that impinge on area and community development. All viewpoints—"national, regional, state and local"—must be considered in planning federal or federally aided development projects, in the words of the act, "to the maximum extent possible, consistent with national objectives, all federal aid for development purposes shall be consistent with and further the objectives of state, regional and local comprehensive planning."

Section 102 of the National Environmental Policy Act (considered more thoroughly in chapter 15) established the requirement of writing "environmental impact statements" for all federally assisted projects. An environmental impact statement reviews the ecological costs and benefits of any project that uses federal money, and any project may be stopped (or, more precisely, denied federal funds) by any citizen on the basis of an inadequate impact statement or evidence of too much environmental degradation resulting from the project.

All these acts and programs, plus Section 701 of the Urban Planning Assistance Act of 1954, which allocates grants to local planning agencies for purposes of coordination, were drawn upon when the Office of Management and Budget wrote its Circular A–95 in 1969 and later broadened its scope significantly in 1971. OMB Circular A–95 encourages a process of review and comment by promoting intergovernmental planning for a variety of federal development programs, provides a means of coordinating federal development projects with state and local planning agencies, and furnishes methods for securing environmental impact statements for federal or federally funded projects. The means of accomplishing all this intergovernmental planning and policy coordination is the establishment of "clearinghouses," to use the term employed in Circular A–95—state clearinghouses designed by the governor or by state legislation, metropolitan clearinghouses of a nonmetropolitan nature inaugurated by the governor, by state legislation, or by interstate agreements. By providing the coordinative mechanisms needed for comprehensive planning throughout the nation, OMB Circular A–95 exemplifies as much as any other document a public policy made by public administrators.

In actuality, state clearinghouses are generally administered from the governor's office, metropolitan clearinghouses are made up of urban planning boards and Councils of Governments, and regional clearinghouses include economic development districts and state-operated rural planning agencies. The major impact of A–95 and the legislation it coordinated, however, is felt by the metropolises. By 1970 the National Service to Regional Councils reported that 99 percent of metropolitan clearinghouses either were COGs or regional planning commissions and, as Mogulof has observed, the policies coordinated by Circular A–95 have "almost overnight established the potential for evolving 'a new level of government.' " [13]

COGs are designed to rationalize particular kinds of metropolitan governmental activities according to areal administrative criteria. These include: those activities that involve large numbers of people and many political boundaries (such as transportation planning); those activities in which the action (or lack of action) by one jurisdiction may undercut the effectiveness of programs in another jurisdiction (such as antipollution programs); and those activities involving economies of scale (such

---

13. Melvin B. Mogulof, *Governing Metropolitan Areas; A Critical Review of Councils of Governments and the Federal Role* (Washington, D.C.: Urban Institute, 1971), p. 1.

as time-sharing arrangements between governments on a single computer, or areal water supplies).

Stanley Scott and John Bollens have stated that the COG "is the mildest of all approaches" to these interjurisdictional dilemmas, "building on the status quo without disturbing its formal organization." [14] Still, the resultant funding patterns stemming from the newly designated review-and-comment authority of COGs certainly bodes ill for the forces of ultralocalism and splintered autonomies. Mogulof concluded that the "differences it has made as a new institution of government are real and important"; COGs have created regional senses of community, sharpened the interdependencies of governments, questioned the utility of establishing more single-purpose government agencies in regions, and been effective in coordinating governmental programs. Mogulof has noted further that COGs have evolved into two distinct identities: the "services-oriented COG," which tries to aid localities as much as possible with federal assistance, and the "planning/implementation-oriented COG," which has a more independent point of view.[15]

Even so, the central problem confronting all COGs at this point in their continuing development is that of willingness to be authoritative on regional issues. To gain greater authority over its member governments will require some changes of attitude by COG officials, greater coordination between HUD (which controls "701" planning funds) and OMB (which administers the funding process through Circular A–95), increased popular representation at local levels, and more staff members in all levels of government. Overall, as the National Research Council (NRC) in its study of the metropolis, concluded: "The Councils of Governments, however, are generally forms in which local officials protect the autonomy of their jurisdictions." [16] If that is the case, and the National Research Council believes it is, then it is a dubious proposition that COGs will evolve into a new level of government as some have predicted. Nevertheless, it can be reasonably argued that COGs have facilitated the intergovernmental process more than they have hindered it.

Local and regional policy councils

A final type of federal stimulus designed to aid in the coordination of programs conducted by local governments is the virtual creation by

14. Stanley Scott and John C. Bollens, *Governing a Metropolitan Region: The San Francisco Bay Area* (Berkeley, Calif.: Institute of Governmental Studies, 1968), p. 2.
15. Mogulof, *Governing Metropolitan Areas, op. cit.*
16. National Research Council, *Toward an Understanding of Metropolitan America* (San Francisco: Canfield, 1975), pp. 124–125.

the federal government of local and regional policy councils. These councils have the power to set policy goals and to implement them. Often they are county-wide agencies that share a common interest in that policy is controlled by local governments with an emphasis on intergovernmental planning in a particular area, such as health planning, manpower planning, criminal justice planning, and economic development.

Unlike COGs, regional planning commissions are not voluntary associations of governments, but are public planning bodies authorized by state legislation (often as the result of pressure from the national government), and are primarily responsible for comprehensive planning. They tend to come in three varieties: county planning commissions, city-county planning commissions, and multi-jurisdictional planning commissions, an arrangement favored in metropolitan areas covering two or more counties. Walker and Richter observe that since the implementation of the Metropolitan Development Act of 1966, notably its Section 204, most regional planning commissions "began to acquire a COG-like character with 50 percent or more of their membership composed of local elected officials." [17]

There are more than six hundred regional councils of all types. By 1972, 30 percent could be considered COGs while the remaining 70 percent were policy councils of various kinds: 46 percent were regional planning councils, 14 percent were economic development districts, and 10 percent were other kinds of area-wide policy councils. Almost half of the councils were located in nonmetropolitan areas.

GRASSROOTS FEDERALISM

So far we have been discussing federalism from the viewpoint of the government in Washington. But the states have active governments, too, and in this section we review their relations with each other and involvement (or lack of it) in the business of their cities, counties, and towns.

Interstate cooperation

States have been known to cooperate and not cooperate with each other, although the Constitution requires that "full faith and credit shall be given in each state to the public acts, records, and judicial proceedings of every state." Since the clause applies only to civil matters and not necessarily to criminal violations, we occasionally witness states harboring fugitives from other states if public officials feel that the fugitive has been treated unjustly in the state from which he or she fled. Other

17. Walker and Richter, *op. cit.*, p. 15.

modes of cooperation between the states involve the creation of inter-state compacts and interstate agencies. By 1971 there were 169 interstate compacts in operation, and 47 of these were adopted in the 1960s. Their popularity is rising; between 1789 and 1900, only 24 such compacts were made. Interstate compacts are distinctive in that they normally require congressional approval to be set into motion. Many interstate compacts have evolved into ongoing interstate agencies, and in 1976 there were sixty-one such agencies dealing with educational concerns, river basin management, transportation, waterfronts, fisheries, and energy. Perhaps the most notable example of what an interstate agency can become is the Port Authority of New York and New Jersey. Established in 1921 and headed by six commissioners appointed by the governor of each member state, the Port Authority is in charge of virtually all transporta-tion in the New York and New Jersey areas; it has eight thousand em-ployees, the highest number of employees of any interstate agency (few interstate agencies exceed fifty, and a number have none).

The states tame their "creatures"

While the states can cooperate with each other as equals, their rela-tionships with their own local governments are quite different. Indeed, the phrase "creatures of the state," was used by Judge John F. Dillon in 1868 and is now known as "Dillon's rule." "Creatures of the state," a concept upheld by the U.S. Supreme Court in 1923, simply means that such units of government as counties, towns, townships, special districts, multipurpose districts, cities, and villages have no independence other than what they are granted by their state governments. It is the state government that determines the areas of political and administrative dis-cretion that its subsuits of government may or may not have. As Edward Banfield and James Q. Wilson note in *City Politics*, "This means that a city cannot operate a peanut stand at the city zoo without first getting the state legislature to pass an enabling law, unless, perchance, the city's charter or some previously enacted law unmistakably covers the sale of peanuts." [18]

State legislatures achieve this kind of control through the type of charter that they grant a city. Most city charters are quite long (New York's, for example, is several hundred pages) because the states often want to retain minute degrees of control. There are four general types of charters: special act charters, general act charters, optional charter laws, and home rule charters.

The *special act charters* are charters that have been drawn specifi-

---

18. Edward C. Banfield and James Q. Wilson, *City Politics* (Cambridge: Harvard University Press, 1963), p. 65.

cally for a particular city. Cities with special act charters remain completely under state legislative control and often these charters facilitate state legislatures passing laws that are written specifically for a particular city. Banfield and Wilson quote by way of example an ordinance stating that "Fall River be authorized to appropriate money for the purchase of uniforms for the park police and watershed guards of said city." [19]

General act charters tend to categorize cities by population size and then apply state legislation to all cities in each size classification. Usual divisions are according to cities with less than 10,000 people, with populations of 10,000 to 25,000, and so on.

Optional charter laws provide relatively more free choice for city governments. They offer optional forms of government that a city may wish to adopt, such as council–manager, commission, or whatever.

Finally, home rule charters are perhaps on the farthest end of the continuum in that they do provide cities with self-governance. Even so, home rule charters are furnished by the state legislature or the state constitution and may be taken away by the state as easily as they are granted. Home rule got its start in 1875 in Missouri and now more than 50 percent of the states have constitutional clauses that provide for the issuance of home rule charters. Roughly two-thirds of the cities in this country with populations of more than two hundred thousand people have some kind of home rule. Political battles over acquiring urban home rule often are bloody ones, usually pitting good-government groups, city mayors, and city managers against rural legislators and large municipal taxpayer groups. In any case, regardless of the type of charter a city may have, the point remains that these charters are granted according to the discretion of the state polity; Judge Dillon's rule stands—all cities and other units of government remain the creatures of the state.

The "mixed bag" of state urban policy

As the foregoing review of city charters implies, states can treat their creatures with severity or laxity. Joseph Zimmerman has observed that states may play the roles of inhibitor, facilitator, or initiator in their relations with their own local governments, and the role most frequently played, in Zimmerman's view, unfortunately is the first. [20] Nonetheless, the states have made some limited strides in constructively contributing to urban government. For example, forty states have developed more than five hundred regional planning and development districts that are

---

19. Ibid., p. 66.

20. Joseph F. Zimmerman, "The Role of the States in Metropolitan Governance," paper presented at Conference at Temple University, Philadelphia, Pennsylvania, August 27, 1973. Cited in Bollens and Schmandt, op. cit.

designed to aid metropolitan areas and urban counties, and these districts represent a growing perception by state governments of the need to handle certain kinds of public problems on a regional basis.

A number of states have established offices specifically endowed with responsibilities pertaining to local or metropolitan affairs. Virtually all the states now have such an office, although there were only five prior to 1966. They provide advisory services and assist the state administration in coordinating local administrative functions. Most are concerned primarily with regional planning; relatively few have direct programmatic responsibility such as urban renewal, housing, and poverty. In a few states these and related offices are beginning to take on a genuine policy-making role for their urban and local governments. Texas, for example, has been active in discouraging the separate incorporation of satellite cities, as have Indiana and Minnesota, although to a lesser degree. According to the National Research Council, other areas in which states are assuming urban functions include water service, sewage, transportation, and air pollution; Massachusetts, New York, Connecticut, and Delaware have been the leaders in this trend. Connecticut is particularly noteworthy because in 1968 it abolished counties as a unit of government. The NRC predicts that "state government may in effect become the metropolitan governmental unit in Connecticut, since Connecticut transferred county functions to the state." [21]

What of the larger panorama of relationships between the states and their local governments? Do the states have a declining role? The overall view expressed in literature is that the states are more of a hindrance than a help to their local governments. For example, Susan Furniss found that in Colorado, suburban and rural state legislatures combined against big-city interests, notably Denver, to prevent legislation that would be beneficial to that city. [22] Bollens and Schmandt concluded that "despite the increasing amount of effort that they have devoted to urban affairs, the states have continued to evidence little desire to intervene in metropolitan governmental reorganization—with the important exception of school districts." [23] And the National Research Council observed as well that "Although states have increased their aid to local governments, such aid generally has not gone to the areas of greatest need." [24]

It is not surprising in this light that a survey taken in 1970 of local officials of cities with populations of more than one hundred thousand

21. National Research Council, *op. cit.*, p. 109.
22. Susan W. Furniss, "The Response of the Colorado General Assembly to Proposals for Metropolitan Reform." *Western Political Quarterly* 26 (December 1973): 765.
23. Bollens and Schmandt, *op. cit.*, p. 58.
24. National Research Council, *op. cit.*, p. 108.

found that approximately two-thirds of those officials believe the national government to be more responsive to their problems than the government of their own states. "The most startling and far-reaching change in American federalism is the emergence of the national government as a focus for discussion of urban and metropolitan affairs," [25] and Daniel R. Grant has noted that "if one were to use the past as the basis of fore-casting the future role of the state and local government reorganization, the prospects for a new, affirmative role would be exceedingly dim." [26] Grant's assessment is probably quite accurate: the future place of the state in its relations with its own local governments will be "a highly mixed bag with contents varying all the way from states which continue the present position of grudging involvement and passive indifference, to a small and select group of states which takes the bull by the horns and restructures metropolitan area government. . . ." [27]

URBAN FEDERALISM

Direct federalism: the feds and cities

If anything, the federal government has a greater political impact on localities than on states. The formal linkage between local governments and the national government has often been called "direct federalism," indicating the bypass that frequently is made around state governments. Nevertheless, the major impact of the federal government on local governments is more accidental than planned. For example, RAND Corporation studies have shown that federal officials often may have more control over the shape and economy in a particular locality than do local officeholders. The RAND studies indicated that in St. Louis federal housing and highway policies attracted many central city residents to the suburbs; in San Jose federal military procurement procedures accelerated the local growth rate; and in Seattle Federal Civil Aviation policies likely affected detrimentally the area's major employer.[28] Bollens and

25. Victor Jones, "Representative Local Government: From Neighborhood to Region," *Public Affairs Report* (Berkeley: University of California, April 1970).

26. Daniel R. Grant, "Urban Needs and State Response: Local Government Reorganization," in Alan K. Campbell, ed., *The States and the Urban Crisis* (Englewood Cliffs, N.J.: Prentice-Hall, 1970, pp. 59–84.

27. *Ibid.*

28. R. B. Rainey *et al.*, *Seattle: Adaptation to Recession*; Barbara R. Williams, *St. Louis: A City and Its Suburbs*; Daniel Atesch and Robert Arvine, *Growth in San Jose: A Summary Policy Statement.* (All published in Santa Monica, Calif.: RAND Corp., 1973.)

Schmandt, in fact, contend that "federal stimulation produced independent housing authorities, a type of special district, and federal encouragement of the growth of suburbia through underwriting liberal mortgage arrangements indirectly led to the creation of many new suburban governments." They go on to observe that the creation of the federal Department of Housing and Urban Development and the Department of Transportation are "both institutional examples of recognition by the national government of its deep involvement in metropolitan affairs."[29]

Both departments are beneficial in that they at least are sensitive to the needs of coordinating metropolitan policies and reducing political fragmentation but, as Samuel Kaplan and others have argued, "The federal government could help stimulate regionalism, if they wanted to, by enforcing Title IV of the Intergovernmental Cooperation Act of 1968 which requires all federal aid for development purposes shall be consistent with and further the objectives of state, regional and local comprehensive planning."[30] It is Kaplan's contention that the federal government has not enforced this and related legislation in any adequate way.

Interlocal agreements:
cities, companies, and other cities

Another major type of intergovernmental cooperation used in America is that between local governments. By any measure, cooperation among local units of government is burgeoning. In 1972, the Advisory Commission on Intergovernmental Relations and the International City Management Association sent a questionnaire to municipalities with populations over 2,500, inquiring about intergovernmental agreements involving seventy-six different services. Forty percent of the municipalities, or 2,375, responded, and of these, 63 percent had entered into a variety of formal or informal agreements for the provision of services by other units of government or by private firms. The survey found that the more people a city has, the more likely it is to enter into agreements with other units of government. Most of the service agreements are among local governments only, but a considerable number also involved state governments or private firms. Of those cities and towns that "farmed out" their personnel administration services through intergovernmental agreements, 50 percent received those services from the state. Such personnel services include training of policemen and fire fighters, criminological services, and so forth.

29. Bollens and Schmandt, *op. cit.*, p. 60.
30. Samuel Kaplan, *The Dream Deferred* (New York: Seabury Press, 1976), p. 160.

The private sector plays a big role in these "intergovernmental" agreements. Eighty-eight percent of the municipalities responding had contracted with private firms for refuse collection; 85 percent had contracted with private companies for engineering services; 84 percent for legal services; 79 percent for street lighting; 67 percent for public relations services; and 64 percent for microfilm services.[31] The line between the private and public sphere, when it comes to local agreements, is indeed a fine one.

These cooperative agreements between local governments share certain characteristics. First, most such agreements are between two governments over a single activity, such as police services. Second, these agreements pertain to services rather than to facilities; cities prefer to build their own buildings, but will frequently enter into service arrangements with other governments. Third, these agreements are not always permanent ones, and often contain provisos for the renegotiation or termination of the agreement by either party at a particular date in the future. Fourth, many of these interlocal agreements are of a stand-by

Federalism and the Metropolitan Morass

In the following passage, a former Secretary of Health, Education, and Welfare, former Chairman of the Urban Coalition, and former Chairman of Common Cause explains why a reconsideration of federalism is vital to understanding and dealing with the traditional (but increasingly unviable) concepts of "city." His analogies of "half-sunken battleships" and a "decerebrate frog" are well taken.

Within the past 20 years the urge on the part of large numbers of people to pile into the cities has become wholly anachronistic.

For 10,000 years, people had excellent reason to crowd themselves into cities. The massing of people and resources in one place served useful purposes. Creativity, for example, depends on the presence of a large number of heterogeneous elements in a situation that permits free combination and recombination of those elements. Thus from earliest days the cities were creative centers. Diverse cultural strains from the countryside met, clashed, and produced significant new combinations.

And the massing of resources made it possible to do things on a scale that would not otherwise have been feasible. The economic and military advantages that accrued to the earliest urban centers were considerable.

31. National Research Council, *op. cit.*, p. 121.

Today, thanks to advances in communication, transportation, and the arts of organization, we can provide the advantages of centralization at any point on the map that strikes our fancy. We have not yet absorbed all the implications of that fact. We are not in a position to make the word "provincial" obsolete.

It is a mistake to suppose that this would weaken our greatest cities. It would strengthen them to be nerve centers in a farflung and varied pattern of human settlements in which vitality is distributed through all parts of the system. The great cities have certainly not been strengthened by the centripetal forces operating in recent decades.

If we recognize the new flexibility that is possible in human settlement, then we should be asking these questions: How can we best use the land space of the Nation? What patterns of settlement and open space best serve our purposes? How can we preserve areas of natural beauty, revitalize rural areas, create new cities, and overhaul existing cities in ways that serve human needs and the requirements of economic vitality?

The best that can be said today is that we are beginning—to think in those terms. Neither at the Federal nor at the State and local levels have we made provision for such thinking on any adequate scale. It is an interesting fact that our national planning for wilderness areas and parks is far ahead of our planning for areas of settlement.

One area of effort which is highly relevant—and in which we have made good beginnings—is regional economic development. I have long believed the Federal Government could and should do more along these lines. I have been particularly interested in the recent talk of economic development efforts in southern rural areas, to stem the deterioration that leads poor people to migrate to the already overburdened city.

If you consider, as I was forced to consider when I was Secretary of Health, Education, and Welfare, the conditions in the Mississippi Delta region that stand as obstacles to human fulfillment, you find that you cannot imagine tackling the problems in one city or town alone nor can you imagine tackling one kind of problem—for example, health—alone. What is needed is a regional approach covering health, education, employment, housing, industrial development, and so on.

And it is significant that one of the most effective barriers to the launching of such an effort is the lack of coordination of the Federal departments that would have to participate in the program.

Large-scale regional economic development schemes can probably only stem from the Federal Government, but any city can begin tomorrow to "think regionally." Not long ago the leading citizens of a medium-sized city came to me to seek help in thinking about a long range plan for the development of their community. To my surprise their thinking was limited to the city itself. They said it would be entirely possible to include the suburbs, but I told them they would have to go far beyond that, to the point of seeing their city as part of a pattern of settlement that included two much larger cities less than 100 miles away, and a dozen or more smaller towns that were in fact satellites of their city. I told them that if they would study that larger pattern they would discover innumerable lines of interdependence that would have to be explored. Transportation and communication were obvious topics for study; other dimensions were less immediately apparent. To what extent, for example, should the hospitals, clinics, and medical school of this medium-sized city be related to the greater medical centers 100 miles away? To what extent should this city regard its own medical personnel and facilities as a resource to the small towns 10 to 20 miles away? Such satellite relationships are certain to be a part of our future. We had better think about them.

The problem of developing such patterns of creative interdependence is much the same in every field—health, education, industry, and so on. It is complicated by the absolute necessity of doing two seemingly contradictory things: (a) availing ourselves of the enormous benefits that come from overall patterns of organization and (b) preserving diversity and human-sized communities.

On the one hand we must go *beyond* the city to area-wide planning if we are ever to solve the problems of air and water pollution control, transportation, open space, and the like. But at the same time that we reach out to create larger systems, we must do everything possible to revive the old-fashioned neighborhood, and to create human-sized communities within the metropolitan mass. . . .

I have looked at all the various problems of the city—the snarled traffic, the polluted air and water, crime, overcrowded schools, inadequate health services, breakdowns in public order, and so on and on. And I have listened attentively to the special explanations as to why each of these problems has arisen. But out of all these crises a conclusion begins to emerge that is more alarming than any one of them: Our greatest cities have lost command of themselves and their future. They lie helpless as the multiple waves of crisis roll over them, like half-sunken battleships battered by heavy seas.

Why? As we review the problems of the city today, I believe we must conclude that there is one which outweighs all others. And that problem is that most cities are monstrosities from a governmental standpoint. The typical metropolitan area is fragmented nonsensically into dozens, even hundreds of political jurisdictions. City officials are typically underpaid. The mayor or city manager rarely has either the authority or money or personnel to do an adequate job of governing. The machinery of city government is typically antiquated. City ordinances are riddled with provisions designed to favor or protect vested interests. The city officials of this Nation deserve medals for the patience and stamina with which they tend the outworn machinery.

One particularly regrettable deficiency is the lack of any adequate planning capability in our great cities. Like a decerebrate frog, the city

> can twitch its muscles in response to specific stimuli, but it cannot think ahead.
>
> JOHN W. GARDNER
> *Science & Technology and the Cities*

nature and come into effect only when certain conditions arise. Such an agreement is known as a *mutual aid pact* and goes into effect when some disturbance, such as a fire or a riot, occurs. Finally, most interlocal agreements are permitted by specific state legislative authorizations that permit cooperation among local governments in one particular field. States have a propensity for specifying that their local governments may cooperate only in the areas that they stipulate, thus limiting interlocal agreements to special functions. Recently, as noted earlier, states gradually are moving away from this idea and permitting interlocal cooperation along a broad variety of fronts.

BOUNDARIES, PEOPLE, POLICIES, AND POWER

Matching people, politics, and political boundaries in such a way that the needs of the citizens are best met is one of the overriding dilemmas of American government. Reorganizing the structure of local governments and redrawing jurisdictions is not an easy task, and political boundaries can be matched with the needs of the citizenry in many ways. How public administrationists would like boundaries and people brought together depends very much on the values those analysts hold. There are at least three different approaches to the boundary question in metropolitan affairs: (1) ultralocalism; (2) gargantua; and (3) compromise.

Ultralocalism:
the status quo and the status quo ante

There is a large and growing sentiment in public administration circles which argues that what is really needed is the current state of fragmentation of local governments, or perhaps even more fragmentation of local governments. This school of thought is called "public choice" or "political economy," and we reviewed it briefly in Chapter 11.

Perhaps the classic expression of public choice as it is applied to intergovernmental affairs is an article that appeared some years ago entitled, "The Organization of Government in Metropolitan Areas: A Theoretical Inquiry," by Vincent Ostrom, Charles M. Tiebout, and Robert Warren. The authors argued for what they termed "polycentric or multinucleated political systems" as the most responsive to the citizenry's needs. The contention is that many units of government, units that often overlap jurisdictionally and are perhaps inefficient economically, are going to be the most responsive to a citizen's demands.

To offer a hypothetical example, suppose you were a resident of an urban area and your house was being broken into by a very mean looking burglar. Your first inclination would be to lock the bedroom door and call the police. The public choice theorists would say that, under the normal system of government, you would have only one option: to call your metropolitan police. Your city's finest might not respond because they would have an effective monopoly on the delivery of the services to you as a citizen. A squad car might be at your door in thirty seconds, or the sergeant answering your call might chuckle at your plight. Under public choice theory, however, you could call (a) your metropolitan police, (b) the county sheriff's office, (c) the state troopers, or (d) perhaps even a private firm offering security protection against burglars. Under the public choice school all of these crime prevention agencies, and perhaps even others not yet conceived, would have overlapping jurisdictions. Hence, if one police department was not up to snuff or was somehow unresponsive to the citizens, another police department could fill that gap. Free market competition thus equals governmental responsiveness. To quote Ostrom, Tiebout, and Warren:

> By analogy, the formal units of government in a metropolitan area might be viewed as organizations similar to individual firms in an industry. Individual firms may constitute the basic legal entities in an industry, but their conduct in relation to one another may be conceived as having a particular structure and behavior as an industry. Collaboration among the separate units of local government may be such that their activities supplement or complement each other, as in the automobile industry's patent pool. Competition among them may produce desirable self-regulating tendencies similar in effect to the "invisible hand" of the market.[32]

Perhaps it is because of this kind of analogy that critics of the public choice school argue that it is a highly conservative political theory that can work against the dispossessed. Members of the political economy camp argue that it is just the opposite.

Regardless of criticism, however, when it comes to urban governance it seems apparent that "minigovs" are required for much the same rea-

32. Vincent Ostrom, Charles M. Tiebout, and Robert Warren, "The Organization of Government in Metropolitan Areas: Theoretical Inquiry," *American Political Science Review* 55 (December 1961): 831–842, as reprinted in Jay S. Goodman, *Perspectives on Urban Politics* (Boston: Allyn & Bacon, 1970), pp. 100–101.

sons as are "unigovs." In 1968 the National Commission on Urban Problems reported that "the psychological distance from the neighborhood to City Hall has grown from blocks, to miles, to light years. With decreasing communication and sense of identification by the low-income resident with his government have come first apathy, then disaffection, and now—insurrection." [33] Similarly, middle-class residents of "bedroom" suburban communities have become disaffected with town councils controlled by local construction interests that zone the town for their maximal profit and ensure that questions of public concerns are placed on the agenda of council meetings for consideration during the wee hours of the early morning on weekdays. It is an unusual town meeting that is attended by a significant portion of the town's people.

From a practical viewpoint, the adoption of a public choice concept in the real administration of metropolises probably is best expressed in the movement begun in the mid-1960s toward neighborhood governments.

Much of this movement is a reaction against what is perceived as the condescension of "professional managers" in the urban bureaucracy, and the very existence of the movement—which advocates a limited disannexation of neighborhood communities rather than outright secession from city hall—does not do credit to public administrators in big cities. Foremost among its proponents are Joseph Zimmerman, Milton Kotler, and Alan Altshuler.[34]

Gargantua

"Gargantua" is used in the same sense that Robert C. Wood used it several years ago: "the invention of a single metropolitan government or at least the establishment of a regional superstructure which points in that direction." [35] A number of public administrationists, in complete contrast to the public choice school, argue that the consolidation of the many splinters of metropolitan government is vital if the public is to acquire effective and efficient public services. Notice here that the emphasis is not on "responsiveness," it is on "efficiency." Often, of course,

---

33. National Commission on Urban Problems, *Building the American City* (Washington, D.C.: U.S. Government Printing Office, 1968), p. 11.

34. See Joseph F. Zimmerman, *The Federated City: Community Control in Large Cities* (New York: St. Martin's Press, 1972). Milton Kotler, *Neighborhood Government* (Indianapolis: Bobbs-Merrill, 1969). Alan A. Altshuler, *Community Control: The Black Demand for Participation in Large American Cities* (New York: Pegasus, 1970).

35. Robert C. Wood, "The New Metropolis: Greenbelt Grass Roots versus Gargantua," *American Political Science Review* 52 (March 1958): 108–122.

"responsiveness" and "efficiency" are synonymous, as most taxpayers prefer getting the biggest bang for their buck, but they are not always the
same. For example, quickly getting a police car to your house, which is
being burglarized, may be very important to you at the time of the
burglary, but when you are filling out your local property tax form you
may object vociferously to the "waste" engendered by many overlapping
units of government, even though this "waste" may have facilitated that
police car speeding to your house when you needed it. It is this latter
value that has been countenanced by such groups as the Committee for
Economic Development, a business-dominated organization, which recommended in 1966 the reduction in the number of the nation's local
governments by a whopping 80 percent (to sixteen thousand), and consolidating the country's twenty-seven hundred nonmetropolitan counties
into no more than 500, although four years later the committee modified
its view and recommended what amounted to a compromise reorganization of metropolitan governments.[36] Similarly, the National Commission
on Urban Problems in 1968 urged governmental consolidation, but less
for the sake of fiscal economies and more to encourage the construction
of new housing and greater responsiveness to other kinds of urban crises.

Economic waste is commonplace and unavoidable in overly small
governments.[37] For example, the 46,000 citizens of Sullivan County, New
York, paid $20.8 million in 1961 to the governments of their fifteen
towns, ten special districts, and six villages, and 20 percent of their taxes
paid purely administrative expenses. In the opinion of a 1960 study team
in Illinois, the liquidation of *all* town governments in the state and consolidation of its 102 counties into 24 would reduce taxes by as much
as 40 percent. The more than 80,000 governments in the United States,
many of which are of Lilliputian dimensions, are managed by some
500,000 elected and appointed officials. Consider, for instance, Blue Earth
County, Minnesota, whose 44,000 residents are governed by 155 units
of local government, 105 state bureaus, and 38 federal agencies; or
Allegheny County, Pennsylvania, which contains 129 municipalities, 78
boroughs, 23 first-class townships, 24 second-class townships, 116 school
districts, as well as the governments of the city of Pittsburgh and Allegheny County. Still another example is the awesomely bureaucratized
communities of Wilton, New Hampshire, whose 60 officials administered
a total of 1,724 citizens in 1960, and Bayfield County, Wisconsin, with

36. Committee for Economic Development, *Modernizing Local Government* (New
York: C.E.D., 1966), and Committee for Economic Development, *Reshaping
Government in Metropolitan Areas* (New York: C.E.D., 1970).

37. The following examples of governmental fragmentation at the local level are
drawn from Reuss, *op. cit.* While dated, the examples remain representative of
the problem.

less than 12,000 people in 1964 but governed by 100 elected legislators in various legislatures, assemblies, and councils and nearly 200 additional elected officials, including 29 treasurers, 29 assessors, and 29 tax collectors. More than 85 percent of all local governments in the United States have fewer than 5,000 people, and less than 50 percent contain even 1,000 constituents.

Delivering public services to the citizenry can be obstructed to the point of absurdity in jurisdictionally fragmented regions. For example, a few years ago there was a fire in a house less than three blocks away from a fire station in Las Vegas. Under orders from their superior the Las Vegas firemen watched the house, which was located just beyond the city limits, burn until county fire engines arrived. The city firemen had been instructed to prevent the fire from reaching city property. Angry neighborhood residents hurled rocks at the immobile city fire engines, causing substantial damage. Similarly, the forty thousand independent police jurisdictions in the United States render coordinated law enforcement action difficult. For instance, in 1965 St. Louis County plainclothes detectives conducting a gambling raid were arrested by police from the town of Wellston, who were staging their own raid. Coordinated and effective programs in air and water pollution control, public health, and highways are impeded or prevented by the irresponsibility, diseconomies, and buck-passing enabled by a plethora of tiny governments.

It has been contended that the argument for governmental consolidation is the product of an "efficiency mentality," which prefers dictatorial efficiency to democratic due process, participation, and representativeness. But making government services more effective and less costly through administratively rational consolidation does not necessarily mandate the establishment of a supercentralized bureaucracy unhindered by popular preferences and insensitive to the subtleties of neighborhood values. Nor is the implicit argument of the defenders of ultralocalism adequate—that is, that the status quo assures governmental responsiveness to local needs. Indeed, it is becoming increasingly apparent that Americans are apathetic when it comes to local politics (an average of only 30 percent of the eligible voters vote in local elections, in contrast to 50 to 60 percent in presidential elections), and the use of the long ballot arrangement in many localities is of questionable service to democratic ideals, since it diverts voter attention from the policy-making offices. For example, a woman got herself nominated for the coroner's office in a 1962 New Jersey primary by persuading nine of her friends to write in her name on the ballot, publicly proclaimed herself unfit for the office, and won the election by eighty thousand votes because she was the candidate of the dominant party. The voters of Milton, Washington (to their subsequent embarrassment) elected a mule to the Town Board. No doubt at least a portion of this profound lack of popular concern over local governance is attributable to a belief by Americans that their local governments are incapable of responding to their needs.

The argument for gargantua is not as unsophisticated as it might appear at first glance. Elinor Ostrom, in a review of much of the research on economies and diseconomies of scale (a term which means that some functions, such as garbage collection, are more efficient when conducted by a single organization over a large region rather than by many small agencies over the same area), concluded that only in the smaller cities, those with twenty-five thousand to two hundred fifty thousand people, could economies of scale be attained by broadening the scope of government. In cities with more than two hundred fifty thousand people it appeared that to expand the scope of government further produced *dis*economy of scale and lower levels of service to the public when calculated on a per capita basis.[38] Although these kinds of findings are unlikely to hold hard and fast for every city, the point is aptly made by Ostrom that economies of scale can work two ways.

The compromise approach

The third and final approach to the question of boundaries and power is the compromise approach, which is of course the classic one of the American polity. This accommodation recognizes that efficiency and responsiveness are both beneficial values. On the one hand, the idea is to retain responsiveness in those areas where responsiveness ought to be retained, such as planning, community/police relations, complaint systems, recreational activities, schools, public health clinics, building and housing code inspections, and a variety of operations that necessitate quick, responsive, and personal reactions by governments. On the other hand, certain other kinds of functions that governments perform should be centralized for greater economy and, in this sense, belong in the gargantuan category of metropolitan government. These functions include, at least potentially, environmental planning, pollution control, tax collection, sanitation, fire protection, computer services, crime control, and a variety of operations that are subject to economies of scale and standardization and that require coordination. Hence both fragmentation and gargantua are reconciled in the compromise approach.

In practice, the compromise approach to urban governance has taken two major tacks: metropolitan districts and comprehensive urban county plans. Let us consider them in turn.

38. Elinor Ostrom, "Metropolitan Reform: Propositions Denied from Two Traditions," *Social Science Quarterly* 53 (December 1972): 474–493.

Metropolitan districts are certainly the least controversial version of the compromise approach. A metropolitan district generally encompasses the entire metropolitan region, or at least a major portion of it; some in fact have waxed into regional governments. Roughly 125 metropolitan districts are now functioning in more than a quarter of the Standard Metropolitan Statistical Areas, and they are particularly popular in the larger cities of more than 500,000 people. They perform such services as managing port facilities, transportation, parks, public housing, water supplies, and so forth. The Port Authority of New York and New Jersey and the Bay Area Rapid Transit (BART) District in San Francisco are among the better known examples of metropolitan districts. They are popular largely because state legal provisions permit their flourishing, at least in comparison to other forms of metropolitan governmental innovation, but they have been criticized as being removed from political accountability to the citizenry, and thus not being responsive to the people. When one realizes that we are talking about a governmental form that generally is responsible only for a single function of government and one that often requires a good deal of expertise, such as water supplies, the problem of popular representation in metropolitan districts becomes a particularly difficult one. In addition to the isolation of metropolitan districts from public accountability, they have been criticized because of their single-purpose organization and the ensuing lack of policy and administrative coordination that often results.

A second variation of the compromise approach is the *comprehensive urban county plan*. The only metropolitan area in the nation using this plan is Miami in Dade County, although that fact does not detract from its more general potential utility, particularly when it is realized that a number of artificial barriers exist that prevent its wide-spread utilization. Cleveland, Dayton, Houston, and Pittsburgh, for example, all have tried to establish such a plan and have failed because of these barriers.

The obstacles to implementing the comprehensive urban county plan include: the lack of legal authorization by states to use this concept; entrenched local officials who may resist what they often regard to be a sweeping renovation of local government; the difficulty in selecting the criteria to be used in structuring the new governmental body of the county; the new duties to be assigned to county government; and inadequate funds to finance the new authority of county governments under such a plan.

That comprehensive urban county plans are useful has been testified to by the Miami–Dade County experience. In that metropolitan region, modern management practices have been put into effect, and a county-wide land use plan has been adopted, including tough regulations on air and water pollution control. Such functions as traffic laws and traffic courts, tax assessment and collection, zoning regulations and enforcement, youth services, and mass transit all have been coordinated and standardized throughout the Miami metropolitan region.

Efficiency or responsiveness: a problem of balance

The matching of political boundaries with political functions always has been a paramount difficulty of American government. Ultralocalism brings with it its attendant inefficiencies and ineffectiveness, but the American populace has tolerated these fiscal and administrative inefficiencies as the price of responsiveness. Indeed, it can be argued that the American people prefer these inefficiencies in that the governmental fragmentation that spawns them is the price of the most effective possible defense against tyranny.

Yet, when the price of ultralocalist government soars too high, the citizens respond accordingly, and we have witnessed this response in the form of taxpayers' revolts against school bond issues. Indeed, as the number of school district consolidations has increased (and more dramatically than any other form of innovation in American government since the 1930s), the number of taxpayers' revolts against school bond elections also has gone up. In the 1970s the number of school bond issues that went down in defeat at the polls exceeded 90 percent, despite the fact that the school districts have consolidated radically for the sake of economy and efficiency. Although there are exceptions to this rule—some citizens' revolts against school districts have been on political rather than economic grounds—these are the exceptions that prove the rule. An example is Kanawha County, West Virginia, which has garnered wide-spread publicity in the resistance of its citizens to certain books being used in its school systems on the grounds that these books were depraved, anti-Christ, and immoral. But the norm, at least if the data are to be read dispassionately, is that Americans will let their children read anything that the system assigns and will let the bureaucracy of public education distance itself from accountability to parents, provided that educational costs can be kept down. But it is only in the schools that Americans seem to prefer efficiency over responsiveness; this preference has not yet made itself felt in other forms of American government such as counties, cities, and towns.

Certainly one way to keep the costs of government relatively hidden, if not down, is to shift the money between governments as quickly as possible. In the last quarter of the twentieth century, American governments having been circulating the money with a vengeance—at least among each other.

FISCAL FEDERALISM

Governments in America give each other money. More often than not, the federal government will give money to states with the understanding that these funds will be channeled to the states' local governments, but states also grant money to local governments on their own. We shall consider first the area of federal transferences of money to state governments, then federal transferences to local governments, and finally state grants to local governments.

A lot of money is involved in these transfers.[39] In 1977 payments by the federal government to state and local governments totalled more than $70 billion, and state payments to local governments totalled more than $50 billion. These kinds of intergovernmental transfers of money have been proliferating for the past forty years, and the probability is that their scope will be enlarged in the future.

The increasing reliance of state and local governments on federal aid is both dramatic and disquieting. In 1902, the first year for which such figures were kept, federal aid to state and local governments amounted to only 2.6 percent of all federal domestic expenditures. By 1977 this proportion had attained nearly a quarter of all domestic, non-defense expenditures. In 1902 all federal aid amounted to only 0.7 percent of state and local general revenues; by 1976 it was almost 28 percent. Most of this money (more than 70 percent) was used for welfare programs. Figure 14–1 indicates the growing dependence by state and local governments on the federal government for money.

Washington, the states, and big money

The 1930s were a period of great expansion in federal grants to state governments, and this expansion became an explosion in the 1960s and 1970s. In 1963 the number of all federal grants to states was 181; ten years later it was more than 500. The cost of these 181 grants in 1963

---

39. The following figures on intergovernmental transfers of money are taken from: Thomas H. Kiefer, *The Political Impact of Federal Aid to State and Local Governments* (Morristown, Pa.: General Learning Press, 1974), p. 9, and Advisory Commission on Intergovernmental Relations, *Significant Features of Fiscal Federalism, 1976–77, Volume II* (Washington, D.C.: U.S. Government Printing Office, 1977), Table 38.

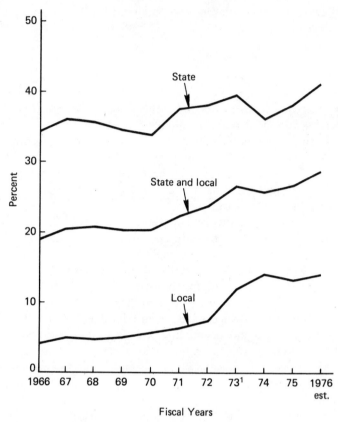

Fiscal Years

¹ Beginning in 1973, includes federal general revenue sharing.

FIGURE 14–1. Federal Aid in Relation to State and Local General Revenue From Own Sources, 1966 through 1976

Source: ACIR, *Significant Features of Fiscal Federalism, 1976–77,* vol. 2, p. 31.

was $8 billion, 324 million or $44 per person; by 1973, this amount had grown to $43 billion, 121 million, or $204 per capita. Table 14–3 indicates the shifts in federal grant policies toward state governments and their purposes from the postwar years to 1973. In 1973 more than 80 percent of total federal intergovernmental transfers were in the form of grants-in-aids.[40] Federal grants were used largely for public assistance—programs for the blind, the disabled, the old, children and the generally needy—followed by public health (notably Medicaid), education, and highways.

40. James A. Maxwell and J. Richard Aaronson, *Financing State and Local Governments,* 3rd ed. (Washington: Brookings Institution, 1977), p. 48.

TABLE 14–3. Federal Grants, 1948, 1963, and 1973

Purpose	Total, in millions of dollars			Percentage distribution		
	1948	1963	1973	1948	1963	1973
Public assistance	718	2,580	7,296	45.4	31.0	20.0
Health	55	442	5,668	3.5	5.3	15.5
Education	120	558	4,348	7.6	6.7	11.9
Economic opportunity	—	334	3,635	—	4.0	10.0
Miscellaneous social welfare	335	912	5,635	21.2	11.0	15.4
Highways	318	3,023	4,724	20.1	36.3	12.9
Other	33	477	5,179	2.1	5.7	14.2
Total	1,581	8,324	36,486 a	100.0	100.0	100.0
General revenue sharing	—	—	6,636			
Total	1,581	8,324	43,121			
	Per capita, in dollars					
All purposes	11.01	44.39	204.04			

Source: James A. Maxwell and J. Richard Aronson, *Financing State and Local Government*, 3rd ed. (Washington: Brookings Institution, 1977), p. 48.

a In 1973, grants-in-aid accounted for over 80 percent of total federal intergovernmental transfers. Small amounts are in the form of shared revenues (most of which go to the states with large acreage), and net loans and repayable advances.

Washington, cities, and suburbs

Direct federal assistance to local governments, as opposed to state governments, also constitutes a major component of fiscal transfers. In 1973 more than $11 billion was channelled from the federal government directly to local governments, constituting more than 25 percent of total federal aid going to state and local governments. This increasing use of "direct federalism" by Washington is an innovative approach to fiscal relationships among American governments. The major federal legislation authorizing this short-circuiting of state governments in fiscal federalism are the Housing Act of 1949, the Housing and Community Development Acts of 1974 and 1977, and a number of pieces of legislation dealing with air and water pollution and airport construction. Table 14–4 indicates the primary purposes of federal funds going directly to local governments, and their growth between 1968 and 1973.

State capitols feed their "creatures"

A final type of intergovernmental transfer of money deals with funds that the states distribute to their own local governments. Money that states give to their own localities account for more than a third of the typical local government's annual revenues. State money is given to local governments in two ways: straight grants, which are almost always tied

TABLE 14–4. Federal Intergovernmental Transfers to Local Governments, 1968 and 1973 (Millions of dollars)

Purpose	1968	1973
Education (school operation and construction in federally affected areas)	694	1,400
Housing and community development	784	2,025
Model cities	—	653
Airport construction	57	232
Waste treatment and water facilities	284	837
Urban mass transit	—	275
Other	453	1,221
Total	2,272	6,643
General revenue sharing	—	4,424
Total	2,272	11,067

Source: Census Bureau, *Governmental Finances in 1967–68*, table 6, and *in 1972–73*, table 6.

to some specific purpose; and shared taxes. A *shared tax* refers to taxes that state and local governments divide between themselves; one level of government, either state or local, collects the tax and shares it with the other level. The norm is for the state to collect the tax and to share portions of it with its local governments.

Until the mid-1960s, state and local governments collected the same proportion of taxes between them, but around 1965 or so this relationship changed and states began collecting proportionately more taxes from their citizens than did local governments. Figure 14–2 indicates this trend, which is likely to continue and grow. However, local governments have always spent more than state governments, and this trend also seems to be accelerating, although less dramatically. Figure 14–3 indicates this relationship. The conclusion that we can draw from both charts is that states are increasingly reallocating their tax revenues to localities.[41]

And facts support such a conclusion. The most obvious feature of state aid to cities and towns is its incredible growth—up from $52 *million* in 1902 to $52 *billion* in 1975. Most of this growth has occurred during the last quarter century; a $5 billion level was achieved only in 1952.

Local governments have become increasingly hooked on their annual fiscal fixes from the states. In 1913 localities received less than 6 percent of their budgets from their state governments, but in 1975 cities and towns were depending on nearly six times that figure—almost 36 percent—as the state contribution to their budgets. Currently, however, the state aid component of local budgets appears to be stabilizing at about one-third of local revenue resources.

41. *Ibid.*, pp. 82–84.

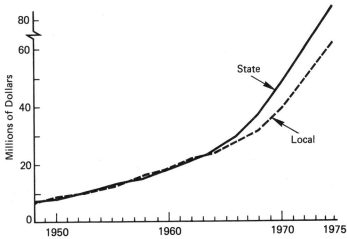

FIGURE 14–2. Tax Collections of State and Local Governments, 1948–75. *Sources:* U.S. Bureau of the Census, *Historical Statistics of the United States: Colonial Times to 1957* (Washington, D.C.: U.S. Government Printing Office, 1960), pp. 727 and 729; and Census Bureau, *Governmental Finances,* annual issues.

Most state aid to local governments is used for education—more than half of the states' money has gone to local education since 1952. This use, however, has been declining in recent years, just as local use of state aid for building highways has been diminishing over a much longer time period. The resulting slack has been taken up by public welfare, which now amounts to more than 15 percent of the state aid received by localities. California and New York, however, are responsible for much of this percentage—these two states alone account for two-thirds of all state aid used for welfare payments by local officials. Table 14–5 traces the growth of state aid to local governments (excluding shared taxes) during this century and shows how these grants were used by local officials.

PURCHASING PUBLIC POLICY: THE LOCAL IMPACT OF NATIONAL DOLLARS

It is obvious from the foregoing overview that big money is involved in transfers among American governments, and the largest portion of these transferences is in the form of federal money going to state and local governments. What is federal policy toward the allocation of dollars to state and local governments? Does federal policy in this area of vital

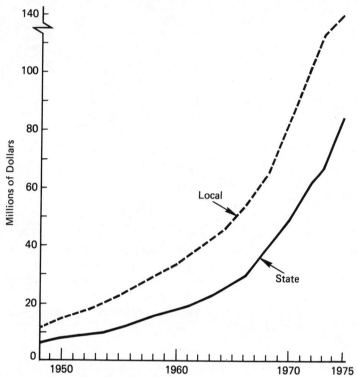

FIGURE 14–3. General Expenditures of State and Local Governments, 1948–75. *Source:* Census Bureau. *Historical Statistics of the United States: Colonial Times to 1957* (Washington, D.C.: U.S. Government Printing Office, 1960), pp. 728 and 730; and *Governmental Finances,* annual issues.

concern to the conduct of the public's business have an impact on the formulation of state and local public policies themselves? With federal grants to state and local governments accounting for more than a quarter of all state and local revenues, it is clear that federal policy in fiscal transferences has a major impact on state and local public policy.

As we have noted, the grants-in-aid system has burgeoned in recent years, but since 1960 it has also changed in ways that have had a major impact on the very nature of state and local governments. First, that year marks the point at which the federal government began shouldering a more substantial share of the financial burden. In most of the grants-in-aid programs enacted after 1960, the federal government began picking up half or more of the tab. Second, and as James L. Sundquist has pointed out, after 1960 federal grants-in-aid became forthrightly national

TABLE 14–5. Composition of State Aid, 1902–1975 (In Millions of Dollars)

Year	Total		General Local Government Support		Education		Highways		Public Welfare		All Other		Health and Hospitals Only	
1975	$51,978	100.0%	$5,129	9.9%	$31,110	59.9%	$3,225	6.2%	$8,101	15.6%	$4,412	8.5%	N.A.	N.A.
1974	45,941	100.0	4,803	10.4	27,107	59.0	3,211	7.0	7,369	16.0	3,451	7.5	N.A.	N.A.
1973	40,822	100.0	4,280	10.5	23,316	57.1	2,953	7.2	7,532	18.5	2,741	6.7	N.A.	N.A.
1972	36,759	100.0	3,752	10.2	21,195	57.7	2,633	7.2	6,944	18.9	2,235	6.1	$955	2.6%
1971	32,640	100.0	3,258	10.0	19,292	59.1	2,507	7.7	5,760	17.6	1,823	5.6	751	2.3
1970	28,892	100.0	2,958	10.2	17,085	59.1	2,439	8.4	5,003	17.3	1,407	4.9	567	2.0
1969	24,779	100.0	2,135	8.6	14,858	60.0	2,109	8.5	4,402	17.8	1,275	5.1	446	1.8
1968	21,950	100.0	1,993	9.1	13,321	60.7	2,029	9.2	3,527	16.1	1,080	4.9	371	1.7
1967	19,056	100.0	1,585	8.3	11,845	62.2	1,861	9.8	2,897	15.2	868	4.5	301	1.6
1966	16,848	100.0	1,281	7.6	10,177	60.4	1,725	10.2	2,882	17.1	783	4.6	275	1.6
1964	12,968	100.0	1,053	8.1	7,664	59.1	1,524	11.8	2,108	16.3	619	4.8	235	1.8
1962	10,906	100.0	839	7.7	6,474	59.4	1,327	12.2	1,777	16.3	489	4.4	189	1.7
1960	9,443	100.0	806	8.5	5,461	57.8	1,247	13.2	1,483	15.7	446	4.7	176	1.9
1958	8,089	100.0	687	8.5	4,598	56.8	1,167	14.4	1,247	15.4	390	4.8	150	1.9
1957	7,439	100.0	668	9.0	4,212	56.6	1,083	14.6	1,136	15.3	340	4.6	142	1.9
1956	6,538	100.0	631	9.7	3,541	54.1	984	15.0	1,069	16.4	313	4.8	132	2.0
1954	5,679	100.0	600	10.6	2,930	51.6	871	15.3	1,004	17.6	274	4.8	N.A.	N.A.
1952	5,044	100.0	549	10.9	2,523	50.0	728	14.4	976	19.3	268	5.3	N.A.	N.A.
1950	4,217	100.0	482	11.4	2,054	48.7	610	14.5	792	18.8	279	6.6	N.A.	N.A.
1948	3,283	100.0	428	13.0	1,554	47.3	507	15.4	648	19.7	146	4.5	N.A.	N.A.
1946	2,092	100.0	357	17.1	953	45.6	339	16.2	376	18.0	67	3.2	N.A.	N.A.
1944	1,842	100.0	274	14.9	861	46.7	298	16.2	368	20.0	41	2.2	N.A.	N.A.
1942	1,780	100.0	224	12.6	790	44.4	344	19.3	390	21.9	32	1.8	N.A.	N.A.
1940	1,654	100.0	181	10.9	700	42.3	332	20.1	420	25.4	21	1.3	N.A.	N.A.
1932	801	100.0	140	17.5	398	49.7	229	28.6	28	3.5	6	0.7	N.A.	N.A.
1927	596	100.0	98	16.4	292	49.0	197	33.1	6	1.0	3	0.5	N.A.	N.A.
1922	312	100.0	35	11.2	202	64.7	70	22.4	4	1.3	1	0.3	N.A.	N.A.
1913	91	100.0	5	5.5	82	90.1	4	4.4	—	—	—	—	N.A.	N.A.
1902	52	100.0	5	9.6	45	86.5	2	3.8	—	—	—	—	N.A.	N.A.

N.A.—Not available.
Source: U.S. Bureau of the Census, *Census of Governments, 1972*, Vol. 6, No. 3, *State Payments to Local Governments* (Washington, D.C.: Government Printing Office), 1974; *State Government Finances in 1973–74* (Washington, D.C.: Government Printing Office), 1975.

in purpose; prior to that year, grants-in-aid were used chiefly as a means of achieving state and local objectives.[42]

The federal grants-in-aid program, therefore, is considerably more than a means of alleviating the state and local financial burden. Michael D. Reagan has listed these major purposes of the national grants-in-aid system: (1) the establishment of minimum national standards and certain programs for all states; (2) the equalization of resources among states, which Reagan aptly dubs "the Robin Hood principle"; (3) the improvement of state programs; (4) the establishment of "critical mass" programs in certain states to circumvent duplicate efforts (for example, air pollution research grants); (5) the stimulation of program experimentation and testing; (6) the improvement of state and local public administration; (7) the promotion of unrelated social missions, such as the standard antidiscrimination clause present in all grants to states and localities; and (8) the minimization of the federal government's role in the implementation of programs. Of this final goal of grants-in-aid, Reagan states,

> Perhaps the most important political achievement of the grants system is to have solved the apparent dilemma arising from the American electorate's contradictory desires, (a) to attack problems that the state and local governments lacked the resources to handle while, (b) not enlarging the federal government.[43]

The federal government transfers money to state and local governments on the basis of two principles. One is that of *recipient autonomy.* How much latitude and discretion permitted the government that is receiving federal money becomes the crucial question. When the federal government wants to limit a state or local government's latitude in deciding how to spend the money it receives, then it issues *categorical grants.* A categorical grant is given for a highly specific purpose and extremely little discretionary action is granted to the receiving government; an example would be the types of grants administered by the U.S. Environmental Protection Agency relating to sewage treatment facilities. In 1976, 442 of 448 federal grants were categorical grants, and they accounted for $51 billion out of a total grants budget of $68 billion in 1977.

When the feds feel that it would be expeditious for a recipient to have more freedom in determining how money is spent, then it issues *block grants.* Block grants are tied to a general area of concern, such as education or community development, and federal money may not be

---

42. James L. Sundquist and David W. Davis, *Making Federalism Work* (Washington, D.C.: Brookings Institution, 1969).

43. Reagan, *op. cit.,* p. 75.

used for purposes beyond that stated area. Nevertheless, the amount of discretionary authority yielded to the recipient is considerably greater than with categorical grants. In 1976 (aside from revenue sharing) there were five block grant programs. These programs were funded under the Partnership for Health Act of 1966, the Omnibus Crime Control and Safe Streets Act of 1968, the Comprehensive Employment and Training Act of 1973, the Housing and Community Development Act of 1974, and the 1974 amendment (Title XX) to the Social Security Act of 1935.

The other criterion that the federal government uses in determining how a grant should be issued is that of *how funds should be distributed,* whether on the basis of some formula or tied to a specific project. A *formula grant* distributes money among all eligible recipients on the basis of some prearranged method; there is virtually no discretionary authority, either by the granting government or by the recipient government. An example of the formula grant is provided by the program of public assistance for the blind: The national government matches state payments to blind citizens on the basis of the number of persons certified by the state as eligible; the payments are distributed equally to all those persons on the roster as a "right." Formula grants are a type of categorical grant, and about one-third of categorical grants are formula grants.

At the other end of the continuum are *project grants.* A project grant is designed to alleviate some particular problem, and in no fixed proportions or formula. Because federal administrators are in a substantially more advantageous position to decide which problems need federal money to solve them than they are under a formula grant arrangement, the project grant system permits a considerable degree of discretion. Project grants comprise about two-thirds of all federal categorical grants, both in terms of number and funds disbursed.

PROBLEMS OF THE GRANT-IN-AID SYSTEM: INEQUITY, DISTORTION, AND CONFUSION

A major difficulty of the grants-in-aid system as administered by the federal government (and very likely as administered by state governments as well) is that project grants and categorical grants tend to undermine the objectives of equitably distributing federal resources among state and local jurisdictions. Those governments that have professional staffs who are more adept at grantsmanship and that have the tax bases to support such staffs are more likely to get the project grant and even the categorical grant.

Second, and relatedly, grants-in-aid, especially formula grants, tend to warp state and local budgets. Budgetary decision makers will favor those public programs that are eligible for "free" federal funds, rather than developing budgets that more accurately reflect their own local needs.

By way of indication, a questionnaire was sent in 1975 to all cities and counties in the United States; more than 32 percent of the cities and almost 23 percent of the counties surveyed responded. Seventy-three percent of the cities and 81 percent of the counties said that they had received a grant from the federal government during the year. About two-thirds of these cities and roughly 80 percent of the counties indicated that they would have made different budgetary allocations had the categorical grants they received from the federal government permitted them to do so. More than 75 percent of each group would have made moderate or substantial changes, and the cities and counties with large populations tended to be more adamant in wishing greater freedom to reallocate funds transferred to them by Washington. Interestingly, more than two-thirds of the city officials and 77 percent of the county officials thought that their governments would shift local funds to other efforts if federal categorical grants suddenly were cut off.[44] Such a finding implies that local officials are making policy decisions to a large extent on the basis of what federal money is available, rather than on the basis of what their real local needs are.

Third, the proliferation of categorical grants for specific programs has created administrative confusion in states and localities; the classic example is the town that ended up with a freeway *and* an urban renewal project planned for the same neighborhood.

Fourth, grants-in-aid of all types do not help states and localities in resolving public problems beyond the scopes of their stated purposes.

Fifth, there is a lot of red tape involved in applying for a grant, and state and local public administrators have increasingly come to resent it. By way of example, the appropriately named town of Lazy Lakes, Florida, a community of fifty residents, turned back (or at least tried to turn back) the check for $1,198 that it received in federal revenue-sharing funds on the grounds that it neither needed nor wanted the money, nor did it want the added cost and paperwork created by revenue sharing—a fiscal transference, it should be noted, that probably is simpler than virtually any other insofar as state and local administrators are concerned. The mayor of Lazy Lakes, incidentally, found that

44. Albert J. Richter, "Federal Grants Management: The City and County View," *The Municipal Yearbook, 1977* (Washington, D.C.: International City Management Association, 1977), pp. 183–184.

it was much more difficult to return revenue-sharing money than to accept it.[45]

SOLUTIONS! SOLUTIONS!
REVENUE SHARING AND BIGGER BLOCK GRANTS

The saga of revenue sharing

Because of these problems in the grants system, Congress in 1972 passed the State and Local Fiscal Assistance Act, better known as revenue sharing. It provided $3.2 billion to be distributed to states and localities over a five-year period, and by 1977 the Office of Revenue Sharing in the Treasury Department had distributed more than $23 billion to more than thirty nine thousand state and local governments.

Public support for revenue sharing was pronounced when it was enacted. A Gallup Poll conducted in 1971 reported that 77 percent of the public endorsed revenue sharing, and that this support transcended party lines.[46]

If everyone was for revenue sharing, then what is it? Revenue-sharing funds are distributed according to the proportion of federal personal income tax funds provided by state and local units of government; thus, richer units of governments, as defined by their tax bases, tend to be favored. New York, California, Pennsylvania, Illinois, Texas, Michigan, and Ohio generally are the leading recipients of revenue-sharing funds in any given year. Roughly one-third of revenue-sharing funds go to the states, while the other two-thirds go to county commissions, city halls, and Indian tribal councils. The complex formula that Congress devised to disburse revenue-sharing funds was more the result of politics—that is, whose district would get what—than of fiscal rationality, and it has resulted in a situation in which financially marginal units of government are supported while governments which are in desperate need of additional cash, notably the big cities, are often underfunded.

This situation was the result of two basic and opposing themes within Congress. On the one hand, a group within Congress insisted that revenue sharing be computed on the basis of need. Under such a concept, only a reading of the poverty levels and the number of people at or below the poverty level would be necessary to develop the formula. On the other hand, there was a large body within Congress that believed

45. Associated Press, July 3, 1977, syndicated nationally.
46. Parris N. Glendening and Mavis Mann Reeves, "Federal Actions Affecting Local Government," *The Municipal Yearbook*, 1977, *op. cit.*, p. 50.

revenue sharing should be an incentive to state and local governments to do more for themselves. This group reasoned that those governments that did more for themselves, by deriving greater revenues from their people, should be rewarded by federal money through general revenue sharing. Obviously, the two points of view were contradictory. The final result was a compromise toward a middle position. Consequently, the formula finally adopted, while very complex, nevertheless did resolve the problem by accommodating both the "need" and the "incentive" factors.

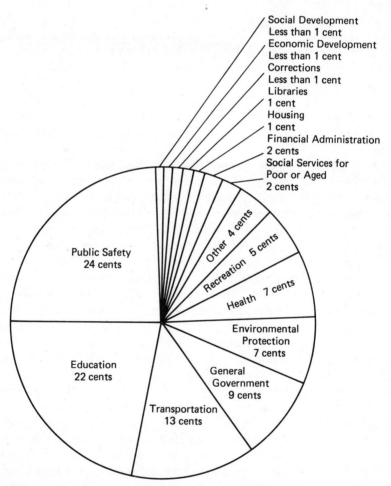

FIGURE 14–4. How the Average General Revenue-Sharing Dollar was Spent July 1, 1974–June 30, 1975.

Source: Office of Revenue Sharing, Department of the Treasury, *Reported Uses of General Revenue Sharing Funds 1974–1975* (Washington, D.C.: U.S. Government Printing Office, 1976), p. 7.

In other words, there was consideration of "need" by determining the number of families at or below the poverty level, but there was also recognition that state and local governments that taxed more and did more for themselves would also be rewarded.

State and local governments may use revenue-sharing dollars for capital expenditures, maintenance, and operating costs in areas including public safety, environmental protection, transportation, health, recreation, libraries, social services for the old and the poor, and financial administration. Figure 14-4 illustrates how state and local governments spent their revenue-sharing money in the mid-1970s.

The chart, however, does not tell the whole story. Analyses of revenue sharing by the Brookings Institution [47] that have been conducted since 1972 conclude that, although small cities and towns use about three-quarters of their revenue-sharing funds for new spending programs (mostly for capital projects), bigger urban areas with one hundred thousand people or more use only half of the money for new spending programs; the remaining half goes to keep taxes down or to avoid borrowing. Among the states only a third of shared revenues is used for new programs, and the tendency of both state and local governments to use shared revenues to keep a muzzle on the tax bite rather than to initiate new spending programs appears to be increasing over time. One reason for this trend is that inflation slashed the real purchasing power of revenue-sharing dollars by 17 percent between 1972 and 1979; thus, state and local governments must use the money mainly to keep their fiscal heads above water by maintaining existing services without raising taxes.

In 1976 revenue sharing came up for renewal in Congress and the issue quickly turned into a political brawl. Many members of Congress had strong misgivings about the program, arguing that it eventually would prove to be a drain on the treasury; that minorities and other deprived groups received a better shake under the categorical grants system rather than under revenue sharing, simply because the grant approach was more likely to embody national, rather than local, values; and that revenue sharing did not press for the administrative reform of local governments to achieve more efficient and responsive public management. In 1975 the Advisory Commission on Intergovernmental Relations reported that only 55 percent of the public supported the program; [48] contrast this to the 77 percent who supported the program in

47. Richard P. Nathan, Allen C. Manvel, Susannah E. Calkins, and Associates, *Monitoring Revenue Sharing* (Washington, D.C.: Brookings Institution, 1975), and Richard P. Nathan and Charles F. Adams, Jr., and Associates, *Revenue Sharing: The Second Round* (Washington, D.C.: Brookings Institution, 1977).

48. Advisory Commission on Intergovernmental Relations, *Changing Public Attitudes on Governments and Taxes* (Washington, D.C.: ACIR, July 1975), p. 2.

1971. The Brookings' studies lend credence to some of these congressional concerns in that they found that fiscally hard-pressed governments were likely to merge revenue-sharing funds with other revenue sources (thus reducing the political visibility of federal fiscal assistance); that traditional patterns of political power were retained in most cities despite revenue sharing (and that, if anything, the clout of entrenched special interests increased); and that, contrary to widespread speculation, revenue sharing had not forced changes in the structure of state and local governments (in fact, it seemed to reinforce those often inefficient structures).[49]

Those in favor of continuing revenue sharing in 1976 were largely Republicans, and the vanguard of the lobby to maintain the program consisted of a coalition of the National Governors Association, the National Conference of State Legislators, the National League of Cities, the U.S. Conference of Mayors, and the National Association of Counties. Democrats represented a looser analgam of resisters to revenue sharing, and ultimately the program was retained and extended through 1980.

The bias of block grants

We have seen how the traditional grant approach permits national policy makers to maintain greater control over state and local public programs, while the newer revenue-sharing and expanded block grant approaches permit governments at the state and local level greater discretion in determining and implementing their own policies.

Real policy differences result, and to summarize these differences crudely but effectively, we can say that national officials, using the traditional grant approach, tend to be more attuned to the needy, whereas state and local officials tend to be more sensitive to the middle class. For example, when seven basic national programs were consolidated under the Housing and Community Development Act of 1974, essentially converting them from categorical to block grants and thereby giving local leaders more control over how the funds underwriting these programs were used, the Brookings Institution found that poverty neighborhoods had fared better under the old model cities program, initiated during the 1960s, than under the new Community Development Programs. (Model cities was one of those programs subsumed by the Housing and Community Development Act.) The Brookings Institution concluded that there had been a shift, both in funding and decision making, away from the poorest people in neighborhoods to more mixed patterns, and that programs had changed from an emphasis on social servies,

49. Nathan and Adams, *op. cit.*

such as health and education, to short-term capital spending for projects such as parking lots and downtown renewal. Social services spending was found to be low under the Community Development Program.[50]

On the other hand, when national officials do retain control they tend to opt for the needy, when possible. This is true even in the case of block grants, which give greater control to local administrators. For example, while the Housing and Community Development Act (a block grant program) did devolve authority to state and local officials in contrast to previous programs, it nonetheless had built into it a formula that favored, and still favors, "needy" cities in the North and Midwest in comparison to the relatively vibrant cities in the South and West. This favoritism was accomplished by distributing the $3.2 billion in community block grant funds on a formula that favored housing age, defined as the number of houses built before 1939, and "population lag," defined as either population dips or increases that fall short of the national growth rate. Since the cities in the North and Midwest are older than those in the South and West and are losing people to those regions, the "needier" cities are favored. Similarly, the Department of Housing and Urban Development (HUD) allocated $400 million to be distributed at the discretion of the secretary for economic development, specifically in large eastern and midwestern cities.

SNOWBELT VERSUS SUNBELT: THE GRANTS WAR

As a result of these national policies concerning how the federal government gives money to state and localities, sharp words were exchanged during the 1977 national meeting of the U.S. Conference of Mayors. The mayor of Albuquerque was quoted as stating that HUD's policies were "Blatant efforts in the so-called war between the frostbelt and the sunbelt," and a number of mayors of major western cities opposed a resolution endorsed during that conference to give special consideration to the need of cities in sixteen northern states.[51]

The tensions between Snowbelt and Sunbelt cities over whom should get federal goodies are tightening in Congress as well. Nearly half of the members of the House of Representatives have joined the Northeast-Midwest Economic Advancement Coalition, which is a congressional

50. Paul R. Dommel, Richard P. Nathan, Sarah F. Liebschutz, Margaret T. Wrightson, and Associates, *Decentralizing Community Development: The Brookings Institution Monitoring Study of the Community Development Block Grant Program* (Washington, D.C.: Brookings Institution, 1978).

51. Jana Bommersbach, "Sunbelt Mayors Tired of U.S. Fund Rules," *Arizona Republic*, June 13, 1977, p. 8.

group designed to promote the flow of federal funds to those regions of the country; Sunbelt representatives complain that the coalition has successfully rigged federal funding formulas to its own advantage.

Various analyses of the regional distribution of federal money have drawn varying conclusions about who gets more than whom. A recent Library of Congress study was essentially accurate, however, when it stated that most defense and public works dollars go to the Sunbelt (with 83 percent of all defense personnel, 63 percent of all defense procurements, and 80 percent of all defense installations), while most antipoverty and economic development grants go to the Snowbelt.[52]

In terms of all federal grants-in-aid, the Northeast receives the largest overall share, but if welfare grants are excluded, then the Northeast drops to third place, below the West and South. When regions are ranked according to grants per person, grants per $1,000 of personal income, and the percentage of state and local revenues that are obtained from Washington, the Northeast leads, followed by the South, West, and Midwest, in that order. Figure 14–5 shows how much federal grant

---

52. Library of Congress Report, 1977. Cited in Ellen Hume, syndicated column, *Los Angeles Times*, November 23, 1977. The best analyses to date of regional shifts in power and people are: (1) a series of seven articles in the *New York Times*, beginning with Robert Reinhold, "Sunbelt Region Leads Nation in Growth of Population Section's Cities Top Urban Expansion," (February 8, 1976), pp. 1, 42; Jon Nordheimer, "Sunbelt Region Leads Nation in Growth of Population Area Spans Southern Half of Country," (February 8, 1976), pp. 1, 42; James P. Sterba, "Houston, as Energy Capital, Sets Pace in Sunbelt Boom," (February 9, 1976), pp. 1, 24; Wayne King, "Federal Funds Pour into Sunbelt States," (February 9, 1976), p. 24; Roy Reed, "Sunbelt Still Stronghold of Conservatism in U.S.," (February 10, 1976), pp. 1, 22; Roy Reed, "Migration Mixes a New Southern Blend," (February 11, 1976), pp. 1, 30; and B. Drummond Ayres, Jr., "Developing Sunbelt Hopes to Avoid North's Mistakes," (February 12, 1976), pp. 1, 24. (2) "The Second War Between the States," *Business Week* (May 17, 1976), pp. 92–114. (3) Joel Havemann, Rochelle L. Stanfield, and Neal R. Pierce, "Federal Spending: The North's Loss Is the Sunbelt's Gain," *National Journal* (June 26, 1976), pp. 878–891. (4) John Ross and John Shannon, "Measuring the Fiscal 'Blood Pressure' of the States: Some Warning Signs of our Federal System and Alternative Prescriptions," paper presented at the Conference on State and Local Finance, University of Oklahoma, 1976. (5) Carol L. Jusenius and Larry C. Ledebur, *A Myth in the Making: The Southern Economic Challenge and Northern Economic Decline* (Economic Development Administration, U.S. Department of Commerce, 1976). (6) Robert W. Rafuse, Jr., *The New Regional Debate: A National Overview* (Washington, D.C.: National Governors Conference, 1977). There are others.

Because of various factors (such as the fact that the country's regions are never defined in precisely the same way by the studies), different conclusions result. Perhaps it is worth recalling here George Washington's concern about "a spirit of jealousy which may become dangerous to the Union, towards the Eastern States." (*Writings*, Volume 31, p. 28.)

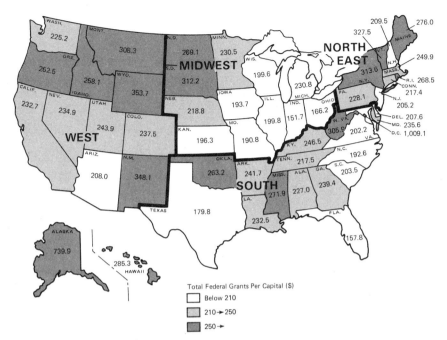

FIGURE 14–5. Total Federal Grants Per Person by States, 1970–1975.

money per capita that each state got during the first half of the 1970s. During the 1970s, however, the average dollar differences between regions narrowed, implying a fairer regional distribution of grant money by Washington.[53]

In brief, the ways in which governments, and especially the federal government, distribute money to other governments not only has an impact on what public policy is and becomes in states and localities, but it can be a divisive or unifying force for the nation as a whole.

FEDERALISM AND THE PYRAMIDING OF POWER

A final summing up is warranted on the nature of relations between governments in the United States, and the summing up points to one conclusion: that governmental power in this country is centralizing despite Americans' ultralocalist leanings.

Perhaps the clearest indication that such is the case can be derived from financial data. Using the quite legitimate measures of financial re-

53. Charles L. Vehorn, *The Regional Distribution of Federal Grants-in-Aid* (Washington, D.C.: Academy for Contemporary Problems, 1978).

sources, services, and manpower, G. Ross Stephens, among others, found that power of all levels of government is *centralizing*, which means that local autonomy is being eroded. The nation's nearly 19,000 municipalities raise less money today than the nation's fifty state governments, and considerably less than the national government. Although money is paid to the national government and part of it is sent back to the state and local governments through revenue sharing and block grants, this practice connotes, at least in the view of some, a centralization of governmental power at the national level. But Stephens' research indicated that such centralization may also be happening at the state level. By ranking the local proportions of financial resources, services, and manpower by state, Stephens found that certain states were quite centralized in relation to their local governments; others were relatively decentralized. Stephens concluded that there is a tendency for larger states to be decentralized governmentally, and for smaller states to be more centralized.[54]

There is additional evidence besides that of fiscal relationships to show that governments are centralizing. A comprehensive study commissioned by the Advisory Commission on Intergovernmental Relations (ACIR) in 1976, which covered 3,319 municipalities, concluded that functional and political responsibilities in all governments were shifting, and principally upward.[55] Nearly a third of the municipalities responding had permanently transferred responsibility, either voluntarily or involuntarily, for a particular function to another governmental unit. Normally, the functions transferred dealt with solid waste collection and disposal, law enforcement, public health, sewage treatment, taxation and assessment of property, building and safety inspections, planning, and the broadly generic area entitled "social services." The larger cities and towns generally shift their governmental responsibilities more frequently than smaller ones; indeed, more than a third of the responding local governments with populations of more than five hundred thousand people had transferred responsibilities for five or more major functions during the past ten years, and these city functions normally went to counties and special districts. Counties in particular received transferences of solid waste collection and disposal, law enforcement, and public health, while special districts generally took over transportation and sewage collection and treatment. States were the recipients of social services transfers. The reasons usually cited for these transfers by government officials were economies of scale, elimination of duplication, sharing of facilities and equipment, and easing of fiscal restraints. Initiatives by the states rarely

54. G. Ross Stephens, "State Centralization and the Erosion of Local Autonomy," *Journal of Politics* 36 (February 1974): 67.

55. Advisory Commission on Intergovernmental Relations, *Pragmatic Federalism: The Reassignment of Functional Responsibility* (Washington, D.C.: ACIR, 1976).

were a factor; most local governments transferred functions to other governments through cooperative arrangements rather than as a consequence of state mandates.

As noted, the major trends in these transferences were the shifting of urban responsibilities for service functions to the county and to the state. The ACIR survey indicated that the states were the recipients of 14 percent of the functions that were shifted by local governments, and these were primarily in the area of social services, which accounted for a third of all transfers by local governments to the states. Fifty-six percent of the services transferred by municipal governments went to the counties, and almost 25 percent of these transfers were in the areas of solid waste collection and disposal.

The ACIR survey also indicated that municipalities have taken over a number of services previously managed by private firms. Almost half of the functions assumed by municipalities previously had been performed by private corporations, especially in the big cities (those with more than five hundred thousand people); indeed, 64 percent of these cities had done so.

A number of functions had been transferred to special districts and these kinds of transfers constituted 19 percent of all the transfers of powers between governments. The county, of all units of government, is that which is the most preferred by urban officials as the government to which powers should be transferred. The Advisory Commission in Intergovernmental Relations predicts that in the future the county and the "urban state" are going to become increasingly important units of local government. So, in terms of political, administrative, and financial arrangements, the "bottom line" of intergovernmental relations in the 1980s is that governmental power will centralize in this country.

SUPPLEMENTAL BIBLIOGRAPHY

BUCHANAN, WILLIAM, "Politics and Federalism: Party or Anti-Party," *The Annals of the American Academy of Political and Social Science,* 359 (May, 1965), 108–112.

ELAZAR, DANIEL J. et al, eds., *Cooperation and Conflict: Readings in American Federalism.* Itasca, Ill., F. E. Peacock, 1969.

FARKAS, SUZANNE, *Urban Lobbying: Mayors in the Federal Arena.* New York: New York University Press, 1971.

GRAVES, W. BROOKE, *American Intergovernmental Relations.* New York: Charles Scribner's Sons, 1964.

GRODZINS, MORTON, *The American System: A New View of Government in the United States.* ed., Daniel J. Elazar. Chicago: Rand McNally, 1966.

———, "American Political System," *Western Political Quarterly,* 13 (December 1960), 12–17.

HAIDER, DONALD H., *When Governments Come to Washington: Governors, Mayors, and Intergovernmental Lobbying*. New York: The Free Press, 1974.

LEACH, RICHARD H., *American Federalism*. New York: W. W. Norton, 1970.

RIKER, WILLIAM H., *Federalism: Origin, Operation, Significance*. Boston: Little, Brown, 1964.

SCHEIBER, WALTER, "Regionalism: Its Implications for the Urban Manager," *Public Administration Review*, 31 (January/February 1971), 42–46.

SEIDMAN, HAROLD, *Politics, Position, and Power*. New York: Oxford University Press, 1970.

The Federal System as Seen by Federal Aid Officials. A Study Prepared by the Sub-Committee on Intergovernmental Relations of the Committee on Government Operations, U.S. Senate, 89th Congress, December, 1965. Washington: U.S. Government Publishing Office, 1965.

TRUMAN, DAVID B., "Federalism and the Party System," in *Federalism: Mature and Emergent*, ed. Arthur W. MacMahon, pp. 113–136. New York: Russell and Russell, 1962.

WEIDNER, EDWARD W., *Intergovernmental Relations as Seen by Public Officials*. Minneapolis: University of Minnesota Press, 1960.

WINKEL, JOHN W., III, "Dimensions of Judicial Federalism," *Annals of the American Academy of Political and Social Science*, 416, No. 4 (November 1974), pp. 67–76.

WRIGHT, DEIL S., *Federal Grants-in-Aid: Perspectives and Alternatives* Washington: American Enterprise Institute for Public Policy Research, 1968.

———, "Intergovernmental Relations in Large Council-Manager Cities," *American Politics Quarterly*, 1 (April, 1973), 163–168.

———, "The States and Intergovernmental Relations." *Publius: The Journal of Federalism*, 1 (Winter, 1972) 40–57.

managing growth

chapter 15

What used to be called the "environmental crisis" collided, during the mid-1970s, with the "energy crunch." As the realization dawned that some environmentally beneficial public policies were simultaneously detrimental to energy conservation measures, policy makers attempted to reconcile the needs of a ravaged earth with the demands of an energy-fixated technoscientific superculture. Increasingly, this effort is being dubbed "growth management."

Growth management is not easy. It is difficult to conceive of two questions more important than the environment and energy. On the one hand, Americans' use of energy resources, such as oil, coal, and nuclear fission, has resulted in a crisis that threatens the biosphere itself. On the other hand, to abandon the use of energy would be the equivalent of a return to the tribe. Thus, environment and energy, as political issues and as physical and economic realities, express more dramatically and succinctly the tensions involved in achieving the good life; the bureaucracy articulates the politics of this tension more profoundly than perhaps any other public entity.

Before delving into what American governments have done to balance environmental questions and the energy crisis, let us consider some developments in the global environment that relate directly to energy use. As the following review indicates, pollution does not respect political boundaries, and there is more to managing the environment than planting a tree, a shrub, or a flower.

The population explosion

Certainly among the unavoidable realities of the environmental crisis is the growth of the world's population, a reality that affects even the smallest American hamlet. The global population now doubles roughly every thirty years; currently, there are more than 4 billion people on earth and, at present exponential growth rates, that number is estimated to hit 7.5 billion by 2000. It is estimated that the "carrying capacity" of earth will be exceeded in the next century, bringing on starvation and pestilence on a global scale.[1]

Population growth of the United States is slower than that of the world at large but, even so, in 1915 only 100 million people lived in the country; today the nation has more than 210 million. Present projections indicate that the country could have 265 million to 322 million people by the end of the century. In the unlikely event that the nation achieved a zero population growth today (currently, the U.S. birthrate is 1.8 births per 100 people), it still would be many years before the national birth rate levels off, probably around the year 2040.

It is a regrettable fact of earthly life that more people use more precious energy resources and thus generate more pollution, and the resulting kinds of environmental degradation that have the most relevance to American governments are water pollution, air pollution, and solid waste disposal. We consider these in turn.

People, pollution, and water

There are two major types of water pollutants. One type is biodegradable, and includes substances such as those emitted from sewage. Biodegradable substances increase the biochemical oxygen demands, or BOD, of rivers and lakes, thereby reducing the level of oxygen available to sustain

1. Donella H. Meadows, Dennis L. Meadows, Orgen Randers, and William H. Behrens, III, *The Limits to Growth* (New York: Universe Books, 1972).

plants and fish in the water. This reduction causes *eutrophication*, or what most of us know as "dead" lakes and streams, such as large portions of Lake Erie. The other major type of water pollutant is known as suspended solids, or material that does not biodegrade in the water.

Until quite recently, it was unknown precisely how many pollutants were being discharged in the nation's waterways. In 1975 the National Academy of Sciences conducted a survey of all 3,111 counties in the United States. It concluded that most water pollutants came from miscellaneous and scattered sources (or what the academy called "nonpoint sources"); the next largest sources of water pollution were industries and the cities themselves, in that order. Pollution from nonpoint sources is the most voluminous, but is also the least dangerous in that such pollution is less likely to cause critical problems in a particular body of water, simply because it is less concentrated.[2] Figure 15–1 indicates these sources of pollution.

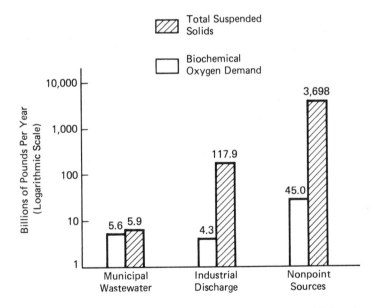

FIGURE 15–1. Estimated Nationwide Water Pollution by Major Sources. Estimates refer to calendar year 1973. Loadings from municipal and industrial sources tend to produce acute local water quality problems, more than loadings from nonpoint sources which are more diffuse (*Source:* National Residuals Discharge Inventory)

2. Council on Environmental Quality, *Environmental Quality*, Seventh Annual Report of the Council on Environment Quality (Washington, D.C.: U.S. Government Printing Office, 1976), pp. 256–261.

People, pollution, and air

A second area of environmental concern is that of air pollution. Air pollutants are found as both gasses and particulates, and more than 200 million tons of them are spewed into America's skies every year. Automobile exhaust, the largest single source, makes up 42 percent of this total, and approximately 6,000 American communities are affected by pollution. When what is known as an *inversion* (that is, unusual weather that prevents the normal dispersion of pollutants) occurs over an air-polluted town, disaster can result. "Killer smog," the combination of an inversion layer and higher levels of pollution, has been known to kill hundreds or even thousands of people in such scattered areas as London, Tokyo, and the Meuse Valley in Belgium. This occurred in the United States in 1948 when twenty people died in Sonora, Pennsylvania, and nearly half of the town's fourteen thousand residents fell ill because of killer smog.[3]

High levels of air pollution can cause interesting weather modifications, such as increasing rain and fog. The classic example is La Porte, Indiana, which is fifty miles downwind from the steel-producing city of Gary. As a result of Gary's steel mills seeding the sky with particulates, rainfall in La Porte is 31 percent above the average, hail storms are 230 percent more frequent, and cloudy weather is more prevalent than normal. Cities generally have about twenty times more particulates than the countryside and receive up to 30 percent less sunlight.

Studies indicate, however, that even though cities receive less sunlight they are hotter than the countryside. The buildings of inner cities act as a windbreak, reducing breezes by as much as 40 percent in the core areas, thus preventing wind from blowing away pollutants. The prevalence of concrete buildings and blacktopped parking lots coupled with the lack of greenery in inner cities causes residents to breathe hotter, drier, and dirtier air than their counterparts in the suburbs.[4]

Garbage: easier to make than destroy

The remaining major area of environmental pollution that is of particular relevance to American governments is that of solid waste disposal. Americans find it far easier to create garbage than to decide where to put it. The nation's municipal trash pile exceeds 145 million tons every year. The generation of waste in the United States is burgeoning at nearly 8 percent every year, reflecting, in the view of some observers, the country's "throwaway mentality." The nation's municipal trash heap includes 17 billion cans, 38 billion bottles and jars, 4 million tons of plastic, 7.6

3. Louis J. Battan, *The Unclean Sky* (New York: Anchor, 1966), pp. 1–13.
4. Associated Press, September 19, 1976, syndicated nationally.

million television sets, 7 million cars and trucks, and 35 million tons of paper. These tons of trash generated by cities do not even include industrial wastes (estimated at 340 million tons a year), mining wastes (1.7 billion tons annually), and agricultural wastes (2.3 billion tons each year)! Among these enormous piles of garbage there are anywhere from twenty million to fifty million tons of materials every year that are clearly and directly hazardous to human health—substances such as Kepone, a chemical which in 1976 rendered serious nerve damage to workers in a Virginia factory.[5]

It is increasingly apparent that such traditional practices as burning trash, dumping it into landfills or, perhaps worst of all, dumping garbage at sea, as New York City does, must be replaced by recycling systems that are not only more environmentally sound, but economically productive as well.

Clearly, the pollution problem is enormous—perhaps overwhelming. But what are governments doing about it?

REGULATING THE ENVIRONMENT: RELUCTANT STATES, TIMID TOWNS

Prior to 1965 state and local governments hardly were at the forefront in protecting Mother Earth, especially in guarding against air pollution. In 1963 research sponsored by the U.S. Senate found that thirty-three of the states and territories had some type of air pollution control laws and eighteen did not; only two states in the entire nation—California and Oregon—had established any sort of air quality and emission standards that were enforced on either a local or statewide basis. Water pollution efforts fared somewhat better in 1963; all states and territories had some sort of program to keep the water clean, and thirty-five states were deemed to have adequate water control standards.[6]

At the local level as well, success in meeting the environmental challenge was negligible. Why? One view is that urban governments do not have the political capacity to make environmental decisions. Mat-

5. Council on Environmental Quality, *Environmental Quality*, Eighth Annual Report of the Council on Environmental Quality (Washington, D.C.: U.S. Government Printing Office, 1977), p. 50.
6. U.S. Senate, Committee on Public Works, *Study of Pollution: Air*, Staff Report (Washington, D.C.: U.S. Government Printing Office, 1963); and U.S. Senate, Committee on Public Works, *A Study of Pollution: Water*, Staff Report (Washington, D.C.: U.S. Government Printing Office, 1963). Both reports are cited in Charles O. Jones, "Regulating the Environment," *Politics in the American States,* 3rd ed., Herbert Jacob and Kenneth N. Vines, eds. (Boston: Little, Brown, 1976). pp. 398–399.

thew A. Crenson, for example, characterized local decision making on pollution control in the 1960s as "non-decision making." Crenson studied fifty-one cities, using as a hypothesis the common-sensical notion that, where the air was most polluted, there was a need for greater pollution control.[7] Yet, Crenson found that those urban interest groups threatened by air quality standards were most effective when they could prevent a decision from ever being made. Because no city councilmember wished to be on record as being for dirty air (which the councilmember could be, if forced to vote on the matter), industrial interests worked assiduously to prevent the issue from ever being placed on the city council's agenda. It was this phenomenon that Crenson called "non-decision making," although perhaps Charles O. Jones puts it in more pithy terms when he remarks that, "what passes as state [or local] environmental policy will normally be no more than some form of limited 'pollution control.'"[8]

Jones, in his cogent analysis of state pollution control efforts, notes that "there are two principal causes of pollution, people and production."[9] Relying on this premise Jones has developed a list of states that are the most likely to have the most severe pollution problems. In all, Jones identifies twenty-nine states as having severe pollution problems, with Michigan, Ohio, Pennsylvania, California, Illinois, Texas, Indiana, New York, and New Jersey leading the way; seven additional states are listed that have high potential for experiencing major pollution problems, and another thirteen states Jones identifies as "special cases," or states that have peculiar characteristics that could result in severe pollution for those states' inhabitants. For example, Maine, which most people do not associate with high levels of pollution, nevertheless ranks second in paper production and fifth in cement production, both of which are high pollution industries.

Are these states budgeting for pollution statement in proportion to their environmental problems? Not according to Jones's analysis. Table 15–1 matches the level of state expenditures (as of 1972) on air quality control and water quality control with their rank ordering on Jones's index of potential pollution level. Using Jones's standard, it is clear that the states are a mixed bag when it comes to spending relative to their total pollution problems. Only four of the nine states with the highest pollution potential, and only one of the next eleven states with a slightly less severe pollution potential, ranked among the top fifteen states in air and water pollution expenditures for the years measured. From reading

7. Matthew A. Crenson, *The Un-Politics of Air Pollution* (Baltimore: Johns Hopkins Press, 1971).

8. Jones, *op. cit.*, p. 392.

9. *Ibid.*, p. 418.

TABLE 15–1. Environmental Expenditures (thousands of dollars) of States with High Pollution Potential, 1970–1971

State	Air quality control				Water quality control			
	Expend-itures	Rank	% of total expend-iture	Rank	Expend-itures	Rank	% of total expend-iture	Rank
Group I								
Michigan	421	18	.011	43	9,381	9	.23	15
Ohio	743	9	.024	25	17,316	4	.56	11
Pennsylvania	997	6	.020	33	15,618	5	.31	14
California	6,194	1	.058	5	12,556	8	.12	21
Illinois	885	8	.020	34	2,191	20	.05	36
Texas	584	14	.016	36	5,053	12	.14	19
Indiana	162	34	.009	45	15,556	6	.89	4
New York	2,317	2	.022	29	81,331	1	.78	6
New Jersey	2,236	3	.085	2	1,315	23	.05	35
Group II								
Alabama	145	37	.010	44	159	46	.01	50
Florida	666	10	.028	22	1,626	21	.07	25
Massachusetts	1,138	5	.044	13	17,957	3	.69	9
North Carolina	446	16	.022	30	1,160	24	.06	30
Virginia	390	21	.022	28	2,771	16	.16	18
Louisiana	354	23	.020	32	360	38	.02	48
West Virginia	329	24	.038	16	451	35	.05	33

Adapted from data in U.S. Bureau of the Census, *Environmental Quality Control,* State and Local Government Special Studies 62 (December 1972) (Washington, D.C.: Government Printing Office).
Source: Charles O. Jones, "Regulating the Environment," *Politics in the American States,* 3rd ed., Herbert Jacob and Kenneth N. Vines, eds. (Boston; Little, Brown, 1976), p. 420.

Table 15–1, then, it appears that very few states with tough pollution problems are really working to correct those problems.

POLLUTION AND POLITICS: THE NATIONAL EFFORT

Because pollutants of water and air blithely ignore political jurisdictions and municipal boundaries, regulating the environment must be, by definition, a national concern. Thus, it is perhaps natural that the federal government has had a disproportionate impact on environmental policies. Table 15–2 indicates the major federal environmental legislation.

Federal legislation and state implementation

Although federal legislation affecting the environment is extensive, not all the national laws listed in Table 15–2 have a consistent impact on state and local governments. Among those federal laws enacted since

431

TABLE 15–2. Major Federal Environmental Legislation, 1965–1977

Year	Legislation	Effect
	1. Comprehensive Planning and Coordination	
1969	National Environmental Policy Act	Established Council on Environmental Quality (C.E.Q.); required impact statements.
1970	Environmental Quality Improvement Act	Established an Office of Environmental Quality to support C.E.Q.
1970	Reorganization Plan No. 3	Established Environmental Protection Agency.
1970	Reorganization Plan No. 4	Established National Oceanic and Atmospheric Administration.
	2. Air Pollution Control	
1960	Air Quality Act	Required states and cities to set standards and submit implementation plans.
1970	Clean Air Amendments	Set national standards and required states and cities to implement them.
1977	Clean Air Amendments	Modified existing programs.
	3. Water Pollution Control	
1965	Water Quality Act	Required states and cities to establish and enforce standards for interstate waters.
1966	Clear Waters Restoration Act	Grants for sewer systems construction.
1970	Water Quality Improvement Act	Limited additional effect.
1972	Federal Water Pollution Control Act	Established national standards for states and cities to administer under federal guidelines.
	4. Solid Waste Management	
1965	Solid Waste Disposal Act	Grants for planning.
1970	Resource Recovery Act	Demonstration grants, technical assistance.
1976	Resource Conservation and Recovery Act	Required federal and state control of hazardous waste.
	5. Noise Abatement	
1970	Clean Air Amendments	Established Office of Noise Abatement in the EPA.
1972	Noise Control Act	Extensive federal regulation and setting of noise control standards.
	6. Pesticide Control	
1972	Federal Environmental Pesticide Control Act	Extensive federal regulation.
1976	Toxic Substances Control Act	Extensive federal regulation of toxic substances.
	7. Land Use	
1975	Amendments to Section 701 of the Housing and Urban Development Act	Required a land use element in all urban planning.
1976	Federal Land Policy and Management Act	Ended policy of conveying public lands into private hands.
1976	National Forest Management Act	Administrative guidelines set for national forests.

1965 that are having a major affect on state and local governments are these:

The National Environmental Policy Act of 1969, which requires agencies to prepare for all "major federal actions significantly affecting the quality of the human environment" a detailed statement concerning the environmental impact of those acts, particularly irreversible and unavoidable impacts, and to list alternative courses of action

The Environmental Quality Improvement Act of 1970, which states that "primary responsibility for implementing" national environmental policies "rests with state and local governments"

The amendments of 1970 to the Clean Air Act, which stipulate that "the prevention and control of air pollution at its source, is the primary responsibility of State and local Governments"

The Noise Control Act of 1972, which contends that "primary responsibility for control of noise rests with State and local governments"

The amendments of 1972 to the Federal Water Pollution Control Act, which state that "it is the policy of the Congress to recognize, preserve, and protect the primary responsibilities and rights of States to prevent, reduce, and eliminate pollution"

The amendments of 1970 to the Solid Waste Disposal Act, which mandate that "the collection and disposal of solid wastes should continue to be primarily the function of States, regional, and local agencies"

The Resource Conservation and Recovery Act of 1976, which encourages the states to regulate the safe disposal of hazardous solid wastes under federal guidelines

In brief, it seems clear that Congress has placed a large responsibility on state and local governments for managing the environment. Indeed, it can be argued that Congress has goaded state and local governments into some action concerning the environment.

The federal impact

After 1965 the situation in environmental policy and pollution control at the state and local levels began changing considerably, and much of the reason behind this change was the enactment of the new federal laws reviewed in Table 15–2. Jones has itemized these changes, noting that the federal government, first of all, set up the framework to plan and coordinate in the area of the environment by creating the Council on

Environmental Quality, enacting the National Environmental Policy Act, which required environmental impact statements, and establishing the Environmental Protection Agency (EPA) through Executive Order. A second development was the enormous expansion of national authority, especially in the areas of air and water pollution control (and, more recently, solid waste disposal). Jones points out that with the passage of the Clean Air Amendments of 1970 and the Federal Water Pollution Control Act of 1972, state and local governments "became administering agencies for federal policies." [10] Finally, federal authority was broadened to cover a number of other environmental areas besides air and water pollution, notably solid waste disposal, noise pollution, and the control of toxic substances.

All this federal activity has had a major impact on the state and local governmental scene. State environmental protection programs have been developed where none existed; state and local agencies have been organized (or, in some cases, reorganized) to meet new responsibilities and to coordinate local policies with federal requirements; and finally, state and local policies designed to meet not only federal regulations but also to coordinate the use of environmental impact statements as required by the National Environmental Policy Act have been enacted.

Perhaps the most succinct indication of the impact that federal legislation has had at the grassroots can be shown by the rise in level of expenditures. Table 15–3 indicates the substantial increase in total state

TABLE 15–3. Total State Expenditures for Selected Environmental Control Programs, 1961–1962, 1968–1969, 1970–1971 (thousands of dollars)

	Years reported			
	1961	*1962*	*1968–1969*	*1970–1971*
Air pollution	2,040 [1]		17,092	27,605
Water pollution	—	8,163	153,058	258,123
Solid waste	N.A. [2]	N.A.	2,438 [3]	6,299 [4]

[1] Total of seventeen states spending over $5,000.
[2] N.A., not applicable.
[3] Total of thirteen states with measurable expenditures.
[4] Total of forty-two states with measurable expenditures.

Source: Charles O. Jones, "Regulating the Environment," *Politics in the American States,* 3rd ed., Herbert Jacob and Kenneth N. Vines, eds. (Boston; Little, Brown, 1976), p. 409. As derived from U.S. Senate, Committee on Public Works, *A Study of Pollution—Air,* Staff Report, September 1963, 32; U.S. Senate, Committee on Public Works, *A Study of Pollution —Water,* Staff Report, June 1963, 75; U.S. Bureau of the Census, *Environmental Quality Control,* State and Local Government Special Studies 57 (April 1971) and Special Studies 62 (December 1972) (Washington, D.C.: Government Printing Office).

10. *Ibid.,* p. 407.

expenditures for selected environmental control programs from 1961 through 1971; water pollution expenditures, for example, grew by a phenomenal 776 percent between 1961 and 1971, and similar growth is found in the area of air pollution. Prior to the passage of the Clean Air Act in 1963, only nine states had adopted any kind of air pollution control legislation. By the end of 1970, however, all states had some sort of legal basis for controlling air pollution, and this development largely was attributable to the model set by the federal government.

Meeting the federal mandate:
the trial of states and cities

States and big cities have had a difficult time meeting the requirements of federal legislation, particularly for air and water quality. The 1970 Amendments to the Clean Air Act set forth a two-fold strategy for cleaning up the nation's air. The first part of the strategy was for the federal Environmental Protection Agency to establish air quality standards; the second part required all the states and thirty-four cities to develop implementation plans indicating how they would achieve these national standards. The EPA is required under the amendments to approve the state and metropolitan implementation plans, and this approval, in effect, makes these plans a part of federal law. The Environmental Protection Agency elected to approve each implementation plan on a case-by-case basis because each region of the country had such different air quality problems. Still, the states and big cities have failed to meet the standards set by the amendments; as of the mid-1970s, no state or metropolitan air pollution control plan had been approved in its entirety by the EPA. EPA has given notice to cities and states that are unable to deliver emission control plans acceptable to EPA that the agency will develop a plan itself and force the state or city to implement it.

Just as the federal government is having a major impact on air pollution, it is having a similar influence in the area of water pollution. The 1972 Amendments to the Federal Water Pollution Control Act of 1948 established for the first time discharge requirements that called upon industrial polluters to attain the "best practicable treatment control technology currently available" by 1977, and "the best available technology economically achievable" by 1983. Cities, also major polluters of the nation's waterways, were required to construct secondary treatment facilities for municipal sewage discharges by 1977 and to attain the best practicable waste treatment technology by 1983. The final goal of the amendments is to eliminate all pollutants into navigable waters by 1985, a goal that many have criticized as being unrealistic. Fortunately the 1972 amendments increased by substantial amounts ($18 billion over a five-year period) the level of federal aid available to local governments for constructing municipal waste water collection and treatment systems. Until 1972 federal grants only covered up to 55 percent of municipal construction costs, and annual appropriations were running at about $1 billion.

Needless to say, the nation's waterways were not clean by 1977. Although many lakes and rivers had been rendered "fishable and swimmable" by that year, as the legislation demanded, less than a third of the country's thirteen thousand municipal sewage treatment plants had secondary treatment facilities by 1977, and six hundred of the four thousand major industrial water polluters had not complied with the law.[11] Even if the 1972 Amendments had been fully met, the nation's waterways, for the most part, could not have been considered "fishable and swimmable."

STATE AND LOCAL GOVERNMENTS ENCOUNTER THE ENVIRONMENT

Since 1960 both state and local governments have assumed increasingly active roles in regulating the environment. Only five states still have separate agencies to administer air quality programs, water pollution programs, and solid waste management. All the rest have consolidated or at least partially consolidated these functions. More than thirty states have reorganized their environmental management programs since 1967. Sixteen states include their pollution control programs within a public health department, a dozen additional states have followed the federal lead and have established a statewide equivalent of environmental protection agency, and fifteen states have created an environmental "superagency" that combines pollution control with the states' conservation programs or natural resource management programs. Again, following the federal lead, by 1976 twenty-six states had their own environmental impact statement requirements. In some states these environmental impact statements are even tougher than those required by the national government; California, for example, requires that a discussion of energy consumption be included in certain types of environmental impact statements.[12] According to a 1973 survey by the International City Management Association (ICMA), 30 percent of the 1,115 responding cities had formal requirements for environmental impact statements. An environmental impact statement is favored very heavily by western cities, where some 70 percent of the responding cities had such requirements.[13]

11. Council on Environmental Quality, *Eighth Annual Report, 1977, op. cit.,* p. 36.
12. Council on Environmental Quality, *Seventh Annual Report, 1976, op. cit.,* pp. 135–136.
13. Steve Carter, Lyle Sumek, and Murray Frost, "Local Environmental Management," *Municipal Yearbook, 1974* (Washington, D.C.: International City Management

In our discussion of the environment, we have been emphasizing the role of the national and state governments. The reason for this is apparent; governments with jurisdiction over larger amounts of land are going to have more environmental problems. A special word, however, ought to be said about the activities of local governments. Local government officials, according to the ICMA survey, consider the environment to be an important issue in their communities, but not the most important issue. Only a third of the local officials responding classified the environment as either the most important or the second most important issue facing their cities. Most local government officials tended to rank taxes, housing, urban deterioration, and education as more important than the environment, although urban administrators in the West thought the environment to be more important than officials in other parts of the country, and the suburbs ranked it more highly than did the inner cities.

Local administrators break down the environmental issue along the following lines: First and foremost are problems relating to land use, with growth and solid and liquid waste disposal problems tied for second. The importance of environmental questions as they pertain to controlled growth is reflected in the fact that a fourth of the responding cities indicated that there was an environmental section in their comprehensive city plan. Indeed, almost 20 percent of all the cities had imposed some sort of moratorium within the past two years on urban growth and land use decisions in an effort to control potential environmental degradation. Nearly a quarter of the cities had created a citizens' commission on the environment, which often possessed a broad legal mandate to investigate local problems pertaining to pollution control.

Despite some intensive local efforts at upgrading the urban environment, it should be noted that, because of state and national pressure, a number of cities have let the enforcement of various pollution ordinances lapse, or at least have not taken it upon themselves to create their own regulations concerning environmental quality. The ICMA survey, for example, found that "with the increased role of the federal and state governments in setting environmental quality standards, many cities have eliminated their environmental standards or have not developed any. Some states prohibit local governments from adopting their own standards."

THE SAGA OF SOLID WASTE RECOVERY

Until now, we have been concentrating on air pollution and water pollution as areas of environmental concern. Among the many other areas of

---

Association, 1974), p. 263. The following data on local environmental policies are drawn from *ibid.*, pp. 255, 258, 260, 263.

concern at the state and local levels the most important ones are solid waste management and land use.

In stark contrast to air and water pollution, little national legislation deals with solid waste management.

The federal government has enacted the Solid Waste Disposal Act of 1965 and the Resource Recovery Act of 1970, both of which do little more than permit grants for planning solid waste disposal and demonstration projects with minimal technical assistance. In 1976 the Resource Conservation and Recovery Act was enacted, and ultimately it will bring the federal government into managing the disposal of hazardous substances. States and localities have dealt with their garbage by burning it, burying it, or dumping it into the ocean, and it is becoming increasingly clear to state and local officials that none of these methods will suffice in an era of "spaceship" earth. The problem is very real. There are an estimated 16,000 land disposal sites for solid waste, of which only 5,800 meet state health regulations.[14]

At the state level interest in solid waste management has increased markedly in recent years and has focused on the development of regional systems for disposing of solid waste and providing technical assistance to local governments. The newest development in solid waste management, at both the state and local levels, is the establishment of resource recovery systems—that is, developing garbage disposal systems that pull out valuable items or recycle waste into new and useful substances. Cans and bottles can be salvaged from solid waste; organic matter can be transformed into mulch or even, in some cases, fuel. By the mid-1970s eleven states had loan or grant programs for cities constructing resource recovery systems or municipalities regulating resource recovery activities through guidelines and other requirements. Even more states had the authority to create agencies to operate resource recovery systems; most of the 9 million tons of waste that is recovered (90 percent) is paper.[15] Connecticut, among the most innovative states in this area, has established a statewide Resources Recovery Authority, which will build ten facilities by 1985 that are expected to process 84 percent of the state's municipal waste for use as fuel by Connecticut's utilities companies.

A related effort deals with what is known as "source reduction," by which is meant reducing the amount of garbage that must be processed by state and local sanitation agencies. Toward this end legislation has been introduced in all the state legislatures and in a number of county and city councils to encourage the recycling of waste products by individual citizens. Three states—Oregon, South Dakota, and Vermont—

14. Council on Environmental Quality, *Eighth Annual Report, 1977, op. cit.,* p. 50.
15. *Ibid.,* p. 54.

have placed restrictions on beer and soft drink containers and Minnesota enacted legislation that affected all major types of packaging. Oregon's 1972 law, the most famous, requires that a minimum of two cents be refunded for beer bottles and five cents for all other containers. In addition, no beverages in flip-top containers can be sold in the state.[16] Some of the most significant advances in resource recovery have been made at the local level. As late as 1971 there was only one resource recovery plant in operation in the nation (in Franklin, Ohio). Today there are twenty-five, some of which can handle up to three thousand tons of waste per day, in operation or under construction. In New Orleans, for example, the city's "Recovery I" takes in six hundred fifty tons of trash daily and converts into a clean land fill that will make more than one thousand acres of currently unusable land available for industry. New Orleans has been able to close five incinerators that polluted the air and convert those sites into recreation centers or parks. Eventually, Recovery I will reclaim fifty tons each of steel and glass and three tons each of aluminum and newsprint per day.[17]

LAND USE:
STATES AND LOCALITIES AS ENVIRONMENTAL INNOVATORS

The nation's effort to enact more enlightened policies for solid waste disposal by slowly moving away from land fills leads us into a more general discussion of land use policy. Use policy remains largely the purview of state and local governments. Although Congress passed legislation in 1976 that involved more stringently regulating federal lands and in 1975 enacted some modest urban land use policies as they applied to the "701" planning process (see Table 15–2), these statutes are hardly comprehensive. Indeed, significant national land use policies have been defeated by special interests at every turn; in 1974 the important Land Use Policy Act was voted down in the House, and the Strip Mining Act was vetoed by the president. Hence, state and local governments have come to grips with the land use question more forcefully than have the feds.

Zoning for limited growth

Zoning, believe it or not, is as close as America comes to having a comprehensive land use policy. At root, zoning simply is a plan determining

16. The data on state programs for the environment in this paragraph are drawn from "Natural Resources and Environmental Management," *Book of the States,* 1976–1977 (Lexington, Ky.: Council of State Governments, 1976), pp. 472–473.

17. Neal R. Peirce, "Trashing Garbage, Not Whether but How," syndicated column, September 30, 1977.

how certain sections of the community may be used—whether for stores, residences, recreations or whatever. Houston stands alone as a major city that does not have and has never had zoning. In recent years, zoning has been used to discourage growth in communities.[18] From an environmental perspective, at least in some cases, restricting growth through zoning can be advantageous, but from the perspective of social equity such use of zoning becomes extremely controversial.

The movement to limit municipal growth through zoning can be traced to the town of Ramapo, a suburb of New York City. Between 1960 and 1970 Ramapo grew from thirty-eight thousand to seventy-eight thousand people, and the land being taken up by those additional Ramapoans was destroying what many felt was the character of the village. Consequently, Ramapo developed an unusual eighteen-year, "delayed-growth" model that permitted the phased development of various service facilities such as water, power lines, and sewers. In effect the town rationed building permits to developers. Ramapo's policy quickly was challenged in the courts (*Golden v. Planning Board of Ramapo*); Ramapo lost the first round, but then won in the New York court of appeals. In 1972 the United States Supreme Court refused to review the decision, thus upholding the position of Ramapo.

Ramapo was an indirect inspiration to the citizens of Petaluma, a town near San Francisco. Petaluma had grown from fourteen thousand people in 1960, to twenty-five thousand in 1970, and to thirty thousand by the end of 1971. Petaluma was more straightforward in its policy to limit growth than Ramapo, and flatly rationed the community's growth to five hundred new residential units a year for the next five years; the city council's policy was ratified by Petaluma's voters in 1973 and the city's ordinance soon was challenged in the courts (*Construction Industry Association of Sonoma County v. City of Petaluma*). Petaluma's lawyers contended that adding more Petalumans would overburden the city's sanitation and school facilities, thus forcing the citizens to vote for increased taxes. The U.S. district court held against Petaluma, ruling that "neither Petaluma's city officials nor the local electorate may use their power to disapprove bonds at the polls as a weapon to define or destroy fundamental constitutional rights," notably the rights of people to travel and settle.

By this time Petaluma was becoming a symbol, with environmental and urban interests taking the side of the city and with civil rights groups and construction interests—banding against Petaluma. Petaluma took its case to the federal appeals court, which reversed the decision of the lower court, stating that Petaluma had a right to use its zoning power "in its

---

18. The following discussion of *Ramapo* and *Petaluma* is drawn from Samuel Kaplan, *The Dream Deferred* (New York: Seabury Press, 1976), pp. 77–79.

own self interest" by employing zoning as "lawfully delegated to it by the state." The judges observed that "the federal court is not a superzoning board" and "should not be called on to mark the point at which legitimate local interests are outweighed by legitimate regional interest."

Since *Petaluma*, a number of local governments, notably San Diego, have wrangled over civil rights and status quo. This controversy is in part racial and economic since, by restricting new housing, local governments are limiting the number of new residents that may join their communities and often such limitations can amount to de facto segregation of whites and blacks, rich and poor. Nevertheless, zoning for no-growth, or for controlled growth, is not the same as "exclusionary zoning," which often amounts to a flat ban on low-income housing (but not on higher-grade housing) in an effort to keep out minorities.

Cities, of course, may enact land use controls beyond those permitted by traditional zoning ordinances. In a survey conducted in 1973 by the International City Management Association of all municipalities with ten thousand people and more, it was found that of nine possible types of land use controls, only 17 percent of the 1,115 responding cities had not enacted any of them.[19] The single most popular land use control was that of requiring developers to install public facilities (such as sewer lines), with 83 percent of the cities having enacted such ordinances. Roughly a quarter of all the responding cities had passed ordinances regarding architectural appearance, growth limitations, and historical preservation, and from a third to a half of the cities had ordinances that zoned for flood planes, open spaces, and natural resources; 12 percent had marsh land controls.

Toward statewide land use planning

The states increasingly are gearing up comprehensive land use plans, and many have established creative working relationships with their towns and cities in evolving comprehensive land use programs.

By the mid-1970s twenty-seven of the states had a total of thirty-eight general land use programs, and five of these states had created ground-breaking comprehensive state programs permitting state officials to deal directly with local developers. In addition all of the thirty eligible states participate in the federal coastal zone management program, and five of these states had enacted special laws to protect their shorelines. Forty-two states have passed preferential tax policies that encourage farmers and other owners of large parcels of land to retain their holdings, and thus resist selling out to real estate developers; thirty-four states have

19. Carter, Sumek, and Frost, *op. cit.*, p. 259.

legislation that deals with the siting of power plants, and thirty-eight states regulate strip mining.[20]

Although the states have not been shy in their desire to encourage the planning of land use, enacting measures that grant governments regulatory authority to control land use is another matter, and most states have ceded a large portion of that authority to their local governments. Indeed, the local government normally is given the flexibility to plan for particular state objectives as well as particular local goals, so the state develops the comprehensive plan and leaves the enforcement, by and large, to the local government.

California may become an exception to the rule that states generally pass down authority in land use matters to local officials. In 1977 Governor Jerry Brown proposed a sweeping reform of California's laws concerning urban growth, amounting to what some have called the most comprehensive proposal for land use management in the nation. Brown rejected the development of new towns, noting that his state had become "the symbol of urban sprawl throughout the world," and instead concentrated on reviving existing cities and suburbs, protecting prime farmland, distributing industry and other commerce more equitably, and providing housing, employment, and public services to the 4 to 8 million new residents expected to migrate to California—already the nation's most populous state—over the next twenty years. Rich communities would be required to share revenues from their sales and property taxes with poorer communities on a regional basis; cities and counties would be ordered to adopt five year rehabilitation programs; slumlords would be replaced by court appointed "receivers" to manage rehabilitation; and other comparatively "radical" strategies also were proposed. California, the symbol of sprawl and perhaps the most urbanized state in the country with 90 percent of its 22 million people teeming in a mere half-dozen metropolitan areas, will be carefully watched to see whether it adopts or rejects such a plan and whether or not it implements it.[21]

THE REVOLUTIONARY ROLE OF THE COURTS

While legislative bodies and bureaucracies have concerned themselves with the environment in varying degrees, state, local and national courts may have made an even larger impact on regulating man's relationship with earth. Several new judicial doctrines have strengthened the role of the courts in enforcing environmental protection. One such development

20. Council on Environmental Quality, *Seventh Annual Report, op. cit.*, p. 67.
21. Gladwin Hill, "California Growth: Sprawl Control Suggested," *New York Times*, June 12, 1977.

is the willingness of the courts to enforce the provisions of the National Environmental Policy Act, notably the judiciary's recognition that the adequacy of environmental impact statements may be questioned in court at the suit of private citizens. Another is the shift in burden of proof obligations in pollution control cases; now a polluter must prove that his emissions are *not* a health hazard. A third is the right of citizens to sue federal agencies for the right to seize sensitive environmental data under the federal Freedom of Information Act of 1967, as well as under the state equivalents of freedom of information acts. Yet another new court doctrine is the right of citizens to participate in agency policy making for the environment, under not only the national Administrative Procedure Act, but also under the authority of various "sunshine laws" at the state and local levels. A final judicial development is the newly recognized right of citizens to sue industrial polluters under the public nuisance doctrine of common law, which is contained in virtually every state and local code.

Of these developments, perhaps the last is most important. Traditionally, a private citizen had no standing in court when lodging a public nuisance claim. A private citizen could bring only a claim of "private nuisance"; in other words the citizen had to show that he or his property was being damaged uniquely by a polluter's emissions, which, of course, he could not, since the overall community was being damaged "equitably" by the polluter. As for bringing a public nuisance suit, a private citizen had no legal standing because he did not legally represent the public; in the court's eyes, only publicly elected officials represented the public and only these officials could lodge public nuisance suits. This was a *Catch-22* situation, because elected officials could easily be pressured in industry-dominated communities with threats of employee layoffs as a result of local government pressure to reduce emissions. The courts began recognizing a private citizen's right to lodge public nuisance suits against industrial polluters, largely on the grounds that the plaintiff was not demanding monetary damages but only prospective relief. Occasionally, as in Michigan, legislatures have written this new standing of the citizen in public nuisance suits into the state's code, thereby strengthening the court's usefulness in protecting the environment.

ENERGY, THE ENVIRONMENT, AND LIFE

The environment, energy, and the biosphere are intimately intertwined on this planet and, as we enter our discussion of energy policy, the intertwining becomes increasingly apparent. For example, if we were to eliminate fossil fuels tomorrow and switch over to nuclear power, we would still have powerful pollution problems. Thermal pollution, from the heat generated as a result of various industrial processes, would increase enormously with nuclear power, particularly heat transfers into rivers and streams. Similarly, disposing of radioactive wastes is a major problem; the mass of radioactive fission products is almost equal to the mass of fuel consumed and the average period of harmfulness of these wastes exceeds six hundred years. While continued use of fossil fuels promises pollution on a global scale, nuclear reactors also will probably always present the hazards of contamination, but of a different kind. For example, if we were to electrify all urban transit (in other words, convert cars and trucks from burning gas to using electricity), such a conversion would likely increase electrical power requirements by at least one-third—an eventuality that, if nuclear-based, obviously could entail pollution problems of a serious order.[22] As the Council on Environmental Quality concluded, "the environmental benefits of slower energy growth cover a wide range; for example, better air quality, less land disturbed for strip mining, fewer oil spills, less radioactive waste to manage." [23]

Energy is closely associated with the food supply; in this country 13 percent of our energy is devoted purely to food production. Between 1940 and 1970 the amount of energy used directly on U.S. farms increased by more than four times, the amount of energy used by the food processing industry by almost three times, and the amount of energy used in preparing food increased by nearly three times. In all cases, the energy requirements used in farming, food processing, and preparation are still rising.[24]

ADIOS OIL, GOODBYE GAS

It is apparent that energy, environment, and life itself are closely interrelated. But where does the energy come from? Most of the world's energy is derived from fossil fuels (oil, gas, and coal), and these are running out.

On the Environmental/Energy Balance

Balancing the frequently conflicting pressures of environmental quality and cheap energy is a challenge worthy of the Flying Wallendas.

22. Howard Bucknell, III, *The Political Economy of Energy: Analyzing U.S. Energy Policy,* from the manuscript, with the permission of the author.
23. Council on Environmental Quality, *Seventh Annual Report, 1976, op. cit.,* p. 192.
24. John S. Steinhart and Carol E. Steinhart, "Energy Use in the U.S. Food Systems," *Science* 184 (April 19, 1974): 307–316.

Even the Council on Environmental Quality, formed in 1969 with the mandate of "cleaning up" the environment, now recognizes that growth management is the real issue and, as the following passage indicates, an increasingly sophisticated one.

Protection of environmental quality is no longer in its infancy. In the 8 years since the Council has reported on our environment, the nation has made strenuous efforts to control pollution, use land wisely, protect the physical and social fabric of communities, and preserve a magnificent natural heritage.

Some of these efforts have achieved a large measure of success. There have also been failures and compromises. And sometimes there have been adverse, unexpected effects from well-meant programs, for example, the urban sprawl generated by overambitious sewer projects which drew their inspiration and funds from the federal program to clean up the nation's waters.

The successes that we have recorded in this and earlier reports are gratifying, but even the half-successes and failures are a necessary part of our environmental learning. Through trial, evaluation, correction, and persistence toward our goals, we are progressing. . . .

With oil and gas supplies dropping, demands rising, and oil imports increasing year by year, we would clearly benefit from new, secure sources of energy. The need is not confined to the United States; world energy demand is expected to double in 2 or 3 decades, and at the same time oil production is likely to level off.

The choice of technologies to meet the need for alternative energy sources is now the subject of intense debate, and two opposing points of view have emerged— the "hard" and the "soft" energy paths.

The "hard" path opts for redoubled efforts to develop all current energy sources, with a highly centralized, highly electrified energy future. For the near term, this approach calls for more of the same thing we have now, for as long as we can make it last. If natural liquid petroleum and gas are running out, then make more synthetically from coal and oil shales. At the same time, meet an increasing share of rapidly increasing energy needs with growth in electricity supply based on coal and nuclear power.

This view recognizes that eventually the fossil fuels may become too scarce, too expensive, or too environmentally damaging for continued use. But meanwhile, nuclear power will have come to maturity. The advocates place their confidence either in the breeder reactor, assuming that its safety and economic problems will be solved reasonably soon, or in the eventual success of nuclear fusion as an almost illimitable source of power. This view is imbued with the technological optimism that has been so much a part of the U.S. character for a century or more.

The "soft" path embodies the fundamental view that nature imposes limits on growth and that it is possible to live comfortably within those limits. Conservation is an indispensable part of this approach. Its advocates believe that greater efficiency can save large amounts of energy, but they also recognize that conservation may require at least moderate changes in habits and lifestyles. This approach emphasizes renewable, relatively nonpolluting, often decentralized, and small-scale sources of energy. Environmental effects of the technologies are described as tractable, reversible, and relatively small. More speculatively, advocates assert that job opportunities will be greater with the nonconventional technologies. And they believe that smaller energy enterprises near the communities which they serve will enhance self-reliance, a greater sense of civic responsibility, and a feeling of being in charge of one's destiny.

Obviously the two sides represent extreme positions. In fact, the paths that they describe are not necessarily mutually exclusive, and it is possible for the nation to adopt some elements of both. It is also evident that the arguments marshaled by both sides go beyond technical, environmental, and socioeconomic conditions to basic ethical values. In a democratic society, such questions can be decided only through the political process.

Council on Environmental Quality
Eighth Annual Report.

The horror of "Hubbert's Pimple"

Figure 15–2 illustrates worldwide energy use and supply over historical time. The curve is derived from geologist M. King Hubbert's research and pertains primarily to the earth's dwindling petroleum reserves, which first

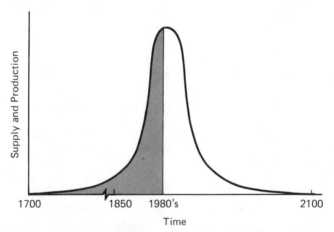

FIGURE 15–2. Hubbert's Pimple: Worldwide Supply and Demand for Nonrecoverable Energy Resources.

started being tapped around 1850 at the advent of the Industrial Revolution. Because the curve illustrates so vividly the historical uniqueness of our century's reliance on fossil fuels, it has gained renown as "Hubbert's Pimple." As Hubbert notes, "the epoch of fossil fuels can only be a transitory and ephemeral event—an event, nonetheless, which has exercised the most drastic influence experienced by the human species during its entire biological history." [25]

The end of the American energy era

For its part the United States runs essentially on only two fuels, which together provide three-quarters of all the roughly thirty-eight million barrels of oil (and its equivalent) that are consumed each day by the United States. These two fuels are natural gas and oil. The remaining equivalency of 9.5 million barrels of oil per day are provided by coal, hydroelectric power, and nuclear fission. Figure 15–3 indicates the primary sources of energy in the United States.

In a mere twenty years, the United States reversed its role as an ex-

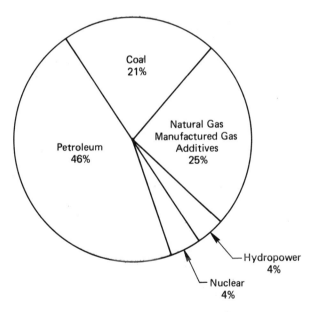

FIGURE 15–3. Primary Sources of Energy in the United States.

Source: Federal Energy Administration 1976, Adjusted for early 1977 trends.
25. M. King Hubbert, "Energy Resources," in *Resources and Man,* Preston Cloud, ed. (San Francisco: W. H. Freeman, 1968), p. 180.

porter of energy and now imports 15 percent of its total energy and a whopping 35 percent of its petroleum. The U.S. population has grown by only about a third since 1950, but its use of energy has doubled, growing at an average annual rate of about 3.5 percent from 1950 to 1965, and then speeding to a 4.5 percent rate until the Arab oil embargo of 1973–74. During this time domestic production of energy grew at only 3 percent per year between 1950 and 1970 and has shown little or no growth since 1970. This decline in domestic energy production was particularly evident for oil, an area in which imports tripled from 1960 to 1973. Between 1947 and 1962 domestic coal production fell by 36 percent. Similarly, nuclear energy, long touted as the long-run saviour for America's energy lifestyle, ran into unexpected snags and has never taken off to the degree initially anticipated.[26]

Figure 15–4 illustrates U.S. gross energy consumption between 1900 and 1975 and projects consumption to the year 2000. The high side of

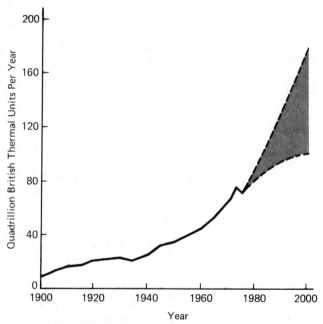

FIGURE 15–4.   U.S. Gross Energy Consumption for 1900–1975 and Range of Projections to the Year 2000.
Source: Council on Environmental Quality.

26. Council on Environmental Quality, *Environmental Quality*, Sixth Annual Report of the Council on Environmental Quality (Washington. D.C.: U.S. Government Printing Office, 1975), pp. 109–110.

the projection is what would happen if Americans continued using energy at their present pace. The low side indicates energy consumption if stringent conservation measures were enacted.

The most alarming consumption is that of oil and gasoline. Figure 15–5 shows the dependence of the United States on both domestic and imported oil. The figure indicates U.S. domestic production is falling and our reliance on imported oil is rising to the point that it now accounts for more than a third of all U.S. oil consumption.

Enter the Arabs

At the time of the Arab oil embargo in 1973–74, America was importing about 6 million barrels of oil each day, but only five years later, in 1978, U.S. imports of oil had risen to 9 million barrels a day and the projection indicated that by 1985, barring any kind of conservation measures, the figure will have risen to 12 million to 15 million barrels per day. It is estimated that by 1985 foreign oil will have at least doubled in price, costing the United States about $100 billion every year in 1978 dollars.[27]

The uses of oil

How does America use its energy supplies? Industry uses approximately 31 percent; electric utilities, 27 percent; transportation, 25 percent (al-

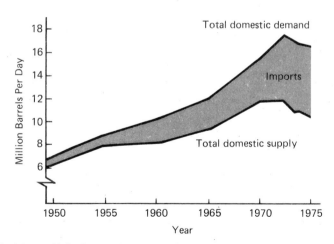

FIGURE 15–5. U.S. Dependence on Imported Oil.
Source: Federal Energy Administration.

27. David S. Broder, "U.S. Still Living in a Fool's Paradise," syndicated column, January 3, 1978.

though about 15 percent of our total energy consumption is used purely for the gasoline demands of the automobile). Residential use accounts for 12 percent, and commercial use roughly 5 percent. Of these uses, perhaps that of transportation strikes the closest to the heart of state and local governments. According to the more refined estimates about 53 percent of all petroleum consumed in the United States is used by transportation (by contrast, in Europe the figure is 28 percent), and more than half of this is consumed by automobiles. Trains, trucks, and buses use substantially less petroleum, chiefly because approximately 80 percent of all passenger miles travelled in America are travelled by automobile.[28]

ALTERNATIVES TO OIL

Conservation, anyone?

The most obvious alternative to the national need for a constant "petroleum fix" is to use less. If all of America's eighty thousand governments initiated stringent conservation policies, the estimated savings could be anywhere from 7 million to 16.5 million barrels of oil per day (or its equivalent in other energy sources) by 1990. Perhaps a better notion of what energy conservation would mean can be derived from the experience of other countries. Although various factors make comparison difficult, it nonetheless stands that a number of countries with a Gross National Product similar to ours—notably Denmark, West Germany, Norway, Great Britain, Austria, France, and Japan—have significantly lower per capita rates of energy consumption. A comparison of per person energy consumption between the United States and Sweden found that Swedish methods of energy conservation could result in a savings of about 30 percent of the total energy used in the United States.[29]

Coal and synthetic fuels

Of course, there are other alternatives to keeping the American economy on a rational energy track besides conservation, and among these are the development of synthetic fuels such as synthetic gas, coal, liquefaction, and shale oil. While not economically competitive at this time, these synthetic fuels have a high energy potentiality, although reliance on coal and oil synthetics could result in severe environmental and health problems. For example, a 1977 study by the National Academy of Sciences found that as many as twenty-one thousand people died prematurely

28. Bucknell, *op. cit.*
29. Council on Environmental Quality, *Seventh Annual Report, 1976, op. cit.*, p. 193.

every year east of the Mississippi River because of pollutants spewed into the air by power plants burning coal and oil; these people died anywhere from one to fifteen years short of their expected life spans. The study examined pollutants emanating from 266 power plants in the eastern half of the United States (power plants that burn, for the most part, dirtier, sulfur-bearing fuels) and analyzed the impact of these power plants on health in 110 eastern cities. The scientists concluded that, if the nation turned to coal as its principal alternative source of electricity, it could expect as many as thirty-five thousand premature deaths by the year 2010, instead of the estimated twenty-one thousand occurring in the mid 1970s as a result of pollution by power plants. To quote the study, "the implications for the increased use of coal are grim. We recommend that these implications be viewed and studied at the highest levels of government." [30]

Solar

A far cleaner alternative than synthetic fuels or coal is the prospect of using solar energy, or the direct use of the sun's rays, to produce energy. One estimate by the U.S. Energy Research and Development Administration suggested that by the year 2020 solar energy could supply as much as 25 percent of the total American energy demand.[31] Although much of solar energy development has been in the private sector, by 1976 not many more than two hundred houses across the entire nation were using solar heating systems.

Nevertheless, solar's potential is enormous. Not only is it a clean source of energy, it is renewable, unlike coal, oil, gas, and uranium. Research in solar energy (notably in the area of photovoltaic cells) remains in its infancy, and the Carter administration, short-sightedly, has not emphasized solar in its energy policy.

The nukes: fission, breeders, and fusion

Perhaps the most widely known alternative to fossil fuel is nuclear power. Nuclear power is among the most sensitive of political issues, chiefly because of concerns over safety and the problem of radioactive waste. An even larger concern in recent years has been the breeder reactor. A breeder reactor is capable of producing more nuclear fuel than it consumes, thus extending the supply of limited uranium. Nevertheless, be-

30. The National Academy of Science, cited in Thomas O'Toole, "Lung Disease may be Price of Coal Use," *The Washington Post*, July 19, 1977.

31. U.S. Energy Research and Development Administration, cited in Council on Environmental Quality, *Seventh Annual Report, 1976, op. cit.*, p. 117.

cause the breeder reactor was considered potentially more dangerous to the surrounding community (there appears to be a higher possibility that it could literally blow up, in contrast to the standard water-cooled plant), plus the recent discovery that a breeder reactor is more likely to take a century to double its usable fuel than the heretofore estimated decade, President Carter discontinued the breeder reactor program in 1977. Both standard and breeder reactors have resulted in major political confrontations, particularly at the state and local levels. Rather than discuss these issues here, we consider them later in this chapter.

Another type of nuclear power that has great potential but at this time is of little practical consequence, is that of fusion power. Both standard water-cooled reactors and breeder reactors are based on the technology of fission power (a process in which the atom is "split"). Fusion power, on the other hand, gives us all the hope of virtually unlimited—and environmentally safe—fuel resources with relatively minute danger of an accidental explosion occurring. In contrast to fission power, fusion power is based on the principle underlying the hydrogen bomb and uses as fuels deuterium, derived from sea water, or tritium, which is bred in the fusion reactor itself. Unfortunately, the engineering and scientific problems surrounding the development of practical fusion power are enormous. It took only three years to develop a fission reaction after it was theoretically conceived; with fusion more than twenty years have passed since theoretical conception, and we still do not have a genuinely workable demonstration of the theory.

Tides, earth heat, water, and wind

There are some other possibilities that should be discussed in terms of alternatives to fossil fuels. *Ocean power*, which involves harnessing the energies available in the movement of the tides; *geothermal power*, in which the natural heat of the earth is used to generate electricity (as is being done in California, for example); and *water power*, if completely harnessed, could match the current production of electricity generated by fossil fuels; however, this would also necessitate building dams and dikes literally everywhere and, in any case, the reservoirs created by those dams eventually would fill up with sediment in about a century or two. *Wind energy*, which, like tidal power, is a version of solar energy, can also potentially be harnessed. Technologically advanced windmills are being developed (experiments are going on in New Mexico) that could contribute to the nation's energy supply.

All of these possible alternatives to gas and oil as the bases for America's technoscientific superculture are, with the exceptions of nuclear and possibly solar energy, limited. Geothermal power, tidal power, and wind energy could not account for much more than a small fraction of the country's total energy needs. Solid waste combustion could generate significant energy, however, and a number of cities and states are investigating this option; we discuss it later in this chapter.

THE FEDS AND THE PHENOMENAL ENERGY FUMBLE

For a variety of reasons, the national government logically should be the primary focus for a discussion of energy policy and politics in America. This is because only the national government is working in tandem with the private sector and together, have the resources needed to develop wholly new sources of energy.

A " moral equivalent of war"

President Nixon's "Project Independence" proposal of 1973 called for total energy self-sufficiency by 1980, but amounted to little more than a spasmodic reaction to the Arab oil embargo of 1973–74. President Carter first called Americans' attention to the energy crisis in a far more realistic fashion in 1977 when he stated that, "with the exception of preventing war, this is the greatest challenge that our country will face during our lifetime. The energy crisis has not yet overwhelmed us, but it will if we do not act quickly. . . . the oil and gas that we rely on for 75 percent of our energy are simply running out." [32]

Do Americans understand energy?

American reaction to President Carter's energy message was revealing. Prior to his speech, Americans were awash in ignorance about energy and were particularly uninformed about oil. In 1975 a major survey revealed that no more than 4 percent of the general public considered energy to be a serious national problem, and, even in early 1977, a Gallup poll revealed a similar level of energy ignorance on the part of the American people.[33] With Carter's "moral equivalent of war" speech on energy, however, popular knowledge rapidly increased, and a variety of polls subsequently indicated that more than half the respondents registered at least some concern over energy. Nevertheless, public opinion concerning the energy dilemma still does not appear to be realistic; according to a

32. Jimmy Carter, address to the nation, April 18, 1977.
33. See J. P. Reilly, ed., *American Public Opinion and U.S. Foreign Policy* (Chicago: Council on Foreign Relations, 1975), and "World Opinion Survey," *U.S. News and World Report*, January 1977, as cited in Bucknell, *op. cit.*

poll taken in late 1977 only 48 percent of the people know that we still must import oil to meet our needs. Another survey indicated that only 26 percent of the people who do not have a high school diploma, in contrast to 58 percent of college graduates, believed that there was an energy shortage. Those Americans who do believe in an energy shortage are also the most willing to take conservation measures, are the most likely to use less hot water, insulate the attic, and to join car pools or buy compact cars.[34]

Federal energy policy: the politics of timidity

If public opinion concerning the energy crisis is discouraging to those who believe that the crisis is real, there is even less reason for them to be encouraged by congressional action. The national government has taken a desultory initiative by setting up the machinery to deal with that crisis, and this legislation is briefly detailed in Table 15–4. In addition to the major legislation concerning energy reviewed in Table 15–4, Congress has passed a number of less significant and modestly funded energy bills concerning research in nonnuclear energy resources such as solar power, geothermal power, and other technologies.

TABLE 15–4. Major Federal Energy Legislation, 1973–1977

Year	Legislation	Effects
1973	Emergency Petroleum Allocation Act	Allocated fuel to regions on a need basis.
1974	Energy Reorganization Act	Abolished the Atomic Energy Commission; created Energy Research and Development Administration (ERDA) and Nuclear Regulatory Commission; centralized federal R & D in energy.
1974	Federal Energy Administration Act	Established Federal Energy Administration (FEA) to advise president and Congress on energy policy.
1975	Energy Policy and Conservation Act	Reduced domestic oil prices; set fuel economy standards for cars and consumer products; permitted FEA to grant funds and assistance to states for energy conservation purposes; ordered power plant conversions from oil to coal.
1976	Energy Conservation and Production Act	Extended FEA and established Office of Energy Information and Analysis within FEA.
1977	Act to Establish a Department of Energy	Established Department of Energy incorporating ERDA, FEA, and Federal Power Commission.

34. Philip H. Abelson, "Public Opinion and Energy," *Science* 197 (September 30, 1977), editorial page.

Thus far, we have been concentrating on the national energy crisis, but it must be noted that the national energy picture is by no means the same as the state and local one. Although energy indeed ties this country together, this binding is by no means uniform, and a variety of knots are used.

The energy crisis of 1974: the
grassroots' response

In 1974 the Arab oil embargo made its full force felt at the grassroots, and its impact was profound. In the Northeast and the Midwest, automobiles were lined up literally for miles in front of gas stations waiting to get what gas they could. In New England, heavily dependent upon foreign petroleum, the costs of a barrel of oil rose 300 percent—from $4.04 in May 1973 to $12.50 by February 1974—resulting in a $2.5 billion price tag to the New England economy; industries have already begun leaving the region in search of more stable energy sources.[35]

In response to the 1973–74 embargo Washington, through its Federal Energy Office, set up a system of ten regional allocation offices to redistribute petroleum reserves within their own regions, and this system was copied by most of the states. The federal government had mandated a 10 percent cutback of all gasoline distribution to the states, and, as a consequence, every state had set up an energy allocation office by the end of 1974; twenty states had adopted gasoline sales plans or some related restriction on the purchasing of gasoline supplies. In Georgia Jimmy Carter, then governor of the state, created an Energy Office that operated directly out of the governor's office without the benefit of legislation or formal funding and which directly represented Georgia's fuel needs to the Federal Energy Office. So effective was Carter in this endeavor that the state was relatively flooded with gasoline, to the detriment of neighboring states.[36]

Girding for energy

By the late 1970s more than thirty states had established some sort of framework for energy planning and data collection, and ten western states had formed the Western Governor's Regional Energy Policy Office, which researches ways of producing low-cost energy, protecting the environment, and developing energy storage systems and encourages an

35. *Ibid.*, p. 16.
36. Bucknell, *op. cit.*

overall energy policy for the region. A number of states have initiated tax incentive plans designed to encourage energy conservation, the most common form being a partial property tax exemption for homeowners who install solar energy devices. Several states have entered the energy research and development business. Ohio, Kentucky, and Iowa, for example, have appropriated several million dollars to study and develop coal reserves in their states. New Mexico, Colorado, Florida, Arizona, and Hawaii, for obvious reasons, are exploring the possibilities of solar energy, while well-forested Vermont has a research and development program to consider using wood for electrical generation.[37] Table 15–5 summarizes the activities of the states in the areas of energy planning, research and development, and tax incentives, as well as other areas that the states have explored in the way of meeting the energy crisis.

The regional energy quandary

It is especially important to realize that there is no typical American community when it comes to energy. While the Northeast may be eager for petroleum, the West Coast, for example, is awash in oil. On the one hand, the northeastern states receive the great bulk of their energy supplies in the form of foreign oil products, and these states are the major users of the nation's imported oil. On the other hand, California, which already has its own oil wells, has more oil being poured into it by vessels that have loaded the oil gushing from the Alaska pipeline. If America's Alaskan oil is to reach the Northeast, where it is most needed, it must be transported by a number of small tankers because, first, there is no pipeline over the Rocky Mountains and, second, the new "supertankers" being built are far too large to navigate the Panama Canal. If this predicament were not enough, oil for the midwestern states is largely supplied by Canadian sources. The point is that different regions of the United States have different patterns of energy use, and especially in terms of oil. For example, the Northeast, for all intents and purposes in terms of energy, is almost a foreign country.

At the local level, similar dilemmas exist. New York City, which has the largest mass transportation system in the country, faces very different problems than Los Angeles, which is almost entirely reliant on the automobile.

Regrettably, national policy makers have absolutely failed to recognize these kinds of regional and local disparities of energy consumption.

37. Theodore J. Maher and Tom Hauger, "The Energy Crisis," in *Book of the States,* *1976–77* (Lexington, Ky.: Council of State Governments, 1976), pp. 508–510, and Council of State Governments, *op. cit.*, p. 20.

The infamous Project Independence, conceived by Presidents Nixon and Ford, did not take these differences in energy supply and demand into account whatever beyond a discussion of variations in energy pricing among nine arbitrarily selected regions, and President Carter's national energy plan does not mention these disparities at all.

The federal energy impact:
Alaskan oil and offshore drilling

It is obviously crucial that these regional and local differences in energy use be given major consideration in the evolution of a national energy policy, but whether or not the federal government adequately considers the realities of these variations in forming a national policy, the fact remains that what the federal government does in the field of energy has a major impact not only on the governments of states and localities but also on their citizens' lives as well. Consider two examples, the Alaska pipeline and offshore drilling policies.[38]

In the case of the Alaska pipeline, it is clear that the nation needs that state's oil. The North Slope reserves are estimated to hold between 10 billion to 15 billion barrels of oil, in comparison with a total national reserve of an estimated 31 billion barrels prior to the discovery of the Alaskan fields. The pipeline disgorges 1.2 millions a day to tankers on the coast.

The state of Alaska received from petroleum companies $900 million in oil leases on the North Slope in 1969, but by 1977 it had spent most of this money on new schools and similar facilities needed to service the boom construction communities that sprang up as a result of the pipeline. In fact, the government of Alaska was faced with severe fiscal problems as a direct result of the pipeline, despite the oil money it received. Workers on the pipeline received enormous salaries for their skills (or, in many cases, in spite of having no skills) and this disparity had a major impact on inflationary forces in the state. So high was the rate of inflation that the Alaskan government had to raise $50 million in revenue anticipation bonds before the pipeline opened to meet the additional cost of servicing the sixteen thousand to twenty thousand workers associated with the pipeline who were residing in Alaska.

Of course, this discussion on the adverse economic impact of the Trans-Alaska pipeline on that state does not even consider the potentially catastrophic environmental impact of the pipeline. Although the na-

38. The following examples are drawn from: Council of State Governments, *State Growth Management* (Washington, D.C.: Office of Economic Planning and Development, U.S. Department of Housing and Urban Development, 1976), p. 22.

tional debate that raged over the pipeline did bring many needed facts to light concerning its potential environmental effects, it nonetheless will be several years before the actual effects can be determined.

A second example of federal influence on state and local energy programs is national policies regarding oil drilling on the outer continental shelf of the United States—an area of deep concern to state governments. In 1975 the U.S. Supreme Court ruled in the case of *United States* v. *Maine* that the original colonial charters of the eastern seaboard states, which claimed 200 miles of offshore sovereignty, no longer were valid and further held that the Atlantic coast states owned only three miles of the outer continental shelf; the remaining 197 miles belonged to the federal government. Maine, in cooperation with other states, had launched its suit chiefly because of environmental concerns relating to the potential impact that offshore oil drilling might have on the states' coastlines, particularly in the form of potential oil spills. After the Supreme Court confirmed that the federal government and not the states controlled offshore drilling rights, the Atlantic coast governors asked that the federal government take adequate precautions against oil spills. The western states also have expressed their deep concern over the prospect of oil drilling on the outer continental shelf, and in the mid-1970s the governor of Alaska testified before a congressional committee that his state needed more time "to prepare for the statewide impacts which we fully expect will dwarf anything we have experienced to date including the Trans-Alaska pipeline."

The power plant problem

Another major energy policy problem for the states concerns locating power plants. Table 15–5 itemizes those states that have had to confront the problem of "energy facilities siting," or where to put the power plants, both nuclear and conventional. Power plant siting has become one of the major controversies of state and local politics in the 1980s. Of the sixty-eight power plants granted construction permits in 1976, fifty-three of them had been delayed by public resistance—and these plants all were of the relatively uncontroversial, nonnuclear variety.[39]

More than half of the states have created some kind of facility siting process that mandates prior review by central authorities of proposals for building a wide range of energy facilities, ranging from oil refineries to transmission lines. Review procedures for siting power plants vary from state to state. In Minnesota and Montana, for example, the state governments are directly involved, whereas in New Hampshire and Maine, the

39. Council on Environmental Quality, *Seventh Annual Report, 1976, op. cit.,* p. 119.

TABLE 15–5. State Energy Actions.

State	Energy planning	Emergency powers to Governor	Subsidized research & development into alternate energy sources	Tax incentives for alternate energy	Energy facility siting process	Consumer advocacy
Alabama	★	—	—	—	☆	—
Alaska	—	—	★	—	☆	—
Arizona	—	—	★	★	★	—
Arkansas	★	—	—	—	☆	—
California	★	—	—	—	★	—
Colorado	—	—	★	★	☆	—
Connecticut	★	★	—	—	☆	—
Delaware	★	★	—	—	—	★
Florida	★	—	★	—	☆	★
Georgia	★	—	—	—	—	★
Hawaii	★	★	★	—	—	★
Idaho	★	—	★	—	—	—
Illinois	—	—	★a	★	—	—
Indiana	—	—	★	★	—	☆
Iowa	★	★	★a	—	—	—
Kansas	★	—	—	—	—	—
Kentucky	★	—	★a	—	☆	—
Louisiana	★	—	—	—	—	—
Maine	★	★	★	—	★	—
Maryland	—	★	★	★	☆	☆
Massachusetts	—	—	—	—	☆	—
Michigan	★	—	★	—	—	—
Minnesota	★	★	—	—	☆	—
Mississippi	—	—	—	—	—	—
Missouri	★	—	—	—	☆	★
Montana	★	—	—	★	★	★
Nebraska	★	—	★	—	☆	—
Nevada	—	—	—	—	☆	—
New Hampshire	★	—	—	★	★	—
New Jersey	★	★	★	—	—	★
New Mexico	★	—	★	★	☆	—
New York	—	★	—	—	☆	★
North Carolina	★	—	—	—	—	—
North Dakota	★	—	★	★	★	—
Ohio	★	—	★	—	☆	—
Oklahoma	★	—	★	—	—	—
Oregon	★	★	—	★	☆	—
Pennsylvania	★	—	—	—	—	—
Rhode Island	—	★	—	—	★	☆
South Carolina	★	—	—	—	—	—
South Dakota	★	★	—	★	—	—
Tennessee	—	—	★	—	☆	—
Texas	★	—	—	—	—	—
Utah	—	—	—	—	—	—
Vermont	—	★	★	—	★	☆
Virginia	—	★	—	—	—	—
Washington	—	★	★	—	☆	—
West Virginia	★	★	★	—	—	—
Wisconsin	★	★	—	—	☆	—
Wyoming	—	★	—	—	★	—

★ Indicates action in 1974–75 biennium.
☆ Indicates action prior to 1974–75 biennium or undetermined date.
a Includes research into conventional sources.

Source: Council of State Governments. *Book of the States, 1976–1977.* Lexington, Ky.; Council of State Govt's, 1976, p. 514.

emphasis is on local government review of sitings in their jurisdictions. California has among the most comprehensive legislation dealing with power plant siting; the review procedure is integrated with an overall energy plan and is administered by the Energy Resources Conservation and Development Commission.

Urban energy policy: conservation and conversion

Local governments, like the states, of necessity have become interested in developing alternative energy sources. In this slowly evolving area of urban energy policy, conservation and solid waste conversion have been emphasized.

The city of Seattle stands as an unusual example of a metropolis that has initiated its own comprehensive energy policy. In 1976 the Seattle City Council decided that its chief municipal utility, Seattle City Light, would not involve itself in nuclear projects; instead, Seattle would try to conserve energy by using less electricity. The community judgment was that nuclear power was too expensive, so Seattle launched a massive energy conservation offensive, directing its fire inspectors to advise businesses and industries on ways to conserve, making aerial photographs available to homeowners to show where they were losing energy, and embarking on an ambitious advertising campaign lambasting energy "hogs" and "power junkies." Seattle's objective is to keep electric demand within the present hydroelectric capabilities of Seattle City Light, since the major cost of power generation to utilities is their investment in new facilities. Seattle's program is showing remarkable success, with savings of 11 percent in its first year attributable to conservation measures.[40]

Perhaps the energy policy most favored by cities is that of converting solid waste to fuel, an option that has been encouraged by the scarcity of sanitary landfill sites and soaring energy and resource prices. Roughly 70 to 80 percent of residential and commercial solid waste can produce energy, and each ton of solid waste has an estimated energy potential of approximately nine million British thermal units. The Council on Environmental Quality has estimated that if all the solid waste in the United States were converted to energy, the energy would equal more than 206 million barrels of oil each year and that this energy equivalency should grow as the population grows.[41] As noted earlier about twenty-five communities across the country already have established resource recovery

40. Grant E. Smith, "Seattle Program to Save Energy Starting to Pay Off," *Arizona Republic*, October 15, 1977.

41. Council on Environmental Quality, *Seventh Annual Report, 1976, op. cit.*, p. 56.

facilities, or at least have put them out for bid; another two dozen have feasibility studies under way.

NUCLEAR POWER AND THE POLITICS OF DISTRUST

If there is an overriding crisis of energy other than the shortage of fossil fuels, it is that of nuclear power.

Turning point: Three Mile Island

In early 1979, this dilemma was brought to a dramatic head when a pump failed at the Three Mile Island nuclear plant near Harrisburg, Pennsylvania. The pump's failure, plus a jammed release valve, caused the reactor's cooling system to overheat, and ultimately produced a bubble of hydrogen gas inside the reactor itself. The actual escape of some radioactive gas plus the risk of a "China syndrome" occurring—that is, of the fuel rods melting and thus causing the radioactive mass to ooze through the reactor's floor—was sufficient to the point that the Governor of Pennsylvania asked children and pregnant women within a five-mile radius of the facility to evacuate the area.

Eventually, the Three Mile Island plant was cooled. But the incident quickly became a symbol of the problem of nuclear power. "No one was killed or injured. . . . Yet, there were casualties from the nuclear reactor accident. . . . Foremost was the loss of public trust in the safety of nuclear power, in the veracity of utility officials, and in the effectiveness of government safeguards." [42]

No to nukes: public resistance to atomic energy

In point of fact, the public has never been especially trustful of the nuclear option. Numerous surveys conducted before the accident at Three Mile Island indicated with some consistency that roughly 40 percent of Americans had concerns about the safety of nuclear energy,[43] and the Three Mile Island episode appears to have nudged many of the formerly "pro-nukes" into an undecided category.

Environmentalists and other citizens have been effective in expressing their distrust of nuclear power. By 1976 twenty-three of thirty-eight reactors that had been approved or announced publicly had been

42. Elaine S. Knapp, "Fallout Begins from Atomic Accident," *State Government News*, 22 (May, 1979), p. 3.
43. Christoph Hohenemser, Roger Kasperson, and Robert Kates, "The Distrust of Nuclear Power," *Science* 196 (April 1, 1977), p. 28.

delayed by public protests, and of the seventy-three reactors under review by the federal Nuclear Regulatory Commission, forty-nine had been delayed. Between 1976 and 1978, because of public resistance to nuclear power, not a single nuclear plant had been ordered to begin construction. Pre-Three Mile Island estimates placed the construction time of a typical nuclear plant from the point of making the decision to build it to finishing construction at no less than a dozen years.[44] In 1977 the nation's first civil disobedience in the antinuclear movement occurred in Seabrook, New Hampshire, when 117 members of the Clamshell Alliance were arrested for sitting in at a nuclear plant construction site.[45]

Public concern over nuclear power plants has been felt most strongly by the grassroots governments. By the mid-1970s no less than twenty-eight states were considering antinuclear initiatives of some kind,[46] and in 1975 Vermont became the first state to require legislative approval prior to the construction of a nuclear power plant.

In 1977 public initiatives calling for a moratorium on nuclear development were defeated in Arizona, California, Colorado, Ohio, Oregon, Montana, and Washington, although similar initiatives concerning moratoria were being prepared in an additional nineteen states.[47] The California initiative was the most widely publicized, and it could have severely restrained nuclear power plant construction until satisfactory waste disposal and safety methods had been assured. After it was defeated by a two-to-one margin by the voters of California, the state legislature enacted three bills that prohibited additional nuclear reactor expansion until certain questions regarding waste disposal and breeder reactors had been answered to the government's satisfaction.[48]

Toward intergovernmental nuclear policy

The interesting aspect of all this anti-nuclear activity at the grassroots is that state and local governments increasingly are demanding greater accountability from the federal government. No doubt this demand will intensify as a partial consequence of Three Mile Island, although the states are in a disadvantageous legal position relative to the U.S. Nuclear Regulatory Commission. In 1971, in the case of *Northern States Power Company* v. *State of Minnesota*, the U.S. Supreme Court struck down the nuclear safety standards developed in Minnesota, which were stricter than those developed by the Atomic Energy Commission (the predecessor

44. Council on Environmental Quality, *Seventh Annual Report*, 1976, *op. cit.*, p. 119.
45. Council on Environmental Quality, *Eighth Annual Report*, 1977, *op. cit.*, pp. 74–75.
46. Council on Environmental Quality, *Seventh Annual Report*, 1976, *op. cit.*, p. 120.
47. Hohenemser, Kasperson, and Kates, *op. cit.*, p. 25.
48. Council on Environmental Quality, *Seventh Annual Report*, 1976 *op. cit.*, p. 120.

of the Nuclear Regulatory Commission), on the grounds that the Atomic Energy Act preempted state control over nuclear facilities. In 1977, however, Congress effectively modified this ruling by writing a proviso into the Clean Air Amendments which stipulates that states can establish and enforce air pollution standards for radiation that are tougher than those by the feds. Since all nuclear plants release some radiation, it is possible that this legislation could terminate future nuclear development.[49]

More pointedly, however, is the concern over nuclear energy that is beginning to be expressed by the nuclear energy industry itself. One difficulty is that nuclear power still is not economically competitive with other energy sources. According to the Atomic Industrial Forum, which is the nuclear industry's chief trade association, atomic power from new plants cost about 20 percent more than power from coal-fired plants in 1976. But more ominously, utilities seemed to be backing away from the atomic alternative even before Three Mile Island, with orders for new nuclear plants decreasing precipitously since 1973. In 1973, American manufacturers took orders for thirty-four nuclear facilities; in 1978, they received two, and foreign manufacturers also were experiencing declines. Consequently, predictions made by the Atomic Energy Commission in 1972 that nuclear power would constitute 12 percent of the national electricity supply by 1975 fell woefully short—coming closer to 9 percent. It follows that the Nuclear Regulatory Commission's projection for 1985 of 33 percent also will fall short.[50]

With the possible exception of a China syndrome occurring, the problem of how to dispose of obviously dangerous radioactive waste generated by nuclear power plants is perhaps the aspect of the nuclear question that is the most worrisome to the public at large. Wastes from both commercial and government nuclear facilities, which are stored in major federal installations in Idaho, South Carolina, and Washington, constitute a significant potential hazard to the environment. The duration of this hazard depends on the type of nuclear waste. Plutonium, for example, has a half-life of no less than 25,000 years (a half-life is the time required for a given amount of any element to disintegrate into one-half of its original quantity), and physicists now recognize that radioactive wastes must be stored for many half-lives before they become harmless. One federal study concluded that as many as twenty-three nuclear power plants may have to close unless new storage sites for radioactive materials are found, and the Department of Energy is evaluating potential nuclear waste burial sites in thirty-six states. By the end of 1977 there were 3,400 metric tons of spent nuclear fuel in storage (a

49. Knapp, *op. cit.*, p. 9.
50. Barry Commoner, "Reflections: The Solar Transition—I," *The New Yorker* (April 23, 1979), p. 95.

metric ton equals 2,200 pounds), and the Nuclear Regulatory Commission was projecting that the amount of commercial waste would increase at the rate of 1,000 metric tons each year.[51]

Regardless of how the nation resolves the nuclear dilemma, America's commitment of the 1960s and 1970s to develop its atomic alternative will remain. Figure 15-6 shows the extent of this commitment. With seventy-two nuclear generating stations in operation in 1979, more than 130 planned or under construction, and a number of nuclear processing plants and waste storage sites scattered across the country, that commitment is real—but not irreversible.

THE PROFUNDITY OF GROWTH MANAGEMENT

The deeper implications of growth management have been recognized only belatedly. The fundamental difference between growth administration and other kinds of administration is that we no longer are talking about regulating relations between men, but instead we are attempting to regulate the relations between men and earth. Moreover, and inescapably, we may be confronting the most important public affair of all: humanity's survival. In short, growth management may indeed be something new under the sun.

When one examines the concepts that thinking about growth entails, one is uncomfortably aware that many of these concepts are wholly new—or, at least, apart from the mainstream in their intellectual thrust. In epistemology, specialized and reductionist thinking must yield to synthesizing and holistic thinking. In economics the theory of growth must give way to the prospects of nongrowth (an especially difficult concept for Americans). In ethics the traditional man-to-other-men morality must now include a man-to-other-creatures and a man-to-earth morality as well. And in public administration the implicit belief that mankind is ultimately perfectable has come under a new and refreshingly serious questioning.

Economics presents a particularly good illustration. In the twentieth century most economists have dismissed Thomas Malthus's predictions on the fate of the world as unnecessarily gloomy and have tried to avoid the appellation of being practitioners in the "dismal science." Malthus, son of a Methodist minister, reasoned that man on earth, given time, would be left only the choices of misery or sin: misery, because the earth's people eventually would outnumber its capacity to feed them; or sin, because the only way to avoid misery would be to make love without the intention of having babies. (Since Malthus's time, however, concepts of sin have changed in a number of circles.)

51. J. P. Smith, *Washington Post* (October 24, 1977), syndicated column.

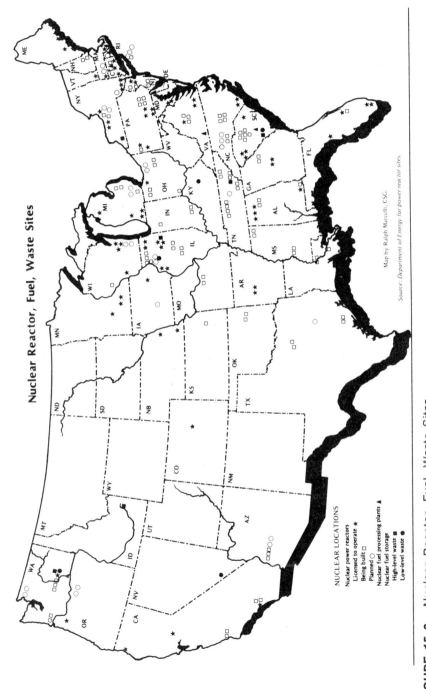

Nuclear Reactor, Fuel, Waste Sites

NUCLEAR LOCATIONS

Nuclear power reactors
Licensed to operate ★
Being built □
Planned ○
Nuclear fuel processing plants ▲
Nuclear fuel storage
High-level waste ■
Low-level waste ●

Map by Ralph Marcelli, CSG.

Source: Department of Energy for power reactor sites.

FIGURE 15-6. Nuclear Reactor, Fuel, Waste Sites.

Source: *State Government News*, May 1979, p. 7.

Modern economists, with some notable exceptions (Kenneth Boulding, John Kenneth Galbraith, Alvin Kneese, and E. J. Mishan, for example), have deemphasized Malthus's basic assumption of a finite earth. Instead, and rather than assuming the opposite hypothesis, that the earth's resources are infinite, they assume that man's capacity (intellectually, politically, and technologically) to deal with the problems of limited resources is infinite. Malthus, of course, did not. He, along with Herbert Simon, thought that man had limited cognitive abilities.

Not only do mainstream economists have different values from "no-growth" economists, but they also have a different operational model of the economic system. As Kenneth Boulding has pointed out, mainstream economists envision a "throughput" system, in which raw materials, manufactured products, and waste are perceived as occurring in a straight line; waste is never viewed as potential "new" raw material. Limited growth economists, on the other hand, use an "input-output" model; materials, products, and waste are seen as a circular system, one that is self-sustaining; a feedback conceptualization replaces a linear conception.[52] These are radically different theoretical perspectives.

Boulding has phrased it particularly well in his notion of a "cowboy economy" versus a "spaceship economy." With the former we can imagine a rodeo rider, laissez-fairing it over the limitless range and winning his bronc-busting prize regardless of consequences. With the latter we envision an astronaut-like strain of human being in a homeostatic state, in control of his environment, his energy, his technology, and his emotions and, above all, vitally concerned about where his garbage goes. Administrators would prefer to manage astronauts rather than cowboys; the question they may have to ask, however, is whether spaceship earth can afford to cater to cowboys.

No-growth economics, also in contrast to mainstream economics, leads to speculation about societies without growth. This is a very new idea. One asks: What kinds of economic patterns would prevail in a society in which "zero population growth" has been achieved? What would be the effects on consumption, for instance? On employment? A former premier of Japan (the most crowded country in the world), for example, urged the modification of his nation's aggressive birth limitation policies on the ground that the national economy would suffer. Former Vice President Spiro T. Agnew classified nongrowth promoters in much the same fashion as he categorized similar "nattering nabobs of negativism," reflecting the sentiments of a large portion of the American population.

The most significant analysis of a nongrowth society has come from the Club of Rome in its study, *The Limits to Growth*. The book is a

52. Kenneth E. Boulding, "The Economics of the Coming Spaceship Earth," in *Environmental Quality in a Growing Economy*, Henry Jarrett, ed. (Baltimore: Johns Hopkins, 1966), pp. 3–14.

literate version of a computer run, in which a number of professors from the Massachusetts Institute of Technology projected the consequences of five variables interacting over time and their combined effects on earth. According to the researchers, the variables—world population, industrialization, pollution, food production, and resource depletion—should result in "a rather sudden and uncontrollable decline in both population and industrial capacity" within the next one hundred years and on a worldwide basis, provided present trends continue.[53] Needless to say, *The Limits to Growth* has been severely criticized by economists and others as naive and simplistic (as well as scary). In the words of the Council on Environmental Quality, the study is "very simplified and does not adequately describe at least two key variables—technological development and price changes. The model, in effect, assumes that the problems grow exponentially while ability to deal with them grows linearly." [54]

The nongrowth advocates, whether right or wrong in their views, have brought up certain questions about the nature of man that are discomfiting to public administrators and public administrationists: If a nongrowth culture is essential to humanity's long-range existence, can man establish it? Is man, as a species, too avaricious and too violent (to his earth as well as to his fellow men) to survive? Does man contain the seeds of his own destruction? Are smoke plumes and oil slicks the fruits of those seeds? Stanley Kubrick began his movie, *2001: A Space Odyssey*, with a scene of missing-link-type apes fighting over a waterhole and the killing of one man-ape by another man-ape. The point is made that death is the essence of *Homo sapiens*, the meaning of meaning for the species. Is this the prophecy to be fulfilled in our age, the age of the "technoscientific superculture"?

CONCLUSION

Energy and the environment are among the most sweeping of issues confronting public administrators in the 1980s. How they make decisions about them will shape the American future. Even more important, how mankind will use public administration—its enormous powers of coercion and persuasion—to preserve and conceivably enhance his place in the universe depends only on man. If, indeed, public administration represents theories of politics, techniques, and ethics applied, then observing the state, its embodied values, how it works, and what makes it work may yield us a glimpse of ourselves and even our meaning.

53. Meadows *et al.*, *op. cit.*, p. 23.
54. Council on Environmental Quality, *Environmental Quality*, Third Annual Report of the Council on Environmental Quality (Washington, D.C.: U.S. Government Printing Office, 1972), p. 53.

SUPPLEMENTAL BIBLIOGRAPHY

ANDERSON, WALT, ed., *Politics and Environment*. Pacific Palisades, Calif.: Goodyear, 1975.

CALDWELL, LYNTON K., ed., "Environmental Policy: New Directions in Federal Action: A Symposium," *Public Administration Review*, 28 (July–August 1968), 301–341.

——, *Environment: A Challenge for Modern Society*. Garden City, N.Y.: Natural History Press, 1970.

——, *Man and His Environment*. New York: Harper & Row, 1975.

COMMONER, BARRY, *Science and Survival*. New York: Viking, 1966.

DAVIS, CLARENCE J., *The Politics of Pollution*. New York: Pegasus, 1970.

DAWSON, FRANK G., *Nuclear Power: Development and Management of a Technology*. Seattle: University of Washington Press, 1976.

EDMUNDS, STAHRL, and JOHN LETEY, *Environmental Administration*. New York: McGraw-Hill, 1973.

ESPOSITO, JOHN C., *The Vanishing Air*. New York: Grossman, 1970.

FOIN, THEODORE JR., *Ecological Systems and the Environment*. Boston: Houghton Mifflin, 1976.

FOSS, PHILLIP O., ed., *Politics and Ecology*. Belmont, Calif.: Duxbury Press, 1972.

GORDON, MORTON, and MARSHA GORDON, eds., *Environmental Management: Science and Politics*. Boston: Allyn & Bacon, 1972.

HASKELL, ELIZABETH H., and VICTORIA S. PRICE, *State Environmental Management: Case Studies of Nine States*, p. 283. New York: Praeger, 1973.

KNEESE, ALLEN V., "Strategies for Environmental Management," *Public Policy*, 19 (Winter 1971), 37–52.

LEIBER, HARVEY, "Public Administration and Environmental Quality Controls," *Public Administration Review*, 30 (May–June 1970), 277–286.

MAKIELSKI, S. J., JR., *The Politics of Zoning: The New York Experience*. New York: Columbia University Press, 1966.

MANDELKER, DANIEL, *The Zoning Dilemma*. Indianapolis: Bobbs-Merrill, 1971.

MCEVOY, JAMES III, *The American Public's Concern with the Environment*. Davis, Calif.: Institute of Government Affairs, University of California, 1971.

MEEK, ROY L., and JOHN A. STRAAYER, *The Politics of Neglect*. Boston: Houghton Mifflin, 1971.

MILES, RUFUS E., *Awakening from the American Dream: The Social and Political Limits to Growth*. New York: Universe Books, 1976.

MUMFORD, LEWIS, *The Urban Prospect*. New York: Harcourt, Brace and World, 1968.

NAGEL, STUART S., ed., *Environmental Politics*. New York: Praeger, 1974.

ROSENBAUM, WALTER A., *The Politics of Environmental Concern* (2d ed.), New York: Praeger, 1977.

SAX, JOSEPH L., *Defending the Environment: A Strategy for Citizen Action*. New York: Knopf, 1971.

APPENDIXES

appendix a

PATH ANALYSIS: AN INTRODUCTION TO BASIC CONCEPTS

In Chapter 6 we noted that path analysis, also known as Performance Evaluation and Review Technique (PERT) or the Critical Path Method (CPM), was worthy of more consideration than space there permitted. In this Appendix we attempt to convey the basics of PERT and CPM in a very simple manner, but one that nonetheless should prove useful in dealing with managerial situations.

Recall from Chapter 6 that a PERT chart is an attempt to clarify the sequence of events and activities of a project for the sake of maximizing coordination and allocating resources and time with the greatest possible efficiency. Hence, we shall begin our review with a definition of what "event" and "activity" mean in the context of PERT.

An *event* in a PERT network is the start or completion of a task. In our PERT chart, events will be represented by a circle. Events do *not* consume resources in any way; they only mark time.

An *activity* indicates the order of events, and is represented by an arrow. Activities consume time, manpower, material, space, effort, facilities, and resources of all kinds. No activity can be completed in a

FIGURE 1

network until the event preceding it has occurred, and no event can be completed until *all* the activities leading to it are completed. Consider the PERT chart in Figure 1.

If we use a cocktail party for our example, Event 1 (*e.g.*, the decision to have a cocktail party) marks the beginning of the project, Activity A indicates the time and money spent to buy glassware and liquor, Event 2 marks the completion of those purchases, Activity B indicates the time and money spent to mail invitations, and Event 3 marks the completion of the project, or the party itself. Incidentally, the numbers and letters identifying the events and activities could be rearranged with no effects on this sequence; it is the *order of the arrows* that matters.

Certain kinds of PERT charts are impossible, given the logical requirements of sequential ordering. Consider the example in Figure 2.

The loop (events 2,3,4,5, and activities B,C,D,E) destroys the PERT network. It is logically impossible; activity F can never get started so that Event 6 may be completed. On the other hand, the network shown in Figure 3 is quite reasonable.

There is no loop. Activity F and Event 6 can be completed. Loops in a PERT network will bring any project to a grinding halt.

With these concepts in mind, we now can turn to the arithmetic of developing time estimates for each activity. This is done by a very simple method: The person most familiar with a particular activity is asked to submit an *optimistic time* (identified by *a*), a *most likely time* (*m*), and a *pessimistic time* (*b*) that he thinks it will take to complete the activity from start to finish. For example:

a = optimistic time, *e.g.*, 12 days (estimate)
m = most likely time, *e.g.*, 18 days (estimate)
b = pessimistic time, *e.g.*, 30 days (estimate)

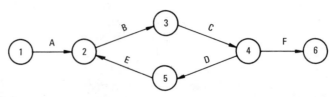

FIGURE 2

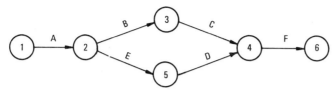

FIGURE 3

Once these estimates are collected, the administrator then must calculate the *average time* that it will take to complete the activity in question. The average time (or t_e, or time estimated) is the average value of the three times $(a, m, \text{ and } b)$, repeated on many occasions. The formula for calculating the average time (t_e) to complete an activity is:

$$t_e = \frac{a + 4m + b}{6}$$

In terms of our previous numerical estimates, this would calculate out as:

$$t_e = \frac{12 + (4 \times 18) + 30}{6} = 19 \text{ days}$$

The wider the separation (*i.e.*, the range of distribution) between the optimistic (a) and pessimistic (b) time estimates, the greater the *uncertainty* that is associated with the activity. This uncertainty is called *variance* (represented by σ^2). The greater the variance, the more uncertain the administrator ought to be about how long it will take to complete the activity. The formula for variance is:

$$\sigma^2 = \left(\frac{b - a}{6}\right)^2$$

Consider the example in Table 1. In it, we are assuming the administrator has two different sets of time estimates, and wants to use the

TABLE 1

Estimate	Optimistic Time (a)	Most Likely Time (m)	Pessimistic Time (b)
I	2 days	4 days	6 days
II	8 days	10 days	11 days

estimate that is the more certain, or precise, according to the standards of PERT.

For estimate I, we would calculate:

$$\sigma^2 = \left(\frac{6-2}{6}\right)^2 = .67^2 = .45$$

For estimate II, we would calculate:

$$\sigma^2 = \left(\frac{11-8}{6}\right)^2 = .50^2 = .25$$

The variance for estimate II (.25) is smaller than for estimate I (.45). Hence, estimate II is more "certain," more "precise," and the administrator likely would use it in his PERT chart.

Once we have decided what average times we want to use for each activity, we then can establish the times that it will take to reach the events in the network. The time that it takes to reach an event is called the *expected time* of completion, and is symbolized by T_E. The expected time (T_E is the earliest possible time that an event can be reached; it is computed by adding together the average times (t_e) for each activity leading to the particular event. Thus:

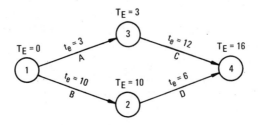

FIGURE 4

As you can see, the expected time (T_E) for completing Event 4 is found by adding the average times (t_e's) of activity B (10 days) and of activity D (6 days). The T_E for Event 4 equals 16 days. You might have noticed that by adding the t_e's of activity A (with a value of 3 days) and activity C (with a value of 12 days), we would end up with 15 days, or 1 day less than the combined B and D activity paths. Of the two figures (15 and 16 days), however, *we must select the larger one for calculating our expected time* (T_E) for Event 4. This is a rule as inflexible as that of avoiding loops in a PERT network, and it goes back to our original statement that "no event can be completed until *all* the activities leading to it are completed." Thus, even though the A–C activity path is finished a day ahead of the B–D activity path, Even 4 must wait the full 16 days before it can be completed. Because of this, the B–D activity path becomes the *critical path* in our simple, two-path PERT chart.

We could stop this discussion of PERT right now and have the basics of the idea; in fact, not even the notion of variance is essential in terms of comprehending the rudiments of PERT and CPM. Nevertheless, a few more computations are worth noting before we conclude our discussion; they are features of every network analysis, and they also amplify the concept of the critical path.

One such calculation is that of the *latest allowable time* (or T_L) that an event can be completed and still keep the project on schedule. The latest allowable time is derived from a "given," which is the previously-established *contractual obligation date*, symbolized by T_S (and which, presumably, stands for time scheduled, although T_S may represent a Freudian slip). Only Event 4 would have a T_S calculation, because it is the "end event" of the network—it represents the termination of the project. Thus, let us say:

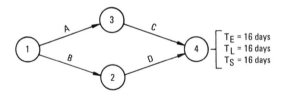

FIGURE 5

In Figure 5, our expected time to complete the project (T_E) is 16 days, our latest allowable time to complete the project (T_L) is 16 days, and our contractual obligation date to complete the project (T_S) is 16 days. If, on the other hand, our expected time of completion was, say, 10 days, that would indicate cheating (or, at least, a very favorable arrangement) on our part because presumably we would be getting paid for a 16-day contract. Obversely, if our expected time was 20 days, we would be cheating ourselves, because we still would be getting paid for only 16 days. In both instances, the latest allowable time for Event 4 remains the same because it is determined by the critical path (activities B and D).

For the other events (Events 2 and 3), the latest allowable times $(T_L$'s) are computed in exactly the opposite fashion from the way that we computed the expected times $(T_E$'s). That is, we start from the last event (Event 4) and work back toward the first event by subtracting the values of the estimated activity times (t_e's) from the values of the latest allowable times (T_L's) of the successor events; if more than one T_L is obtained, the smallest value always is selected. Thus we have the situation shown in Figure 6.

As you can see, the T_L of Event 3 (which is 4 days) is found by subtracting the t_e of activity C (which has a value of 12 days) from the T_L of Event 4 (which has a value of 16 days). Likewise, the T_L of Event 2 (which is 10 days) is found by subtracting the t_e of activity D (which has a value of 6 days) from the T_L of Event 4 (which has a value of 16 days).

This brings us to the notion of *slack*. Just like the concept of slack in organization theory, slack in a PERT network refers to the "looseness" of the system or, more specifically in terms of PERT, "the period of grace" that the administrator has in which to complete his project. As a computation, the slack of an event is found by subtracting the expected time (T_E) from the latest allowable time (T_L); thus: Slack $= T_L - T_E$. In our very simple network, Events 1, 2, and 4 have "zero slack," or no period of grace; in each case, $T_L - T_E = 0$. But Event 2 has a slack time of 1 day. As Figure 7 indicates, the T_E of Event 3 (3 days) subtracted from the T_L of Event 3 (4 days) equals 1 day. The slack time for Event 3 is 1 day of "positive slack." That means if activity A falls behind schedule for 1 day, Event 3 can still be completed "on time"—that is, the delay will not hold up the completion of the entire project. "Negative slack" also is a possibility. Negative slack occurs when the value of the expected time (T_E) of an event exceeds the value of the latest allowable time (T_L) of the event. *Negative slack* indicates that your project is suffering from a lack of adequate resources or is behind schedule; *positive slack* means your project has too many resources or is ahead of schedule; *zero slack* shows that your project has precisely enough resources, is on schedule, and is operating with optimal efficiency.

The less the slack (*i.e.*, the more negative the slack) in an activity path, the more *critical* that path becomes. Thus the concept of *critical*

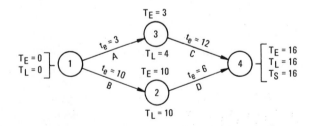

FIGURE 6

path which was mentioned briefly earlier, reemerges. We are now ready to express the critical path idea in more formal terms: the *critical path in a PERT network is the path of minimum slack.* In our example, activities B and D represent the critical path because each event on that path has zero slack, while the A–C activity path has a positive slack of 1 day (Event 3).

As can be seen in Figure 7, the critical path requires the most time to get from the initial event (Event 1) to the final event (Event 4). Any event on the critical path that slips in time or resources will cause the final event to slip in time or resources by the same amount. This is not the situation with the other path, and it is for that reason the critical path is just that—critical.

For the sake of brevity we can conclude our review of PERT and CPM here. (We have not, incidentally, considered the mathematics of ascertaining the probability of attaining "strategic events," *i.e.*, the events along the critical path, but such a review may be foregone without undue sacrifice.) Note, however, that, at root, all the arithmetic we have reviewed rests on out-of-the-hat estimates—nothing more. While PERT is a very valuable tool for clarifying interdependencies in a system and allocating resources accordingly, it nonetheless rests on some fellow out in the field scratching his head and taking a shot at how long it might take and how much it might cost to complete some activity. If our fellow in the field knows what he is doing, those optimistic, most likely, and pessimistic estimates may be superbly accurate; if he does not and must rely on "guesstimates," no amount of algebra is going to help. While PERT may succeed in making those initial estimates look very impressive and

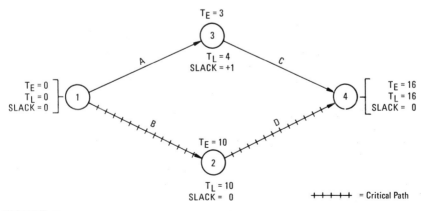

FIGURE 7

scientific to the uninitiated, all the projections of PERT go back to some people making guesses. At best, those guesses may be educated and based on experience; at worst, they may be fabricated from thin air. While PERT can be extremely useful to the public administrator, its foundation of guesswork should never be obscured by its superstructure of techniques.

appendix b

TOWARD SPEEDIER RESEARCH:
INFORMATION SERVICES AND BIBLIOGRAPHIES
IN PUBLIC ADMINISTRATION AND RELATED FIELDS

The following list identifies and describes seventy-eight information services and bibliographies (annotated bibliographies, for the most part) in public administration and related fields. These sources are extremely useful to the researcher in public administration. Learning how to use them will not only reduce the researcher's library time by a considerable number of hours, but it will most likely result in more comprehensive and improved research.

Most older bibliographies (pre-1960) have been omitted, as have bibliographies found in standard public administration textbooks. The sources are arranged alphabetically according to ten subject areas. Although subject areas overlap in many instances, they should provide helpful initial guidelines.

The subject areas are:

1. Sources Relating Directly to Public Administration and Public Affairs

2. Sources Relating to Specialized Areas of Public Administration: Comparative Administration, Development Administration, Human Resources Management, Intergovernmental Relations, Personnel Administration, and Science Policy
3. Sources Relating to Political Science and Government
4. Sources Relating to Management Science and Organization Theory
5. Sources Relating to Other Fields Bearing on Public Administration: Economics, Law, Psychology, Sociology, and the General Behavioral Sciences and Humanities
6. Sources Relating to U.S. Government Publications and the Organization of the Federal Government
7. Sources Relating to the American States
8. Sources Relating to Urban and Metropolitan Affairs
9. General Information Sources of Potential Usefulness
10. Miscellaneous Sources: Careers and Grants

1. Sources Relating Directly to Public Administration and Public Affairs

Administration: A Select Bibliography. London: Ministry of Overseas Development, 1967. ———, *Supplement,* 1968–. A bibliography of general, comparative, national, and special studies dealing with government administration, planning, development, etc. Also lists periodicals and bibliographies dealing with public administration matters. No annotations.

Mars, David, *Suggested Library in Public Administration.* Los Angeles: School of Public Administration, University of Southern California, 1962. ———, *Supplement,* 1964. Lists over 2,300 publications. No annotations.

McCurdy, Howard E., *Public Administration: A Bibliography.* Washington, D.C.: College of Public Affairs, American University, 1973. A thousand books are listed, and each book is rated according to the frequency with which it is cited by forty representative scholars in the field. Annotations accompany the 200 most frequently cited books.

Public Administration Abstracts and Index of Articles. New Delhi: Indian Institute of Public Administration, 1957–. Indexes articles from a few selected journals relating to public administration. Issued monthly without cumulations. The coverage is limited, but still useful for long abstracts of major articles and some emphasis on administration in developing areas.

Public Administration Service, *The Administration of a Public Affairs Library: A Report on the Joint Reference Library Collection.* Chicago: Public Administration Service, 1970. Lists more than 500 periodicals and 200 references in public affairs by title, author, publisher, and price.

Public Affairs Information Service Index. New York: Public Affairs Information Service, 1915–. This index, with annual cumulations, unifies a wide variety of sources concerned with public affairs. It lists books, pamphlets, periodicals, and government documents. Most articles include brief explanatory items.

Public Policy: A Yearbook of the Graduate School of Public Administration, Harvard University. Cambridge: Harvard Univ. Press, 1940–. Each volume contains several essays on various subjects, emphasizing public administration.

Publications on Governmental Problems. Chicago: Joint Reference Library of the Public Administration Service, 1932–. A semi-monthly publication listing all material received by the Joint Reference Library. More than 5500 publications are listed annually.

Sage Public Administration Abstracts. Beverly Hills, Calif.: Sage, 1974–. A quarterly publication that lists and abstracts more than 1000 publications in the field annually. Abstracts are indexed by author, title, and subject, and a year-end cumulative index is published.

Universal Reference System. Edited by Alfred De Grazia. New York: Metron, Inc., 1967–. A superb series of computer-produced bibliography-indexes covering ten sub-fields of political science. URS publishes basic bibliographical volumes, called Codexes, which cover the significant literature —including periodical articles, books, and documents—of each sub-field. The Codexes are supplemented by "Quarterly Gazettes" bringing coverage up-to-date, with an annual cumulation for each gazette at the end of the year. The Universal Reference System issues Codexes and "Quarterly Gazettes" in the following subject areas (asterisks indicate those volumes of particular interest to public administrationists):

International Affairs

Legislative Process, Deliberation, and Decision Making

*Administrative Management: Public and Private Bureaucracy

*Current Events and Problems of Modern Society

Public Opinion, Mass Behavior and Political Psychology

Law, Jurisprudence, and Judicial Process

*Economic Regulation, Business, and Government

*Public Policy and the Management of Science

*Comparative Government and Cultures

Bibliography of Bibliographies in Political Science, Government and Public Policy

Volume 4 of the Universal Reference System (*Administrative Management*) is an annotated list of 2407 publications which are intensely indexed. The volume identifies 358 unannotated bibliographies and 182 annotated bibliographies relating to public or private management. Other descriptors provide access to works dealing at least in part with intergroup relations, relations between governments, budgeting and fiscal planning, international organizations, labor unions, planning, individuals holding executive positions, participation in decision-making, etc.

2. Sources Relating to Specialized Areas of Public Administration: Comparative Administration, Development Administration, Human Relations, Personnel Administration, and Science Policy

BICKER, WILLIAM, et al., *Comparative Urban Development: An Annotated Bibliography.* Washington, D.C.: Comparative Administration Group,

American Society for Public Administration, 1965. An annotated bibliography of over 600 books and articles published since 1950.

CALDWELL, LYNTON K., *et al.*, *Science, Technology, and Public Policy: A Selected and Annotated Bibliography*. Bloomington, Ill.: Department of Government, Indiana University, 1968–1970, Vols. I and II. A superb set on science and public policy. Volume I abstracts whole issues of journals, books, and government documents; Volume II treats journal articles from 1945. The works were sponsored by the National Science Foundation and consider computer science, environmental management, and related topics. Both volumes are updated intermittently to include more recent works.

HEADY, FERREL, and SYBIL STOKES, *Comparative Public Administration: A Selective Annotated Bibliography* (2nd ed.), Ann Arbor, Mich.: Institute of Public Administration, University of Michigan, 1960. Lists and annotates over 900 books and articles relating to comparative administration.

Michigan Index to Labor Union Periodicals. Ann Arbor, Mich.: Bureau of Industrial Relations, Graduate School of Business Administration, University of Michigan, 1960–. Covers about 50 publications and issued monthly with annual cumulations.

PEGNETTER, RICHARD, *Public Employment Bibliography*. Ithaca, N.Y.: New York State School of Industrial and Labor Relations, Cornell University, 1971. A useful general guide.

Poverty and Human Resources Abstracts. Ann Arbor, Mich.: Institute of Labor and Industrial Relations, University of Michigan and Wayne State University, 1966–. A bimonthly journal containing long abstracts of articles, books, reports, congressional publications and other materials on economic, political, and social conditions of the poor.

SPITZ, ALAN A., *Developmental Change: An Annotated Bibliography*. Lexington, Ky.: University of Kentucky Press, 1969. An updated version of the *Development Administration* bibliography by Spitz and Weidner.

SPITZ, ALAN, and EDWARD W. WEIDNER, *Development Administration: An Annotated Bibliography*. Honolulu: East-West Center Press, 1963. Annotated listing of about 300 articles relating to administration in developing areas published between 1945 and 1960.

U.S. Civil Service Commission Library, A *Bibliography of Public Personnel Administration Literature*. Washington, D.C.: Civil Service Commission, 1949–. An exhaustive bibliography of books, articles, documents, etc., on all aspects of public personnel administration. A basic volume was published in 1949, and eight supplements were issued covering materials up through 1958. Since then, the bibliography can be supplemented through *Personnel Literature*.

U.S. Office of Personnel Management Library, *Personnel Bibliography Series*. Washington, D.C.: U.S. Government Printing Office, 1970. A comprehensive annotated listing of books and articles on themes of relevance to public personnel administration. Each issue concerns a particular theme, such as "Scientists and Engineers in the Federal Government," or "Managing Human Behavior." Although the series began earlier, only titles beginning in 1970 are presently available.

U.S. Office of Personnel Management Library, *Personnel Literature*. Washington, D.C.: U.S. Civil Service Commission, 1958–. A monthly annotated listing of a wide range of public personnel materials.

U.S. Department of Agriculture, Economic Research Service, *A Selected Bibliography on Interlocal Governmental Cooperation.* Washington, D.C.: Department of Agriculture, 1964. Annotated listing of articles and documents on relations among local governments, stressing rural areas.

3. Sources Relating to Political Science and Government

ABC POL SCI: Advance Bibliography of Contents: Political Science and Government. Santa Barbara, Calif.: American Bibliographical Center-Clio Press, 1969–. Published eight times a year, it reproduces the tables of contents of about 260 journals in political science, public administration, law, and related fields. An annual subject index and an author index appear in each issue and are cumulated twice a year. An article copying service is available to subscribers.

Brock, Clifton, *The Literature of Political Science: A Guide for Students, Librarians and Teachers.* New York: R. R. Bowker, 1969. An excellent volume that functions as a bibliography of bibliographies of political science. There is a chapter on "Public Administration, State and Local Government."

CQ Guide to Current American Government. Washington, D.C.: Congressional Quarterly Service, 1963–. Issued twice a year as an "up-to-date handbook for the study of American government." Contains material that appears in the *Congressional Quarterly Weekly Report,* "rearranged and rewritten for classes and study use."

Holler, Frederick L., *The Information Sources of Political Science.* Santa Barbara, Calif.: American Bibliographical Center-Clio Press, 1971. A useful compendium covering information sources in the discipline by subfield and by type of source (*e.g.,* guidebooks, dictionaries, book review indices, etc.). Chapter IX is devoted to public administration.

International Bibliography of Political Science. Paris: UNESCO, 1954–. This reference is published annually by the International Committee for Social Sciences Documentation under the auspices of the International Political Science Association.

International Political Science Abstracts. Oxford: Basil Blackwell, 1951–. Prepared quarterly, each volume contains about 350 abstracts, including 150 abstracted journals. In the first volume, a very broad subject group is arranged with an author and subject index. Subsequently, the arrangement is alphabetical by author, with cumulated subject and author indexes in the fourth issue of each year.

Wynar, Lubomyr R., *Guide to Reference Materials in Political Science.* Rochester, N.Y.: Libraries Unlimited, 1968. Consists of two volumes of an extensively annotated guide to bibliographies.

4. Sources Relating to Management Science and Organization Theory

Business Periodical Index. New York: H. W. Wilson, 1958–. A subject index to articles in about 170 business periodicals. Published monthly, cumulated quarterly and annually. The *Industrial Arts Index* provides index coverage of business periodicals from 1913 to 1957.

Current Contents: Behavioral, Social and Management Sciences. Philadelphia: Institute for Scientific Information, 1969–. Published weekly, reproduces the tables of contents to about 700 journals in various social science disciplines, along with an author index and article copying service.

Eisenstadt, S. N., "Bureaucracy and Bureaucratization: A Trend Report and Bibliography," *Current Sociology*, 7, No. 2 (1958). Contains long articles analyzing bureaucracies, plus an annotated bibliography of over 600 books and articles.

International Review of Administrative Science (Revue Internationale des Sciences Administratives). Brussels: Institut Internationale des Sciences Administratives, 1928–. Each quarterly issue has a "Bibliographical Section," which contains abstracts of recent books on administration, plus a list of periodical articles.

Jones, G. N., and R. N. Giordano. *Planned Organizational Change: A Working Bibliography.* Los Angeles: School of Public Administration, University of Southern California, 1964. A short bibliography on early works in organization development.

Management Research. Amherst, Mass.: University of Massachusetts School of Business Administration, 1968–. An annotated bibliography of considerable use, covering periodical articles dealing with administration, organization, social responsibilities, personnel policy, manpower planning, personnel testing and selection, motivation and performance, human behavior, human resources development, etc. Also contains a list of new books and editorial notes about periodical publications. Issued monthly.

Mayntz, Renate. "The Study of Organizations: A Trend Report and Bibliography," *Current Sociology*, 13, No. 3 (1965). Analyzes large-scale organizations, with an annotated bibliography of over 500 articles and books. Has section on administrative organizations.

Wasserman, Paul., *Decision-Making: An Annotated Bibliography.* Ithaca, N.Y.: Graduate School of Business and Public Administration, Cornell University, 1958. Bibliography of major books and articles, stressing business decision making. A *Supplement* has been issued covering the period 1958–1963.

5. Sources Relating to Other Fields Bearing on Public Administration: Economics, Law, Psychology, Sociology, and the General Behavioral Sciences and Humanities

ABS Guide to Recent Publications in the Social and Behavioral Sciences. Beverly Hills, Calif.: Sage Publications, 1965–. This is a cumulation of abstracts appearing in the "New Studies" section of the *American Behavioral Scientist.* The first volume contains the abstracts that appeared from 1957 through 1964. Annual cumulative volumes have been issued since 1966. The abstracts are listed alphabetically by author, with a subject and methodological index.

American Behavioral Scientist. Beverly Hills, Calif.: Sage Publications, 1957–. Each monthly issue of *ABS* contains an insertion section entitled "New Studies: A Guide to Recent Publications in the Social and Behavioral Sciences." This consists of brief abstracts of articles selected from over 300 journals, plus significant new books.

Index to Legal Periodicals. New York: H. W. Wilson, 1908–. A subject index to articles in over 250 legal journals. Covers all the law reviews.

Journal of Economic Abstracts. Chicago: American Economic Association, 1963–. A quarterly journal containing lengthy abstracts of articles in the major economic periodicals, both English and foreign. Supplemented by a five-volume *Index of Economic Journals* (Homewood, Ill.: Irwin, 1961–62) which indexes, but does not abstract, economic articles published from 1886 to 1963.

Psychological Abstracts. Washington, D.C.: American Psychological Association, 1927–. Covers all the significant literature of psychology, carrying over 15,000 abstracts of articles, books, and reports per year. Its coverage of the literature of social psychology is most relevant. Published monthly, with author and subject indices in each issue which are cumulated annually. A cumulative subject index covering the years 1927–1960, as well as cumulated author indices covering 1927–1963, have been published by the G. K. Hall Co.

Reference Books in the Social Sciences and Humanities (2nd ed.), Rolland E. Stevens, ed. Champaign, Ill.: Illinois Union Bookstore, 1968. Offers an annotated list of reference materials on a number of topics, including public administration.

Sills, David, ed., *International Encyclopedia of the Social Sciences*, 15 vols. New York: Macmillan and Free Press, 1968. This work supplements the old *Encyclopedia of the Social Sciences*, published in the early 1930s. A synthesis and summary of the "state of the art" in all the social sciences. Consisting of original articles contributed by leading social scientists, it covers the disciplines of Anthropology, Economics, Geography, History, Law, Political Science, Psychiatry, Psychology, Sociology, and Statistics. There are a number of articles on organization theory, administrative science, and one on public administration by Dwight Waldo.

Social Sciences and Humanities Index. New York: H. W. Wilson, 1907–. A subject and author index to over 200 major scholarly journals in the social sciences and humanities. Published quarterly, with two-year and five-year cumulations. Until 1965, its title was *International Index.*

Sociological Abstracts. New York: Sociological Abstracts, Inc., 1952–. Carries about 3,300 abstracts per year of articles and books in sociology, and covers all the major sociological journals. Abstracts are classified into 21 subject sections, with subclassifications. Particularly useful for its coverage of the literature of bureaucracy. Published eight times a year, with an author index in each issue and an annual cumulative author and subject index.

White, Carl M., et al., eds., *Sources of Information in the Social Sciences: A Guide to the Literature* (2nd ed.), Chicago: American Library Association, 1973. Besides general reference works, this source offers a separate treatment of history, economics, business administration, sociology, anthropology, psychology, education, and political science. Each chapter has an introduction, important studies, bibliographies, and data sources. The volume is designed for an interdisciplinary and behavioral approach to the social sciences. The first edition was published in 1964.

6. Sources Relating to U.S. Government Publications and the Organization of the Federal Government

Directory of Information Resources in the United States. The National Referral Center for Science and Technology of the Library of Congress, Washington, D.C.: U.S. Government Printing Office. Published irregularly. This directory contains material available to the public on request only, and when the supply is exhausted it is unobtainable. Supplies a strong list of most federal and federally sponsored agencies and describes their activities and the types of data available from each. Most of the material comes in the form of printed government documents and in typewritten and mimeographed reports. Two volumes are particularly helpful to the public administration student: *Social Sciences,* 1965, and *Federal Government,* 1967

Federal Register. Washington, D.C.: U.S. Government Printing Office, 1936–. A daily compilation of executive orders, administrative regulations, and decrees emanating from executive agencies. Has monthly, quarterly, and annual indices, which are cumulative.

JACKSON, ELLEN, *Subject Guide to Major Government Publications.* Chicago: American Library Association, 1968. Gives an annotated bibliography of key government documents on general topics, as well as suggested cross-references.

Praeger Library of U.S. Government Departments and Agencies. New York: Praeger, 1967–. A series of books on federal departments and agencies. Each volume analyzes and describes in detail one bureau.

SCHMECKEBIER, LAURENCE F., and ROY B. EASTIN, *Government Publications and Their Use* (2nd rev. ed.), Washington, D.C.: Brookings Institution, 1969. An excellent guide that describes the basic guides to government publications, indicates the uses and limitations of available indices, catalogs, and bibliographies, explains the systems of numbering, notes outstanding compilations or series, and directs the student in the various ways of obtaining the publications.

Selected United States Government Publications. Washington, D.C.: U.S. Government Printing Office, 1928–. A monthly list of the thousands of pamphlets, books, and periodicals published by the Government Printing Office. One may place one's name on the free mailing list by sending name and address to: Superintendent of Documents, United States Government Printing Office, Washington, D.C. 20402. The order form is attached to the lists.

United States Government Organization Manual. Washington, D.C.: U.S. Government Printing Office, 1935–. The "official organization handbook of the Federal Government," published annually. Has descriptive sections on all government agencies, including statement of purpose or authority and lists of key officials. Includes organization charts and appendices listing abolished or transferred agencies and the major publications of the various agencies. A valuable source.

United States Government Publications: Monthly Catalog. Washington, D.C.: U.S. Government Printing Office, 1895–. Since 1940, this has been the only general list of federal documents. Issued monthly, it lists all publications received by the U.S. Documents Office during the previous month. Documents are listed under the government departments and agencies responsible for their publication, with complete bibliographical information given for each document.

U.S. Bureau of the Budget. *Statistical Services of the United States Government* (rev. ed.), Washington, D.C.: U.S. Government Printing Office, 1968. This describes the statistical program of the government, with a list and description of the major statistical publications of federal agencies.

U.S. Department of Commerce. Clearinghouse for Federal Scientific and Technical Information, *U.S. Government Research and Development Reports*. Washington, D.C.: U.S Government Printing Office, 1946–. All nonclassified Research and Development reports of the federal government are listed and abstracted on a semi-monthly basis under twenty-one subject fields. Field 5 concerns "Behavioral and Social Sciences" and emphasizes public administration.

WISDOM, DONALD, and WILLIAM P. KILROY, *Popular Names of U.S. Government Reports*. Washington, D.C.: Library of Congress, 1966. While many significant reports are popularly known by the names of the responsible officials, their name is seldom part of the official titles. This guide leads you to the exact citation when all you have to work on is something such as "The Ash Report."

7. Sources Relating to the American States

Book of the States. Chicago: Council of State Governments, 1935–. Published biennially and "designed to provide an authoritative source of information on the structures, working methods, financing and functional activities of the state governments." Has sections on "Administrative Organization," "Finance," "Intergovernmental Relations," and "Major State Services." Contains descriptive and statistical data. Two supplements are issued, one a directory of "State Elective Officials and Legislatures," the other a directory of "Administrative Officials Classified by Functions."

Monthly Checklist of State Publications. Washington, D.C.: U.S. Government Printing Office, 1910–. There is no complete list of all state documents, but this is the most extensive listing available. About 20,000 publications are listed each year, arranged alphabetically by state, with an annual index. Publications issued by regional organizations and associations of state officials are listed in a special edition.

U.S. Bureau of the Census. *Directory of Federal Statistics for States: A Guide to Sources*. Washington, D.C.: U.S. Government Printing Office, 1967. A subject listing of sources containing data on the state level.

8. Sources Relating to Urban and Metropolitan Affairs

BOOTH, DAVID A., *Council-Manager Government, 1940–1964: An Annotated Bibliography*. Chicago: International City Managers' Association, 1965. Annotated listing of books and articles on the council-manager plan published since 1940.

County Yearbook. Washington, D.C.: International City Management Association and National Association of Counties, 1975–. A useful counterpart to the *Municipal Yearbook*. Valuable, original research on county problems and government.

HALASZ, D., *Metropolis: A Select Bibliography of Administrative and Other Problems in Metropolitan Areas Throughout the World*. The Hague: Nijhoff, 1967. Publications dealing with administrative problems in metropolitan areas throughout the world, with the exception of the U.S. and Canada, are listed under a geographical arrangement.

Metropolitan Area Annual. Albany: Graduate School of Public Affairs, State University of New York at Albany, 1966–. An annual reference volume with section entitled "Metropolitan Area Bibliography," which lists recent books, articles, and pamphlets, plus a "Metropolitan Surveys" section listing studies in progress or recently completed on metropolitan problems.

Metropolitan Area Problems: News and Digest. New York: Conference on Metropolitan Area Problems, 1957–. Each bimonthly issue has a section entitled "Recent Publications on Metropolitan Area Problems," which contains a selective listing of books and articles.

Municipal Yearbook. Washington, D.C.: International City Management Association, 1934–. Provides "information on current activities and practices of cities throughout the United States." Contains extensive data on Governmental Units, Personnel, Finance, and Municipal Activities. Includes directories of city officials. Has bibliographical sections that refer to additional sources.

Public Administration Service, *Metropolitan Communities: A Bibliography with Special Emphasis upon Government and Politics*. Chicago: Public Administration Service, 1956–1970. A series of five volumes covering more than 20,000 publications on urban government.

Urban Affairs Annual Reviews. Beverly Hills, Calif.: Sage Publications, 1967–. A series of "annual reference volumes designed to present critical analyses" in various fields of urban studies.

U.S. Bureau of the Census, *County and City Data Book*. Washington, D.C.: U.S. Government Printing Office, 1949–. Contains selected statistical series, based on census data, for each county in the U.S., Standard Metropolitan Statistical Areas, and cities with more than 25,000 population. More than 140 items are presented for each unit.

U.S. Bureau of the Census, *Directory of Federal Statistics for Local Areas*. Washington, D.C.: U.S. Government Printing Office, 1966. A guide to sources of federal statistics for metropolitan areas, counties, and urban areas.

U.S. Senate Committee on Government Operations. *Metropolitan America: A Selected Bibliography*. Washington, D.C.: U.S. Government Printing Office, 1964. Annotated listing of the most significant literature on metropolises.

9. General Information Sources of Potential Usefulness

Bibliographic Index. New York: Wilson, 1937–. A subject index to separately published bibliographies as well as bibliographies included in books and periodicals.

Dissertation Abstracts. Ann Arbor, Mich.: University Microfilms, 1952–. A monthly compilation of abstracts of doctoral dissertations completed in about 160 universities. Covers all subject fields, but has a section on "Political Science" with a subsection on "Public Administration." For each dissertation listed, there is a 300–400 word abstract. The dissertations themselves may be purchased from University Microfilms, either in photocopy or microfilm. Each issue of Dissertation Abstracts has a subject and author index that is cumulated annually. University Microfilms has a computer-based search called DATRIX, through which an individual can request a "keyword" search of all dissertations listed in Dissertation Abstracts.

Masters Abstracts: A Catalog of Selected Masters Theses on Microfilm. Ann Arbor, Mich.: University Microfilms, 1962–. A highly selective listing of masters theses, with abstracts, available from University Microfilms. Issued quarterly, with a cumulative subject and author index.

WINCHELL, CONSTANCE M., ed., *Guide to Reference Books* (8th ed.), Chicago: American Library Association, 1967. Divides 7,500 titles into five categories: general reference works; humanities; social sciences; history and area studies; and pure and applied sciences.

10. Miscellaneous Sources: Careers and Grants

BRIER, DONALD E., *A Guide to Federal Internships for Students.* Washington, D.C.: National Institute of Public Management, 1978. A useful guide.

Directory: Programs in Public Affairs and Administration. Washington, D.C.: National Association of Schools of Public Affairs and Administration, 1972–. Published biennially, the *Directory* is a rich information resource on graduate programs in public administration in the United States and Canada.

Federal Career Directory: A Guide for College Students. United States Office of Personnel Management. Washington, D.C.: U.S. Government Printing Office, 1956–. This is one of several guides to federal employment. The OPM's regional offices also publish separate local guides.

Grant Data Quarterly. Los Angeles: Academic Media, Inc., 1967–. "A journal devoted to the collection and dissemination of grant information and opportunities." Four issues, with each revised once a year: I. Selected Overview of Grant Support; II. Government Support Programs; III. Business and Professional Organization Support Programs; IV. Foundation Support Programs. Each issue has a section on political science.

Policy Grants Directory. Urbana: Policy Studies Organization, 1977. Describes public and private funding sources for policy studies research.

Policy Studies Directory (2nd ed.). Urbana: Policy Studies Organization, 1976. An inventory of university-based policy studies units.

appendix c

The following list identifies and describes 90 journals that are particularly germane to public administration on a general level. That is, it encompasses such areas as public policy analysis, public personnel administration, budgeting, and so forth, but does not delve deeply into those journals identified with fields of tangential relevance to public administration, such as political science, economics, and sociology.

There are a number of new journals bearing on public administration that, while worthwhile, are not well known. These have been included, as have foreign journals published in the English language.

Academy of Management Journal. A high-quality publication on general management with a mathematical and behavioral orientation.

Administration. Devoted to Irish administration with an occasional article on Western European administration.

Administration & Society. Formerly the *Journal of Comparative Administration,* its articles are still reflective of the comparative public administration school.

Administration Management. A quantitatively directed journal with an operations research emphasis.

Administrative Science Quarterly. Perhaps the foremost journal in administrative theory and in organizational theory of special relevance to public administration.

Advanced Management. Originally a scientific management journal, it has been steadily broadening its scope in recent years.

American Journal of Public Health. Concerns policy and administration aspects of public health in the U.S.

American Journal of Sociology. Publishes occasional articles relevant to public administration theory and public policy. Excellent book-review section.

American Political Science Review. Occasional articles on public policy making and the political aspects of public organizations. Book reviews on boundary topics.

American Sociological Review. Has articles relevant to administrative behavior, bureaucracy, organization theory, and social issues. Quality book reviews.

Annals of the American Academy of Political and Social Science. Each issue concentrates on a specific area in the social sciences, and produces an extensive book review and notes section covering the social sciences.

Bureaucrat, The. Articles on public administration, usually on a theme for each issue. Regular features include a public policy forum, professional development articles, and humor column.

Business and Society Review/Innovation. A journal that absorbed *Innovation* and began publication in 1972. Published quarterly, it addresses the "role of business in a free society."

California Management Review. A high-quality journal in the style of *Harvard Business Review,* but more data-conscious.

Canadian Public Administration. Devoted to Canadian public administration and comparative analysis.

Chinese Journal of Administration. Devoted to Taiwanese development administration.

Civil Service Journal. Published quarterly by the U.S. Office of Personnel Management. Each issue contains five to eight sections of interest to the civil service and the working public, and sections on legal decisions and legislation. Includes a one- or two-page annotated bibliography of primarily government-published materials on employee training, personnel management, and related topics.

Data Access News. Issued six to eight times a year, this bulletin covers the various statistical bureaus of the federal government.

Economic Development and Cultural Change. Concerns research findings in development.

Environment. The major journal dealing exclusively with environmental science and public policy.

Evaluation. An experimental magazine focusing on program evaluation issues.

Federal Accountant. Concerns public finance and budgeting.

Futures. An international journal of forecasting and planning.

GAO Review. Published quarterly by the U.S General Accounting Office, this is a journal of high-quality focusing on the whole spectrum of accountability in government.

Good Government. A journal very much in the tradition of civil service reform, with articles that reflect that tradition.

Government Finance. A quarterly journal devoted to issues in municipal finance.

Harvard Business Review. Concerns a variety of administrative processes. An outstanding journal of quality.

Human Relations. A behavioral journal of excellent quality, often dealing with organization theory.

Indian Administrative and Management Review. Devoted to administrative aspect of policy and development in India.

Indian Journal of Public Administration. Relates to administration in India, comparative analysis, and development administration.

Industrial and Labor Relations Review. Devoted to industrial relations in both public and private sectors. Substantial book review section.

International Development Review. Published quarterly by the Society for International Development. Short articles devoted to development. Comprehensive book review section. Research notes.

International Journal of Public Administration. A new journal with a comparative bent.

International Organization. Occasional articles on international administration.

International Review of Administrative Sciences. Devoted exclusively to comparative public administration and international administration.

Journal of African Administration. Deals with problems of public administration in Africa.

Journal of Administration Overseas. Concerned with development administration.

Journal of the American Institute of Planners. Devoted to public planning.

Journal of Applied Behavioral Science. Devoted to applied behavioralism and organization development.

Journal of Criminal Law, Criminology and Police Science. Devoted to policy and administration of law enforcement.

Journal of Management Studies. A Scottish journal that concerns applied behavioral theory.

Management Information Service Report. A monthly publication on local government that is practitioner oriented.

Management Review. Monthly publication, first put out by the American Management Association in 1914. Includes survey of books for executives, critical reviews of between 10 and 20 recent works, and a listing of recent publications received from publishers. Books cover topics of labor relations and human relations, arbitration of labor disputes, union-management relations, etc.

Management Science. Oriented to mathematics, systems, and scientific method in administration.

Maxwell Review. A public policy journal with a distinctly philosophic orientation. Each issue covers a theme, such as "Mass Communications."

Midwest Review of Public Administration. A journal dealing with American public administration, often focusing on education issues in public administration.

Minerva. A philosophic journal devoted to the relationships among government, higher education, and science policy.

National Journal. Founded by a group of editors and reporters in 1970 who left *Congressional Quarterly* because they felt it did not pay enough attention to bureaucratic decision making. The journal is published weekly and designed as a monitor of all government actions. It analyzes details surrounding such actions, focussing mainly on the relationships among the various agencies. It also contains in-depth reports on federal programs, biographical information on government officials, and analyses of congressional districts.

New Zealand Journal of Public Administration. Devoted to New Zealand administration.

Organizational Behavior and Human Performance. A high-quality journal focussing on interaction in small groups, conflict resolution, and the social psychology of organizations.

Personnel. Short articles on personnel; published monthly by the American Management Association.

Personnel Administration. Useful for public personnel administration.

Personnel Management. A journal that concerns public personnel administration, often with a comparative orientation.

Philippine Journal of Public Administration. Devoted to Southeast Asia administration, comparative analysis, and development administration.

Policy Sciences. Concerns public policy theory and methodology.

Policy Studies Journal. Generally features overview pieces on public affairs and the policy sciences.

Political Quarterly. Devoted to public policy issues and public administration in England.

Public Administration. Devoted to British administration and comparative analysis. Lists recent British government publications.

Public Administration. Devoted to Australian administration.

Public Administration in Israel and Abroad. Articles on Israeli administration and comparative administration.

Public Administration Newsletter. Published by the Public Administration Division of the United Nations, the newsletter contains occasional articles in development administration, but is devoted principally to reports of field projects conducted by UN officials in developing countries.

Public Administration Review. The most significant American journal concerned with public administration. Review articles are of high quality; research notes are provided.

Public Administration Survey. A bimonthly publication of the Bureau of Governmental Research at the University of Mississippi.

Public Administration Times. A newsletter with employment opportunities.

Public Affairs. A public affairs, public policy journal.

Public Choice. A policy journal with a political economy orientation.

Public Employment Practices Bulletin. Published by the International Personnel Management Association, it is designed as a reference series for public personnel agencies.

Public Finance. Devoted to comparative public finance.

Public Finance Quarterly. A journal emphasizing economic approaches to budgeting in the United States.

Public Management. Short articles devoted to urban administration. Published monthly by the International City Management Association.

Public Personnel Review. Short articles devoted to public personnel administration. Published quarterly by the International Personnel Management Association.

Public Policy. Excellent articles on public policy and public affairs.

Public Interest, The. High quality articles on public policy issues.

Public Welfare. Devoted to policy and administration of public welfare in the United States.

Publius. A journal devoted to intergovernmental relations and federalism.

Research Management. Concerns problems of managing research-and-development units in large organizations.

Revenue Sharing Bulletin. A monthly publication of the Revenue Sharing Advisory Service that provides information and technical aid on federal revenue sharing.

Review of Public Data Use. A quarterly journal designed "to encourage the use of publicly-available data for research or analysis applied to local, regional, or National problems." Representative articles include "American Statistics Index: Key to Government Statistical Data," "The Utilization of Criminal Justice Statistics," "Evaluating Distribution of General Revenue Sharing Funds," and "Use of Census Data as a Management Tool in a Large City."

Sage Professional Papers in Administrative and Policy Studies. Twelve academic papers are published annually in three issues, devoted to the administrative sciences.

Science. The major science journal of the nation; extremely useful for articles and reports on public science policy.

Science Policy. A British-based journal dealing with comparative and international science policy and administration.

Society (formerly *Trans-action*). Applies social science research to contemporary social and public policy problems.

Southern Review of Public Administration. A new journal of good quality.

State Government. Devoted to state government problems in the U.S. Published quarterly by the Council of State Governments.

State Government Administration. Conversational articles that concern public administration in the states.

State Government News. A useful monthly publication that reviews current state legislation and policy. Published by the Council of State Governments.

Student Review. Reflects student thinking in the administrative sciences, both public and private.

Urban Affairs Quarterly. Devoted primarily to sociological and political treatments of urban areas.

Urban Research News. A biweekly newsletter for the urban specialist that "reports on current developments—personnel, meetings, research projects, publications, etc.—at over 200 centers engaged in urban research."

Washington Monthly. A liberal-journalistic publication of high quality. It focusses on the injustices of the public bureaucracy, as well as on policy issues.

Western City. Articles on urban administration in the West; published monthly.

appendix d

The following national groups all have a direct relevance to public administration. Virtually all of them publish journals and newsletters on topics of interest; you may wish to contact some of them for their materials. The organizations, together with a brief description and their addresses, are listed in alphabetical order.

Academy for Contemporary Problems. 1501 Neil Avenue, Columbus, OH 43201. A "think tank" specifically oriented towards state and local governmental problems.

Advisory Commission on Intergovernmental Relations. Washington, DC 20575. Founded in 1959, the ACIR publishes significant studies of the federal system.

American Academy of Political and Social Science. 3937 Chestnut Street, Philadelphia, PA 19104. Publishes the *Annals* of the American Academy of Political and Social Science.

American Association of School Administrators. 1801 North Moore Street, Arlington, VA 22209. The largest association of school managers.

American Association of State Highway and Transportation Officials. 444

North Capitol Street, Washington, DC 20001. The major association of state transit officials.

American Institute of Planners. 1776 Massachusetts Avenue, N.W., Washington, DC 20036. A major association of public planning officials.

American Political Science Association. 1527 New Hampshire Avenue, N.W., Washington, DC 20036. The chief academic association of political scientists.

American Public Welfare Association. 1155 Sixteenth Street, N.W., Washington, DC 20036. The major organization of public welfare officials.

American Society for Public Administration. 1225 Connecticut Avenue, N.W., Washington, DC 20036. The major organization of academics and professionals in public administration at all levels of government.

American Society of Planning Officials. 1313 East Sixtieth Street, Chicago, IL 60637. An important organization of public planning officials.

American Public Transit Association. 1100 Seventeenth Street, Washington, DC 20036. The major association of public officials interested in mass transit.

Brookings Institution. 1775 Massachusetts Avenue, N.W., Washington, DC 20036. A major academic think-tank with important concerns in state and local public affairs.

Center for Community Change. 1000 Wisconsin Avenue, N.W., Washington, DC 20007. Provides technical assistance to communities.

Center for Science in the Public Interest. 1779 Church Street, N.W., Washington, DC 20036. A coalition of scientists interested in the impact of public policy on science and society.

Center for the Study of Democratic Institutions. P.O. Box 4068, Santa Barbara, CA 93103. A high level study group devoted to advancing democratic theory.

Coalition for Human Needs and Budget Priorities. 2030 M Street, N.W., Washington, DC 20036. A liberal coalition designed to change the federal budget for the benefit of human needs.

Committee for Economic Development. 477 Madison Avenue, New York, NY 10022. A private group that studies issues relating to business and public policy.

Common Cause. 2030 M Street, N.W., Washington, DC 20036. An organization of more than 300,000 members dedicated to political reform.

Conference of Minority Public Administrators. 1225 Connecticut Avenue, N.W., Washington, DC 20036. The major national association of minority public administrators.

Congressional Quarterly Service. 1735 K Street, N.W., Washington, DC 20006. Publishers of *Congressional Quarterly* and other publications relating to congressional action.

Council of State Community Affairs Agencies. 1612 K Street, N.W., Washington, DC 20006. The major association of state community affairs officers.

Council of State Governments. Ironworks Pike, P.O. Box 11910, Lexington, KY 40511. Publishers of *The Book of the States* and other publications relating directly to state governments.

Environmental Action, Inc. 1346 Connecticut Avenue, N.W., Washington, DC, 20036. Environmentalists who are interested primarily in solid waste disposal.

Environmental Defense Fund. 1525 Eighteenth Street, N.W., Washington, DC 20036. Environmentalists concerned with toxic substances and noise pollution.

Freedom of Information Center. School of Journalism, University of Missouri, P.O. Box 858, Columbia, MO 65201. Conducts studies on the public's uses of federal, state, and local Freedom of Information Acts.

Institute of Public Administration. 55 W. 44th Street, New York, NY 10036. A public affairs research group.

International Association of Chiefs of Police. 11 First Field Road, Gaithersburg, MD 20760. The major organization of police chiefs.

International City Management Association. 1140 Connecticut Avenue, N.W., Washington, DC 20036. The major organization of city managers and other individuals interested in city management.

International Personnel Management Association. 1313 East Sixtieth Street, Chicago, IL 60637. The major organization of public personnel administrators at all levels of government.

Movement for Economic Justice. 1609 Connecticut Avenue, N.W., Washington, DC 20009. An organization concerned with utility rate increases, real estate practices, and property taxation.

Municipal Finance Officers Association. 1313 East Sixtieth Street, Chicago, IL 60637. The major organization of budgetary and taxation officers in local governments.

National Association for the Advancement of Colored People. 733 Fifteenth Street, N.W., Washington, DC 20005. The most prestigious political organization of blacks.

National Association of Counties. 1735 New York Avenue, N.W., Washington, DC 20036. The major organization of county officials, and publishers of research on county government.

National Association of Housing and Redevelopment Officials. 2600 Virginia Avenue, N.W., Washington, DC 20037. The major association of state and local officials concerned with community development.

National Association of Regional Councils. 1700 K Street, N.W., Washington, DC 20036. The major organization of Councils of Governments and related organizations.

National Conference of State Legislatures. 1405 Curtis Street, Denver, CO 80202. The major association of state legislatures.

National Committee Against Discrimination in Housing. 1425 H Street, N.W., Washington, DC 20005. A national organization dedicated to ending racial discrimination in housing.

National Governors Association (formerly the National Governors Conference). 444 North Capitol Street, Washington, DC 20001. The organization of American governors.

National Institute of Public Management. 1612 K Street, N.W., Washington, DC 2006. A research organization in public administration.

National League of Cities. 1620 Eye Street, N.W., Washington, DC 20006. One of the major associations of urban governments.

National Municipal League. 47 East 68th Street, New York, NY 10021. One of the major associations dedicated to improving urban governments.

National Planning Association. 1606 Connecticut Avenue, N.W., Washington, DC 20009. A major organization of planning officials.

National Welfare Rights Organization. 1420 N Street, N.W., Washington, DC 20005. Works to improve and expand welfare policy.

National Civil Service League. 1825 K Street, N.W., Washington, DC 20006. An organization dedicated to civil service reform.

Public Administration Service. 1313 East Sixtieth Street, Chicago, IL 60637. An organization conducting significant research on public administration questions.

Rand Corporation. 1700 Main Street, Santa Monica, CA 90406. A major think tank concerned in part with public problems.

Tax Foundation, Inc. 50 Rockefeller Plaza, New York, NY 10020. A private association concerned with tax issues.

Urban Environment Conference. 1609 Connecticut Avenue N.W., Washington, DC 20009. Coordinates civil rights groups and labor organizations on land use issues.

Urban Institute. 2100 M Street, N.W., Washington, DC 20037. A research organization devoted to urban issues.

United States Conference of Mayors. 1620 I Street, Washington, DC 20006. The major association of American mayors.

Water Pollution Control Federation. 2626 Pennsylvania Avenue, Washington, DC 20037. A national organization of environmentalists dedicated to control of water pollution.

appendix e

CORRECT FORMS OF ADDRESS FOR PUBLIC OFFICIALS

Information, like money, is one of those things of which there is never enough. When you need information on a public issue that is not publicly available, it often is a good idea to write and ask someone who knows. A correct form of address can add to the effectiveness of your request to a public official, so this final Appendix lists the proper ways of addressing public officials.

Public Official	Form of Address	Salutation
alderman	The Honorable John Green	Dear Mr. Green:
assemblyman	—see *representative, state*	
associate justice, Supreme Court	Mr. Justice Green The Supreme Court of the United States	Dear Mr. Justice:
Cabinet officers (as the Secretary of State *and* the Attorney General)	The Honorable John (or Joan) Green Secretary of State The Honorable John Green Attorney General of the United States	Dear Sir: (*or* Dear Madam:)

Public Official	*Form of Address*	*Salutation*
chief justice, Supreme Court	The Chief Justice of the United States	Dear Mr. Chief Justice:
commissioner	The Honorable John Green	Dear Mr. Green:
councilmember	The Honorable John Green	Dear Mr. Green:
former U.S. president	The Honorable John Green	Dear Mr. Green:
governor	The Honorable John Green Governor of—	Dear Governor Green:
judge, federal	The Honorable John Green United States District Judge	Dear Judge Green:
judge, state or local	The Honorable John Green Chief Judge of the Court of Appeals	Dear Judge Green:
lieutenant governor	The Honorable John Green Lieutenant Governor of—	Dear Mr. Green:
mayor	The Honorable John Green Mayor of—	Dear Mayor Green;
president, U.S.	The President	Dear Mr. President:
representative, state (same format for assemblyman)	The Honorable John Green House of Representatives State Capitol	Dear Mr. Green:
representative, U.S.	The Honorable John Green The United States House of Representatives	Dear Mr. Green:
senator, state	The Honorable John Green The State Senate State Capitol	Dear Senator Green:
senator, U.S.	The Honorable John Green United States Senate	Dear Senator Green:
speaker, U.S. House of Representatives	The Honorable John Green Speaker of the House of Representatives	Dear Mr. Speaker:
vice-president, U.S.	The Vice-President United States Senate	Dear Mr. Vice-President:

Acknowledgements, continued

work. The New Yorker Magazine for "Poetic Larks Bid Bald Eagle Welcome Swan of Liverpool" by Hendrik Hertzberg; © 1972 The New Yorker Magazine, Inc. Oxford University Press for *From Max Weber: Essays in Sociology* edited and translated by H. H. Gerth and C. Wright Mills, Copyright 1946 by Oxford University Press, Inc.; Renewed 1973 by Dr. Hans H. Gerth. Reprinted by permission. Frederick Herzberg, "One More Time: How Do You Motivate Employees?" *Harvard Business Review,* XLVI (January-February, 1968), 53–57. "The 1978 Nobel Prize in Economics," March, J. G., *Science,* Vol. 202, pp. 858–861, 24 November 1978. Oxford University Press and Chatto and Windus Ltd., Publishers, for two extracts from *Only Connect: On Culture and Communication* by Richard Hoggart. Excerpt from *The Making of a Counter Culture* by Theodore Roszak. Copyright © 1968, 1969 by Theodore Roszak. Reprinted by permission of Doubleday & Company, Inc. The World Publishing Company and George Weidenfeld and Nicolson (Publishers) for Lord Russell of Liverpool, "Introduction," in *Commandant of Auschwitz* by Rudolph Hoess; English translation Copyright © 1959 by George Weidenfeld and Nicolson Ltd. Translated from the German by Constantine FitzGibbon, New York: Popular Library, 1959, pp. 8–19. Houghton Mifflin Company and John Murray (Publishers) Ltd. for C. Northcote Parkinson, *Parkinson's Law,* pp. 78, 79–82. John Kidner, *The Kidner Report: How to Operate in Bureaucracy at ½ Horsepower,* Washington, D.C. 20009: Acropolis Books, Ltd., 1974, pp. 107–109. Nicholas Henry, "Bureaucracy, Technology, and Knowledge Management," *Public Administration Review,* 35 (November/December, 1975), pp. 572–573. Table 12–1, p. 316 reprinted by permission of the *Journal of the American Institute of Planners,* Vol. 43 (July 1977), p. 235. Samuel Kaplan, *The Dream Deferred: People, Politics, and Planning in Suburbia.* New York: The Seabury Press, 1976, pp. 193–196. Richard P. Nathan and Paul R. Dommel, "Understanding the Urban Predicament," *The Brookings Bulletin,* Vol. 14, Nos. 1 & 2, Spring-Summer 1977, p. 20. Copyright by the Brookings Institution. James A. Maxwell and J. Richard Aronson, *Financing State and Local Governments,* 3rd ed., Washington: The Brookings Institution, 1977, p. 48. Copyright by the Brookings Institution. Alan Lupo, in Alan Lupo, Frank Colcord, and Edmund P. Fowler, *Rites of Way: The Politics of Transportation in Boston and the U.S. City,* pp. 9–10. "Carter Finding Power Limited," November 11, 1977, © 1977 by The New York Times Company. Reprinted with permission.

index

503